Great American City

GREAT AMERICAN CITY

Chicago and the Enduring Neighborhood Effect

ROBERT J. SAMPSON

THE UNIVERSITY OF CHICAGO PRESS CHICAGO AND LONDON

The University of Chicago Press, Chicago 60637
The University of Chicago Press, Ltd., London

Paperback edition 2013
Printed in the United States of America

22 21 20 19 18 17 16 15 14 13 7 8 9 10 11

ISBN-13: 978-0-226-73456-9 (cloth)
ISBN-13: 978-0-226-05568-8 (paper)
ISBN-13: 978-0-226-73388-3 (e-book)
10.7208.9780226733883

Library of Congress Cataloging-in-Publication Data

Sampson, Robert J.
Great American city : Chicago and the enduring neighborhood effect / Robert J. Sampson.
p. cm.
Includes bibliographical references and index.
ISBN-13: 978-0-226-73456-9 (cloth : alkaline paper)
ISBN-10: 0-226-73456-0 (cloth : alkaline paper)
1. Chicago (Ill.)—Social conditions.
2. Neighborhoods—Illinois—Chicago. I. Title
F548.3.S26 2011
977.3′11—dc23
2011029350

♾ This paper meets the requirements of ANSI/NISO Z39.48-1992 (Permanence of Paper).

CONTENTS

FOREWORD

WILLIAM JULIUS WILSON

Robert Sampson's *Great American City: Chicago and the Enduring Neighborhood Effect* will not only change the way we think about neighborhood effects, it also sets a new standard for social scientific inquiry. Indeed, in my judgment, *Great American City* is one of the most comprehensive and sophisticated empirical studies ever conducted by a social scientist. The scope of this very readable and precisely worded book boggles the mind. As Sampson points out, "this book is at once an intellectual history of an idea, the story of a major research project, the tale of an iconic city, a systematic theory of neighborhood effects, an empirical account of community-level variations in a range of social processes, an analysis of competing schools of social inquiry, and a sustained empirical analysis that was designed to uncover new facts while adjudicating and integrating existing hypotheses."

Great American City examines two fundamentally different ways of looking at the world—one sees life in terms of independent self-maximizing individuals, the other focuses on the important collective processes in contextual settings rooted in shared understanding. The first image is powerfully reflected in contemporary America, not only in popular belief systems but also in recent developments in social science disciplines (for example, rational choice models of human behavior). This book's theoretical thrust brilliantly elevates the second idea by revealing how the mechanisms of social causality are profoundly shaped by the spatial logic of urban life. In the process the book does not inherently begin at the top (social structure) or bottom (individual behavior) but rather creatively integrates individual, neighborhood, and structural dynamics.

Sampson is a quantitative social scientist who understands the logic of scientific inquiry and therefore the importance of integrating the structure of explanation, the meaning and significance of concepts, and the nature of evidence. Sampson's research, empirical measures of concepts, and analysis of data are theoretically motivated. And he fully exploits his very rich data sets by taking a "pluralistic stance on the nature of evidence to assess causation." His pathbreaking findings flow mainly from a comprehensive research endeavor called the Project on Human Development in Chicago Neighborhoods (PHDCN). Using the iconic city of Chicago as a laboratory, the PHDCN collected longitudinal data on children, families, and neighborhoods. It is one of the most ambitious and creative research projects in the history of social science inquiry. A typical question will be raised about how representative Chicago is of other American cities. That is the wrong question to ask. This is a theoretically driven study, and Chicago happens to be an excellent laboratory for testing theoretically derived hypotheses.

Based on his incredibly rich and diverse data sources, Sampson argues that neighborhood contexts are, in themselves, important determinants of the quality and quantity of human behavior. In so doing, he not only clearly specifies the structural and cultural dimensions of neighborhood effects, he also gives attention to the choices and perceptions of individual residents, as well as the impact of larger structural forces. With the skillful use of ecometrics, the method of empirically assessing ecological settings, Sampson provides a comprehensive roadmap for the study of context and convincingly demonstrates that collective phenomena like neighborhoods demand their own measurement logic and are not reducible to individual-level traits.

Since Sampson's empirical measures of various aspects of neighborhoods are theoretically derived, his approach stands in sharp contrast to the typical studies that highlight or search for the "correct" operational definition of neighborhoods, a measurement that is often arbitrarily selected independent of any theoretical considerations. Indeed, Sampson's multiple measures of neighborhood effects reflect his broad and flexible theoretical framing of the variable interactions, perceptions, and institutional forces manifested in large and small ecologically specified areas. And his comprehensive longitudinal data set allows him to "examine a family of neighborhood effects across a wide range of social phenomena."

Great American City demonstrates the powerful effects of ecologically concentrated disadvantage on individual outcomes as well as rates of behavior across neighborhoods. These effects—including joblessness, poverty, and single-parent families with children, verbal ability, violence, incarceration, and collective efficacy—are magnified by racial segregation. Sampson reveals that poverty and its correlates are especially persistent in poor black neighborhoods. Indeed, his systematic presentation of evidence on the durability of neighborhood stratification—despite urban social transformations and macro economic and political changes in the late twentieth century and gentrification in the early twenty-first century—is one of the major contributions of this book.

Sampson carefully points out that historical, macroeconomic, and global forces have indeed impacted urban neighborhoods; however, they do not negate the potent "lower order" mechanisms of neighborhoods that help to account for variations in concentrated inequality. These include social psychological mechanisms that interact with broad cultural processes (e.g., stereotypes and shared expectations and perceptions of disorder) and have played a role in shaping the long-term identities and trajectories of neighborhoods. And this research leads me to strongly concur with his contention that the role of collectively shaped perceptions of disorder and moral and legal cynicism "may be underappreciated causes of community wellbeing and of continued racial and economic segregation in the United States, and perhaps cities elsewhere."

Another important and original contribution of *Great American City* is Sampson's powerful critique of studies that place special emphasis on self-selection bias, a term used in research to describe the effect of people grouping themselves together on common characteristics. Proponents of self-selection bias argue that the effects we attribute to poor neighborhoods may instead be caused by the characteristics of families and individuals who end up living there. In other words, they believe that disadvantaged neighborhoods might not be the cause of poor outcomes; rather families with the weakest job-related skills, with the lowest awareness of and concern for the effects of the environment on their children's social development, with attitudes that hinder social mobility, and with the most burdensome personal problems are simply more likely to live in these types of neighborhoods. Some even go so far as to deny the importance of neighborhood effects.

Sampson does not dismiss the role of individual selection effects. Rather he points out that neither higher-order structures nor neighborhood mechanisms are subservient to individual selection. Indeed, argues Sampson, "individual selection is embedded in social contexts" and is itself a neighborhood effect. Neighborhoods, he contends, affect individual decisions (selection) and perceptions, which in turn influence mobility and ultimately neighborhood composition and social dynamics. Selection and mobility also have an effect on extraneighborhood (e.g., spatial proximity) processes as well as higher-order (nonspatial) links. Accordingly, "in a fundamental sense," Sampson proclaims, "individual selection is both a neighborhood effect and embedded in a process of 'structural sorting,' bringing full circle the findings of the book that integrate individual, neighborhood, and ultimately structure."

I found Sampson's special emphasis on social structure in the study of neighborhood effects particularly appealing. Of the roughly 3,500 empirical studies that have cited or addressed arguments in my book *The Truly Disadvantaged*, the focus has been overwhelmingly on individual outcomes, despite the book's structuralist orientation. Many of the more rigorous studies of neighborhood effects highlight experimental causation. Sampson's book, in sharp contrast, brings structure back in. Indeed, Sampson contends that theoretical arguments incorporating social structure by their very nature challenge the assumptions of experimental causation for two essential reasons. First, a nonsocial world is created by randomization, at least momentarily; and, second, causal inferences reside at theoretical levels and do not directly emanate from data or particular methods (however elegant or rigorous). Accordingly, locating or displaying causal mechanisms using statistical or experimental results provide clues, he argues, not answers to theoretical questions. "Sometimes qualitative empirical data can even be more informative than what at first glance appear to be more rigorous quantitative data."

In the various chapters of this book, Sampson demonstrates how his flexible conception of causality stands in sharp contrast to the "crucial individual experiment." Rather than a single effect, *Great American City* features a holistic "contextual causality" that captures neighborhood social processes. A family of neighborhood effects is theoretically interpreted, described, observed, and analyzed using a variety of methodologies, including the creative use of ecometrics.

Great American City also provides a framework for raising crucial questions about the "cultural turn" in the social sciences in the last few decades, particularly in the discipline of sociology, that highlight the importance of concepts such as "tool kits" and "scripts." Although recognizing the positive contributions of this development, Sampson points out that the applications of these dominant concepts seem to be individualistic and are therefore not very suitable for understanding persistent macrohistorical continuity, cultural mechanisms, and deeply embedded structures. Given the findings of *Great American City*, Sampson raises the following question: "If individuals have so many tool kits to choose from, why is there so much consistency (structure) and intersubjective agreement on basic mediators of neighborhood social reproduction?" What is clearly demonstrated in this book is that unlike tool kits and scripts that are interchangeable and can be readily accessed or discarded by individuals, norms and shared understandings are persistent (or reproduced) across a variety of social settings, including neighborhoods.

The incredible scope of *Great American City* is also seen in Sampson's analysis of data from the Chicago Collective Civic Action Project in chapter 8. With use of these data Sampson carefully examines the impact of nonprofit organizations under a variety of conditions including racial segregation, concentrated poverty, residential stability, population density, as well as a number of other varying social processes ranging from friend/kinship ties to voluntary associations. Sampson finds that the density of nonprofit organizations has a notably positive effect on neighborhoods regardless of racial segregation, poverty, or other social conditions that make life in these settings so difficult. What should be emphasized in this connection is that Sampson's robust findings on the impact of nonprofit organizations relate to his earlier theoretical and empirical discussion concerning the importance of neighborhood collective efficacy. Basically, Sampson argues, neighborhoods that posses a rich organizational life enhance informal social control and embedded shared expectations that reinforce and promote trust. These findings have important implications for social policy dealing with neighborhood interventions, such as President Obama's Promise Neighborhoods—a point that is elaborated further in Sampson's discussion of the policy implications of his overall findings, as I will soon illustrate in my closing comments.

In the penultimate chapter 16, Sampson revisits the city of Chicago after the economic crisis of 2008 and provides a fascinating discussion of his analytic strategy and entire set of analyses applied to present-day Chicago. In this chapter he returns to the narrative structure and methods discussed in chapter 1 of the book. He zooms in on these neighborhoods with a bird's-eye view—starting with a walking tour of the same neighborhoods in 2010, armed with observations, photos, and field notes, as well as recent quantitative data on foreclosures, crime, and a new letter-drop study. Thus the original data in this remarkable book covers the period from 1995–2010, with census data analysis going back to 1960. His findings in chapter 16 not only confirm but also extend the thesis of the book under new and significantly different macroeconomic conditions.

In the concluding chapter 17 he revisits Zorbaugh's 1929 classic study *Gold Coast and Slum* and specifically "Death Corner," the area that now sits in the center of the space occupied by the former Cabrini-Green housing project. He went back multiple times in the summer of 2010 and again as late as October 2010, with the goal to narrate the thesis of the book from the perspective of this one place. And he uses the Cabrini-Green demolition, surrounding Death Corner, to segue into the chapter's final section on policy implications.

Based on the theoretical arguments and empirical findings of this book, Sampson advocates a different approach to policy interventions for distressed areas of the city. Instead of moving people out of troubled neighborhoods, he makes the case for community-level interventions, as well as holistic policy interventions that recognize the important interconnected social fabric of neighborhoods in American cities. And, consistent with the theory and research of *Great American City*, this policy initiative would include a focus on strategies to integrate public safety intervention—such as regular meetings of local police and residents to co-identify problems—with broader noncrime policies that address the mediating social processes of social organization—such as opportunities to enhance citizen participation and mobilization. This initiative would also include other theoretically relevant projects that are inextricably linked to neighborhood-level dynamics, such as community economic development and citywide or metropolitan programs of mixed-income housing that are connected with the dynamics of neighborhood migration. All of these policy proposals are consistent with Sampson's focus on how government action—ranging from zoning decisions to interconnected housing and school policies—affect concentrated poverty, residential segregation, neighborhood stability and, most recently, home foreclosures.

Sampson argues that given the historical evidence that community structures are highly patterned, policies focusing on community-level interventions, and based on research knowledge about the mechanisms of urban change, are more feasible and indeed more cost effective over the long term than targeting individuals. For all these reasons he sees the need to broaden our perspective of policy evaluation, which tends to focus almost exclusively on individual actions. Since meaningful change depends on understanding the impact of ongoing neighborhood dynamics and social structures, these social processes should be an essential part of any program of evaluation. Sampson contends that there is no intrinsic reason why social policy cannot address the realties of individual choice while intervening at the scale of the community and citywide social connections.

I began this foreword by arguing that *Great American City* will change the way we think about neighborhood effects and that it sets a new standard for social scientific inquiry. I say this without exaggeration. This book will be debated and discussed for years and will become a standard reference for social science disciplines. However, despite the incredible documentation and precise scientific arguments, it is also accessible and will attract the attention of general educated readers as well. Indeed, Sampson's study and engagement with the streets of Chicago will lead readers to appreciate, in his words, "the logic and power of neighborhood effects."

ACKNOWLEDGMENTS

There are many people and institutions that made this book possible. I begin with a special thanks to the core Project on Human Development in Chicago Neighborhoods (PHDCN) team. Felton (Tony) Earls, Steve Raudenbush, and Albert J. Reiss Jr. stand out as my closest colleagues in the early years. Tony's leadership was essential in keeping the PHDCN from imploding in perilous times, and Steve has been a collaborator from the very beginning of my involvement with the project. I am especially grateful that I have been able to count on Tony and Steve for their friendship and intellectual wisdom over the years. Although Al is no longer with us, I will not soon forget his iron will and headstrong opinions no matter what the prevailing mood. The memories of many meetings and too many hotels have blurred, but not the rewarding intensity with which the idea of PHDCN was collectively pursued.

A number of other scholars were part of the PHDCN team of scientific leaders or external advisors. In addition to those noted in chapter 4, I would like to acknowledge Temi Moffitt, Steve Buka, Jeanne Brooks-Gunn, Michael Tonry, Al Blumstein, and David Farrington for their central roles in helping shape the PHDCN, and Doug McAdam for his efforts in helping launch the civic participation project described in chapter 8. I have also had the pleasure of working with a number of smart graduate students on various analyses, papers, and ideas stemming from the PHDCN and its spinoffs, including Jeff Morenoff, Dave Kirk, Heather MacIndoe, Simon Weffer, Chris Browning, Corina Graif, Patrick Sharkey, Charles Loeffler, and Ann Owens.

From this stellar cast I am pleased to acknowledge the following colleagues for their contributions to chapters where I build on prior collaborative efforts: Steve Raudenbush (chapter 6); Tony Earls and Steve Raudenbush (chapter 7); Doug McAdam, Heather MacIndoe, Simon Weffer, and Kaisa Snellman (chapter 8); Jeff Morenoff and Corina Graif (chapter 10); Pat Sharkey (chapter 11); Corina Graif (chapter 13); and Corina Graif and Dave Kirk (chapter 14). Ann Owens and Carly Knight provided superb GIS research assistance in the last year, and Genevieve Butler kept the organization of multiple components of the research effort under control.

Institutions figured greatly in the making of PHDCN. The John D. and Catherine T. MacArthur Foundation and the National Institute of Justice provided the major funding at the outset and stuck with the project despite a rough early going and series of challenges. I know that Tony and Steve share my wish to acknowledge publicly their indispensable roles in sustaining the project. The NIMH provided later funding for data collection, as did the American Bar Foundation and the Chicago Community Trust. Grants that supported analysis and writing were received from the NIH (P01 AG031093), the Robert Wood Johnson Foundation (Grant #052746), and the Russell Sage Foundation. I also thank the Center for Advanced Study in the Behavioral Sciences and the Russell Sage Foundation for providing pleasant and supportive sabbatical settings for getting work done. Last but not least, I wish to acknowledge my intellectual home bases. For a total of twenty years I have been fortunate enough to claim two wonderfully idiosyncratic universities—the University of Chicago and Harvard University. I thank them both for their uniquely different and intense cultures, administrative support, and intellectual colleagueship. Without a committed set of institutional lifelines, the PHDCN and this book never would have been accomplished.

Large projects like the one mounted by PHDCN take an enormous effort and extract a personal toll that goes well beyond published scholarship. But dedication and long hours do not tell the full story—a strong dose of expertise was essential to mounting the Chicago field effort. In particular I want to acknowledge John Holton (site director), Alisú Schoua-Glusberg (survey director), the project managers—James "Chip" Coldren, Cynthia Coleman, Jan Dunham, Pat Lau, Kelly Martin, Nancy Sampson, and Lorrie Stone—and the rest of the incredible PHDCN team in Chicago, at one point numbering more than 150 people. Collectively, the PHDCN unit at 651 West Washington Street pulled off a heroic feat of data collection. NORC at the University of Chicago also carried out the difficult Systematic Social Observation and Key Informant studies with expertise and innovation. Despite considerable hardship in the field, ABT Associates together with PHDCN staff managed to pull off the first Community Survey. The University of Michigan's ISR completed the second.

Toting up one's intellectual debts is an impossible task, especially when they involve friends, colleagues, institutions, and family. I shall thus be brief and apologize for those I leave out. For comments on various chapters, related papers, presentations, or the penultimate draft, and for grounding my various obsessions, I would especially like to thank Tony Earls, John Laub, Doug McAdam, Steve Raudenbush, Nancy Sampson, Gerry Suttles, Per-Olof Wikström, Chris Winship, and Bill Wilson. Not only has Bill been the touchstone toward whom all urban scholars aspire, he has been an inspiring colleague ever since the exhilarating first days of my time on the faculty at the University of Chicago. His work has been an exemplar, and I am honored that he graciously agreed to write the foreword to this book. I can only hope that I have done justice to his efforts.

For early comments on my work, I thank James F. Short Jr., a true intellectual and standard bearer of the Chicago School. He read the manuscript in rough form but has been an enthusiastic supporter from day one of my community-level project. The readers for the Press also gave me more insights than they probably realized on the initial proposal and ideas. Claude Fischer and Andrew Abbott correctly warned that my incomplete vision would take time to refine, but I am grateful for their confidence and sage advice in tackling the early phases of the book's evolution. Discussions with Rob Mare on selection and neighborhood change have been helpful as well and have led me to new ways to think about future work.

Doug Mitchell has steered many University of Chicago Press books to publication, and this one is no exception. His enthusiasm for the idea of the project was evident in the early stages, and it sustained my efforts to craft a final product. In addition to Doug, I would like to thank Tim McGovern, Kate Frentzel, Rob Hunt, and the rest of the staff at the Press for their efforts in helping to bring the book to its final form.

This book is dedicated to the efforts of all those who helped carry out the PHDCN and the thousands of Chicagoans who took part in the study as participants over the years, from the smallest infants and their caretakers to the most powerful movers and shakers in the city. Their contributions are everywhere in the pages that follow.

PART I **SETTING AND THESIS**

1 Placed

Imagine a world where distance has died, where globalization and high-tech wonders have rendered place irrelevant, where the Internet, Blackberries, and planes are the coin of a global realm, not local difference. From the North End of Boston to the North Beach of San Francisco, imagine cities where neighborhood difference is an anachronism, a victim of "placelessness."

On the surface this thought experiment matches common experience. Who doesn't know a teenager wired to everything but her neighborhood? It seems everyone nowadays is traversing the urban metropolis while chatting away on a cell phone, plugged into an iPod, or perhaps even "tweeting."[1] As for the idyllic urban village said to characterize communities of yesteryear, few of us have the time or energy for dinner with our neighbors anymore. Americans are notoriously individualistic and roam widely, so what then is the relevance of place? Globalization is everywhere triumphant according to the dominant narrative, rendering us "elsewhere" rather than placed. Thus according to the social theorist Anthony Giddens, we need not imagine at all, for the very essence of high modernity and contemporary conditions can be captured in the idea of place as "phantasmagoric."[2] Neither does the public intellectual Thomas Friedman need a thought experiment, because for him the world is already "flat," or at the very least, flattening.[3]

These influential thinkers and this common wisdom about the effects of technology are right at some fundamental level. Universal forces create places that are similar no matter where we go. The strip malls that line cities and suburbs across the country come quickly to my mind, uniformly ugly in the same way no matter where they alight. Even cities as a whole are thought by many to be interchangeable; if we can be anywhere, then nowhere in particular stands out. And even if we cannot literally be anywhere, we can be elsewhere aided by profound advances in technology.

Setting aside the suspicion that only the privileged elite enjoy a global playing field, there are also good empirical reasons to take seriously the questioning of place and concepts like neighborhood or community. Social-network theorists have shown us that urbanites create nonspatial communities that cross-cut geographic ones. Metropolitan dwellers might not know their neighbors on an intimate basis, but they are likely to build viable sets of social relations spread across the city, state, country, and increasingly the world.[4] In an influential paper in the late 1970s, Barry Wellman referred to this as "community liberated," or what might be thought of as community beyond propinquity.[5] Perhaps place *is* phantasmagorical and community lost.

With all the emphasis on new forms of alienation from traditional forms of community, it may come as a surprise to learn that intellectual and public concern with the decline of community is longstanding and finds vigor in every historical period. Today's manifestations might be unique but not the perceived problem. In the most abstract version the theme of declining community and yearning for renewal finds its roots in the Judeo-Christian tradition: Eden became sin city and salvation still awaits. Karl Marx was secular but the promise of community after the overthrow of capitalism was unmistakable and launched societal revolutions. The entire discipline of sociology, in fact, was founded on the upheavals of the late nineteenth century widely thought to have frayed the social fabric of "Gemeinschaft" (community).[6] The presumed decline of traditional forms of personal association in small towns besieged by the advance of widespread urbanization and industrialization became the central problematic for other noted scholars such as Émile Durkheim, Georg Simmel, and Max Weber. Louis Wirth later expanded these concerns by arguing that large population size, density, and ethnic heterogeneity were socially disintegrative features that characterized rapidly changing cities. Wirth famously asserted in 1938 that these defining elements of urbanism made social relations "anonymous" (like

Internet surfing? blog comments?) and "superficial" (like texting? Facebook?), with estrangement undermining family life and ultimately the bonds of solidarity thought to reflect community.[7] One can read Wirth today, insert technology as the villain, and get a familiar result.

This classic thesis of decline—aptly described as "community lost"—thus posits the idea that the social ties of modern urbanites have become impersonal, transitory, and segmented, hastening the eclipse of local community and feeding processes of what became known as "social disorganization."[8] A well-known book in the middle of the twentieth century adroitly captured the collective urging of the times: *The Quest for Community*.[9]

The beat went on and never stopped. The contemporary manifestation of community lost is exposed by the intense attention focused on the notion of Americans "bowling alone" and "hunkering down." Robert Putnam's thesis of a decades-long decline in voluntary associations, trust, and informal neighborly exchange captured the imagination not just of social scientists but the public at large.[10] The concept of community lost has also been frequently invoked in scholarly debates across a range of fields, including "social capital,"[11] civil society,[12] social movements,[13] and in the public intellectual world of communitarians.[14] As if to underscore these concerns, a widely reported and earnestly discussed finding in 2006 argued that the core discussion networks of Americans decreased by a third from the mid-1980s to the present, with notable declines for voluntary associations and neighborhood contacts.[15] More recently came a warning of the "downside of diversity," with evidence pointing to increasing immigration and ethnic heterogeneity as a potential source of mistrust in one's neighbors.[16]

An interesting irony is that the placelessness and globalization critique finds an affinity with the longstanding narrative of community lost in the idea that personal ties to the local community have withered away.[17] The difference is that the globetrotting modernist says good riddance (community liberated!), whereas "communitarianism" can be seen as a sort of resistance movement to counter the bowling-alone scenario of decline and inspire a renewal of community.[18] Either way, the implication many public intellectuals and scholarly pundits alike have taken away is that places—especially as instantiated in neighborhoods and community—are dead, impotent, declining, chaotic, irrelevant, or some combination thereof.

Observing Chicago

Chicago is the great American city.

Norman Mailer, *Miami and the Siege of Chicago*.[19]

Enter contemporary and, yes, global Chicago.[20] Logic demands that if neighborhoods do not matter and placelessness reigns, then the city is more or less a random swirl. Anyone (or anything) could be *here* just as easily as *there*. Identities and inequalities by place should be rapidly interchangeable, the durable inequality of a community rare, and neighborhood effects on both individuals and higher-level social processes should be weak or nonexistent. The effects of spatial proximity should also be weak. And so goes much contemporary scholarship.[21]

By contrast, the guiding thesis of this book is that differentiation by neighborhood is not only everywhere to be seen, but that it is has durable properties—with cultural and social mechanisms of reproduction—and with effects that span a wide variety of social phenomena. Whether it be crime, poverty, child health, protest, leadership networks, civic engagement, home foreclosures, teen births, altruism, mobility flows, collective efficacy, or immigration, to name a few subjects investigated in this book, the city is ordered by a spatial logic ("placed") and yields differences as much today as a century ago. The effect of distance is not just geographical but simultaneously social, as described by Henry Zorbaugh in his classic treatise *The Gold Coast and the Slum*.[22] Spatially inscribed social differences, I argue, constitute a family of "neighborhood effects" that are pervasive, strong, cross-cutting, and paradoxically stable even as they are changing in manifest form.

To get an initial feel for the social and physical manifestations of my thesis and the enduring significance of place, walk with me on down the streets of this iconic American city in the first decade of the twenty-first century. I begin the tour in the heart of phantasmagoria if there ever was one—the bustling "Magnificent Mile" of Michigan Avenue, the highly touted showcase of contemporary Chicago.[23] As we start southward from the famed Water Tower, we see mostly glitter and a collage of well-to-do people, with whites predominant among the shoppers laden with bags from the likes of Louis Vuitton, Tiffany's, Saks Fifth Avenue, Cartier, and more. Pristine stores gleam, police officers direct traffic at virtually every intersection throughout the day, and construction cranes loom in the nearby distance erecting (or in anticipation of) new condos. There is an almost complete lack of what James Q. Wilson and George Kelling famously termed "broken windows," a metaphor for neighborhood disrepair and urban neglect.[24] As I walked south on a midmorning in January of 2006, street sweepers were cleaning both sides of an already clean street as if to make the point. Whatever "disorder" exists is in fact socially organized, whether the occasional homeless asking for money in approved locations (near the river is common; in front of Van Cleef & Arpels or the Disney Store is not) or groups with a cause pressing their case with pamphlets, signs, and petitions. A favorite blip around the holidays is charity appeals mixed with the occasional hurling of abuse (or ketchup) at shoppers emerging from the furrier. I see nothing on this day but many furs. Other warmer times of the year bring out a cornucopia of causes.[25] On a warm day in late March of 2007, a homeless shelter for women presses its cause alongside an anti-Obama crusader (the latter getting many glares, in this, Obama country).

As we near the Chicago River, Donald Trump announces his vision. It is not subtle, of course, but rather a symbolic shout; in the city of skyscrapers the cranes here are busy erecting the self-described world's tallest future building, one in which "residential units on the 89th floor will break a 37-year world record held by the John Hancock Center for the world's highest homes off ground level."[26] Chicago is once again a "city on the make," as Nelsen Algren put it well,[27] and so it seems perfectly fitting that Trump chose Chicago for this particular behemoth.[28] On a cold day in March with barely a hole in the ground, international tourists were busily snapping pictures of the spectacle to be. A year later at fifteen stories and rising, and then later at almost ninety, the shutters of the tourist cameras continued to flap. In April 2009, only the height had changed and Trump's vision was complete. Here, status is in place.

After crossing the Chicago River from the Near North Side into the Loop and passing the clash of classic architecture and Trump's monument to the future in its midst, one begins to see the outlines of the new Millennium Park in the distance, the half-billion-dollar extravaganza long championed by the second Mayor Daley and built considerably over cost with cries of corruption and cronyism.[29] Yet there is no denying the visual impact and success of Millennium Park, a Disney-like playground, all shiny and new. Even on a cold winter day there is public activity and excitement in the air. People mill about, skaters glide across the rink, and film-projected faces of average citizens stare out of the fountain's facade. Looking west from the park the skyline and bustle of the Loop stand out in a different way than the Near North—more workers and everyday business activity against the backdrop of landmark buildings and institutions.

Continuing south along Michigan Avenue past Roosevelt Road one sees more action, but with a twist. The architecture and historical pulse of the southern part of Chicago has always been different from points north. Despite its proximity to the Loop, the community of the "Near South Side" was marked by vacant rail yards, vagrants, dilapidated SRO (single-room-occupancy) hotels frequented by transients, penny arcades, and warehouses. The latter are now being redeveloped for lofts and one old SRO building after another is being swept away for new condos and chic restaurants. Unlike the cumulative advantages being piled high atop the long-stable Gold Coast, renewal is the order of the day. Alongside and in some cases atop former railroad yards, the Near South development rose to prominence in the mid-1990s when Mayor Richard M. Daley and his wife moved there from the storied political neighborhood of Bridgeport in 1994.[30] Other developments soon took off and today flux is readily apparent where decay once stood. Few Chicagoans just ten years ago would have imagined eating smartly at South Wabash and 21st, the former haunts of hobos and the homeless.[31] Whereas the Magnificent Mile has long anchored development and moneyed investment, the Near South Side tells a story of real change.[32]

Further down Michigan Avenue between about 35th and 47th Streets in the communities of Douglas and then Grand Boulevard, the scene is jarringly different. The transformation of the Near South has given way to what sociologists traditionally called the "slum." In a walk down Michigan Avenue in 2006 I saw what appeared to be a collapsing housing project to the left, broken glass in the street, vacant and boarded-up buildings, and virtually no people. Those I observed were walking quickly with furtive glances. On my walk in 2006 and again in early 2007, no whites were to be found and no glimmering city parks were within sight. The cars were beat up and there was little sign of collective gatherings or public activity, save perhaps what appeared to be a drug deal that transacted quickly. Yet even here there were stirrings of change, symbolized most dramatically by vacant lots to the west of where there once stood hulking and decaying projects built expressly to contain the city's black poor.

In fact, the South Side of Chicago once housed the most infamous slum in America. Chicago showed it knew how to build not just skyscrapers but spectacular high-rises for the poor; the Robert Taylor Homes alone once held over twenty-five thousand residents–black, poor and isolated,[33] outdoing Cabrini Green, another national symbol of urban despair. As described by the Chicago Housing Authority itself, Robert Taylor apartments were "arrayed in a linear series of 28 16-story high-rises, which formed a kind of concrete curtain for traffic passing by on the nearby Dan Ryan Expressway."[34] The wider neighborhood of the projects—"Bronzeville," as it was named by St. Clair Drake and Horace R. Cayton in *Black Metropolis*—became infamous as one of the most dangerous and dispossessed in the country in the latter half of the twentieth century.[35] Yet in a short ten-year span the Robert Taylor Homes have been demolished (literally, blown up with dynamite) and former residents scattered throughout the metropolitan area. The tragic mistake of designed segregation became too much for even the Chicago City Council to ignore. Officially recognized as a failed policy, the last building of Robert Taylor was closed at the end of 2006.

I visited the area in March 2007 after the last building was destroyed. It was eerily quiet as I paused to contemplate and observe vast open spaces where grinding poverty once reigned amid families making the best they could out of an unforgiving environment. An especially haunting reflection came to mind, a visit in 1995 to the Robert Taylor Homes on the same exact block. Passing inoperable metal detectors and walking up urine-stenched stairs because the elevators were broken, the physical signs of degradation were overwhelming. Yet a group of us entered an apartment that was immaculate, where we met two single mothers who told a story of survival and determination to see a better day. Both of their sons had been murdered and they had knitted a quilt with one-foot by one-foot squares honoring every other child who had also been murdered in the projects. The unfurled quilt extended nearly the length of the room. Shaken, I remember thinking at the time that surely anything would be an improvement over the prisonlike towers. On this spot one sees almost a verdant green expanse, with downtown far in the distance (fig. 1.1). The "problem" is now out of sight and for many, including city leaders, out of mind.

Heading slightly east and progressing toward the lake, one sees the emergence of a thriving black middle class amid the rubble and vacant

FIGURE 1.1. In the former shadows of the projects: where the Robert Taylor Homes once stood. Photo by the author, September 13, 2007.

lots adjacent to the former projects. Hard as it might be to imagine, $500,000 homes are being erected next to boarded-up buildings at the center of what was a low-rise slum just years earlier. Riders arriving by train into Chicago between the 1960s and the recent past would witness concentrated poverty up close—abandoned buildings and all the signs of decline appeared to the west of the tracks on the South Side in the small community of Oakland, which sits just north and east of Grand Boulevard. Nearby at the corner of Pershing and Langley, new homeowners are beckoned by a sign for the "Arches at Oakwood Shores"—a country club–like name where prostitutes once roamed freely and physical destruction was rampant.[36] Vacant lots serve as reminders of the transition still in progress. At Drexel and 43rd on a day in March of 2007, a group of homeless men sit around a fire on a trash-strewn lot. At 47th and Wabash sits a huge boarded-up building, menacing in feel. Although still a work in progress, the areas in Oakland and around parts of Bronzeville represent one of the most stunning turnarounds in urban America today.[37] How and why this happened takes on significance considering that most slums in Chicago, as shown in chapter 5, remain slums.

Soon after heading south from this surreal transformation to the likely "Black Gold Coast" of the future, one finds stately mansions in Kenwood and then the integrated and stable community of Hyde Park, home to passionate intellectuals and a dense organizational life. Adopted home and inspiration to President Barack Obama and other movers and shakers, almost nothing happens in Hyde Park without community input and institutional connections, visible in signs, churches, bookstores, petitions, and a wide variety of community organizations. People instantly know what you mean when you say you live in Hyde Park; the name swims in cultural meaning. It was no accident that Obama was a "community organizer," as chapter 8 explains.

Just west of Hyde Park, however, stark differences appear again. Across Washington Park sits a community of the same name that has seen hard times and still struggles mightily. Along the major thoroughfare of Garfield Boulevard stand burned buildings, gated liquor stores, and empty lots. At the corner of Michigan Avenue, we could not find a more apt portrayal of the second part of Zorbaugh's contrast. The inverse of Michigan Avenue north of the Loop, here we find dead spaces permeated by a sense of dread. At midday, groups of men hang out, bleary eyed and without apparent purpose. As we head further south into Woodlawn we see block after block of what most Americans would consider the classic ghetto. Black, visibly poor, and characterized by physical disrepair, west Woodlawn looks bleak to the eye. Zorbaugh might not have imagined the *Black Gold Coast and the Slum*, but today it is apparently here.

Continuing the patchwork quilt, if we head eastward to the area south of the University of Chicago, renewal announces itself once again. First one witnesses a stretch of open land where tenements once stood. Then east of the elevated tracks and former strip of decay on 63rd Street, new homes start sprouting. Around 63rd and Kimbark it looks almost like a suburb with back decks, grills, and lawns on display. On Kenwood Avenue, just south of 63rd, sit more new homes in a row. Tidy and neat, the middle class is moving in to reclaim the slums.

Heading further south to Avalon Park and Chatham we find the neighborhoods where a stable black middle class has existed for decades. Along street after street south of 79th and west of Stony Island one can see neat brick buildings, myriad neighborhood associations, and children playing happily in the streets. No new developments, no dramatic changes, and little media glare like that chronicling the disrepute of the slums. For years and like many neighborhoods across the U.S., this area has seen families raising their kids, tending to their homes, and going about quietly living the American Dream. At almost every block a sign announces a block club and shared expectations for conduct.[38]

If we head west past the Dan Ryan Expressway we find more stability, albeit an impoverished one. Here we confront concentrated poverty stretching for hundreds of blocks. Outsiders are often surprised at how far one may drive in certain areas of Chicago's South Side and see marked signs of deterioration. Stability of change thus rules again, where neighborhoods maintain their relative positions in the overall hierarchy. Why these neighborhoods and not the ones like Oakland?

And so it goes as one continues on through the highly variegated mosaic of twenty-first-century Chicago—or Boston, New York, Los Angeles, or any other American city. Venturing down the streets of our cities, the careful observer sees what appear to be "day and night" representations of community life. There are vast disparities in the contemporary city on a number of dimensions that are anything but randomly distributed in space. Perhaps more important, the meanings that people attribute to these places and differences are salient and often highly consensual. Our walk also reveals that important as was Zorbaugh's work, the Gold Coast and the slum is not the only contrast. No matter which direction one turns in Chicago, the result will be to encounter additional social worlds—perhaps the teeming immigrant enclave of Little Village, bohemian Wicker Park, white working-class Clearing, yuppified Lincoln Park, the upper-class white community of Norwood, the incredibly diverse Uptown, or the land that time forgot, Hegewisch.

Thus while some things remain the same from Zorbaugh's day, other things have changed. The intersection of West Oak and North Cambridge in the west part of the Near North Side was considered "Death Corner" in the 1920s by Zorbaugh.[39] That maintained for decades and the area around the infamous Cabrini Green homes was still dicey on multiple visits in the decade of the 2000s, a swelter of contradictions. Decay was present in many blocks with a large number of boarded-up buildings near Oak and Hudson. On Locust near Orleans it was common until recently to see high-rise projects with unemployed men hanging out during the day. Yet the Cabrini Green projects are in the process of being razed to be replaced by low-rise, hopefully mixed-income housing. The area sends mixed messages and its future is one to watch, however painfully. On a brisk day in March of 2007 I witnessed a clearly emaciated and drug-addled woman begging for money a short stroll from Cabrini units near a large sign announcing new condos and a gym on North Larrabee St. with the unsubtle proclamation: "Look Better Naked." I revisit Death Corner in 2010 in the final chapter.

For now it is clear that Chicago possesses neighborhoods of nearly every ilk—from the seemingly endless bungalow belt of working-class homes to the skyscrapers of the Loop, the diversity and disparities of Chicago are played out against a vast kaleidoscope of contrasts. Indeed, The Gold Coast(s) and the slum(s)—and everything in between represent a mosaic of contrasts that reflect the twenty-first-century city and its diversity of interrelated parts.

A Bird's-Eye View

Neighborhoods differ dramatically in their quality, feel, sights, sounds, and smells—that much is experienced in our walks. But equally remarkable is the diversity of behaviors and social actions that cluster together in space and that define the social organization of the city. At a macro level the inverse of placelessness is ecological concentration and disparity. Layering independent empirical data on top of the street observations above, I thus zoom out to take a bird's-eye view.

Consider first the apparent anomaly of the ecological concentration of disparate aspects of wellbeing across the neighborhoods of Chicago.[40] Whether the measure is homicide, low birth weight, infant mortality, teen pregnancy, physical abuse, or accidental injury, there is compelling evidence pointing to geographic "hot spots" of compromised health. Figure 1.2 provides a vivid example, displaying the geographical ordering of homicide incidents and the expected health outcomes of infants over six years (2000–2005) based on the poverty rate of each of seventy-seven community areas in Chicago.[41] At first blush, what could be more different than a woman giving birth to a baby weighing less than 2,500 grams and the murder of another human being, typically by a young male? Yet homicide is highly concentrated in the same communities scoring low

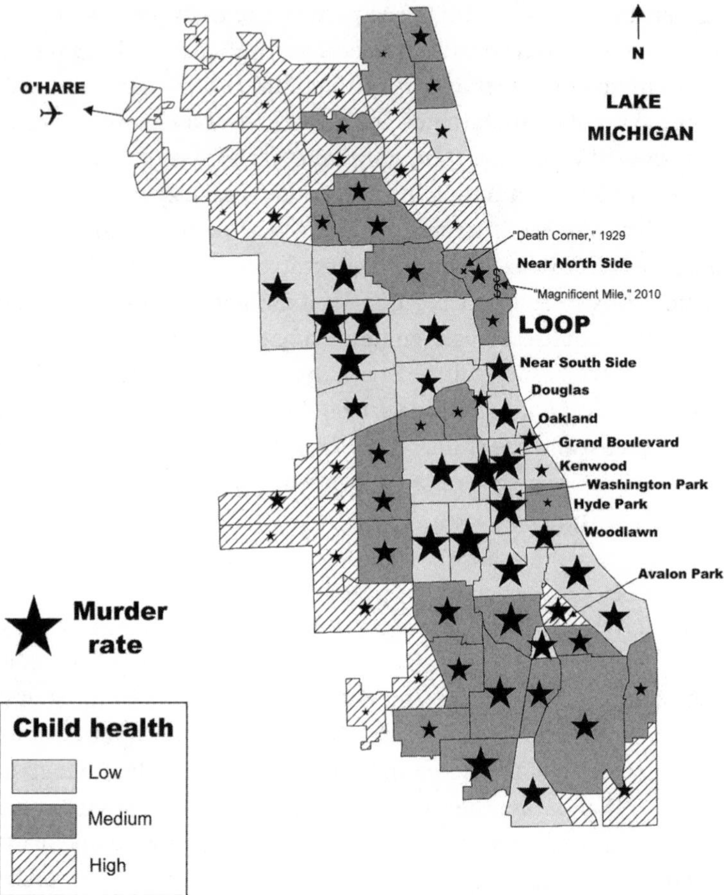

FIGURE 1.2. The ecological concentration of compromised wellbeing in Chicago communities: homicide predicts poor infant health, 2000–2005, poverty adjusted. Stars are proportional to homicides per hundred thousand population. Adjusted child health scores are classified into equal thirds.

on infant health, with a clustering or corridor of compromised wellbeing on the Near South Side (e.g., the Grand Boulevard and Washington Park communities of our walk earlier), Far South Side (e.g., Riverdale, West Pullman, Roseland), and West Side (e.g., North Lawndale, West Garfield Park, and, to their south, Austin). By contrast, neighborhoods on the north and southwest sides fare much better, including some working-class communities (e.g., Portage Park), diverse communities (e.g., Lakeview), and some geographically close to high poverty and violence (e.g., Beverly, McKinley Park, and Clearing).

The reader may suspect that this spatial pattern is simply a poverty story. It is not: the infant health classification in figure 1.2 is adjusted for concentrated poverty, and alternative procedures replicate the basic pattern.[42] And as we shall learn in later chapters, other commonly invoked suspects—from individual attributes and vulnerabilities on the one hand, to race/ethnic composition on the other—are insufficient to explain this stark phenomenon.[43] Equally impressive, the concentration of "death and disease," as Drake and Cayton put it over a half century earlier in *Black Metropolis*, is longstanding.[44] As shown in their original publication in 1945, whether manifested through insanity, infant mortality, delinquency, tuberculosis, or "poverty and social disorganization," the city of Chicago was highly stratified by disadvantage and ecological risk, with many high-rate communities then overlapping with those in figure 1.2. The specific communities may change but the broader pattern of concentration is robust.

The modernist critic might give ground but view crime and disease as outliers, something out of the old "social disorganization" playbook of urban sociology.[45] So let us turn things around and look instead at the American political equivalent of "apple pie"—collective civic engagement. Figure 1.3 displays the enduring association and neighborhood concentration of collective civic events such as community festivals, fund drives, parades, blood drives, and PTA meetings over three decades.[46] The data suggest that civic life is not dead but rather highly differentiated and spatially ordered, with clear evidence that the clustering of civic engagement goes well beyond chance and keeps reappearing in the same places. Areas that generate traditional civic engagement appear host to public protests as well, such as marches against the Vietnam or Iraq wars and protests against police brutality. Moreover, the intensity or rate of activity from 1970 to 1990 (classified into thirds) strongly predicts the initiation and location of collective civic events in 2000 that are represented as dots in figure 1.3. As will be shown later, this pattern of collective civic action is best explained not by race or class but the density of organizations in the community. Modern society writ large may well be an organizational one, but its manifestation has clear local imprints that are anything but random.

Perhaps collective civic engagement, even impassioned protest, is not

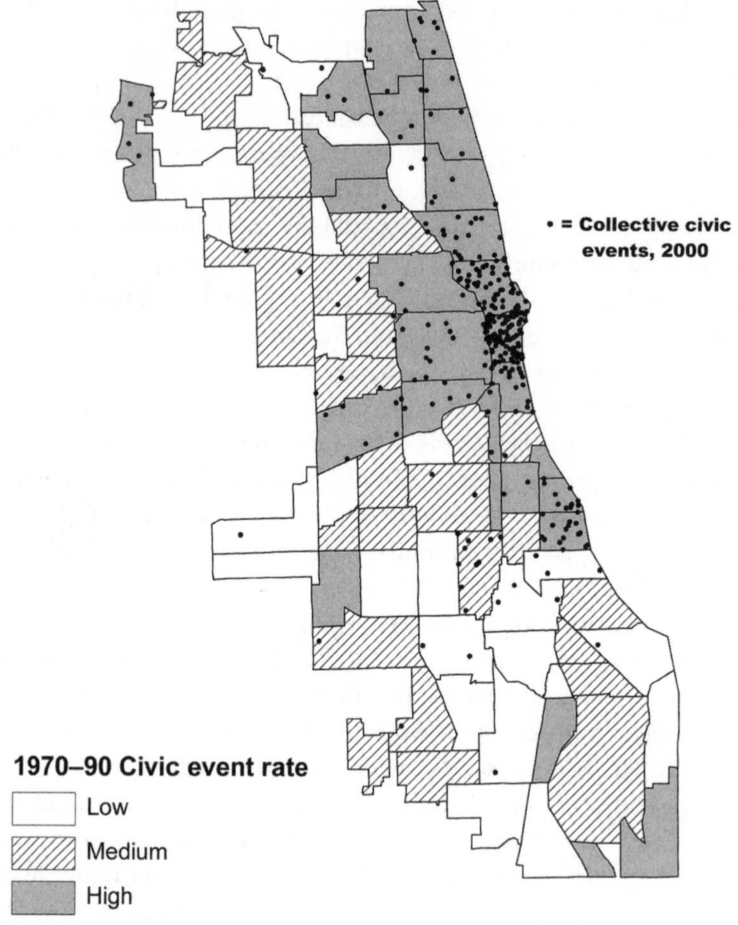

FIGURE 1.3. Spatial concentration and long-term endurance of collective civic engagement in Chicago communities, 1970–2000

fully modern either. Maybe networks are where globalization instantiates the potential to destroy community differences.[47] As a preview of results to come, I display in figure 1.4 the pattern of "connectivity" among people to whom key leaders in two Chicago communities go to in order to get things done. Each dot in the figure represents a leader, and connecting lines denote a direct or indirect tie between them.[48] In South Shore, the ties among relevant actors are either absent, shown as "isolates" along the left (almost half of the entire set), or they collapse into one of three distinct "cliques" that are disconnected from each other. By contrast, in Hegewisch ties are very dense, with only three isolates and over 90 percent of leaders deeply embedded in an overlapping structure of ties. Chicago is composed of marked variations in structural configurations such as these, with consequences for key dimensions of city life, especially including political power and the allocation of resources (e.g., funds for economic development, parks, and cultural affairs).

As a further and distinctly contemporary example, figure 1.5 maps the distribution of income-adjusted Internet use in 2002 alongside the concentration of "bohemians" (artists and related workers, designers, actors, producers and directors, dancers and choreographers, musicians, singers, writers and authors, and photographers) in Chicago in 2000. The economist Richard Florida posits bohemians as a leading indicator of the "creative class," that group of intellectuals, writers, artists, and scientists who seek to live alongside other creative people.[49] According to Florida, the creative class is the driving engine for economic growth—one that is transforming work, leisure, and community. Whatever one makes of this causal claim about growth, figure 1.5 clearly reveals that they cluster together—cyberspace use and the creative class reflect residential sorting into distinct spatial communities. Like the other social phenomena considered so far, this concentration is highly nonrandom

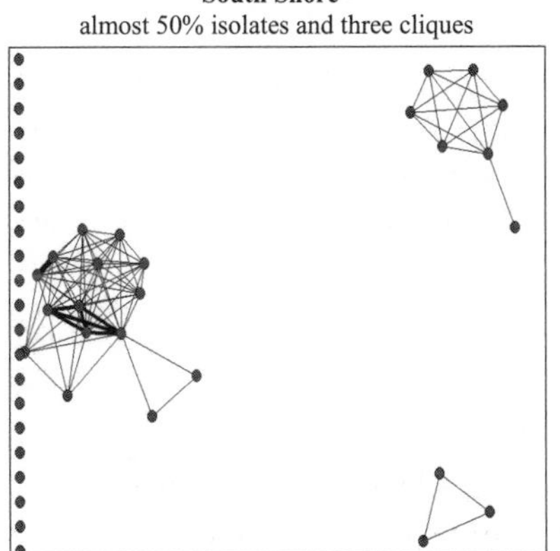

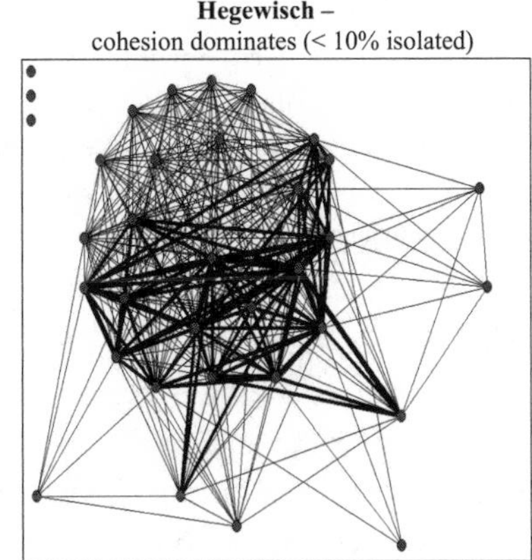

FIGURE 1.4. Community variation in network connectivity of leadership

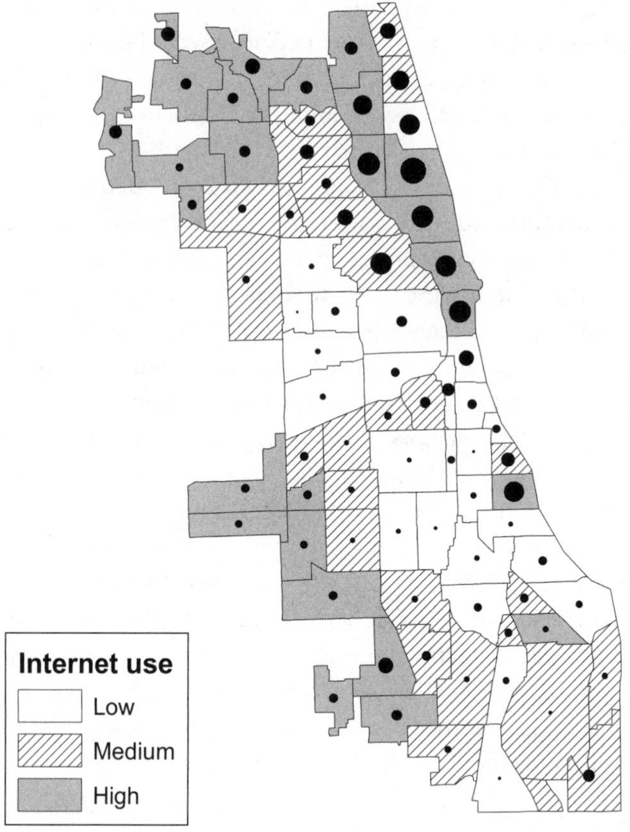

FIGURE 1.5. Local cosmopolitans: income-adjusted Internet use and "Bohemia." Communities classified in equal thirds according to Internet usage reported in 2001–2 community survey, from 0–9 percent (light), 9–17 percent (medium), and 17–50 percent (dark) using Internet more than five hours per week. Internet use rate adjusted for median income and median rent of the community in 2000. Circles proportional to "bohemians" per hundred thousand, defined as artists, designers, actors, producers and directors, dancers and choreographers, musicians, singers, writers and authors, and photographers.

and the story is not reducible to economics. One might worry about differential access to the Internet, for example, the so-called digital divide. But figure 1.5 shows the frequency of Internet use that is expected based on the community's income level and median rent. When we remove these economic correlates in further analysis, a persistent connection remains.[50] A form of cultural sorting appears to be present. Even the distribution of Starbucks in Chicago is similarly clustered and tracks closely the density of bohemians, perhaps much to their chagrin.[51]

A final example takes us out of the Windy City. Even though my earlier observations of neighborhood disparity and social distance by place reflect several dimensions, and despite the bird's-eye maps of the city thus far, the stubborn reader might still object that this is just a Chicago story. Or perhaps a peculiar "state" effect of American policy rather than a neighborhood effect.[52] So let us peek ahead and compare Chicago to an exemplar of modern efficiency, cultural sophistication, state planning, and cutting edge technology—Stockholm, Sweden. It is hard to imagine two cities more different than Chicago and Stockholm, not to mention the countries within which they are situated. Stockholm certainly doesn't have concentrated poverty the likes of Chicago, and more people are murdered in Chicago in a single year than over the last fifty years in Stockholm. But surprising similarities emerge despite the radical differences in state policies.

As an initial demonstration, I assess whether concentrated poverty is similarly related to violence, each defined the same way, in both cities. Figure 1.6 shows a similar decreasingly positive association of violence with disadvantage in both cities. To be sure, there are many more disadvantaged neighborhoods in Chicago, where the association with violence begins to tail off. There are also more concentrated *affluent* neighborhoods in Chicago as well (note the areas to the left of the graph). In this sense, figure 1.6 reflects "inequality compression" in Stockholm, characterized by restricted variation in disadvantage and lower violence. Indeed, Chicago "sits atop" Stockholm at virtually every level of disadvantage, and its extended range of concentrated disadvantage is pronounced. Yet as disadvantage rises, violence does as well in both cities in a nonlinear way, a distinct pattern unlikely to arise by chance.[53] Detailed research by Swedish criminologists further shows the concentration of homicides (albeit fewer in number, of course) in a disproportionately small number of neighborhoods, just like Chicago.[54]

These distinct ecological patterns provide a tantalizing hint that larger principles of societal organization, such as equality of housing and racial stratification, are etched in place and that they may explain city differences in violence. It remains to be seen how well this framework stands up to further tests, but it appears that there is something

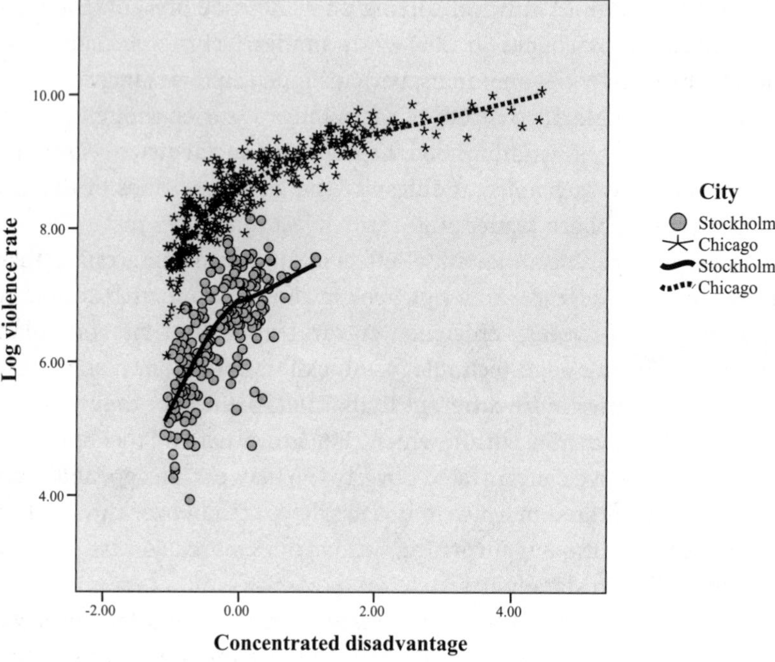

FIGURE 1.6. Similar prediction of violence rates by concentrated disadvantage in highly divergent contexts: Chicago and Stockholm neighborhoods

fundamental about place stratification and violence that cuts across international boundaries and yet is locally manifested in its distributional form. The larger point is that Chicago is not just a lens through which to view contemporary American cities; instead it can provide a platform for investigating cross-national or comparative questions as well. I will revisit Stockholm later in the book to explore other social characteristics and look to emerging research from Australia, England, and other countries for further patterns.

Thesis and Plan of This Book

Our walk through Chicago, layered with a bird's-eye empirical view, communicates with images the central thesis of this book. Despite globalization's march and plausible claims about the death of distance and place, neighborhood differentiation remains durable in American society. Any real estate agent will tell you that it is still about location, location, and location, but even for Starbucks what matters is location. Not only is this symbol of globalization concentrated in contemporary cities the world over, bad locations mean bad business and thus franchises are concentrated in particular parts of cities as well.[55] Social ecological differentiation is everywhere.

Fascination with globalization has tended to deflect attention from the persistence of local variation, concentration, and the spatial logic of inequality. The popular belief that the world is "flat," in particular, has clouded our thinking on neighborhood effects.[56] This is not to say that globalization theorists are wrong about economic markets or that the facts of ecological concentration are incompatible with the placelessness of many aspects of life. To the contrary, one strand of globalization theory suggests that, if anything, the reverse is true. As Manuel Castells puts it boldly, "most of New York, in fact most of Manhattan, is very local, not global."[57] The key to theoretical progress is to recognize that the stratification of people and resources across urban areas remains entrenched and evolves in new ways as globalization proceeds. Paradoxically, in fact, inequality among neighborhoods in life chances has increased in salience and may have been exacerbated by globalization.[58] As noted above and documented in chapter 2, the concept of community more generally also thrives despite the global turn.[59]

I thus reject the common idea that technology, dispersed social networks, state policy, and the accoutrements of (post)modernity explain away neighborhood inequality and a focus on spatial forms of social organization and community. The implication I draw instead is that the main storyline to be explored is *enduring neighborhood inequality* and the community-level manifestations of social change that persist and may be accelerating. In this sense I argue that a durable spatial logic organizes or mediates much of social life, with neighborhoods and local communities a key component. In so doing I expand the traditional definition of neighborhood effect: we react *to* neighborhood difference, and these reactions constitute social mechanisms and practices that in turn shape perceptions, relationships, and behaviors that reverberate both within and beyond traditional neighborhood borders, and which taken together further define the social structure of the city. As motivated by the images of this chapter, neighborhood effects are thus simultaneously local and extralocal in nature, and reciprocally related to individual actions.

At the broadest level, then, the present study is an effort to show that neighborhoods are not merely settings in which individuals act out the dramas produced by autonomous and preset scripts, or empty vessels determined by "bigger" external forces, but are important determinants of the quantity and quality of human behavior in their own right. It is, in other words, an effort to specify the structural and cultural dimensions of neighborhood effects. The term "effects" is meaningful in both verb and noun forms—at least in theory, neighborhood is consequence and cause, outcome and producer. In the following chapters I will expand on this theoretical claim through concepts and analyses that reveal the multiple layers of the neighborhood-effects picture.

The Nature of the Challenge

At this point the reader might plausibly ask: Neighborhood effects on what? Is it not impossibly broad to think of the social structure and spatial logic of the city? Here I must confess. Although I am not much of a TV watcher, an episode of *Seinfeld* came to mind in thinking about describing the content of the chapters to follow. In pitching their idea to TV network bureaucrats, Jerry and George blurted out the idea for their show—it was to be "about nothing." This book is nearly the opposite—it is more about everything, or at least almost everything social about the city. Admittedly this is still a tall order. Unlike the *Seinfeld* episode, this thought is more frightening than funny, possibly even foolhardy in that the division of labor in the academy is one of specialization. The common approach is to divide problems by disciplines that set a priori "master variables"—demographers study infant mortality and low birth weight, criminologists study crime, social movement researchers study protest events, medical sociologists and public health researchers study health, network aficionados study networks, political scientists study political participation and community power, and so on. When one starts with a set paradigm or variables, answers are often automatic.

I reject this approach by giving priority to the spatial nature and larger social ordering of the phenomena themselves rather than a prior commitment to the hypotheses of a single discipline or theory. Although in some sense radical, I seek an opportunity to draw together, in one analytic framework, the diversity of the contemporary city. This move requires me to transgress the narrow confines of disciplinary fields and canonical variables, and embrace instead a more holistic and systemic approach that gives priority to general social mechanisms and processes. It implies an empirical approach that will be pursued in later chapters, where I draw on demographic, criminological, organizational, social movement, cultural, network, and other perspectives to investigate how things "hang together," rather than only splitting them apart artificially. The goal of a "neighborhood-based" rather than variable-based approach is to understand the configuration of social dynamics and causal processes—the "everything" of the city. This is not just a Seinfeldian conceit; rather, the data introduced in this chapter show that any lesser motivation risks intellectual error. It is better to forge ahead and fail than to ignore the hard questions.

This book shows that a "kinds of people" or compositional explanation of neighborhood disparities and social processes that turns on individual selection fails to answer the questions. While taking individuals seriously, my approach focuses on social mechanisms and processes that are supraindividual in nature, perhaps even crossing cultural and societal boundaries as figure 1.6 suggests. This approach highlights a class of contextual questions. What, for example, accounts for the ecological stratification and social ordering by place of multiple and seemingly disparate phenomena like crime, collective civic engagement, the allocation of public goods, altruism, poor health, protest, and disorder? How do we account for neighborhood stability and social reproduction? What explains neighborhood change? What neighborhood factors best predict the civic health and wellbeing of citizens? How do individual choices combine to create social contexts that then constrain choices? In short, what are the social pathways by which neighborhood effects are transmitted in the contemporary city?

These are big questions, to be sure, but the data presented to this point motivate a sustained effort to provide answers. At the very least they undercut the common wisdom of placelessness and the death of distance by painting an initial picture of city life as a multidimensional mosaic. As Thomas Gieryn puts it, "social processes (difference, power, inequality, collective action) happen *through* the material forms that we design, build, use, and protest."[60] The goal of this book is to paint the big picture of a broad class of "neighborhood effects," accomplished through a systematic examination of the continuing (if not increasing) significance of place in a global and iconic American city.

Project on Human Development in Chicago Neighborhoods

To assess these arguments I present an integrated set of original data sources that I helped design in order to address the questions and puzzles highlighted in this chapter. The book's empirical base builds on a large-scale interdisciplinary study launched in the early 1990s—the Project on Human Development in Chicago Neighborhoods (PHDCN)—and continuing today in new forms. From its early planning phase to the present, the entire project was designed and carried out with a core theoretical idea in mind—to test neighborhood effects and developmental processes simultaneously, hence motivating the project's name. By embedding individuals in context, and insisting on the study of neighborhood context as a goal in its own right, the project, but especially this book, seeks to reject the increasing reductionist thrust of much of modern social science that starts and ends with individuals.[61] If the 1990s comprised the scientific "decade of the brain" with all the advances in neuroscience and genomics, maybe with a nudge from this book and the data produced from PHDCN we will look back on the early decades of the twenty-first century as the "era of context."

As described in more detail in the chapters to come, the PHDCN research enterprise consists of multiple interweaving approaches that include, among others:

- a longitudinal cohort study of 6,200 children and families followed wherever they moved in the United States over approximately seven years
- a representative community survey of more than 8,000 Chicago residents in 1995 and another survey in 2002 of over 3,000 residents
- a systematic social observational study (through videotaping) of more than 20,000 street segments in a sample of neighborhoods purposely chosen to vary by race/ethnicity and SES, along with a follow-up observational study by raters seven years later across the entire city

- a Network Panel Study of more than 2,800 key leaders in forty-seven communities, interviewed in 1995 and again in a 2002 follow-up of over 1,000 leaders
- a study of more than 4,000 collective action events in the Chicago metropolitan area from 1970 to 2000
- a "field experiment" in 2002 and 2010 designed to measure community-level differences in the propensity of people in public settings to mail back "lost letters"

These data sources were combined with archival records on health (e.g., mortality, birth weight, and teenage pregnancy), crime, violence, housing, organizations, and a wealth of population characteristics from the U.S. Census across several decades. I also spent many years observing and thinking about the city during my daily rounds, and I conducted interviews with community leaders up to 2008. The PHDCN and its several spin-offs represent a long-term commitment and collective investment of labor to a larger theoretical vision. That so many people stepped up to the plate and sacrificed considerable time and energy was no small feat, propelled largely by a shared vision of the importance of social context to our understanding of human development. Add to that a Chicago can-do attitude and the recipe for a study that many thought could never get off the ground was born—a "project on the make."[62]

Roadmap

Following this chapter's introduction of my theoretical orientation and proposed empirical solution to the problem, chapter 2 provides an assessment of the evolution of one of the book's animating ideas: *neighborhood effects*. This idea has considerable import for understanding PHDCN and the connections among multiple urban phenomena like those shown in the figures presented in this chapter. It also serves as the flashpoint for an ongoing debate in the social sciences over the proper unit of analysis—"micro" (individual) or "macro" emergent properties (such as neighborhood and nation)—and level of causal explanation. The idea of neighborhood effects is often confused in recent literature, not least by what seems to be a collective amnesia about the past and interference of a related idea: community. Chapter 2 corrects this oversight by commencing with the innovative work of European epidemiologists in the 1800s, reviewing key theoretical developments and empirical findings, and offering a historically situated analysis of how ecological approaches to the city evolved to the present day. Fortunately, there are many intellectual giants on whose shoulders I stand.

In part 2 I turn to the principles and methods that underlie the book's contribution. Chapter 3 builds on past research on neighborhood effects and community to articulate a theoretical and analytic approach to the study of the contemporary city. It lays bare the theoretical underpinnings that guided and continue to guide the PHDCN. Chapter 4 presents the making of PHDCN and its sequelae. Because of the central importance of the PHDCN to the book and its goal to provide data to the wider public for scholarly use, I provide an intellectual history of its origins along with details of the data collection and evolution of the project to its present-day form. Consistent with the idea that all data are theory, I thus subject the project itself, which was a huge undertaking, to a form of social analysis. In so doing I also answer head on the question of "Why Chicago?" Norman Mailer is only one in a long line of observers who have claimed Chicago as the great American city, but I argue that what is most important to this book are the corollary advantages that Chicago offers as a site of social science research and a platform on which to build a contextualized theory about contemporary urban life.

The guts of the empirical and theoretical contributions to this goal are found in parts 3 and 4. Part 3 focuses on social phenomena that vary across neighborhood and community levels of analysis ("side by side"), with a focus on social processes and mechanisms. Chapter 5 examines *legacies*—the surprising stability of neighborhood inequality across a diverse array of phenomena and across multiple decades, along with the systematic nature of change. Chapter 6 continues to probe the dynamics of inequality but with a new look at the powerful concept of *disorder* in recent urban discourse and social policy. Contrary to the influential "broken windows" theory that asserts disorder as a cause of crime, I probe the conditions under which disorder (and our perceptions of it) emerges. I take a cognitive turn, as it were, in thinking about how we observe the city, which in turn leads me to conceptualizing disorder as a key mechanism helping to explain why the stability of inequality described in chapter 5 is typically strong.

Chapter 7 begins with the classical concept of social disorganization promoted by the early Chicago School, an idea not far from disorder theory. However, I build on the legacy of disorganization theory and offer instead an elaboration of a newer concept—*collective efficacy*—defined as social cohesion combined with shared expectations for social control. I describe a measurement scheme for neighborhood-level processes—*ecometrics*—and analyze collective efficacy in multiple ways that extend beyond Chicago to Stockholm, Sweden, as a means of assessing its generality as a neighborhood concept. Chapter 8 lays out the *organizational* and civic dimensions of neighborhood effects and in the process one answer to the question of where collective efficacy comes from. The organizational side of the story has been largely neglected in neighborhood studies, but chapter 8 shows, as President Obama discovered in Hyde Park and earlier on the Far South Side of Chicago, that the organizational life of a community is central to our understanding of collective action and dimensions of community-level collective efficacy. I show how collective efficacy is formed and that it is related to a neighborhood's organizational history more than the makeup of its current residents. This chapter corresponds to a recent move to bring organizations back into the picture of urban studies.[63]

I conclude part 3 of the book with a consideration of justice, social altruism, and the "good community." Once we grant that neighborhoods and community reflect a fundamental feature of urban social organization, it behooves the social scientist to think about how or whether they better humanity and contribute to the common good. In chapter 9 I thus explore philosophical notions of the good community and how they might connect to the empirical findings of the book. To ground the argument, I examine novel data on other-regarding behavior linked to social mechanisms of collective efficacy derived from previous chapters. Informed by the philosophy of John Rawls, I argue that the provision of CPR to heart attack victims and the mailing of lost letters constitute an unambiguous public good, albeit one that varies systematically across place and that constitutes a fundamental part of a community's social character. This framework provides a way to conceptualize and operationalize the good community, its interrelated parts, and its structural antecedents. Key features of neighborhood social structure introduced in prior chapters contribute to the altruistic character of a community and thus wellbeing.

Part 4 moves beyond "local" neighborhood-level processes to explore interlocking mechanisms that knit together, or keep apart, the varied segments of the American city. I begin in chapter 10 by recasting the findings of the previous chapters in spatially informed ways, beginning with the concept of *spatial interdependence*. I show that for many important social processes, what happens in one neighborhood is tightly connected to adjacent neighborhoods, creating a "ripplelike" effect that encompasses the entire city. Moreover, using new methods, I am able to show how some social processes work differently in different spatial areas of the city, creating a form of spatial heterogeneity of causal processes. Spatial spillover and heterogeneity provide insights on how regimes of spatial advantage and disadvantage are reinforced.

The next three chapters push the logic further by analyzing the sources and consequences of residential mobility. The movement of individuals across neighborhoods over time is quite prevalent and a crucial part of how the social structure of the city is created and inequality reproduced. Chapter 11 revisits the influential Moving to Opportunity (MTO) housing experiment in Chicago that randomly assigned vouchers to families that subsidized moving to low-poverty neighborhoods. I show what happened to these families and how the experiment reshapes our understanding of the social reproduction of inequality. Unlike in the movies, trading places takes on new meaning in a stratified metropolis because opportunities are predefined by a larger structure and not just individual choices. Individual moves also transform the social context—in this case the treatment itself. I compare the moves of the MTO participants to the PHDCN as well and find surprising commonalities in basic processes of residential mobility.

Chapter 12 expands the PHDCN analysis to the sources and consequences of residential mobility. I examine not only race and social class but how previously unexplored factors such as an individual's depression and criminality shape residential mobility and have a bearing on hypotheses about "drift" and neighborhood selection on vulnerability. Results on upward and downward mobility do not conform to standard accounts that emphasize individual choice. Moving itself is also shown to have detrimental consequences depending on the larger geographical location of the destination and not just the internal neighborhood characteristic.

In chapter 13, I push the logic a notch higher by considering the structure of residential mobility as a key mechanism that lies behind urban stratification and hierarchies of place. I do so by examining neighborhood networks of residential exchange that are produced by individual mobility. Analyzing dyadic relations among neighborhoods in the citywide networks of residential migration, I find that similarity in social processes such as perceived disorder and friend/kinship ties predict interneighborhood connections beyond the more standard sorting mechanisms of racial composition and income. In chapters 11 through 13, *selection is a social process* with emergent outcomes. My ultimate argument is thus that selection is not a "bias" but rather part and parcel of a dynamic social process—another form of neighborhood effect.

The last contribution in part 4, chapter 14, examines organizational and political networks among elites that cut across community boundaries in ways that go beyond spatial proximity, helping to explain the larger structural context of how resources and information are differentially allocated by place. I create new measures of *elite social networks* that can be compared across time, community, and type of organizational domain (e.g., politics, law, and education), allowing me to examine networks not just as a metaphor but as a property of communities that defines both their internal structure (e.g., the cohesion of ties within a community) and location in the wider social structure (e.g., the centrality of contacts of a given neighborhood in the citywide playing field). I show that leadership networks to key actors vary widely across communities and are not determined simply by material resources or composition, but the nature of shared expectations and social cohesiveness. Both internal characteristics and external ties that differentially connect communities to the outside world thus matter. Importantly, I also examine how spatial networks of neighborhood residential exchange defined in chapter 13 are linked to the informational and organizational networks created by community elites. They are directly related in a way not explained by internal composition, providing a crucial piece of evidence on the previously hidden ways that the American city is structurally interconnected.

Part 5 concludes the book with an eye to present and future implications. In chapter 15, I revisit the core theoretical principles laid out in chapter 3 and synthesize the analysis in chapters 5–14. I do so by highlighting the guiding ideas that tie together the individual chapters and that taken together define the book's contributions. Drawing on the book as a whole I also take a unifying stance on social inquiry that motivates a pragmatic understanding of "contextual causality" in a way that respects but is not subordinated to individual choice. The logic of social inquiry cannot be divorced from the nature of how the social world works, which means ultimately a change in how we construct and evaluate explanations. I thus offer the foundations of a theory of neighborhood effects and the city, with implications for the development of a contextual social science.

I then return in chapter 16 to the streets and neighborhoods encountered in this introduction. Not only do I revisit the same places in 2010, I collect new data from communities across the city in an effort to examine how the social organization and structure of Chicago has changed (or not) after the economic crisis of 2008 and the massive public-housing transformation that occurred in the middle part of the decade. I combine my personal observations and community-level variations gathered in 2010 to ground the more abstract concepts that I analyzed in empirical depth with the PHDCN for the years leading up to the social "shocks" that Chicago and other cities faced in 2008–9. I show that in multiple domains—including housing foreclosures, violence, poverty, and altruism—the neighborhood social ordering of Chicago endures, helping us better understand how external or "outside" forces are mediated by context and experienced on the ground.

Chapter 17 completes the story based on multiple returns to the most famous contrast of all, the twenty-first-century Gold Coast and slum of Zorbaugh's Near North Side. Here the multiple meanings and mechanisms of this book take palpable form and provide insight into the future of the American city. Equally important, they suggest novel directions for community-level (and higher) interventions that counteract the individual-level dominance of current policy. I thus hope that the alternative ideas of this book provide the motivation for the next generation of research and policy on neighborhoods, the city, and human behavior generally understood.

2 Neighborhood Effects

The Evolution of an Idea

While the twenty-first-century city has been declared spatially liberated, I argue that it remains place-based in much of its character. As chapter 1 contends, social science needs revised conceptual approaches and methodologies to chart this reality. In this book I attempt to meet the challenge, taking as my laboratory the social landscape and continued vitality of Chicago and guided by the inspiration of more than a century of careful scholarship.

The reader will be forgiven for suspecting my approach is in important respects a descendant of the well-known "Chicago School" of urban sociology, which many triumphantly consider dead.[1] There are now LA Schools, NY Schools, French schools, the "new urban sociology" that originated in the 1970s, and undoubtedly more to come. Now is not the time to review claims of intellectual supremacy. Besides, Chicago was not even the first to seriously engage the idea of neighborhood effects, and I agree with Harvey Molotch's exasperated reaction—"School's Out"—to a recent Chicago-LA School shootout.[2] My position is that there are many nuggets of insight worth preserving from our intellectual predecessors and that the goal should be to transcend tradition rather than view it as something to flee altogether. What matters is not whether a theoretical approach is old or new (or what "school" it belongs to) but whether it is productive for the question at hand. I thus discard what proved to be clearly wrong in the old Chicago School of urban sociology but preserve its key insights and draw upon newer schools and paradigms (e.g., political economy, social networks) when they are clearly right for the task. I also strive to recognize the changing nature of the city in global (or cyber) society in ways that take advantage of modern technology to collect new forms of data on community.

Although many publications have told the "Chicago School Story," the threads have not been connected to the main plot in a systematic way that derives productive implications rather than just criticism. As a result I aim for breadth rather than depth about the Chicago School, painting it in broad strokes with an eye toward highlighting the long-term evolution of intellectual thought about neighborhood effects and extracting principles for moving forward.[3] Although historical exegesis is not my goal, getting the sequence of facts right is central to any social inquiry. It helps that the facts are interesting and, for the pre–Chicago School history, often neglected. As one set of authors put it more generally (over seventy years ago), "The enthusiasm of social scientists often leads them to attribute greater originality to contemporary studies and less value to the old than is actually warranted by the facts in the case."[4] I thus begin the journey overseas where pioneers in criminology and epidemiology set the stage for modern social inquiry into the city.

Origins

The ecological concentration of a broad sweep of human conduct and general wellbeing has a venerable history that predates Chicago's founding. Contextualized approaches appear to have originated with social statisticians intrigued by crime patterns. In 1833 André-Michel Guerry published *Essai sur la Statistique Morale de la France* and the cartographic method of presenting the statistical distribution of crime. Using judicial statistics based on the quarterly returns of the local public prosecutors, Guerry was one of the first researchers to empirically document the variation in crime rates within a country. Contrary to the then prevailing assumption derived from the notion of individual free will—that crime was randomly distributed—Guerry demonstrated that crime and other social behaviors occurred disproportionately in certain areas and at certain times. Guerry also analyzed the distribution of crime among geographical units (administrative departmental units) in relation to what are now standard sociological variables, such as education, income, urbanization, and density. He found that units with the greatest concentration of manufacturing industries had the highest rate of property crime. Like Durkheim, Guerry's inquiry aimed to demonstrate that social facts influenced human behavior independent of individual biology and psychology. Guerry's quantification of social data and ecological analysis served as a stepping stone for ecological researchers of the twentieth century, earning him the title of "the first of the social ecologists."[5]

Adolph Quetelet followed in Guerry's tradition and expanded the use of statistics to analyze differences in crime type between France, Belgium, and the Netherlands. Quetelet found that the greatest number of convictions for crime occurred in Southern France and in the southern part of Belgium and the Netherlands.[6] Like Guerry, Quetelet found that there was a stronger "le penchant au crime" (propensity to crime) against persons in Southern France and a stronger propensity to crime against property in Northern France. Quetelet interpreted his data as supporting the concept of "social physics," which was a milestone in the theory of sociological ecology according to Morris.[7] Although Quetelet's ideas are probably better known than Guerry's, Quetelet was only marginally interested in the study of the spatial relations of people and institutions within a given habitat. Still, both Quetelet and Guerry were able to demonstrate in convincing fashion that crime was not a randomly distributed phenomenon but rather was concentrated disproportionately in the same areas over time.

Rawson shifted Guerry and Quetelet's geographical focus of analysis from France to the distribution of crime in England and Wales. He argued that since "the employments of the people exert the most important influence upon their physical condition,"[8] occupation should be an important determinant of their moral and social character. Dividing counties of England and Wales into four occupational types (agricultural, manufacturing, mining, and metropolitan London workers) on the basis of the 1831 census, Rawson found that crime prevailed to the greatest extent in metropolitan occupational areas. He found a low incidence of crime in the small mining counties and the mountainous districts of Northern England and Wales, and no differences in the crime rates between manufacturing and agricultural counties. Rawson's strategy was one of the first examples of the typological approach in ecological analysis, which resurfaced over a century later in what came to be known as "social area analysis."

As impressive as the work of these scholars was, a major turning point in the study of the nineteenth-century city came in the form of now classic works in London by Henry Mayhew[9] and Charles Booth.[10] Both scholars provided detailed documentation and early visual portrayals of the neighborhood context of multiple indicators of "pathology." In the same vein as Clifford Shaw's *The Jack-Roller*,[11] Mayhew provides a unique picture of London in its historical and ecological setting. Based on scores of interviews and ecological analysis, Mayhew claimed that crime was learned and passed down in areas characterized by poverty, drunkenness, bad housing, and economic insecurity.[12] Mayhew foreshadows the idea of "cultural transmission" put forth later by Shaw and Henry McKay, who documented the transmission of delinquent values across generations in areas characterized by social disorganization.[13] Mayhew also linked the incidence of crime to the opportunities that areas characterized by taverns and lodging houses afforded thieves and prostitutes. In effect, he called for studies of crime to focus on the ecological distribution of environmental opportunities that are presented to potential offenders.

Booth's empirical efforts were even more impressive and stand the test of time in terms of methodological detail and multimethod inquiry of social context. Indeed, perusing the many volumes of *Life and Labor of the People of London* is both a humbling and invigorating experience. Well before the advances offered by modern research technology, Booth painstakingly captured the wide ecological variability that Dickens's London offered up. The Booth collection holds more than four hundred original notebooks from his surveys and observations, which include detailed assessment of the environments in which Londoners lived, as well as interviews with policemen on their beats, factory owners, ministers, and a diversity of city dwellers. Booth's *Inquiry* mapped poverty and wealth street by street.[14] It is worth noting as well that the oft-cited discovery of the etiology of cholera in London by the physician John Snow in the 1850s was inextricably intertwined with mapping the ecological unfolding of the disease.[15] Taken together Booth and Snow represent an early example of neighborhood logic in action.

The Green Bible (a.k.a. *Introduction to the Science of Sociology*)

Although a social-ecological approach to cities flourished in Victorian London, the approach of sociologists at the University of Chicago brought neighborhood-centered research to the fore of the discipline during the early twentieth century. This is one of the most well-known turning points in sociology and, more generally, social science research.

Before World War I and well into the twenties, Robert Park, Ernest Burgess, and a number of their students took to the streets to investigate the ecological contexts of a wide range of social behavior.[16] The famous concentric zone map, with its central business district forming the core of an expanding city, still fascinates and adorns the seminar room to this day at the University of Chicago. The "Green Bible" of Park and Burgess served as a touchstone to generations of scholars.[17] The Chicago School proposed that cities were divided into numerous functioning "natural areas," which exhibit distinct physical and cultural characteristics. Park's human ecological framework focused on the interaction between the processes of human nature and the "metes and bounds" set by the physical geography of the city.[18] Familiar ecological terms such as *competition*, *invasion*, *succession*, *segregation*, and *symbiosis* stemmed from his analysis of the interrelations between the biotic and cultural levels of community. The concentric zone map derived from Burgess's hypothesis that social differentiation in cities was expressed ecologically as a radial expansion from the business district outward.[19]

Clifford Shaw, one of the most noted criminologists of the twentieth century, operated within the theoretical framework of Park and Burgess. The ideas put forth by Park and Burgess and a group of largely unsung social workers[20] set the stage for the publication of Shaw's *Delinquency Areas*, in which he proposed that "the study of such a problem as juvenile delinquency necessarily begins with a study of its geographical location."[21] To accomplish this, Shaw studied the distribution of delinquent boys and girls brought before the Juvenile Court of Cook County from 1900 to 1927. He utilized basic statistics to measure the delinquency rate (ratio between the number of delinquents and the total population of the same sex and age groups) and was one of the first American sociological researchers to demonstrate the marked variations within a major city. With his later associate Henry McKay, Shaw showed that the highest delinquency rates in Chicago were located in deteriorated zones in transition next to the central business and industrial district. Rates of delinquency decreased as distance from the center of the city increased, the exceptions being areas also characterized by industry and commerce. These findings led Shaw and McKay to conclude that delinquent behavior was closely related to the growth processes of the city as outlined in Park and Burgess's masterwork, *The City*.

Community environments were a focus of early research in the field of epidemiology as well, with an exemplar found in the early twentieth-century research of Joseph Goldberger and his colleagues on the vitamin deficiency known as pellagra.[22] In a study of the distribution of pellagra in cotton-mill villages of the South, Goldberger and colleagues found that its contraction was related not only to individual-level socioeconomic status but also to the availability of nutritional foods in villages. They amassed an impressive array of both individual- and village-level data relating to food supply and malnutrition that included village-level measures of the prevalence of retail grocery establishments and home-provided foods, and contrasts in the type of agriculture in farm areas surrounding the villages. Their study also provided early evidence of an interaction between individual- and community-level health risks: in villages with fewer supplies of nutritious food, family income was "less efficient as a protective factor than in other similar localities with better conditions of food availability."[23] Goldberger's work was widely influential and illustrative of a much broader tradition of epidemiological research on the ecological context of health that dates back to the early nineteenth century. His work stands as testament to the fact that the clustering of disease and the notion of "concentration effects" have long been with us even if their significance has been neglected.[24] Neighborhood effects on health have been rediscovered and now make up a booming area of research.[25]

Social Disorganization Theory

In their major work published in 1942, *Juvenile Delinquency and Urban Areas*, Shaw and McKay extended Park and Burgess's ecological theory of cities to include neighborhood characteristics and mediating social factors to explain their importance. They identified low economic status foremost, but ethnic heterogeneity and also residential instability as the three consistent predictors of delinquency rates. They discovered that high rates of delinquency in Chicago persisted in low-income, heterogeneous (usually immigrant) areas over many years. Moreover, the same Chicago neighborhoods characterized by poverty, residential instability, and high rates of crime and delinquency were also plagued by high rates of infant mortality, low birth weight, tuberculosis, physical abuse, and other factors detrimental to child development. Shaw and McKay argued that delinquency "is not an isolated phenomenon"[26] and went on to document the close association of delinquency rates with a host of social problems.

In a similar vein, Robert E. L. Faris and H. Warren Dunham[27] applied the ecological idea to mental health, showing that areas in transition with high rates of poverty had higher rates of hospitalization for mental disorders. Like Shaw and McKay, Faris and Dunham observed that high rates of adverse outcomes tended to persist in the same communities over time, despite the movement of different population groups through them. The teamwork of Faris and Dunham and Shaw and McKay formed the precursor to the general conceptual point and supporting maps shown by Drake and Cayton in *Black Metropolis* several years later.[28]

Guided by these findings, the Chicago School sociologists asserted that neighborhoods possess relatively enduring features and emergent properties that transcend the idiosyncratic characteristics of particular ethnic groups that inhabit them. Shaw and McKay specifically argued that criminal behavior was transmitted intergenerationally in neighborhoods characterized by "social disorganization." The concept of social disorganization was defined as the inability of a community to realize the common values of its residents and maintain effective social controls.[29] This definition later came to be operationalized in so-called systemic terms—that is, the disorganized community was viewed as suffering from a disrupted or weakened system of friendship, kinship, and acquaintanceship networks, which were seen as crucial for ongoing processes of socialization.[30] Poverty, heterogeneity, and rapid population turnover were also thought by social disorganization theorists to reflect at the neighborhood level the larger processes of urbanization, industrialization, and social change emphasized by fellow Chicago School theorists such as Wirth. These neighborhood-level dynamics were thought to undermine personal ties, voluntary associations, and local institutions, which in turn were hypothesized to weaken the infrastructure necessary for socialization and social control, thus eventually leading to outcomes such as crime, delinquency, homelessness, and educational dropout. In this way the Chicago School theorists attempted to trace how macrolevel forces worked their way down to the local level in terms of community-level processes of social control and regulation.[31]

The theory of social disorganization did not go unchallenged. In *Street Corner Society*, William F. Whyte famously argued in 1943 that what looks like social disorganization from the outside is actually an internal organization.[32] He discovered through extensive fieldwork an intricate pattern of social ties embedded within the social structure of the low-income Italian area of Boston's North End; there were organized gangs and an integration of illegal markets with the routines of everyday life. Noting the relative nature of organization in the community, he maintained that the real problem of "Cornerville" was that its social organization failed to mesh with the larger structure of society around it. Whyte's research came to be seen as a repudiation of the prevalent theory that slum communities were inherently "disorganized." A bit later, circa the 1950s and 1960s, ethnographic research discovered thriving urban communities and ethnic enclaves where kinship and friendship solidarities flourished.[33] Especially in poor urban neighborhoods, the evidence of dense social networks and local identification remained strong.[34]

Despite these criticisms, social disorganization theory survived and was even revitalized in later years, or reinvented, some might say, by the popular idea of "social capital." Although there are many definitions of the term, social capital is typically conceptualized as a resource embodied in the social ties among persons—networks, norms, and trust.[35] The connection of social disorganization to social capital theory was articulated by Robert Bursik to mean that neighborhoods lacking social capital, indicated by depleted social networks, are less able to realize common values and maintain the social controls that foster safety and efforts to promote social goods.[36] Dense social ties thus play a key role in both social capital and disorganization theory. Perusing recent works on social capital reveals little that was not said in slightly different language by sociologists of the city from the birth of the discipline onward. Also like social disorganization, social capital as a concept has come under attack but continues to influence research on neighborhood effects.[37]

I will revisit some of these issues in chapter 7, but for now I would claim that what makes the Chicago School framework of the pre–World War II era of continued relevance to the study of neighborhoods is less its specific emphasis on disorganization (or, later, social capital) and more (a) its general emphasis on the characteristics of *places* rather than *people*, (b) its emphasis on neighborhood-level structural differentiation, (c) its notion of what we would now call "mediating social mechanisms," (d) its focus on the concentration of multiple and seemingly disparate social phenomena, (e) its emphasis on the importance of dynamic processes of social reproduction over time, and (f) its recognition of larger macrosocial forces. One can admit to a concern over the concept of disorganization (which I do) while appreciating this broader Chicago School outlook.

Post-War Challenges

Theoretical work on neighborhoods leveled off and declined after the retirement of the Chicago School leaders and Whyte's seminal critique. An empirical stumbling block also appeared at midcentury in the form of Robinson's famous critique of the "ecological fallacy."[38] Robinson argued that individual-level relationships could not be accurately inferred from aggregate or ecological correlations. The main example he used was literacy rates and percent foreign born, where the state-level correlation was opposite (positive) that of individuals (negative). A backlash followed against ecological research, but for misleading reasons. Robinson's mistake, and that of many readers, was to assume that ecological researchers only cared about individual-level inferences. Rather than arguing against ecological or neighborhood-level research, the right message was to make clear distinctions among units of analysis and to appropriately frame analytical questions, an early version of what we now call "multilevel" analysis. It follows that if the main goal is to explain *rates of variation* across neighborhoods rather than individual differences, Robinson's critique does not hold. Moreover, worry about the ecological fallacy distracted attention from the "individualistic fallacy"—the often-invoked and also erroneous assumption that individual-level relations are sufficient to explain collective outcomes.

Despite the Robinson detour, empirical research in the mid-twentieth century documented the continuing ecological differentiation of American cities in the Chicago School tradition. In an influential work of this period, Eshref Shevky and Wendell Bell developed three constructs to reflect social differentiation and stratification in urban, industrial society: social rank, urbanization/family status, and segregation.[39] Using government census tracts as units of analysis, *social rank* was measured by the configuration of occupation, education, and rent; *urbanization/family status* by single-family versus multiple-dwelling units, fertility, and female labor force participation; and *segregation* by the proportions of racial and ethnic groups living in relative isolation. Typologies based on this scheme came to be known as "social area analysis," reflecting the idea that social stratification was manifested in geographical areas. Although criticized for reasons that go beyond present concerns, many other independent studies of American cities during this postwar period largely confirmed the Chicago School prediction that spatial differentiation occurs along dimensions of socioeconomic, family, and ethnic status.[40]

Political Economy of Place and the State

Another important objection to the Chicago School model, circa 1970 onward, turns on the idea that neighborhoods are deeply shaped by extralocal processes having their roots in economic and political structures. Ecological conceptualizations of the black ghetto as a naturally occurring phenomenon came under withering criticism.

It is hard to overemphasize the early influence of the notion of a "natural area" that conceived neighborhoods as dynamic, adaptive systems driven by free-market competition that existed between businesses for land use and population groups for affordable and desirable housing.[41] Borrowing concepts from Darwinian theory, Park and Burgess focused on the "balance of nature" and argued that natural forces were responsible for the initial distribution, concentration, and segregation of urban populations.

In the 1970s a Marxian approach to the urban question, often called the new urban sociology, was launched by scholars such as Manual Castells, David Harvey and Mark Gottdiener.[42] At around the same time the "political economy of place" perspective emerged, culminating in the work of John Logan and Harvey Molotch.[43] These interventions repudiated market-based assumptions and the biotic model, arguing that the Chicago School paradigm ignored capitalistic production and political forces beyond the borders of the local community. From this view, neighborhood inequality in American cities is shaped directly and indirectly by the logic of capital accumulation and the "growth machine" of the city, especially the collusion of public officials and businesses. Structural or institutional racism was also implicated in the persistence of racial segregation, a direct critique of the spatial assimilation model of the Chicago School that seemed to imply that ethnic ghettoes were temporary and thus that the black ghetto would disappear.

The political economy story was powerful. It claimed that the decline and rebirth of many central-city neighborhoods in the postwar era was facilitated not only by individual preferences or voluntary migration, but by incentives for suburban growth in the form of tax breaks for developers and private mortgage assistance, highway construction and urban renewal, economic disinvestment (or not) in central cities, and zoning restrictions on land use.[44] For example, consider public housing and the legacy of urban renewal in the crucial period of inner-city decline. Bursik has shown that the construction of new public-housing projects in Chicago in the 1970s was associated with increased rates of population turnover, which in turn predicted increases in crime independent of the area's population composition.[45] Wesley Skogan argued that urban renewal and forced migration contributed to the wholesale uprooting of many urban communities; a good example is how freeway networks driven through the center of many cities in the 1960s destroyed viable, low-income neighborhoods.[46] The state has also been posited as a causal force through the differential provision by government of city services, public housing, and human welfare resources to some and not other neighborhoods. Loïc Wacquant's comparative analysis of American black urban ghettos (typified by those on the west and south sides of Chicago) and French banlieues maintained that the decline of American urban centers after the 1960s is explained by the withdrawal of state resources, or "desertification."[47]

Thus with the purposeful segregation of low-income public housing, withdrawal of needed services, government subsidized development by the private sector, zoning, red-lining, blockbusting, or something so simple yet powerfully symbolic as gated communities with no sidewalks, it is no longer possible to think of neighborhoods as purely natural areas created by the aggregation of individual preferences alone. Government, business, and the wider political economy along with processes of place stratification thus matter to our understanding of what communities can and cannot supply. So too do globalization and international forces such as migration. From this view, neighborhoods may be seen as mediating extralocal social forces. This does not mean that neighborhoods lose analytic value any more than individuals do in an interconnected world. It means that they take on a more complex, situated role and that our job is to examine both the internal and articulating mechanisms that tie neighborhoods to the larger social order. The next intellectual intervention made such an attempt.

The Truly Disadvantaged and "Concentration Effects"

In the latter part of the twentieth century, highly visible publications brought neighborhood-based research to the forefront once more. This time there was an even clearer focus on macrolevel forces that the early Chicago school researchers had tended to gloss. The best-known effort to accommodate the large-scale social changes seen in the latter decades of the twentieth century is William Julius Wilson's notion of the "concentration effects" that arise from living in a neighborhood that is overwhelmingly impoverished.[48] *The Truly Disadvantaged* marks another turning point in the study of neighborhood effects after the classic studies of Victorian London, the paradigmatic intervention of the Chicago School, and the political economy critique.[49]

Wilson argued that the social transformation of inner-city areas in the decades of the 1970s and '80s resulted in an increased concentration of the most disadvantaged segments of the urban black population—especially poor, female-headed families with children. The consequences of these various ecological distributions are profound because they mean that relationships between race and individual outcomes are systematically confounded with important differences in community contexts (in fact, chapter 5 will demonstrate the virtual absence of white low-income communities, not just in Chicago but nationwide). Wilson argued that this racialized concentration of poverty and joblessness resulted from macrostructural economic changes related to the deindustrialization of central cities where low-income minorities were disproportionately located.[50] These changes include a shift from goods-producing to service-producing industries, the increasing polarization of the labor market into low-wage and high-wage sectors, and the relocation of manufacturing out of the inner city, all of which can be linked to global economic trends. According to Wilson, the exodus of middle- and upper-income black families from the inner city also removed an important social buffer that could potentially deflect the full impact of prolonged joblessness and industrial transformation.[51] The increasing stratification among blacks differed significantly from the environment that existed in inner-city neighborhoods in previous decades. Wilson argued that income mixing within communities was more characteristic of ghetto neighborhoods during previous decades, whereas inequality among communities today has become more pronounced as a result of the increasing spatial separation of middle- and upper-income blacks from lower-income blacks.[52] The result was the "social isolation" of the ghetto poor from mainstream America.[53]

Douglas Massey and Nancy Denton picked up the thread of Wilson's work in 1993, but focused on racial segregation as a primary causal variable.[54] They describe how increasing social differentiation caused by economic dislocation interacts with the spatial concentration of a minority group to create a set of structural circumstances that reinforce the effects of social and economic deprivation. In a segregated environment, economic shocks that cause a downward shift in the distribution of minority income not only bring about an increase in the poverty rate for the group as a whole but also cause an increase in the geographic concentration of poverty. This geographic intensification of poverty occurs because the additional poverty created by macroeconomic conditions is spread unevenly over the metropolitan area.[55] Thus the greater the segregation, "the smaller the number of neighborhoods absorbing the shock, and the more severe the resulting concentration of poverty."[56] Segregation by race and poverty, then, is the key causal force in Massey's conceptual scheme. Along with *The Truly Disadvantaged*, *American Apartheid* stands out as one of the dominant pieces of scholarship at the closing of the twentieth century. Although these books posited different causal mechanisms, both were powerful statements on neighborhood effects.[57]

The Ideology of Community Lament

No discussion of neighborhood effects can be complete without confronting the concept of "community." Across the entire history of intellectual thought about neighborhoods, a persistent refrain has been what Robert Nisbet aptly described in the mid-twentieth century as the "ideology of lament"—a widespread concern that something essential had been irrevocably lost by the apparent shredding of community bonds.[58] As introduced in chapter 1, the notion of "community lost" has morphed over time to take on different forms but the basic message is seemingly always the same: community is in decline and must be recovered.

Today, lamentation for community lost is as strong as ever but with a twist. Calls for a return to community values and neighborhood governance have been voiced across an unusually diverse spectrum. Whether from elite politicians on the Left or Right, local government officials, communitarians, private foundations, real estate developers, or social scientists, the appeals to community have been many. For example, the move to community-based approaches has penetrated broadly in the foundation world and criminal justice policy, from well-known efforts to increase community policing to community-based prosecution policies and community corrections.[59] Although it is not surprising that philanthropic foundations have embraced community as an ideal, real estate developers are also on board. Taking heed of modern discontent with suburban sprawl and anonymity, the "new urbanism" has promoted visions of architecture that promote neighborliness, local interaction, and common physical space in an attempt to restore elements of community.[60] Even the World Bank has adopted concepts of community and social capital to alleviate poverty around the globe.[61] The communitarian perspective also landed at both the Clinton and second Bush White Houses, and themes of community organization serve as a backdrop to the Obama administration.[62]

Whatever the ultimate source, once again in our intellectual history there has emerged a widespread belief that a return to "community" is needed.[63] Indeed, the appeal of community has never lapsed, and the idea of a shared vision and collective approach to solving human problems is a deeply social yearning. The problem is that much of the discussion around community is normative and nostalgic rather than analytic, impeding progress on how research should proceed.[64] Thus despite widespread interest across multiple disciplines, the nature, sources, and consequences of community in contemporary society remain ambiguous and largely disconnected from serious inquiry. Appropriation of social capital and communitarian ideals, for example, tends to romanticize the idea of community rather than pose hard questions subject to empirical scrutiny. If community has come to mean everything good, as a concept it loses its analytical bite and therefore means little.

We must also be careful to incorporate the possibility of a darker side to communal life and reflect on empirical evidence that a generation of community-building efforts came up empty-handed.[65] In particular, what do we stand to lose by a return to community and the idea of "community organizing" and control—what does such a communal life potentially *deny*?[66] As Thomas Sugrue's research on postwar Detroit has taught us, neighborhood associations, while often a force for good, were nonetheless exploited by whites to forcibly keep blacks from moving into white working-class areas by resorting to arson, threats, and violence.[67] This is not what communitarians mean by neighborhood cohesion. Justice and inequality must in the end be part of discussions of the idea of community (chapter 9). Put differently, the shared content of what passes through social networks matters as much as their structural configuration—cohesion or efficacy cannot be "read off" from the simple density of networks.

Ultimately, then, the equation of neighborhood with traditional community has done the field a disservice, for with this equation neighborhoods seem to have declined by definition. As described in chapter 3, by taking an alternative approach we can escape prior traps of community ideology yet retain what is most relevant—variability in the spatial social organization of everyday life. With this move neighborhoods have not declined by definitional fiat; moreover, aspects of what we think of as community are variable over time and space and, depending on the problem, still conceptually relevant. As I will later argue, shared understandings constitute a major aspect of community that need not be about private ties and therefore can be analytically applied in the contemporary city.

Neighborhood Effects at the Turn of the Twenty-First Century

By the dawn of the twenty-first century the literature on neighborhood effects was enormous. When my colleagues and I attempted a comprehensive review circa 2000 we discovered hundreds of studies and since then hundreds more have appeared.[68] It was impossible to review them all then and would be even more so now. We did, however, summarize in broad form a core set of themes that have emerged—what we termed "neighborhood facts": *first*, there is considerable social inequality between neighborhoods, especially in terms of socioeconomic position and racial/ethnic segregation. *Second*, these factors are connected in that concentrated disadvantage often coincides with the geographic isolation of racial minority and immigrant groups. *Third*, a number of crime- and health-related problems tend to come bundled together at the neighborhood level *and* are predicted by neighborhood characteristics such as the concentration of poverty, racial isolation, single-parent families, and to a lesser extent rates of residential and housing instability. *Fourth*, a number of social indicators at the upper end of what many would consider progress, such as affluence, computer literacy, and elite occupational attainment, are also clustered geographically (as shown in chapter 1).[69] I think this broad characterization still stands.

While these facts may seem relatively straightforward and noncontroversial, their theoretical implications are not. The reason is that while the urban ecological tradition has yielded a treasure trove of correlates and the knowledge base of facts is considerable, the social mechanisms and dynamic processes accounting for neighborhood effects have remained largely a black box. We have known for at least a hundred years the demographic correlates of all sorts of community indicators of general wellbeing, especially the aggregated characteristics of individuals. But by focusing on correlates of outcomes at the level of community social composition—most notably poverty and fixed categories of race—prior research has tended toward a risk-factor rather than an explanatory approach. Why, to take the most notable example of the past several decades, does concentrated poverty (which is, after all, the concentration of poor *people*) matter? Wilson has promoted the idea of social isolation as a social process mediating the effects of concentrated poverty, while others have emphasized moral cynicism and the erosion of collective efficacy. Consistent with the original Chicago School, the larger idea is that if neighborhood effects are not merely the reflection of individual characteristics then presumably they stem from social-interactional and institutional processes that involve collective aspects of community—emergent properties, in other words.

It is from this idea that in recent decades we have witnessed another turning point in the form of a renewed commitment to uncovering the social processes and mechanisms that account for neighborhood (or concentration) effects. Social mechanisms provide theoretically plausible accounts of *how* neighborhoods bring about change in a given phenomenon.[70] Mechanisms are by and large a theoretical claim about explanation—mechanisms can only rarely be observed or manipulated causally in an experiment. Rather, social mechanisms make up the hypothesized links in the pathway of explanation from a theoretically manipulable cause to an outcome. The goal is to develop indicators of the sets of practices, meanings, and actions that reflect hypothesized mechanisms. This commitment has led to programs of research designed to directly assess theoretically motivated social processes and cultural properties that vary at the neighborhood or extralocal level (e.g., through spatial dynamics of diffusion) and thus go beyond the simple aggregation of individual traits. My colleagues and I have referred to this shift in focus as the "process turn" in neighborhood-effects research; this book and the PHDCN-related studies as a whole stand as a renewed effort in this direction.[71]

There have been counterdevelopments as well, most notably a shift in some quarters to individual-level accounts of social life, highlighted by increased concerns about causal inference and what has become known as "selection bias." In fact, much of the newer literature has redefined neighborhood effects in ways that have led to stylistic modern convention, whereby the analytic focus is the direct effect of the neighborhood on some individual behavior. While important, this leaves much of interest out of the picture. From the European epidemiologists to the Chicago School and its followers, the main unit of analysis and inference has not been the individual but *rates of social behavior* that varied by neighborhood-level cultural and social structure. A key intervention that shifted the unit of interest to the individual came from Christopher Jencks and Susan Mayer, who can be considered the foremost source of late twentieth-century anxiety over the dilemma posed by individuals selecting environments. In a widely cited set of critiques, they asked the question: How do we know that the neighborhood differences in any outcome of interest are the result of neighborhood factors rather than the differential selection of adolescents or their families into certain neighborhoods?[72] They concluded that we did not know the answer and that the only way to address the question rigorously was to conduct controlled experiments.

As a result, recent years have witnessed a vigorous debate over the role of experiments in social research in general and neighborhood effects in particular. Many have responded to the call for experiments and more emphasis on the estimate of single causal parameters. The belief that experiments promise a superior research strategy for assessing causality has become dogma in many quarters and has led to a kind of experimental hegemony of thought. The most widely promoted efforts of this new turn hail from criminology, epidemiology, and the Moving to Opportunity (MTO) housing studies. MTO randomly allocated housing vouchers to poor families to induce movement to low-poverty neighborhoods, motivated by the idea that causal neighborhood effects on later outcomes could be estimated in an unbiased manner. But I argue in chapters 11 and 15 that the MTO experiment, while seductive, does not answer important theoretical questions that I ask, including how individuals select themselves into neighborhoods and how individual perceptions (and in turn selection itself) are influenced by neighborhood characteristics. MTO also randomized *individuals* rather than neighborhoods to a treatment, and the offer of a voucher does not tell us the social mechanisms that account for *why* neighborhoods have effects on individuals, if in fact they do. Causal explanation requires theory and concepts that organize knowledge about (typically) unobserved mechanisms that bring about the effect, a challenge that simultaneously demands a base of rigorous observational evidence.

This book therefore advances the processual and social-mechanistic turn of the late twenieth century in ways that respect causal logic but that take context seriously and steer clear of individually reductionist accounts. Experiments can tell us a lot and experimental logic—especially what James Woodward calls a "manipulability theory" of causal explanation—helps improve our thinking about observational evidence.[73] But causal questions are not the only ones, and the experimental method alone is ill-equipped for the study of neighborhood-level phenomena and macrolevel social processes that unfold over long periods of time. This is not to say that individual choice or causal inference are unimportant—to the contrary, I describe in the next chapter an analytic approach to neighborhood effects that draws on the lessons of past research to engage contextual explanations at the level of both neighborhood (and higher) processes and individual selection.

PART II **PRINCIPLES AND METHOD**

3 | Analytic Approach

The ideology of community lament set a snare from which neighborhood-effects research has never fully escaped. As a result, the decline of "community" has long been confused with the decline of place. But definitions of these concepts can be separated, and I start by teasing out the idea of neighborhoods in the physical or spatial sense rather than as a form of social solidarity. The broad definition of neighborhood that was provided by Park and Burgess was that of people and institutions occupying a spatially defined area that is conditioned by a set of ecological, cultural, and political forces.[1] In a utopian-like way Park went so far as to claim that the neighborhood formed "a locality with sentiments, traditions, and a history of its own."[2] He also viewed the neighborhood as the basis of social and political organization.

Park's definition overstated the political distinctiveness of residential enclaves, and the criticisms of the Chicago-School idea of the natural area are well known. Neighborhoods are not monolithic in character or composition, and market forces are not the only force behind the formation of community. Still, criticisms of the natural area concept may have themselves been overstated. As Gerald Suttles reads Park and Burgess rather than their caricature, "they meant to emphasize the ways in which urban residential groups are not the planned or artificial contrivance of anyone but develop out of many independent personal decisions based on moral, political, ecological, and economic considerations."[3] In the current era it is reasonable to think this describes many if not the majority of neighborhoods, even allowing for important nonnatural processes or constraints. The problem with the political economy or any purely structural critique is that it brackets individual choice and assumes more unified macrolevel control over individual behavior than seems warranted. Pure "top-down" thinking is not better than pure "bottom up."

Hence there are some aspects to Park's reasoning worth preserving. One is the recognition that neighborhoods are spatial units with variable organizational features, and the second is that neighborhoods are nested within successively larger communities. Neighborhoods vary in size and complexity depending on the social phenomenon under study and the ecological structure of the larger community. This notion of embeddedness is why Choldin emphasized the fact that the local neighborhood is integrally linked to, and dependent on, a larger whole.[4] For these reasons, I prefer to think of residential neighborhoods as having a "mosaic of overlapping boundaries" emphasized by Suttles, or what Reiss called an "imbricated" structure.[5]

The socially constructed nature of the local community is another essential idea that postdates the Park-Burgess model. Suttles identifies what might be thought of as a cultural mechanism (which I will return to in the chapters to follow) when he posits that "residential groups are defined in contradistinction to one another."[6] It is the nature of community that it matters differentially, and so residents sort themselves and identify themselves with broad groupings, especially along race, ethnic, and class lines. It is for this reason that neighborhoods are still salient in the contemporary city: they are markers for one's station in life and are frequently invoked for this purpose. This does not mean neighborhoods are homogenous, only that they gain their identity through an ongoing commentary between themselves and outsiders, a collective version of the "looking-glass self." Community identities are both positive (Gold Coast, Upper East Side, Happy Valley) and pejorative (Jew Town, Back of the Yards, Skid Row), underscoring the collective determination of the symbolic nature of community and its physical boundaries.[7] In this sense neighborhoods and larger residential communities often take on a distinct sense of place that embodies a set of meanings that go well beyond physical location.[8] This pattern is consistent with the hypothesis that the cultural principle of difference is layered onto the ecological landscape. The broader inference we can draw, initially, is that one of the mechanisms of enduring spatial inequality in the United States is "homophily," or the tendency of people to interact, associate, and live near others like themselves and to maintain distance from those disvalued.[9] One might think of this as the demand side of inequality—leading to what we can think of as a spatial form of *hierarchy maintenance*, a mechanism I explore in later chapters. Actions taken by individuals and institutions to maintain privileged positions produce the sorts of structural constraints typically emphasized by sociologists. But cultural principles of identity are also at work in the selection of places that inscribe social distance into neighborhood difference.

An extension of the social construction of community is the "defended neighborhood." According to Suttles, the defended neighborhood arises from a perceived threat of invasion from outside forces.[10] As such, defended neighborhoods can only be understood in relational terms. One of the paradoxes of community cohesion is that it is often generated by external threat, a point recognized by Coleman fifty years ago in his defense of a macrolevel conception of social disorganization.[11] Racial turnover is the classic case that comes to mind, but perhaps political threats may be equally important, for example when Chicago mayor Richard M. Daley announced in 1990 that he planned to build a new airport in the southeastern community of Hegewisch. Under siege and faced with physical destruction, Hegewisch became the quintessential defended neighborhood, mobilizing to defeat city hall and developers with many millions of dollars at stake. In this case a latent sense of community was ignited and reinvigorated by an external threat, leading residents to defend their common interests.

We are confronted, then, with a complex social phenomenon. Neighborhoods are both chosen and allocated; defined by outsiders and insiders alike, often in contradistinction to each other; they are both symbolically and structurally determined; large and small; overlapping or blurred in perceptual boundaries; relational; and ever changing in composition. Suttles's concept of the defended neighborhood also unveils the potential interaction between boundaries and socially constructed meaning—ecological boundaries can be perceived as either sacrosanct or meaningless, and therefore must ultimately be socially understood. Moreover, apropos of the "community liberated" argument, social networks are potentially boundless in physical space. This characteristic of social networks allows groups to share identity and exist anywhere—they may or may not be spatially bounded by neighborhoods. It therefore can be seen that neighborhood invokes two meanings in the literature—physical proximity or distance (as in "neighbor") and variable social interaction, usually considered in face-to-face terms.

These conceptual conundrums are often glossed over in the futile search for a single operational or statistical definition of neighborhood. I begin instead by conceptualizing neighborhood in theoretical terms as a geographic section of a larger community or region (e.g., city) that usually contains residents or institutions and has socially distinctive characteristics. This definition highlights the general characteristic of neighborhoods from ancient cities to the present—they are analytic units with simultaneous social and spatial significance.[12] An empirical test is implied that the review in chapter 2 of various operational definitions rejected—if there is no ecological differentiation (or clustering) by social characteristics, there is no neighborhood in the socially meaningful sense. But as we have seen, there is considerable neighborhood social inequality or differentiation, and more will be shown. My conceptualization also views neighborhoods as nested within larger districts or local communities that are recognized and named by institutional actors and administrative agencies.[13] In many cases both residents and institutions identify neighborhoods and local communities interchangeably—for example, Hyde Park in Chicago is considered by most of its residents and by the University of Chicago as a neighborhood, but it is also rather large (about thirty thousand residents) and simultaneously considered a local community.

These analytic moves avoid conflating neighborhood and local community with the existence of strong face-to-face intimate, affective relations that are thought to characterize primary groups.[14] Such a primary-group assumption probably always has been false. Henry Zorbaugh, a contemporary to Louis Wirth, wisecracked back in the 1920s: "Along the Gold Coast, as elsewhere in the city, one does not know one's neighbors."[15] But this did not imply then the analytic irrelevance of how spatial proximity interacted with social distance or the social sorting of groups into different neighborhoods. Nor does it now, and even in today's more interconnected world it remains the case that some neighborhoods *are* tight knit and characterized by frequent social interaction. Neighborhoods are conditioned by a *varying* set of ecological, sociodemographic, institutional, cultural, and political forces, as are many other subjects of social inquiry. How family is defined is the subject of considerable contention, for example, but this does not mean that family is a social construct void of causal power.[16] The political borders of societies are also variable, and many people within those borders do not maintain a national identity. But as Rogers Brubaker argues, nationalism is a legitimate object of scientific inquiry that is rooted in everyday practices and institutionalized forms, even if "nation" is a socially contingent concept.[17] Groups do not lack causal power because their boundaries are socially constructed or they lack internal cohesion.

The logical implication of my approach is that sometimes neighborhoods make a community in the classical sense of shared values, solidarity, and tight-knit bonds, but often they do not. What some might call "neighborhoodness" (e.g., dense social interactions, place identity, or exertion of social control) is a contingent or variable event. The extent of structural or cultural organization (and for what) is an empirical question, leaving the extent of solidarity or social interaction within (and across) neighborhoods as subjects for investigation.[18] It is the intersection of practices and perceptions in a spatial context that is at the root of neighborhood effects. When formulated this way, social factors—whether network ties, shared perceptions of disorder, organizational density, cultural identity, or the civic capacity for collective action—are variable and analytically separable not only from potential structural antecedents (e.g., economic status, segregation, housing stability) and possible consequences (e.g., crime, wellbeing), but from the definition of the units of analysis. This conceptualization allows empirical research to proceed without tautology and, as we shall see, offers a scalable menu of options for measuring theoretical constructs across ecological units of analysis.[19]

Out of the Ghetto

What we might call the "poverty paradigm" has dominated the urban research agenda at least since Wilson's classic, *The Truly Disadvantaged*.[20] Concepts such as the "inner city," "underclass," and "ghetto" have dominated intellectual debate. While important, poverty is a relational concept that requires an understanding of the middle and upper echelons of society. "Inner-city" poverty is also no longer valid ecologically—many of the poorest neighborhoods are in the far flung corners of U.S. cities or the suburbs, and Chicago is no exception, as we shall see. Yet the poverty paradigm has directed many surveys to focus solely on poor individuals, and the majority of ethnographies are on poor communities. Recent decades have seen an outpouring of excellent urban ethnographies, but virtually all of them are located in black or poor ethnic communities.[21] That much of urban sociology has focused on the lives of the poor and downtrodden is quite striking in its implications—neighborhood variation across the full range of structural contexts and social mechanisms remains a limited topic of inquiry.

In this book I thus move beyond the confines of the "ghetto" and focus on social mechanisms theoretically at work across a broad spectrum of factors such as informal control, network exchange, homophily, selection, and organizational capacity. As introduced in the last chapter, I conceptualize a social mechanism as a plausible contextual process that accounts for a given phenomenon, taking as its central goal the empirical study of the sources and consequences of social behaviors that vary across neighborhoods. It follows that I take a comparative approach, investigating multiple neighborhoods over time, whenever possible. This strategy counterbalances the tendency in some of the ethnographic literature to make comparative claims based on single cases and in some of the quantitative literature to focus on cross-sectional or one-shot studies. Starting with William F. Whyte, for example, a common refrain by critics of social disorganization theory is that they see evidence of organization in the neighborhoods they are studying. Most recently, Martin Sanchez-Jankowski writes in this tradition, saying that in his long stays in high-poverty neighborhoods he "only once experienced (and only briefly) social disorganization."[22] Setting aside how different observers might define (dis)organization or whether they would see the same thing in the same neighborhood, the issue is not some absolute level of social organization but rather its *variation across communities and time*. Sanchez-Jankowski might thus be right, but we would need to know the level of organization in *other* neighborhoods (say, upper or middle income as opposed to only poor) and how they also changed in order to make claims about neighborhood-level theories of social organization.[23] The advantage of a comparative framework, which in principle can be ethnographic or not, is the ability to directly make such comparisons.[24]

A focus on comparative social mechanisms should not be read to imply a neglect of cultural and symbolic processes or a search for universal covering laws. The approach of this book and its study design allow me to simultaneously probe what may be the most powerful role for neighborhoods in the contemporary city—perceptual (or cognitive) social organization. Neighborhood studies have often been conceptualized in terms of objective structural variables that could be implanted anywhere. When social organizational factors, such as networks and control, are studied directly, they are also often considered to be analytically separate or independent from the perceptions and interpretations that give them meaning. But as Gerald Suttles and Albert Hunter, and Walter Firey before them, have shown, places have symbolic as well as use value.[25] Places are also interpreted and narrated—"imagined"[26]—and these symbolic gestures in turn reinforce the idea of place. Tom Gieryn has argued that places are not just abstract representations on a geometric plane; they take on social significance through the interaction of material form, geography, and inscribed meaning.[27] When Mayor Daley II moved out of Bridgeport and "up" north, it was cause for widespread handwringing in Chicago not just because of either the place's race or working-class composition, but because of what the move stood for symbolically and politically—a concession to the "Lake Side Liberals." Many other neighborhoods in Chicago convey a distinct stereotype, just as in other cities. Beacon Hill, the Tenderloin, Hollywood, Bed-Stuy, Kensington, and the Left Bank, to name a few, convey a distinctive meaning and sense of place. Neighborhoods have reputations that may well be sturdier than individuals.

In short, people act *as if* neighborhoods matter, which is a fact of profound importance in the social reproduction of inequality by place. Consideration of both the cultural and structural mechanisms that make neighborhoods meaningful is a central task of this book.

Ecometrics

What has hindered the analysis of social processes and mechanisms? Theory plays a role because theory guides the production of methodological tools and analytic approaches. Here is where sociology stumbled in the "decontextualization" phase of the mid-twentieth century, when the Chicago-style tradition of research was slowly overtaken by the increasing dominance of individual-centered questions and survey research.[28] The focus in sociology turned narrowly to individuals, both as units of data collection and targets of theoretical inference. Although this dominance has been challenged, especially by ethnographers, it persists despite the resurgence of interest in neighborhood effects. Not only does most research continue to focus largely on the ghetto poor and negative outcomes at the traditional bottom of the heap, quantitative research in particular usually treats social context as just one more characteristic of the individual used to predict individual variations.

By contrast, I argue that we need to treat social context as an important unit of analysis in its own right. This calls for new measurement strategies as well as a theoretical framework that do not treat the neighborhood simply as a "trait" of the individual. However, unlike individual-level measurements, which are backed up by decades of psychometric research into their statistical properties, the methodology needed to evaluate neighborhood properties is not widespread. For this reason Stephen Raudenbush and I proposed moving toward a science of ecological assessment, which we called "ecometrics," by developing systematic procedures for measuring neighborhood mechanisms, and by integrating and adapting tools from the field of psychometrics to improve the quality of neighborhood-level measures.[29] Setting aside statistical details, the important theoretical point is that neighborhood, ecological, and other collective phenomena demand their own measurement since they are not stand-ins for individual-level traits. I believe this distinction is crucial for the advancement of theoretically motivated neighborhood research. Underlying this book's conceptual emphasis on neighborhood social processes is therefore a simultaneous quest for the development of methodological tools that serve theoretical goals—a metric for the social-ecological contexts of the city.

"Extralocal" Processes and the Larger Social Order

The idea of ecometrics leads naturally to another challenge—that of linking neighborhoods and places together in the larger social order of the city. Prior research on neighborhood effects has focused largely on the idea of "contained" or internal characteristics, assuming that neighborhoods are islands unto themselves. This approach is surprising given that a workhorse of urban ecological thinking is spatial interdependence. Recently have we seen advances in spatial techniques that I capitalize on, allowing me to capture the interdependence of social processes through spatial networks, and thereby mechanisms such as diffusion and exposure.

It remains true, however, that previous approaches have largely limited their focus to how internal neighborhood characteristics are associated with the internal characteristics of a "neighborhood's neighbors"—spatial proximity or geographic distance has been the defining metric for the recent advances in spatial social science. While important, the ways in which neighborhood networks are themselves tied into the larger social structure of the city in nonspatial ways are not well understood and rarely studied. Ironically, the classic work of Robert Park and Ernest Burgess envisioned research on the ecological structure where neighborhoods only were pieces of the mosaic of the city.[30] The political economy critique made a similar point as did the social network theorists: nonspatial relationships are just as important theoretically as internal neighborhood characteristics and therefore studies of place cannot proceed by considering their *indigenous* qualities only. It is not just city-level processes that are at stake—national and global forces can influence place stratification. As Wilson argued in *The Truly Disadvantaged*, deindustrialization and the shift to a service economy was disproportionately felt in the inner city.[31]

How do we go about documenting the extralocal layers of these kinds of macrolevel influences? What might be the biggest hurdle to neighborhood-effects research is the simple fact that neighborhoods are themselves penetrated by multiple external forces and contexts. Acknowledging this and studying it are two different things—critiques of the Chicago School are legion but convincing empirical demonstrations of the effects of "larger" structures are thin. Motivated by this concern, I explore in this book the implications of thinking in terms of interconnected and multilevel social processes that go beyond the idea of an isolated urban neighborhood. My strategy is to examine how residential mobility, organizational ties, and elite social networks differentially connect neighborhoods to the cross-cutting institutions and resources that organize much of contemporary economic, political, and social life.[32] This strategy is pursued through analysis of moving trajectories across neighborhoods and in the Key Informant Network Study, a panel study of the networks among leaders, organizations, and ultimately neighborhoods of Chicago. These data permit me to address one of the most basic but untested propositions in the literature, in which the unit of analysis is *relations* between and across neighborhoods—not merely as a function of geographical distance (e.g., ties in adjacent neighborhoods) but of the actual networks that cross-cut neighborhood and metropolitan boundaries. For example, I examine the network structure of the citywide pattern of residential migration and informational exchange among leaders. I also examine how the structural pattern of ties among key community actors is related to variation in organizational and social resources.

A caveat is nonetheless in order. My project is not one that attempts to reveal the full workings of the global economy or other macropolitical forces on neighborhood effects. This is not to say global or "State" effects are unimportant, only that it is not possible with my research design to do them justice in their own right analytically. But I do claim that macrolevel processes are lived locally and experienced on the ground in everyday life, a claim that perhaps ironically has its roots in the nonquantitative method of ethnography. The implication for strategy is that I attempt to connect multiple scales of influence wherever possible. Especially in part 4, this multitiered approach attempts to lay bare the connections to and from larger-scale political, network, economic, and organizational processes that operate beyond local boundaries but that have implications for community *and* individual life. Such higher-order links among communities constitute a different kind of neighborhood effect that is rarely considered, one that forms a key analytic goal of this book.

Individual Selection Reconsidered

The reader at this point may suspect I am a structural determinist. But this study should be read as saying that individuals matter too. How neighborhoods change and how city dynamics are brought about are considered not just from the structural view or from the "top down" but also from the "bottom up." In *Foundations of Social Theory* James Coleman presented a heuristic that illustrated the different analytic links

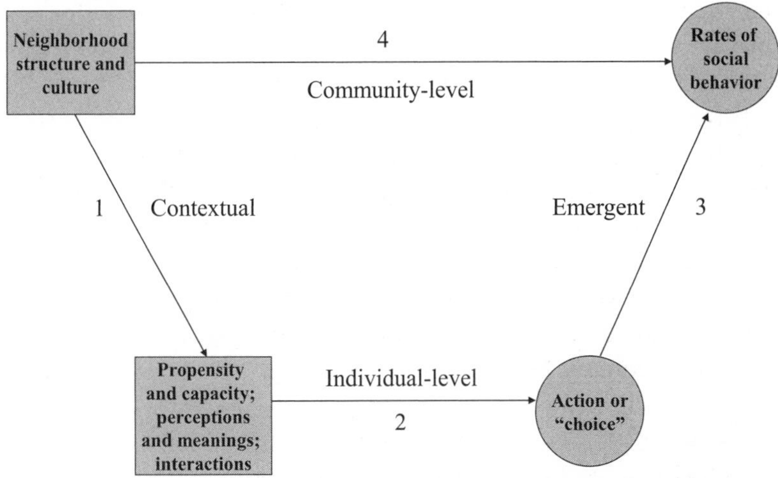

FIGURE 3.1. Conceptual model of neighborhood micro-macro links

in studying micro and macro processes that connect the "top" and individuals at the "bottom." Although I do not accept or apply his underlying rational choice framework and I reject the rigid strictures of "methodological individualism," I believe it is productive to consider Coleman's analytic scheme for understanding micro and macro links and apply it to our present concern with neighborhood effects to see how far it can take us.

In figure 3.1 I graph across the top the macrolevel connections emphasized in chapter 2, what I call "side-to-side" analysis (e.g., *between-neighborhood* associations of concentrated poverty with crime rates). These are also represented as the link-4 connections. Link 1 reflects "contextual effects," in this case of neighborhoods, on individuals ("top down"), especially on their propensities and capacities and the kinds of social interactions and meanings that influence behavior—"action" in the Coleman sense.[33] Most social science operates at the individual-level link 2, whereas research in the Chicago School tradition tends to operate either at the "macro level," theorizing connections "side to side" across the top of the Coleman "boat" (link 4), or at the contextual level of link 1. The task of this book is to better understand the mechanisms that connect the entire process through the various multilevel links, including side-to-side or community-level links and both bottom-up and top-down links. My task is also to better define and study the role of context, what I consider the main failure of methodological individualism.

This strategy leads me to a reconsideration of the common wisdom regarding the role of individuals and the current popularity of experiments. In chapter 2, "selection bias" due to individual sorting was a ubiquitous concern in the literature on neighborhood effects.[34] There is widespread concern that because individuals make choices and sort themselves by place, nonrandomly, estimates of neighborhood effects on social outcomes (most commonly crime, teenage childbearing, employment, mortality, birth weight, social disorder, and children's cognitive development) are therefore confounded. By and large the response to this critique has been to take selection as a statistical problem to be controlled away rather than as something of substantive interest. As chapter 2 revealed, the usual method in neighborhood-effects research using observational data is to control away many individual-level variables. A more recent approach has been to conduct experiments in order to obtain more unbiased causal inferences.

James Heckman has recently articulated what he calls the "scientific model of causality," in which the goal is to confront directly and achieve a basic understanding of the social processes that select individuals into causal "treatments" of interest.[35] Although I do not adopt a formal model or economic theory and while I do not adhere to an overly "scientistic" stance, I do think that studying the individual sorting and selection into neighborhoods of varying types is an essential ingredient in my larger theoretical project of understanding neighborhood effects. Relying on randomization through the experimental paradigm sets aside the study of how these mechanisms are constituted in a social world defined by the interplay of structure and purposeful choice. In this book I therefore focus on a key aspect of selection—neighborhood location or choice—and treat the neighborhood outcome achieved by the individual as problematic in its own right. This approach allows me to examine the sources and consequences of sorting for the reproduction of social inequality in the lives of individuals, and for the reproduction of the stratified urban landscape (links 1 and 2 in fig. 3.1). Equally important, by taking selection and the micro to macro link 3 seriously, rather than defining it away, leads me to study how individual choices in the form of residential movement lead to "upward" consequences

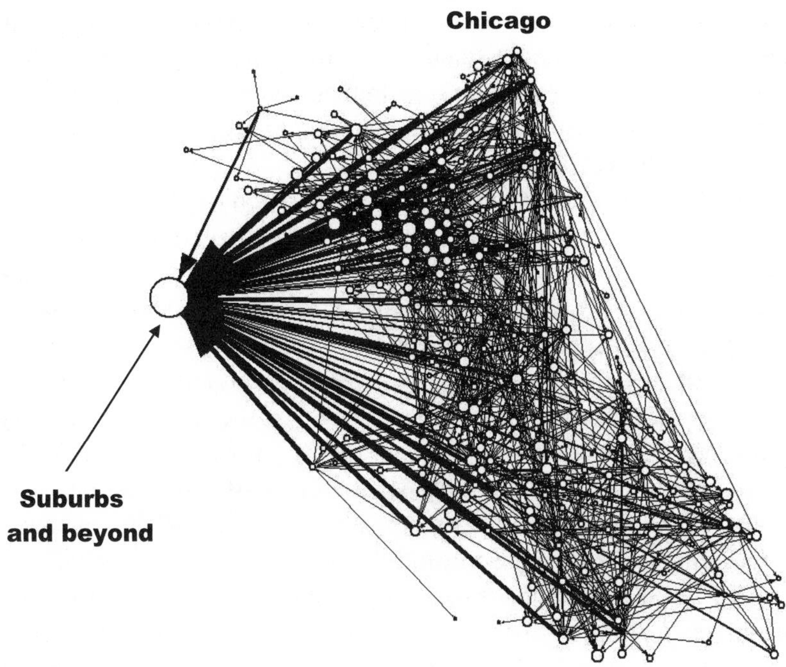

FIGURE 3.2. Dynamic residential mobility flows, 1995–2002

that ramify across the city and beyond (and, in turn, back to link 4). These are connections that define the demography of the wider city. Individual actions are constitutive of the bird's-eye view, in other words.

To use a simple example and motivate the idea of the interconnected city, consider that if I move from community A to B I engage in an individual action but at the same time I establish a connection or exchange between these two places. Structural consequences ensue. In figure 3.2 each line represents a connection created by a move between an origin and destination neighborhood of families within the Chicago study soon to be described in detail. Neighborhoods are denoted by circles, and the thickness of lines is proportional to the volume of flows between neighborhoods. One can see that the individual moves create an emergent social structure of "exchange" among neighborhoods. Some flows reflect white flight, others the increasing diversity of formerly black areas, and still others moves to the suburbs. I explore in Chapters 11–13 how these and other types of "micro" actions yield social structural connections between neighborhoods of different racial, economic, and social makeup, helping us to better understand the reproduction of persistent urban inequality. In chapter 14 I examine individual and cross-neighborhood connections of a different sort—key informant networks—and how they constitute Chicago's social structure.

Unlike many research efforts on neighborhood effects that privilege a hierarchically nested or top-down effect of neighborhoods on the individual, I thus consider side-to-side, bottom-up, and bird's-eye orientations along with issues of ecometric measurement, social causality, extralocal spatial processes, perceptions as causation, and selection bias all as a way to address the scheme in figure 3.1. I also firmly believe that macrolevel mechanisms (link 4) have their own social logic and are not reducible to individual actors in the ways that methodological individualists imply.[36] My argument is thus that there are many ways to conceive of neighborhood effects, with the dominant top-down pathway important but far from the only link worth considering. Even when contextual link 1 is at issue, its conceptualization is typically narrow, and mediating pathways from neighborhood context are inappropriately controlled away, as in the ubiquitous notion of attempting to render "all else equal." If neighborhood conditions are implicated in cognitive perceptions and evaluations, for example, they are causally implicated in individual behavior and social structure alike. Although social life may be said to be emergent, its structure is produced by a complex set of relations among individuals that are shaped by macrolevel and often durable neighborhood processes.[37] My analytic approach therefore moves back and forth between the various "levels" of the social structure of the contemporary city, with an eye to explaining and integrating the multiple causal processes that reflect a broad conception of neighborhood effects.

Theoretical Principles

Backed by over a decade's worth of original data collection from the Project on Human Development in Chicago Neighborhoods, my goal is to place contextual processes on a theoretical foundation that recognizes the ways in which metropolitan life has been transformed over the years. As noted, what unites all the chapters is a concern with the social mechanisms and dynamic processes of place in the contemporary city—in this case, Chicago. The Chicago School of urban sociology that nourished me as a scholar provides a grand tradition for such work, but it must also be reinvented—just as Chicago the city is currently being reinvented.

I propose ten active elements of what I view as a general theoretical approach to the study of neighborhood effects and the contemporary American city.[38] I refer here not to specific hypotheses that will come later, but to the larger or more abstract principles of Chicago School–inspired social inquiry that are operationalized and expanded upon in this book:

1. Relentlessly focus first and foremost on *social context*, especially as manifested in urban inequalities and neighborhood differentiation.
2. Study neighborhood-level or contextual variations in their own right, adopting an eclectic style of data collection that relies on multiple methods but that always connects to some form of empirical assessment of social-ecological properties, accompanied by systematic standards for validation—*ecometrics*.
3. Across ecological contexts and guided by ecometric principles, focus on *social-interactional, social-psychological, organizational, and cultural mechanisms* of city life rather than just individual attributes or traditional compositional features like racial makeup and poverty.
4. Within this framework, integrate a life-course focus on the temporal dynamics of neighborhood *change* and the explanation of neighborhood trajectories.
5. Invoke a simultaneous concern for processes and mechanisms that explain *stability*, highlighting forms of *neighborhood social reproduction*.
6. Embed in the study of neighborhood dynamics the role of *individual selection* decisions that in turn yield consequences for neighborhood outcomes—treat selection as a social process, not a statistical nuisance.
7. Go beyond the local. Study neighborhood effects and mechanisms that cross or spill over local boundaries to yield larger *spatial (dis) advantages*.

8. Go further still and incorporate macro processes beyond the influences of spatial proximity, building a concern with the social organization of the city or metropolitan area *as a whole*, integrating variations across constituent neighborhoods with higher-order—or nonspatial—networks that connect them.

9. Never lose sight of human concerns with public affairs and the improvement of city and community life—draw implications for *community-level interventions* as a scientifically principled alternative to the individual disease model of medicine.

10. Finally, emphasize the integrative theme of *theoretically interpretive empirical research* while taking a pluralistic stance on the nature of evidence and causation. The disjuncture that often exists between theory and empirical research, akin to the so-called two cultures problem[39] of quantitative versus qualitative, seems never to have had much force at Chicago. It should not today.

These ten principles entail a number of modi operandi that I build or infer from the Chicago School and adapt to the contemporary social world. In essence I argue that the *activities* if not the thoughts of the Chicago School yielded agreement on a "contextualist paradigm," premised on the notion that "no social fact makes any sense abstracted from its context in social (and often geographic) space and social time."[40] This is a robust approach to social life that links theory to operational concepts to make sense of the empirical world of the ever-changing city (not other theorists). My approach thus attempts to unite method and theoretical principle, viewing theory in its classic form—the analysis of a set of empirical facts in their relation to one another, organized by a set of guiding explanatory principles and hypotheses. The specific theoretical claims and hypotheses are laid out in the individual chapters that follow.

A Note on Style

As the next chapter will reveal, the PHDCN is a large effort that has evolved in multiple directions. Its tentacles are to be found in many places, and future investigators will undoubtedly take the project in other directions not yet known.[41] But at present almost fifteen years' worth of research and publications now need to be brought together in one place and synthesized. There are also many new results to report and previously unanalyzed data sources that I tap. While I do not attempt to cover all prior material produced from PHDCN, one learns from cumulative experience, including both its progress and mistakes. The challenge is that the published articles on PHDCN so far are like unassembled pieces of a jigsaw puzzle, scattered in many different places and written with different voices. Given the public nature of much of the project and its eventual data, I thus consider it incumbent on me to assemble these diverse pieces and describe in an integrative way and in one voice how past work set the stage for the framing of my subsequent empirical work. Against this backdrop I then present new data and findings accompanied with a synthetic and revised portrait of the overarching theoretical framework.

In particular, I focus in this book on dynamic processes and longitudinal data collected in the PHDCN follow-ups at both the individual and the neighborhood and community levels, in addition to cognate panel studies of other-regarding behavior, collective civic engagement, organizations, and elite networks. I also rely on personal interviews with community leaders and field observations I recorded over the course of the study in strategically chosen neighborhoods. The result is that virtually all of the empirical findings and observations that I highlight, especially in figures, reflect original analysis. The remainder reinterprets prior results from a longer-term perspective, with each chapter dipping into topics, data sources, or analyses not previously explored. This integrative strategy requires me to revisit prior findings and places, interrogate them with longitudinal data, and then revise them again, culminating in a set of final field visits and data collection strategies conducted in Chicago in 2010. These revisits engage not just with PHDCN-related material but entail a dialogue with an ongoing stream of studies that were conducted in Chicago over the last century and that have enriched social science.[42]

The study of neighborhood effects and urban social structure is complicated and raises a hornet's nest of methodological challenges. It is thus not surprising that a great deal of technical material has been produced from the PHDCN. The challenges are not minor, and I have spent years with my colleagues trying to solve one or another empirical problem. The details behind much of this groundwork can be found in peer-reviewed journals, supplemental materials, and footnotes to this book, but I will keep the focus here on painting the big picture. As a result this book is largely "coefficient free" and nontechnical. In fact there are no tables. At the same time, data are important to see and I do not believe readers should simply trust authors. Herein lies the dilemma of presenting scholarly and at times densely researched findings in an accessible way. My solution in this book is to include for the reader a large number of maps and figures that are meant to portray visually the theoretical ideas and empirical regularities that have been vetted back and forth with more complicated methods. I believe this strategy is warranted by the scope of the inquiry and hope the journey is worth any challenges to the reader. Those who wish to retrace my steps, pore over evermore details, or dig deeper into method may do so by following the roadmap provided in the footnotes, online sources, and citations.[43]

4 The Making of the Chicago Project

With a general analytical framework and motivating questions now in place, this chapter describes what I will call the Chicago Project. I emphasize a number of connected studies, all of which focus on Chicago circa the late twentieth and early twenty-first centuries. The effort that unites them and the empirical base of this book is the Project on Human Development in Chicago Neighborhoods (PHDCN). But the PHDCN contains multiple components that in turn spawned cognate studies with independent intellectual standing and that I integrate in this book; hence the name "Chicago Project."

To make sense of the whole, I describe the overarching research design of PHDCN and its rationale, the different kinds of data ultimately collected, and some of the operational challenges we faced when the study hit the streets. Many social science studies appear rather antiseptic in their description, as if data cleanly appeared on the analyst's computer screen without any blood, sweat, or tears. The PHDCN generated lots of the latter, and I believe that the story of its making is relevant to an understanding of how social science works, how cities work, and the interplay between them in producing a human outcome. The role of scientific investigators in such endeavors is usually overlooked, as is the process by which ideas generate the construction of data. Paraphrasing Goethe, one might say that "data are theory." Also underappreciated are the twists, turns, and compromises that researchers encounter once the research design texts are closed and data collection commences. I thus make an effort to breathe life into those key moments in the project. I begin with the intellectual backdrop to PHDCN, which might be subtitled: "What happens when social science gets into bed with big science?"[1]

Intellectual History

The story begins in 1982, when a study group funded by the John D. and Catherine T. MacArthur Foundation was appointed to make recommendations for a major new study, a kind of "Framingham" for criminology.[2] The makeup of the study group reflected the intellectual tensions that were to move the project forward. The members were Richard Ogilvie, former governor of Illinois, the legal scholar Herbert Wechsler, James Q. Wilson, then at Harvard, Lloyd Ohlin, also at Harvard, Norval Morris of the University of Chicago Law School, and Daniel Glaser of the University of Southern California. Based on personal conversations and a study of project archives, my interpretation is that the two key players in this early group turned out to be James Q. Wilson, a leading political scientist who at the time was writing *Crime and Human Nature* with the psychologist Richard Herrnstein at Harvard, and Lloyd Ohlin, a sociologist best known for his classic book with Richard Cloward, *Delinquency and Opportunity*.[3] The tensions, not surprisingly, revolved around a vision of crime as an individual trait, perhaps biologically rooted as suggested by Wilson and Herrnstein, versus crime as a social and thus contextual phenomenon, favored by Ohlin.[4]

Another relevant backdrop was the appointment of a National Academy of Sciences (NAS) panel, Research on Criminal Careers, chaired by Alfred Blumstein, an operations researcher at Carnegie Mellon University. The NAS issued a highly visible report in 1986, shortly after the publication of *Crime and Human Nature* in 1985. Together these works set forth the notion of the "career criminal," foreshadowed by the work of Marvin Wolfgang. In *Delinquency in a Birth Cohort*, Wolfgang and colleagues reported that 6 percent of the members of a Philadelphia birth cohort had committed about two-thirds of the offenses of the entire cohort.[5] Crime was produced, it appeared, by relatively few individuals. Wolfgang had identified the "career criminals" retrospectively, and a consensus emerged that the field needed to design a major new *prospective* study of criminal careers. The policy motivation rested on the idea of prediction and selective incapacitation. As John Laub argued in his presidential address to the American Society of Criminology in 2003, these events were major turning points in the study of crime in the United States.[6] The provocative arguments put forth by Wilson, Wolfgang, Blumstein, and others set in motion a research agenda on "career criminals" (later "super predators") and in particular a widespread return to what had been an early focus in criminology—prediction.[7]

The final backdrop is hard to fully appreciate by present conditions. Barely twenty years ago American cities were said to be dying, under siege by record levels of violence, disrepair, and outmigration. Violence in urban areas skyrocketed in the late eighties and early nineties, and the tenor of the times was one of despair. As we mounted the project, the *Chicago Tribune* ran a Pulitzer Prize–winning series in 1993 called "Killing Our Children," which documented the murder of every child under age fifteen in the metropolitan area. Children were being murdered in unconscionable numbers, and headlines in the *Chicago Tribune* were unrelenting as in other major cities around the country. A representative headline read: "Caught in Violence and Poverty: City Kids at Risk." Another declared a population flight to the suburbs: "Second City to Suburbs: More Chicagoans Find It Isn't Their Kind of Town."[8] There was a public outcry for solutions to the violence problem in cities, and the PHDCN was conceived as a scientific effort to provide empirical evidence in support of urban crime policies.

With support from the MacArthur Foundation and later the National Institute of Justice, the initial investment of the study group led to a 1986 book by David Farrington, Lloyd Ohlin, and James Q. Wilson titled, appropriately, *Understanding and Controlling Crime: Toward a New Research Strategy*.[9] Inspired by the intellectual energy and the pressing nature of problems in the city, the MacArthur Foundation was convinced to host a large working conference in Dallas in February of 1988 to hash out the details of an actual design. From what I have been able to determine (I was not there) there were dozens of invited guests—a virtual *Who's Who* of the leading lights in the behavioral sciences at the time. Opinions differ on what transpired, but several sources told me the meeting did not foster intellectual cohesion. The picture that emerges from these reports is one of considerable disagreement, cacophony, and in some cases expression of naked self-interest in advice for how to move forward. In apparent unhappiness, MacArthur retreated to the drawing board. It took time for the dust to settle, and action was needed for further progress. It fell to the intellectual and personal savvy of Norval Morris at Chicago to work the back rooms. He and a small group of others spearheaded an effort to convince MacArthur to try again, this time with peer review, matching federal support from the National Institute of Justice, and a smaller group of chiefs.

It eventually worked, and phase I of the project was born later in 1988, with working groups chaired by Lloyd Ohlin, David Farrington (psychology, Cambridge), and Felton Earls (child psychiatry, Harvard), and the overall effort directed by Michael Tonry (law, University of Minnesota). The original title deliberately laid emphasis on crime and individual development: Project on Human Development and Criminal Behavior. The emphasis on crime reflected the widespread challenge that cities were facing, and the individual developmental focus reflected the increasing influence of what would later become known as the decade of the brain—a medical model conception of human behavior. These twin foci foreshadowed intellectual battles to come. The planning effort envisioned a prospective study of thousands of youth in multiple cities, ages zero to twenty-five, in a cohort-sequential longitudinal design and hopefully an experimental component. The measurement plans were heavily tilted to individual difference constructs, psychiatric diagnostic criteria, and family processes. Sociological factors and community were nodded to, but the latter in particular appeared perfunctory and in service of providing just another variable to add to the prediction of individual differences.

A key turning point for my personal situation came with the appointment of Albert J. Reiss Jr. to the steering committee later that year. This appointment came at the urging of Lloyd Ohlin. Reiss, who had recently retired from the Yale University sociology department, obtained his Ph.D. in sociology at Chicago in 1949, and served for a time on its faculty.[10] Steeped in Chicago sociology, Reiss urged the inclusion of contextual and sociological features in the study. It helped that he had recently edited *Communities and Crime* for the University of Chicago Press and (for me) that I had written a commissioned article in the volume.[11] Reiss enlisted my help, and in late 1988 I began serving on a planning committee.

That's when my hair began to turn gray, as I learned that interdisciplinary "big science" was as painful as it was exhilarating. I had to listen to neurobiologists and read behavioral genetics while interacting with leading scholars. Arguing over beers with a behavioral geneticist can also be a great deal of fun.[12] There were many battles, but the main flare-ups centered on the proper role of individual and contextual factors in the etiology of crime. James Q. Wilson and a diverse group of criminologists and developmentalists favored a design that would include biological factors, while Lloyd Ohlin and other sociologists championed a focus on contextual factors. Al Reiss and I argued for community-level factors, and, in the end, we prevailed in at least getting the issue a place at the table. This was no small feat, considering the diversity of the committees, funding sources, and intellectual backdrop. Many more details could be elaborated, but it is sufficient to say that after much haggling and input from dozens of scholars, a design finally emerged.[13] It was to be an "accelerated longitudinal" or cohort sequential design, from ages zero to eighteen, each followed for up to eight years. In other words, the idea was to follow multiple cohorts of different ages over the same historical time. In turn the cohort study was to be embedded in a community design, with independent data collection on the social organization of communities. The victory, from my view, was a commitment to the study of contextual variations as an important endeavor in itself, *prior to and independent of* the study of individual pathways to crime. Equally important, the study shifted from a focus on crime to a more general and interdisciplinary investigation of human development across the life course.

A key turning point in the project came with the intellectual and administrative intervention of Felton ("Tony") Earls, a child psychiatrist at Harvard with a longstanding interest in child development and adult wellbeing as opposed to just crime. Earls brought a broad set of intellectual interests, wisdom, and a deep commitment to seeing the project succeed. The marriage of a developmental approach to child wellbeing with a contextual or population-based approach to urban life was cemented when Earls was named the principal investigator and the project was institutionalized at the Harvard School of Public Health. Stephen Buka, a colleague of Earls's at Harvard, also in public health, was the coprincipal investigator. At that time I became a scientific director along with Albert Reiss, Terrie Moffitt, and Stephen Raudenbush.[14]

The original plan was to carry out the study in several U.S. cities, but budgetary and pragmatic concerns quickly intervened. Only one city could realistically be studied intensively, so we searched for the ideal fit. Data were collected on numerous aspects of candidate cities, including LA, Chicago, Baltimore, NYC, and New Orleans. These included primarily census data, health records, and crime records. After site visits to each city that included meetings with local officials, Chicago was officially selected and the collaboratively constructed research design was finalized.[15]

Why Chicago?

I am an American, Chicago born—Chicago, that somber city—and go at things as I have taught myself, free style, and will make the record in my own way: first to knock, first admitted; sometimes an innocent knock, sometimes a not so innocent.

Opening proclamation in Saul Bellow's *The Adventures of Augie March*

Chicago has inspired passion in writers and scholars of the city, and, most recently, a president. Our choice of site, however, was not an effort to locate the study in the home turf of the Chicago School of urban sociology. Many issues came into play, from the theoretical to the pragmatic. A major goal from the outset was to obtain sufficient representation of the three largest race/ethnic groups in American society—blacks, Latinos, and whites—combined with variation in socioeconomic status (SES). That eliminated most cities, and the remaining ones were ranked according to intellectual resources, cooperation from a variety of local officials, available archival data, estimated costs, and an established record of prior study that could be used as a comparative frame for understanding contemporary city life. Chicago emerged as the obvious choice, with its unparalleled history of community research being the icing on the cake.

There is another less tangible factor too, and that is simply the notion that Chicago is arguably the quintessential American city. As Saul Bellow, Nelson Algren, Norman Mailer, and a long line of literary, political, cultural, and criminal characters attest, Chicago captures the full range and intensity of American passions. Even the diehard New Yorker and renowned British historian Tony Judt weighed in on Chicago's leading role in American urban life. In a moving tribute to his adopted New York just before he died, Judt observed like Mailer that while New York is a world city it looks outward: "It is not the great American city—that will always be Chicago."[16] To be great is hardly to be flawless, of course. Quite to the contrary and to the dismay of would-be boosters, some of the worst excesses of American life, such as inequality, violence, racial segregation, and corruption, are on major exhibit in Chicago. Disasters are a regular part of the landscape as well, including deadly heat waves, crippling snowstorms, and the infamous Great Fire. Perhaps for these reasons Chicago has motivated deep social scientific study as well as literary, intellectual, architectural, and political passions, and has emerged on the international stage as the place that introduced Barack Obama to politics and produced his world views.[17] Chicago is not absolutely average, to be sure, and I do not claim "never a city so real."[18] But Chicago has faced the dynamics that have confronted all the major cities in the country—growth, decline, riots, crime, and boom times. In this sense Chicago is both unique and broadly representative, grounded in a thoroughly documented history and context that helps us understand key patterns. My goal is to interpret the contextual contingencies unique to Chicago (or at least thought to be) against the backdrop of more general social processes.[19] Throughout the book I describe real places and people, with attention to detail if it helps ground concepts that have some level of generality.

While attuned to observations and keeping closely grounded to contextual nuances, my goal is thus to identify what is typical rather than merely unique—to study regularities and structural patterns, in other words, with comparison to other cities wherever possible. This balancing between abstract principles and concrete instantiations is the most compelling intellectual route to take, I believe.[20] It is not the pure lab model of scientists, where reality is kept at bay, or the type of field ethnography that focuses on particularistic knowledge only. Warts and all, Chicago is my exemplar of "truth spot" to work out empirical processes and theoretical ideas. Certainly the place is an interesting one that, like Bellow's Augie March, is knocking its way headlong into the twenty-first century.[21]

The Data

Following several more years of fundraising, protocol development, pretesting, and open bidding for pieces of the large-scale data collection, a research shop was eventually set up in 1994, under the title Project on Human Development in Chicago Neighborhoods. The name was changed to reflect the integration of the two major themes of the study: *development* and *context*. Phase II of the project got started and the really hard work began.

To study neighborhoods we needed operational definitions. In chapters 2 and 3 I presented a theoretical definition and reviewed the debate over the idea of neighborhood in the contemporary city. In Chicago as elsewhere, there exist communities that have well-known names and usually distinctive borders, such as freeways, parks, or major streets. Chicago has seventy-seven such "community areas" that average about thirty-seven thousand persons and that were constructed to correspond to socially meaningful and natural geographic boundaries.[22] Although these boundaries have been critiqued and in a few cases names have undergone change over time, Chicago's community areas are nonetheless widely recognized by the media, administrative agencies, local institutions, service providers, and residents alike.[23] Community distinctions thus have both political force and symbolic value that have been reinforced over time in a kind of self-fulfilling prophecy. Census tracts refer to smaller and more socially homogeneous areas of roughly three thousand to five thousand residents on average. Although defined for administrative purposes, census tract boundaries attempt to take into account major streets, parks, and other geographical features. A third and even smaller area is the block group—a set of blocks averaging approximately one thousand residents. The smallest units typically used in research are "face-blocks" (the area including the two sides of the street facing one's home).[24]

Ecological units such as local community areas, census tracts, block groups, and face-blocks offer diverse operational definitions for empirical research. These geographical units are reasonably consistent with the notion of overlapping and nested ecological structures, and generally they possess more integrity with respect to geographic boundaries, land-use patterns, and social homogeneity than cities or metropolitan areas. They have also been put to the test successfully and pragmatically in a wide range of empirical research. In this study, I therefore do not enforce one and only one operational definition. Because communities are socially constructed for various purposes, one needs flexibility in research procedures depending on the outcome in question. As foreshadowed in chapter 3, I rely on the imbricated structure notion of Reiss and will report on multiple levels of analysis, including block groups, tracts, community areas, and relational patterns that cut across neighborhood boundaries.

But the PHDCN had to start somewhere. We decided that community areas were too big and heterogeneous to anchor the neighborhood sampling design, yet we were leery of relying only on census tracts, many of which we found, based on observation, might be too small. As a compromise we began by carving up the city into 343 neighborhood clusters (NCs)—groups of two to three census tracts that contain approximately eight thousand people. Major geographic boundaries (e.g., railroad tracks, parks, freeways), knowledge of Chicago's local neighborhoods, and cluster analyses of census data guided the construction of NCs so that they were relatively homogeneous with respect to racial/ethnic mix, socioeconomic status, housing density, and family structure. A total of eighty sampled neighborhood clusters were then randomly selected for intensive study after stratifying across twenty-one cells defined by the cross-classification of socioeconomic status (SES) and race/ethnicity. Census data were used to define the two stratification variables: racial/ethnic mix (three homogeneous strata and four heterogeneous strata) and a SES scale divided into equal thirds. Reflecting the pattern of segregation that is predominant in American society, the number of NCs falling into the twenty-one strata created by the cross-classification of racial/ethnic mix and SES was uneven. Although the aim of the PHDCN was to obtain nearly equal numbers of NCs from each of the strata, three of the twenty-one strata came up empty and an additional three cells had fewer than five NCs.[25] Thus in these three cells all NCs were selected (the population). In other strata, NCs were selected systematically after sorting by SES and housing density. The resulting probability sample of eighty NCs capitalized on, to the extent possible, the range of race/ethnic diversity and SES stratification in the city of Chicago.

Figure 4.1 displays the final selection of sampled neighborhoods by social type. One can see the wide variety and dispersal of neighborhoods across the city. The intended heart and soul of the PHDCN was the Longitudinal Cohort Study (LCS), which was designed to be embedded in these neighborhoods. Thus within the eighty NCs of figure 4.1, children falling within seven age cohorts (ages 0, 3, 6, 9, 12, 15, and 18)

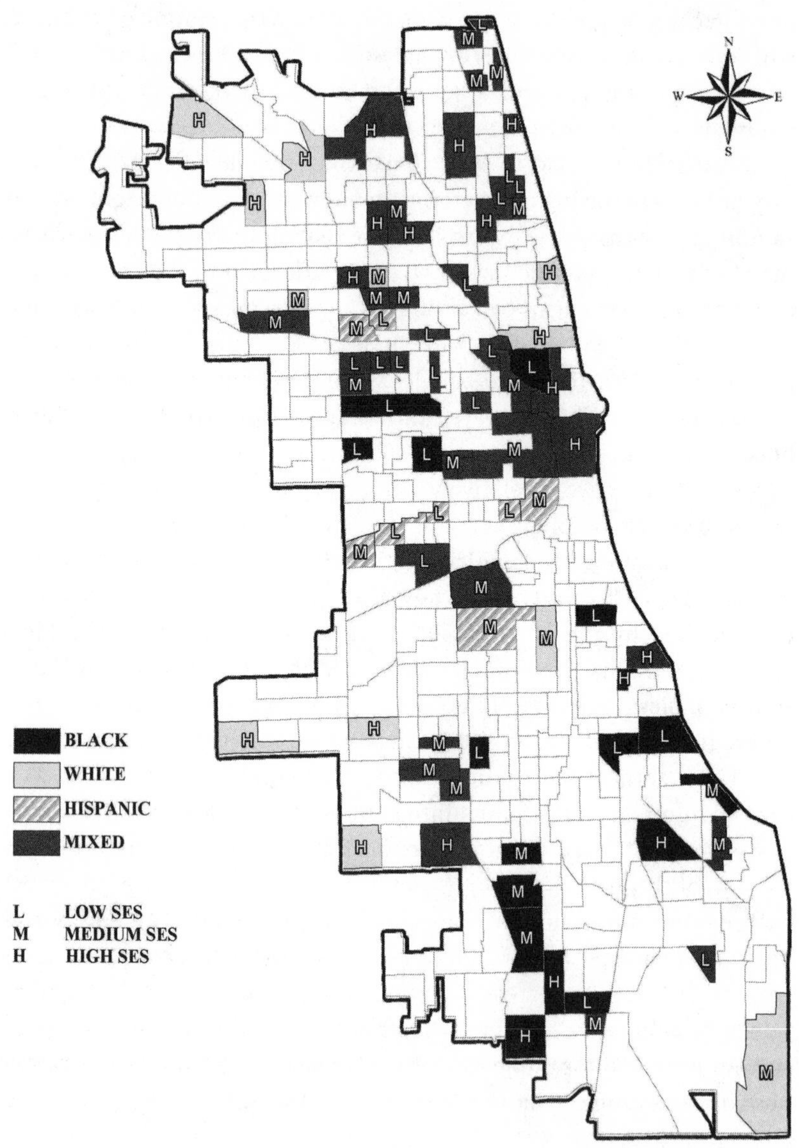

FIGURE 4.1. PHDCN-sampled neighborhood clusters by SES and race/ethnicity, 1995

were sampled from randomly selected households. The cohorts range in size from 1,262 in cohort 0—a representative, household-based, prenatal cohort—to 631 persons at age 18. This effort required the individual screening of over forty thousand households for pregnant women or age-eligible children to obtain the desired sample. Dwelling units were selected systematically from a random start within enumerated blocks. Within dwelling units, all households were listed, and age-eligible participants (the target was household members within six months of age 0, 3, 6, 9, 12, 15, or 18) were selected with certainty. As a result, multiple siblings were interviewed within some households. Participants are representative of families living in a wide range of Chicago neighborhoods (16 percent European American, 35 percent African American, and 43 percent Latino) and evenly split by gender.

Extensive in-home interviews and assessments were conducted with the sampled children and their primary caregivers. Rather than farm out the data collection for the cohort study, the decision was made to create a research and administrative staff dedicated to the study over a number of years. At one point some two hundred people were employed with a base in rented office space in the West Loop area of downtown Chicago.[26] Data collection took place over about eight years on a rolling basis at three points in time, at roughly two-and-a-half-year intervals (wave 1 in 1994–97, wave 2 in 1997–99, and wave 3 in 2000–2002). The subject and parental assessments were intensive and in most cases conducted separately by two interviewers depending on age. Types of information gathered include health, temperament, personality, cognitive functioning, ethnic identity, moral development, social competence, exposure to violence, substance abuse, delinquency, family structure and process, and peers. In the infant cohort, some five hundred babies were randomly selected for participation in a repeated observational study in which children and parents were videotaped and observed as a means to capture aspects of temperament and personality.

Owing largely to the dedication and hard work of the local staff, participation rates and retention were excellent for an urban sample in this time era. The PHDCN managed to enroll over 70 percent of the hardest-to-reach eighteen year olds, and over 76 percent of the birth cohort; the overall participation rate was 75 percent of the intended target at wave 1. Many of the children and families moved frequently after the first visit, both within and outside Chicago. In fact, over 40 percent of

PHDCN members moved, covering virtually all of Chicago and extending throughout the metropolitan region as shown in figure 4.2. Each move was geocoded to an address, and I exploit these residential mobility flows in the analyses to come.

PHDCN families were followed wherever they moved in the U.S. and beyond, such as Mexico. These destinations are revealed in figure 4.3. PHDCN staff spent a considerable effort tracking people down despite the widespread movement and managed to achieve a follow-up retention of 87 percent at wave 2 and 76 percent at wave 3.[27] In the contemporary era of urban data collection, this retention rate is rather remarkable. Specific measures from the data collected will be introduced as they are used in the chapters to come. For now I simply want to portray the flow of the data sources as the study took place.

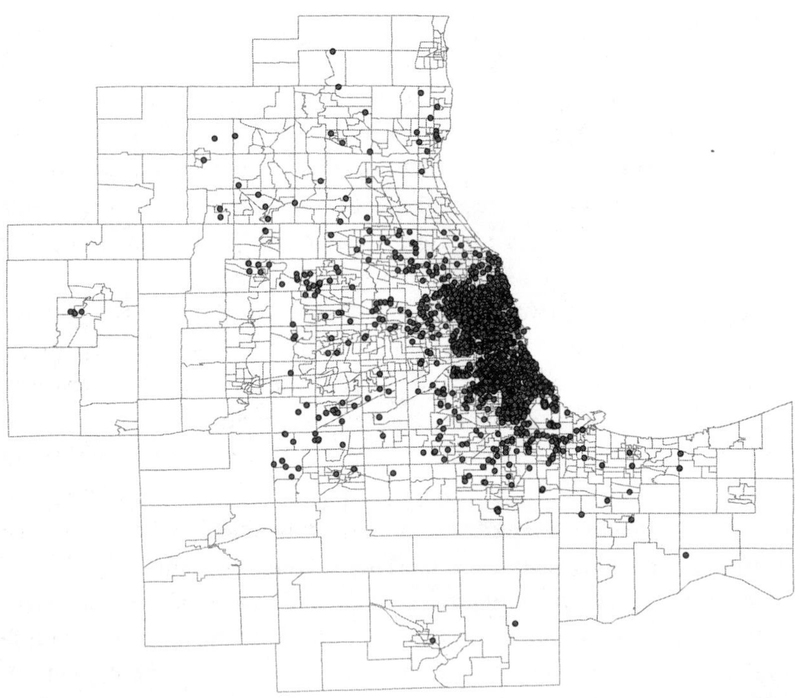

FIGURE 4.2. PHDCN residential destinations at end of follow-up in the Chicago metropolitan area, circa 2002

FIGURE 4.3. PHDCN national residential mobility and beyond

Community Survey

We executed three independent community studies apart from the families studied in the seven age cohorts. The largest leg of the community design was a survey in which the goal was to use residents as informants about their neighborhood using a "clustered" or multistage sampling approach. Since there had been a lot of work in community psychology and urban sociology relevant to our goals, we convened a workshop in Chicago in the fall of 1990 to gather advice on how to go about asking questions. Major scholars offered generous advice that continues to guide the study.[28] A key outcome of the meeting was ratification of the idea to treat neighborhoods as independent sampling units and not simply an appendage of the cohort members. A number of core concepts were proposed, such as social control and disorder, and leading scholars presented their experiences in how best to measure them across neighborhoods.

Following this meeting it was left to Al Reiss and me to construct the community survey and design the specifics of the sampling plan.

This charge sounds deadly dull but in fact the process turned out to be an intellectual treat that reached its apex in a marathon session at the Yale Club in NYC. My memory of this event is especially vivid. Reiss and I worked almost nonstop until we hashed out a blueprint. Questions were written by day over a large wooden table in a windowless library study, and progress evaluated over dinner and single-malt scotch late into the night. At marathon's end we produced a draft survey protocol and sampling plan to measure a number of concepts such as social cohesion, informal social control, friend/kinship ties, moral cynicism, organizational participation, and still others to be described later.

The Community Survey (CS) was a multidimensional assessment by residents of the structural and cultural organization of their neighborhoods. Our objective was to assess *all* Chicago neighborhoods, whether the individuals in our core sample resided in them or not. This was partly motivated by the expectation that many subjects would move within Chicago and that we would want to be able to characterize the receiving neighborhoods. But it was also done because of our affirmative focus on processes of neighborhood change and spatial mechanisms involving neighborhoods that adjoined the neighborhoods where LCS subjects resided. Thus, the Community Survey used the same NC sampling frame as the LCS, but independent data were collected on all 343 Chicago NCs. In total, 8,782 individuals eighteen years of age or older were interviewed in their homes in 1995, with an average of twenty-five individuals per NC (average of fifty interviews conducted in eighty target NCs and average of twenty interviews in nontarget NCs).[29]

We also conducted two other studies within the sample of eighty focal NCs linked to the LCS. The biggest non-survey component of the community design was the Systematic Social Observation (SSO) of all the street segments within the eighty NCs. A third and somewhat separate component was the Key Informant Study, composed of interviews with approximately 2,800 community leaders representing the institutional domains of business, law enforcement, community organizations, education, political, and religion. I describe each of these components below. But before I do, it is important to sketch out some of the challenges we faced in carrying out the community survey and initial enrollment of the PHDCN cohort members. They are tied in interesting ways to the characteristics of the neighborhoods and the city we set out to study.

Challenges and Solutions, Chicago Style

The naked truth of the origins of the PHDCN is that it was on the brink of failure at the starting gate. Not only did the project risk failure, each of the major investigators fell into despair in the early stages, certain that the project was about to come crashing down.

Things started in earnest when a national survey firm won a national bid to carry out the household listing, screening, identification of eligible participants for the cohort study, and the Community Survey. These tasks entailed a massive undertaking with a budget in the millions. Yet neither the contractor nor PHDCN senior investigators fully comprehended how difficult a challenge awaited as data collection "ramped up" and attempted to hit stride in 1995.[30] Readers from Chicago may remember 1995, for it spawned the most intense heat wave in the city's history.[31] It was miserable much of the summer, with temperatures reaching a hundred degrees on a number of consecutive days. Some seven hundred people died. The contractor hired to do the screening for cohort participants and the Community Survey stumbled badly, and in addition it turned out later that they had underbid the project. Things simply broke down. The survey firm ran out of money with only about ten thousand households screened and the community survey incomplete.

This turn of events led to one of the more unpleasant and bizarre experiences of my academic career. Lawsuits and lawyers entered the picture; at one point we found ourselves in a room arguing details of research design before attorneys and corporate administrators. A painful settlement was eventually reached—the survey firm would finish the community survey at an apparent financial loss (future grants were at stake), and we would have to pick up the pieces and do the screening and listing for the cohort study ourselves. Things looked disastrous as PHDCN lost about a year's time and costs spiraled.

Even when data collection was back on track, it ran into the realities of both old and new Chicago. Interviewers not only (literally) collapsed in the heat, some were robbed at gunpoint, others sexually harassed. Two research assistants on the way to a cohort interview came across a drive-by shooting and witnessed a dead body on the sidewalk. This was Chicago in the mid-1990s. Yet contrary to what many would expect, response rates were high in the "inner city." What nearly broke the back of the project was the North Side lakefront. Residents of the new Chicago in lakefront high-rises—typically white, affluent, childless, professional, busy, and assertive—had effectively sealed themselves off from the neighborhoods west of them. As network theorists might have predicted, the lives of many of these people were extralocal in nature. Yet, paradoxically, local space was crucial, and it manifested itself in doormen to block outside entrance, elaborate security devices and gates, and powerful condo or homeowner associations vigilantly guarding property values and local conditions. It was not that the local neighborhood was unimportant—how could it be with seven-digit real estate values and development galore? Rather it was that these neighborhoods were tightly defended, more by hired security guards than by residents. In screening households and interviewing for the CS, the project was thus at one point "locked out."

In response to the obstacles posed by residents' reclusiveness and the building security, the survey firm resorted to another Chicago tradition—they bribed or flattered the doormen to let them into the building. The clincher was an outside team known as "The Travelers," two women, one from New England and the other from the South. According to field notes from one of our interviewers and compiled by the site director, these women were in their forties, petite, charming, dressed in the latest fashions, and "utterly elegant—adorned with jewelry, diamond earrings, and pearl necklaces." They were high energy, fast thinking, and able to cross race and class boundaries with savior faire. Working as a team, they cracked the North Side.[32]

Data collection was also virtually halted in one Southwest Side community. Residents there refused to answer the door, much less the questions. Instead they directed us to the local alderman, again in good Chicago form. After repeated attempts at contact, the alderman informed us that he had to first read the interview to see what information was being collected before he would put out the word that we were to be trusted. If this is not a measure of power and social organization, I don't what is. He also offered to "consult" with us on adding questions of interest to his constituents. This situation required lots of ego massaging, negotiation, and some quid pro quo to get back on track. Even so, our participation rate in that NC was only 65 percent. To play good politics we had to brief the mayor's office, police department, and on down the line before going into any neighborhood.

There was more. One morning we woke up to an ominous headline in the *Chicago Tribune* to the effect that a massive federal initiative on crime had targeted Chicago. An activist from Washington was quoted as linking us—inaccurately and without any evidence—to the so-called Violence Initiative, an ill-fated attempt by Fred Goodwin, who was head of the National Institute of Mental Health (NIMH), to coordinate research activity on crime and focus on biological determinants. We were charged with seeking to draw blood from participants to identify biological markers so that we could eventually identify and incapacitate criminals from the inner city. Another story charged that our goal was to sterilize black women. A group of local activists called the Chicago Coalition against the Violence Initiative soon joined the fray and called for the study to shut down operation and for residents to refuse participation.[33]

Fortunately, we were blessed with strong leadership and had recruited a committed, ethnically representative, and streetwise local staff. Our site director, an African American, was appalled at the scurrilous charges and led a counterattack that took enormous social organizational effort. He and other project staff gave presentations and seminars throughout the city and met with community organizations over the course of many months. Aldermen were also brought in on the plans, along with key church leaders in the lower-income communities. The principal investigator, Tony Earls, spent countless hours articulating the scientific goals of the project and navigating a thicket of challenges both political and administrative.

In the end we received the strongest support from the citizens in the very neighborhoods that many activists sought to represent. We even received an endorsement from the *Defender*, Chicago's oldest and biggest black newspaper, along with the Left-leaning *In These Times*. I should note too that our design—with equal measure black, white, *and* Latino areas, low *and* upper SES, belied the charges of limiting the study to the inner city or "ghetto"—in fact the design might be read as an implicit criticism of the underclass "poverty paradigm" in urban sociology (see also chapter 3). It is also ironic that attempts to shut us down were followed by support from community activists. At one point I was approached by a campaign manager for someone running for mayor against Richard Daley. As an aspiring politician, he had warmed to the idea of appropriating the concept of "collective efficacy" for his campaign. I declined to get involved in politics, but having seen the project be criticized by the Left and Right, I came to the conclusion that we must be doing something right.

There was one major substantive casualty to the design. For a variety of reasons, biological measures were considered but dropped from the final data collection plans.[34] James Q. Wilson left the project soon thereafter, I suspect partly because of this turn of events. Some have claimed the study is flawed for not being on top of recent advances in biology. Although at the time I felt that sociology had in a sense won a battle, I no longer feel that way, and have come to the broader conclusion that sociology's typical position on biology risks its credibility in the interdisciplinary world that characterizes recent trends in science. Disciplinary barriers are breaking down fast, and in ten years the way we currently cut up the academic landscape may have little relevance for understanding human behavior. Moreover, because context is necessary for the expression of genetic variation, sociology should be an intellectual player in the explanation of gene-environment interactions.[35] That said, the PHDCN could not be everything.

These are just a few examples of the challenges of large-scale social science research in the modern city. A confluence of factors—race/ethnic segregation, suspicion of different paradigms, high-rise towers, fears of eugenics and biological determinism, gated communities, anonymity, and old-fashioned politics—conspired to make household interviewing and comprehensive assessments of individual development a difficult art. Yet the project overcame these challenges, hit its groove, and ended up pulling off both the community survey and longitudinal cohort studies with a better than anticipated cooperation rate.[36]

Systematic Social Observations

A major linchpin of the community design rested on observation rather than on what people say. In the spirit of the early Chicago School of urban sociology, the project directors believed that direct observation was fundamental to the advancement of knowledge. As Abbott emphasized, one of the hallmarks of the Chicago School was its concern for observing public places—not just abstract variables but the sights, sounds, and feel of the streets.[37] More than twenty-five years ago Albert J. Reiss Jr. advocated systematic social observation as a key measurement strategy for natural social phenomena. By "systematic," he meant that observation and recording should be done according to explicit rules that permit replication. He also argued that the means of observation, whether a person or technology, must be independent of what is observed. By "natural social phenomena," Reiss meant that "events and their consequences, including properties of organization, can be observed more or less as they occur."[38] Although he studied police-citizen encounters in his own research, Reiss noted the general import of the systematic social observation (SSO) method for assessing the physical conditions and social interactions within neighborhood settings that survey respondents may be incapable of describing.

One of the primary obstacles to our bringing independent and systematic social observation to bear on this conundrum is methodological uncertainty. This uncertainty includes not just how to properly conduct such observations but also how to properly assess their measurability at the neighborhood level. Another concern is cost, although direct observations are potentially less expensive than household surveys, since listing, screening, broken appointments, and response rates are eliminated. To address these issues we developed systematic procedures for collecting observational assessments of public space.

Between June and October 1995, observers trained by NORC at the University of Chicago drove a sport utility vehicle (SUV) at a rate of three to five miles per hour down every street within the stratified probability sample of eighty NCs. The geographic unit of recorded observation was the "face-block": the block segment on one side of a street. For example, the buildings across the street from one another on any city block comprised two separate units of observation. At each intersection a unique geographic identification code was assigned so that adjacent face-blocks could be pieced together to form higher levels of aggregation. To observe each face-block, our team fielded a driver, a videographer, and two observers. As the SUV was driven down the street, a pair of video recorders, one located on each side of the SUV, captured social activities and physical features of both face-blocks simultaneously. At the same time, two trained observers, one on each side of the SUV, recorded their observations onto an observer log for each block face. The observers added verbal commentary when relevant (e.g., about accidents or a drug bust), and that was captured by an audio recorder. One may wonder how we managed to do all this without suspicion. The answer is twofold: the windows were tinted, and even by 1995, SUVs had become commonplace. Despite our fears, no one seemed to notice. This became apparent upon viewing video extracts.

Observing and videotaping face-blocks took place between the hours of 7 a.m. and 7 p.m. The SSO team produced videotapes, observer logs, and audiotapes for every face-block in each of the eighty sampled NCs. In all, 23,816 face-blocks were observed and videorecorded for an average of 298 per NC and 120 per tract. The data collected from the 23,816 observer logs focus mainly on land use, traffic, the physical condition of buildings, and evidence of physical disorder. Unlike the observer logs, which could be directly entered into machine-readable data files, the videotapes required the expensive and time-consuming task of first viewing and then coding. We selected a random subsample of all face-blocks for coding. A total of 15,141 face-blocks were sampled for videotape coding, an average of 189 per NC and 77 per tract. From the videotapes, 126 variables were coded, including detailed information on physical conditions, housing characteristics, businesses, and social interactions occurring on each face block.[39]

Much like the original Chicago School of urban sociology, SSO takes researchers to the streets and provides the sights, sounds, and feel of everyday life. As James F. Short Jr. has argued, summoning the legacy of Park and Burgess, the essential spirit of the Chicago School was to "observe and record social life in every conceivable setting, and to generalize its forms and processes."[40] Through new technologies and methodological strategies, coupled with a theoretical lens that recognizes the changing nature of the city, PHDCN tried to keep this spirit alive and well in community research.

Follow-Ups

The data collection for PHDCN was virtually constant from 1994 to 2002. Just as the cohort study was winding down, however, a second Community Survey was conducted in 2001–2 in collaboration with the Chicago Community Adult Health Study (CCAHS) of the University of Michigan's Institute of Social Research (ISR). A new (repeated) cross-sectional sample of all persons aged eighteen or over living in the 343 NCs defined by PHDCN and thus covering all of Chicago was defined, and 3,105 randomly selected, in-person, adult (eighteen or older) interviews were carried out.[41] A second and revised SSO was also conducted in the collaboration between PHDCN and the University of Michigan health study. Observational data were collected across the entire city, this time based on the administration of observer logs for the block around each community survey respondent's house.[42] More details on both the second CS and SSO will be described when analyzed, but what these follow-ups mean in simple terms is that the PHDCN and its spin-offs produced the potential to measure in new ways the social mechanisms that make up neighborhood stability *and* change in Chicago. These dynamics and variations across neighborhoods in key social interactional and cultural properties lie at the heart of this book.

Cognate Studies

So far I have described how, in the community design of the PHDCN, we interviewed residents of Chicago and carried out systematic social observations of the city's streets in order to capture important social and physical characteristics that are unavailable in standard methods that assess individuals. Linked to the community-level design are a number of cognate efforts to assess community context through an alternative lens or in new settings. Some of these data sources derive from administrative or public records that, while not original to PHDCN, nonetheless provide important sources of information, such as census data (e.g., on income, racial composition, and home ownership), police and court records (e.g., on violence rates and incarceration), health statistics (e.g., rates of infant mortality, teen births), phonebook fiches (used to assess the density of churches), and tax records that are used to study nonprofit organizations. Variability by community in a select few of these dimensions was introduced in chapter 1.

There are also projects in Australia, England, Colombia, Sweden, China, and Africa, to name a few places, that are examining community-level processes inspired by the Chicago Project. One in particular was mounted in the mid-1990s in an international collaboration with Per-Olof Wikström at the University of Cambridge that would make possible the systematic comparison of data on Chicago and Stockholm neighborhoods. Owing to a fortunate set of circumstances, we were able to design a study including interviews with several thousand residents of Stockholm living in more than two hundred neighborhoods. The substance of the Stockholm protocol was designed to be comparable to the community survey of PHDCN. As I will show in chapter 7, this design allowed us to examine similarities and differences in how neighborhood collective efficacy and the stratification of socioeconomic resources account for crime rates in Chicago and Stockholm.

There are three other original and, I believe, novel efforts that round out the Chicago Project and that will be described more fully in later chapters. These include the Chicago Collective Civic Participation Project, which collected data on over four thousand public events of civic engagement in the Chicago area over three decades (analyzed in chapter 8), and the lost letter experiment, in which the rate of return for randomly dropped stamped envelopes was measured in 2002 and 2010 (analyzed in chapters 9 and 16). The lost-letter field experiment allows a direct but unobtrusive measure of altruistic or other-regarding behavior. The largest cognate study is a longitudinal effort to examine the community-level context of connections among the city's movers and shakers—the Key Informant Network Study (KeyNet). In 1995, we interviewed more than 2,800 community leaders and experts in six institutional domains—law, politics, education, business, religion, and community organizations. Based on their public positions, the sampled leaders in these domains were expected to have specialized knowledge of, and responsibility for, community social action. We also conducted a "snowball sample" to identify additional key actors who might not be detected in public records. Then in 2002 we returned to over a thousand of the respondents from the 1995 Key Informant study to interview them or those new to the original position.[43] In chapter 14 I describe these data in more detail and derive theoretically motivated measures (for example, the density and cohesion of leadership among elites) that are linked back to the other community concepts, such as collective efficacy. A panel-based positional approach to the study of community dynamics also allows for the direct measurement of stability and change in leadership structures and ultimately a glimpse into mechanisms of community governance and the interlocking structures of leadership networks that go beyond any one community.

Conclusion

The result of over a decade's worth of data collection, the Chicago Project resembles a web of data deliberately spun from theoretical ideas about community-level processes and contextual effects on individuals in the modern city. This book integrates and exploits this complex web of data in service of a theoretically guided assessment of how cities, neighborhoods, and individuals interact. But the contextual, intellectual, and historical backdrop of the data collection is itself an important part of the story, prompting me to present in this chapter an overview of the project's social origins and evolution. In fundamental respects, data are theoretical—they only take on meaning within a conceptual framework and guiding question. In my opinion research design is thus theoretical and takes precedence over statistical analysis. PHDCN and the emergent Chicago Project reflect an empirical embodiment of this core idea.

Finally, I should disclose that I spent eighteen years living in Illinois and consumed with all things Chicago. For twelve of those years I taught at the University of Chicago and observed the city's neighborhoods (especially from downtown and the Near North Side to the far South Side and reaching into the southern suburbs) on a daily basis as part of my normal rounds.[44] Obviously this is not ethnography, but I was immersed, and local knowledge of place helps to make sense of the larger picture. I also personally led focus groups, carried out selected interviews with community leaders, and took field notes and pictures of city streets on numerous occasions over the years. The bulk of the data to come are nonetheless more quantitative and systematic in nature, and I "detached" myself as a regular from Chicago (both the university and the city) in 2002, perhaps to better appreciate it from a distance and reflect on personal biases.[45] Like Howard Becker, however, ultimately I believe that the canonical distinctions made between qualitative and quantitative research are not sustainable.[46] I would further argue that key principles and impulses that motivate ethnography can guide quantitative work. What counts is the quality of empirical information and the veracity of inferences and claims drawn from it.

PART III **COMMUNITY-LEVEL PROCESSES**

5 Legacies of Inequality

In 1945, St. Clair Drake and Horace R. Cayton's *Black Metropolis* brought a disturbing pattern to the attention of scholars and the wider public. Whether through "disease and death" or "poverty and social disorganization," the city of Chicago by the mid-twentieth century was deeply stratified by a racialized hierarchy of wellbeing.[1] Drawing on the work of Louis Wirth, Robert E. L. Faris, H. Warren Dunham, and others in the Chicago School, the maps in *Black Metropolis* suggested a synergistic connection among seemingly disparate dimensions of place-based disadvantage.

Twenty years after *Black Metropolis*, Daniel Patrick Moynihan became famous (and simultaneously infamous) by calling renewed attention to the racialized configuration of the American city. With an unflinching eye, Moynihan's view of history led him to forecast key social trends and identify multiple challenges confronting urban America in the decade following *Brown vs. Board of Education*. Nothing in his view was more salient than the "tangle of pathology" in the black ghetto, by which he meant the strong clustering of numerous social problems.[2] The language was blunt and ignited a firestorm of protest that was not soon forgotten.[3] To this day the term "pathology" is avoided by social scientists.[4]

Yet many of the underlying facts Moynihan confronted remain unchanged today. Almost seventy years after Drake and Cayton's portrayal of Chicago, this chapter will show that while specific neighborhoods have shifted or traded places, with poverty moving outward from the inner city, the general force of ecological concentration and neighborhood racial stratification continues to have a strong grip on the city. In chapter 1, I showed a preliminary demonstration of this pattern. Looking back at figure 1.2, the reader will see scarcely any difference in the ecological distribution of homicides and low-birth-weight babies despite the seemingly distinct etiological origins of these two phenomena. Unfortunately, then, it appears that not much has changed, requiring us to face this overlooked stability and confront uncomfortable facts.

My goal in this chapter is to get beyond the pathology debate and focus on the larger issues that motivated Moynihan and other students of the city who came before him. Like Kenneth Clark, my take is that Moynihan wanted social policy to focus primarily on the inequality that resided at the structural and social-ecological level and not just the individual or family. That is a core idea that runs counter to much of the individual reductionism (or behaviorism) that characterizes contemporary social science and public policy. A host of social problems and dislocations that Moynihan highlighted are undeniably clustered for many of those in society who lack the resources to escape communities of disadvantage. My reading is thus that he was pointing to a *neighborhood* tangle of inequality—one inextricably tied to race—and that he emphasized its *durability without government intervention*.[5] Moynihan was insistent on this point, and in the most important chapter of his famous (but never published and often unread) report "The Case for National Action," he argued against the "variable" approach and called for a more holistic approach to both explanation and policy:

> It is our view that the problem is so inter-related, one thing with another, that any list of program proposals would necessarily be incomplete, and would distract attention from the main point of *inter-relatedness* (emphasis added). We have shown a clear relation between male employment, for example, and the number of welfare dependent children. Employment in turn reflects educational achievement, which depends in large part on family stability, which reflects employment. Where we should break into this cycle, and how, are the most difficult domestic questions facing the United States.[6]

More important, Moynihan coupled interconnectedness with *durability* and suggested the idea of reinforcing cycles of disadvantage or what might better be called *poverty traps*.[7] He noted in the beginning of his report that "so long as this situation persists, the cycle of poverty and disadvantage will continue to repeat itself." In the final policy chapter, he warned that "three centuries of injustice have brought about deep-seated structural distortions in the life of the Negro American" and that the "present tangle of pathology is capable of perpetuating itself without assistance from the white world. The cycle can be broken only if these distortions are set right."[8] Otherwise, he argued that once set in motion, racially linked poverty is a trap that reinforces itself and can be broken only by structural interventions.

Integrating the scope of thinking spanning the nineteenth-century London epidemiologists (to whom I return in chapter 6), the Chicago School, *Black Metropolis*, and the Moynihan report, I argue that a structural logic emerges that implies three broad ideas or theses that are interlinked:

1. The "tangle of pathology," or what today we would call social dislocations or social problems, has a deep neighborhood structure and connection to concentrated inequality.
2. Neighborhood social disadvantage has durable properties and tends to repeat itself, and because of racial segregation is most pronounced in the black community. I would add a related implication or subthesis: black children are singularly exposed to the cumulative effects of structural disadvantage in ways that reinforce the cycle.
3. The "poverty trap" cycle can be broken only with structural interventions of the sort that government or other large organizational units (e.g., foundations) are equipped to carry out.

The purpose of this chapter is to pursue these and related arguments, setting the stage for later analyses. I emphasize the big picture by showing both stability *and* change in neighborhood stratification and by showing that Chicago is not as unique as some claim. Inequality is durable and multiplex but not inevitable or natural, generating direct implications for theories of community-level processes, the social reproduction of inequality, individual selection bias, neighborhood interventions (thesis 3), and causality in the social world. Let me now lay out the essential facts of spatially inscribed inequality.

Things Go Together

As Clifford Shaw and Henry D. McKay argued in the Chicago of the 1920s and 1930s, Drake and Cayton in the mid-twentieth century, and William Julius Wilson and Douglas Massey near century's end, many social problems typically considered "outcomes" cluster together.[9] This pattern continues. Violence, a leading indicator of neighborhood viability, remains concentrated in early twenty-first-century Chicago and cities as different as Stockholm, as I showed in chapter 1 (fig. 1.6). Incidents of low birth weight map onto the location of violence (fig. 1.2), and when I extend the data through 2005 this same relationship remains (correlation of 0.77, $p < 0.01$). Other indicators of wellbeing tell the same story. For example, the infant mortality rate is correlated 0.76 with the teenage birth rate, which is in turn highly correlated with the homicide rate at 0.89 (both $p < 0.01$). There is a deep and divided structure in the concentration of wellbeing across multiple dimensions of the contemporary city.

What are often considered *sources* of compromised wellbeing—such as unemployment, segregation, poverty, and family disruption—are equally clustered in space. The basics of these patterns are common to many cities and extend across multiple ecological units of analysis ranging from census tracts to metropolitan areas and even states.[10] I illustrate and update this phenomenon here by considering empirical patterns for a core set of socioeconomic indicators in both Chicago and the U.S. I argue that disadvantage is not encompassed in a single characteristic but rather is a synergistic composite of social factors that mark the qualitative aspects of growing up in severely disadvantaged neighborhoods. My colleagues and I investigated this idea by examining six characteristics of census tracts nationwide,[11] taken from the 1990 and 2000 censuses, to create a measure of concentrated disadvantage: *welfare receipt, poverty, unemployment, female-headed households, racial composition* (percentage black), and *density of children*. These indicators all loaded on a single principal component we called "concentrated disadvantage" in both decades and both Chicago and the rest of the U.S. (altogether some sixty-five thousand census tracts).[12] The main difference of note between the U.S. and Chicago neighborhoods is that the exposure of children under eighteen years of age to concentrated economic disadvantage and racial segregation is more pronounced in Chicago.[13] The data thus confirm that neighborhoods that are both black *and* poor, and that are characterized by high unemployment and female-headed families, are ecologically distinct, a characteristic that is not simply the same thing as low economic status. In this pattern Chicago is not alone.

To probe the implications of this point in a different but more concrete way, I calculated the per capita income in the year 2000 in black compared to white neighborhoods in Chicago (defined here as census tracts with 75 percent or more of each group). The result was that *not one* white community experiences what is most typical for those residing in segregated black areas with respect to the basics of income—the entire distribution for white communities (mean = $42,508) sits to the right of the mean per capita income of black communities ($12,276).[14] Trying to estimate the effect of concentrated disadvantage on whites is thus tantamount to estimating a phantom reality. Latino and mixed-race communities are better off, but even there the mean is well below white areas. The bottom line is that the racial stratification of Chicago's urban landscape precludes a simple estimation of a single causal effect of disadvantage for all racial groups, as commonly attempted in the literature.[15] As Massey and Denton argue more generally, while race and poverty are obviously distinct concepts, a set of "allocation mechanisms" lead race and other dimensions of disadvantage into overlapping ecological units.[16]

It follows from these data and the spatial logic of the "tangle of pathology" thesis that the knot of inequality is far greater in the black community than the white community. Another way to test this thesis is to examine how the relationship between the unemployment rate and poverty varies by the racial status of the neighborhood. Unemployment in the black community was seen by Moynihan as one of the central drivers of poverty, which he felt was intensified over time by discrimination and segregation. The implication is that alternative resources available in white communities would be able to offset, to some extent, the connection of unemployment with welfare dependency, another core feature of Moynihan's analysis and at the center of much of the poverty debate both past and present. Consistent with this argument, I find that there is no significant relationship between unemployment rates and economic dependence in white communities—surprisingly, in fact, *a simple flat line emerges*. Yet in mixed and minority areas the correlation is strongly positive and significant.[17] This finding demonstrates the much tighter connection among economic-related indicators in minority areas, a process that contributes to the synergistic intersection of racial segregation with concentrated disadvantage.

Concentrated Incarceration: A New "Pathology"?

There is a new kind of social distortion that has come to characterize the national scene that might surprise even Moynihan, were he alive today. From the 1920s to the early 1970s, the incarceration rate in the United States averaged 110 inmates per one hundred thousand persons. This rate of incarceration varied so little both here and abroad that many scholars believed that the nation and the world were experiencing a stable equilibrium of punishment. But beginning in the mid-1970s, the incarceration rate in the United States accelerated dramatically, reaching the unprecedented rate of 197 inmates per one hundred thousand persons in 1990 and the previously unimaginable rate of 504 inmates per one hundred thousand persons in 2008.[18] Incarceration in the United States is now so prevalent that it has become a normal stage in the life course for many disadvantaged young men, with some segments of the population more likely to end up in prison than attend college. Scholars have broadly described this national phenomenon as *mass incarceration*.[19]

Yet, in fact, mass incarceration has a local concentration, what Charles Loeffler and I have called "Punishment's Place."[20] Obscured by a focus on national trends are profound variations in incarceration rates by communities within cities, especially by their racial composition. Like the geographically concentrated nature of criminal offending by individuals, a small proportion of communities bear the disproportionate brunt of U.S. crime policy's experiment with mass incarceration. In Chicago, we can see this by calculating the rate of incarceration for each census tract in Chicago and comparing it to the level of concentrated disadvantage and percent black.[21] The correlation of incarceration rates in 1990–95 with concentrated disadvantage and percent black at the neighborhood level in 1990 is 0.82 and 0.75, respectively. The corresponding correlations for 2000 disadvantage and percent black predicting incarceration in 2000–2005 are 0.80 and 0.74. The persistence over time at the census-tract level is, by implication, very strong (0.86, all coefficients $p < 0.01$). Because of this ecological concentration, large swaths of the city, especially in the southwest and northwest, are relatively untouched by the imprisonment boom no matter which period we examine, with almost no one sent to prison in some areas. By contrast, there is a dense and spatially contiguous cluster of areas in the near west and south central areas of Chicago that have rates of incarceration many times higher. This pattern of concentration results in a racialized configuration of the city—the correlation between concentrated disadvantage and the incarceration rate in white areas is no different than zero, but in black, Latino, and mixed areas the correlation is over 0.6 ($p < 0.01$).

Once again, then, "things go together," but the strength of the connection, especially among social dislocations like poverty, crime, infant mortality, low birth weight, incarceration, and unemployment, is decidedly stronger in communities of color.

Poverty Traps: Social Transformations Revisted

The continued concentration of poverty, crime, incarceration, and general disadvantage is an intriguing puzzle, because residential moves ensure that different individuals make up the same neighborhoods over time. Consider the residential mobility introduced in chapter 3 that defines contemporary Chicago as it does other cities (fig. 3.2). Almost 50 percent of the PHDCN sample moved at one point, and virtually every neighborhood in the city is connected through residential mobility flows. A substantial number of moves are also to the suburbs of Chicago and beyond.

These patterns motivate deceptively simple questions. How much stability or change in concentrated neighborhood inequality is generated over time given the dynamic flows of people? The question is not how individuals change but whether and to what extent the geographic concentration of poverty became increasingly entrenched in certain urban neighborhoods. We can extend this line of reasoning to other dimensions as well, perhaps even those that can change quickly. For example, how tenacious is the hold of high rates of violence on select urban neighborhoods? When crime goes down, or up, are the trends similar for all places? How stable are social processes over time? What predicts neighborhood change? Does it take a planned intervention to bring about true structural change? This section examines stability and change over important periods of Chicago's history from the 1960s to the present.

William Julius Wilson and others have stressed the "social transformation" of the concentration of poverty during the 1970s and 1980s.[22] Still others have written on "The New Chicago" in the decade of the 1990s.[23] The data, however, tell a story of both stability and change in neighborhood poverty during this historical time. At the neighborhood level, for example, Jeffrey D. Morenoff and I reported a very high correlation ($r = 0.87$) between neighborhood poverty rates in 1970 and 1990. Neighborhoods that were poor in 1970 generally continued to be poor in 1990.[24] Most of the variance in poverty (67 percent) was due to differences *between* neighborhoods rather than differences over time *within* neighborhoods. The implication is that between-neighborhood differences in poverty were quite stable over time. The most significant secular change was that the poverty rate for the average neighborhood in Chicago increased from 11 percent in 1970 to 20 percent in 1990—a change induced by broad social and global economic forces. This change was most pronounced at the upper tail of the neighborhood poverty distribution. The seventy-fifth percentile of the distribution corresponded to a poverty rate of only 14 percent in 1970, but by 1990 it had more than doubled, increasing to 30 percent. Despite the growth (or change) in poverty between 1970 and 1990, then, there was stability in the relative rank order of neighborhoods—poverty was persistently concentrated by neighborhood while increasingly prevalent.

Figure 5.1 extends the examination of the social transmission of concentrated poverty from a decade earlier—1960—and the dawn of the civil rights era—to a decade later and the census of 2000. It also shifts the analysis to the community-area level and gives names to places (e.g., Hyde Park, Grand Boulevard, South Shore, and Lincoln Park) that serve as markers of difference and symbolic value.[25] Community areas have political and social reputations that continue to this day.[26] It is also of relevance that Wilson's thesis of concentration effects was developed on data from the community areas of Chicago.

Figure 5.1 shows that concentrated poverty is surprisingly stable

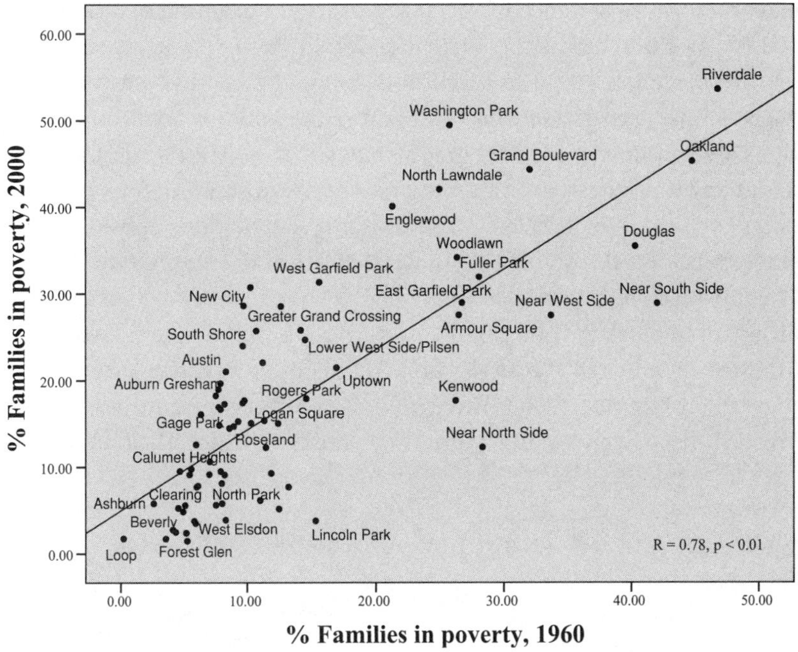

FIGURE 5.1. Persistence and change in poverty across forty years

over the long period of forty years. In a time of rapid social change, riots, crime-rate swings, racial change, economic recessions, and gentrification at the end of the twentieth century, concentrated poverty is stubborn in its concentration. Note the high correlation between poverty in 1960 and 2000 of 0.78. For over forty years, Riverdale and communities in the "black belt" on the South Side stand out as "poverty carriers" in contrast to the largely white and well-off communities such as Norwood and Edison Park in the upper west corner of the city. Beverly on the Southwest Side remained economically healthy despite its proximity to the black belt and increasing racial heterogeneity. Overall, then, the data reveal that if we know the poverty level of a neighborhood at one point in time it is possible to quite accurately forecast its outcome up to four decades later. It is not obvious that this should be possible given that people move in and out of neighborhoods that are constantly in flux. How do we account for this stability amid change?

The link of race to poverty suggests a logical next step. To further elaborate the persistence of racial segregation I examine *changes* in racial composition across the same four-decade period, plotting in figure 5.2 the percentage of a neighborhood's population that was black in 2000 against percent black in 1960, before the major urban transformations Wilson described. This graph shows that where racial change is abundant it is structured in an asymmetric way, yielding four types of neighborhoods. The first two reflect durable segregation—those that are stably black (upper right) and those that are stably white (lower left). The third type reflects transitional neighborhoods that went either from all white to black ("white flight") or partially black to segregated black (up the left side and across the top). That is not a surprise, although it may be hard for people in Chicago to imagine that communities such as West Englewood and Auburn Gresham were once white. The fourth type

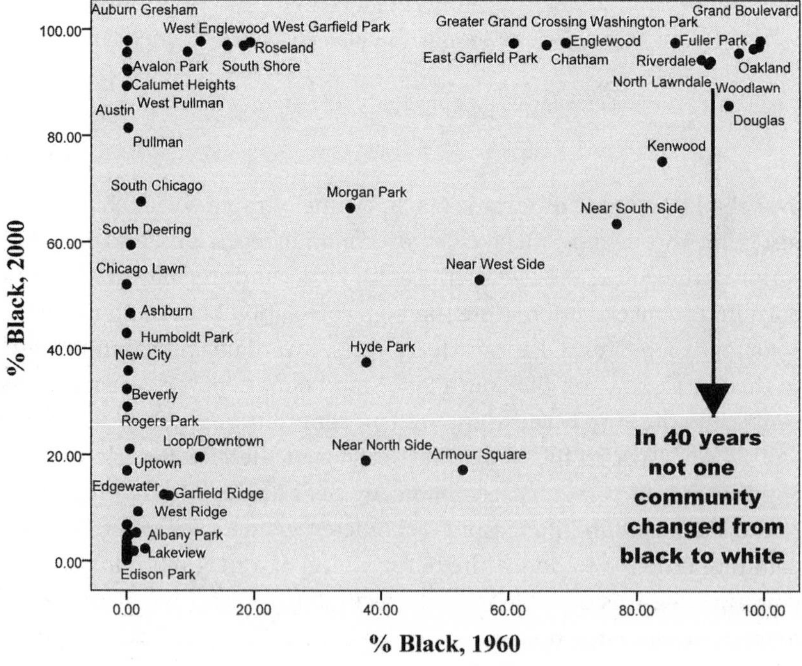

FIGURE 5.2. Stable asymmetry of racial change across forty years

is the small number of integrated communities that have remained so, such as Hyde Park and the Near West Side.

What is startling is the missing type—in the third-largest city in America, *not one neighborhood transitioned from predominantly black to predominantly white*. The lack of observations in the lower right quadrant of the graph indicates that none of the areas that had large percentages of black population in 1960 lost significant shares. In fact, there appears to be a threshold effect of around 50 percent black, above which all neighborhoods either maintained or increased their share of black population. Only one or two communities (notably Hyde Park and the southern part of Kenwood, home to President Barack Obama) maintained a reasonable black-white integration over this period.[27] Figure 5.2 thus tells a story of change within a relatively stable social-ecological structure: there were great shifts in neighborhood racial composition from 1960–2000, but neighborhoods that were initially black stayed that way over time, while at the same time many areas of the city remained off limits to blacks. In light of this pattern, Chicago has the distinction of being not just one of the most racially segregated cities in America, but it appears to be durably so.[28] Is this an anomaly?

What about the Economic Boom? And Is Chicago Unique?

I turn now to a closer focus on the decade of the 1990s, the decade for which complete data are currently available and a period considered by many students of the city to be characterized by profound gentrification and a changed urban landscape. These were, of course, the boom years of economic growth, real estate growth, increasing globalization, high tech, and investment bank adventures to be followed by an economic crisis. It was also the period when incarceration rates reached unprecedented and previously unimagined levels. Does preserving rank or stability still hold? The typical answer nowadays is no. A recent look at the "new urban renewal" in Chicago and New York, for example, concludes that "countless neighborhoods are being monumentally altered."[29] But what about the bird's-eye view that takes into account all neighborhoods and thus does not select on change itself? What about the constellation of factors that motivate this book's focus? And what about the first decade of the twenty-first century that ushered in a new set of social upheavals?

In probing this issue I confront head on a constant refrain I have heard over the years: Chicago is unique. Malcolm Klein argued that Chicago is "just weird."[30] A recent book argues that single-city studies are "biased."[31] Mario Small more politely asked if Chicago is merely an "outlier."[32] After all, the racial dynamics seen in the previous figure would seem to say yes.

The full data provide a different and surprising answer. For basic parameters of social stratification by neighborhood, it seems that, if anything, *it is the U.S. that is unique or weird.* First, I have already demonstrated that the clustering of factors that make up concentrated disadvantage are the same whether we look at all census tracts in the U.S. or just those in Chicago. In a recent study I went a step further by plotting the relationship predicting concentrated disadvantage in 2000 from 1990 disadvantage.[33] Whether in the city of Chicago or for the sixty-four thousand census tracts across the rest of the U.S. (with Chicago removed), disadvantage has strong inertial tendencies at the ecological level. The correlation is above 0.9 at both the local and national level with an identical pattern.

I consider here a further test. The census years 1990 and 2000 are important for a number of reasons, not least because a huge national experiment took place when the Clinton administration dismantled welfare as we knew it. What does the ecological concentration of public assistance look like pre- and post-welfare reform? Figure 5.3 provides the answer. In both Chicago and the U.S. there is a strong linear relationship, with welfare concentration highly stable over the decade despite a macrolevel policy intervention. Chicago is parallel to the national scene, and the correlations at the neighborhood level are identical. What is unique is not Chicago, apparently, but U.S. cities compared to non-U.S. cities (fig. 1.6).

Perhaps it is racial composition that is different in Chicago and the U.S. Chicago has a long history of racial segregation, and its segregation indices are higher than the national average. But when we consider the stability of percent black in the period of the 1990s, a decade of considerable change and gentrification in the U.S., a sobering picture

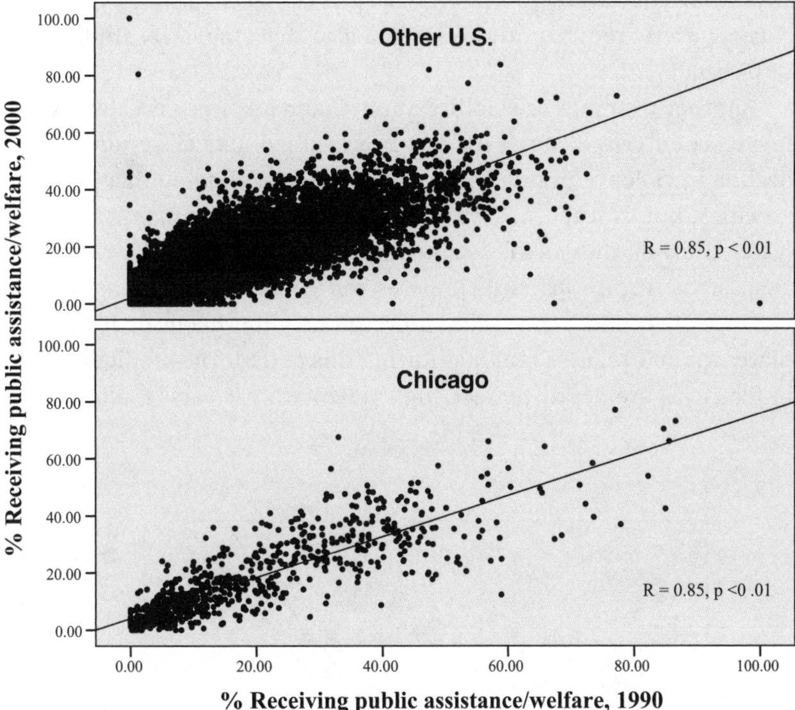

FIGURE 5.3. Chicago is not unique: durability of concentrated welfare dependence before and after federal policy to "end welfare as we know it": Chicago (N = 844) and the U.S. (N = 64,902), 1990–2000

emerges. There is a 0.96 correlation between percent black in 1990 and percent black in 2000, statistically no different than in Chicago, where the correlation is 0.98. What's more, the asymmetry of change evident in figure 5.2 emerges at the national level as well.[34] Literally thousands of neighborhoods nationwide transitioned from white to black, but *in the entire U.S, out of some sixty-five thousand tracts, only about ten went from over 60 percent black to substantially (60 percent or more) white*. Two did in Chicago, but the base is less than one thousand tracts. Overall, then, racial stratification is profoundly stable in terms of relative positioning, as is concentrated poverty. And Chicago is hardly unique—a general nationwide process is at work, and the picture of stability and change is largely identical. A book devoted to comparing neighborhood structural dynamics across many U.S. cities comes to the same basic conclusion, even though motivated by the idea that single-city studies may be biased.[35]

Another example of stability amid change can be revealed by the incidence of crime. Much ink has been spilled about the unexpected decline in violence in the U.S. during the 1990s.[36] I do not have data on all cities, but Chicago was no exception. Robbery and homicide rates, which are well measured, declined nearly 50 percent in Chicago from 1995–2006. Figure 5.4 superimposes the general downward trend in violence over time. Remarkably, however, neighborhoods do not switch places in their relative rankings during this period. The prediction lines in figure 5.4 are nearly perfect: high violence areas persist and low vio-

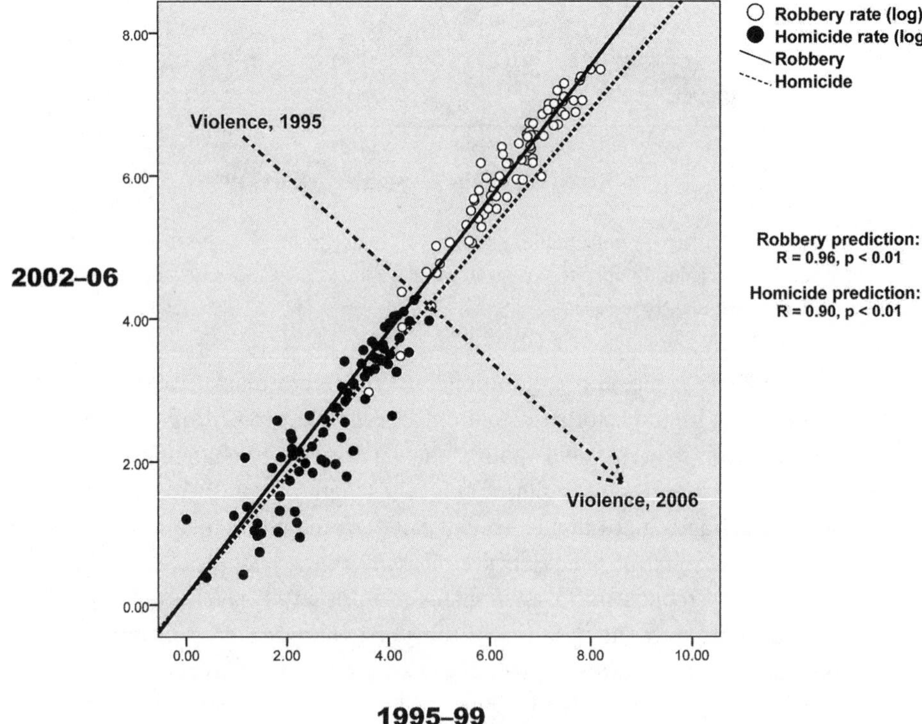

FIGURE 5.4. Stable homicide and robbery profiles during a sharp secular decline in violence, Chicago, 1995–2006

lence areas remain so. There is almost no relative change in position, yet violence plummeted and virtually all neighborhoods benefitted by experiencing fewer robberies into the mid-2000s.

Post-2000 Trends

The persistent critic might still argue that while the stability of change held in the twentieth century, after 2000 things finally tipped to wholesale change. Here the argument would be that gentrification post-2000 constitutes a unique or truly transformative phenomenon. The Census Bureau has taken on a major new procedure and post-2000 will not be strictly comparable with prior decades. As readers who filled out the 2010 census probably noted, perhaps with surprise, the new short form was basically only a headcount of household members and their race. The usual suspects from the "long form" of censuses past were not asked about and were instead collected by the American Community Survey (ACS) using a sample for small areas such as census tracts and over a rolling number of years. Detailed data were not available before 2010.

I nonetheless was able to take advantage of two data sources that were released as I completed the present analysis. One was interim population estimates made available in 2009 from what is known as the Public Use Micro Samples (PUMS) that the ACS released, based on representative samples of communities with more than twenty-five thousand in population in the years 2005–7.[37] For Chicago, local officials defined nineteen areas made up of contiguous community areas, most of which are socially similar. For example, one North Side PUMS area brings together Rogers Park, Edgewater, and Uptown, while Roseland, Pullman, West Pullman, and Riverdale make up a Far South PUMS.[38] Poverty, income, immigration, and racial composition indicators were defined in the same way for both the 2000 census and 2005–7. The PUMS is analytically strategic because it gives us panel data over a half decade after the 2000 census that includes the economic bubble and a period of continuing gentrification. If wholesale social transformation is not visible in this era or the 1990s, it is hard to imagine where to find it. Although entailing only nineteen areas, the data are incontrovertible in their verdict: stability's grip has not loosened. For percent black, the correlation is in effect unity ($r = 0.99$), meaning that when it comes to the city's racial structure, the spatial ordering of segregation remains in check with respect to larger clusters of community areas. Poverty, median income, and foreign born are highly stable over time as well, with correlations of 0.87, 0.88., and 0.99, respectively (all $p < 0.01$). The median income stability is noteworthy in light of the gentrification that occurred in areas adjacent to and in the Loop.

Second, I examined the connection of poverty in 2000 and the poverty rate averaged from 2005–9 and linked to the smaller geographic unit of census tracts. These data also come from the American Community Survey, released in December of 2010. I was able to correlate the poverty data and found that across census tracts the poverty rate from 2000 predicted the 2005–9 poverty rate at 0.74 ($p < 0.01$). When I moved back up the geographic scale and constructed a poverty rate for community areas, the correlation increased to 0.91 ($p < 0.01$). Moreover, the predictive correlation of poverty from 1960 to nearly fifty years later was a durable 0.60 ($p < 0.01$). The newer data thus did not change the story but rather reaffirmed the main plot. Indeed, once again inequality's spatial distribution is intact across multiple scales of neighborhood, this time almost to the year of this book's publication and despite differences in census procedures.

The data, then, are consistent by demonstrating the deep structure induced by legacies of inequality. *Namely, communities can be said to inherit their positional inequality*. The common practice of focusing on absolute changes in one or a handful of communities is misleading, for when it comes to a bird's-eye view of the spatial dynamics of an entire city or nation, a remarkable process of the reproduction of inequality is taking place just as it has in the past.

Racial Inequality

Another implication of Moynihan's reasoning and the spatial logic advanced in this book is that the grip of neighborhood inequality—the "tangle"—is amplified, more durable, and qualitatively distinct in the black community. The expectation is that we should see more persistence of disadvantage in minority or black communities than white ones and the durability of nonoverlapping neighborhood distributions. Chicago, with its segregated urban structure, affords an opportunity to assess this notion within relatively homogeneous subgroups. I disaggregated the city into four race/ethnic strata—predominantly white, black, Latino, and other (mixed). In minority areas the continuity of concentrated disadvantage during the 1990s is much higher, but the result is especially striking when comparing segregated black neighborhoods, where the correlation is 0.83, to white neighborhoods, where the stability correlation is only 0.24.

This divergence is even more evident for the durability of unemployment that Moynihan emphasized and documented again in Wilson's *When Work Disappears*.[39] This can be demonstrated by considering the prediction of neighborhood unemployment rates in 2000 from unemployment rates in 1990 for predominantly black neighborhoods compared to predominantly white neighborhoods. In Chicago, at least, the correlation of unemployment over time is relatively high (0.64) and significant in the black community but nonexistent in the white community (−0.05). The distributions are virtually incomparable—most white neighborhoods sit to the left of where the black distribution starts.[40] The data thus confirm that blacks and whites live in different social worlds of work. As Moynihan worried in 1965, unemployment appears to recycle itself in the black community.

So too does imprisonment, a new "social distortion" that did not exist in Moynihan's time to anywhere near the extent that it does today. There has always been incarceration, of course, but in the post-Moynihan era the U.S. has witnessed a form of what many call mass incarceration. I argued earlier, however, that mass incarceration is "placed" in certain communities, a pattern that I now show visually in figure 5.5. The stability of incarceration's spatial distribution over time is virtual unity (correlation of 0.98), but what is most striking in figure 5.5 is the incommensurability of mass incarceration in black compared to white communities. There is no overlap in the distribution and a clear gap between the "highest incarcerated white community" and the "lowest" for black communities. West Garfield Park and East Garfield Park on the city's West Side stand out as the epicenter of the modern incarceration regime. If we transform the log scale into simple rates of imprisonment per hundred thousand, a disturbing fact is revealed. West Garfield Park has a rate *over forty times higher* than the highest-ranked white community on incarceration, Clearing (4,226 vs. 103 per 100,000). This is a staggering differential even for community-level comparisons—a difference of kind, not degree.

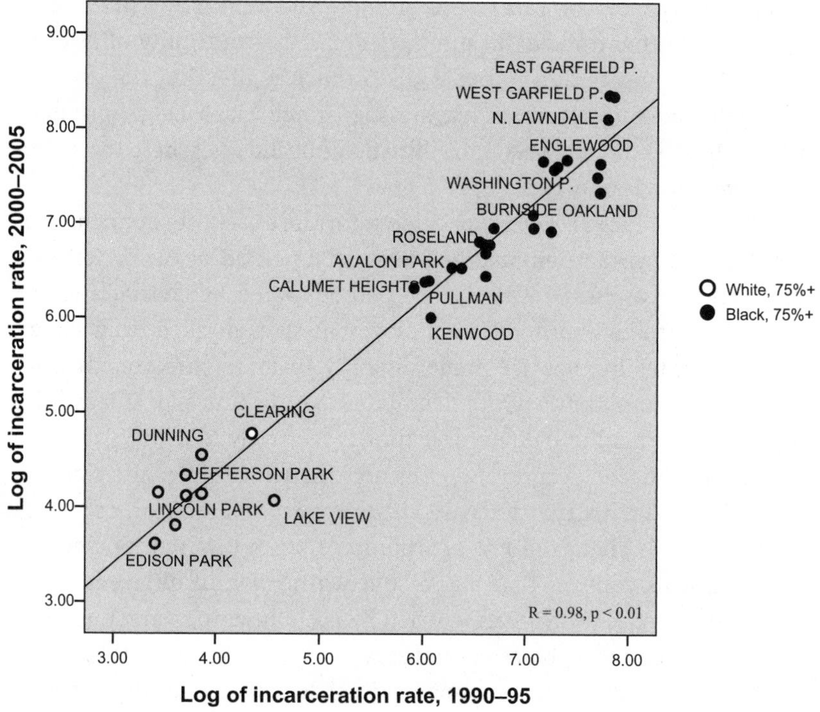

FIGURE 5.5. Incarceration in black and white: persistence of spatially concentrated incarceration by the racial status of Chicago communities, 1990–2005

In a similar vein, the data reveal that the rate of male unemployment, which Moynihan and Wilson were most concerned about, is much more predictive of incarceration in the black communities of figure 5.5 than white communities. The correlation in white communities is nonsignificant, whereas for black communities the male unemployment rate in 2000 predicts later incarceration (0.53, $p < 0.01$). This interaction suggest that incarceration is part of the cycle of disadvantage behind the "poverty traps" that I have shown in this chapter, traps that find their most intense manifestation in segregated and racially isolated communities. There is likely a reciprocal feedback, in which imprisonment removes males from the community while at the same time unemployed males drive the incarceration "input," thus reinforcing a vicious cycle.

This modern-day distortion implicates, and complicates, policy operations of the government.

Changing Contours of Poverty's Spread

I have argued that a key to understanding the pathways of neighborhood change is racial geography. I assess this claim further by examining whether residual changes in neighborhood poverty over time occurred in a spatially random fashion or whether they are concentrated within certain areas of the city. If spatial logic does not matter, but only a neighborhood's internal history of poverty does, then a good predictor of a neighborhood's current poverty rate would be its past poverty rate, and variations in poverty from the predicted rate would not have a strong spatial pattern. After all, I have just shown how poverty is relatively stable over time.

Figure 5.6 evaluates this notion by plotting *residual* poverty for each neighborhood in Chicago from 1960 to 2000 against the baseline racial composition in 1960.[41] Predominantly black neighborhoods in 1960 were geographically clustered at the core of Chicago's black belt in community areas such as Grand Boulevard and Oakland to the south, and in North Lawndale on the West Side. But residual increases in poverty from 1960 to 2000 form just three contiguous clusters that pushed out from the core of Chicago's black ghetto to adjacent areas and along the city's periphery. Communities like Woodlawn, South Shore, and Englewood saw rapid unexpected increases based on past poverty, as did North Lawndale and Austin on the Far West Side (which eventually became virtually all black) and Riverdale on the Far South Side.

So change is clearly evident, especially the growth in "outer-city" and suburban poverty.[42] Yet from a macrolevel perspective the change is structured—figure 5.6 captures the growth of urban poverty as a spatial process, revealing that most of the unexpected change in poverty in a historical sense occurred in close geographic proximity to the classic black ghetto and then radiated outward in systematic fashion rather than following a placeless process. Neighborhoods like Englewood and Austin were already vulnerable to increasing concentration effects because of their spatial position and relative lack of resource advantage.

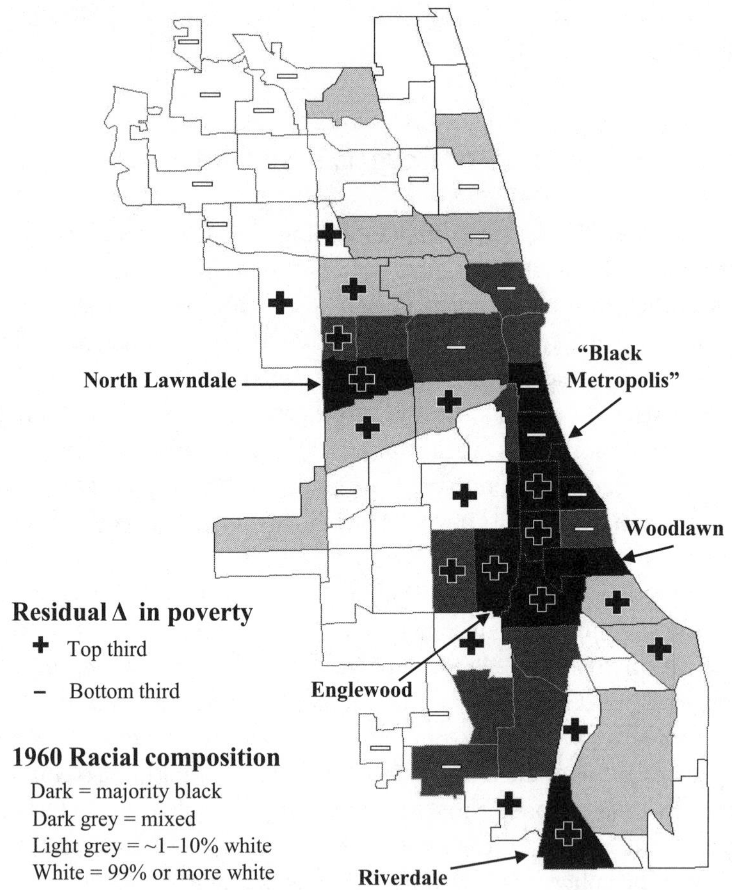

FIGURE 5.6. Original "black metropolis" and growth in concentrated poverty from 1960 to 2000, unaccounted for by baseline poverty

Left largely untouched by the growth of urban poverty were areas of the North and Northwest sides, which actually saw *decreases* in poverty beyond what would be normally expected. In a spatial example of the "Matthew Effect," the rich tended to get richer building on their initially advantaged position. And those spatially proximate to the rich became better off too. This reinforcing pattern appears to have lock-in effects, or, one might say, "lock-up effects," when it comes to the intense incarceration removal on the city's West and South sides (fig. 5.5).

Structural Interventions: Breaking the Trap?

Inequality is stubbornly persistent even though change is constantly taking place. How can the durable inequality I have documented be changed in possibly transformative ways? This question is the hardest of all, and, as Moynihan sensed, there are no easy answers. This is especially true in a culture in which freedom of choice to move anywhere one can afford is highly valued.

Although the evidence is insufficient at this point to support a strong causal claim, it is notable that communities undergoing robust interventions saw unexpected declines in the rate of concentrated poverty as predicted from 1990 levels alone. Looking again at figures 5.1 and 5.6, and considering changes from 1990 to 2000 in particular, communities below the regression line of continuity share a similar profile. Places like Douglas, Oakland, and the Near South Side were mainly poor black communities that witnessed structural changes from the outside, including the dismantling of segregated high-rise public housing by the Chicago Housing Authority and considerable investment by the city and institutions such as the University of Chicago in both the physical infrastructure and educational system (e.g., charter schools). The Near West Side also saw considerable investment by the city and economic developers, and along with the Near South and Near North sides, saw a relative improvement in median income in the very recent past. These communities are part of the "New Chicago" that have seen, literally, new neighborhoods spring to life.[43] Dearborn Park in the South Loop is a notable example introduced in chapter 1, but there are others in the near- to mid-south area, especially where the teardowns of public housing have led to gentrification by the black middle class.[44] The Near West Side saw the destruction of the famed Maxwell Street, the expansion of "University Village" near the old "Chicago Circle" campus, and the construction of the United Center amid former devastation.

Individual choice in migration decisions should not be overlooked either. There has been a return to cities across the country, and Chicago is no exception. The city saw growth in its population overall and a number of formerly poor areas became attractive to bohemians and the so-called creative class (fig. 1.5). Gentrification may be overstated in some cases, but it is real. Other communities, for example, Wicker Park, Bucktown, and the Near South Side, saw gentrification that was not driven by large-scale policy intervention. The West Loop and Near West Side have also been hot, with trendy restaurants sprouting like wildflowers, Oprah's studio, and considerable gentrification that has crept into the heart of the Latino Pilsen district. I will return in later chapters to a detailed analysis of interneighborhood migration patterns, but for present it is apparent that positional stability is persistent but not inevitable.

Reversal of community fortune is thus possible, but in the case of Chicago, at least, it appears that structural levers are needed to spur or sustain change in deeply distressed minority communities that have experienced a history of subjugation. There are any number of ongoing planned interventions that have attempted to change the trajectory of concentrated poverty, such as mixed-income housing redevelopment, tax-financed economic development zones, and community policing. I will address these further in terms of policy implications in the final chapter, but for now the data suggest that in an ongoing process with durable or self-reinforcing properties, macro interventions of the sort government is uniquely suited to mount, or support through zoning changes, need to be at the top of our policy considerations and evaluation efforts. Moreover, from the mid to late 1990s to the present was an especially propitious time for structural interventions because a natural change has been taking place across much of the country—crime and violence rates have been falling sharply. In the next chapter we learn how in earlier eras, crime and violence drove down central city populations and contributed to the widespread sense of urban decline. Recent times have been less plagued by crime and a renewed appreciation for the viability of cities has emerged. In places like Chicago and cities nationwide, neighborhood renewal is occurring in the heart of some of what were previously high-crime, very poor, and often devastated areas. No one factor can be credited with this change, but it appears that smart local decisions that capitalize on secular changes are benefiting cities even though the benefits remain spatially concentrated. I return to this theme and an exploration of what explains the success of certain high-risk communities in the final section of the book.

Conclusion

Glasses half full are of course also half empty. How then should we view the twin processes of stability and change? The first lesson is that cities and neighborhoods are constantly changing, and in no inherent direction. Chicago lost population in the 1970s, but reversed itself in the 1990s, for example. Many other cities are back from the gloom-and-doom years of the '70s and '80s as well, with many high-crime neighborhoods seeing a turn to increased safety. Yet we have simultaneously seen inequality increasing in society at large and evidence of neighborhood social reproduction that disproportionately affects minority groups.[45] Poverty and its correlates are persistent in terms of neighborhood concentration, especially for black areas. Despite urban social transformation in the post-Moynihan era, in other words, most neighborhoods remained stable in their relative economic standing despite the inflow and outflow of individual residents. The second lesson is thus that there is an enduring vulnerability to certain neighborhoods that is not simply a result of the current income of residents. Although not studied directly in this chapter, neighborhoods possess reputations that, when coupled with certain residential selection decisions, reproduce existing patterns of inequality.

The change that does occur reveals strong patterns of asymmetry by race and class, suggesting that once a neighborhood is beyond a certain threshold or "tipping point" of either percent black or percent poor—but especially the former—further change is in the direction of greater racial homogeneity and more poverty. Not one neighborhood in Chicago more than 50 percent black in 1960 became predominantly white forty years later (fig. 5.2). By contrast, a large number of white neighborhoods turned black even as the polar extremes (all-black and all-white neighborhoods) remained the dominant pattern. Neighborhoods in general also tended to stay in the same poverty category or move to a higher-poverty category over time. Therefore the third lesson I have shown is that upgrading (or gentrification) does not topple stability of the ecological structure even in the 1990–2007 period. Whether we consider concentrated disadvantage in Chicago or the U.S. as a whole, this pattern holds—Chicago is not an outlier.

These findings resonate with the earlier concerns introduced at the outset by Moynihan and scholars such as Kenneth Clark.[46] The pattern may not be encouraging, but it does signal a distressing reality that some forty-five years since the original Moynihan report, the language has changed but the same questions must be raised again. Moynihan did hypothesize a partial solution in the form of structural government interventions. The jury is still out, but the preliminary data presented here suggest a glimmer of hope that cycles of poverty can be broken, providing examples of poor communities that are repositioning themselves on an upward trajectory. But how pervasive the phenomenon is remains to be seen, and research so far has not systematically examined the consequences of change in one community on changes in other, perhaps even distant communities that may be receiving new burdens. In the case of Chicago, for example, the tens of thousands of poor residents uprooted from the Robert Taylor Homes on the South Side had to go *somewhere*. If most of these vulnerable families moved to other poorer communities further south, as the evidence explored in chapter 11 suggests, then it may be that the burdens of poverty are simply being redistributed rather than solved.

In the meanwhile, however, I turn in chapter 6 to a closer examination and revision of a leading theory of urban decline that bears on continuity and change—the famous "broken windows" theory of urban disorder. A close cousin of the "social disorganization" theory introduced in chapter 2, the broken windows theory posits that cues of disorder increases crime. But perceived disorder and its associated attributes may also have corrosive effects on the social fabric of communities. I examine the idea that certain neighborhoods get locked into dynamic processes that generate stigmatizing reputations, selective outmigration, reduced civic involvement, and eventually a deepening of poverty and further crime and disorder. To evaluate this thesis I begin with an overview of disorder theory and its critics, and then ask not what disorder causes but what forms our perceptions of it in the first place.

6 "Broken Windows" and the Meanings of Disorder

> When they approach me they see only my surroundings, themselves or figments of their imagination—indeed, everything and anything except me.
>
> Ralph Ellison, *Invisible Man*

Scholars of the city have long interpreted signs of disorder in public spaces in ways that constitute powerful forces of social differentiation. From observers of London in the 1800s, such as Charles Booth and Henry Mayhew, to Jane Jacobs's 1961 *The Death and Life of Great American Cities*,[1] concerns over "broken windows," crime, and other signs of disorder have been taken as symptomatic of city life. Social disorder is commonly understood to mean public behavior that is considered threatening, like verbal harassment, open solicitation for prostitution, public intoxication, and rowdy groups of young males on the streets. Physical markers of disorder typically refer to graffiti on buildings, abandoned cars, garbage in the streets, and the proverbial broken window.

Booth's detailed investigations and maps of Victorian London provide an early illustration of disorder's role in the social ranking of places. His meticulous portrayal of this vast city included color codes for the economic and social makeup of its streets.[2] The lowest classes, coded in black, were described as not just poor but living in "squalor" with public displays of alcoholism. Expressing a view that most still hold (if silently), Booth unabashedly labeled the lowest-class category as "vicious, semi criminal," with the lowest grade "inhabited principally by occasional labourers, loafers, and semi-criminals—the elements of disorder."[3] What Booth discovered, then, was a pattern of ecological classification and with a potent moral evaluation that might be considered the precursor to the contemporary "underclass." This was a consequential intellectual move, for the designation of areas as disreputable and disordered, I argue, sets in motion long-term processes that reinforce stigmatized areas and contribute to the durability of concentrated inequality shown in chapter 5. In this chapter, I thus probe beyond the purely economic and structural dimensions and attempt to highlight some of the perceptual and cultural bases of social inequality.

The *Economist* recently provided intriguing examples of the enduring social character of neighborhoods in London from Booth's day to the present, down to the micro-ecological level. South of the Thames in Stockwell and nearby Brixton lie some of the most racially mixed neighborhoods in London. The object of several police raids after the 2005 London bombings, racial tensions have flared in these neighborhoods for several years. A century ago, however, just east of Stockwell Road, Booth and his research team "found a pocket of filth and squalor, with rowdy residents and broken windows." The *Economist* reports that since then the area has been physically transformed but still replicates important features of the past: "Dismal two-storey cottages have been swept away and replaced by grass and the apartment blocks of the Stockwell Park Estate. But the appearance of the neighbourhood has changed more than its character. Julie Fawcett, who lives in one of the blocks, characterises her neighbours as 'the mad, the bad and the sad.'"[4] Unemployment is double the city average and "heroin alley" lies around a corner.

Perhaps Booth's crude distinctions are not so antediluvian after all. Contrary to the expectations of those who claim the world is flat because of globalization and place is "phantasmagorical," the quote by Ms. Fawcett reveals that it is not just economic or racial status but identities and morally laden evaluations that remain durable. How stable is visual disorder and the inference of concentrated poverty? What predicts perceptions of disorder and what are its consequences? In addressing these questions, my thesis is that perceptions of disorder constitute a fundamental dimension of social inequality at the neighborhood level and perhaps larger areas. At first this might seem counterintuitive considering that dominant stratification theorists take a structural stance in analyzing the material bases of inequality. Demographers do likewise in thinking about urban change. Whether expressed by Charles Booth or our Stockwell contemporary in London, perceptions about disorder are likely to be dismissed in favor of presumed weightier causes linked to objective material conditions.

By contrast, I argue that the grounds on which perceptions of disorder are formed are contextually shaped by social conditions that go well beyond the usual signs of observed disorder and poverty, starting a process that molds reputations, reinforces stigma, and influences the future trajectory of an area. "Seeing" disorder, like seeing Ralph Ellison's narrator, is intimately bound up with social meaning at the collective level and ultimately inequality. This conceptualization resists the tempting strategy of reifying disorder as a natural part of the environment. If believing is seeing rather than the reverse, such resistance is necessary.

A Brief History of Disorder

The importance of visual disorder appears in the early writings of the Chicago School. Louis Wirth seemed to see disorder and disorganization everywhere, and a consequence of increasing urbanization. More recently, Richard Sennett argues in *The Uses of Disorder* that our concern with disorder is fundamentally a concern about the loss of control in an increasingly urbanized world. He argues as well that our concern is an attempt to restore the myth of a "purified community" and an effort to keep unknown and disorderly events at bay.[5] For Sennett, anxiety over disorder is rooted in psychological needs for control and at a general theoretical level, to efforts aimed at restoring an imaginary community of solidarity.[6] The community of solidarity never existed, of course, but our longstanding obsession with controlling disorderly people and things in urban spaces remains prevalent throughout history.

Tangible manifestations of disorder, or what Hunter called "incivilities,"[7] were argued by another Chicago School theorist as central to a neighborhood's public presentation of self. Erving Goffman pointed out the obligation in medieval times to keep one's pigs out of the streets to demonstrate how the norms regulating public order covered not just face-to-face interaction among strangers or acquaintances, but the visual ordering of the physical landscape.[8] He also showed how shared expectations formed around the maintenance of public spaces and keeping the streets free of refuse. In figure 6.1, we see that even *The New Yorker* recognized the salience of public cues of disorder, here in the mid-twentieth century (and, as always, with humor). Jane Jacobs's

"This neighborhood certainly is going to pot."

FIGURE 6.1. Perceiving disorder, 1950s style. Illustration by Whitney Darrow Jr., published in *The New Yorker*, January 10, 1959.

observation of urban life also in the 1950s evoked a concern with the impact of disorder on neighborhood civility, especially the negotiation of public encounters.

These observers did not consider disorder in literal or essentialist terms, nor did they propose disorder as somehow random or chaotic. Disorder can be spatially patterned and socially organized. What was important to Goffman and Sennett, I believe, were the expectations and perceptions surrounding signs or cues, the rules of urban social order, as it were. These expectations are as powerful as the signs themselves, motivating theoretical and empirical interrogation. The fundamental importance of public observation in the process of social order was well stated by the American urban theorist Lynn Lofland: "The answer to the question of how city life was to be possible, then, is this. *City life is made possible by an 'ordering' of the urban populace in terms of appearance and spatial location such that those within the city could know a great deal about one another by simply looking.*"[9] The key to Lofland's argument is that social ordering in a "world of strangers" is a visual process that involves classification. People divide the urban world into manageable bits, with one of the most important differentiating characteristics being signs of disorder. But there is more than meets the eye here. The human tendency to quickly categorize racial and other groups, our ability to easily observe skin color, and our sensitivity to the opinions of others in the form of reputations or identities that stigmatize areas, makes for a potent combination.

The Current Scene

Debates about disorder and diversity in the urban context continue to inspire passion, but with new twists. Diversity and the increasing presence of minority and immigrant groups in cities around the world has led to a growing social anxiety, with some scholars proposing a direct link between diversity and declines in public trust.[10] Disorder in cities has also produced a theory about crime and institutionalized police action. According to the well-known "broken windows" theory of urban decline, James Q. Wilson and George Kelling argued that public incivilities—even if relatively minor, such as drinking in the street and graffiti—attract predatory crime because potential offenders assume that residents are indifferent to what goes on in their neighborhood. At its core, the broken windows theory sees visual cues as objective and obvious in their meaning—signs of disorder serve as a signal of the unwillingness of residents to confront strangers, intervene in a crime, or call the police.[11] Proponents thus assume that physical disorder and social disorder provide important environmental cues that entice potential predators and, eventually, crime.

Few ideas are more influential than broken windows in the urban policy world, with police crackdowns on elements of social and physical disorder in numerous cities. New York City is the best-known example of aggressive police tactics to control public incivilities.[12] The tactics of broken windows policing and a neoliberal approach to public order have been exported around the world, including liberal Paris and, most recently, England. The Blair government's attempt to "soothe the savage beast" and tamp down antisocial behavior led to a declared "war on incivility" that remains in place.[13] In the Stockwell neighborhood, the London police keep an "aggressive" watch, which has apparently proven "a comfort to many Londoners" yet provoked anger within the neighborhood.[14]

The concept of disorder has also influenced the study of mental and physical health. Following the broken windows theory, again the argument is that cues of disorder are negative, with harmful consequences for individual health and overall wellbeing. A number of recent studies have linked perceived disorder to physical decline, depression, psychological distress, and perceived powerlessness.[15] Residents are thought to read signs of disorder as evidence of a deeper neighborhood malaise, undermining personal health and trust.

Even if we wish it were untrue, disorder theory itself may be self-fulfilling by triggering attributions and predictions in the minds of insiders and outsiders alike. It changes the calculus of prospective homebuyers, real estate agents, insurance agents, investors, the police, and politicians, and may shape the perceptions of residents who would consider moving out or moving in. Evidence of disorder may also dampen the effectiveness of residents seeking neighborhood improvement, and it may discourage activism. Physical and social disorder in public spaces therefore appears fundamental to our understanding of how urban neighborhoods work.

Does Disorder Cause Crime?

Most research on disorder turns on whether disorder causes crime, and whether the aggressive policing of disorder reduces crime. I have weighed in on this debate in a paper published with Stephen Raudenbush.[16] Instead of conceiving of disorder as a direct cause of predatory crime, we considered first whether or not disorder is part and parcel of crime itself. Consider items commonly used to define social disorder, such as solicitation for prostitution, loitering, and public use of alcohol or drugs. Or consider "incivilities" such as graffiti, smashed windows, and drug vials in the streets. All of these are evidence either of crimes themselves or ordinance violations, meaning that in one sense the broken windows theory is saying that crime causes crime. Contagion theories have their place but cannot explain the concentration of effects in the first place. When cast in this light, the broken windows theory takes on a different and, in my view, less compelling explanation of crime.

Second, although ordinance violations like drinking in public and many "soft crimes" like graffiti may not be judged as particularly serious, the factors that produce them may be the same factors that produce more serious crime. It may be, then, that public disorder and predatory crimes are manifestations of the same process at different ends of a seriousness continuum. Other noncriminal elements of disorder such as garbage in the street and abandoned housing may also stem from violations of an ordinance (as in littering, slumlord abandonment), thus sharing similar causal features and predicted by shared community-level processes.[17]

One of the processes hypothesized in the following chapter as an inhibitor of both disorder and crime is "collective efficacy," defined as the linkage of cohesion and mutual trust among residents with shared expectations for intervening in support of neighborhood social control. Other commonly hypothesized sources of disorder and serious crime include concentrated disadvantage, density, and the land use of neighborhoods. If the "broken windows" thesis is correct, the association of a lack of collective efficacy, concentrated disadvantage, and other structural features of the environment with serious crimes ought to be mediated by social disorder. The alternative hypothesis is that disorder is an independent manifestation of crime-relevant mechanisms. From this viewpoint, collective efficacy and socioeconomic resources should reduce both disorder *and* violence by disempowering the forces that produce both.

We thus tested whether disorder is an essential link in the pathway that leads to predatory crime, or, by contrast, whether both crime and disorder are rooted in the same neighborhood structural characteristics, such as concentrated disadvantage, land use, stability, and neighborhood collective efficacy. Of course, disorder and collective efficacy can also be reciprocally related to the extent that disorder undermines efficacy. Exploiting the community survey, systematic social observation (SSO), archival records, and census described in chapter 4, we showed that public disorder in urban spaces can be reliably measured at the neighborhood level using systematic observational procedures.[18] In turn, concentrated poverty and mixed land use (business and residential) significantly forecasted observed physical and social disorder. Collective efficacy predicted lower observed disorder after controlling not only sociodemographic and land-use characteristics, but perceived disorder and prior rates of predatory crime as well. Collective efficacy also predicted lower rates of violent crime after adjusting for the feedback effects of violence itself.

By contrast, the results for observed disorder did not match the strong theoretical expectations set up by the main thesis of "broken windows." Disorder, despite its definitional overlap with crime, was only a moderate correlate of predatory crimes like burglary and homicide, and it varied consistently with prior neighborhood characteristics like poverty and land use. Once these characteristics were taken into account, the connection between observed disorder and crime was reduced in the majority of tests—including for homicide, which is arguably the best measure of violence. The overall results support the inference that public disorder and most predatory crimes share similar features and are consequently explained by the same constructs at the neighborhood level, especially the concentration of disadvantage and lowered collective efficacy.

Figure 6.2 graphs a heuristic that portrays an extended interpretation, using as a visual backdrop a scene from a Chicago neighborhood that I photographed in October of 2010. By many accounts the graffiti on the garbage pails and building wall are a signal of disorder. But even if we grant that the graffiti is a cue of disorder, unless created by the building's owner it was simultaneously an act of crime by Chicago law—defacement of public or private property (vandalism). Like the earlier empirical findings in Chicago, this implies that the link between cues of disorder and crime may be spurious (bottom line with question mark in fig. 6.2), either by definition or as the result of common third causes. Although figure 6.2 questions the strong version of the broken windows thesis, it does not in any way imply the theoretical irrelevance of disorder. For one thing, we found a direct association of disorder with police-recorded robbery rates. Robbery offenders apparently respond to visual cues of social and physical disorder in the neighborhood. The picture that emerges is then that disorder entices robbery, which in turn may undermine collective efficacy, leading over time to yet more disorder and ultimately robbery.[19]

Moreover, as I elaborate in the next section, physical and social elements of disorder comprise highly visible cues to which neighborhood observers differentially respond under certain social conditions,

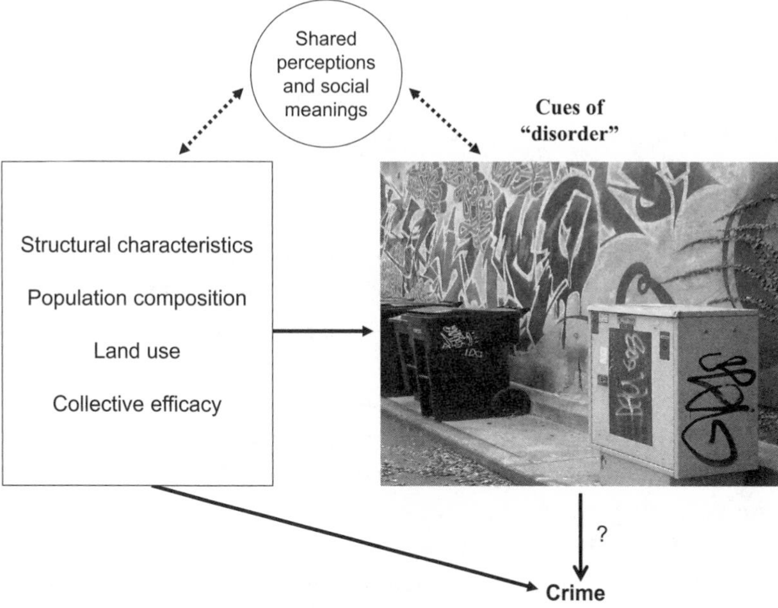

FIGURE 6.2. Reconsidering the "broken windows" theory of crime

potentially influencing migration patterns, investment by businesses, reputations of places, and thus overall neighborhood viability. Disorder has *social meaning*, in other words, and may work in a cascading feedback loop by encouraging people to move (increasing residential instability) or by leading to a stigmatized neighborhood and possibly future increases in concentrated poverty. Perceptions of disorder may also discourage efforts at building collective response to crime and thus indirectly have a feedback effect on crime. If I am correct, the link between cues of disorder and crime is deceptively misleading, and policies to eradicate disorder through law enforcement techniques are misplaced because they leave common origins untouched and assume that perceptions of disorder are in themselves uniformly unproblematic. Thus while disorder might not form the causal link to crime, as is often assumed, it follows that the meanings of disorder and its contextual moorings need to be a central part of our understanding of neighborhood change. It is to this issue that I now turn.[20]

Interrogating Perceptions

A matter of the construction of their inner eyes, those eyes with which they look through their physical eyes upon reality.

Ralph Ellison, *Invisible Man*

I have argued that at one level the broken windows theory is on the right track by emphasizing the salience of visual cues. It seems natural to assume that graffiti or drug-addled revelers are a problem. But imagine a situation in which these same cues are not evaluated negatively. Perhaps the partiers are students on a bender, or the graffiti is on the streets of the local arts district or campus town. Does this still cause crime or urban decline? Or might it be perceived instead as "colorful" and "edgy"? Walking along the south side of the Seine in Paris recently, I observed a long stretch of graffiti against the backdrop of couples strolling peacefully. Why is this "disorder" not seen as problematic and why is Paris thriving? One wonders, are there neighborhoods in Amsterdam where parked bikes surrounded by a mark of temporary graffiti are *not* viewed as a conflict of norms? These questions suggest that the broken windows theory needs to be reconceptualized by probing what triggers our shared perceptions of disorder in the first place.

The prevailing view seems to be that seeing disorder is a straightforward matter of observing cues in the environment that are visible to our eyes. From this view perceived disorder is a characteristic of the neighborhood, an objective place that generates consensus.[21] But it is one thing to perceive, more or less accurately, what is in the objective environment, and another to assign it meaning or to weigh its seriousness. Here language and cognition are central, for the dominant method of asking (thinking?) about disorder is to have respondents assess "how much of a problem" it is. Can we separate what is in the environment from how it is interpreted or perceived and how much it matters to the observer "as a problem"? We can also ask about the context of "disorder": Is the perception of disorder filtered or altered by the presence of stigmatized groups or its location in disreputable areas? Does seeing disorder as a problem depend on the collective judgments of others?

To recognize subjective variations in perception and the assignment of meaning is not to give up on systematic social inquiry. To the contrary, as Goffman classically argued, how we frame social situations may be seen as a fundamental aspect of social life.[22] I specifically argue that collective (or intersubjectively shared) perceptions form a context that constrains individual perceptions and social behavior. As Anthony E. Bottoms and Paul Wiles have also argued, perceptions of order and safety are part of culture in the sense of being rooted in shared understandings of the nature of particular areas and public spaces.[23] Lamont makes a similar point in her call for studies to assess social meaning in the form of "institutionalized cultural repertoires" and "publicly available categorization systems."[24] What is the "the mad, the bad, and the sad" if not a cultural repertoire and, potentially even more consequential, a widespread categorization system?

Implicit Bias and Racialized Meanings

"In the first instance, 'race' is a mode of perceptual categorization people use to navigate their way through a murky, uncertain world."[25]

Cultural attributions about disorder are prevalent in American society and increasingly in cities internationally as a result of exported American policies, feeding the hunger that humans carry for social information that will reduce uncertainty. Stereotypes become especially tempting when, as is almost always the case, residents are not trained to question them as systematic observers. If cultural stereotypes are pervasive and residents have uncertain information, then they may, acting like "Bayesians," augment that information with contextual cues about people who can be seen on the streets.[26] Mounting evidence from cognitive science reveals that we make decisions habitually and without much introspection. Although we prefer to think of ourselves as sentient beings that are rational and pursue goals consciously, what dominates is *hidden* rather than explicit reasoning.[27] It follows that individuals may be quick to draw on their priors in perceiving disorder as a problem—combining uncertain evidence with widespread beliefs underwritten by cultural stereotypes.

Categorical distinctions are particularly important for the organization of information in everyday life, and the categories of relevance are hardly random.[28] A considerable body of research shows that Americans hold persistent beliefs linking blacks, disadvantaged minorities, and recent immigrant groups to many social images, including crime, violence, disorder, welfare, and their undesirability as neighbors.[29] Beliefs about disorder are reinforced by the historical association of nonvoluntary racial segregation with concentrated poverty, which in turn is also linked to institutional disinvestments and neighborhood decline.[30] While race may be widely dismissed as a biological classification, dark skin is an easily observed and salient trait that has become a marker in American society, one imbued with meanings about crime, disorder, and violence, in turn stigmatizing entire categories of people.[31] The use of race to encode disorder does not imply "irrationality," nor is it simply prejudice in the sense of conscious group hostility. Suppose that someone without racial animus has nonetheless been exposed to the historically and structurally induced inequality that is urban America: on average, for example, rates of violence such as homicide *are* higher among blacks than whites. The problem arises when this person automatically concludes from such a statistical generalization that a specific black person, without corroborating evidence, is violence prone. The power of cultural stereotypes is that they operate beneath the radar screen of our conscious reasoning, forming what has been termed *implicit bias*.[32] Research shows that automatic racial stereotypes can persist regardless of conscious or personal rejection of prejudice toward blacks, leading to what some call "laissez-faire" and others "institutionalized" racism.[33]

Consider the effect of race in a vignette study in which experimental subjects were told to shoot armed targets and not to shoot unarmed targets. Participants made the correct decision to shoot an armed target more quickly if he was African American than if he was white.[34] The magnitude of this racial bias in shooting decisions varied with perception of cultural stereotypes but *not* with personal racial prejudice. In fact, the study revealed equivalent levels of shooting bias in African American and in white participants. This finding underscores the potentially far-reaching consequences of statistical discrimination and cultural stereotypes that lie below the level of conscious racial prejudice. As the authors argue, race can influence the decision to shoot because cultural traits associated with African Americans, such as "violent" or "dangerous," act as a schema to influence perceptions of an ambiguously threatening target. Moreover, African Americans are exposed, as is everybody, to dominant cultural stereotypes and thus implicit bias.

Contextualizing Disorder

Implicit bias and statistical discrimination theory are limited, however, in their tendency to adopt either a psychologically reductionist or a rational choice model of decision making, both of which neglect the context and meaning of perceptions. A contextual stance was taken some time ago by Carl Werthman and Irv Piliavin, who argued that the police divide up the territories they patrol into readily understandable, and racially tinged, categories.[35] The result is a process of what they called *ecological contamination*, whereby all persons encountered in a "bad" neighborhood are viewed as possessing the moral liability of the neighborhood itself. This process has general implications if citizens themselves impute the character of disreputability to neighborhoods containing stigmatized minorities, immigrants, and the "rabble class."[36] Although Goffman's concept of stigma[37] was originally advanced at the individual level, its contextual forms are what I find compelling. Such stigmatization appears to be an enduring mechanism going back at least to Charles Booth's lower-class London with its "loafers and semi-criminals."

The social structure of everyday life is tied to the race and class of both persons and places, reinforcing the production of disrepute.[38] As Arthur Stinchcombe argued over forty years ago, access to private space is structured such that disorder by the disadvantaged often consists of doing many things in public that would be (and are) legitimate in private (e.g., drinking, hanging out).[39] Because privileged status increases private access, it reduces everyday exposure to public disorder. The perception and meaning one attributes to disorder, then, will vary by one's social position. The resulting social structure of public spaces also confirms the stereotype that disorder is a problem mainly in poor, African American communities. This stereotype feeds racial stigma and the creation of a durable spoiled identity for the modern American ghetto.[40]

Ethnographic work underscores the symbolic importance attached to the intersection of race and disorder. In a study of a white working-class Chicago neighborhood, Maria Kefalas sought to understand the fastidiousness with which residents kept up their property and why they seemed to be obsessed with physical signs of order. She found that homeowners fretted about "the last Garden" and the threats that disorder were thought to bring on the neighborhood.[41] No act of vandalism was too minor, no unkempt yard too trivial to escape notice. Kefalas argued that residents were especially threatened by the encroachment of blacks, which they associated with decline preceded by visual cues of disorder. In many ways the residents of Kefalas's Beltway had a broken windows theory in mind, but one with a decidedly black face.

None of this is to assert that the average city dweller is somehow irrational or merely ignorant. The rational basis of beliefs lies in a social history of urban America that links geographically isolated minority groups and recent immigrants with poverty, economic disinvestment, and visible signs of disorder. Visual cues of disorder can be disturbing even to those who study them for a living.[42] The problem is that predictions become self-confirming when stigma and spoiled identity intercede, leading to actions that increase the statistical association between race and the observable behavior. If affluent residents use a neighborhood's racial composition as a gauge for the level or seriousness of disorder, unconsciously or consciously, they may disinvest in predominately minority areas or move out. Such actions would tend to increase physical disorder in those neighborhoods. In this way implicit bias leads to self-enforcing mechanisms that perpetuate the connection of race to disorder.

The general framework of my argument is portrayed in figure 6.3, showing the multiple influences of social position, observed disorder, racial stigma by place, and implicit bias in interpreting the effect of concentrated minority groups and immigration on perceptions. Indicated by Booth's depiction of the Irish in Victorian London, racial and ethnic categories subject to hierarchical classification are historically variable. My argument is not just about blacks or Latinos, in other words. In many U.S. cities circa World War I, it was the Irish and Italian immigrants who constituted the dangerous and disorderly class.[43] In present-day London, moreover, social distinctions within the white working class may be nearly as pernicious as black-white distinctions in the U.S. Narratives of disorder (e.g., homelessness, "filth," public alcoholism) linked to the white working class/poor appear to create social boundaries and status differentials by neighborhood in the council estates of Camden.[44]

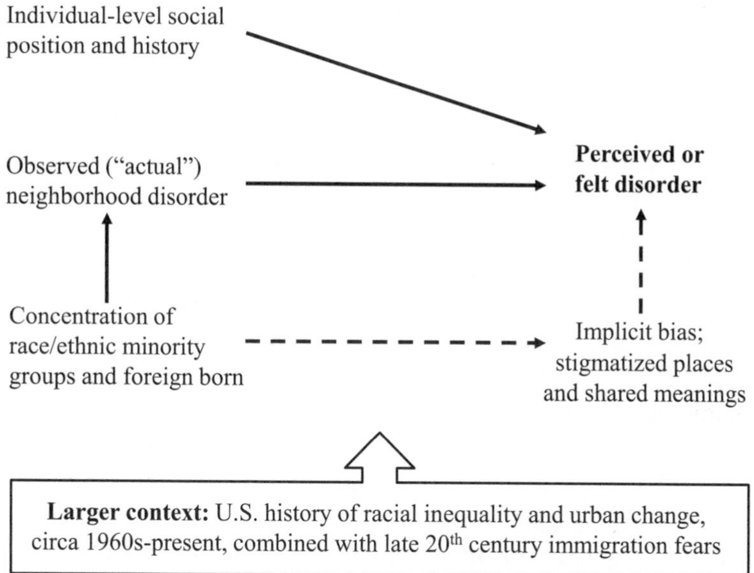

FIGURE 6.3. Believing is seeing: the social basis of perceiving disorder

Hypotheses and Approach

Little research bears on the general theoretical argument in figure 6.3 that social and cultural settings trigger perceptions that disorder is a problem. To address this gap I put forth and assess the proposition that perceptions of neighborhood disorder are socially mediated, relatively stable, and contextually shaped by much more than actual levels of disorder. I do this by first replicating and extending with data over time my earlier study with Raudenbush.[45] According to the logic of broken windows theory, the perception of disorder is governed by actual, observed levels of disorder. We therefore reasoned that residents *within* any given neighborhood should be largely in agreement on perceived disorder. Their views of disorder in the neighborhood should not, for example, vary systematically and substantially by social class or other markers of social position. Furthermore, we should find few if any variations in perceived disorder *between* neighborhoods that are linked to population characteristics once actual disorder, systematically observed, is accounted for.

Figure 6.3 suggests an alternative scenario. Because skin color is easily observed and carries established stereotypes, we hypothesized that racial composition would loom large not just in observed levels of disorder but for people's reporting of disorder. For some respondents, the racialized context of the neighborhood might go well beyond observed disorder, especially in a city like Chicago with a troubled history of racial strife in its recent past that etched in the city's collective memory an implicit association of disorder with blackness. Figure 6.3 thus incorporates the historical and contemporary association between racial composition and observed disorder. The notions of stigma and implicit bias also suggest that if there is an association between racial composition and perceived disorder, it ought to be independent of the race or ethnicity of the observer (consider, for example, the black citizen who crosses the street at night to avoid a group of approaching young black males).

Our data began with the comprehensive neighborhood survey of Chicago residents described in chapter 4, who lived in approximately five hundred block groups where detailed videotaped observations were taken. Census block groups average about 1,300 residents, compared to about 4,000 for the average census tract, and appear to reflect the layout of pedestrian streets and patterns of social interaction. Interviews were based on over 3,500 randomly chosen adult residents within households who were asked six questions about physical disorder (e.g., litter, graffiti, vacant housing) and social disorder (e.g., public drinking, fighting, drug dealing). They were asked, "Are these a big problem? Somewhat of a problem? Not a problem?" From these questions we constructed scales of disorder at the level of the individual and block group. From the neighborhood survey we also examined a large set of personal demographic and background characteristics that might anchor one's perception of disorder, including age, sex, home ownership, and a composite measure of socioeconomic status that took into account education, income, and occupational prestige.

From the separate study of community positional leaders and key informants, we relied on over one thousand interviews with representatives of the educational, political, business, religious, community organizational, and law enforcement domains. Leaders were asked detailed questions about their personal characteristics and social network ties in addition to their perceptions of disorder in the communities they represented or worked in. For the block groups in our study we also collected independent information from the U.S. census that was likely to have bearing on perceptions of disorder: the proportion of families in poverty, population density, and the proportion black and Latino. Then from Chicago police records of violent offenses such as robbery, homicide, rape, and aggravated assault, we constructed the violent crime rate in each block group per hundred thousand residents. The last and I believe most innovative method was systematic social observation (SSO) of streets as described in chapter 4. From the SSO, multiple scales accounting for measurement error in observed disorder were created and validated.

Overall our initial results supported the general theory in figure 6.3. Racial and immigrant concentration proved more powerful predictors of perceived disorder than did carefully observed disorder. This disparity was not necessarily "irrational" or a reflection of simple prejudice. Skin color is not only visual but psychologically salient in a society with a long history of slavery, segregation, and racial conflict. That the findings need not reflect pure racial prejudice was supported by a key pattern in the data: blacks were no less likely than whites to be influenced by racial composition in predicting disorder. If racial prejudice was determining the association between percent black and perceived disorder, this association ought to be much stronger for whites than for blacks: few would contend that blacks are as prone to antiblack racial prejudice as whites. Although blacks perceive less disorder than whites living in the same block group, this tendency was *not* linked to the percent of black residents.[46]

Further, we examined the main finding on the independent data on perceptions of disorder collected from key leaders in 2002 (see chapters 4 and 14 for details). We selected leaders who lived *outside* the community they worked in in order to remove as much as possible the role of inside information or local knowledge. Yet racial composition strongly predicted leaders' evaluations of disorder, controlling for observed disorder, a pattern similar to that found for residents. Moreover, perceptions of disorder by the residents themselves independently predicted leaders' perceptions, presumably mediated through complaints, stigma, and broader reputational processes that have staying power. The meanings attached to disorder among residents rather than its mere presence is thus bound up with the views of community leaders.

Seeing Disorder over Time

I now consider pathways to and from disorder, beginning with a replication and multipronged extension of the Sampson and Raudenbush paper based on the follow-up studies in 2002 that provide longitudinal data on the prediction of disorder.[47] My goal is to assess whether the key findings on racial and immigrant context stand up. They do. The data reveal an almost complete replication using independent data on all of the core measures that were repeated in the 2002 community survey and SSO. Once again, for example, whites perceived more disorder than blacks, Latinos, and Asians/others even when they lived in the same neighborhood and thus were exposed to the same context. A new finding is that third-generation immigrants perceived more disorder than otherwise similar first-generation immigrants within the same neighborhoods.

I present a visual sense of these results in figure 6.4, derived from a comprehensive model that adjusts for a host of both individual and neighborhood factors measured on over a thousand block groups. In the top panel, note the higher levels of perceived disorder among whites compared to blacks, adjusting for neighborhood racial composition and other confounding factors. In the bottom panel, note the higher levels of perceived disorder among third-generation and higher immigrants compared to first-generation, adjusting for the prevalence of Latinos.[48] Graphed differences are all significant and fully adjusted at the mean for all covariates.[49] A virtually identical pattern of within-neighborhood race/immigrant differences holds when census tracts are substituted, so the "anchoring" effects of social position are stable across units of analysis.[50]

Perhaps more important, figure 6.4 shows that both whites and blacks perceive more disorder as percent black increases *across* neighborhoods, adjusting for observed levels of disorder. Low-percent black is defined as the bottom quartile and high-percent black, the upper quartile. For both blacks and whites and after controlling for other differences, we see that moving from the lower to upper quartile of percent black is associated with about a 0.4 increase in individually perceived disorder, more than half a standard deviation. Similarly for first-generation immigrants and those in the third generation, neighborhoods higher in

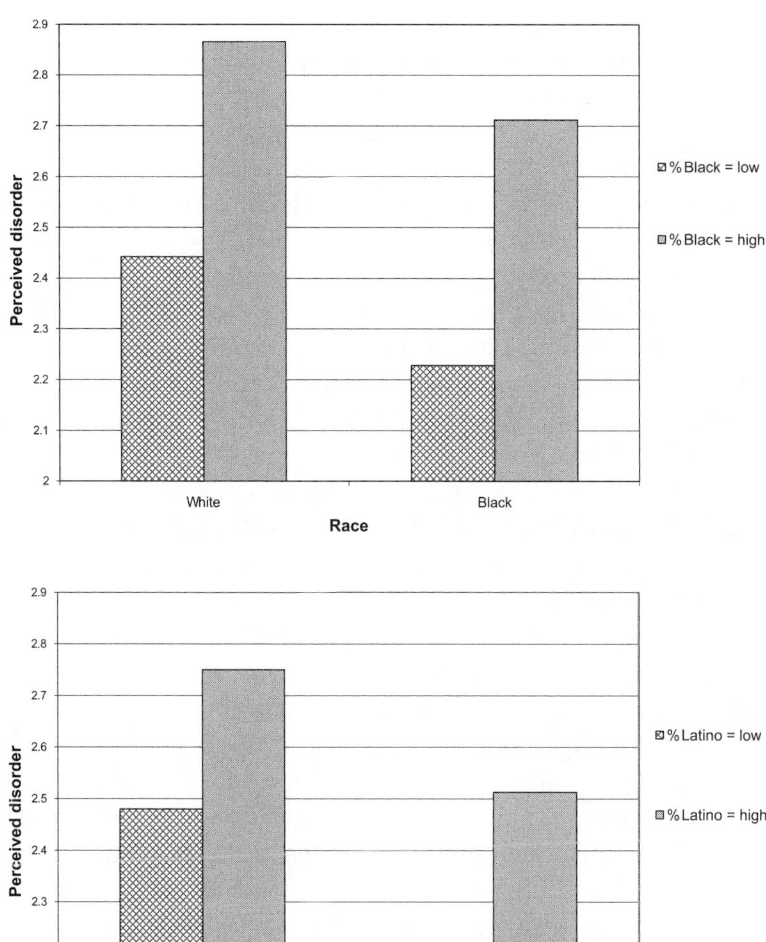

FIGURE 6.4. Black-white and immigrant differences in perceived disorder by neighborhood race/ethnicity. 2002 Chicago Survey (N = 3,105) at the block-group level, with individual and neighborhood characteristics controlled.

the concentration of Latinos (and immigrants) are associated with significantly greater perceived disorder. Some twenty-five individual-level covariates were adjusted and thus cannot plausibly explain these large disparities. The effect of race/ethnic composition on perceived disorder is also independent of multiple and highly reliable measures of observed disorder. Moreover, there are no significant differences between blacks and whites or immigrant generation in the nature of the prediction of perceived disorder from percent black (or concentrated immigration), further supporting the notion of implicit bias associated with neighborhood racial context. Specifically, there is no significant interaction of neighborhood racial composition with respondent's race in predicting individually perceived disorder.[51] The influence of racial composition is thus direct and strong.

I present next the hypothesized relationship between the group dynamics of social disorder and individual perception. The question here moves beyond racial/ethnic composition versus systematically observed disorder to how observed disorder and *intersubjective* or shared perceptions of disorder matter for the development of an individual's perceptions. It is important to recall that the sample I use to measure shared perceptions is independent from and seven years prior to that used to measure individual variations. If the mechanism is largely statistical discrimination, then percent black should remain a predictor and shared perceptions should be less important than observed disorder. But if social meaning and cultural attributes are also at work, as argued above, it stands to reason that shared neighborhood perceptions—the prior intersubjective variance component—should have a direct association with an independent current assessment by any individual. Collective or unconsciously coordinated perceptions are the embodiment of reputation and through social interaction are passed down and reproduced over time.[52]

Despite stringent controls for dozens of individual-level characteristics, including fear of crime, age, race, sex, home ownership, social class, friendship ties, fear, victimization, and even perceptions of collective efficacy, which are correlated with perceptions of disorder, there is a large effect of collectively perceived disorder in 1995—*but not 2002 levels of observed disorder*—on an individual's perceptions.[53] I conducted a complete replication of this analysis in the 2002 survey, controlling for systematically observed disorder in 1995 as well, obtaining similar results. For example, at the tract level, shared perceptions of perceived disorder strongly predicted concurrent "subjective" disorder, but prior observed ("objective") disorder was insignificant. I examined a number of additional neighborhood-level controls as well, including the violence rate, age structure, and collective efficacy, all with similar results.

Perhaps it is the community-area level where shared perceptions take on their most tenacious hold because it is here that well-known names and reputations are most pronounced. To assess this I examined a series of relationships across the seventy-seven community areas of the follow-up survey and in the subset of community areas (N = 47) where systematic videotaped observations were conducted in 1995. To ensure a conservative test I included the violence rate for the four years leading up to and including the second survey. Key results with magnitudes of association are graphed in figure 6.5. Adjusting for the twenty-five individual factors by which communities vary in their composition (N = 77) and adjusting for between-community differences in census-based poverty, immigrant composition, and violence rates, one can still see the relative strength of shared past judgments of disorder in predicting individual outcomes. The magnitude of the racial composition effect is greater than systematically observed disorder (compare the bottom

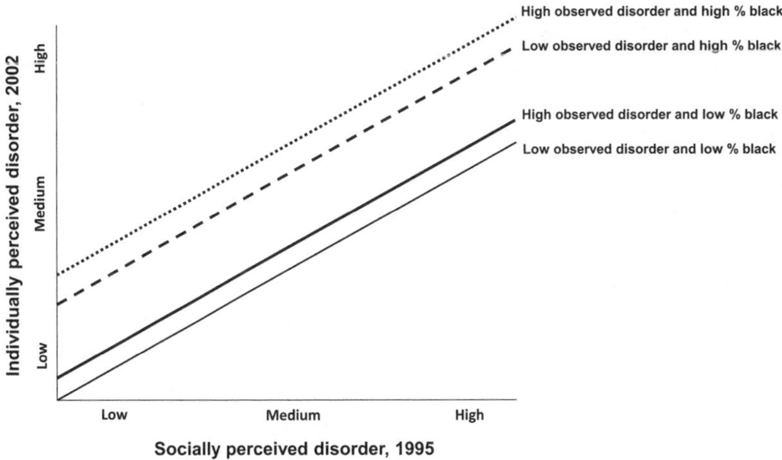

FIGURE 6.5. Comparison of systematically observed disorder, racial composition, and socially perceived disorder. 2002 Chicago Survey (N = 3,105) at community-area level, with individual and community characteristics controlled.

two lines representing the twenty-fifth and seventy-fifth percentiles in observed disorder within low-percent-black areas), and in turn the effect of shared prior perceptions is greater than both racial composition *and* observed disorder.[54] By contrast, increases in perceived disorder associated with concurrently observed disorder are much smaller and not significant. When I also control for measureable *prior* differences in observed disorder along with *concurrent* disorder, the picture does not change.[55] Perhaps surprisingly, collective prior perceptions again retain the same predictive power and prior observed disorder is insignificant.

Finally, I replicated the analysis on perceptions of disorder among leaders who worked in the community but lived outside of it. In doing so I included new controls for concentrated disadvantage and systematically observed (or SSO) disorder measured both prior to *and* concurrently with key leaders' perceptions in 2002. Once again, observed disorder took a back seat in the entire process, and shared perceptions of disorder many years earlier had by far the strongest effect on elites' perceptions of community disorder in 2002. For example, the raw correlation between residents perceptions in 1995 and the views of outside leaders in 2002 is 0.83, and the standardized coefficient for this relationship controlling for confounding factors was 0.70 ($p < 0.01$), approximately ten times larger than the effect of concurrently observed disorder (0.07, not significant). Concentrated disadvantage and residential stability were not predictive in this same model. What matters most for community leaders is apparently what matters most in the minds of community residents. The durable effect of shared perceptions is a clear indicator of the power of reputational processes that extend even to those who do not live in the community.

That social perceptions have such persistent and strong predictive power adjusting for current and lagged observed levels of disorder is rather remarkable and suggests the sensitivity of humans to the evaluations of others and adds new meaning to the truism that past judgments matter. Because we are hungry for social information, encoded social perceptions are "sticky" and appear to be eagerly accepted and consumed liberally. Might the stigma of disorder have additional ramifying costs or impacts on a community? At the other end of the spectrum, might a reputation for being a clean, orderly place lead to cumulative advantages? I now provide a direct look at the social dynamics of the legacy of disorder.

The Role of Disorder as a Dynamic Force

Beginning about 1965, which Robert Putnam argues is the point of decline of American civic life, crime rates began to explode in American cities.[56] They rose to unprecedented heights and fluctuated at high levels in the 1970s and 1980s, a period also of increasing concentration of poverty. Going back to figure 6.2, I believe that crime and especially disorder have been overlooked in the feedback processes that helped to perpetuate poverty traps, especially in precipitating selective outmigration from central cities burdened with high rates of victimization. Violence and robbery may also prompt the withdrawal of businesses and middle-class families from inner-city areas, which may have fueled more crime and a deepening of poverty. As I have argued, neighborhoods high in crime and "signs of disorder" are especially prone to developing reputations as "bad" and best avoided. The consequences of stigmatization combine with the historical legacy in U.S. cities, where racial segregation and poverty are bound up with patterns of disinvestment. A form of self-fulfilling prophecy takes place.[57] Residents acting on their perceptions of disorder undertake actions that have the effect of only increasing that disorder. It is impossible to study empirically all these feedback loops in one study (or perhaps any number of studies), but I can begin to break down their constituent parts.

To date, the evidence on these links is mostly about crime rates. Studying Chicago neighborhoods, for example, Bursik found that "although changes in racial composition cause increases in the delinquency rate, this effect is not nearly as great as the effect that increases in the delinquency rate have on minority groups being stranded in the community."[58] In a study of forty neighborhoods in eight cities, Wesley Skogan found that high rates of crime and disorder were associated with higher rates of fear, neighborhood dissatisfaction, and intentions to move out. Jeffrey Morenoff and I showed that increases in violent crime and proximity to violence contributed to population loss and decline of neighborhoods in Chicago. The effect of crime on population loss is also observed at the city level. In a study conducted over twenty years ago, I showed that increases in homicide were strongly associated with population decline and increases in the poverty of the black population in major U.S. cities. These results are independent of the usual demographic predictors of urban change. A later study found that robbery rates also played a significant role in white flight from central cities, therefore increasing racially segregated poverty.[59]

What about disorder? If shared perceptions of disorder predict later poverty better than observed disorder, crime, and perhaps even prior poverty, this is evidence in favor of the cultural aspects of the social reproduction of inequality and the persistence of poverty traps. On the basis of these findings I believe that socially evaluated disorder is firmly implicated in how the character of a neighborhood evolves over time. Consider first the stability of perceived disorder over time at the neighborhood level. The extended theory outlined here implies a "poverty trap" effect for neighborhood social processes, where shared perceptions reinforce later disorder and potentially still more concentrated poverty. Neighborhood variations in perceived disorder are not only large, but neighborhoods by and large maintain their relative positions over time. The correlation of perceived disorder at the community-area level is a very high 0.89 ($p < 0.01$), with "pockets" of high disorder that are quite durable and apparently hard to overcome. This finding implies that the cultural and social aspects of neighborhood disorder are coherent, durable, and potentially of causal relevance in explaining the puzzle of stability amid change.

To assess this idea I examine the prediction of poverty from prior socially perceived disorder at the community-area level, where perceptions and reputations are most likely to be reinforced institutionally. In initial examination there was a nonlinear trend in the data, with an increasing correlation of perceived disorder with later poverty.[60] Figure 6.6 presents the linear form of the relationship. The pattern is striking, with a correlation unusual in social science even for community-level data (0.91). Communities such as Washington Park and Riverdale on the Far South Side stand out as deeply entrenched in poverty and stigmatized as "disordered."[61] Of course, a number of factors that predict perceived disorder are also predictive of poverty and might confound the pattern. I therefore controlled for key known predictors, including prior (1990) racial and immigrant composition, the violence rate for the five years leading up to the 2000 decennial census, prior observed disorder, and the prior poverty rate, which we know from chapter 5 is a strong link to continuing poverty. I also assessed the robustness of the results by

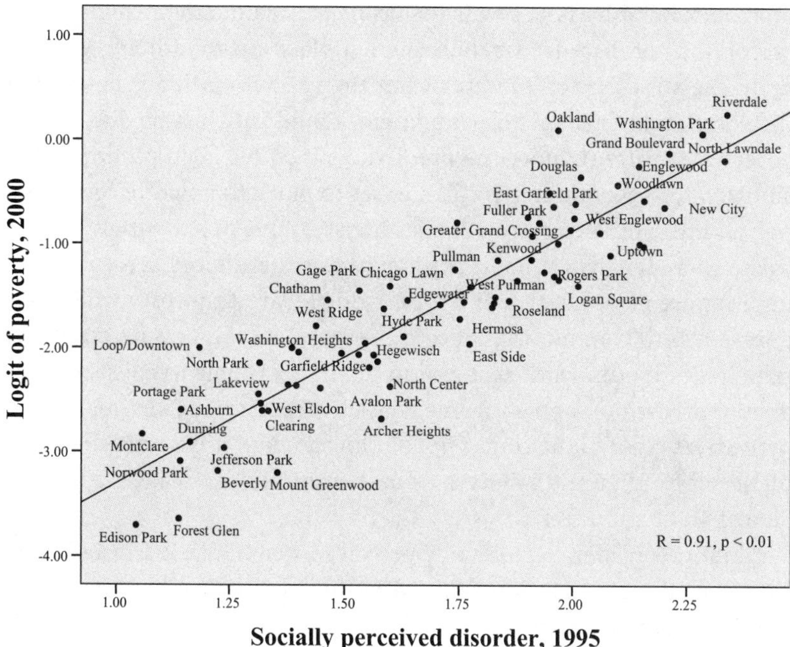

FIGURE 6.6. Socially perceived disorder strongly predicts later poverty at the community level

repeating the analysis on block groups, tracts, *and* community areas, obtaining similar results.

The result was as striking as the pattern in figure 6.6. Systematically observed disorder had *no independent association with later poverty*. More relevant, shared perceptions had a predictive relationship with later poverty that rivaled population composition by race and immigrant status. Moreover, shared perceptions of disorder had essentially the same magnitude of association with later poverty levels as the inertial path dependence for which the indicator of prior poverty serves as a direct proxy. Violent crime had no effect next to perceived disorder.[62]

Another piece of evidence supports the theoretical framework of this chapter. I divided the sample of census tracts into those that are predominantly (75 percent or more) black and those that are predominantly white. I used tracts rather than community areas to obtain a sufficient number of cases in each racial type. A clear pattern showed that black neighborhoods bear the brunt of the underlying dynamics—perceptions of disorder foretell where a black neighborhood will end up in the stratification hierarchy, but the prediction line is flatter and the correlation smaller for white areas. Could this just be due to past poverty? Apparently not—the prediction slope for 2000 poverty when adjusted for 1990 poverty is still steeper in black than white communities, and the adjusted correlation is almost double in magnitude.[63] Once again, then, the data support the hypothesis that shared perceptions of disorder are more consequential for a downward trajectory when they intersect with communities of color. Perhaps we can now better appreciate how the "disorder" pictured in figure 6.2 is able to exist in a predominantly white, upper-income, and elite section of Chicago, just off 57th Street close to the University of Chicago. And it is no accident that the humor of figure 6.1 derives from its otherwise upscale, Upper East Side of Manhattan feel.

Finally, consider the effect of perceived neighborhood disorder on changes in population. I examined both raw population change and ecological shifts in population that were deviations from the overall trend in Chicago over the decade of the 1990s. Both strategies produced similar results at three levels of ecology with the same measures and models. Controlling for prior violence, race, immigrant concentration, observed disorder, *and* the poverty rate, collective priors on "problem disorder" significantly predicted residual and relative declines in population size.[64] Thus whether one is seeking to predict future poverty or outmigration, perceptions of disorder are equally, if not more significant than the usually cited structural variables.[65]

Summary

This chapter uncovered a consistent pattern pointing to the relevance of social psychological mechanisms interacting with cultural processes to explain a phenomenon previously dominated by structural determinism. Namely, *shared perceptions of disorder rather than systematically observed disorder appear to be a mechanism of durable inequality*. I have thus shown that disorder rooted in intersubjectively shared historical assessments—rather than simply the current cues themselves—form a meaningful definition of the neighborhood environment that influences individual perceptions and further social outcomes. By this account, the perceptual basis of action is contingent on neighborhood context, which in turn plays a role in shaping the long-term trajectories and identities of places. I revisit this claim in later analyses of residential mobility and its consequences for structural networks of mobility that connect different parts of the city (chapters 12–13). In the meantime, I suggest that collectively shaped perceptions of disorder may be one of the underappreciated causes of continued racial and economic segregation in the United States and perhaps cities elsewhere. At the very least, shared perceptions of disorder appear to matter for reasons that extend far beyond the presence of broken windows or the physical structure of the built environment.

It is instructive at this point to reconsider what predicts crime—observed cues of disorder or shared perceptions thereof? Whether lagged or concurrent, the data studied here reveal that historical perceptions carry the predominant explanatory weight. In 2002, for instance, collectively perceived disorder but not observed disorder predicts the homicide rate from 2002–6, all else equal. Shared judgments (1995 socially perceived disorder) significantly predict later homicide but *concurrently observed disorder does not*. If the broken windows theory is correct, it is apparently perversely so, and not for the original reasons hypothesized by its authors. Indeed, by popularizing the idea that signs of disorder lead to decline, the theory may have unwittingly promoted self-reinforcing actions in this very direction (e.g., outmigration, increasing poverty), thereby producing what it seeks to avoid.

But if crime is only tangentially related to physical cues of disorder, its past presence is central to the study of neighborhood health and wellbeing. The next chapter takes up this broad issue, pursuing a critique of disorganization theory in order to theorize the kinds of social processes that deter crime and promote wellbeing. Empirical analyses of neighborhood crime reaffirm the importance of traditionally cited suspects like concentrated disadvantage and residential instability, but also provide significant backing to a newly theorized concept—collective efficacy—which, as we shall see, plays a significant role in mediating structural characteristics and that may serve as a community protective factor. I also continue to focus on the long-term consequences of durable inequality and how certain neighborhoods get locked into a social dynamic that generates further stigmatization, disorder, outmigration, crime, civic withdrawal, and eventually the deepening of poverty. Equally important, however, is how some communities break out of poverty traps and the mold of stigmatizing perceptions. Collective efficacy and organizational action provide a clue.

7 | The Theory of Collective Efficacy

The previous chapter demonstrated that the concept of disorder has played a dominant role in our thinking about the social milieu of cities. Despite frequent attacks, so too has the similar concept of social disorganization. As demonstrated in chapter 2, William F. Whyte attempted to relegate social disorganization theory to the intellectual dustbin in the 1940s. But rather than going away, it actually experienced a vigorous resurgence in the late twentieth-century focus on neighborhood effects. Robert J. Bursik and Harold Grasmick provide a revealing anecdote in their *Neighborhoods and Crime*. Recalling a conversation at the annual meeting of the American Society of Criminology in the late 1980s, they were told by a respected but unnamed colleague that "social disorganization is the herpes of criminology . . . once you think it is gone for good, the symptoms flare up again."[1]

Although I have several suspects in mind as the source of this comment, the late Yale sociologist Albert J. Reiss Jr. is at the top of my list. Ever the ornery intellectual, in an opening essay, "Why Are Communities Important for Understanding Crime?," Reiss trained his critical eye on social disorganization theory.[2] Against a backdrop of admiration for the efforts of Shaw and McKay and others in the social-disorganization tradition, Reiss pointed out that in many so-called disorganized slums, there coexisted criminal networks, organized gangs, and often a complex density of social ties. Surely it would be a mistake to consider Whyte's North End, to use Reiss's example, as simply "disorganized." Yet it did have high crime rates, and many of the features of Shaw and

McKay's delinquency areas. Characteristically, then, Reiss raised a paradox: high-crime areas often seem to be both organized and disorganized simultaneously, yielding an uneasy coexistence within the same boundaries. Wouldn't it be best, as Bursik and Grasmick's critic implied, to simply eradicate social disorganization theory once and for all? At the very least it seems that promoting the reformulation of this classic framework on communities and crime is a risky business. At the same time, I believe that the theory has been unfairly maligned and that the hypothesis lurking underneath the theory is worth saving—*community-level variations in social control contribute to varying crime rates.*

Thus my position is that we should recognize what is useful about social disorganization theory while modifying or discarding what is no longer relevant. I agree that there are good reasons to question the definition of disorganization and to rethink the role of dense personal ties in generating low crime rates. The definitional issue has been a perennial problem. As Bursik noted, a number of early scholars defined disorganization in terms of what they hoped to explain—what better indicator of social disorganization than crime?[3] But if crime (or disorder) is simply a marker for disorganization, then we have defined the cause in terms of outcome-related factors and have not identified any independent explanatory mechanism. For this reason social disorganization research shifted in recent decades to measuring its key construct in terms *independent* of crime, most notably with respect to what is commonly referred to as a "systemic" notion of the density of personal ties.[4] Although this was a necessary move away from tautology, other conceptual problems remained in the theory's treatment of social ties.

First, there is evidence that in some neighborhood contexts strong personal ties may impede efforts to establish social control. Wilson, for example, has argued that residents of very poor neighborhoods may be tightly interconnected through personal networks but without necessarily producing collective resources or social regulation.[5] He argues that ties in the inner city are excessively personalistic and parochial—socially isolated from public resources and role models in the "mainstream culture." Although total social isolation from the media-driven aspects of our larger culture is probably rare, restricted networks and nontraditional coping mechanisms in deprived neighborhoods do appear to yield an uneasy relationship to public institutions of social control such as the police, schools, and courts.[6]

Second, networks connect not just do-gooders but the underbelly of social life, from drug dealers to gang members to crooked politicians. In her study of a black middle-class community in Chicago, Mary E. Pattillo-McCoy addressed the limits of tight-knit social bonds in facilitating social control.[7] She argues that although dense local ties do promote social cohesion, they simultaneously foster the growth of networks that impede efforts to rid the neighborhood of organized drug- and gang-related crime. Sudhir Alladi Venkatesh finds a similar pattern in a low-income neighborhood of Chicago.[8] Thus dense social ties potentially have both positive *and* negative ramifications, reminding us that it is important to ask what is being connected—networks are not inherently egalitarian or prosocial in nature. Christopher Browning extends this idea to explore the conditions under which dense social ties *inhibit* crime control.[9] This argument has a long pedigree in the urban sociological and gang literature, going back at least as far as *Street Corner Society*.[10]

Third, and perhaps most important, shared expectations for social control and strategic connections that yield effective action can in principle be fostered in the absence of thick ties among neighbors. As Mark Granovetter argued in his seminal essay on "weak ties," less intimate connections between people based on infrequent social interaction may nonetheless be critical for establishing social resources such as job referrals because they integrate the community by bringing together otherwise disconnected subgroups.[11] Consistent with this view, there is evidence that weak ties among neighbors, reflected in middle-range rather than either nonexistent or intensive social interaction, are predictive of lower crime rates.[12] Dense social ties are thus not always predictive of better outcomes, as commonly expected.

Finally, as introduced in chapter 1, in contemporary cities the idyllic "urban village" endures largely in myth. Even given ample time or energy, I suspect most people do not want to be close friends with their neighbors. They desire trust with them, not necessarily to eat dinner with them. When ties are "thick," it may even be that outcomes are worse rather than better. More important, there is the mathematical impossibility of relying on friendship or other close personal ties to achieve social order in the contemporary (or any) city—there are simply too many people to know. Indeed, this is the essence of a city as Louis Wirth classically emphasized: one cannot know more than a tiny fraction of one's neighbors on a personal basis. The law of numbers and the nature of everyday social relations therefore force us to think about how social integration, cohesion, and other aspects of social organization can be achieved in a fully urban world.

From Social Disorganization to Collective Efficacy

To address these conceptual issues, my colleagues and I have proposed a theory of collective efficacy. The concept of collective efficacy draws together two fundamental mechanisms—*social cohesion* (the "collectivity" part of the concept) and *shared expectations for control* (the "efficacy" part of the concept).[13] Our premise accepts the basic idea of social disorganization theory that social control is a collective challenge not attributable to the characteristics of individuals alone and that it constitutes a major source of variation in crime rates and general wellbeing across neighborhoods.[14] But we relaxed the traditional disorganization assumption that the ideal contextual setting for social control is necessarily one characterized by dense, intimate, and strong neighborhood ties (e.g., through friends or kin). This theoretical framework recognizes the transformed landscape of contemporary urban life and assumes that while community efficacy may depend on some level of working trust and social interaction, it does not require that neighbors or local police officers be one's friend. Institutional mechanisms may be sufficient.

Following this logic, we focused on the everyday strategies by which residents address challenges. Examples of informal control strategies include the monitoring of spontaneous play groups among children, sharing information about other children's behavior, willingness to intervene in preventing acts such as truancy and street-corner "hanging" by teenage peer groups, and doing something about persons who are exploiting or disturbing public space. Even among adults, violence regularly arises in public disputes, in the context of illegal markets (e.g., prostitution, drugs) and in the company of peers. The capacity of residents to exercise control (which includes calling the police) is thus expected to be a mechanism influencing opportunities for interpersonal crime in a neighborhood. Informal social control also generalizes to broader institutional issues facing the wellbeing of neighborhoods, such as the ability to extract resources and respond to cuts in public services (e.g., police patrols, fire stations, garbage collection, housing code enforcement).

Collective efficacy then elevates an active view of social life that goes beyond the accumulation of stocks of personal resources, such as those found in local ties or civic memberships. This conceptual orientation is consistent with the redefinition of "social capital" by Alejandro Portes in terms of "expectations for action within a collectivity."[15] Distinguishing between the resource potential represented by personal ties, on the one hand, and the shared expectations for action represented by collective efficacy, on the other hand, helps to clarify why dense networks are not sufficient for the exercise of control. For this reason we posited an analogy between individual efficacy and neighborhood efficacy: both entail the activation of latent resources to achieve an intended effect. Expectations of action are crucial.

We also argued that just as self-efficacy is situated rather than general (one has self-efficacy relative to a particular task), a neighborhood's efficacy exists relative to specific tasks and is embedded in conditions of mutual trust and social cohesion. There is good reason to hypothesize that humans will be less likely to expect engagement in acts of social control in contexts (whether neighborhoods or everyday situations) where there is no expectation of future contact or where participants mistrust one another. As Russell Hardin argues, trust is constituted by shared expectations.[16] Collective efficacy theory goes further to argue that repeated interactions, observations of interactions, and an awareness of *potential* interactions that could be invoked all establish shared norms (a sense of the "we") beyond the strong ties among friends and kin.[17] Put differently, a person can perceive trust and infer shared expectations about public behavior without having to know their neighbors in the "urban village" sense of cohesion.

The logic of collective efficacy theory is not disproven by the intermingling of criminal and noncriminal networks that Whyte, Pattillo, Venkatesh, and Martin Sanchez-Jankowski found. Over fifty years ago Solomon Kobrin noted how delinquents had contacts with nondelinquents and vice versa. The development of values and goals simultaneously are exerted in both directions.[18] Shouldn't we expect to find that delinquents have brothers, sisters, grandmothers, and neighbors that know them well? That they defend and love them even as they may condemn their behavior? I suspect that middle-class parents are no more or less likely than lower-class parents to disown their children when they get in trouble with the law. The difference is that the disadvantaged are more exposed to the realities of crime, and the proximity of black middle-class communities to high-crime areas means that on a day-to-day basis, their residents must negotiate their way among the "street-wise" and potentially criminal encounters.[19] What matters ultimately is the relative weight of social controls directed toward reducing crime.

What Influences Collective Efficacy?

As with individual efficacy, collective efficacy does not exist in a vacuum. It is partly "endogenous" or contingent on the challenges at hand, cultural contexts, and the stratification of places by key structural characteristics. Existing theory has focused mostly on the role of concentrated poverty, racial segregation, immigrant enclaves, and residential stability. As noted in chapters 2 and 5, economic segregation by race increases the concentration of cumulative disadvantage, intensifying the social isolation of lower-income, minority, and single-parent residents from key institutional resources that support collective social control. Equally salient is the influence of racial and economic exclusion on perceived powerlessness. Research has demonstrated that an individual's socioeconomic status is positively linked to his or her sense of personal control, efficacy, and even biological health.[20] A similar process may work at the community level, where alienation, exploitation, and dependency wrought by resource deprivation act as a centrifugal force that stymies collective efficacy. Even if personal ties are strong in areas of concentrated disadvantage, they may be weakly tethered to collective actions.

The evidence also suggests that newer immigrant groups are less active in local civic affairs and that rapid population change can undermine neighborhood social organization. A high rate of residential mobility, especially in areas losing population or characterized by rapid immigration flows, may weaken expectations for collective life because the formation of trust and social ties takes time. Home owners have a vested interest in supporting the commonweal of neighborhood life when compared to renters. Thus residential tenure and home ownership are likely to promote collective efforts to maintain social control.

Based on these ideas, we tested the hypothesis that collective efficacy is lowered by concentrated disadvantage, immigration, and residential instability. In turn, we asked whether collective efficacy helped explain the association of structural features of the urban environment with rates of interpersonal violence. Specifically, we hypothesized that collective efficacy has independent explanatory power above and beyond the composition of the population and that it partially mediates the effects of neighborhood structural features.

Prior Results

Ecometrics is rooted in the idea that we have to take seriously the measurement of community-level properties in their own right.[21] Stephen Raudenbush and I have argued that without a coherent strategy for evaluating the quality of ecological assessments, a serious mismatch arises in studies that aim to integrate individuals and neighborhoods. The assessment of individual differences, building on decades of psychometric research, employs measures that have withstood rigorous evaluation. This is especially true of measures of cognitive skill and school achievement, but extends as well to measures of personality and social behavior. These measures have been thoroughly evaluated in many studies; each scale includes many items; ill-performing items have been discarded; and psychometric properties have been found to hold up in many contexts. Without comparable standards to evaluate ecological assessments, the search for individual and ecological explanations is likely to overemphasize the individual component.

We further argued that it is tempting at first to describe the challenge as one of needing to understand "the psychometric properties of ecological measures." But this awkward phrasing reveals the individualistic bias of modern social science, underscoring the need to take ecological assessment seriously as an enterprise that is conceptually distinct from individual-level assessment. Ecological constructs are not merely the aggregate of individual characteristics, leading to what we termed the "ecometric" rather than psychometric properties of social-ecological measures. Ecometric assessment, while borrowing tools from the rich tradition of psychometrics, has its own logic and treats neighborhoods as important units in their own right. I set aside the statistical details here and focus on the basics of how emergent properties such as collective efficacy and other neighborhood social processes can be measured.

Based on the Community Survey of 8,782 residents of 343 Chicago neighborhoods in 1995, we first developed a theoretically motivated measurement strategy. To capture shared expectations about social control, we designed vignettes. Residents were asked about the likelihood that their neighbors could be counted on to take action if: (1) children were skipping school and hanging out on a street corner, (2) children were spray-painting graffiti on a local building, (3) children were showing disrespect to an adult, (4) a fight broke out in front of their house, and (5) the fire station closest to home was threatened with budget cuts. Our measurement relied on vignettes because of the fundamental unobservability of the capacity for control—the act of intervention is only observed under conditions of challenge. If high collective efficacy leads to low crime, then at any given moment no intervention will be observed precisely because of the lack of need. Like Bandura's theory of self-efficacy, the argument is that expectations for control will increase behavioral interventions when necessary, but the scale itself taps shared expectations for social action—in our case ranging from informal intervention to the mobilization of formal controls.[22] The emphasis is on actions that are generated "on the ground" rather than top down. It turned out that residents varied sharply in their answers both within and across neighborhoods. After adjusting for individual differences, our strategy was to measure between-neighborhood patterns in informal social control.

The "social cohesion/trust" part of the measure taps the nature of community relationships and was measured by coding whether residents agreed with the following propositions: "People around here are willing to help their neighbors," "People in this neighborhood can be trusted," "This is a close-knit neighborhood," "People in this neighborhood generally get along with each other," and "People in this neighborhood share the same values." As hypothesized, social cohesion and social control were strongly related across neighborhoods and were combined into a summary measure of collective efficacy, yielding an aggregate-level reliability in the high 0.80s.[23] Individual differences *within* neighborhoods in the ratings of collective efficacy as a result of social position (e.g. age, race, sex, social class, home ownership) were controlled for, and the key question turned on variance *between* neighborhoods.

We found that collective efficacy varied widely across Chicago neighborhoods and was associated with lower rates of violence measured by independent methods, while also controlling for concentrated disadvantage, residential stability, immigrant concentration, and a comprehensive set of individual-level characteristics (e.g., age, sex, SES, race/ethnicity, home ownership) as well as indicators of personal ties and the density of local organizations. Whether measured by homicide events or violent victimization reported by residents, neighborhoods high in collective efficacy consistently had significantly lower rates of violence. This finding held up controlling for prior neighborhood violence, which was negatively associated with collective efficacy. This pattern suggests a dynamic process in which prior violence depresses collective efficacy (e.g., because of fear or cynicism), while collective efficacy helps stave off future crime. We found that after adjusting for the prior-violence link, a two standard-deviation elevation in collective efficacy was associated with a 26 percent reduction in the expected homicide rate.[24]

Another key finding was that the association of concentrated disadvantage and residential instability with higher violence declined after collective efficacy was controlled, suggesting a potential causal pathway at the community level. This pathway is presumed to operate over time because collective efficacy is undermined by the concentration of disadvantage, racial segregation, family disruption, and residential instability, which in turn fosters more crime. A follow-up study that considered additional factors showed that the density of personal ties was associated with higher collective efficacy and hence lower crime, although the former did not translate directly into lower crime rates—its association with crime was indirect.[25] These findings are consistent with the hypothesis that collective efficacy helps explain the effect of both structural deprivation and the density of personal ties on crime rates. As noted at the opening of this chapter, however, we must bear in mind that social ties are neutral in the sense that they can be drawn upon for negative as well as positive goals. A study by Browning and colleagues extended Al Reiss's concern by showing that dense networks attenuate the effect of collective efficacy on crime, adding another twist to the idea that strong ties are not necessarily a good thing.[26] In what is termed a *negotiated coexistence* model, collective efficacy is negatively associated with the prevalence of violent crime in urban neighborhoods, but the density of exchange networks interacts with collective efficacy such that as network density increases, the regulatory effect of collective efficacy on violence declines.

What are the kinds of structural and normative contexts that promote (or undermine) collective efficacy and nonexclusive social networks other than those already considered? This is a question that cannot be answered easily and that I will come back to in chapter 8. But there are clear hints in our data that the civic infrastructure of local organizations and voluntary associations helps sustain a capacity for social action in a way that transcends traditional personal ties. Organizations are equipped to foster collective efficacy, often through strategic networking of their own or by creating tasks that demand collective responses.[27] Whether disorder removal, school improvements, or police responses, a continuous stream of challenges faces contemporary communities—challenges that no longer can be met by relying solely on individuals. I thus conceive of shared expectations for control and effective social action as depending in part on organizations and connections that do not directly reflect the density of personal ties in a neighborhood. PHDCN-related research supports this position by showing that the density of local organizations as reported by residents and their involvement in voluntary associations predicts higher levels of collective efficacy, controlling for poverty, social composition, and prior crime rates.[28] The following chapter and chapter 14 will reconnect with the organizational story by exploring a new perspective on collective civic action and the ways in which networks of ties among community leaders and organizations knit together collective efficacy.

In the meanwhile, the data from the PHDCN and other studies of neighborhood social process are for the most part consistent with the inference that collective efficacy is an independent source of variation in crime rates and that it partially mediates the effect of neighborhood characteristics like concentrated disadvantage, residential stability, and local network ties. Travis Pratt and Frances Cullen conducted an independent review of more than two hundred empirical studies of neighborhood and crime rates from 1960 to 1999.[29] Using the technique of meta-analysis, they found that collective efficacy had a mean correlation of −0.303 (on a scale of −1 to 1) with crime rates in relevant studies (the 95 percent confidence interval is −0.26 to −0.35). By meta-analysis standards this is a robust finding, and when weighted by sample size the authors rank the magnitude of collective efficacy ahead of more traditional suspects such as poverty, family disruption, and race. Although the number of studies directly measuring social processes is much smaller than for factors like poverty (under twenty-five), and while there is considerable variability in the specification of measures, we can conclude that collective efficacy has a consistent negative association with crime rates.[30]

The Reach of Collective Efficacy

It is important to emphasize that the original social disorganization theory and collective efficacy theory were both designed mainly to explain variations across neighborhoods in rates of crime and other behaviors. I have been addressing the evidence on this question. Asking whether the collective efficacy of one's residence reaches further to explain how neighborhoods influence the criminal behavior of individuals no matter where they happen to be at the time or in later years is a compatible but logically different question. In this case neighborhoods would have developmental or lagged effects. The separation of types of explanation is important to consider because residents often traverse the boundaries of multiple neighborhoods during the course of a day. Adolescents, for example, typically occupy different neighborhood contexts outside of home, especially when it comes to schooling and hanging out in the company of peers. It is thus possible for the prevalence of participation in some crimes to be spread fairly evenly across neighborhoods, even as crime events are ecologically concentrated.

Research on the Chicago PHDCN data that I have led finds that collective efficacy in the neighborhood of residence does not have a direct association with the self-reported violence of adolescents.[31] It appears that whereas collective efficacy predicts the event (or location) rate of violence in a neighborhood, it does not necessarily predict the violent offending propensity of neighborhood youths that may occur elsewhere in the city. This pattern suggests that collective efficacy is situational when it comes to crime. But this does not imply causal irrelevance, of course, because the earlier results logically suggest that neighborhood collective efficacy consistently influences the probability of crime within its borders. The offending of PHDCN adolescents may thus still be influenced by the collective efficacy of the *nonresidential* neighborhoods in which they hang out. A study of robbery locations in Chicago supports this idea—low collective efficacy is an "attractor" for robbery offenders even if they do not live in the neighborhoods.[32] A further study of routine activities and ecology in England shows that individual delinquency by crime-prone adolescents is significantly deterred by the collective efficacy of neighborhoods where the adolescents spend their leisure time.[33] Consistent with the routine-activity approach, studies based on the PHDCN have reported direct effects of collective efficacy on unstructured socializing with peers and early initiation of sexual behavior. The contextual influence of collective efficacy on teenage sexual behavior among Chicago adolescents suggests a broad role for neighborhood-level supervision or regulation.[34] A recent study also argues that neighborhood collective efficacy is significantly associated with adolescents' unstructured socializing with peers, and that this relationship must be accounted for when studying violence. In particular, a significant negative effect of collective efficacy on violent behavior by neighborhood adolescents became evident "only upon including the effect of unstructured socializing with peers."[35] This finding implies that the influence of collective efficacy on individual violence was suppressed in our earlier study.

Taken together these results suggest that much more than "street crime" is at stake. In fact, Christopher Browning argues that collective efficacy reduces domestic violence "inside the home" as well, through the hypothesized mechanism of disclosure by women at risk of partner abuse to third parties in neighborhoods characterized by high collective efficacy.[36] PHDCN-related research by others has also documented significant links between collective efficacy and rates of *asthma, birth weight, self-rated health,* and *heat-wave deaths*.[37] Collective efficacy thus reaches out to capture a number of health-related dimensions that go well beyond the original application of the theory to street crime.

A sketch of the argument made to this point is shown in figure 7.1. I argue that inequality in resources and other structural forces outside the immediate control of residents (e.g., organizations) bear on the production of collective efficacy. By this account collective efficacy theory is not an attempt to shift the burden of social regulation solely onto residents (or to "blame the victim," as some would have it). Macrolevel and spatial processes beyond the local neighborhood also matter, as do individual selection processes—these are represented in dotted boxes outside the circle of present findings. I defer empirical examination and

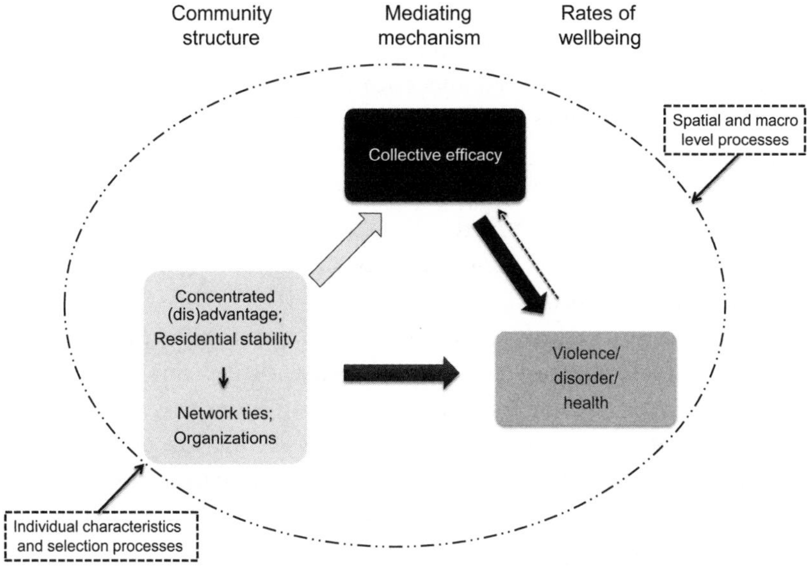

FIGURE 7.1. Conceptual framework of collective efficacy theory and community wellbeing

theoretical elaboration of these dynamics to a later chapter, but to anticipate one finding, the pathways in figure 7.1 hold up after I account for spatial interdependence. Recall also that the results described above account for the compositional makeup of neighborhoods. I will address selection bias and hypothesized reciprocal or feedback effects later, but would note that while most research is unidirectional, the bulk of studies control for prior violence or other neighborhood challenges and thus anticipate a feedback loop (dotted arrow). Figure 7.1 is meant to convey a parsimonious but empirically supported conceptual scheme reflecting how neighborhood socioeconomic resources (or the lack thereof), organizations, and the density of ties influence rates of violence and wellbeing in part through the mediating role of collective efficacy.

Comparative Ecometrics: Sweden and Beyond

The logic of collective efficacy is not limited to specific cities, the United States, or any country, for that matter. Just how far can we push collective efficacy theory? Is it applicable in societies like France, where republican values and strong norms that the government bears responsibility for intervention might conflict with the idea that neighbors should take some responsibility for action? Does it hold in welfare states where concentrated disadvantage is less tenacious, or in former Soviet states where public spiritedness is allegedly on the wane? Our comparative knowledge base is unfortunately limited—very few studies have been carried out with the explicit goal of cross-national comparison of crime rates and community social mechanisms.

I have attempted one comparison by systematically studying Chicago and Stockholm in collaborative work with Per-Olof Wikström.[38] This choice of cities is, at first blush, counterintuitive—why Chicago and Stockholm? After all, Sweden and the U.S. are worlds apart along a number of dimensions, including the concentration of poverty, welfare support, the planned nature of housing, and, not least, violence. Compared to Stockholm, Chicago is very violent, segregated, and characterized by great economic inequality. Yet from a comparative perspective, this is analytically strategic if our goal is to examine whether there are social characteristics that transcend cultural and national boundaries. Following the simple but efficient "most different" research design for comparative studies,[39] our motivation was to discover whether there are common relationships in these highly disparate cities, and if so, along what dimensions. Chicago and Stockholm not only fit the bill, they represent the third-largest and largest city in the U.S. and Sweden, respectively.

To accomplish this goal we integrated census data on structural differentiation, geocoded police records on violent events, and coordinated surveys of individual characteristics and neighborhood context. The Stockholm study was designed to replicate key portions of the PHDCN community survey and was carried out within a year of the first wave, in 1996. Questionnaires were administered to a random sample of five thousand residents of the county of Stockholm, which includes both the inner city and Greater Stockholm suburbs. Based on a response rate of 80 percent, the final sample was composed of 3,992 people. These respondents are spread across geographic neighborhoods (average size = 5,000) where boundaries were constructed by city-planning authorities based on family status, housing tenure, transportation access, and other land-use considerations. Stockholm neighborhoods with at least five survey respondents (representing over 90 percent of the original sample) were selected for the comparative analysis, yielding two hundred areas compared to 343 neighborhood clusters in Chicago.

In both the Chicago and Stockholm surveys, the design was explicitly multilevel, so that respondents were asked about personal and household characteristics along with a set of questions designed to assess neighborhood context. At the individual level we constructed core measures in both sites in a way that was directly comparable: *age*, *sex*, *college education*, *length of residence* in the household, *home ownership*, *married*, residence in *public or government housing*, and *unemployment*. Each respondent was also asked whether he/she had been victimized by a violent crime in the neighborhood in the six months prior to the survey. We were therefore able to examine individual-level risk of violent crime in addition to the effect of neighborhood social context on rates of violent crime measured by police records.

Racial or ethnic status is a different matter when it comes to cross-national comparison. Nevertheless, at a broad level it is possible to examine the ecological distribution of what we can think of as the disadvantaged group with respect to discrimination or "outgroup" status in each country. In Chicago, as in the U.S. at large, African Americans have long been segregated by neighborhood, and a long line of research including prior chapters suggests they are a disadvantaged minority group. In Sweden, race/ethnicity make little sense as a concept, but immigration from Turkey and the former Yugoslavia in particular is increasing, and there is emerging evidence of spatial clustering and segregation of the non-Swedish-born. We thus created an indicator in Stockholm of foreign-born status, which we selectively compare to African American status in Chicago. They are not tapping the same manifest characteristic, of course, but they tap a larger and more interesting factor, namely the ecological segregation of minority groups that are disadvantaged or discriminated against by the societal mainstream.

To save on costs, a reduced set of collective efficacy items was asked in the Stockholm study, two from the cohesion scale ("People around here are willing to help their neighbors" and "Neighbors can be trusted") and two from efficacy/control (about children spray-painting graffiti and fighting in front of a house). At the neighborhood level these constructs are strongly and similarly related, with a correlation in excess of 0.7 in both cities. We thus created a modified collective efficacy scale that combined the constituent items that were highly reliable across areas.

Although the community surveys measure key aspects of social stratification, we chose to collect independently measured census characteristics. *Concentrated disadvantage* is defined, as it was for Chicago, by the percentage of families with low income, percentage of families receiving public assistance, and percentage of families with children that are female headed. These indicators covary in a similar pattern in both cities—areas that are high in public assistance are also low income and characterized by the concentration of female-headed families. *Residential stability* is defined as the percentage of residents five years old and older who lived in the same house five years earlier, and the percentage of homes that are owner-occupied.

Finally, we collected independent event data from the Chicago and Stockholm police on violent offenses. Locating the occurrence of the crime, we tallied the counts of all interpersonal violence (homicide, aggravated assault, and robbery) matched to the years of the survey. For total violence, we examined the log of the event rate per hundred thousand persons at risk.

Although the focus of this chapter is collective efficacy, it is important to note that the stigmatized minority group in each city faces ecological dissimilarity with respect to socioeconomic resources, but the disparity is much greater in Chicago than Stockholm. As foreshadowed in chapter 5, there are considerably more segregated minority areas in Chicago than in Stockholm, and these areas are more sharply related to concentrated disadvantage. But even in egalitarian Stockholm, as the percentage of immigrants goes up, so does their socioeconomic spatial isolation.[40] One wonders what will happen as the pace of immigration increases in this and other European cities. Will a threshold be passed? The logic of this analysis predicts that tensions in places like Stockholm are likely to increase given their relatively homogeneous past.

Chapter 1 presented an initial look at the association of concentrated disadvantage with increasing violence in both cities (fig. 1.6). Further analysis reveals that this pattern holds for each component of disadvantage and when controlling for residential stability and disorder.[41] Concentrated disadvantage also predicts lower collective efficacy in both cities, albeit with a trailing off, nonlinear pattern. After controlling for neighborhood stability and individual-level characteristics, collective efficacy sharply declines in both Stockholm and Chicago as concentrated disadvantage increases, up to about one standard deviation above the

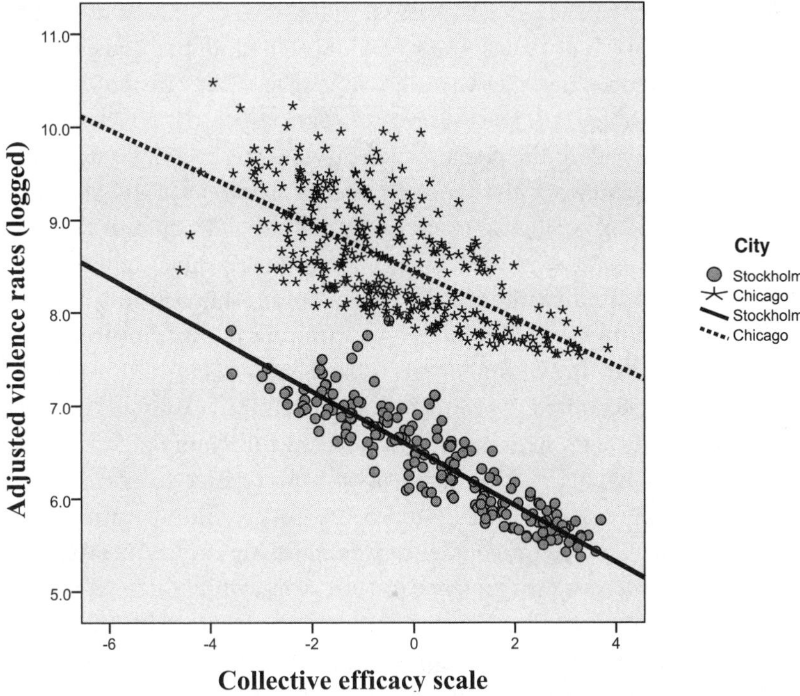

FIGURE 7.2. Similar prediction of violence in Chicago and Stockholm neighborhoods from collective efficacy, adjusting for concentrated disadvantage, percent black/immigrants, and residential stability

mean. As seen in figure 1.6, after that point no more Stockholm neighborhoods are represented. Only in Chicago is severe concentrated poverty found, and it is in these "truly disadvantaged" areas that disadvantage shows a weakened relationship with both violence and collective efficacy. One might say that the damage has already been done, with further disadvantage not registering.

Figure 7.2 graphs the negative relationship between collective efficacy and the expected rate of violence based on a neighborhood's disadvantage, stability, and minority/immigrant composition. The slope of the collective efficacy–violence relationship is clearly negative and similar in each city despite the fact that Chicago sits "atop" Stockholm across the board because of higher levels of violence. The multivariate results show that collective efficacy is directly linked to lower violence in both cities, mediating a portion of the proposed influence of structural antecedents. The collective efficacy–violence link is also robust to additional controls at the neighborhood level, including a conservative test in which social disorder was adjusted.[42] The direct effect of concentrated disadvantage still looms large, however, especially in Chicago.

These data reflect the social order of violence in a cross-national, comparative framework and support the conclusion that neighborhood-level variations in ecological structure, collective efficacy, and violence accord with theoretical predictions in a reasonably consistent fashion in two cities with a vastly different makeup and history. Indeed, Chicago and Stockholm could not be more different in most respects, and the data confirm important differences in how social resources are ecologically distributed. Despite the ecological disadvantage encountered by immigrants with respect to poverty, for example, Stockholm is much more equal at the neighborhood level relative to Chicago and most other U.S. cities. Yet the nature of the relationship between community social structure and violence is remarkably similar. Because the same features account for violence in both cities, while these very same features are differentially allocated according to larger principles of societal organization, the results tap into a macrolevel or societal explanation of city differences in violence. It remains to be seen how well this framework stands up to future tests, and the "Chicago effect" remains large after controlling for disadvantage, possibly owing to deep cultural differences.

Replications and extensions of the Chicago Project are now underway in Los Angeles, Brisbane (Australia), England, Hungary, Moshi (Tanzania), Tianjin (China), Bogotá (Colombia), and other cities around the world. The results so far point to a significant cross-cultural role for collective efficacy. A recent publication based on a direct replication of PHDCN and modeled after the Chicago-Stockholm study shows that collective efficacy predicts lower crime across communities in Brisbane, controlling for the density of social ties and other compositional features.[43] Lorraine Mazerolle and colleagues report that despite cultural differences between the United States and Australia, collective efficacy is a significant mechanism in explaining the spatial distribution of crime. In the very non-Western culture of China, a recent study based on PHDCN items finds that collective efficacy has a direct negative association with burglary victimization in Tianjin, controlling for characteristics of both households and neighborhoods.[44] Felton Earls of PHDCN took the ideas of collective efficacy to Africa to mount an AIDS and sexual abuse prevention trial. As part of this study, a community survey measuring collective efficacy was administered to both adults and children. Early results reveal that an intervention to improve children's health behaviors was significantly associated with perceptions of increased collective efficacy.[45] In the United Kingdom, the PHDCN survey was replicated and integrated with the Environmental Risk Longitudinal Twin Study directed by Terrie Moffitt. A paper from this study finds that neighborhood collective efficacy is negatively associated with levels of children's antisocial behavior at school entry for those living in deprived neighborhoods. This relationship held after controlling for neighborhood problems and family-level risk factors.[46] In Hungary, a national survey used PHDCN items to measure collective efficacy. Controlling for confounders, collective efficacy showed the second-strongest association (after education) with reduced mortality among both men and women.[47]

Latin American countries may prove to be the exception. Research in Brazilian neighborhoods suggests that poverty concentrated in the *favelas* leads to higher and not lower cohesion, perhaps aiding survival.[48] A similar relationship appears to be emerging in Bogotá, Colombia, where resistance to armed militias and corrupt police in poor areas creates a unique challenge that shapes the association of collective efficacy with violence in a manner apparently quite different than other countries.[49] One might also expect collective efficacy to serve a different function in regions of Mexico where drug cartels control many low-income neighborhoods and the police are considered corrupt. Intervening in such contexts means risking one's life. Here, collective efficacy may serve something of a survival function by which residents band together to protect each other from the organized forces of drug violence.

Back in the U.S., PHDCN replications are being designed by the new National Children's Study[50] and in several cities around the country. The largest city study is the Los Angeles Family and Neighborhood Study (LAFANS). Early reports from LA based on over eight hundred adolescents in sixty-five neighborhoods find that collective efficacy is directly associated with lower rates of obesity measured in three different ways.[51] Using the same data, another LAFANS study finds that collective efficacy significantly predicts lower teen birth rates in Angelino neighborhoods with less than 50 percent Hispanics. In areas of concentrated immigration, however, the same relationship is attenuated, suggesting an interaction of collective efficacy with Latino culture.[52]

In sum, although the manifestation of collective efficacy is dependent on societal culture and local challenges, creating a relationship with crime and health that is variable rather than invariant, what is striking is the fact that large community-level variations can be detected and ecometrically assessed in such divergent country settings. Wherever people have looked so far, the emergence of variation in collective efficacy beyond that expected based on the aggregated composition of individuals suggests that the capacity for social control is a basic social property, one that transcends poverty and race and in many cases predicts lower violence and enhanced public health. Similar to the message of chapter 5, at a broad conceptual level Chicago is not as unique as many seem to assume when it comes to a comparative international context. In the next section I show that collective efficacy has enduring properties that cut across time as well.

Stability and Change

It is ironic that studies of community social processes are largely static despite the "process" logic underlying key concepts. To confront this challenge I examine the dynamics of collective efficacy, analyzing both its long-term sources and its own predictive power in explaining crime-rate variations up to the middle part of this decade, using the most recent data available. I begin by examining a deceptively simple question: How stable is collective efficacy? The answer is that it is surprisingly durable, more than I had originally expected. As explained in chapter 5, the evidence points to social reproduction amid a period of overall change.

The data come from the two community surveys described in chapter 4, with identical items asked at each wave. The difference in the two surveys is sample size, with the second survey interviewing less than half as many people as the original (3,105 vs. 8,732). The empirical result is that collective efficacy (CE), and virtually all other neighborhood processes, are measured less reliably in 2002 than 1995.[53] The latter values are higher because of the larger sample within community areas than clusters at both waves. Tract reliabilities are the lowest, at 0.58 and 0.37 in 1995 and 2002, respectively, but tracts provide more than ten times the number of analytic units as community areas, and overlap ("multicolinearity") is lower. Hence there is a direct tradeoff—community-area measures are more reliable but the units are bigger and less numerous. I manage the tradeoff by analyzing relationships across multiple levels and focusing on the consistency of findings in light of theoretical considerations.

Despite the varying reliabilities and independent (or repeated cross-sectional) samples at the different points of time, communities scoring highly in 1995 on collective efficacy look quite similar seven years later. This result is robust, holding whether we look at census tracts, neighborhood clusters, or community areas, and despite changing population composition. To get a simultaneous visual and statistical sense of this relationship, figure 7.3 presents the correlation for community areas arrayed by low, medium, or high in percent black—a simple indicator of relative racial heterogeneity. Figure 7.3 first reveals that collective efficacy seems to be transmitted across years, even as residents fluctuate in or out of the community (recall fig. 3.2). That is, despite rapid movement of individuals in and out of the neighborhood, and despite a separate sample of residents in the two community surveys, collective efficacy is correlated at 0.73 over time. Communities that are high tend to stay high, and vice versa.[54]

Second, stability is patterned across the full spectrum of racial composition and ethnic diversity. The social disorganization tradition leads us to expect more unfavorable outcomes as ethnic homogeneity declines, but the data have not supported this prediction and neither does figure 7.3. For example, one sees that areas in the middle range of percent black are represented at the *top* of the scale at both periods. This being Chicago, truly integrated communities are rare, and a full third of the city's communities are essentially all white. Mount Greenwood is no exception, but it is nonetheless in the middle third of the race distribution and produces high collective efficacy while proximate to what is widely thought of as the "South Side ghetto." Beverly is a stable middle-class area proximate to the same ghetto, and one third of its residents were black in 2000, probably more like 40 percent by mid-decade. Yet Beverly stands out as the most efficacious community in Chicago in 1995 and second best in 2002 after Mount Greenwood. Figure 7.3 shows

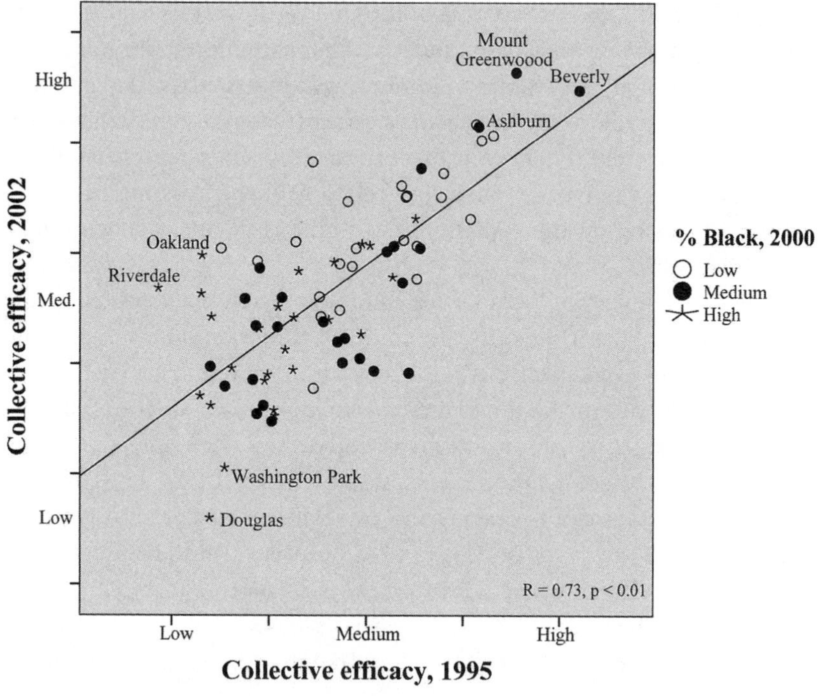

FIGURE 7.3. Stability of collective efficacy across time, by racial composition

that Ashburn is also a mixed-race community (43 percent black, 37 percent white, and 17 percent Latino) and high in collective efficacy. At the other end of the spectrum are the depressed and homogeneously black communities of Washington Park and Douglas, although they are not far from the communities above. That the extremes of the collective efficacy distribution are all on the widely denigrated South Side and that the high end comes not from all-white communities underscores my emphasis in the book on social processes over composition.

Third, even though there is no information about collective efficacy earlier than 1995, we can go back in time to measure key structural aspects of inequality that the last two chapters suggest portend a legacy for later social processes like collective efficacy. It turns out that concentrated poverty in 1970 has a long reach, and its traces have not been easily overcome. Figure 7.4 maps this phenomenon. With few exceptions, most communities above the median in 1970 poverty appear in the lowest third of collective efficacy. Although a few high-poverty communities in 1970 have a high level of collective efficacy in 1995, they experienced some of the highest *decreases* in poverty between 1970 and 2000 along with the highest increases in collective efficacy from 1995 to 2002 (data not shown). This picture of the systematic nature of change—the "stability of change"—is embedded within a pattern of spa-

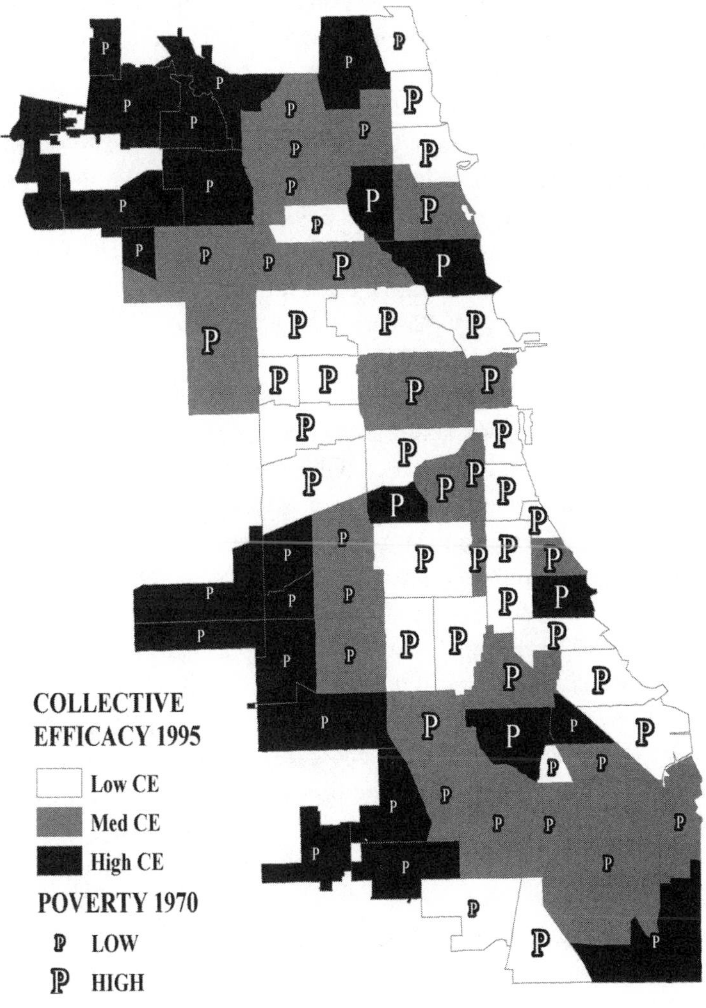

FIGURE 7.4. Legacy of concentrated poverty for collective efficacy twenty-five years later

tial clustering, where communities with low levels of collective efficacy are proximate to each other and overlap with poverty clusters, combining into what appear to be unfortunate traps of spiraling vulnerabilities and reinforcing spatial risks. I will return to this spatial mechanism in greater detail in chapter 10.

For now, the data support the argument that the durability of structural deprivation is interwoven with sharp differences in the construction and maintenance of collective efficacy. What about alternative explanations? To assess this question, I examined the predictive power of concentrated disadvantage across several decades, alongside residential mobility, population diversity, and spatial interdependencies in collective efficacy. I found that poverty from the 1970s had a resilient and significant negative association with collective efficacy extending to 2002. To the extent that the 1970 level of poverty is highly associated with more recent levels of community poverty (chapter 5), this finding is not entirely unexpected. Interestingly, however, *1990 poverty is less strongly associated with contemporary collective efficacy than 1970 poverty*, a strong empirical indication of a cumulative "Matthew Effect" of poverty. Perhaps more unexpected was the durable effect of 1970 poverty on *recent decreases* in residents' trust and collective efficacy, controlling for increases in poverty that also predicted decreased efficacy. It appears that poverty and its associated pitfalls, such as perceived disorder and violence, may have a lasting and cumulative effect on collective memories, distorting a community's reputation and perceived "local character," fostering a spiral of further disadvantage and mistrust.[55]

The other major finding is that after controlling for poverty and residential stability, diversity in 1970 and changes in diversity across three decades do not significantly predict collective efficacy in 1995 *or* change in collective efficacy from 1995 to 2002, respectively.[56] This finding suggests that any zero-order association between racial diversity and lower collective efficacy is accounted for by a common association with poverty and stability.

Overall then, we can see that there is a great deal of continuity in collective efficacy and its sources: there is a legacy to inequality and to inequality's relationship with collective efficacy. Considering the measurement imprecision inherent in the enterprise at hand, figures 7.3 and 7.4 indicate an impressive persistence in a community's character that is related to residents' trust and shared expectations for control, and its prior levels of disadvantage. The change that does occur, moreover, is structurally patterned and not random, an issue to which I will return in the final section with updated data.

Explaining Crime, 1995–2006

As a final assessment, I examine the ability of collective efficacy to predict variations in crime rates in a dynamic fashion. Guided by the results above, we know that collective efficacy is relatively stable, which implies that change is relatively rare and not measured with great precision. Preliminary analysis also showed a similar negative relationship between collective efficacy and crime rates in both surveys. I combine these two pieces of information to form a pooled neighborhood panel with two "levels" of analysis—time and neighborhood. At the first level, the unit of observation and the predictors vary over time *within* each neighborhood. An example would be the collective efficacy of the same neighborhood in 1995 and 2002. In the second level, the unit of analysis is *between* neighborhoods, and the goal is to estimate the average within-neighborhood effect of collective efficacy on crime rates.

The panels were set up as parallel in their measurement strategy. In the first panel collective efficacy and other social processes from the 1995 survey, along with census predictors from 1990, are used to model variations in crime in the late nineties. For the second wave, collective efficacy from 2002 and structural characteristics from the census 2000 are used to predict crime rates from 2002 onward. My main outcome is the homicide rate per hundred thousand residents, which is very well measured across time and space. Every homicide event known to the Chicago Police Department was geocoded to census tracts for the individual years 1995 to 2006.[57] I estimate a predictive model to reduce the risk of feedback effects and pool homicide across years to stabilize rates and increase precision of estimates.

I begin with a basic model that includes key structural predictors so far—concentrated disadvantage, residential stability, and population density. Capitalizing on the panel-based community survey, I also adjust for density of friendship ties and the moral/legal cynicism among residents.[58] All predictors are measured prior in time to the outcomes, and I estimate models both with and without a control for lagged crime.[59] By pooling the data, I draw strength from the two surveys and am able to estimate a single and more reliable estimate of the average effect of collective efficacy, adjusting not only for structural characteristics and other social processes, but for period effects on crime.[60] I focus here on an overview of results that emerged as consistent across crime types and specifications. First, we know that crime declined in the late nineties and then leveled off (recall fig. 5.4), and that this is reflected by the significant negative effect of the wave 2 time indicator in all models. Second, concentrated disadvantage had a large and positive association with violence across the board as well, whereas the pattern for residential stability was inconsistent. Third, the main factor of interest, collective efficacy, directly predicted lower homicide after accounting for prior homicide (coeff. = -0.87, t-ratio = -3.04). Legal cynicism was also directly linked with higher homicide (t-ratio = 3.04). A subsequent study using the PHDCN replicated both the collective efficacy and cynicism findings.[61]

To illustrate the main results in a more straightforward way, figure 7.5 displays the estimated homicide rate for neighborhoods in the lowest and highest quartile of collective efficacy, by time period and adjusting for the effects of poverty, stability, density, friendship ties, moral cynicism, and prior challenge in the form of violence. Hence the figure represents the average association of collective efficacy with homicide, expressed for clarity to show rates per 100,000. For the highest quartile of collective efficacy in the first wave, homicide rates are approximately 10.4 per 100,000. By contrast, in lower efficacy neighborhoods, the rates are over 16 per 100,000, more than a 50 percent increase. To put this in perspective, one can also see that the "period effect" is about the same, a 50 percent reduction in the homicide rate. In terms of body counts, given the size of Chicago overall the data translates to an estimated 168 fewer killings associated with high collective efficacy. By any standard this is a large estimated effect.

I also repeated these procedures on official rates of robbery and burglary and survey-reported violence rates. Overall the results were consistent with the homicide rate patterns. For example, collective efficacy had a direct negative association with robbery rates *after* adjusting for prior robbery (which is highly stable) and all other covariates.[62] Perceived violence was strongly predicted by collective efficacy as well controlling for the total crime rate in the prior period. Similar results were obtained at the community-area level.

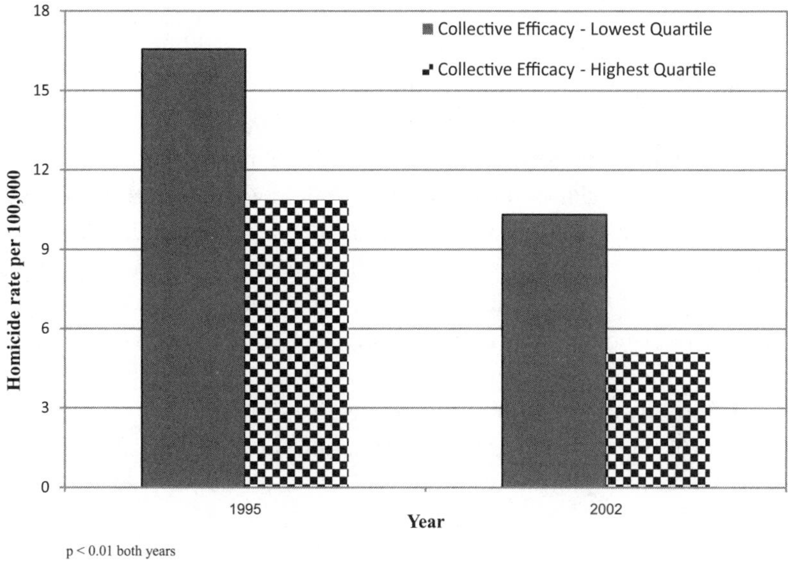

FIGURE 7.5. Association of collective efficacy and time period with homicide rates, controlling for concentrated disadvantage, residential stability, population density, friend/kinship ties, legal/moral cynicism, and prior homicide

I then took advantage of the time series data on crime and looked at annual variations from 1996 to 2006, after the 1995 survey.[63] I thus can explicitly assess change in a key subset of predictors—disadvantage, stability, diversity, and collective efficacy—in an attempt to decompose stability and change effects. Collective efficacy in 1995 predicts a lower mean level of homicide during this period adjusting for stability, diversity, and concentrated disadvantage. Moreover, although relatively stable overall, *change* in collective efficacy is associated with a greater *decrease* in homicide in this period, and homicide in disadvantaged neighborhoods declined at a slower clip than those not suffering from concentrated disadvantage. Figure 7.6 graphs the trajectories of the collective efficacy and disadvantage relationship based on the full model with all controls. The bottom line shows how the greatest declines in homicide are found in neighborhoods that experienced *increases* in collective efficacy and *decreases* in disadvantage. By contrast, the top line shows that increasingly disadvantaged and low efficacy neighborhoods declined less rapidly in homicides. Collective efficacy appears to exert a protective factor in confronting change.

It is important to remember here that collective efficacy is a social process hypothesized to be variably related to challenge, and crime is one of the ultimate challenges in a free society. As I and others have argued, crime may reduce later expectations for control, and observations of what happens when crime is witnessed may also lead residents to update their prior beliefs in a Bayesian-like way.[64] It is thus not surprising, for instance, that the average resident in Stockholm perceives greater collective efficacy than her counterpart in Chicago—the latter is demonstrably more violent. I have controlled for prior crime rates in the above models, but a more direct way to test this feedback process is to conduct cross-lag analyses that get at reciprocal associations. Put differently, I have shown that collective efficacy predicts crime in future years, but does the reverse hold—does crime predict collective efficacy in future years as well? Or is collective efficacy driven largely by

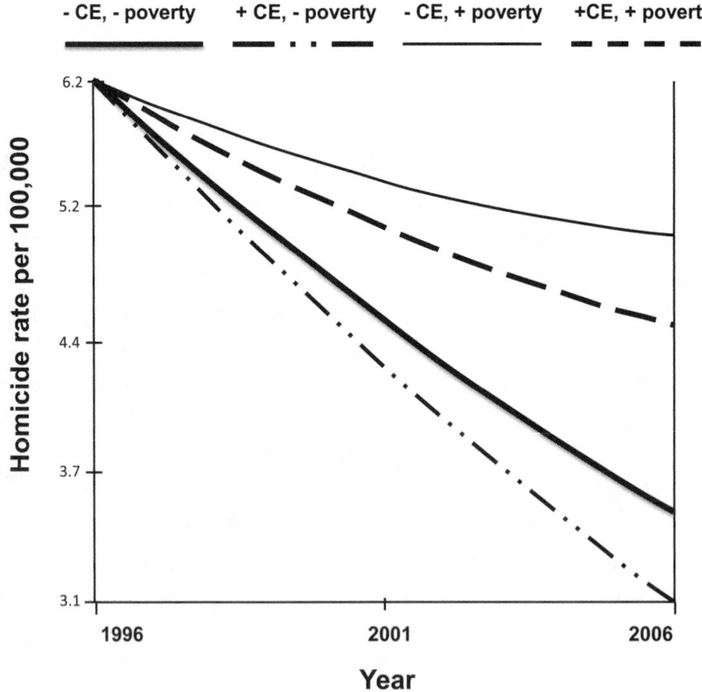

FIGURE 7.6. Changes in collective efficacy (CE) and concentrated poverty explain trajectory of homicide decline in Chicago neighborhoods, 1996–2006

structural conditions? I examined this question by reversing the above procedures and considering collective efficacy in 1995 and 2002 as the simultaneous outcomes in the hierarchical panel framework. The predictors were lagged census characteristics, prior crime, contemporaneous friendship ties, and moral cynicism.

The results support the idea of a reciprocal feedback loop (fig. 7.1). Collective efficacy increased over time in Chicago and is significantly higher in neighborhoods characterized by residential stability (t-ratio = 8.29), friendship ties (t-ratio = 7.01), lower moral cynicism (t-ratio = −4.63), lower density (−8.44), and lower concentrated disadvantage (−8.28). The total crime rate in the neighborhood prior to the survey, net of these important predictors in their own right, was associated with lower collective efficacy (t-ratio = −6.05). Moreover, when I controlled for lagged collective efficacy, prior crime continued to be important, suggesting that *changes* in collective efficacy over time are in part a response to prior experiences with crime. For example, the t-ratio for the effect of lagged homicide (five-year average) on collective efficacy in 2002 was −3.12 with a standardized coefficient of −0.12. This result holds for yet other crimes and is consistent with the updating and feedback notion underlying how efficacy works over time. Nonetheless, concentrated disadvantage was the strongest predictor. It was more than three times larger in magnitude than prior crime (standardized coeff. = −0.36, $p < 0.01$). These findings suggest that while prior violence should be accounted for, concentrated disadvantage is the ultimate challenge in large part because it is more visible as a social construct (chapter 6).

Conclusion

The research on collective efficacy cuts across a number of different studies, investigators, specifications, time periods, outcomes, and more. Limitations of data and method are always present. For these reasons I focus on commonalities that are unlikely to be dependent on any single estimate. Overall the results presented here and by others in a growing number of studies around the world suggest that in communities that are otherwise similar in composition, those with higher levels of collective efficacy exhibit lower rates of crime. There is also evidence that collective efficacy is relatively stable over time and that it predicts future variations in crime, adjusting for the aggregated characteristics of individuals and traditional forms of neighbor networks. Although more infrequently studied, highly efficacious communities seem to do better along a number of dimensions besides crime, such as birth weight, teen pregnancy, asthma, and mortality, suggesting a link to the general concept of population wellbeing.

When I examined what predicts collective efficacy that may help explain the results, I demonstrated that prior experiences with violence typically reduce later expectations for control. This finding makes sense from expectations rooted in self-efficacy theory and our individual lives—past experience matters. But concentrated disadvantage mattered more, and I showed that traces of poverty from prior decades independently predicted current collective efficacy. Institutional and cultural mechanisms are apparently at work in social reproduction, inducing another form of legacy. How do these legacies—both good and bad—get passed on, despite the high rates of residential mobility that characterize city life? And how also to account for neighborhoods like Beverly and Mount Greenwood in Chicago, which maintain high levels of collective efficacy in spite of the structural challenges they face? The next chapter takes up these and related questions by exploring a new perspective on collective civic action and how organizational life bears on collective efficacy and other aspects of the urban social fabric.

8 Civic Society and the Organizational Imperative

> To outsiders, the men and women gathered inside a sleepy West Side restaurant may have seemed unlikely power brokers: a janitor, a real estate agent and others hardly known outside their circuit of neighborhood dances and back-yard barbecues.
>
> *Chicago Tribune*, April 6, 2007[1]

The attack on "community organizing" by the Republican ticket in the 2008 national election generated sharp debate on the value of Barack Obama's experience to the presidency. Much was made of Obama's roots in the South Side of Chicago, especially his early years organizing the poor at the Altgeld Gardens Project in Riverdale.[2] The image painted by the conservative Right was that community organizing was socialist in leaning and subversive of American ideals.

The irony is that community organizations and the nonprofit organizational sector more generally are the unsung heroes tilting against the narrative of "community lost" that has long worried observers of civil society, especially traditionalists.[3] While we might know fewer of our neighbors than in the past, every day thousands of nonprofit organizations around the country are busy organizing and creating opportunities for new associations. Community nonprofits and voluntary associations also span the political spectrum, from allegedly Left-leaning community organizers a la Obama to conservative church groups, community recreation centers, after-school programs for children, fraternal societies, block associations, and more. What could be more American than organizing the annual Fourth of July block party?

This chapter probes the social, organizational, and spatial contexts that produce collective civic events. We know little about this type of community organizational life in the contemporary era, surprisingly so, given the national prominence of the "civic society debate" in America. Across a wide field of commentators, a dominant argument has been that participation in civic life has plummeted dramatically over the last three decades. Whether the indicator is a decline in voting, reduced trust in others, lower membership in the parent-teacher association, or slipping attendance at public meetings, Americans are thought to be "bowling alone" more than ever.[4] But on deeper inspection, the alarm bells that Putnam set off had little to do with bowling club memberships per se or the Benevolent and Protective Order of the Elks. Relying on Tocqueville's classic insights from the 1800s, political theorists and social critics have been most concerned with the negative consequences of civic disengagement for democratic capacity and the collective health of the American polity. Yet in a potential misreading of classic concerns, recent studies on civil society have centered largely on the perceptions, memberships, and behaviors of *individuals* rather than the production and realization of *collective* action.

As part of the Chicago Collective Civic Participation Project, one of the augmentations to the PHDCN, Douglas McAdam and I addressed this theoretical disconnect by turning our attention to what we categorized as *robust civic action* in the form of collective civic events.[5] Drawing on insights and lessons learned from the social movements literature, we gathered a sample of over four thousand collective action events in the Chicago metropolitan area—both civic participation *and* protests—for selected years from 1970 to 2000. Through detailed coding of these events, we constructed a database that allowed us to chart the variable nature and community-level structure of collective action during the period of rising concern over American civic decline. In shifting the focus from individuals to collective public events that bring two or more people together to realize a common purpose or specific claim, predictions of a decline in civil society were not upheld. We found instead a surprising stability in the rate of collective civic action and the nature of public claims over a long period of time. Charity, education, the arts, children, the environment, and local government policy dominated collective action across all three decades. The typical form of organized collective action was also not the stereotypical protest, lawsuit, or rally. The top five forms were charity events, community festivals, public meetings, recreational activities, and workshops. Hardly radical—in fact many conservative events emerged in the data. Most important for this book, collective civic action is concentrated ecologically and better explained by the density of community organizations than individual social ties or membership in traditional civic groups.

This chapter builds on my work with McAdam to reframe the civil society debate in terms of collective, rather than individual, action. The overarching thesis is that collective civic engagement has changed rather than declined, with sources that are organizational and spatial rather than interpersonal in nature. After describing the data and methods designed to assess this thesis, I briefly summarize key results previewed above and then turn to new analyses and findings, including those that incorporate a virtual census of nonprofit organizations and a separate study of churches, a traditional source of support for community organizing in the black community. These analyses confirm the importance of the nonprofit sector but uncover further surprising findings on the widely assumed efficacy of the black church. Taken together I believe the project's findings contribute to a rethinking of our assumptions about community civic life and point to the organizational imperative underlying effective response to social challenge.

From Protest to Collective Civic Participation

The scholarly field of social movements has tended to privilege a stylized form of contention—featuring disruptive protests linked to broad national struggles waged by disadvantaged minorities—over far more numerous, if less visible, kinds of collective engagement.[6] But "mundane" forms of collective civic action may be no less important, and, given the organizational and personal style of American life, they may even be better.

Social movement scholarship nonetheless offers important building blocks that can be used to transcend its traditional focus. McAdam is one of the field's leaders, and on the happy occasion of overlapping at the Center for Advanced Study in the Behavioral Sciences, we struck up a conversation over lunch one day on shared intellectual interests. The conversation kept going all year and ended up yielding a major collaboration. Conceptually, we began by drawing on the major strengths of social movement research. One is its decisive empirical shift from individual civic participation to a focus on *collective action events*, which logically, we argued, is essential to the underlying phenomenon at the heart of the civil society debate. A second strength concerns the honing of a methodology consistent with an event-based focus, which I describe below. A third strength, more theoretical in nature, concerns the central importance assigned by movement analysts to an understanding of the social processes that give rise to and help sustain collective mobilization and action, an intellectual move that rejects the idea that collective action results simply from the aggregation of individual civic propensity.[7]

It became clear to us upon reflection that social movements and collective efficacy theory as elaborated in previous chapters share a common orienting framework—a focus on the mobilization (or capacity thereof) of action for an intended purpose. This framework argues for a direct focus on civic events that are collective in nature and that bring together members of the community. Events such as blood drives, community festivals, pancake breakfasts at the local fire hall, fundraisers for cultural causes, block parties, or neighborhood crime watches, for example, go straight to the heart of civic capacity. The collective nature and spatial concentration of such phenomena has been overlooked in the social capital debate; instead attention was focused on national trends in things like group membership, social ties, trust, voting, routine meeting attendance, giving, and television viewing. The collective efficacy framework in this book is obviously sensitive to neighborhood context and the idea of collective events, but to this point its measurement has relied on survey questions about trust and shared expectations. The social movement literature focuses on nonroutine events but eschews much concern for neighborhood variation and concentrates on explicit "protest" agendas such as the antiwar, civil rights, labor, and environmental movements.

Seeking to bridge these gaps and leverage a more general conception of collective civic action, McAdam and I borrowed different elements of each theoretical approach, first by replacing the individual-level focus of most social capital arguments with an event-based approach to examining collective civic behavior. Second, we adopted the task-oriented and spatially informed framework of collective efficacy theory. Third, we expanded the protest agenda of traditional social movement research by including an explicit focus on collective *civic* events. Restated within the basic thesis of this book, we hypothesized that collective action events in the contemporary city are (a) highly concentrated geographically and (b) explained by systematic variations in community-level characteristics. But which ones? When the social ecology of neighborhoods has been considered, it has typically been viewed through the lens of the urban-poverty paradigm articulated in William Julius Wilson's *The Truly Disadvantaged*. Robert Wuthnow, for example, a leading student of civil society, argues that because the new urban poverty is defined in terms of its geographic concentration, "the character of civic involvement must be understood in terms of the social ecology of entire neighborhoods, rather than as an attribute of individuals or families alone."[8] Although Wuthnow's directive is taken up in this chapter and throughout the book, restricting the focus to poor neighborhoods or concentrated poverty is an analytically narrow approach (see also chapter 3). So is the dominant counterthesis on civic decline, namely that the (declining) density of local ties and memberships in local voluntary associations constitute the main force generating civic action.[9]

Rather than poverty or civic memberships, we emphasized the proposition that the capacity for sustained collective action is conditioned mainly by the presence of established institutions and organizations that can be appropriated in the service of collective action goals. Proponents of the political process model of social movements have previously emphasized the role of established institutions or organizations in the onset of contention. As McAdam argues, "Absent any such 'mobilizing structure,' incipient movements [are] thought to lack the capacity to act even if afforded the opportunity to do so."[10] It is worth reiterating that this emphasis is conceptually different from claims that turn on rates of individual participation in voluntary associations and related civic activities as emphasized in the social capital literature. The main difference is that movements and related protest events are not simple aggregations of individual participants; rather, they are social products born of complex interactive dynamics played out within established social settings. Thus while high rates of individual participation and dense personal ties may be related to organizational infrastructure, conceptually they are not the same thing. Imagine, for example, an "urban village" with intense participation by its residents in only one local organization, compared to another community with a lower prevalence of memberships spread across a multiplicity of institutions. Even when membership and institutional density are coincident, high rates of individual participation are likely to be an outgrowth of existing organizational structure, not the reverse. From this perspective, emergent collective action is seen as a product of extant institutions and organizations working through interactional processes taking place within them. Individuals (the micro level) are the necessary conduit, but individual civic endowments and levels of participation are not a sufficient driver.

Blended or Hybrid Forms of Civic Action

Integrating the social movements and urban community literature suggests a further revision in the social capital–civic society debate. The insight to be gleaned is to view forms of protest not as inherently problematic, but as both an expression and catalyst of community building. Protest, after all, is a form of collective action that Tocqueville himself might have admired for its democratic underpinnings. Putnam seems to agree: "Whether among gays marching in San Francisco or evangelicals praying on the Mall or, in an earlier era, autoworkers downing tools in Flint, the act of collective protest itself creates enduring bonds of solidarity."[11] Along these lines, a recent analysis of democracy by a political scientist claims that social conflict and civic engagement have a symbiotic relationship in a well-functioning democracy.[12] As uncomfortable as it may be for some, this is the essence of community organizing as Saul Alinsky, the father of community organization, demonstrated so well in his early Chicago days.[13] This theme has endured and expanded, reflected in venues as diverse as marches supporting democracy in Iran and immigration rights. An impressive example of a collective response in the heart of Chicago's Loop is shown in figure 8.1, as thousands of participants gathered in 2006 to promote the rights of immigrants.

We thus took the next logical step of conceptualizing a largely unrecognized but potentially transformative type of activity. We combined the metaphorical bowling league with civic action by examining events that combine community gatherings (e.g., parades, festivals, barbecues) with claims for social change. Similar to the hybrid suggested in the opening quote of this chapter, consider an event reported in the *Chicago Tribune* under the headline: "Spearheads Playground Battle: Community Group Demands Playground Facilities for Youth at Park District." This article describes a collective event in which a community action group called Let's All Get Together and Work arranged a meeting with the

FIGURE 8.1. March for immigration rights in Chicago, 2006. Photograph by Michael L. Dorn. Reproduced under Attribuition-ShareAlike 2.0 Generic Creative Commons license.

Park District to demand that a vacant lot be converted to a playground for children. Or consider another event reported under the headline: "Neighbors' Library Plea Is Granted: Community Residents and Students Lobby for Temporary Library Facility." In this event, community residents and a group of middle-school students attended a board meeting of the public library to request that a temporary library site be found to service the community during the two years it would take to restore a neighborhood library destroyed by fire.

These *hybrid* events represent examples of "blended social action." This form of action blurs traditional boundaries by combining common types of civic participation, such as festivals or neighborhood association meetings, with a stated claim and an organized public event that seeks change. In other words, hybrid collective events combine protestlike "claims" for change with civil society "forms," such as the successful library protest that grew out of a neighborhood association. Rather than assuming that membership in neighborhood organizations triggers social action, we looked instead to concrete public claims and collective action behavior. Blended events, neither wholly civic nor wholly protest, provide a key to understanding the seeming paradox of decline in traditional civic memberships amid durability in collective civic engagement. The hypothesis that blended forms of social action constitute an increasing form of collective civic action in the United States is further motivated by the fact that community-based nonprofit organizations have grown over time and are increasingly embedded in the contemporary political process through the mediation of publicly funded services.[14]

In short, a focus on community-based organizational structures, especially the nonprofit sector, unifies a dual theoretical concern with temporal trends and community-level variations. Temporal change is seen from the lens of a changing organizational form, and the concentration of the events themselves is theorized as rooted in the density of local organizational activity.

The Chicago Collective Civic Participation Study (CCCP)

The data consist of detailed information collected over four years on collective events occurring in the Chicago metropolitan area between 1970 and 2000. We collected event data by extending a well-established methodology of social movement research—gathering and coding reports of protest events from newspaper archives.[15] We selected the *Chicago Tribune* as the main paper of record because it has the largest circulation and is the most influential paper published in the Chicago area. Collection of newspaper data has typically relied on keyword searches of newspaper indices. Although more time consuming, our project read the entire newspaper, searching for candidate events. We chose this approach in order to collect all forms of collective civic action, not just highly visible protest events, and because pretesting revealed that selecting events through an index keyword search failed to yield the broad types of collective action events of theoretical interest. To maximize resources and cover as long a temporal frame as possible, we sampled every third day of a given year. With this strategy no one day is privileged and we were able to cover three decades' worth of events. The event-identification process was identical for each day that events were collected, ensuring a representative sample of newspaper sections, days of the week, and days of the month across all years of the study.

Five primary criteria were used to distinguish articles that reported collective action events from other news stories, articles, and listings. First, prospective events had to be public. Second, they had to involve two or more individuals (though usually many more). Third, we only collected events with a discrete time occurrence that could be identified within a two-week time window on either side of the newspaper date. Fourth, we excluded routine political activity initiated by the State or formal political parties (e.g., political party dinners, speeches, and rallies). Such regular or ongoing political activity does not arise from emergent claims-making or civic capacity of citizens, but develops instead from the initiative of political actors and professionals. Typical examples would be a speech by a mayoral candidate, regular city council meetings, or party-sponsored rallies held for a state senator. Routine political lobbying by groups like MADD or the Sierra Club, while important, is continuous in nature and does not fit with our definition of discrete events of civic participation. A politically oriented march, like the one in figure 8.1, would count. Fifth and finally, we excluded profit-oriented events and regularly scheduled gatherings that are typical fare in any large city, such as professional sports games, live entertainment (e.g., rock concerts, theater), school swim meets, church services, university classes, and meetings of self-help groups such as Alcoholics Anonymous or weight-loss groups. Self-help groups, classes, and regular public meetings initiated by professionals or as part of an organization's mandate—like routine political activity—do not provide a direct or robust indicator of collective civic action or capacity.[16]

Classifying Events

Trained project personnel systematically read each page of the *Tribune*, collecting all articles that contained a collective public event.[17] The team then coded nine distinct categories of information: date/time; event type (protest, civic, or hybrid); frame of reference (e.g., national, state, city, neighborhood issue); claims/purpose (specific nature and intent of event); forms (e.g., a sit-in, march, community breakfast, fundraiser); location of event (by address, neighborhood, and/or municipality); intensity (e.g., number of participants, size, arrests, injuries, damages, deaths); event initiator information (e.g., community location and organizational type); and event target information. Based on our theoretical framework and using this information we also classified each triggering event as *protest*, *civic*, or *hybrid*. This classification was accomplished by examining the claims or purpose of events as well as their functional forms. Claims were defined as a demand for either a change in society or an avowed desire to resist a proposed change. Forms were defined as the manner in which action is undertaken by event initiators (e.g., rally, sit-in). Protest is when individuals collectively make a claim or express a grievance on behalf of a social movement organization or social category. In other words, a protest event explicitly states a claim to bring about or prevent a change in policy or services (e.g., civil rights and gender equality). Examples of protest forms include rallies, sit-ins, and marches, as well as petitioning, letter-writing campaigns, and class action lawsuits. Although protest events present a challenge to the existing social order and sometimes entail disruption or violence (by either protestors or responding authorities), most are orderly and peaceful, such as those reflected in civil disobedience or symbolic displays.[18]

Perhaps most interesting theoretically are *hybrid* events, which represent a blending or blurring of civic and protest types of collective action. Hybrid events typically exhibit a claim or grievance, but instead of a protest form (such as a march or rally), hybrid events exhibit a form that is typically associated with civic action. An example of this sort of event is a neighborhood art fair that doubles as a protest regarding current AIDS policy. In other words, claims of this sort grow out of traditional forms of civic life and not from social movement organizations or from other organizations defined a priori in terms of their claims.

Methodological Challenges

The CCCP addressed the challenges associated with the collection of newspaper data by using the local paper of widest coverage as the main source for events, employing a uniform sampling method across the time period of the study, and following a strict protocol for event identification and coding of information. Nonetheless at least two new issues were introduced to the standard methodology of newspaper event coding. The first is that we expanded event analyses to include not only less standard forms of protest but civic forms such as fundraisers, petition drives, and celebrations—exactly the type of events that are systematically excluded from research on traditional social movements. By including both civic and hybrid events we captured the full range of collective civic action—as shall be seen, pure protest is in the minority.

A second issue is that many of the theoretical questions of interest turn on coding the location of events in geographic space. Potential spatial bias is related to the more traditional issue of temporal consistency in newspaper coverage. Does the *Tribune* cover certain neighborhoods more than others? Does the paper consistently report events over time? Prior evidence shows that papers choose stories about protest based on their "newsworthiness," but many civic events are not that newsworthy in the traditional sense, and so the role of temporal and geographic bias is unknown. Based on interviews with *Tribune* staff, along with an extensive search for changes in paper policies toward civic reporting, we found no evidence that particular times or particular neighborhoods were systematically favored over others.[19]

Because of the importance of these issues, however, the CCCP collected independent data from the *Chicago Defender*, the nation's largest black newspaper. Virtually the inverse of the *Tribune*, the *Defender* validates key findings and allows a unique analysis of an important but neglected phenomenon from a comparative perspective—black civic society. This strategy is discussed below. For now, the claim is not that the systematic sampling and coding scheme produced an exact count without error, but rather that it achieved a credible sample and representative picture of collective civic and protest events for Chicago during the study period.

Initial Trends and Patterns

My primary purpose in this chapter is to describe the sources and manifestations of community-level variations in collective civic engagement. Long-term temporal trends for the Chicago metro area are important as a backdrop, however, so I begin with a brief overview.

The first pattern to note is that the trend in protest and civic action does not align with claims regarding the inexorable decline of civic life in the United States over the past three decades. While there was a sharp decline in protest and civic events between 1970 and 1980, the level of activity for 1990 and 2000 was higher than near the height of the New Left "protest cycle" in 1970, suggesting a continuing vitality to civic/political life in metropolitan Chicago that is at odds with the decline account of social capital. Second, and probably to the surprise of many steeped in the social movement tradition, protest—the classic type of collective action—constitutes only a small segment in the CCCP data. *In fact, civic events amount to nearly 80 percent of all events in Chicago over the years in question and protest just 15 percent.* Located between the highly visible worlds of electoral politics (studied primarily by political scientists) and sociological studies of social movements, this vibrant arena of collective civic life lies under the screen of most researchers, but it accounts for the vast majority of events.[20] The third pattern concerns the increase in hybrid forms of social action that combine traditional civic pursuits with claims-making. The percentage of *hybrid* events increased from under 4 percent of the total counts in 1970 to over 12 percent in 2000, more than a threefold increase. The hybrid-event rate per capita more than doubled, meaning that shifts in population size cannot explain the basic trends.

What types of collective engagement claims motivate Chicagoans? A durable pattern of collective action for public goods emerges. Across all decades, the predominant focus or claim of activity was charity, which never dropped lower than fifth in the rankings of claims. Education ranked consistently high, as did claims related to children, youth, and the arts. By contrast, the kinds of claims traditionally associated with social movements, such as the environment, women's rights, civil rights, and housing, were not the top-ranked issues. With the exception of the environment, these movement-type claims did not even rank in the top ten.

Although protest marches and rallies dominate our image of collective action forms, the narrative of civic decline turns on the loss of the simple public meeting. But ranked second in 1970 and first in 2000, the public meeting as a form of collective action consistently rose to the top echelon along with charity events. Moreover, "community festivals" climbed steadily from ninth place in 1970 to the third-most-common form of collective action in 2000. The community festival is a broad-based form that allows a plethora of activities to flourish—including protest. One example of its versatility was reflected in a Fourth of July celebration that included a special time set aside for a "human chain" composed of residents displaying signs, t-shirts, and buttons advertising the causes they support. This and many other examples suggest that the community festival embodies many other-regarding qualities of civil society.

Community-Level Findings

The long-term temporal trends indicate that collective civic life remains active. The community-level results do as well, but like everything else in this book, the main story to be told is about concentration. Collective civic engagement is differentially produced and consumed.

To explain variations in rates of collective action across communities, we compared the empirical power of competing explanatory perspectives by capitalizing on the PHDCN community survey integrated with the newspaper event data. Our key indicator of the density of *organization-based resources* was a multi-item index of the mean number of survey-reported local organizations and program resources in the neighborhood—community newspaper, neighborhood watch, block group or tenant association, crime prevention program, alcohol/drug treatment program, family planning clinic, mental health center, youth center, afterschool recreational programs for youth, counseling or mentoring services (e.g., Big Brother), crisis intervention center, and mental health clinics for children. This survey-based measure assesses the extent of organizational resources in the community, with results that agree with independent "local knowledge" of the social organization of Chicago communities. Consider Hyde Park, the neighborhood surrounding the University of Chicago, which is usually considered one of the most, if not the most, organizationally rich areas in the city. As noted in chapter 1, adopted home of President Barack Obama and other leaders, Hyde Park is thought to be dense with community organizations and institutional connections. It makes sense, then, that in the survey-based data, Hyde Park is in the ninety-ninth percentile of the organizations scale. Only one community—Beverly—scores (slightly) higher, and it too is known for its strong community organizational base.[21]

Civic membership was also recorded in the PHDCN community survey, allowing us to create a separate indicator of community-level voluntary associations. In each community we took the mean score of whether residents (or a household member) belonged to (1) religious organizations; (2) neighborhood watch programs; (3) block groups, tenant associations, or community councils; (4) business or civic groups such as Masons, Elks, or Rotary Club; (5) ethnic or nationality clubs; and (6) political organizations such as a neighborhood ward group. These groups represent the sorts of voluntary associations and memberships emphasized by civil society scholars. But they correlate very modestly ($r = 0.17$, not significant) with the organizational density of resources at the community level, permitting us to assess their independent contributions to predicting collective action events.[22] We also used the survey to assess two other key dimensions typically posited as sources of resident-based social capital—the *density of friend/kinship networks* and *reciprocated exchange* among neighbors.[23]

Controlling for confounding demographic and need-based economic factors, the data revealed that a community's organizational service base directly predicted later collective civic engagement and blended social action.[24] Kinship ties were associated with lower rates of blended or hybrid action and reciprocated exchange was associated with lower collective civic engagement. It is possible that there are determinants of collective action correlated with a community's organizational base that might produce spurious results. To assess this concern, we controlled for the rate of collective action events in 1990 in an attempt to adjust for determinants of collective action that were not tapped by our measures but that were correlated with organizations. The results were revealing on two counts. First, the stability in collective action was surprisingly robust across types of events—a strong and significant predictor of collective engagement events in 2000 was the rate of such events in 1990, whether traditionally civic or the newer hybrid form. This finding underscores the predictive validity of the data and is further evidence of the continuity in collective civic engagement—the past character of a community matters, once again. Second, after prior activity was adjusted, the only predictor of both traditional civic and hybrid social action was the density of organizational resources.[25]

A critic might wonder whether civil society is best conceptualized in terms of the location of collective action. Many Chicago events occur in the Loop or downtown area as a matter of strategy and thus may not tap the collective "production capacity" of the communities that actually *initiate* the events. For example, if a group from Hyde Park on the

South Side of Chicago regularly initiates protests or civic events in the Loop, we would be remiss not to examine such generative capacity. Or recall chapter 1's walk down Michigan Avenue, where we encountered a Tibetan protest. No doubt it was planned elsewhere. To gain leverage on this issue, we reexamined the community location of the initiating organization or group responsible for each event, regardless of where the event itself took place.[26] The results were nearly identical—a threefold increase in collective engagement rates was associated with a one-standard-deviation increase in prior organizational resources even after controlling for the 1990 rate of collective engagement. By contrast, economic factors, population density, and violent crime failed to predict the intensity of initiating activity. Friend/kinship ties were irrelevant as well, and reciprocated exchange was linked to a modestly *lower* rate of initiating activity. Combined with the findings of chapter 7, it appears that local ties promote collective efficacy but not wider participation in public events or an institutional readiness to address social problems.

I visualize the key results thus far in figure 8.2 by graphing the spatial concentration of collective civic action events in Chicago in 2000 by the organizational density and resources measure from the 1995 PHDCN community survey. I bring into the picture as well whether communities are in the top quartile of voting in the last Chicago mayoral election (denoted by the boxed √) as measured in the second PHDCN community survey. I do so to contrast the organizational dimension of community civic life from the individual but powerful form of civic action reflected in voting. Communities in the upper quartile of collective civic events are denoted with the "linked hands" symbol. We see that high-intensity collective civic action tends to occur in a relatively narrow band of communities running from the Loop up along the lake all the way to Rogers Park that are characterized by a dense organizational profile. There is a similar cluster on the West Side (such as Near West, Little Village, Pilsen, North Lawndale) and the South Side communities of Hyde Park and Kenwood that are rich in organizational life, and as a result, the data suggest a disproportionate share of collective action. Importantly, I have shown that the organizational resources and services of these areas matter above and beyond their population composition, income, and density of personal ties.

We can also see that while the top voting communities do overlap slightly with those high in collective action, the pattern is not isomor-

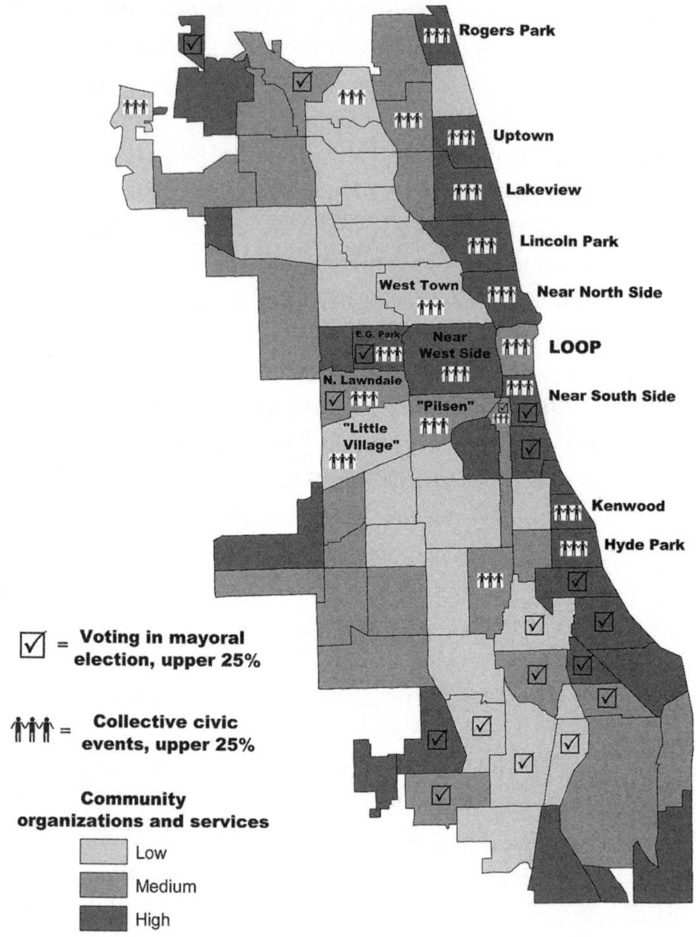

FIGURE 8.2. Density of organizational services in 1995 and collective-action events in 2000, by voting behavior of community residents

phic. In fact, only three communities in all of Chicago are in the top quartile of both voting and collective civic action, less than 5 percent of the total. A number of communities on the Southwest and Northwest sides that are "traditionally civic" in terms of voting are curiously absent on the collective action front. I consider shortly whether these communities make up for their absence in other ways, perhaps more informally through the collective efficacy among residents. But for now figure 8.2 confirms that whereas voting is obviously civic, it does not define the collective civic engagement character of the neighborhood.

It is not just voting and civic events that diverge. Communities such as Hyde Park and Uptown, while at or near the top of the organizational rankings, sit much lower on the scale of individual civic memberships, further supporting the contention that the prevalence of membership is distinct from the breadth or density of organizations. In fact, Uptown is in the bottom one-third of the civic membership distribution. Other communities, such as Avondale, are near the middle of the civic membership distribution but near the very bottom of organizational density. The lowest-scoring civic neighborhood in membership is Oakland (just north of Kenwood), but it nonetheless fares well in the organizational resources picture (seventy-second percentile). These two dimensions of community social organization are conceptually distinct, and Chicago communities vary considerably in their profiles of civic memberships versus organizational density. Apparently, some communities are able to achieve an active organizational life without the dense civic memberships of the past.

One of the reasons may be that membership in groups such as the Elks, the Rotary Club, and neighborhood tenant groups are more aimed at instrumental goals tied to self-interest than to the promotion of social goods. Another and perhaps more likely reason is that corporate actors—themselves organizationally constituted—often provide the economic underpinnings of support for community-based organizations, a mechanism distinct from civic membership.[27] This scenario suggests multiple pathways to collective action and, by implication, collective efficacy. A renewed consideration of the role of organizations is in order.

The Role of Nonprofit Organizations

This section revisits the claims above with longitudinal data on nonprofit organizations and churches along with additional data on community activism. Surveys are important, but the first wave of PHDCN tapped organizational resources that are visible and perceived by residents. The underlying "objective" infrastructure of organizations is not necessarily the same thing.

To address this issue, the CCCP project gathered data on *nonprofit organizations* from the National Center for Charitable Statistics (NCCS), core files based on the IRS's annual RTFs (return transaction file) for nonprofits that are required to file Form 990. Organizations with less than $25,000 in gross receipts are excluded even if they had filed Form 990. Congregations, foreign organizations, or those that are generally considered part of government are also excluded by NCCS. Overall, the NCCS thus provides a nearly complete census of all but the very smallest nonprofit, nongovernmental organizations other than churches. Nonprofit counts were matched to census tracts using the nine-digit zip code provided by the NCCS, and then rates per hundred thousand constructed for each community area to capture nonprofit density as of January 1 for the calendar years 1990, 1995, 2000, and 2005. Data on community-level density of *churches* were collected separately using phone microfiches and geocoding for the same years as nonprofits.[28]

A major and perhaps surprising finding is the strong stability in nonprofit organizational density that extends more than a decade. The rate of nonprofits in 1990, for example, is correlated at 0.87 ($p < 0.01$) with the density of nonprofits in the same community fifteen years later, as of 2005. The ten-year correlation is over 0.90. The corresponding fifteen-year stability coefficient for church density is 0.93 ($p < 0.01$). Figure 8.3 displays the prediction graph of nonprofit organizations during the decade of the 1990s, shaded by the combined initiation and collective-action event rate of Chicago communities. There is an unusually strong linear pattern, with nonprofits at the beginning of the decade sharply predictive of a community's organizational profile at the millennium. Moreover, where nonprofit density is high, the rate of collective action events is similarly high. Communities such as the Loop and its neighbors (e.g., Near West, Near North), along with Hyde Park (once again), stand out as very organizationally dense—this time determined by independent data from the IRS on nonprofits—and high in collective civic action. At the bottom of the nonprofit density and collective action nexus are a majority Hispanic enclave (McKinley Park) and two black communities (Riverdale and Burnside).

It is intriguing that communities like Hyde Park and the Near West and South sides are high in collective action, for they contradict stereotypes that racially and ethnically diverse communities depress civic life. According to the present data, it appears that nonprofits may be serving as a sort of counterweight to the challenges of diversity, perhaps

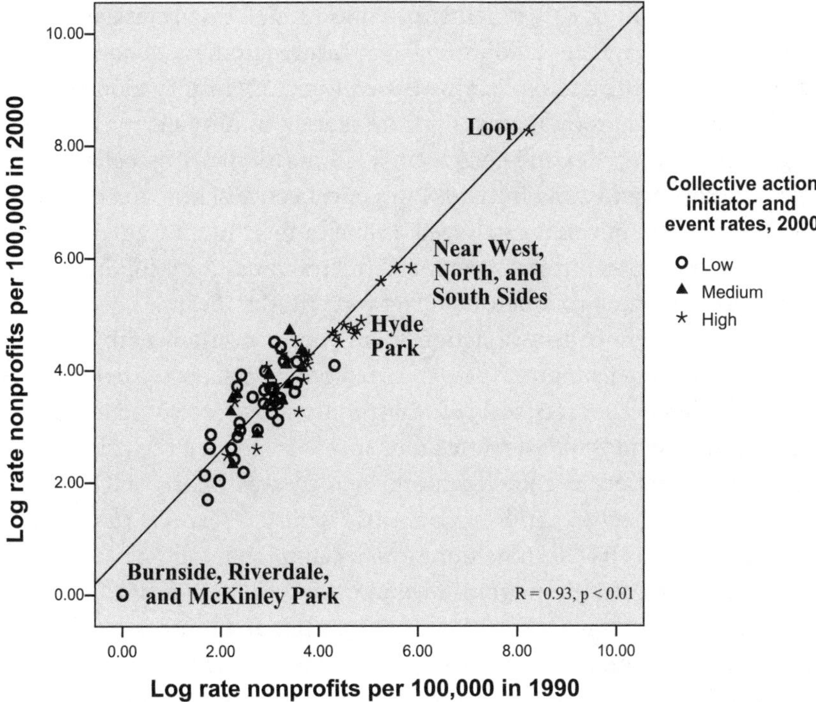

FIGURE 8.3. Long-term stability of nonprofit organizational density, by level of collective civic engagement

even thriving in their diverse contexts. To probe this idea further I constructed a pooled multi-item index from the census measuring diversity in 1990, 2000, and change in diversity over the decade.[29] Although increases in diversity have driven the concern about civic decline, the data instead reveal a clear pattern in which nonprofit density predicts later civic intensity *at all levels of diversity*. Most striking, and consistent with previous observations, communities highest in nonprofit density and collective civic action (e.g., the Loop, Hyde Park, Near South Side) are actually in the highest diversity category. It follows that diversity and collective civic action are not contradictory.

I replicated the basic results linking organizations to collective action by imposing a comprehensive set of controls when examining rates of both event initiation and location. For example, I examined the independent explanatory power of nonprofit density under a variety of specifications, including adjustments for concentrated disadvantage, residential stability, and population density measured from the 2000 census, therefore updating and replicating the earlier CCCP results, along with competing social-process measures from the community survey, including friend/kinship ties and civic memberships (voluntary associations). For both the location and initiator rates of collective action, the density of nonprofit organizations emerged as one of the strongest predictors. When organizational resources tapped by the community survey were controlled, the nonprofit density effect was still significant.

Because where collective action events occur overlaps with where they are initiated (community-level correlation = 0.84, $p < 0.01$), I also formed a single summary scale of what I will call "collective action propensity." In the most conservative model that controlled the prior rate of collective action in 1990, nonprofit density was the second-largest predictor of collective action propensity. The usual suspects in the urban poverty and civic decline literature, most notably concentrated disadvantage and racial/immigrant diversity, were not significant. Friend/kinship ties, voluntary associations, organizational resources, and civic memberships were not predictive either.[30] When it comes to collective events of a public nature, then, the density of formally defined nonprofit organizations emerges as a consistently salient factor across multiple analyses.

At this point the logical question: Does the organizational index from the community survey correlate with the census of nonprofit density? The answer is yes, but modestly so—the correlation is only 0.36. It appears that these indicators are tapping somewhat different elements of a community's organizational life. The indicator of nonprofit density is more structural in nature, reflecting a community's organizational base, while the survey indicator reflects the reported activation of its organizational base for specific services, programs, and purposes, a phenomenon closer to collective efficacy in its nature. A differential effect of these two organizational indicators on collective responses to public challenges is thus a plausible expectation. To assess this idea and tie back to the query posed in chapter 7 about the sources of collective efficacy, I combined the data sources in both chapters, including the second PHDCN community survey. I estimated a number of different models that took into account various demographic/structural characteristics (e.g., concentrated disadvantage, instability, and diversity),

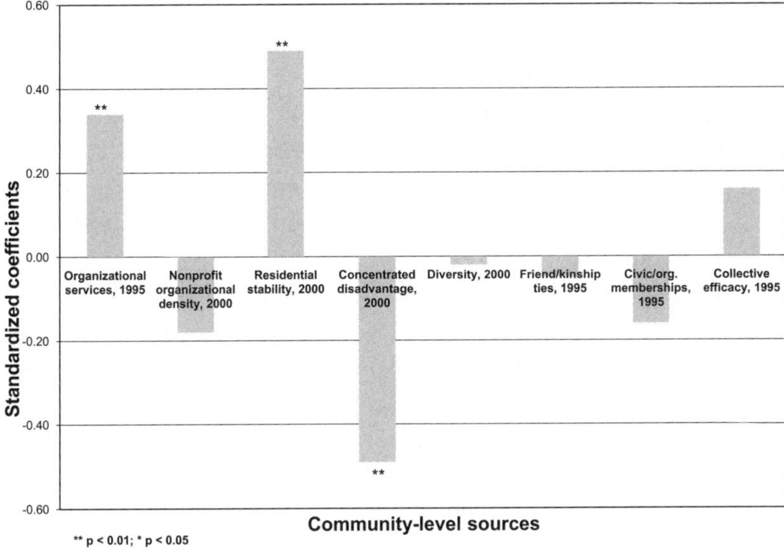

FIGURE 8.4. Sources of collective efficacy in 2002

prior challenge (crime), social capital stocks (friendship ties, voluntary associations), prior levels of efficacy, and the two organizational mechanisms analyzed above.

The results were consistent across different specifications and verified that collective efficacy and collective action events are not the same phenomenon but rather are differentially explained by community-level characteristics. As a summary representation, figure 8.4 displays the magnitude of community-level organizational effects on collective efficacy while simultaneously controlling for key competing determinants. Consistent with chapter 7, residential stability is a strong positive source of collective efficacy even though it apparently depresses collective-action event rates. Concentrated disadvantage, as also expected based on the theoretical framework and results in previous chapters, serves to depress collective efficacy. When it comes to organizational mechanisms, however, the explanatory driver is now resources and not sheer density.[31] This finding is theoretically sensible because collective efficacy is fundamentally about shared expectations. Chapters 6 and 7 revealed that perceptions are central to shared expectations. Because the organizational survey question is rooted in residents' perceptions, it is therefore logical that a sense of collective beliefs about the power to get things done is tied more to this experiential aspect of organizations than sheer nonprofit density.

To be sure, *both* aspects of organizational life are theoretically important, and this chapter has shown empirically that it would be a mistake to elevate one over the other—they do different things and, depending on the task, are differentially relevant in predicting a community's strategy of collective action. Put differently, there appear to be distinct organizational pathways to a community's collective character, with each serving a unique causal function. Collective efficacy among residents appears to be more about informal social control and shared expectations, which are enhanced by the types of organizational resources tapped in the services measure, many of which are informal and not incorporated as nonprofits (e.g., neighborhood watches, block group or tenant associations, afterschool programs). Collective civic events, by contrast, are less spontaneous than informal social control and require forward planning of the sort that is enhanced by the formal incorporation of nonprofit organizations. It would seem that communities possessing a rich set of both types of organizational life are ahead of the curve.

Black Civil Society

In this section I reach further to explore the nature of civic life in the black community. There are at least two major reasons for doing this. One is theoretical and tied to the strong roots of the civil rights movement in collective protest and engagement in the black community, coupled with the mounting evidence in previous chapters on the concentrated disadvantage that black residents commonly experience. I specifically ask whether the substantive framework that has been established has relevance when we restrict the analytic focus to segregated and at-risk black communities, which we know are prevalent in Chicago and nationwide (chapter 5). As Doug McAdam, Cathy Cohen, and Michael Dawson have also argued, black civil society is at once a classic terrain for social movement activity arising out of the civil rights revolution, but it remains understudied in terms of contemporary civic life.[32] I therefore examine the organizational contribution of nonprofits to civic life in the black community, as well as the separate organizational influence of a profound actor in the black community—the church.

A second reason to focus on black civic society is methodological. Chicago is a racially divided city, and the *Tribune* is considered by many to be a conservative paper that caters to one side of the divide. The issue, in brief, is whether the *Tribune* provides a reliable picture of black civil society. I address this concern head on by analyzing data from the *Chicago Defender*, the nation's oldest African American newspaper—a venerable and well-known institution not just in Chicago but "the most important black metropolitan newspaper in America."[33] The *Defender* is explicitly designed to serve the needs of an African American readership, but its coverage is still metropolitan-wide, permitting leverage to see if a different picture emerges of collective action events than in the *Tribune*. At least in principle, all African American *communities* (as distinct from events) should be covered in the *Tribune*, so the key question is whether both papers are capturing the common capacity of communities to generate collective action events, initiating organizations, or both—even if contaminated by a racialized reporting lens. To address these issues the CCCP collected a detailed set of data from the *Defender* using the same basic criteria and methodology that we used for the *Tribune*, with only minor differences in sampling.[34]

As expected, the *Defender* reports more events in African American communities than the *Tribune*. For example, traditional black communities like Douglas, Grand Boulevard, and Englewood rank in the top ten communities for the *Defender* but not the *Tribune*. Communities like the Near West Side, the Loop, and the Near North Side nonetheless rank highly across both papers, indicating some continuity in geographic perspective.[35] While the *Defender* does report more events in the black community, the overall level of agreement with the *Tribune* is surprisingly consistent across space and across three decades. However, it could be that this convergence occurs because of different mechanisms. Each paper could report more or less the same pool of events, or, more interesting, it could be that the papers are tapping into the same capacity of neighborhoods to generate social action, but with a different mix of actual events generating the pattern.

To adjudicate among these possibilities we matched specific events, with the results confirming both scenarios but with a definite leaning toward the second. The *Defender* was much more likely than the *Tribune* to cover collective civic events in smaller African American churches on the South and West sides, whereas the *Tribune*'s coverage in the black community ran more to larger middle-class churches and larger, politically visible events. Still, 18 percent of *Defender* events from 1970 to 2000 were matched exactly in the *Tribune*.[36]

I rely on these findings to conduct a new set of analyses that focuses on the organizational sources of collective civic events within and across the racial divides of Chicago. I begin with community-level correlations between the two newspapers across all communities. The 2000 correlation was 0.50 ($p < 0.01$) for initiator rates and 0.40 ($p < 0.01$) for event rates. Although not terribly high, the correlations are positive and significant despite the inherent errors in measurement, leading me to combine each type of collective action measured separately by the *Defender* and *Tribune*. Based on a principal components factor analysis, some 75 percent of the variation was accounted for by the first component of event initiation rates across sources and 70 percent of variation in event location rates, empirical evidence that the two newspapers tap common variance in an underlying dimension of collective action capacity—whether initiator based or event based.

Building on these results, I tested the ability of the present theoretical framework to explain the shared variance in collective action derived from the otherwise disparate newspaper sources of the *Defender* and *Tribune*. As before, the most conservative assessment adjusts for a community's trajectory or prior history of collective action. Based on theoretical concerns and the analyses throughout this chapter, I also adjusted for concentrated disadvantage/race, residential stability, diversity, civic memberships, and dense ties in the core models. In analyses to assess robustness of results, I examined a number of additional indicators not examined in the original 2005 study, but the pattern was consistent. For parsimony, I present in figure 8.5 the results from a strict test that includes the history of collective action across all Chicago communities. The result is crisp—nonprofit density is clearly the strongest source of collective action propensity, save for the latter's history, with significant and substantial standardized coefficients revealed in predicting both initiator and event rates. There is further evidence in the data that concentrated disadvantage is associated with higher and not lower collective action, yet another sign that the determinants of collective efficacy and the more formal organizational structures of action are

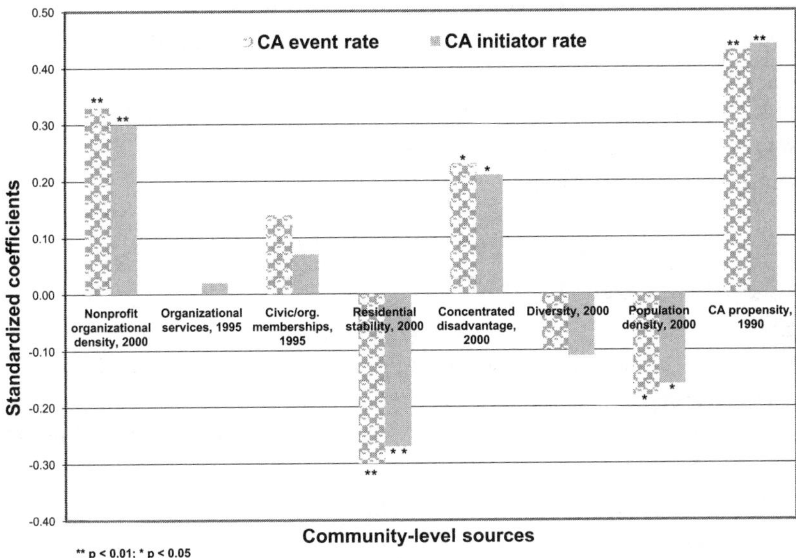

FIGURE 8.5. Sources of propensity for community-area (CA) initiation and occurrence of collective civic action in 2002

different. Residential stability is again negatively related to collective action events.

I consider next the prediction of collective action propensity *within* segregated black communities in Chicago with more than 75 percent black population (N = 25). The same basic picture holds. But because the smaller number of communities reduces statistical power, I restrict the focus to a direct comparison of the two organizational mechanisms controlling for the prior rate of collective action. Subdividing the communities by race in effect also controls for concentrated disadvantage and segregation. Nonprofit density predicts civic action in black communities (coefficient of 0.34; t-ratio = 2.48; $p < 0.05$) but *not* organizational services (coefficient = 0.05, $p > 0.05$). Interestingly, a virtually invariant pattern prevails in nonblack communities (N = 50) for nonprofit density (coefficient of 0.22; t-ratio = 2.50; $p < 0.05$) and organizational services ($p > 0.05$), which suggests a general collective action process despite the different manifestations that resulting events might take by race.

In short, there is broad agreement on the ecological concentration and organizational sources of collective civic action when comparing the *Tribune* and *Defender*—even when the actual events differ and when communities are subdivided by racial composition. Given the divergent nature and organization of the two papers, not to mention the racial segregation in Chicago, this finding lends validity to the earlier results and underlying argument.

Religious Ecology

Nowhere is the promise of organizing more apparent than in the traditional black churches.

Barack Obama, 1988[37]

As President Obama observed during his organizing efforts on Chicago's South Side, no study of black civil society or the black community can avoid the black church. Certainly the civil rights movement is widely considered to have arisen from the pews of the black church. Does it follow that the density of churches is a source of collective action in the black community? Received wisdom based on the civil rights literature would seem to say yes. But as this chapter has shown, the density of organizations is not always consonant with the services rendered by those organizations. Moreover, just because a church is located in a particular community does not mean that its interests coincide with that community. Omar McRoberts's study of the religious ecology of a poor Boston neighborhood shows that the density of churches is problematic when many parishioners come from *outside* the community.[38] Such a mismatch is especially common in low-income black areas that continue to draw middle-class parishioners that have migrated to other residential neighborhoods in the suburbs or far reaches of the city.

I therefore conclude the analysis with a look at the relationships among churches, nonprofit organizations, and collective action events. There are four major patterns in the data relevant to the present chapter. The first is that black and nonblack communities differ greatly when it comes to churches. Figure 8.6 makes the point visually. Black communities are much higher than white communities in church density. Second, as figure 8.6 reveals, the density of churches is only weakly related

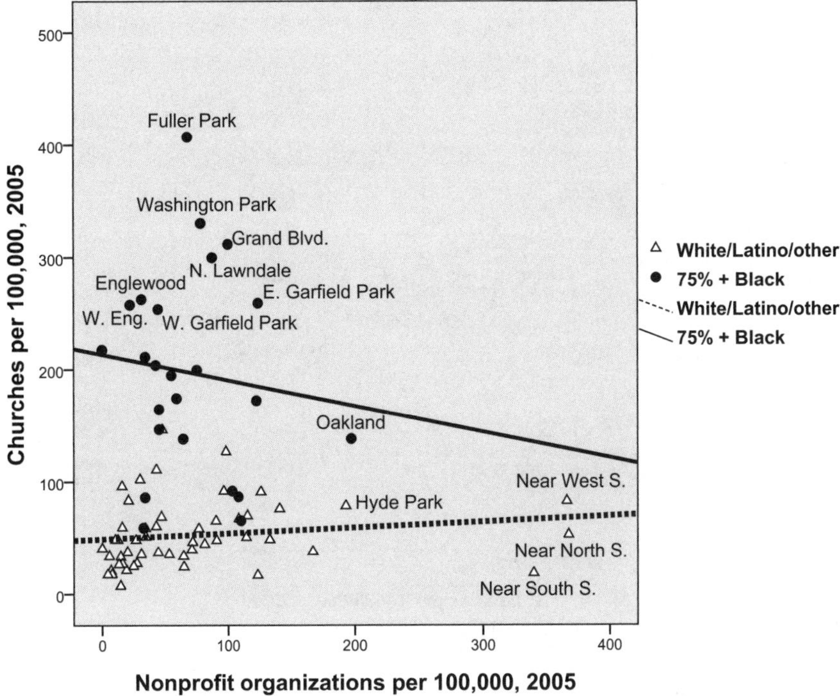

FIGURE 8.6. Religious and organizational ecology by racial composition

to the density of nonprofit organizations in both black and nonblack communities. Third, when I simultaneously examine both of these organizational sources of collective action events in a model that adjusts for prior propensity, church density adds nothing while the effect of nonprofit density remains.[39] Churches are clearly different than other nonprofits, with the religious sector appearing unrelated to "outside" or nonreligious civic engagement defined by the event rate of collective civic action.

Fourth and most surprising, a deeper inspection of the data reveals that the density of churches is *negatively* related to collective efficacy and one of its core indicators—trust. Figure 8.7 shows that in the black communities with the most churches per capita, trust is lowest ($r = -0.74$, $p < 0.05$). Trust in one's fellow man is apparently not enhanced by the church.[40]

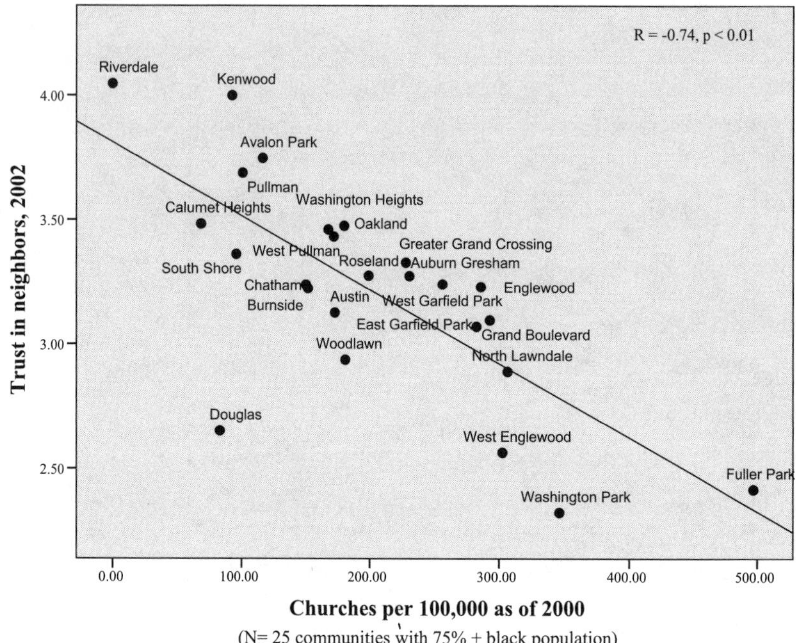

FIGURE 8.7. In God we mistrust man? Trust is inversely related to church density in the black community.

Organizing in America: A New Kind of Politics?

> Do you have gaping potholes on your street and feel the city is not fixing them quickly enough? How about patching them yourself? That's what a group of residents on Chicago's West Side did Wednesday. Members of the South Austin Coalition bought 8 bags of a pavement mix for about $100 and used shovels, rakes and a 250-pound push roller to fill 15 holes . . . "The city's not doing it, so residents need to take the matter into their own hands," said Eric Redmond, an organizer with the coalition.[41]

In a traditional American way, nonprofit and community-based organizations reflect diverse constituencies that organize from the ground up, not the top down. Whether fixing potholes in Austin, sustaining integrated neighborhoods in Beverly, or organizing immigrant clubs on the Lower West Side, as the opening quotation of this chapter noted, organizational civic life is very much alive in Chicago.

Given that community organizations extend across the political and geographic landscape, are the opposite of a federal intervention, and by definition require organizing, the Republicans' broadsided attack in the 2008 election seems misplaced and ironic in retrospect. Former Governor Sarah Palin's appeal to the "small-town mayor" at the Republican convention may help explain the flawed logic. Despite the immersion of the conservative Right, much like the liberal Left, in nonprofit community organizations, the anger likely stemmed from the perception that Democrats and the liberal elite dismiss social problems in small-town America. The problem of concentrated poverty that motivated Obama's original experience in Chicago is perceived as limited to the inner city. But small towns and suburbs across the country have been devastated by economic restructuring and are seeking answers just like their big-city counterparts.[42]

Being a small-town or small-city mayor under such circumstances is a tough job and should not be trivialized any more than a community organizer on the South Side of Chicago. Each in a different way is trying to bring more resources in order to stem the further loss of community life and reinvigorate economic health. Although proposing different solutions, each relies on community organizations to effect change no matter how "mundane." As the data in this chapter show, collective civic events in Chicago and the nonprofit organizations that predict them run the gamut but by and large reflect claims and forms (such as education, charity, and, yes, even fixing potholes) that are supported by the vast majority of the American people no matter what their background. Recall that only 15 percent of collective action in Chicago during the study period is of the social movement—or "protest"—variety that Palin had in mind in formulating her attack.

Another irony is that collective civic action does not stem primarily from race or poverty, the typical public face of the big city. There is a tendency of social movement scholars and even the larger public to adopt the "underclass" paradigm to understand collective action, but this chapter shows the limitation of such an approach. By far the most potent and enduring structural driver of action is a community's organizational density. Collective efficacy is another matter, as it is tied more deeply to shared expectations and trust. It is little wonder that years of poverty and deprivation lead residents to be cynical and lose trust in authorities. The data here and in chapters 5 and 7 reveal the long-term power of concentrated disadvantage in eroding collective efficacy. Given the troubling legacy of deprivation in black communities, the fact that organizational resources predict collective efficacy and that nonprofits produce externalities that foster collective civic action is good news, because it suggests new organizational forms and strategies that can draw in individuals—including the very poor—for collective pursuits. This in no way implies that federal or state policies are unimportant, only that organizational mechanisms in the community have a role to play, perhaps especially in mediating or moderating such policies.

Robert Putnam's last book on civic society must be read in this context. His examples of successful community building all revolve around institutional or organizational structures, from the community newspaper in Mississippi, to branch libraries in Chicago, to a neighborhood organization in Boston, to a church in Southern California.[43] Still more telling is the example from Chicago provided by community policing, where "beat meetings" bring together residents and the police to address local problems.[44] Residents do not attend beat meetings as a result of personal social ties; rather the meetings had their origin in a structural initiative—by organizing, hosting, and supporting beat meetings, the police created an opportunity for civic involvement across the city. In disadvantaged neighborhoods residents typically have fewer opportunities and effective models for involvement in anticrime efforts, but *when* they do, residents are at least as likely to be involved as residents of better-endowed neighborhoods.[45] In an interesting way, Chicago's policing program has helped to even out the opportunities to participate in community governance, with the greatest increase in collective participation by African Americans. As Archon Fung argues, designed institutions of "participatory democratic governance" such as these can spark citizen involvement that in turn generates innovative problem-solving and public action.[46]

The black church, then, may not be the savior of the inner city, as many, including Obama, might have hoped. In the black community, churches are prevalent, but in the current data they do not seem generative of collective action. If anything, church density is related to *lower* trust and collective efficacy (fig. 8.7). What is cause and what is effect is not clear, but either way, the proud civil rights heritage notwithstanding, the density of churches in the black community—in all communities—is unrelated to the major manifestations of collective civic life in the contemporary city. This is perhaps not surprising when the findings in this book are considered as a whole. Black communities in particular have long been devastated economically, as shown in chapter 5. Chapter 6 revealed the unforgiving role that perceptions of disorder play in perpetuating concentrated disadvantage, and chapter 7 showed the long-term negative effects of disadvantage on trust. It apparently takes more than churches to overcome such a legacy.

Conclusion

With inequality eating away at the democratic social fabric in communities everywhere, the results in this chapter provide a hopeful signpost and partial reassurance about the future. For despite persistent poverty, racial diversity, and other social challenges, community-based organizations strongly predict collective efficacy and collective civic action, durably so. It is not just one type of institution, and indeed churches alone are not the answer, contrary to what some believe. It is the totality of the institutional infrastructure that seems to matter in producing healthy communities. Perhaps President Obama's experience in big-city community organizing is not as irrelevant to governance as many critics assert. But the larger point is that civil society is alive and seemingly well from an organizational viewpoint. As I will probe more in the final section, community organizations provide a strategic site for policy intervention, one that is conceptually attuned to the increasingly organizational world that we inhabit.

9 Social Altruism, Cynicism, and the "Good Community"

The summer of 2009 took an unexpected twist one sunny afternoon with the arrest of Henry "Skip" Gates in Cambridge, Massachusetts, a Left-leaning bastion sometimes referred to as the "People's Republic of Cambridge." Gates, a renowned black professor at Harvard, was arrested for disorderly conduct at his own home by a white police officer. The rest, as they say, is history. Culminating with a "beer summit" at the White House, the arrest raised a stormy and hyperpublicized debate about race relations and police profiling in America. But it also raised general questions on core themes of this book, including what defines a good neighbor, cynicism about legal institutions, and ultimately the "good community."

Lucia Whalen was the white neighbor of Gates who placed the original 911 call to the police. Inexplicably, her name was not redacted from the police report and she was quickly vilified in numerous media outlets and the blogosphere. A *Boston Globe* columnist berated Whalen for not recognizing who Gates was, for example, feeding an emerging narrative of a white citizen profiling her neighbors based on racial stereotypes—just like the police officer.[1] What might in theory have seemed a good deed—calling the police to investigate an incident possibly involving crime—became instead grounds for opprobrium. Humiliated and also the target of numerous threats on her personal safety, Lucia Whalen initially retreated in silence.

As is usually the case in media conflagrations, the facts came out after the pundits had rendered their verdict and moved on. But the eventual release of the 911 transcripts revealed that Whalen did not see or know the race of Gates and, when asked by the police, got it wrong.[2] Her almost apologetic 911 call was mundane, a routine act of doing her perceived duty as a citizen to watch out for others, in this case the property of a neighbor and a concerned elderly woman. Whalen later held a press conference to clear her name and proclaim that she would assert her citizenly duties all over again under the same conditions.[3] What was problematic for Gates was thus not Whalen's call to the police but the police sergeant's behavior that followed.[4] Lucia Whalen's roundly criticized intervention, which some might even deem an expression of collective efficacy, brings into sharp relief questions about what behaviors constitute the "common good." Are there theoretical principles or consensus conditions under which we can define acts that constitute other-regarding behavior? What is social altruism and under what contexts does it arise? Is it related to collective efficacy? Trust? Perhaps more difficult from a scientific perspective, can we identify behavioral indicators of other-regarding or altruistic behaviors that are not subject to interpretive work by participants *after the fact*? Or that are not confounded by opportunities for enactment or, as in the case of Gates, by race? How do empirical indicators of other-regarding behavior vary and what are their community-level sources? In short, is Lucia Whalen friend or foe of the common good?

I make the argument in this chapter that there are both philosophical and social science principles that can serve as a framework for conceptualizing what I will abstractly call the "good community." Informed in part by the philosophy of John Rawls, I theorize that there are concrete forms of altruistic behavior that satisfy his classic "veil of ignorance" test and by implication lead us out of the racial snare that trapped Lucia Whalen's critics. I also draw on experimental research showing that contrary to the assumptions of *homo economicus*, people demonstrate other-regarding preferences under a variety of conditions. I then marshal empirical evidence using two independent data sets that permit me to construct direct and what I believe are novel indicators of other-regarding behavior in natural settings: *providing aid to victims of cardiac arrest* and *mailing a lost letter*. I submit that whether "all else equal" or under counterfactual "original conditions," these forms of altruistic behavior are widely desired, adaptive, and surprisingly widespread, given the opportunity for enactment. I further show that altruism systematically varies across neighborhoods in ways that conform to theoretical predictions: behavioral altruism is positively related to independent measures of collective efficacy from the PHDCN, negatively related to concentrated disadvantage and moral cynicism, and independently predicts important indicators of later wellbeing. While examples of "negative" community exist, cohesive neighborhoods appear overall to be other-regarding.

Aligning Justice and the Collective Good

I raised initial concerns in chapter 2 about the potential downside to neighborhood-level social capital and collective efficacy. In the pursuit of informal social control and collective goods, there is the danger that freedoms will be restricted unnecessarily and that individuals will face unwanted or unjust scrutiny. For example, the surveillance of suspicious persons in socially controlled communities can morph into the interrogation and profiling of racial minorities—exactly the initial charge against Whalen in the Gates case. Consider also examples of citizens exploiting dense networks to come together to block the residential entry of a racial minority group. As Thomas Sugrue argues in his research from postwar Detroit, neighborhood associations were sometimes exploited by whites to forcibly keep blacks from moving into white working-class areas (e.g., by means of arson, threats, violence).[5] Such exclusion prompted Gerald D. Suttles to warn of the dark side of "defended neighborhoods."[6] William Julius Wilson's work on neighborhood loyalty signals a similar theme, suggesting that white working-class communities that are both socially organized and exposed to black inmigration are the most likely to resist.[7] There is also related evidence that racial hate crimes are higher in socially organized communities.[8]

These cautionary notes suggest a need to consider a community-level conception of truly *nonexcludable* public goods and, in the process, individual rights. Theories of community cannot simply ignore theories of justice, especially given that conflict is ever present in human affairs even when there is consensus on core values. As the philosopher John Rawls starkly puts it, "Grant and Lee were one in their desire to hold Richmond but this desire did not establish community between them." People generally want the same things, he notes (e.g., liberty, opportunity, shelter, and nourishment), but the pursuit of common goals is fraught with potential conflict and thus must proceed cautiously with a respect for individual rights, diversity of preferences, and limits on State power to counteract what Rawls called the "fact of oppression."[9] It was this dilemma that led to the working out of his well-known "justice as fairness" argument, widely thought to reflect an individually rationalistic basis for deriving "contractarian" principles and institutions that promote justice. Rawls has his critics, certainly, but the theory of justice as fairness was one of the major intellectual achievements of twentieth-century philosophy, one that I believe yields useful insights for thinking about the concept of community.[10] In particular, while criticized for advocating the "right over the good," it is often overlooked that Rawls stressed reciprocity as an intermediary social mechanism and argued for the predominantly social basis of humanity. At the end of the sprawling *A Theory of Justice*, for example, he emphasized "the idea of social union" and argued that justice is grounded in interdependency and *social cooperation* as opposed to the rational actor notion of "private society." Writing as a sociological philosopher might, he argues that "it follows that the collective activity of justice is the preeminent form of human flourishing. . . . Thus the public realization of justice is a value of community."[11]

Achieving common goals in a diverse society has proven especially problematic in an age of individual rights. But even Rawls allows that procedural justice and community are not the contradiction that common wisdom suggests.[12] More than that, the idea of justice as fairness and his intellectual tool of the "original position" allow us to derive social conditions that we can defend as constituting the just, or good, community. The original position is a thought experiment, the essential idea being that individuals do not know in advance their economic or social position, and so must decide future principles in conditions of initial equality and under the "veil of ignorance."[13] Under such hypothetical conditions Rawls derives his principles of justice as fairness and institutional implications for equality and the inclusion of individual rights, which I set aside for present purposes. I wish to argue instead that the counterfactual of the original condition, combined with a conception of justice as rooted in social interdependence, leads to basic principles of socially altruistic behavior, or what we might think of as *urban ethics*. Beyond desiring to live in communities with more social equality rather than less (the distributional question of opportunity), I argue that under a "veil of ignorance" individuals will choose neighbors that respond to those in need rather than ignore them, and neighbors that contribute everyday acts of kindness rather than free riders.[14]

Other-Regarding Norms and Social Context

There is consistent evidence from the social sciences to back up my thus-far philosophical argument. Under experimental conditions where all else is equalized, the data show that humans act in other-regarding fashion far more than theories of selfish or rational man would have it.[15] All of us have had the experience of a store clerk or cab driver returning money when we have inadvertently overpaid. This is no fluke behavior. In recent years social scientists have carried out hundreds of experiments under names like the social dilemma game, ultimatum game, and dictator game. Generally speaking these experiments force subjects to make choices to maximize their own payoffs or help others. In game after game, cooperation is higher and defection rarer than expected, suggesting that other-regarding preferences are commonplace.

Equally common are "cheater-detection" mechanisms and the tendency of humans to punish those who violate social norms of fairness, even if it means self-sacrifice. There is evidence that subjects in experiments fear that others will in turn punish them if they violate norms of fairness, such as making a "lowball" offer.[16] As the legal scholar Lynn Stout puts it, this finding means not only that other-regarding preferences exist, but that we also know that *other* people have other-regarding preferences, ultimately supporting the existence of a social sanction or social norm.[17]

It follows that the social context of the experiment matters in the shaping of other-regarding behaviors. When players are allowed to speak to one another, when group identity is promoted, when the benefits of cooperation are made better known, and when subjects believe that their fellow players will behave fairly, altruistic behavior is increased. One way to restate or generalize these findings is to say that under conditions of cohesion and perceived legitimacy of the experimental context, other-regarding preferences are enhanced. This finding connects to the literature on procedural justice in psychology and on social identity in economics.[18] Simply stated, when people believe that the rules are fair and followed properly, voluntary self-sacrifice and other-regarding behavior is more common. People do not obey the law just because they are afraid of being arrested, for example—the police are few and far between. Rather, people obey the law on most occasions because of a combination of the perceived legitimacy of authority (law), informal social controls, and social norms that support law-abiding behavior.[19]

Altruistic or other-regarding behaviors are not only generally desired under initial conditions of equality or perceived legitimacy; there is good reason to believe that they contribute to the long-term wellbeing of human communities as well. A long line of anthropological, biological, and evolutionary research argues that humans have evolved a capacity for other-regarding or altruistic behavior because it is adaptive. Cooperation that is individually "irrational," that is, can still evolve if it benefits the species, whether family, exchange partners, or related groups. Some biologists thus argue in favor of what is called multilevel or group selection based on altruism.[20] Whether or not we accept the theory of group-based selection, my larger point is that there are evolutionary reasons to argue that other-regarding, altruistic behaviors contribute to the long-term interests of social groups.

Neighborhood Hypotheses

Ironically enough, Lucia Whalen found herself in a Rawlsian position when, not knowing the race or "background" of the actors in question, she based her decision to call the police on the principle of being a good citizen. This is consistent with the notion that altruism is at some general level motivated by the common good.[21] It is likely that most if not all of us would prefer that our neighbors call the police if they suspect a break-in at our home. Furthermore, under conditions of equality at the outset, preferences for such other-regarding acts will dominate without regard to an individual's background (e.g., wealth, race). Even after being arrested, it should be noted, Skip Gates came to the strong defense of Lucia Whalen, without whose call Sergeant Crowley and he would never have met. The injustice in the Gates case was not about the good or bad neighborly act of Whalen, after all, but the institutional response that followed.

But let us accept her critics for a moment and recognize that the police lack legitimacy in many circles and that the invocation of formal police control may not be equally desired nor necessarily a contribution to collective wellbeing. As I argued previously and explore further below, concentrated poverty and racial isolation are linked to legal and moral cynicism, with the police bearing the brunt of much distrust among African Americans.[22] It is thus important to ask if we can imagine concrete acts of altruistic behavior that would satisfy a strict veil of ignorance test and contribute to the common good, or what we might otherwise call the "good community." The challenge is also to find empirical indicators that can be applied to neighborhoods or communities and that satisfy scientific standards of measurement.

I propose two such behaviors: helping behavior with regard to a serious personal health crisis and a more mundane matter, the mailing of a lost letter. My assumption is that the provision of aid to those suffering a cardiac arrest is a direct behavioral indicator of other-regarding and almost classically altruistic behavior that satisfies the Rawlsian test. CPR is not without risks, including both mild (disruption or delay in one's daily rounds; anxiety at performing in public) and serious (guilt or public blame if not performed properly; potential death of the victim). These risks might prompt free riding, but they do not diminish the desirability of providing aid for those in critical need. The provision of CPR more than doubles the probability of surviving a heart attack, so its contribution to the collective good (or, in evolutionary terms, to adaptation) is not in dispute. If someone mistakenly drops a stamped letter on the street, the act of mailing it by a stranger likewise constitutes other-regarding behavior, albeit with less cost and fewer stakes. It takes little time and involves arguably little downside to the intervener, but the benefit to the "victim" is still potentially great (e.g., a letter to employer or an insurance company). One can imagine additional other-regarding behaviors, such as helping a car-accident victim, organ donation, dousing a small fire about to spread to a house, giving directions, and calling a lost child's parents. Manipulating or controlling opportunities for enactment is crucial, however, making it difficult to measure comparable between-community variations based on observational data.[23]

Exploiting two unique sources of data described in the sections that follow, I invoke the spatial and neighborhood-effects logic of this book to investigate community-level variations in giving CPR to heart-attack victims *conditional on a cardiac arrest* and mailing lost letters *systematically dropped by the investigator*. I submit that these two behaviors provide direct indicators of my theoretical object while simultaneously varying in the commitment entailed in the intervention. Lost-letter methods in particular are unobtrusive and were subject to the manipulation of the PHDCN investigators, providing additional benefits in adjusting for opportunity conditions. After proposing a model to assess individual and situational-level determinants, I examine the neighborhood character of altruism. In so doing I test a series of linked hypotheses drawn from this chapter's framework:

1. CPR and letter returns vary significantly across neighborhoods and are geographically concentrated, similar to the structure of the many other behaviors and perceptions analyzed throughout this book.

2. CPR and letter returns are influenced by longer-term dynamics, such that a neighborhood's rate of other-regarding behavior at one time will predict its future rate net of population composition. Social altruism is part of the enduring social character of a community, in other words. I thus test the hypothesis that the rate of CPR predicts lost-letter return rates many years in the future.

3. Behavioral variations in returning lost letters are connected to prior neighborhood trust and collective efficacy, but undermined by moral cynicism and concentrated inequality.

4. Finally, socially altruistic behavior defines a unique marker for the 'good community' that foretells later crime-related and other social outcomes independent of demographic composition, in much the same manner as does collective efficacy.

I thus claim that urban ethics in general and social altruism in particular have concrete consequences that can be studied empirically and not just philosophically, and contextually in neighborhood settings and not just in individual experiments.

The Lost Letter Experiment

A methodological innovation of the second wave of the community study was that it included a "lost letter" experiment, an unobtrusive behavioral measure of other-regarding behavior in the form of social helpfulness. The letter-drop technique derives from the pioneering work of Stanley Milgram of sociometric fame and the father of "six degrees of separation" in network analysis. While many have heard of the Kevin

Bacon game and the "small world" of social networks, an argument can be made that an equally creative invention of Milgram's was his lost letter experiment. In the original study, Milgram and colleagues were interested in unobtrusive measures of political attitudes and varied the addressee list of some four hundred letters that were distributed in New Haven, Connecticut. Two addresses were benign (a generic name for an individual and "Medical Research Associates") while the other two were "Friends of the Communist Party" and "Friends of the Nazi Party." Rates of return were selective, not surprisingly, with only a quarter of the latter group mailed back compared to 70 percent of the first two.[24]

To date there have been few attempts to implement the technique in a systematic way using probability sampling. The 2002 Chicago community survey thus set out to incorporate the strengths of the lost letter technique and adapt it to a sociological context. The idea was to randomly scatter letters across neighborhoods of Chicago and measure the situational aspects of each letter-drop setting and whether the letter was later returned. Specifically, during the interview phase of the second community survey, project staff unobtrusively dropped two preaddressed stamped envelopes on opposite random corners of each home block of study participants who themselves had been randomly selected. Conditions at the time of each drop were recorded. One letter was addressed to a fictional person, Mary Jones, and the other to a fictional company, Universal Services. The delivery address on both letters corresponded to post office boxes at the Institute for Social Research in Michigan, and the return address was a fictional street in Chicago. Some 3,300 letters were dropped, and just over a third were mailed.

My present goal is to examine *neighborhood-level* variation, connecting it to the themes of this chapter's concept of the good community. I first conducted an analysis with the unit being the individual letter, predicting its receipt (yes/no) based on the following characteristics: weather (indicators of rain, wind), time of day, season, whether the letter was dropped before or after the anthrax scare of that period (fall 2001), whether people on the street appeared friendly or suspicious, month (separate indicators from September to February/March), whether the letter drop was observed, whether it was a weekday, type of addressee (Mary Jones vs. Universal Services), whether it was a private apartment or high-rise public housing, and land-use conditions of the block around the letter drop (e.g., parking lot, residential, waterfront area). The probability of receiving the original letter in the mail was unrelated to most of these conditions, but it was lower if the drop was near high-rise public housing or it was windy—the latter a random event. Returns were also lower in the winter months and where interviewers were greeted with suspicion on the street. By contrast, letters were more often mailed if friendly people were observed on the street and in residential (as opposed to commercial or industrial) areas.[25]

As described below, I calculated the lost letter "return rate" (i.e., returned to the mail and delivered to the addressee) for census tracts, neighborhood clusters, and community areas, after adjusting for the influence of letter-drop conditions. There was considerable variation across all geographic units, with return rates ranging from a low of 0 percent to a high of 82 percent. Because the number of letters dropped was quite small for tracts (< 5), I focus primarily on the community area, which averaged about forty letter drops and thus provides more reliable between-community measurement.[26] Interestingly, the community with the highest level of returned letters, at 82 percent, is the heterogeneous community of Lakeview on Chicago's dense and very urban North Side. Apparently, this form of anonymous yet other-regarding behavior is not necessarily inhibited in the big-city environment, as many—going back to Louis Wirth—would predict.

The Cardiopulmonary Resuscitation (CPR) Study

For my second set of data I draw on a study that was originally conducted in the late 1980s in Chicago. During the years 1987 and 1988, the Emergency Medical Service (EMS) unit recorded data on all cardiac arrests that occurred in the city, including detailed information on the characteristics of the cardiac arrest event itself, the victim, and its location. Medical sociologists at the University of Chicago geocoded these data and reported that the rate of giving CPR varied significantly across census tracts.[27] The question that arises in the context of this book is the extent to which rates of CPR vary with key neighborhood processes, especially many years later. In particular, is there an other-regarding social character to neighborhoods that is durable?

To answer these and other questions, I obtained the original data and linked them to various components of the PHDCN family of studies. The incident-level unit of analysis comprised the population of all cardiac events serviced by EMS (N = 4,379 events). Like the original authors, I begin by examining two sets of characteristics central to CPR by a bystander. The first describes the cardiac arrest itself, including where it occurred (at or near home vs. outside block of residence), the time of the 911 call, and whether or not it was witnessed. The second set includes key characteristics of victims—age, race, and sex. It might be that certain types of victims are less likely to be attended to, and as we know from results throughout this book, neighborhoods vary dramatically in their demographic composition. I thus took the event and victim factors simultaneously into account in estimating the probability of CPR within any one community. Consistent with the original study, I found that CPR was more likely if it was witnessed, not at home, and the victim was older or white. There were no gender differences, however, and the race differential disappeared once these other factors were controlled.

I then examined both raw and adjusted CPR rates that took these individual and situational factors into account at the census-tract, neighborhood-cluster, and community-area levels. Although the patterns are similar across these ecological units, the reliability of measurement increases with the sample size, so I again focus primarily on community areas, where over fifty cardiac arrests occurred on average. The adjusted mean probability of CPR across communities is 0.22, meaning that in just under a quarter of the cases of pulmonary crisis in Chicago, a victim received CPR from a bystander circa 1988.

Neighborhood Effects on Altruism

My first empirical test concerns spatial variability: Does where a heart attack takes place matter for receiving critical help? It certainly does. The rate of giving CPR varies from a low of 13 percent to over a third (37 percent) across community areas. I find significant variation across census tracts and neighborhood clusters as well. Thus if we define CPR as a form of social altruism, there is empirical evidence of neighborhood differentiation.

A second but more intriguing question concerns the "reach" or overlap in forms of altruism. Does the CPR rate predict the act of returning a lost letter? Of course, performing CPR in 1988 does not directly cause someone to mail back a lost letter a decade or more hence. But if my theoretical approach is correct, then communities should still exhibit durability in their other-regarding *character* and evidence of "transference" across types of helping behavior. Norms of altruism have self-reinforcing properties, I argue, whether through social learning, institutional support, or mechanisms of reward such as public acknowledgement of unselfish acts. These are the sorts of mechanisms that undergird cultural reproduction.[28] Although mine is a strict empirical test with over a dozen years elapsed between giving CPR and the lost letter experiment, I find that the correlation of the two rates of behavior is moderately positive and significant (0.34, $p < 0.01$). This relationship is graphed visually in figure 9.1. Note the clustering of high-intervention communities in the north and along the lake (e.g., Near North, Edgewater, Uptown) and in the northwest communities of Portage and Norwood Park. By contrast, there is a large cluster of low-intervention areas in the south central areas of the city, although there are a number of socially altruistic communities nearby as well (e.g., Beverly, Morgan Park, West Elsdon). That clusters of altruistic hotspots—and their inverse—exist in 1988 and reappear many years later provides evidence of a durable structure to norms of other-regarding behavior.

The reader might object, because we know from prior chapters that communities differ widely in demographic composition, as do cardiac-arrest victims. Race and age, for example, predict who gets medical help (blacks a bit less, the elderly more), as does who is at home at the time of crisis, which is correlated with lifestyle. More generally, poor or uneducated residents may be less familiar with CPR techniques and so afraid to intervene even if motivated. A poor or dense neighborhood with a concentration of blacks, for example, might then bias the simple correlation, leading to an over- or underestimate of the factors that predict neighborhood variations in altruism. To address these concerns I controlled for poverty, age and racial composition, and population size from the 1990 census, which is most proximate in time to the cardiac arrests. This strategy follows the logic of the original investigators even though anything measured after 1988 is potentially a partial result of the other-regarding character of the neighborhood tapped by CPR. Controlling these later pathways could distort the results. But when I do so and whether at the tract, neighborhood-cluster, or community-area

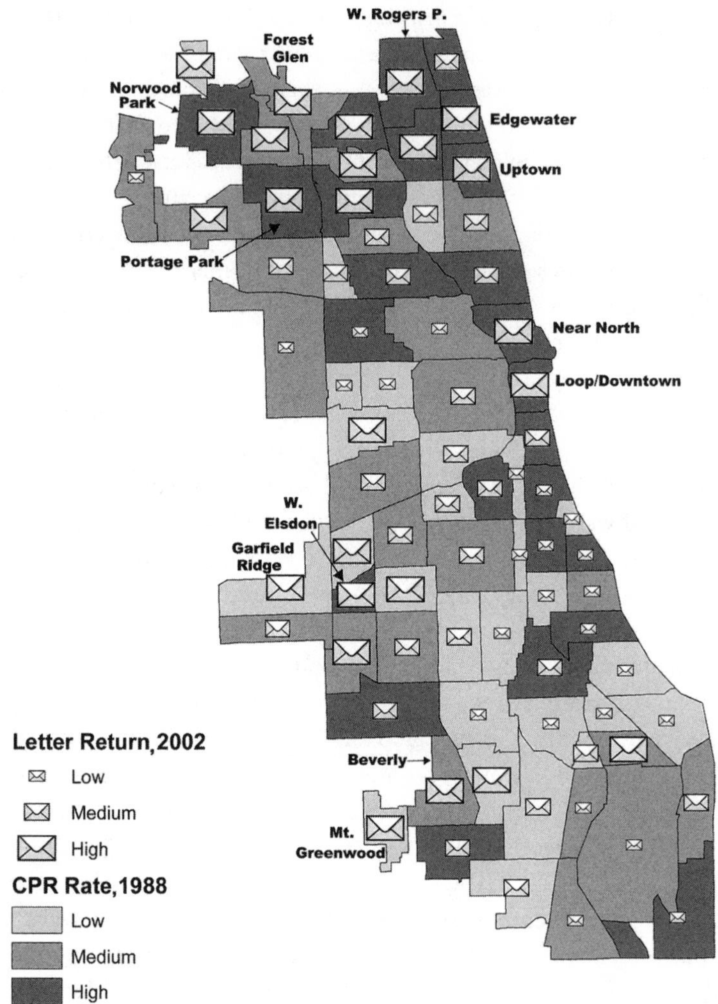

FIGURE 9.1. It matters where you have a heart attack or lose something: spatial inequality in CPR after a cardiac arrest and returning lost letters

level, raw CPR rates still predict higher letter return rates fourteen years later ($p < 0.05$), indicating a noncompositional mechanism.

I then analyzed cardiac arrests taking all types of influence into account. For each arrest I controlled for the effects of the victim's age, race, and sex, the time to a 911 response, where the heart attack occurred (at home or not), and whether the heart attack was witnessed. *When* a heart attack occurs is in effect random, and by implication whether it is witnessed, creating "exogenously" generated variation in social altruism.[29] At the community level I then controlled for concentrated disadvantage, diversity, density, population size, *and* age composition.[30] In the final step I calculated community-level variation in CPR not accounted for by all situational, victim-level, demographic composition, and structural factors. Especially considering that *where* heart attacks occur also has a large random component, my summary indicator taps community-level altruistic tendencies in a direct way.[31]

I still find a long-term connection among altruistic behaviors after all these adjustments. In fact the temporal correlation is not materially different and remains significant (0.32, $p < 0.01$). Consistent with figure 9.1, communities tend to cluster in spatial configurations of other-regarding behavior despite the manifest difference in underlying correlates of CPR and letter-drop returns. Scoring relatively high on social altruism are heterogeneous and seemingly "anonymous" places like the Loop, Rogers Park, West Rogers Park, the Near South Side, and Lakeview, along with more traditionally stable white communities like Jefferson and Norwood Park. Low-scoring communities tend to be poor, racially segregated, and disproportionately located on the South Side (e.g., Washington Park, Burnside). Douglas is a bit of an anomaly—it has one of the lowest letter-return rates of all communities in Chicago at around 10 percent, but its CPR propensity from years back was relatively high. Recall from chapter 5 that this area of Bronzeville on the South Side (e.g., Oakland, as well) witnessed some of the most unexpected changes in the city, perhaps accounting for its unusual position (e.g., fig. 5.6). Overall, however, the data reveal a reasonably durable form of social altruism across communities.

The previous chapter and work reviewed earlier suggest that organizational density may be a community institutional factor that helps sustain both norms and opportunities for altruism, especially in the case of CPR. To test this notion I examined the rate of nonprofit organizational density as measured in the previous chapter for the year closest to the CPR study, 1989. Controlling for population density, population size, and the age, race, and economic composition of the neighborhood in addition to the characteristics of the cardiac event itself (e.g., witnessed, age, race, sex of victim), the rate of nonprofit organizations in the community has a direct and large association with bystander CPR.[32] On the heels of the last chapter, this finding supports the argument that there is an organizational effect on collective civic engagement and a more general norm of social altruism.

My next step was to conduct a rigorous analysis of the letter-drop experiment analogous to that conducted for CPR. The approximately 3,300 lost letters were first analyzed as a simultaneous function of twenty-one situational predictors, such as time of day, month, housing conditions, weather, and more, along with a set of neighborhood-level predictors, including concentrated disadvantage (see chapter 5), ethnic and immigrant diversity, residential stability, and population density.[33] I examined several alternative specifications at the community level, including separate models for poverty, racial composition, population size, and other census-based characteristics, all with similar results. Consistent with the preliminary description earlier, there was significant ($p < 0.01$) variation in the letter-drop return rate across neighborhoods both before and after adjusting for situational factors, from census tracts to community areas. However, the reliability of the letter-drop return rate is highest at the community-area level, at 0.75, signaling that we have substantial ecometric ability to detect between-community-area variations.

I then examined the structural and organizational-level predictors of community-level variations in the rate of returning lost letters, taking into account both microlevel letter drop and local ecological conditions. In severely disadvantaged communities (namely, poor and segregated), the rate of returning letters is significantly lower. The magnitude of association is substantial and perhaps surprising in that there is nothing immediately apparent in a materially deprived community that would prevent someone from returning a lost letter.[34] Cultural or normative factors are quite possibly at work. Also surprising, given common perceptions, heterogeneity made no difference and population concentration (size) was positively linked to altruistic behavior. Louis Wirth would not have anticipated these results.

The second largest factor is organizations, building on chapter 8. Like the bystander CPR findings, the density of nonprofit organizations has a direct association with lost letter returns. The structural predictors of these distinct but correlated other-regarding behaviors are thus similar in nature, again suggesting a latent construct of altruism that persists over time. The data also clearly suggest that an organizational component underlies altruistic communities.

Collective Efficacy and Altruism

The theoretical framework of this chapter and results so far underscore cultural and social interactional factors alongside disadvantage and organizations in explaining altruistic behavior. Extending the ideas articulated earlier, I hypothesize that altruistic intervention is more likely in environments where shared expectations for public intervention are high, people trust their neighbors, and there is little perceived alienation from institutional rules or laws regarding other-regarding behavior. In this section I assess these predictions, starting with collective efficacy.

As we know from chapter 7, collective efficacy is highly stable over time ($R > 0.7$). Thus I employ the mean collective scale from 1995 to 2002 in predicting later lost letter return rates. The correlation is significant (0.41, $p < 0.01$) at the community-area level. Shared expectations for control and trust in neighbors in 2002, which are constituent elements of the collective efficacy scale, also correlate significantly with letter returns at 0.32 and 0.60, respectively ($p < 0.01$). Trust therefore appears to be the most directly related to altruistic behavior in the form of letter returns, a pattern that holds once neighborhood compositional factors are controlled.

"Moral cynicism" is a construct that taps the darker side of human nature. In an effort to gauge general beliefs about the sense in which laws or collective moral rules are not considered binding in the present lives of Chicago residents, we asked respondents to report their level of agreement with statements such as "Laws were made to be broken"; "It's okay to do anything you want as long as you don't hurt anyone"; and "To make money, there are no right and wrong ways anymore, only easy ways and hard ways." In communities with high levels of cynicism and a perceived lack of legitimacy of normative and legal rules, letter-return rates are significantly lower (−0.46, $p < 0.01$). This association is largely explained by disadvantage, however; once it is adjusted, along with stability and diversity, the link between community moral cynicism and letter-drop returns weakens.[35]

There is one set of relationships worth noting for their conspicuous absence in predicting altruistic behavior. I have not said much about dense social networks, such as friendship and kinship ties, reciprocated exchange, and closure among adult-child networks. My reason for this stems from the theoretical argument and lessons learned in chapter 7. There I demonstrated that the active ingredients of collective efficacy were far more salient for outcomes like crime and other public aspects of community wellbeing than the strong ties of friends and family. What about social altruism? The same general story applies. I estimated a number of models whereby previously validated measures of social interaction, ties, and exchange were examined in relation to behavioral altruism in the form of letter-drop behavior. I also examined a measure of general trust to compare against the contextualized measure of trust in neighbors (see above). The general pattern was a weak relationship, whether in simple correlations or more comprehensive multivariate models. Again, what mattered most were disadvantage and organizations, and in the case of letter-drop return, collective efficacy and trust.

Altruistic Propensity and Its Consequences

The results at this point support the theoretical validity of my measures derived from the CPR and letter-drop studies, and further suggest a commonality to these otherwise dissimilar aspects of altruism. Mutual trust in fellow neighbors and shared beliefs about their willingness to intervene appear to be part of the other-regarding community as well—what I have elsewhere called collective efficacy. The final question is, what about consequences?

This is a large question, and no one analysis can hope to be definitive regarding cause and effect. But the results of this chapter motivate what I believe is an innovative strategy capitalizing on the unique nature of the CPR and lost letter experiments. The main idea is to create a unified measure tapping what I conceptualize as the general propensity of communities to exhibit altruistic behavior over time and thereby to promote altruistic norms. Guided by the theoretical framework and results so far, I constructed the first principal component of the *Adjusted CPR* and *Adjusted Letter Drop* scales, a measurement model procedure that captures their shared or common covariation. The first principal component accounts for 65 percent of the common variation in the two observed indicators, even though they are separated by fourteen years.[36] Collective efficacy (CE) taps a theoretically related but distinct construct—it modestly predicts letter-return rates but is only weakly related to CPR altruism from many years earlier. I therefore examined collective efficacy as a separate factor alongside the combined altruism component in the main set of analyses. The advantage of this scheme is that it allows me to examine two broad measures of altruism and other-regarding character—one behavioral (CPR/letter drop) and one more cognitive in nature (shared expectations of CE).

Just as participants in experimental games are more cooperative when trust is high, I have shown that acts of behavioral altruism are higher in contexts of community trust and shared expectations for public intervention. A second question is motivated by this pairing: What happens when we fuse *shared expectations* for action with *behavioral* action in the form of altruism? There are theoretical grounds to argue that combining the behavioral and normative dimensions makes for a different kind of marker of the underlying, unobservable construct of tendencies to altruism. To formalize this notion, rather than controlling for collective efficacy I included it in a second principal component with the 2002 adjusted letter drop because both were measured at the same time (2002) and in the recent past (1995) for collective efficacy. I repeated this procedure with the trust indicator from 1995 to 2002 (average) in lieu of the mean collective efficacy scale from 1995 to 2002. Although the results were consistent across scales, I focus on the collective efficacy–based score to provide greater theoretical continuity across chapters and because of its explicit "intervention" scenario. CPR was considered a separate indicator.[37]

I examined the spatial distribution of my main behavioral indicator of altruistic propensity circa 1988–2002 and homicide rates averaged over later years (2002–6) to improve accuracy and to ensure correct temporal order. There was a clear patterning, with altruistic communities exhibiting significantly lower homicide rates. I also examined relationships with other crime rates and dimensions of health and adolescent wellbeing, such as infant mortality, low birth weight, and teenage childbearing.[38] The correlations were all significant and the spatial patterns similar to homicide—where altruism is higher, children's wellbeing is higher. Teen birth rates are an especially interesting indicator because theoretically we would expect collective efficacy and altruism to be reflected in more social support and greater informal social controls placed on early sexual initiation, thus ultimately resulting in fewer teenage births. Recent research supports this reasoning, showing a direct link between neighborhood collective efficacy and lower rates of sexual behavior among adolescents.[39]

Even though the altruism scale was adjusted for confounders, we still have to worry that compositional differences across communities may be biasing any simple comparisons. To address this concern I examined a series of models that adjusted for economic and demographic factors so as to determine the direct association of social altruism with community outcomes. On theoretical grounds I first focus on the model that separates behavioral altruism from collective efficacy. I examine moral/legal cynicism as a separate construct as well because the data indicated that, while correlated negatively with altruism, cynicism emerges as an independent construct and is not directly predictive of letter-drop returns in the same manner as CPR. Our past work in Chicago has also shown links between cynicism and violence at the individual level, and there is a theoretical rationale for arguing that moral cynicism is a mechanism that lubricates criminal and nonconformist behavior, especially among marginalized groups.[40] I thus hypothesized earlier in the chapter that there is a link between cynicism and violence at the other end of the other-regarding spectrum. Cynicism, after all, is all about how people do *not* care about the norms of others—it is in effect a form of *anti*-altruism.

Figure 9.2 shows the results for homicide and teenage birth rates side by side, with the entries based on standardized coefficients from the full multivariate models. These are obviously very different phenomena, one happening to young girls and involving a live birth, the other involving criminal death, usually by and of males. Yet these two otherwise disparate outcomes are rooted in social interactions and share a similar explanatory profile. They are both predicted foremost by concentrated disadvantage, which yields the largest estimated effect on increased homicide and teen births, a pattern consistent with the story told elsewhere in this book. After accounting for concentrated disadvantage and population diversity by race/ethnicity and immigration, we see three additional patterns. First, where moral cynicism is high, teen births and homicide rates are high. Second, where altruism is high, rates of homicide and teen births are significantly lower. Third, collective efficacy has a strong negative relationship with both homicide and teen birth rates. In addition to collective efficacy (recall also chapter 7), moral cynicism and social altruism are thus directly linked to future community-level

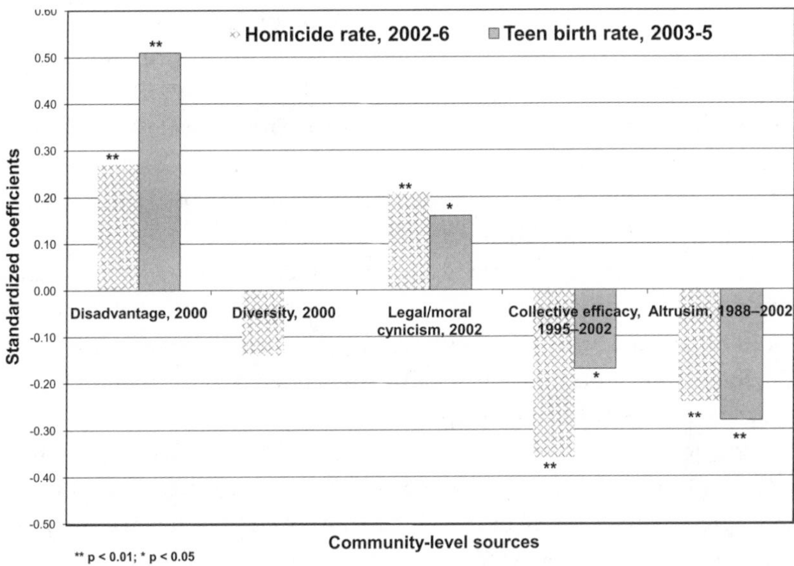

FIGURE 9.2. Social altruism and community wellbeing: links to violence and teenage birth rates in Chicago

outcomes in ways that cannot easily be explained away by population composition.[41]

Another rather strict test is to control the prior history of the outcome in question. I did not have prior teen births available, but I was able to control for the homicide rate across five years (1995–99), in addition to diversity and disadvantage. Post-2002 homicide rates were still associated with the three social processes highlighted in figure 9.2; the t-ratios associated with the effects of altruism, moral cynicism, and collective efficacy on change in homicide were −3.07, 2.75, and −3.15, respectively (all $p < 0.01$). This test, along with the general robustness in the face of alternative controls, suggests that when we adjust for the prior causes of homicide, the consequences of an altruistic, collective, and moral cynical culture are virtually unchanged.

A way to summarize the magnitude of the basic result is to construct a typology of communities based on their altruistic character and later homicide experience after both factors are adjusted for preexisting conditions as just described. Of communities in the top third of altruistic character measured prior to and up to 2002, over half are in the lowest third of homicide vulnerability in 2002–6 that is unexplained by prior homicide. By comparison, only 12 percent of low-altruism communities are fortunate enough to be low in present-day homicide. This relationship is substantial and significant at the community level. If we assume that controlling prior homicide is a conservative adjustment, the data once again point to a fairly robust association of a socially altruistic propensity with the wellbeing of a community.

In further tests I examined the combined collective efficacy and letter-drop scale along with the CPR rate as the sole or "purest" indicator of altruism. I also examined rates of infant mortality and low birth weight as indicators of public health. The collective efficacy and letter-drop index was the strongest predictor of homicide, mediating or absorbing much of the effect of CPR altruism. The result for teen birth rate was broadly similar to the previous pattern, with CPR and CE/letter drop remaining more or less equally important.[42] When we combine the normative and behavioral aspects of altruism in this manner, we see a strong negative association with both crime rates and adolescent births. However, the altruistic propensity of a community did not reveal a direct association with rates of infant mortality or low birth weight once confounding factors were adjusted. Although these health-related phenomena have social roots, they are less directly social interactional in nature than interpersonal violence or sexual behavior as reflected in teen pregnancy. It thus seems that the more social interactional in character the outcome, the stronger the independent role for the latent altruism of a community.

Implications

Evolutionary biologists have long claimed that altruistic behavior is favored in natural selection because of benefits to the group. That may or may not be true, but the proposition has remained elusive to empirical testing, as have many other evolutionary mechanisms. In a very different field, scholars have waxed philosophic about the collective good but without much empirical grounding. I suggest that both altruism and the good are worth empirical scrutiny, providing a framework in which to revisit and synthesize many of the basic themes of this book.

The present chapter could not assess causal pathways in a foolproof way, but I did marshal a set of novel databases to test logically derived hypotheses about altruistic behaviors that we can reasonably say contribute to the "good community," or at least the kind of community I believe most readers would prefer to live in. Consistent with the justice as fairness principle applied to Rawls's idea of the social union, I invoked his "veil of ignorance" thought experiment and linked it to the spatial and neighborhood-effects logic of this book to investigate community-level variations in social altruism and other-regarding behavior. I posited that giving CPR to heart-attack victims and mailing lost letters provide direct indicators of my theoretical conception that pass the Rawlsian test. Lost-letter methods are also unobtrusive and subject to systematic manipulation by investigators, allowing me to adjust for opportunity conditions. CPR conditions were not manipulated, but the nature of heart attacks gives us a type of quasi-natural experiment. The altruism data thus provided me with a unique opportunity to revisit basic empirical patterns and theoretical themes that were presented in earlier chapters.

After proposing a means to assess individual and situational-level determinants, I showed that altruism follows a social and spatial logic similar to many other behaviors and perceptions analyzed throughout this book. This is perhaps the most important finding. Altruism appears to have a neighborhood-level path dependence that is influenced by long-term dynamics, such that a neighborhood's other-regarding behavior at one time sets in motion actions and norms that govern future altruism beyond that expected on the basis of its composition. Social altruism is part of the character of a community, I argue. This was confirmed through the prediction of lost-letter return rates by CPR-administration rates from more than a dozen years previous. Disadvantage and other factors are important, to be sure, but the altruism prediction holds, notwithstanding their effects, and the returning of lost letters is also positively related to localized trust and collective efficacy. These patterns point to an enduring culture that is located on a dimension of social altruism.[43]

The final test supports what we might call the neighborhood effects *of* altruism. I argued that CPR and letter-return rates are behavioral indicators of socially altruistic behavior, forming a distinct marker

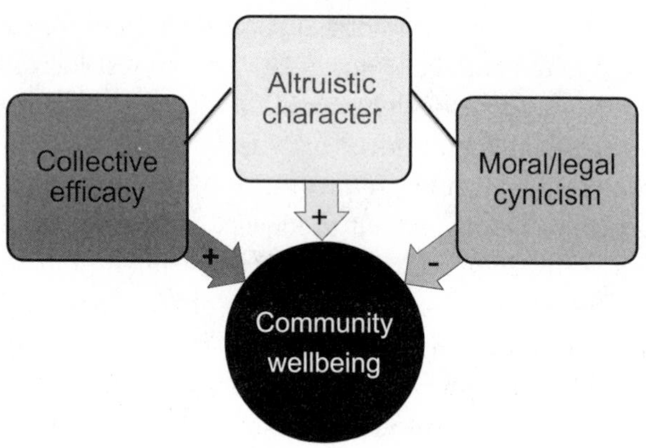

FIGURE 9.3. Core social dimensions of neighborhood context and wellbeing

for the "good community" that foretells later outcomes independent of demographic composition. Although operating at a more cognitive level, collective efficacy is theoretically in the same camp and has an important cultural ingredient in shared expectations for action. Altruism does not explain all outcomes, of course, nor should it. But indicators of altruism and collective efficacy did independently predict violence and teen births, controlling for neighborhood composition, alone and in combination with one another. Independent of the collective efficacy and altruism pathways, the moral cynicism of a community exhibited a positive association with violence and teen birth outcomes, again independent of the economic and racial composition features that dominate current debates.

I conclude that altruistic or other-regarding interventions, moral cynicism, and collective efficacy capture important elements of the social life of neighborhoods that (a) are influenced by but not reducible to materialist explanations or individual properties, and (b) have empirical import for tangible behaviors that shape wellbeing and the perceived "good community"—sometimes with deadly consequences. Figure 9.3 displays a simplified heuristic of this argument. Although this account has never been evaluated in prior research, the empirical findings in this chapter implicate a neighborhood effect in fundamental mechanisms of human culture and urban ethics, whether in favor of helping others in need, fostering shared expectations for producing public goods, or a corrosive moral cynicism that favors disregarding others. In previous chapters I also showed the relevance for wellbeing of civic engagement, organizations, and collectively perceived disorder. How such community-level processes along with structures of neighborhood inequality are embedded in the larger spatial and interlocking context of the city—including that constructed by individual action—is the challenge taken up in the next section.

PART IV **INTERLOCKING STRUCTURES**

10 Spatial Logic; or, Why Neighbors of Neighborhoods Matter

Forty years ago, Waldo Tobler coined what he termed the "first law" of geography—"everything is related to everything else, but near things are more related than distant things."[1] What he thought was an innocuous phrase in a minor paper went on to be cited more than five hundred times since its publication. The idea of a "law" sparked sharp criticism, with the ironic result that for some time geographers discarded what is now considered one of their discipline's classics. As retro as it may at first appear, I will show that Tobler's basic point stands tall to this day, with appropriate caveats observed. In particular, I interpret his invocation of the term "law" in the small sense, referring not to an argument for geographic determinism but rather to a remarkably durable pattern of spatial interdependence that demands empirical and theoretical attention.[2]

The patterns demonstrated in this book so far provide qualified support for the first law of geography. In some fundamental sense, a spatial story has been told in virtually every chapter. Rather than urban processes occurring on a quasi-random or "placeless" field, the reader has been shown examples of the spatial clustering of everything from homicide and low birth weight to the spatial separation of income and racial groups to the concentration of visible signs of disorder and collective civic action to symbols of globalization. Applying Tobler's insight to the current scene thus yields an updated appreciation of the pattern that what is close by geographically is disproportionately similar in character. The task that remains is to formalize the argument and probe more deeply the explanatory mechanisms of spatial inequality.

This chapter does just that, the first of five in a section of the book that considers the bird's-eye view of "higher-order" processes—the social structure of the city. One of these interlocking processes involves spatial dynamics that go beyond the local boundaries of neighborhoods. Having demonstrated the continuing significance of "local" neighborhood effects in previous chapters, my goal here is to examine spatial interdependence at the extralocal level and whether it holds up once we take into account important internal characteristics of the neighborhood, such as poverty and racial composition. The reason for this is that what appear to be spatial effects may reflect neighborhood heterogeneity in disguise. In other words, spatial interdependence may be explained by the differential composition of neighborhood populations. Against this critique, I demonstrate in this chapter that spatial dynamics are significant well beyond what we would normally expect and hold up despite adjusting for multiple characteristics of the neighborhood itself. I also examine how race, crime, and immigration are bound up with spatial inequality, and how the influence of neighborhood characteristics varies according to spatial location, especially spatial "regimes" of the city.

The remaining chapters in this section consider other themes that, taken together, make up a concerted effort to paint a holistic picture of how the contemporary city is linked. This analytic move does not slight the microlevel actions of individuals. Chapters 11 and 12, for example, examine residential mobility and how the moves of individuals are a reaction to spatial context and create interdependent contexts. Chapter 13 examines the social structure of ties between neighborhoods created by residential mobility. Chapter 14 examines the structure of ties between communities that are created by key leaders. In different ways, all five chapters in this section are united by a common concern with interlocking effects and crossing boundaries, addressing head on the criticism that neighborhood-effects research misses the big picture.

The Idea of Spatial Interdependence

Just as individuals are influenced by their friends and perhaps the friends of their friends, neighborhoods are embedded in a larger network of social relations. Contrary to the common assumption of independence of social units, the animating idea is that neighborhoods are *inter*dependent and characterized by a functional relationship between what happens at one point in space and what happens elsewhere—to put it simply, a neighborhood's neighbors matter. Cross-neighborhood spatial ties challenge the traditional "urban village" model that assumes neighborhoods represent intact or insular social systems, functioning as islands unto themselves.

Crime provides an obvious case. Spatial dependence is implicated by the fact that offenders are disproportionately involved in acts of crime near their homes. Without making any assumptions about social interaction, it follows that a neighborhood's crime rate is ratcheted up by geographical proximity to places where known offenders live or exposure to hypothesized causes of crime, such as concentrated poverty and low collective efficacy. After all, offenders are not required to respect the geographic boundaries set by researchers.

But the process of interconnectedness goes deeper. Mundane though it may be, even in today's cyber world the reality is that, whether encountering a potential marriage partner or a criminal offender, social choices are governed by spatial proximity.[3] Opportunities for contact increase with physical propinquity, and social interactions may in turn concatenate along chains of contact, with their influences ultimately felt away from the geographic point of origin. For example, most violent crimes occur among acquaintances and are reactive in nature, such that a homicide in one neighborhood may provide the spark that leads to a retaliatory killing in a nearby neighborhood. More generally, it follows that any behavior transmitted along geographically linked chains of social interaction is subject to spatial diffusion.

To summarize, there is good reason to expect that spatial interdependence arises from processes related to both *diffusion* and *exposure*, with the result being that the characteristics of surrounding neighborhoods influence the social wellbeing of nearby neighborhoods, with nearby effects larger than distant (the "first law"). Diffusion refers to the processes by which behaviors spread over time and space, such as when drug-use networks concatenate over ecological boundaries to spread drug use to a nearby neighborhood, simultaneously increasing high-risk sexual behavior and in turn the incidence of future HIV infection. The concept of exposure focuses on contact with antecedent conditions that in the HIV case might foster the initial drug behavior itself, such as proximity to the concentration of poverty or organized drug markets.

There are pragmatic reasons to think spatially as well. One criticism of neighborhood-level research concerns the artificiality of boundaries; for example, two families living across the street from one another may be arbitrarily assigned to live in different neighborhoods even though they share social ties. This possibility reflects what is known as the "modifiable areal unit problem" that arises when artificial boundaries are imposed on more or less continuous spatial phenomena. Spatial models are designed to address this problem by incorporating spatial errors and interdependencies in operationally defined neighborhood units that are contiguous.

Spatial Patterning versus Randomness

One can assess empirically the nature of spatial interdependence with a simple test known as a Moran scatter plot, which classifies each neighborhood based on its value for a given variable, *y* (say, poverty), and the spatially weighted average of the variable *y* in contiguous or nearby neighborhoods, denoted by *Wy*. In the case of poverty, *Wy* is the average poverty rate for the "neighbors" of a given focal neighborhood. In spatial analysis we can weight our observations by distance or contiguity to a chosen number of "neighborhood neighbors," producing a weights (W) matrix. In Chicago, my colleagues and I examined spatial associations like this for a variety of spatial units (block groups, tracts, neighborhood clusters, and community areas) and with different definitions of spatial contiguity (e.g., adjacency, nearest four and nearest six neighborhoods). Consistent with the maps presented in earlier chapters, previous research with the initial round of the PHDCN has revealed that concentrated disadvantage, crime (especially homicide, robbery, and burglary), and collective efficacy are all highly spatially interrelated in ways that go beyond chance expectations.[4]

I expand previous work by incorporating the most recently available PHDCN, census, crime, and incarceration data. For the sake of parsimony, I do not report the full panoply of results but only highlight the spatial patterning of key neighborhood structural and processual characteristics that emerged in previous chapters. Figure 10.1 displays the relationship between a focal neighborhood's internal characteristics on

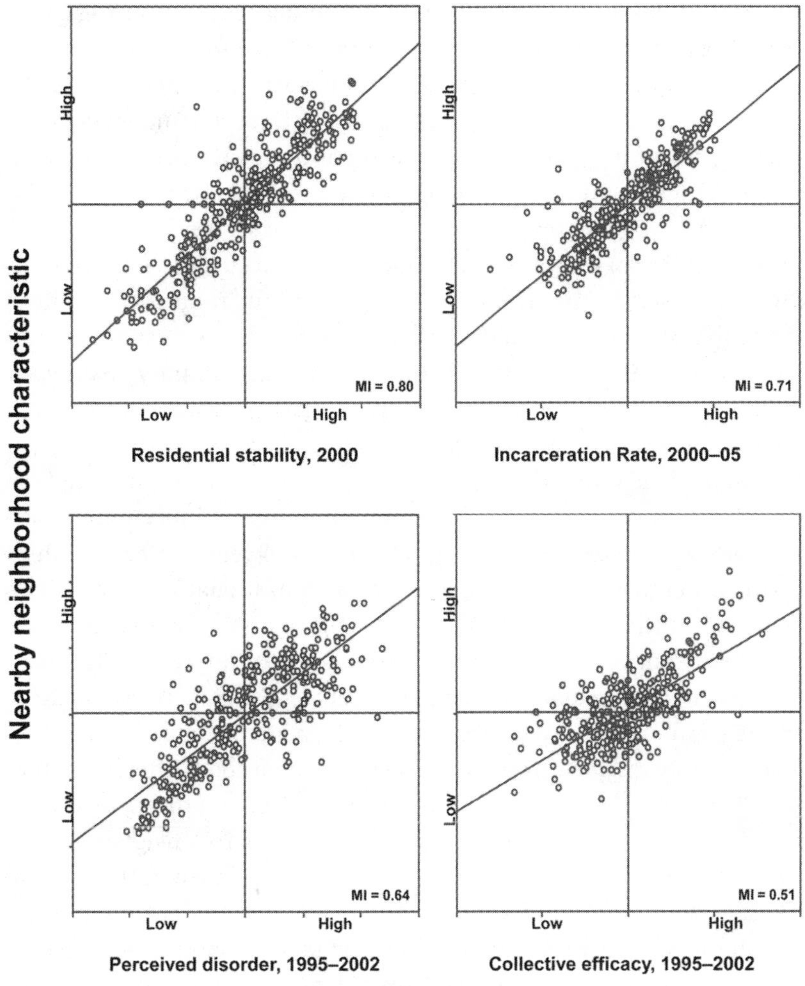

FIGURE 10.1. Spatial interdependence of key neighborhood characteristics

the *x* axis and that of its six closest neighbors on the *y* axis (*Wy*), along with the spatial coefficient of "Moran's I" (denoted MI).[5] Figure 10.1 reveals that whether it is the social-ecological characteristic of residential stability, the intensity of local incarceration removal to state prison, socially perceived disorder, or collective efficacy over seven years, there is a linear relationship and evidence of significant spatial processes at work. Neighborhoods that are high in any of these four characteristics are significantly more likely to be located near other neighborhoods that are also high, generating broad implications for understanding social behavior beyond local ecological borders. Although not shown, concentrated disadvantage, immigration, and crime are also spatially patterned, as anticipated by prior results and chapters 5 and 6, yielding significant Moran's I of 0.66, 0.80, and 0.72, respectively. Thus the "big three" of structural disadvantage, immigration, and residential stability are all spatially interdependent, as are key social processes and criminal justice factors. Other factors not shown that are significantly linked spatially are population density and social altruism.

It is important to emphasize that not everything is spatially interdependent. One might even expect that such an outcome would reflect a methodological artifact. As it happens, a number of social processes are weakly or modestly correlated in the spatial sense. Friend/kinship networks, organizational participation, organizational density, neighborhood cynicism, and reciprocal exchange exhibit signs of positive spatial dependence, but weakly and with no significant results. This pattern may in part be due to measurement error in social processes based on the community survey data, because the general pattern is that the more reliably the measure taps between-neighborhood differences, the greater the significant spatial clustering. Collective efficacy and perceived disorder, for example, are highly reliable across neighborhoods and yield relatively large Moran's coefficients, as do most of the census-based indicators.[6] I conclude then that while the evidence is mixed, overall the trend is toward modest to strong spatial interdependence.

Figure 10.1 permits additional insight on the conceptual value of spatial analysis. In each quadrant of the graphs, we can conceive of neighborhoods that are above the mean on y to have "high" values of y, while neighborhoods below the mean are "low." The same distinction can be made with respect to values of Wy for each neighborhood, resulting in a fourfold classification. To take collective efficacy as an example, consider the following categories: (1) low-low, for neighborhoods that have low levels of efficacy and that are also proximate to neighborhoods with low levels of efficacy; (2) low-high, for neighborhoods that have low levels of efficacy but are proximate to high levels; (3) high-low, for neighborhoods that have high levels of efficacy but are proximate to low levels; and (4) high-high, for areas with high levels of efficacy that are proximate to high levels of efficacy. In a paper I coauthored with Jeffrey Morenoff and Stephen Raudenbush, we used this typology to reveal the high degree of overlap between the spatial distributions of collective efficacy and homicide.[7] Over 70 percent of the Chicago neighborhoods that have spatial clustering of high levels of collective efficacy (category 4) experience statistically significant clustering of low homicide rates. Most of the clustering of low homicide coupled with high collective efficacy occurs in neighborhoods located on the western boundaries of Chicago, particularly on the Far Northwest and Southwest sides. At the other end of the spectrum, there is a strong correspondence between the spatial clustering of high homicide rates and low levels of collective efficacy. Some 75 percent of homicide *hotspots* (defined as high-high, using the spatial classification) are in the low-low spatial category (#1) of collective efficacy. Even the "off-diagonals" of figure 10.1 have meaning. Despite their relative rarity, for example, 15 percent of homicide *coldspots* (low-low) appear in neighborhoods with *low* levels of collective efficacy but that are surrounded by high levels. Fifteen percent of the homicide hotspots are in neighborhoods that have *high* levels of collective efficacy surrounded by neighborhoods with low levels. Neighborhoods where the level of collective efficacy is at variance with surrounding neighborhoods are thus important because they reveal neglected forms of spatial advantage and disadvantage.

Accounting for Alternative Explanations

It is always possible that heterogeneity in the internal characteristics of the neighborhood is driving what appear to be spatial patterns. Although the results above are provocative, perhaps a neighborhood generates spatial clustering simply because it is poor, for example, or has a particular demographic profile. In this section, I address the competing "heterogeneity" challenge both by adjusting for known correlates of the outcome in question and introducing direct measures of spatial interdependence into explanatory models. My overall hypothesis is that, despite internal risks, neighborhood wellbeing is conditioned by the characteristics of spatially proximate neighborhoods, which in turn are conditioned by adjoining neighborhoods in a spatially linked process that ultimately characterizes the entire city. The data support the hypothesis by showing the independent role of spatial proximity in distinct ways.

I consider first a recalibration of the homicide results from previous work. I begin by assessing differences in adjusted mean homicide rate in relation to neighborhood collective efficacy and spatial homicide risk. I obtained updated counts of homicides, pooling data across the years 2002–6 to calculate the average rate per hundred thousand, which I then separately analyzed as a function of the major predictors identified in previous chapters (e.g., concentrated poverty, immigration, racial composition, and residential stability). I then created a standardized residual homicide rate, which may be interpreted as the homicide rate for a focal neighborhood after removing the demographic and economic compositional factors internal to that neighborhood. I then combined the two waves of the community survey to obtain the prior (1995–2002) collective efficacy scores for each neighborhood.

The results in figure 10.2 show that *within* categories of high and low collective efficacy in the focal neighborhood, adjusted mean homicide rates are much higher in neighborhoods that are spatially proximate to high levels of homicide than they are in neighborhoods that are spatially proximate to low levels of homicide. In vulnerable neighborhoods of low collective efficacy, the difference is especially notable, with spatial proximity to danger associated with over a third of a standard deviation increase in the local homicide rate. Consistent with chapter 7, collective efficacy in the focal neighborhood nonetheless remains significant and substantively large, adjusting for spatial proximity and a host of potentially confounding internal characteristics. Particularly when spatially proximate to high risk, collective efficacy emerges as a protective factor (compare the second bar in fig. 10.2 with the rightmost bar). Hence a key finding is that a neighborhood's spatial proximity to danger influences its homicide rate independent of the continuing influence of collective efficacy and other internal neighborhood factors. It follows that pitting the local and extralocal against one another is misleading—*both* types of social processes are at work.

I consider next the role of spatial processes that "ripple" across the geography of the entire city—what is often referred to as spatial spillover. Typically spatial spillover models are examined in one of two ways. The first makes fewer assumptions and is technically referred to

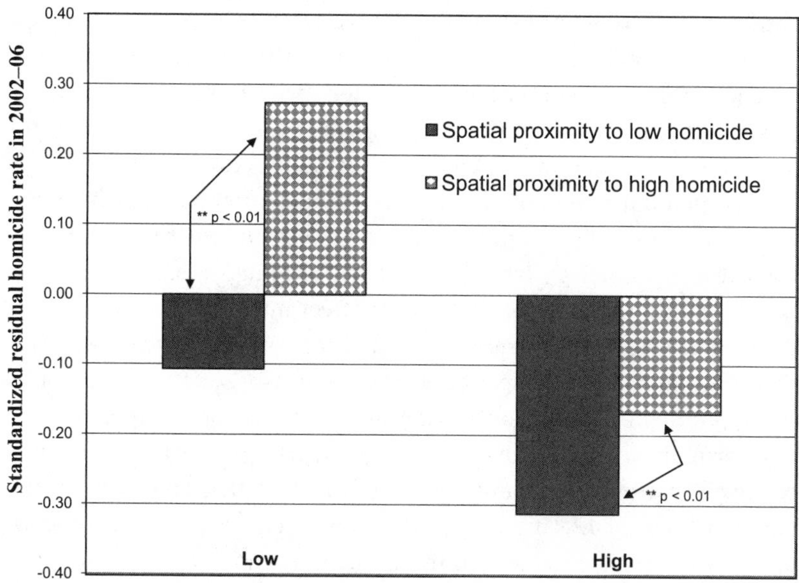

FIGURE 10.2. Adjusted homicide rates (2002–6) by neighborhood collective efficacy (1995–2002) and spatial proximity to homicide (2002–6)

as a "spatial error" model. Here the main idea is that unobserved spatial processes (e.g., spatial correlation in omitted variables or errors in measurement) may bias estimation of traditional models that assume independence among neighborhood units. The solution is to account for spatial interdependencies in the error term when estimating the association of internal neighborhood factors with a given outcome. Using this model is thus a straightforward way to assess the robustness of results to spatial dependencies that may be present. I performed this kind of test on the key results in chapter 6 on disorder, chapter 7 on collective efficacy, chapter 8 on organizational density, and chapter 9 on social altruism—in fact, virtually all analyses in this book were subjected to controls for spatial errors. Unless otherwise noted, the results were very similar despite controlling for spatial dependencies. To take one example from the last chapter, when I estimate the relationships in figure 9.2 after controlling for spatially linked errors, the same pattern obtains for the key predictor of social altruism on both homicide and teen pregnancy ($p < 0.05$). What this result signifies substantively is that local (or internal) neighborhood characteristics continue to matter—in this case, the propensity to help others in need—even when we control for errors introduced by unobservable spatial processes.[8]

A related but more ambitious spatial model attempts to estimate directly the effect of a neighborhood's neighbors in what is technically termed a "spatial lag" regression model, although a simpler label is "spatial effect." The reason the spatial effect model is more ambitious than the error model is that an estimate is generated for the association of a unit change in the spatial proximity measure with the outcome. Using homicide as an example, the interpretation of the spatial lag is that for a given neighborhood, *i*, it represents the effect of a one-unit change in the average homicide rate of *i*'s first-order neighbors on the homicide rate of *i*.[9] This interpretation suggests a diffusion process, whereby a high homicide rate in one neighborhood diffuses outward and affects homicide rates in surrounding neighborhoods.[10] But the spatial lag model also incorporates the idea of "exposure" to causal risk factors reflected in the measured covariates and error terms of spatially proximate neighborhoods.

Although at first this all seems complicated, the basic idea behind both the spatial error and effect model is intuitively simple—*residents of a focal neighborhood are exposed to both the measured and unobserved characteristics of surrounding neighborhoods*.[11] I wish to focus on this larger point in describing the basic spatial patterns arising from the data. Three sets of results deserve mention. First, in prior work we have shown that the demography of population change is strongly linked to changes in the crime rate of surrounding neighborhoods.[12] When crime rates nearby are high or increasing, residents of any given focal neighborhood tend to move out. Second, certain forms of a neighborhood's social fabric are spatially conditioned, as mentioned above. Despite measurement error, we have shown that social control and intergenerational closure (adult-child ties) in the first community survey appear to be significantly influenced by their levels in adjacent areas, even after controlling for race, poverty, and other factors.[13] Third, controlling for measured characteristics internal to a neighborhood, violence is significantly and positively linked to the violence rates of surrounding neighborhoods.[14] These findings suggest a diffusion or exposure process, whereby violence is influenced by the characteristics of spatially proximate neighborhoods, which are influenced in turn by adjoining neighborhoods in a spatially linked process that ultimately reaches throughout the entire city. For example, if neighborhood A's risk is dependent on neighbor B's characteristics, and B's characteristics are in turn dependent on C's, then in effect A is spatially linked to C even if they are not contiguous or if they are possibly miles apart. This process continues in a steplike fashion, incorporating the neighborhood characteristics of successively higher-order neighbors and thus (indirectly) all neighborhoods in Chicago.

The cumulative magnitude of these spatial associations can be large when the spatial multiplier process is fully considered. For example, controlling for a wide variety of other neighborhood characteristics, a one-standard-deviation increase in concentrated disadvantage in a focal neighborhood is linked to a 40 percent increase in the homicide rate in the focal neighborhood according to the Chicago Police data and a 24 percent increase according to the independent homicide victimization rate derived from vital statistics. Yet all else being equal, a one-standard-deviation increase in the average level of concentrated disadvantage *in the first-order neighbors* of the focal neighborhood is associated with an *additional* 9 percent increase in the homicide rate in the focal neighborhood according to the police data and a 4 percent increase according to vital statistics. The effects of disadvantage decrease exponentially with each succeeding level of contiguity. To gauge the cumulative effect, we estimated that a simultaneous one-standard deviation increase in concentrated disadvantage in the focal neighborhood, and in the first-, second-, and third-order neighbors, was associated with a substantial 52 percent increase in homicide according to police data and a 28 percent increase according to the vital statistics. These are large associations, considering that potential confounders in the form of indigenous neighborhood factors (e.g., density, prior crime, residential stability) were explicitly adjusted. A similar spatial pattern emerges for collective efficacy. Cumulatively, a one-standard-deviation increase in collective efficacy in the focal neighborhood along with the first-, second-, and third-order neighborhoods is associated with a 15 percent reduction in the homicide rate of the focal neighborhood according to police data and a 14 percent drop according to the victimization rate.

In short, I have investigated the spatial logic of Chicago using formal tests and find that the main results of this book are fundamentally similar whether I use a so-called spatial error or spatial effect (lag) model. Across different levels of aggregation, measures, outcomes, and specifications, the results converge in revealing the spatial interdependence of neighborhoods and also the continued influence of internal factors examined in previous chapters. What this means is that neighborhood effects are simultaneously local *and* interlocking across the city.

Spatial Inequality and Ecological Dissimilarity by Race

Fifteen years ago, Bill Wilson and I proposed a theory of race and urban inequality to explain the disproportionate representation of African Americans as victims and offenders in violent crime.[15] In the language of this book, the basic idea put forth was that community-level patterns of racial inequality give rise to the ecological concentration of the truly disadvantaged, which in turn leads to structural barriers and cultural adaptations that undermine collective efficacy and ultimately the control of crime. According to this perspective, race is not a distinct or credible cause of violence or other social behaviors, for that matter—rather it is a marker for the constellation of social disadvantages and resources that are differentially allocated by racial status in American society. We pursued this logic to argue that the community-level causes of violence are the same for both whites and blacks, but that racial segregation by community differentially exposes members of minority groups to violence-inducing and violence-protecting social mechanisms, and that this process explains black-white disparities in violence.[16] This has come to be known in the literature as the "racial invariance" thesis. I revisit that thesis here because at root it rests on *racially shaped mechanisms of spatial inequality*.

The first part of the racial invariance thesis points to the substantial variations within black and white neighborhoods that correspond to variations in crime rates. We hypothesized that if the structural sources of variation in crime are not unique by race, then rates of crime by blacks should vary with social-ecological conditions in a manner similar to whites. The data confirm the wide variability in crime rates among white and black communities, along with robust similarity in key predictors.[17] Moreover, although the empirical base is limited, neighborhood factors correlated with race explain a significant proportion of the black-white racial gap in violence among individuals. Using the PHDCN, we found that neighborhoods with an above average proportion of people in professional or managerial jobs were protected against violence, as were neighborhoods with higher concentrations of immigrants. About a third of the black-white gap in violence was explained by these neighborhood factors. Further, we found no systematic evidence that neighborhood or individual-level predictors of violence *interacted* with race, and there were no significant racial disparities in trajectories of change in violence.

The second part of the invariance logic focuses on ecological *dis*similarity by race. Writing in 1995, we asked: "Is it possible to reproduce in white communities the structural circumstances under which many blacks live?" Chapter 5 gave a mostly negative answer, as did our earlier work in 1995, Daniel P. Moynihan in 1965, and St. Clair Drake and Horace R. Cayton in 1945 by drawing on the Chicago School.[18] Ultimately this means that to compare predominantly minority neighborhoods to white neighborhoods is to compare apples and oranges on key social predictors of violence. In other words, to test the racial invariance thesis by selecting on comparable neighborhoods necessarily sets aside the large majority of *non*poor white neighborhoods that have no black counterpart, leading to comparison neighborhoods that are in a real sense "outliers" or phantoms. A paradox of sorts thus emerges—where studies have compared appropriate points in the ecological distribution where blacks and whites are similarly situated, there is little evidence that the neighborhood causes of violence are distinctly different. But these comparisons camouflage the larger reality of how race organizes the spatial dynamics of neighborhood inequality in the metropolitan system.

To better understand how spatial externalities are situated against a regime of racial and ethnic segregation, I examined neighborhoods divided into race/ethnic categories: (1) at least 75 percent white, (2) at least 75 percent black, (3) at least 75 percent Latino, and (4) mixed/other. As Mary Pattillo-McCoy argued in her ethnography of a Chicago South Side community in *Black Picket Fences*, the black middle class is economically disadvantaged compared to the white middle class because of its spatial proximity to the ghetto.[19] The PHDCN data show that this extends across the entire city—even white working-class areas do better than the highest-income black neighborhoods when it comes to the economic status of near neighbors. An important additional finding, however, is that the idea of spatial vulnerability extends to key social processes even *within* the black middle class. Among neighborhoods with high collective efficacy measured using both community surveys (up to 2002), virtually all predominantly white neighborhoods (95 percent) were situated ecologically near other high-efficacy neighborhoods compared to less than half of the black and Latino neighborhoods. Because of larger processes of segregation and migration that will be explored more in the next chapter, minority neighborhoods are thus quite vulnerable spatially even when they have high levels of collective efficacy. Seen from the opposite perspective of what might be called "free-rider" spatial advantage, among neighborhoods with *low* collective efficacy, over half (60 percent) of white neighborhoods were nonetheless still proximate to high collective efficacy, compared to a only quarter of Latino neighborhoods and less than 20 percent of black neighborhoods.[20]

The implication is sobering: when African American neighborhoods (and, to a lesser extent, Latino neighborhoods) generate collective efficacy, or when they achieve middle-class status, their residents still face the added challenge of being situated in a wider spatial environment characterized by social disadvantage in addition to economic disadvantage. The situation of white neighborhoods is nearly the opposite—even when they are at high risk because of internal characteristics, their residents benefit from high levels of control and cohesion in nearby areas, as well as economic privilege. In a real sense, then, the data show that *white neighborhoods are benefiting from their neighbors despite low internal contribution to the collective good.*

Ecological dissimilarity is thus even more important than most previous research would have predicted. The evidence implies that the differing spatial environments of black and white neighborhoods play a role at least equal to that of internal structural characteristics, including concentrated disadvantage, in generating racial inequalities. How do these spatial differences come about? I examine this issue in chapters 11 and 12 by examining how black, white, and Latino residential mobility within and outside of Chicago over time creates spatial flows of racial inequality. As argued in chapter 6, social-psychological mechanisms linked to perceived disorder may be a key to further advances in explaining why people move or choose to stay in neighborhoods of a particular racial or immigrant configuration, in the process contributing to continued spatial disadvantage and ecological dissimilarity by race in the American city.

Immigration as a Spatially Shaped Social Process

The United States is becoming increasingly diverse ethnically, not just in our nation's cities but in suburban and rural areas as well.[21] Latino Americans are now the largest minority group at almost 15 percent of the population, and immigration has neared peak levels historically. Some 12 percent of the current population is foreign born, and over half are from Spanish-speaking Latin America. Although the Sampson-Wilson thesis and the spatial interpretation of it have been mainly about blacks and whites, can the "racial invariance" thesis be applied to ethnicity and crime? And what role does space play? Combining answers, I argue here that Latino immigration is deeply linked to processes of spatial diffusion, with surprising results for cities like Chicago.

The first data of relevance is that homicide among Latino Americans follows the same general pattern as among blacks and whites in terms of the predictive power of concentrated disadvantage, even though other predictors of Latino violence are somewhat unique. In particular, the basic links among economic deprivation and homicide are similar for blacks, Haitians, and Latinos.[22] Thus it appears that the racial invariance thesis may be extended to ethnic invariance in community-level causes of violence, when it comes to disadvantage.

But second, ethnicity and immigration bring in new issues that transcend race and bear directly on the spatial logic of the city. Consider the so-called Latino paradox, whereby Latinos do much better on various social indicators, including violence, than blacks and apparently even whites, given relatively high levels of disadvantage. The concentration of immigrants also appears to tell a very different story with respect to violence than the concentration of African Americans. Using the PHDCN, Jeffrey Morenoff, Stephen Raudenbush, and I found a significantly lower rate of violence among Mexican Americans compared to blacks and whites.[23] A major reason for this is that more than a quarter of all those of Mexican descent were born abroad, and more than half lived in neighborhoods where the majority of residents were also Mexican. In particular, first-generation immigrants (those born outside the United States) were 45 percent less likely to commit violence than third-generation Americans, adjusting for individual, family, and neighborhood background. Second-generation immigrants were 22 percent less likely to commit violence than the third generation. This pattern held true for non-Hispanic whites and blacks as well. Most relevant here, we showed that living in a neighborhood of concentrated immigration was directly associated with lower violence (again, after taking into account a host of correlated factors, including poverty and an individual's immigrant status). Hence immigration appeared "protective" against violence.[24]

The spatial implications of these findings are far reaching when set against the backdrop of one of the most notable social changes to visit the United States in recent decades. Foreign immigration especially from Mexico to the United States rose sharply in the 1990s, as did its concentration in immigrant enclaves in large cities. Overall, the foreign-born population increased by more than 50 percent in just ten years, to over thirty million by 2000. A report by the Pew Hispanic Center found that immigration grew most significantly in the mid-1990s and hit its peak at the end of the decade, when the national homicide rate plunged to levels not seen since the 1960s. Immigrant flows have receded since 9/11 but remain high, while the national homicide rate leveled off and recently has been creeping up.[25] The pattern upends popular stereotypes. Among the public, policy makers, and many academics, a common expectation is that the concentration of immigrants and the influx of foreigners drive up disorder and crime because of the assumed propensities of these groups to commit crimes and settle in poor, presumably disorganized communities. This belief is so pervasive that, as shown in chapter 6, the neighborhood concentration of Latinos strongly predicts perceptions of disorder no matter what the actual amount of disorder or the rate of reported crimes. Yet increases in immigration are correlated with *less* crime, and immigrants appear to be less violent than those born in America, particularly when they live in neighborhoods with high numbers of other immigrants.

The result is that we are witnessing a scenario both similar to and different than early twentieth-century America. Then, too, growth in immigration, along with ethnic diversity more generally, was commonly associated with increasing crime and formed a building block for the "social disorganization" theory a la chapter 2. The nation's largest cities at the time were virtual poster children for the theory, as they received an influx of European immigrants. Yet even then some criminologists questioned the immigration link and pointed instead to social change rather than the criminal propensity of first-generation immigrants.[26] Today immigration flows are radically different in origin, but New York, a leading magnet for immigration, has for a decade ranked as one of America's safest cities. Crime in Los Angeles dropped considerably in the late 1990s and 2000s, as it did in other cities with a large Hispanic population such as San Jose, Dallas, and Phoenix. The same can be said for cities along the border, like El Paso and San Diego, which have ranked as low-crime areas for some time. Cities of concentrated immigration are some of the safest places around and many decaying inner-city areas gained population in the 1990s and became more vital, in large part through the process of immigrant diffusion. Chicago once again is not unique, as crime dropped in the late 1990s as immigration surged. One of the most thriving areas of economic activity in the entire Chicago area, second only to the famed Magnificent Mile of Michigan Avenue, is the 26th Street corridor in Little Village.

These kinds of economic and demographic changes are a major social force, and immigrants aren't the only beneficiaries—native-born blacks, whites, and other traditional groups in the United States have been exposed to the gains associated with lower crime, such as decreases in segregation, decreases in concentrated poverty, and increases in the economic and civic health of central cities, to name just a few. For the first time in New York City's history the income of blacks in Queens has surpassed that of whites, for example, with the surge in the black middle class driven largely by the successes of black immigrants from the West Indies. There are many inner-city neighborhoods rejuvenated by immigration besides Queens and the Lower West Side of Chicago. From Bushwick in Brooklyn to Miami to large swaths of south central Los Angeles and the rural South, to pockets of the North and South sides of Chicago, immigration is reshaping America. It follows that the spatial "externalities" associated with immigration are multiple in character and constitute a plausible mechanism to explain some of the ecological variation in crime rates of *all* groups in the host society.

There are important implications to this line of argument. Simply adjusting for things like economic revitalization, urban change, and other seemingly confounding explanations is not supported from a causal explanation standpoint because they would instead be mediators or conduits of immigration effects—themselves part of the pathway of explanation. To the extent that immigration is causally bound up with major social changes and processes of spatial diffusion that are in turn part of the explanatory process of reduced crime, estimating only "direct" effects of immigration will give us the wrong answer. This in fact is the tack that much research takes instead of carefully defining the mediating pathways of explanation. Moreover, applying a spatial logic of externalities leads to the hypothesis that the salubrious effects of immigration are magnified in certain regions or spatial regimes of the city, such as formerly segregated "ghettos" that are being economically rejuvenated through inmigration. Working- class white areas that have not recently experienced much ethnic diversity may also benefit from increases in immigration. By this account it is not just spatial proximity that matters; rather, spatial location plays a role in strengthening or weakening the effects of immigration diffusion.

A recent paper with Corina Graif supports this line of thinking. The overall pattern we found was that *increases* in immigration and language diversity over the decade of the 1990s predicted *decreases* in neighborhood homicide rates in the late '90s and up to 2006, adjusting for a host of internal characteristics. This is a robust finding based on within-neighborhood comparisons that account for alternative explanations rooted in unmeasured factors about the community.[27] In particular, examining changes in crime associated with changes in immigration, we can adjust for fixed (or stable) effects of the neighborhood. I focus here on language diversity because it more directly taps the idea of diffusion and cultural contact among different groups. Analogous to the concept of "treatment heterogeneity" in the medical literature, our analysis revealed that the *magnitude* of the immigrant diversity effect on homicide varied significantly and quite substantially, in some cases exhibiting countervailing effects depending on spatial location.

Figure 10.3 displays the striking variability in pattern—there is distinct spatial heterogeneity across the city beyond what we would expect based on random variation. The white shading on the map reflects areas of no significant patterning in the data, while the darker areas reflect neighborhoods with increasingly significant associations of changes in language diversity with decreases in homicide, adjusting for disadvantage, residential stability, population density, time-invariant

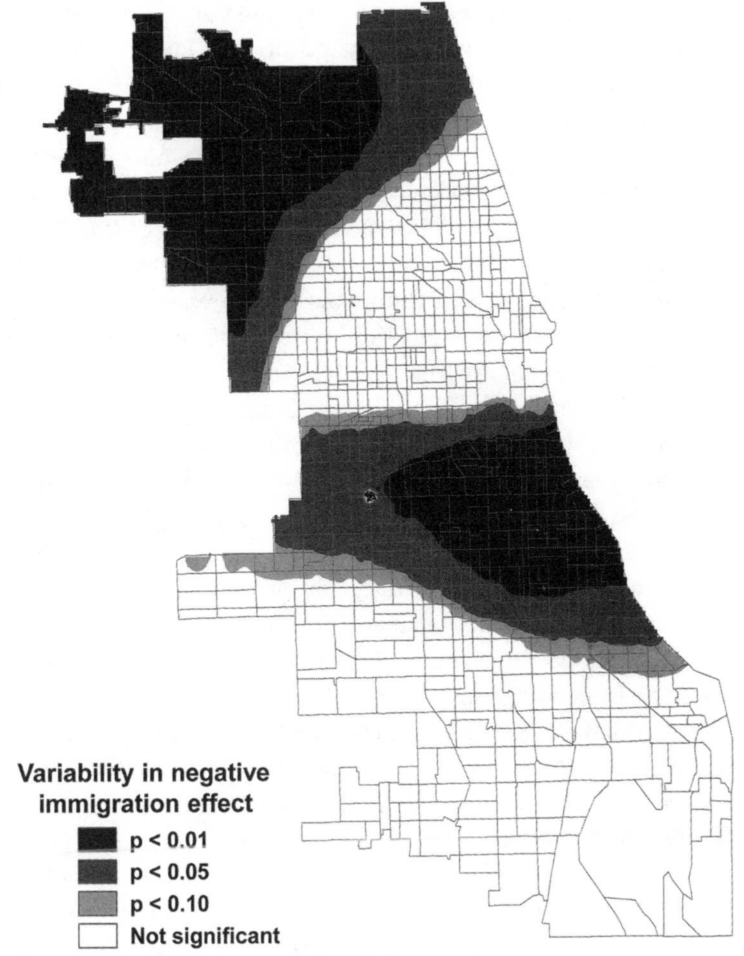

FIGURE 10.3. Spatial variability in the effects of changes in language diversity, 1990–2000, on changes in homicide from 1995 through 2006 (controls for concentrated disadvantage, residential stability, population density, and spatial error)

("character"-based) factors internal to the neighborhood, *and* spatial spillover. Immigration-related increases are linked to the biggest crime decreases in the middle and near southern sections of Chicago that are proximate to the center of Mexican immigration, and in the far northwestern areas of the city that have historically been predominantly white.[28]

Where local coefficients are most attenuated or insignificant tends to be in parts of Chicago with recent histories of Puerto Rican settlement (Humboldt Park, parts of West Town) or black segregation (East and West Garfield Park), or magnets for young urban professionals (Near North, Loop, Lincoln Park). But parts of the white-shaded areas are quite diverse (Uptown, Lakeview) or have long histories of European immigration. One speculation is that for many areas of Chicago's North Side *changes* in immigration simply have less influence in large part because there is already an institutionalized culture and organizational infrastructure supporting population diversity of many stripes. In the traditional black belt of the Near South Side (e.g., Oakland, Grand Boulevard, Washington Park) and in the traditionally white areas of the Far Northwest Side, by contrast, increases in immigration may be relatively more noticeable and consequential for sparking economic improvements and new businesses.

What is puzzling is the large number of areas on the Far South Side that are not diverse historically and many of which remain segregated racially. It is possible that the immigrant diffusion has simply not reached this part of the city yet; the Far South Side is geographically a fairly isolated region and distant from the engines of economic growth that define the bustling Latino centers of immigration in the middle part of the city (e.g., in Pilsen and Little Village). If this logic is correct, the spread from the center of Mexican immigration may soon yield spillover "immigration effects" in areas such as Lawndale, pushing north and further south into Englewood and beyond. Already the Latino population has pushed into the west suburbs, defining the character of places like Cicero. Figure 10.3 is consistent with this prediction. Whatever the mechanisms, the data suggest that in certain communities of Chicago, immigration's effects are muted and in others the influence is heightened, meaning that spatial location conditions the overall relationship between immigration and homicide. This is one more way that spatial context matters beyond local borders, one that may even help us understand national patterns of societal change.

Spatial-Cultural Penetration—Societal Renewal?

Because immigration leads to the spread of diverse and formerly external cultures, this logically implies a cultural overtone to the spatial process of diffusion. Quite simply, immigrant penetration into formerly "native" areas may contribute to lower crime if immigrant cultures are less encouraging of violence and crime. It's no secret, after all, that for a long time the United States has been a high-violence society, with many scholars positing a subculture or code of the streets as its main cause. In one influential version, shared expectations for demanding respect and "saving face" lead participants in the "street culture" of poor inner cities to react violently to perceived slights, insults, and otherwise petty encounters that make up the rounds of daily life.[29] But according to the logic of this theory, if one does not share the cultural attribution or perceived meaning of the event, violence is less likely. Outsiders to the culture, that is, are unlikely to be caught in the vicious cycles of interaction (and reaction) that promote violence.

The penetration of immigrants throughout the United States, including rural areas and the South, represents a process of cultural diffusion with spatial ramifications. A possible result is that American culture is being "diluted." Some of the most voracious critiques of immigration have embraced this line of argument. The late Samuel Huntington is a well-known example of those who claim the very essence of American identity is at stake because of increasing diversity and immigration, especially from Mexico.[30] He may be right, but the diagnosis might not be so bad if one of the defining features of American culture is a frontier mentality that endorses and perpetuates codes of violence. I concede this to Huntington. If immigration can be said to have brought violence to America, it most likely came with another form of spatial diffusion when (white) Irish and Scottish immigrants settled in the rural South in the 1700s and 1800s. Robert Nisbett and Dov Cohen present intriguing evidence that in areas with little state power to command compliance with the law, the tradition of frontier justice carried over from rural Europe took hold, with a heavy emphasis on retaliation and the use of violence to settle disputes, represented most clearly in the culture of dueling.[31]

In today's society, then, I hypothesize that immigration and the increasing cultural diversity that accompanies it generate sorts of "conflicts of culture" that lead not to increased crime but more nearly the opposite. In other words, immigration in the current era may be leading to the greater visibility of competing nonviolent mores that affect not just immigrant communities but diffuse through social interactions to

FIGURE 10.4. Immigrants reject criminal stereotype, Chicago, 2006. Photograph by Seth Anderson. Reproduced under Attribuition-ShareAlike 2.0 Generic Creative Commons license.

depress violent conflict in general.[32] Recent findings showing the spread of immigration to all parts of America, including rural areas of the Midwest and South, give credence to this argument. Figure 10.3 supports a reduced version of this argument when it comes to immigration diffusion in Chicago, with the effects of immigration being magnified in the whiter and blacker areas of the city.

The emerging story is therefore complex but provocative. Although concentrated disadvantage and neighborhood social processes predict rates of violence in similar ways across race and ethnic groups, the patterns for Latino Americans and immigration go against the grain of popular beliefs. A major task for future research is to solve the so-called Latino paradox and explain how immigration makes it a predictor of lower violence. This task is made more difficult by the perceptual biases against immigrant concentration demonstrated in chapter 6 and the radically different but textbook-familiar spatial pattern that dominated early twentieth-century America, where spreading immigration was also thought to be linked with increasing crime and therefore became a founding basis for the social disorganization theory of crime. But the facts show that immigration and diversity do not invariably lead to crime. The spatial diffusion of immigration is instead linked to decreases in crime. Not only are immigrants and Latinos less violent, but this quality is amplified when they live in concentrated immigrant areas. As the Chicago-area protestors in figure 10.4 directly communicate, immigrants are keenly aware of the power of cultural stereotypes and how they serve to reinforce existing dominance hierarchies.

Conclusion

Not everything is spatially linked, but most things are: Waldo Tobler was right. Consistent with findings from earlier chapters but pushing spatial logic in new directions, this chapter has demonstrated five general patterns and yielded implications for understanding the changing city of Chicago and perhaps cities elsewhere.

First, spatial clustering is not just a visual phenomenon or trick of the eye. For a number of key community-level factors, especially economic disadvantage, residential stability, immigration, collective efficacy, altruism, and crime, spatial interdependence is significant, strong, and durable over time using formal tests. Second, these patterns are not simply due to a "kinds of neighborhoods" explanation, which would predict that if we account for the composition and internal characteristics of the neighborhood, then spatial dependence disappears (what is known as a "neighborhood heterogeneity" argument). To the contrary, adjusting for the rich set of neighborhood characteristics developed throughout the book barely puts a dent in the magnitude of spatial dependence. This result tells us that there is something fundamental about social connections and interactions across ecological borders.

Third, although there are limitations of my data, a number of analyses here and in related papers are consistent in supporting the idea that the social characteristics of a "neighborhood's neighbors" independently explain variation in the outcomes of a focal neighborhood. This pattern emerges very strongly for crime, collective efficacy, and disadvantage. Fourth, spatial proximity does not change the pattern of effects of internal characteristics, but it adds a separate layer of explanation. A series of tests controlling for spatially linked autocorrelation revealed that the major results in previous chapters are upheld. "Extralocal" spatial processes can then be considered a new layer of effects added on to the durable community processes identified in section 3 of the book.

The final set of results point to the importance of space in explaining the effects of racial inequality and immigrant diffusion. The "spatial externalities" perspective on racial disadvantage investigates how extra-neighborhood and citywide spatial dynamics create racial inequalities in a wide variety of social processes that are potentially more consequential than the ones already at play within neighborhoods. As I have argued, this view has direct implications for understanding the persistence of violence, disorder, and outmigration in poor black neighborhoods and the ever-present threat of violence in what otherwise would be characterized as middle-class areas. The spatial logic developed in the chapter also bears on the immigration debate. At the neighborhood level in Chicago, immigration increases are linked to *lower* crime, especially in poorer areas and those with histories of racial segregation and exclusion. Comparing figure 10.3 with the data in chapter 5 supports the idea that increasing immigration may be working to reduce segregation among blacks, whites, and Latinos.

Overall, then, spatial processes come in many forms and seem to be a pervasive part of any attempt to take a bird's-eye or holistic view of the contemporary metropolis. But the kinds of spatial processes considered in this chapter were still of a certain kind, looking to the neighbors of neighborhoods. Higher-order links that transcend spatial proximity, such as networks that span miles and leap across adjacent neighborhoods, or residential moves to neighborhoods in the far-flung suburbs, are equally if not more important. The rest of this section therefore probes the knitting together of the city's social fabric, with the next two chapters confronting the social structure of Chicago constructed simultaneously from the bottom up (individual selection) and top down (structurally), both part of the ongoing effects of neighborhood and larger spatial contexts.

11 Trading Places

Experiments and Neighborhood Effects in a Social World

> Why, then, would members of the city's ghettos seek to embrace a pathology of the suburb in exchange for their own?
>
> Kenneth Clark, *Dark Ghetto* (1965)

A foggy picture has emerged from one of the nation's largest attempts to eradicate concentrated poverty. Moving to Opportunity is an experiment designed to lift poor families out of concentrated poverty and into the American Dream.[1] Inspired by the landmark Gautreaux housing program that helped poor families move from Chicago's racially segregated ghetto to the white and presumably better-off suburbs in the 1970s, the federal government initiated a lottery in the mid-1990s in Chicago, NYC, Los Angeles, Boston, and Baltimore. Winners received housing vouchers redeemable only in low-poverty neighborhoods.

Despite high expectations, Moving to Opportunity (MTO) has not had the transformative effects intended. With some exceptions, researchers have reported disappointingly modest or no improvements in the later wellbeing of children, and in some cases perverse effects—boys seem to fare worse in their new neighborhoods in the short run. Moreover, some recent critics assert that the migration of public-housing residents is increasing social problems in destination areas. Writing in the *Atlantic*, for example, Hanna Rosin boldly asserted that the migration of poor public-housing residents from inner-city Memphis had the unintended result of dispersing crime and disorder to new areas on the city's outskirts, potentially setting in motion a new cycle of concentrated disadvantage.[2] Did something go wrong and, if so, why? The answers bear directly on future choices in housing, neighborhood, and economic policy.

The MTO also exposes a deep divide in the social sciences on how to think about neighborhood effects and thus the questions raised in this book. On one side, MTO publications and presentations appear to have cast doubt on the general thesis that neighborhoods matter in the lives of poor individuals. With the weight of the experimental method behind them, broad assertions have been made about the best way to conduct research, the validity of theories of neighborhood effects writ large, and the direction that policy should take. Consider, for example, the assertion that because MTO "used randomization to solve the selection problem," it offers "the clearest answer so far to the threshold question of whether important neighborhood effects exist."[3] Or consider the headline: "Improved Neighborhoods Don't Raise Academic Achievement" from the National Bureau of Economic Research.[4] On another side, critics charge that the small differences in neighborhood racial integration induced by MTO's housing vouchers do not provide a robust test of neighborhood effects in the first place.[5]

MTO therefore motivates me to interrogate further the nature of neighborhood effects, "selection bias," and, on a fundamental level, the social structure of inequality, setting the stage for analyses in the following chapters as well. By examining residential moves that connect far-flung neighborhoods, my analysis in this chapter takes another step toward a bird's-eye view of how the metropolis is interconnected. Ironically, we will see that the individualistic intervention of MTO provides an intriguing vehicle for observing the reproduction of neighborhood inequality.

Unraveling MTO and Its Logic

Families below the poverty line and living in concentrated poverty (40 percent or greater) in five cities in the mid-1990s were deemed eligible to apply for housing vouchers. Those that did so were randomly assigned to one of three groups: experimental, Section 8, or control. The experimental group was offered a housing voucher that, if used, had to be applied toward residence in a neighborhood with less than 10 percent poverty. Counseling and assistance in housing relocation were also provided. Those in the Section 8 group were offered vouchers with no restrictions imposed on where they could move. The controls were given no treatment. The baseline population eligible for the voucher study was not only poor but predominantly black or Latino, and it comprised mainly female-headed families on welfare living in concentrated public housing—or what many would term the "inner-city ghetto"—circa 1995–97.

Five sets of outcomes have been studied—adult economic self-sufficiency, mental health, physical health, education, and risky behavior. No significant differences between experimentals and controls have been reported by MTO researchers for adult economic self-sufficiency or physical health. Significant positive effects of the MTO intervention have been reported for adult mental health, young female education, physical and mental health of female adolescents, and risky behavior (e.g., crime, delinquency) among young girls. Adverse effects emerge for the physical health and delinquency of adolescent males in the MTO sample. And null effects have been reported for a number of outcomes, such as cognitive achievement. Thus the MTO results to date are mixed rather than negative—sometimes neighborhood effects matter, sometimes they do not.

In the counterfactual paradigm implied by MTO, the question is whether an individual residing in a poor neighborhood would follow a different course if he or she in fact resided in a nonpoor neighborhood. Thus individuals are the unit of analysis, and selection bias is the main concern. Randomly allocating individuals to neighborhood treatment is the canonical scientific way to equate otherwise dissimilar people, permitting estimation of an average causal effect. Of course, MTO did not (and could not) assign persons where to live. But they did induce movement through the random assignment of housing vouchers.

A separate question and one of several advanced in this book is how to explain variations in rates of social behavior across neighborhoods. Here the experimental counterfactual and "manipulability" is not about individuals. Rather, neighborhoods would be randomly allocated to treatment and control conditions and a macrolevel intervention introduced. Consistent with ecometrics, this counterfactual takes seriously the analysis of neighborhoods as important units of analysis *in their own right*, especially with regard to social and institutional processes.

It is important to emphasize that a theory aiming to explain concurrent neighborhood-level variability is logically not the same enterprise as explaining how neighborhoods exert long-term effects on individual development. For example, we may have a theory of social control that accurately explains variation in crime event rates across neighborhoods regardless of who commits the acts (residents or otherwise), and another that accurately explains how neighborhoods influence the individual behavior of their residents *no matter where they are*. In the latter case neighborhoods have developmental effects; in the former, situational effects.[6] One is not mutually exclusive of the other. The logical separation of explanation is reinforced by considering routine activity patterns in contemporary cities, where residents typically traverse the boundaries of multiple neighborhoods during the course of a day.

In short, if we want to learn about the effects of neighborhood interventions in an experimental design, the best method is to randomly assign interventions at the level of neighborhoods or other ecological units, not individuals. Examples include the random assignment of neighborhoods to receive a network-based AIDS intervention, community policing, or an effort to mobilize collective efficacy. Here the theoretically implied unit of intervention is the community itself. To this day, even though little heralded, interventions such as the Chicago Area Project survive.[7] If rates of sexually transmitted diseases or public violence were significantly reduced after the randomized interventions, or if dissimilar outcomes in particular were affected (e.g., civic trust, social interactions), we may then speak of an emergent neighborhood-level effect. From a public policy perspective, neighborhood or population-level interventions may be more cost effective than those targeted to individuals, an important point to which I return in the final chapter.[8]

What Is the Question, and for Whom?

Another fact—regardless of the level of intervention—is that MTO restricted itself to a narrow slice of the population. Those eligible to participate in MTO included poor families with children living in public housing and in neighborhoods with over 40 percent in poverty. In cities like Chicago, this meant virtually all black (98 percent), female-headed (96 percent), nonmarried (93 percent), and extremely poor households, with mean total income less than $8,000.[9] To get an idea of how small a slice this restriction reflects, I calculated the falloff from a representative sample after applying an MTO "adjustment" to the PHDCN study of this book. At baseline there was not a good measure of living in public housing, so I selected those families headed by a black, nonmarried female, receiving welfare, and living in a neighborhood with greater than 40 percent poverty. Based on published MTO data this selection characterizes the MTO Chicago site—if anything it is probably a generous definition, as it includes some nonpublic housing families. Out of approximately 4,600 families, 139 fit the MTO bill. When weighted to account for the stratified sampling scheme, 5 percent of the PHDCN population is MTO equivalent. These MTO "equivalents" establish just how far into the extreme tail of the poverty and race distributions the MTO study reaches. It is thus reasonable to conclude that 5 percent of the population does not make a general test of neighborhood effects.

As poor MTO families move from one neighborhood to another, entire bundles of variables are also changing at once, making it difficult to disentangle change in neighborhood poverty from simultaneous changes in correlated structural and cultural features of the environment. Furthermore, because moving is a major and possibly disruptive life event that is associated with negative outcomes for many children, neighborhood change is confounded with the causal effects of moving. As a result, MTO cannot, experimentally at least, separate the impact of moving itself from changes in neighborhood context. For similar reasons the design of the MTO does not permit estimation of the impact of moving into poverty or the effect of neighborhood change that occurs around those families that never move.

We can now better appreciate the causal question MTO asks. The study is designed to answer a policy question: *Does the offer of a housing voucher only redeemable in a lower-poverty neighborhood affect the later outcomes of the extreme poor?* I would add: *and those who have grown up in poverty and may have already experienced its developmental effects?* The MTO question is important and of substantial interest to policy makers who are considering whether to provide vouchers to induce mobility among the very poor. But housing policy for a select group of the population should not overshadow numerous other questions derived from neighborhood-effects theory that are at stake. The claim that MTO is scientifically superior because it experimentally addresses the "threshold" question of whether neighborhoods matter in the first place is only correct to the extent that: (1) we consider the voucher-induced mobility question answered by MTO to be broadly and accurately reflective of neighborhood contextual effects; (2) we stick to individual-level inference and set aside neighborhood-level experiments (whether conceptual or actual); and (3) we bracket theory of the mechanisms that produce neighborhood effects *and* selection into the treatment—the "why" question.

Although the evidence and theoretical logic lead me to reject adopting any of these positions, it remains the case that MTO is a major advance owing to its ability to solve the perceived problem of omitted variable (or selection) bias. Selection bias in observational research raises a hornet's nest of analytic problems, which MTO does address (at the individual level of inference) by balancing or adjusting through randomization "unobserved" characteristics. The randomized design of MTO thus sets it apart from research that posits ex post explanations derived from analysis of observational data that uses control variables to adjust for potential confounding. In evaluating observational studies of this type, social scientists worry mainly about *omitted variable bias* in promoting experiments like MTO. Their concern is that there is some (undefined or unobserved) quantity out there that we have failed to measure or cannot measure.

Yet we should worry as much if not more about what I have called the *included variable bias* problem—one that, while more subtle, wreaks just as much havoc with observational research. Many or most of the covariates that make their way into observational studies represent potential causal pathways by which the neighborhood may influence the outcome of interest. For example, in an attempt to account for characteristics of individuals and families that might influence both selection into poor neighborhoods *and* individual outcomes, observational studies often include control variables such as income, family structure, depression, health problems, criminality, physical disabilities, education, and peer influence. But if one is to interpret resulting estimates as a test of neighborhood effects, one must make the assumption that all such controls are pretreatment covariates—unaffected by an individual's current or prior neighborhood. This is an unwarranted assumption given the research reviewed or reported in previous chapters and a body of theory positing neighborhood effects on health, family norms and composition, adult labor market outcomes, and more. MTO underscores my point by showing that improved neighborhoods lower depression, which in turn is a major predictor of later life outcomes.[10] Controlling for depression in observational studies, which is usually thought to account for selection bias in neighborhood effects, would instead distort a potential pathway by which neighborhoods may influence developmental outcomes, ironically *inducing rather than reducing* bias.[11] The introduction of time-varying adjustments can make things even worse, although there are promising methods that can integrate a dynamic life-course framework with neighborhood effects.

Before turning to this line of inquiry and a revised approach to selection as a social process, it is necessary to assess claims about the MTO treatment. An experiment is only as good as its treatment, after all. Understanding the nature of the treatment in MTO is essential to understanding its meaning and empirical relevance for neighborhood effects.

Moving to Inequality

The change in neighborhood environments among families receiving vouchers has been questioned because the experimental group moved from and to largely segregated black areas subject to the reinforcing disadvantages highlighted in the work of William Julius Wilson and Douglas Massey. The initial experimental-control-group differences in poverty diminished over time as families increasingly moved back into neighborhoods similar to those at baseline. Further, children in the MTO experimental group attended schools that differed little from those in the control group in terms of racial composition, average test score performance, and teacher/pupil ratio. The critics Susan Clampet-Lundquist and Douglas S. Massey were thus not surprised that moving *within* segregated neighborhood contexts, despite improvements in economic status, would produce small effects on adult economic sufficiency. In response, Jens Ludwig et al. claim that large differences in neighborhood poverty were produced—the intended goal of MTO.[12] When asked to respond to this debate, I argued that it is not racial composition itself that matters, but its entanglement with resource deprivation and disadvantage in the American city.[13] As Clampet-Lundquist and Massey similarly note, social allocation processes in the U.S., with its particular history of race relations, has led to persistent sorting along racial-economic cleavages that disadvantage blacks.

To shed light on the race-disadvantage nexus relative to poverty and the MTO debate, I examine two distinct issues and kinds of data. I first analyze the structure of residential moves of MTO participants across multiple social dimensions and levels of neighborhood, both static and dynamic. Second, I consider the implications of social-ecological confounding for selection bias more generally by analyzing patterns beyond the MTO sample. I analyze data from the Chicago MTO site because it permits a strategic comparison with PHDCN. Further, Chicago was the site of much of Wilson's *The Truly Disadvantaged*, which motivated the original design of MTO. My key goal is to examine *neighborhood attainment* as the outcome of the MTO treatment, not individual characteristics such as crime or economic self-sufficiency. This analytic move is consistent with my goal in this section of the book to assess higher-order structural connections, in this case formed by individual decisions and residential moves.

If the MTO intervention made a fundamental or lasting difference in residential location, this will be reflected in where people are living several years out and not just a short time after the experiment, when voucher moves were restricted. To test this, I examine neighborhoods of residence at the follow-up in 2002, about six to seven years after the experiment began. The average number of years lived at the destination address was 3.38 for experimentals and 3.29 for controls, a substantial rather than fleeting amount of time. (The difference between groups is not significantly different.) I start with a measure of concentrated disadvantage by drawing on chapter 5, additional analysis of Chicago and the U.S., and the long line of research reviewed in chapter 2 that demonstrates the clustering of racial and socioeconomic segregation across time and multiple levels of ecological analysis.[14]

MTO began with high-poverty neighborhoods, which in Chicago were clustered in a small number of census tracts on the South Side of Chicago in the Grand Boulevard, Douglas, and Oakland communities—more or less Bronzeville in Drake and Cayton's terms. Where did the take-up families move? First, there was no treatment difference for staying in metropolitan Chicago—92 percent of each group remained in the area. Second, I have shown that even if we consider the entire metropolitan area, there is not much difference in the patterning of where people moved, controls and experimentals alike.[15] Both groups tended to move southward from the inner city to areas slightly better off but still relatively high in concentrated disadvantage.

To sharpen the portrait and provide a more conservative test, I consider here a new look at the experimental "compliers," those who used the MTO voucher to move to a lower-poverty neighborhood. This is a self-selected group that almost by definition should provide the biggest shift away from poverty. Figure 11.1 shows the location of compliers at the end of the MTO follow-up, mapped across the Chicago metro area shaded by the summary index of concentrated disadvantage, split into equal thirds based on the metropolitan distribution. Yet even for compliers—less than half of all those offered a voucher—movers spread outward from the inner city to final destinations that are similarly disadvantaged. Entire swaths of Chicago are simply untouched, as is most of the metro area. Like the controls and noncompliers, MTO compliers tended to move close by to other South Side Chicago communities in the upper range of concentrated disadvantage. Relatively few moved elsewhere, but when they did we see in figure 11.1 that the destinations form a systematic cluster of communities on the Northwest Side and close-in suburbs in the southern part of the metropolitan area, again qualitatively similar in disadvantage. The observed structure of movement is striking in its geographic spread to entrenched pockets of disadvantage. The modal picture for all groups is a dual migration southward along an upside-down T—*a spatial regime of concentrated disadvantage.*

There is thus clear evidence to justify concern about the MTO treatment. It induced residential outcomes over the long run that differ in poverty but not necessarily racial integration or the constellation of factors that define the concentration of disadvantage. I would further argue that even for poverty, the MTO differences are *one of degree, not kind*. For destination tracts, the experimental reduction was from 42 to 37 percent below poverty. This five-percentage-point reduction (or 15 percent, compliance adjusted) is statistically significant and consistent with prior MTO findings, but is the glass half empty or full? Consider that the experimentals were still living in neighborhoods that by most definitions had high poverty rates and at levels the average American will never experience. Aggregated across all five sites, the data also reveal a considerable (> 30 percent average) poverty rate for both groups and a nontrivial 20 percent poverty rate even for compliers. Segregation was barely nudged—both experimental and controls in Chicago lived at destination in areas that were almost 90 percent black.[16] At the other sites, average percent minority shares are over 80 percent for both groups.[17] Consistent with figure 11.1 and earlier results, comparing controls with

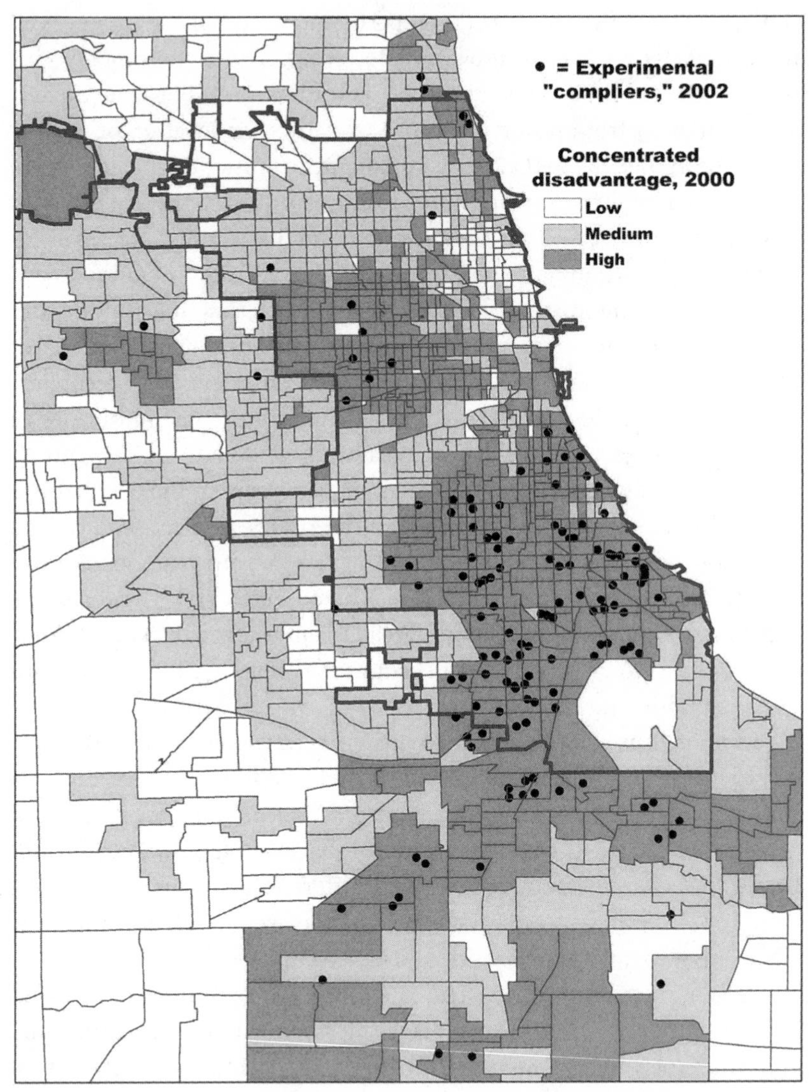

FIGURE 11.1. Residential movement of MTO experimental-group voucher users: destinations in the Chicago metropolitan area in 2002 by concentrated disadvantage

all experimentals, I conclude that while neighborhood poverty differs, as intended, in the end the MTO experimental differences in concentrated disadvantage are marginal overall when compared within the larger structural contexts of inequality.

A major claim of this book is that social and cultural mechanisms matter as much if not more than the standard neighborhood suspects of poverty and racial composition. Until now, the social fabric of neighborhoods has so far not been central to the MTO discussion. Using the community survey of Chicago from PHDCN in 2001–2 that closely matches the time of the MTO follow-up, I created neighborhood-level (vs. individual) measures of collective efficacy, intergenerational closure, legal cynicism, reciprocated exchange among neighbors, friend/kinship ties, tolerance of deviance, organizational participation, victimization, perceived violence, and disorder. For tracts in Chicago where police data were available, I also examined homicide and burglary rates in 2000–2002. Of a dozen characteristics measured independently from MTO, none were significantly different ($p < 0.05$) between the treatment and controls.[18] Limiting ourselves to Chicago reduces differences somewhat, given that experimentals were more likely to leave the city than controls (17 percent vs. 12 percent), but the similarity of neighborhood processes between randomization groups for the vast majority who stayed is evident.[19]

Finally, although neighborhoods are quite durable in their relative positioning over time (chapter 5), that does not imply an unchanging treatment. To date, the debate about MTO has proceeded largely as if the neighborhoods to which people move are sequentially static, like a pill. But neighborhoods have trajectories just like individuals. It follows that we need to consider more than just the level (even if interpolated over time) of neighborhood poverty. I might use a voucher to move to a lower-poverty neighborhood than that of a control member, for example, but that neighborhood may be on a downward trajectory (e.g., with declining house values), whereas the control neighborhood is stably poor. The question is whether there are treatment differences in the rate of change, and ultimately future viability, of neighborhoods. I therefore examine both raw and residual change in percent poverty, percent black, and concentrated disadvantage from 1990 to 2000 and points in between. Residual change offers us the unique advantage of looking at neighborhood-change trajectories after removing the effect of larger metropolitan dynamics.

The dynamic picture tells us a different story than the static. First, there are no significant differences between the treatment and control groups in raw changes in percent black or poverty, nor in residual changes in percent black or poverty. Second, there is a modest difference in changes in concentrated disadvantage, but in a direction that favors controls. On average, disadvantage was decreasing over time in Chicago, but the rate of decrease was *less* for the treatment group compared to the controls. This means that when trajectories of neighborhood change are the outcome criterion, the MTO experiment did not result in the treatment group ending up in better-off neighborhoods. Third, I examined change from 1995 to 2002 in the measures of neighborhood social processes noted above (e.g., cohesion, control). Again, *no change trajectory differed significantly by treatment group*. These results confirm the lack of an MTO treatment effect on contextual processes and dynamics of the neighborhood.[20]

Spatial Disadvantage

As demonstrated in the previous chapter, African Americans, including blacks in the middle class, face a unique risk of ecological proximity to disadvantage that goes well beyond local neighborhoods. The implication is straightforward: while the black poor might be able to move to a better-off census tract with an MTO voucher, that tract is still likely to be embedded in a larger area of poverty and crime, and therefore spatial disadvantage. In chapter 10 I presented strong evidence of neighborhood spillovers.

It follows that we need to consider more than just census tracts in any adjudication of MTO. I do so again by taking advantage of Chicago's local community areas that have well-known names and much more distinctive borders than census tracts, such as freeways, parks, and major streets (chapters 1 and 4). Although some community names and the ecological nature of their boundaries have undergone change, Chicago's community areas are still widely recognized by administrative agencies, local institutions concerned with service delivery, and residents alike. They also carry reputations that are reinforced in the media. I therefore recalibrated the movement in MTO by characteristics of community areas, relying on the finding that the vast majority of moves of both experimental and control groups are clustered within Chicago.

Although concentrated disadvantage was not greatly affected by the MTO treatment, I highlight here the effect on exposure to key social processes. One of the stated motivations of MTO was to reduce "social isolation" and increase social support to families. Another was to increase exposure to healthier environments for children and youth, and another was to move families to neighborhoods with greater capacity for establishing safety and social control. I directly assessed each of these for Chicago's seventy-seven communities. I first created a measure of the social support networks that community residents could draw upon to provide financial aid, job information, and personal advice.[21] Second, I created a measure of what I call "compromised health" based on independent archival records from the Illinois vital statistics. I calculated the infant mortality rate, low birth weight rate, and rate of teen births for 2003–5 for each community and combined them into an overall scale.[22] Third, I examined collective efficacy for each community.

Figure 11.2 displays the spatial network of connections from the MTO baseline tracts of origin. I seek the big picture on differences in outcome, in this case the density of social support in the destination communities (divided into equal thirds of low, medium, and high). I compare controls with experimentals to isolate the causal effect of the intervention, and I map flows both within and between neighborhoods to capture the dynamics of change. What we see again, although in a new light, is a striking social reproduction of social disadvantage among MTO participants, experimental and control members alike.[23] Indeed, the pattern of neighborhood flows is indistinguishable and suggests a profound structural constraint, whereby both controls and experimentals move disproportionately to *low-support areas*. Note also the large "churning" of movement along tracts within the larger community of origin and the dominant flows to areas further south in Chicago—almost all in the lowest third of social support networks. In a pattern of cumulative disadvantage, communities initially low in social support are the places drawing vulnerable MTO families that are in need of support systems. These same communities are highly circumscribed by concentrated disadvantage, as we would expect from figure 11.1.[24] MTO thus cannot be said to have overcome social isolation.

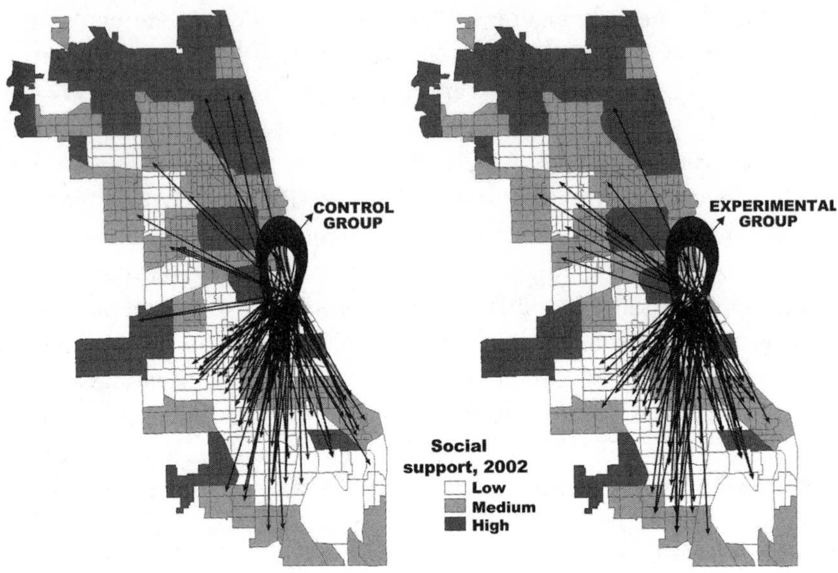

FIGURE 11.2. Residential flows of MTO families from origin to destination neighborhoods, 1995–2002, by density of social support networks in Chicago community areas (2002). Social support is classified in equal thirds. Loop arrows reflecting "churning" within the same neighborhood and ties between tracts are proportional to volume of movement.

The same story holds for the network flows of MTO participants according to compromised health and collective efficacy, factors that are at least as important as poverty and support networks. Maps not shown confirm the overlapping risks that MTO families face whether in the experimental group or not. Areas of the South and West sides that have high rates of infant mortality, low birth weight babies, and teen pregnancy are the attractors for MTO families, almost all of which are composed of single female heads. Another map shows that destination areas of both groups are relatively low in collective efficacy as well. In essence, moves cluster in systematic flows and social processes cluster, as do structural bases of inequality and place stratification. The result is that MTO controls and experimentals both tended to end up in areas characterized by concentrated disadvantage, racial segregation, low social support, compromised public health, and low collective efficacy (among other risks).[25]

Another way to consider population movement is to calculate the number of families each Chicago community area received as in-movers from the experimental and control groups, and then calculate a rank-order correlation. The resulting Spearman correlation is 0.79 ($p < 0.01$). Another is to calculate the "MTO penetration" to each community at risk, which I define as the number of MTO in-movers per hundred thousand residents as of 2000. When we direct our attention to the pure experimental comparison induced by MTO, we find that both groups not only end up in disadvantaged communities, they disproportionately move to the *same exact communities*. Clustering is surprisingly present even at the tract level. Over half (55 percent) of the experimentals ended up in just 4 percent of all possible tracts in the Chicago metropolitan area, while 55 percent of the control group ended up in 3 percent of all tracts. In network terms, the strong spatial concentration indicates the centrality of a relatively small core of neighborhoods that receives the majority of MTO families, regardless of treatment or complier status. At the other end, 51 percent of communities in Chicago received not a single MTO experimental participant. Approximately 57 percent saw no in-movement of the control group.

Correlations and percentages do not do justice to these patterns, so figure 11.3 plots this visually, showing the relationship between the MTO control and experimental-group penetration rate by community. One sees that the association is strongly positive, but dominated by Douglas and Oakland on the Near South Side, which together account for practically all of the moves. Even if I remove these two areas, the correlation is still high (0.70). Woodlawn, Washington Park, and Grand Boulevard, longstanding poor black communities, are next in the receiving line for MTO families. These five communities alone account for over 40 percent of the entire MTO penetration from the origin. The communities that receive experimental members as opposed to controls—such as Fuller Park, Roseland and South Shore—are hardly advantaged. The very poor community of Englewood is also seeing in-movement of voucher users and MTO families. The general mechanism of the poor getting poorer is revisited in chapter 16.

No matter how you cut it, then, the data show that sorting in MTO is highly structured by place. Is this unique to the MTO families? Figure 11.4 suggests not. Here I examine moving trajectories in the independent PHDCN sample *at the same time* among MTO "equivalents" as

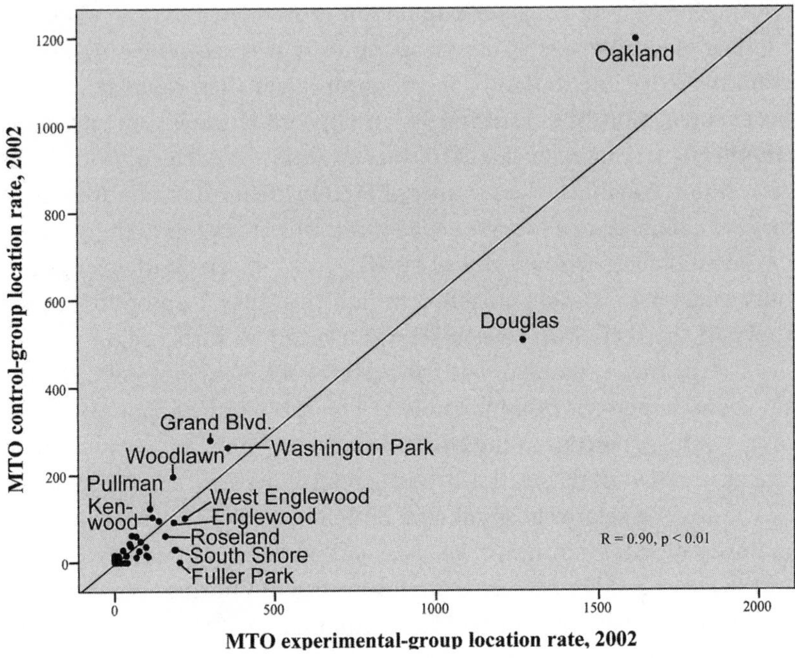

FIGURE 11.3. MTO penetration in Chicago communities by experimental status, 2002.

defined above. For comparison purposes I examined concentrated disadvantage and collective efficacy, with figure 11.4 presenting the latter results.[26] PHDCN poor families show a strikingly similar "churning" within neighborhoods. The origin community of MTO is captured by PHDCN on the Near South Side, where we see considerable within-community circulation, as well as moves further south to other disadvantaged neighborhoods, the same pattern produced by MTO flows. A West Side cluster and a Far North Side cluster are also observed. Not surprisingly, all the origin areas are low collective efficacy and poor. But since there was no voucher to limit where PHDCN families could move, the destination results are surprisingly constrained in neighborhood outcome, with almost all flows to low-collective-efficacy destinations as well.

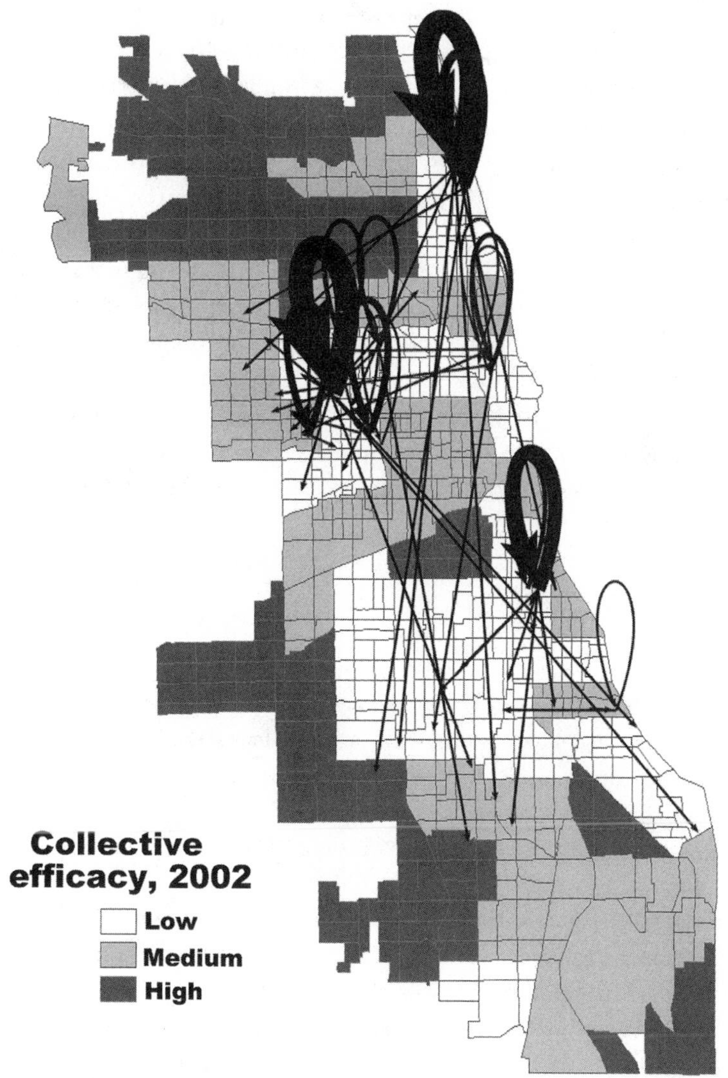

FIGURE 11.4. Neighborhood circulation flows of "MTO-equivalent" poor families in the PHDCN Longitudinal Cohort Study (N = 139), circa 1995–2002, by collective efficacy in Chicago community areas. Collective efficacy (CE) recoded into equal thirds. Lightest shading indicates "low" CE and darkest "high" CE. Loop arrows reflecting "churning" within the same neighborhood and ties between tracts are proportional to volume of movement.

In general, then, the hierarchy of places is enduring in both studies. Chicago is only one city, of course, and its take-up rate was lowest among MTO sites, but the basic pattern holds in the Baltimore MTO study too, and I would hypothesize similar patterns exist elsewhere.[27] At the national level, Sharkey has shown the intergenerational transmission of concentrated disadvantage, further demonstrating the durable lock that segregation by race and class has on trajectories of neighborhood attainment.[28] Whether in the experimental MTO or the observational PHDCN, poor people moved to inequality, with opportunities embedded in a rigid and likely reinforcing dynamic of metropolitan social structure. One way to think about this process is that there is something like a community chain to the movement of the poor. The replicating nature of moving decisions in MTO prompts a reconsideration of the typical ways of viewing selection bias in observational research and compliance in social experiments.

Compliance and Neighborhood Sorting

> It is often remarked how difficult it is to get a family to consent to move out of the slum no matter how advantageous the move may seem from the material point of view, and how much more difficult it is to keep them from moving back into the slum.
>
> Henry Zorbaugh, *The Gold Coast and the Slum* (1929)

As medical experiments have taught us, humans are agents with the decision-making power to accept or reject treatments—they can toss the pill in the toilet instead of swallowing. Statistics on the take-up rate show that a majority of MTO families who were offered a voucher did not actually use it. Families who used the voucher experienced less neighborhood poverty than the noncompliers, but the vast majority remained within a relatively short distance of their origin neighborhood. Moreover, many families moved back into poor neighborhoods that were similar to the ones in which they started, surprising many observers. Yet no one should be surprised. As far back as the 1920s, Zorbaugh noted the "pull" of the slum and how existing social ties kept people returning. As Kenneth Clark's quote at the beginning of this chapter suggests, it is only from a middle-class point of view, or what Zorbaugh called the "budget minded social agency," that the behavior of those who have grown up in poverty seems "incalculable."[29]

Does this self-selection within the treatment group pose problems for valid causal inference? Because of differential compliance, the "intent to treat" effect will significantly underestimate the "treatment effect on the treated" or the effect of actually moving. To cope with this challenge, MTO researchers have used the randomization of being offered a voucher as an "instrumental variable" to identify the impact of actually using the voucher. But in this case, valid causal inference depends on the assumption that the offer of a voucher will affect outcomes *only if participants use the voucher*. If this assumption is plausible, it supports the validity of inferences about the treatment effect on the treated (compliers)—those who would use the voucher if assigned to the experimental condition but who would not use the voucher if assigned to the control group. For example, by weighting the various outcomes according to the proportion of compliers, Ludwig et al. argue that the unbiased overall effect of the "bundled" MTO treatment can still be estimated. Viewed from the perspective of a social world, however, the instrumental variable method applied to MTO is problematic.

First and foremost, social interactions among MTO participants would constitute statistical "interference" in violation of the "stable unit treatment value assumption" (SUTVA) underlying experiments.[30] Ludwig et al. argue that the interference concern is mitigated by the small sample of MTO participants in destination neighborhoods. But the more relevant concern is the strong clustering in the *origin* neighborhoods. Suppose, for example, that I was a complier and moved further south in Chicago, as figures 11.1 to 11.4 showed is common, to satisfy the voucher requirement. If I or my children had friends or family back in the old neighborhood who were voucher eligible, and we complained about the hardship of moving or, to the contrary, expressed enthusiasm about the new neighborhood, these social interactions could have influenced moving decisions, destinations, and outcomes of those in our network—especially given the multiyear window of randomization (and thus lease-up) and the fact that many compliers drifted back to poor neighborhoods. Ludwig et al. assume that the intervention had no effect on noncompliers and that interference is unlikely because "fully 55%" reported no friends in baseline neighborhoods. But this means that 45 percent, or nearly half, *did* have friends in the neighborhood

(35 percent had family), and my calculations reveal that approximately 20 percent of the core residential population at baseline was in MTO, a nontrivial level of saturation.

Second, social influences do not just derive from friends—acquaintances and "weak ties" may be just as important. Perceptions and meanings, as earlier chapters showed, derive from a variety of factors, and reputations of areas are transmitted among strangers, in the press, and in everyday interaction. On this point consider that there were highly publicized events going on in the housing projects in and around the MTO site related to housing decisions, such as the widely reported destruction of the nearby Robert Taylor Homes (with over fifteen thousand units). It is hard to imagine that conversations and discussions about moving, especially among those receiving financial assistance in the way of vouchers, would have been absent.

Third, there is a large and significant difference in compliance—25 percent in the early randomization group took up the offer compared to 42 percent in later groups. The nonprofit organizations administering MTO were said to be more effective in counseling as time went on, but the take-up pattern is equally consistent with social interactional or linked migration flows. Whether compliers communicated their likes/dislikes or otherwise interacted with other MTO members is ultimately unknown.

The larger lesson seems clear. While observational research is often criticized for making assumptions that cannot be proven, experiments are not home free either: they just have to make *different* assumptions. In the present case, assuming asocial MTO participants and a lack of social interactions between participating families that make up 20 percent of the original neighborhood and the other residents is not any more plausible than the assumptions on which observational research is based. As the economist Angus Deaton has argued more generally: "Randomized controlled trials cannot automatically trump other evidence, they do not occupy any special place in some hierarchy of evidence, nor does it makes sense to refer to them as 'hard' while other methods are "soft."[31] Experimental research faces problems just like observational research, especially once we move outside the controlled laboratory and into the social world. Credible knowledge cannot simply be assumed based on the method of origin.

Developmental Neighborhood Effects

At the beginning of the experiment, MTO families living in high-poverty neighborhoods had for the most part grown up there or in high-poverty neighborhoods elsewhere. This yields developmental questions about life-course timing and long-term versus short-term neighborhood effects. In particular, if the effect of disadvantage is cumulative, lagged, or most salient early in life, as recent evidence suggests for cognitive ability and adolescent mental health, then moving out, while still potentially important, does not erase neighborhood influences in early childhood.[32] In this sense, the MTO experiment may be inconsistent with theoretical perspectives that stress early brain development and critical periods in which contextual effects get "locked in."[33] This problem becomes more complex given that most families living in severely disadvantaged neighborhoods have lived in similar environments for multiple generations, raising the possibility that the influence of disadvantage extends across generations.[34] Neighborhood effects are thus in part "developmental" and not just static.

To illustrate this process I considered the lagged effect of concentrated disadvantage on trajectories of verbal ability, which research has shown is a sturdy predictor of a number of life outcomes. Patrick Sharkey, Stephen Raudenbush, and I formulated a strategy designed to estimate the effects of concentrated disadvantage on verbal ability in the case in which the contextual "treatment" (disadvantage), outcome (verbal ability), and confounders *all* potentially vary over time.[35] Our idea was to use information gleaned from analysis of residential selection through time to weight each time period of observation by the inverse probability of receiving the treatment (disadvantage) actually received.[36] The results bear directly on the interpretation of MTO and neighborhood effects more generally.

First, based on the time-varying model of neighborhood change, we estimated that living in severely concentrated disadvantage reduced the *later* verbal ability among African American children by over four points, over 25 percent of a standard deviation and roughly equivalent to missing a year of schooling. This result implies that the neighborhood effect on verbal ability is lagged or lingers on even after a child leaves a severely disadvantaged neighborhood. Second, the life-course framework leads us to expect that influences on verbal skills will be most pronounced during the developmentally sensitive years of childhood.[37] I tested this developmental interaction in another analysis by estimating the influence of neighborhood disadvantage on verbal ability for the youngest African American children assessed in the PHDCN cohorts—six- to nine-year-olds at baseline. I found a full six-point deficit in verbal ability trajectories linked to living in disadvantage at the midpoint of the study, a substantial and significant difference.[38] If we assume for the sake of argument that the selection weighting model I used is reasonable in adjusting for baseline (or "pretreatment") and time-varying confounding of covariates, the implications for MTO and kindred studies are significant.

Consider, for example, the trajectories of verbal ability for black children in Chicago who lived in concentrated disadvantage. If we randomly provided housing vouchers to the families of these children and then compared outcomes at a later time, we might conclude that there are no neighborhood effects if there is no difference between treatment and controls at the follow-up *among those who were previously living in disadvantage (or receiving treatment).*[39] This conclusion is potentially quite misleading, however, because it does not ask the question: What about the lagged or developmental effect of living in concentrated disadvantage compared to those living in an advantaged neighborhood? When I asked this question in the PHDCN, the answer was that there is a substantial estimated neighborhood effect, equivalent to missing well over a year of schooling (a six-point "IQ" deficit), associated with living in concentrated disadvantage. In this model, the effect of concurrent disadvantage was not significant.

It follows that existing studies of children or adolescents living in poverty may provide only a narrow test of the causal effect of neighborhood social contexts. One can examine developmental interactions in studies like the MTO, but selecting on living in poverty sets limits on how far one goes—only 14 percent of the interim evaluation sample was between ages five and seven. Well over half were age twelve or older. Combined with the fact that MTO families were selected on poverty, analyses like those in this chapter are constrained by design.[40]

Summary and Prospects

The MTO is one of the best controlled social science experiments—if not the best at the individual level. By introducing a randomized design that induces the poor to make residential moves to lower-poverty neighborhoods, the MTO design is a breakthrough. So why has there been disagreement on the results and what does MTO portend for the future? Believing it important for social science that the MTO experimental debate end in clarity, I offered what I hoped was a fair summary in a 2008 debate that I update here in light of newer results and the broader findings of the book.[41] I wish to emphasize a dozen interrelated themes.

1. *MTO has distinct inferential limits.* By design, MTO was an *individual-level* intervention that offered housing vouchers to extremely poor, largely minority families. Although this might be a very good policy and humane, nothing can be inferred analytically from MTO about the success or failure of neighborhood-level interventions, and any generalizations about voucher effects now or into the future are restricted to a small segment of the population, namely the very poor.

2. *MTO's treatment was applied to a very restricted range.* The treatment of an MTO voucher induced statistically significant reductions in census-tract poverty (about eight percentage points overall) in comparison with the control group, but within what are usually considered high-poverty areas. While over half of the families who used a voucher to move through MTO (compliers) had tract poverty rates of approximately 20 percent in 2002, the average poverty rate was greater than 30 percent for both the experimental and control groups across sites. What this means is that overall the MTO experiment induced neighborhood poverty differences in the long run *of degree, not kind.*

3. *The treatment effect also weakened over time.* Published results from MTO confirm that the treatment effect on neighborhood conditions weakened up to the interim follow-up in 2002 as participants either moved back to poverty, or the neighborhoods to which they moved increased in poverty around them. A second follow-up of the MTO was undertaken in 2009–10 and HUD is scheduled to release a report in 2011. The logic and theory of this book suggests that the newer MTO results will mirror the trends observed in 2002, with a further decaying

of the original voucher effect on current poverty and therefore decaying neighborhood effects on individual outcomes. The original experiment remains unchanged, in other words, so I predict the basic trends described in this chapter will continue to follow the same trajectory.

4. *Poverty is not all that matters.* Compared to poverty levels, there were smaller differences induced by MTO in *concentrated disadvantage*, defined as the segregation of African Americans in neighborhoods of resource deprivation across multiple domains. Moreover, whether we look at destination neighborhoods or take into account interim moves, both controls and experimentals experienced hypersegregation and there were no meaningful differences in racial composition induced by the treatment. Seen in this light, the overall results are more understandable.

5. *Neighborhood trajectories matter too.* Furthermore, there were no significant differences in the *rate of change* for poverty or for a host of neighborhood-level *social processes* (e.g., collective efficacy, intergenerational closure) in Chicago—whether static or dynamic—by randomization group. As a result, the trajectories of destination neighborhoods turned out to be virtually identical for experimentals and controls, and social organizational features of community were largely unaffected by treatment. The significance (or lack thereof) of differences does not change when complier status is adjusted.

6. *Spatial disadvantage is an additional influence.* Experimental and control families ended up in the same or similar community areas regardless of any differences in neighborhood poverty measured in census tracts. The patterned structure of community-level ties induced by moving, seen in the bird's-eye view of Chicago (e.g., figures 11.2 and 11.3), reveals a near-identical network comparing experimentals and controls. Moreover, community-area differences in social processes were not different by treatment group, nor was spatially lagged poverty or concentrated disadvantage. In particular, low social support, low collective efficacy, and compromised health characterized the destinations for MTO families, whether offered a voucher or not.

7. *Not surprisingly, then, MTO produces mixed results.* At the individual level, MTO has demonstrated mixed results that vary by outcome, site, and subgroup, especially gender. Some effects are comparatively large (e.g., on mental health and girls' behavior), while others, like adult economic self-sufficiency, appear null. Given the design restrictions combined with the modest treatment, the endurance of any significant

findings is notable. In particular, even marginal shifts in the quality of neighborhood environments appear to make a continued difference for mental health, a finding that connects to my argument in Chapter 6 on cognitive processes of inequality.

8. *Moving has causal significance*. The MTO experiment induced neighborhood change only by moving. Hence residential mobility and change in context are intertwined. There may also be mobility-by-neighborhood interactions, perhaps explaining the gender differentials (e.g., boys might be more vulnerable to being the new kid in the neighborhood). Because moving is a life-course event of theoretical importance, it is desirable to separate its effects from neighborhood effects. I describe such an approach in the next chapter.

9. *Developmental neighborhood effects need scrutiny*. Because MTO subjects were selected on living in neighborhood poverty, which is persistent, early developmental effects of concentrated poverty cannot be effectively studied for adults and only in a limited way for children.[42] For the most part, MTO tests whether exits from poverty can overcome previously accumulated deficits. Thus, *any lack of MTO effects does not necessarily imply a lack of durable or developmental neighborhood effects within the lives of individuals*.

10. *Assumptions revisited: social interactions and migration go together*. MTO requires that we invoke strong assumptions about voucher use, some of which, like no interference from social interactions in the experiment, are not convincing for acts of moving. If migration research has taught us anything, it is that moving is embedded in chainlike social networks. The bad news is that overcoming interference requires us to characterize and specify how it actually occurs. Otherwise our causal estimates will combine disparate and possibly countervailing effects in the study population.[43] We need a plausible model of the interference, (observational) data with which to estimate its key features, and a statistical procedure that would produce consistent estimates. There is a growing statistical literature making advances on interference and compliance in randomized experiments, but at present we are left with many unknowns.[44]

11. *Randomization does not solve the causal inference problem*. When randomization at the individual level is invoked and we find evidence for the influence of a voucher offer on individual outcomes, it nonetheless remains unclear what mechanisms link the manipulated treatment

with outcomes. Experiments do not answer the "why" question, and there is no such thing as theory-free inference. The causes of neighborhood effects and social mechanisms have been a black box, and neighborhood-level interventions have been neglected. I return to this point in chapter 15.

12. *Selection in a social world is not a nuisance*. In the social structure that constitutes contemporary life, selection bias is misleadingly thought of mainly in terms of unobserved heterogeneity and statistical "nuisance." This gets it backward. Selection is a social process that itself is implicated in creating the very structures that then constrain individual behavior.

In sum, the validity of a study of two individuals "trading places" depends on the question one wants answered—just like for any other study or even an imagined experiment. In the popular 1983 movie *Trading Places* starring Eddie Murphy and Dan Aykroyd, a rich pair of brothers conducted a cruel experiment to separate individual (nature) and context (nurture). The Hollywood result was amusing, as one would expect given the actors, but in its own way the "design" (or scripted background of characters and nature of treatment) presaged an answer. The real-world MTO asks a specific question that is important, but it is only one of the many questions that a social theory of neighborhood effects should ask. As a century or more of research reveals, neighborhood effects may be conceived in multiple ways at multiple levels of analysis and at varying time scales of influence. Thus experiments like MTO that have posed individual-level questions give us only one kind of answer and do not address the causes or consequences of selection, neighborhood-level interventions, or the study of neighborhood social mechanisms, to name some of the concerns of this book. The next chapter takes up the selection challenge.

12 Individual Selection as a Social Process

In late 2008 the *Chicago Tribune* ran a special series on what they called "Separate Chicagos." Belying the illusory image of harmonious integration beaming from Grant Park on the election-night triumph of Barack Obama, the *Tribune* described Chicago as "America's Most Segregated Big City."[1] The series portrayed in vivid terms how racial lines drawn years ago remain entrenched and reinforced by people's choices.

What seems to be a simple point—that choice matters—is in fact complex and the subject of much controversy among social scientists. One side takes the view that segregation and constraints of inequality override choice, in extreme cases almost as if individuals are pawns in a predetermined game. Another side valorizes choice to the point where it is said to undercut research efforts to investigate the effects of neighborhood context. Individuals "escape" poverty, for example, by differentially allocating themselves nonrandomly according to their ability and preferences. Observational estimates of neighborhood effects on outcomes such as crime, mortality, teenage childbearing, employment, low birth weight, mental health, and children's cognitive ability are, by this logic, confounded and thereby biased. The MTO debate in the previous chapter is the prime case in point of the alleged "curse" of neighborhood selection bias.[2]

The typical response of quantitatively oriented scholars to individual selection is to view it as a statistical problem to be controlled away and not something of substantive interest in itself. For this reason selection pathways are more imagined than they are examined. The most common approach in the literature has been to estimate the effect of a "structural" factor like concentrated poverty on an individual outcome after controlling selected individual-level variables. The other approach, exhibited in the case of MTO, is to conduct a randomized experiment.

As I argued in chapter 11, however, selection is much more than a statistical nuisance when we consider its implications for inequality in neighborhood attainment and broader population or city-level processes. To extend this point, in this chapter I elaborate an alternative view that simultaneously invokes the power of structure and choice—"chains of selection," as it were. I argue that the sorting of individuals by place is not just a technical concern for those studying neighborhood effects, it is a process that knits together and defines the social-ecological structure of the city. This argument is consistent with what the economist James Heckman calls the "Scientific Model of Causality," in which the goal is to confront directly and achieve a basic understanding of the social processes that select individuals into causal "treatments" of interest.[3] As we saw with MTO, experimental randomization does not tell us about how causal mechanisms are constituted in a social world defined by the interplay of structure and purposeful choice by individuals. Although rare in the literature, studying the predictors of sorting and selection into neighborhoods of varying types is therefore an essential ingredient in the larger theoretical project of understanding neighborhood effects.

Building on and extending collaborative work with Patrick Sharkey, this chapter focuses on a key aspect of selection by treating the income level and racial isolation of an individual's neighborhood attainment as problematic in its own right and requiring explanation. Going back to the PHDCN, I highlight the sources and consequences of sorting for the reproduction of racial and economic inequality in the lives of individuals and ultimately for the reproduction of a stratified urban landscape. A focus on life-course trajectories and neighborhood change remains faithful to the idea that individuals make choices about their environment, not only whether to stay put or move to a different neighborhood, but whether to leave the city for the suburbs or beyond. Such decisions are influenced by resources, preferences, and changing life circumstances, but they are also conditioned by the interaction of an individual's race/ethnicity and social behaviors with the wider structural context that governs consequential life decisions.

By simultaneously examining movers and stayers, this approach permits a dynamic conceptualization and allows separation of the competing sources of neighborhood change—that induced when an individual moves, when migration into or out of a community changes the context around an individual who nonetheless remains in place, and when secular changes in wider conditions occur, such as a city-level rise or decline in income. Choosing to remain in a changing or even declining neighborhood is a form of selection, after all, and can be just as consequential as the decision to relocate, a point overlooked in debates about neighborhood effects. Moreover, advancing a mover-stayer model permits me to examine what predicts moving and the developmental effects of moving on later outcomes. In the last chapter the importance of this question was highlighted by the confounding of moving and neighborhood change in the MTO experiment. Based on prior research and theory, there are good reasons to hypothesize that moving itself is a causal factor in the life course, especially for adolescents.

This chapter pursues the moving question in several concrete ways. First, I report findings on selection into neighborhoods that stems from a model of moving that takes account of previously unexamined sources of heterogeneity at the individual and neighborhood levels. I examine factors such as criminality and depression at the individual level, and, drawing on chapter 6, I go beyond the staples of neighborhood poverty and race to examine the effects of collectively perceived disorder on decisions to move away from a neighborhood. Second, I examine upward and downward mobility by race to estimate the prevalence and prediction of this kind of "selection." Third, I consider the effects of moving separate from neighborhood change. The data reveal that moving cannot be understood independent of how neighborhoods are embedded in the larger social structure of the city. The effect of moving, in other words, depends on the destination in the metropolitan area and not just on internal neighborhood characteristics. This analysis thus contributes directly to the overarching goal in this section to articulate a new kind of neighborhood effect defined by supraneighborhood dynamics and bottom-up moves that constitute the social fabric of contemporary cities.

Pushing this theme further, the final goal of the chapter is to introduce the emergent consequences of residential selection. Here the question becomes how individual decisions *combine* to create mobility flows that socially reproduce the ecological structure of inequality, a phenomenon that social scientists and lay people alike have had difficulty explaining within the dominant free market and behaviorist paradigms. The dilemma is an example of the "Coleman phenomenon" of micro-to-macro relations I described in chapter 3. In this chapter I apply the schema in figure 3.1 to an analysis of the structural flows of exchange between neighborhoods of different social positions. I begin with interracial and inter-income "exchange" between neighborhoods based on mobility transitions. I also examine how neighborhoods are connected through flows of movement based on traditionally conceived individual characteristics such as criminal propensity and depression. Chapter 13 then extends the focus to a full network analysis of the sources of what I call "structural sorting." These analyses thus come full circle in probing the social consequences of selection decisions for neighborhood inequality.

Neighborhood Attainment as Outcome

The problem of neighborhood selection can be addressed by studying individual change in neighborhood environments as a multilevel process that unfolds over time. Building on what Richard Alba and John Logan referred to as the "locational attainment" model, a body of research has estimated the association between individual-level characteristics and census measures of neighborhood characteristics, usually the percentage of white (or black) neighbors and the poverty rate.[4] This approach has been used to provide empirical evidence on differences between racial and ethnic groups in terms of the extent to which individual resources and advantages are associated with desired neighborhood outcomes. It is consistent with urban demographic models put forth in early writings of the Chicago School, which assume that members of minority or immigrant groups attempt to translate economic advances into residential advantage by moving out of segregated areas and into areas occupied by members of the dominant race/ethnic group.[5]

Although individual and family differences in socioeconomic status (SES) explain some of the discrepancies in neighborhood environments, a common finding is that substantial gaps between whites and nonwhites remain, even after controlling for multiple dimensions of SES. Places are units of stratification in their own right, contrary to the Chicago School's emphasis on unfettered sorting (or spatial assimilation) among "natural areas." The urban demographic literature thereby shifted to think not only of individual stratification but *place stratification*.[6]

An important question remains, however, regarding the mechanisms and social processes by which place stratification is produced. If individuals are not followed over time, one cannot distinguish the pathways by which a neighborhood changes from individual-level changes in life cycle or economic status and how those in turn relate to neighborhood change. To address this issue, a number of scholars have utilized longitudinal data from the national Panel Study of Income Dynamics (PSID) to assess how different groups of individuals move into or out of poor neighborhoods.[7] This approach represents a step forward by taking a temporal perspective and considering a wider range of individual-level predictors, especially in the form of socioeconomic resources. The results show the continued persistence of race/ethnic gaps in neighborhood income attainment among those who move, with blacks' locational "return" on their social resources and human capital substantially less than whites, accounting for household wealth.[8]

In 2008 Patrick Sharkey and I took the next step of decomposing within-individual trajectories of neighborhood change and then analyzing consequences for both individuals and the larger structure of place-based inequality. We did so by exploiting distinctive characteristics of the Project on Human Development in Chicago Neighborhoods.[9] The PHDCN offers crucial analytic advantages for studying sorting and inequality, adding to the knowledge gained from MTO in the last chapter and the PSID. First, the high levels of immigration into Chicago and its considerable ethnic diversity provide us with a sample that allows for detailed comparisons of whites, blacks, and Latinos, many of whom are recent immigrants, while others have lived in the U.S. for generations. Second, by following people, we can decompose neighborhood change into that arising from residential mobility versus natural change experienced among stayers.

Third and most important, the PHDCN allows us to go beyond research on neighborhood attainment that focuses on a now standard set of predictors *and* outcomes. There is reason to believe that some individuals end up in poor neighborhoods while others end up in more advantaged neighborhoods for reasons that go well beyond the canonical predictors of human capital and demography. Robert E. Faris and Warren H. Dunham, for example, set the stage for the "drift" hypothesis, whereby individuals with cognitive vulnerabilities get stuck or drift into selected disadvantaged environments.[10] Competence and social support systems have also been hypothesized as important predictors of multiple facets of life-course advancement.[11] And at the "outcome" level, it is not just economic attainment but social location broadly defined that is of interest. The extensive data collection in the PHDCN longitudinal study allows us to assess potentially important dimensions of the ability or vulnerability of families (e.g., depression, family criminality, exposure to violence, and social support) in achieving residential outcomes.

Measures and Analytic Strategy

Earlier we saw the clustered nature of the PHDCN multilevel design at baseline in the city of Chicago and the destination of subjects at wave 3 of the study (figs. 4.2 and 4.3). The dispersion and movement is considerable—the third wave covers all of Chicago plus a large swath of the metro area stretching west, north into Wisconsin, and southeast to Indiana. Families moved to many other states as well, but were tracked no matter where they moved. From the parent interviews, we geocoded detailed address information at all three waves of the survey, which we in turn linked to census-tract codes across the U.S. This information was then merged with social and demographic data that were available on all census tracts in the U.S. in both 1990 and 2000, thus permitting examination of stability and change in neighborhood-level attainment over the course of the study. For these tracts, *median income* was our key indicator, expressed in 2000 dollars. Although most studies of neighborhood stratification examine the low end of the distribution in the form of the poverty rate, median income better captures the full distribution of income in the neighborhood and yields a clearly interpretable measure of the economic status of neighborhood residents with a familiar metric—the dollar. Here I also examine *percent black* as an indicator of racial segregation at the neighborhood level.

An extensive set of time-invariant covariates was assessed at the baseline or wave 1 interview, beginning with basic characteristics such as the caregiver's and subject's *age* and *sex*. The caregiver's *race/ethnicity* denotes if the caregiver is white, African American, Hispanic/Latino, or a member of another racial or ethnic group—Asian Pacific Americans are the most common group among individuals in the "other" category. The caregiver's *immigrant generation* is captured by whether she is a first-generation immigrant (i.e., born outside of the United States), second-generation (i.e., at least one birth parent was born outside the U.S.), or third-generation or higher. *Citizenship* indicates if the caregiver is a U.S. citizen. *English language proficiency* taps if the caregiver's language is "good" (the reference group), "fair," or "poor." The caregiver's *educational attainment* is measured with four variables indicating if the caregiver has less than a high school diploma, a high school diploma or GED (the reference group in regression models), some college or professional school, or at least a college degree.

We measured five constructs that tap both the vulnerability and capacity of caretakers in neighborhood choice. On the vulnerability side we include problems with the criminal justice system, violence, and mental health that are known to compromise life-course outcomes. *Family criminality* represents the number of family members with a criminal record. *Domestic violence* represents the sum of responses to nine survey items asking caregivers about violent or abusive interactions with any current or previous domestic partner.[12] Caregiver *depression* is a dichotomous measure based on the Composite International Diagnostic Interview (CIDI) Short Form, coded positively if the caregiver is classified as having experienced a period of major depression in the year prior to the interview.[13] The reliability of the individual survey items used to generate the scale is very high (0.93); also the same measure of maternal depression using the PHDCN is strongly predictive of child mental health problems when controlling for other factors. *Exposure to violence* is measured by whether the caregiver (in the case of the three-year-old and six-year-old cohorts) *or* the subject (in the nine- through fifteen-year-old cohorts) saw someone shot or stabbed in the year prior to the interview. Such forms of violence influence the perceived level of safety in a neighborhood, especially pertaining to children. On the capacity side, *social support* from community members, including friends and family, has long been considered a means by which parents are able to collectively manage childrearing tasks and thus is a potential influence on moving or staying in one's community. The caregiver's perceived level of social support is captured by the mean of fifteen survey items (reliability = 0.77) on the degree to which the caregiver can rely on friends and family for help or emotional support and the degree of trust and respect between the caregiver and his/her support network.

Time-varying Measures

A life-course framework and a developmental focus on neighborhood selection over the life course demands that key time-varying circumstances must also be examined.[14] To do this, we included the *employment status* of the caregiver and the caregiver's spouse or partner (working or not working); a variable indicating if the caregiver is *receiving welfare*; the caregiver's total *household income*, consisting of six variables indicating if total household income is below $10,000, $10,000–$19,999, $20,000–$29,999, $30,000–$39,999, $40,000–49,999, or $50,000 and above; *home ownership*; *household size* (the total number of individuals in the household); *marital status*, consisting of indicators of whether the caregiver is single, cohabiting, or married; and *occupational status* based on the socioeconomic index (SEI). If the caregiver is not employed and has a partner, the partner's SEI score is used. If both the caregiver and a partner are employed, the maximum score is used. All time-varying covariates refer to the subject or family's status at the interview. Collection of detailed time-varying information between waves was not possible across all the variables of interest due to project constraints.[15]

Trajectories

At the beginning of the study, African Americans in Chicago lived in neighborhoods with median incomes roughly $17,700 lower than whites, while the gap between whites and Latinos was more than $18,000. Members of other racial and ethnic groups lived in neighborhoods with median incomes that were about $12,000 lower than whites. The data thus reveal an initial racial and ethnic hierarchy of neighborhoods that is quite large in magnitude—whereas whites lived in neighborhoods with a median income over $54,000, blacks and Latinos lived in neighborhoods where the median income was roughly a *third* lower. Race and ethnicity of the household head explains about a quarter of the between-family variance in neighborhood income.

Over time the gaps between whites and nonwhites grew slightly, but all groups experienced a positive slope of change.[16] The trends are strongly shaped by whether PHDCN families stayed at their original address or moved—and to where. Specifically, the largest changes in neighborhood income occur among movers who leave the city. The difference in the slope of change for white movers who leave the city compared to those who remain in Chicago is almost $6,300 per survey wave—whites who leave Chicago enter neighborhoods with median incomes close to $9,200 higher than their neighborhoods of origin. Over the course of the survey, the total change for white movers who exit the city is a substantial $18,400. The total gain in neighborhood median income for African Americans who exit Chicago is $13,900 from wave 1 to wave 3; for Latinos, the gain is about $17,300.

The counterexplanation for the persistence of racial inequality among each group of movers and stayers is heterogeneity by racial/ethnic groups in economic status, life-cycle stage, or other potential factors that might influence residential choices. This possibility is addressed by adjusting for the extensive set of covariates described earlier. I deemphasize results on individual-level predictors and focus on the overall pattern of neighborhood attainment.[17] Perhaps surprisingly to the reader, including the full set of covariates does not change the basic story. Figure 12.1 graphs a subset of the key results by depicting the trajectories of neighborhood change for *stayers* (top graph) and *movers* out of Chicago (bottom graph), with both adjusted for the full set of covariates. The size of the racial and ethnic gaps in neighborhood income is reduced somewhat from the unadjusted results, but these slight differences are far outweighed by the striking gaps across groups. Stayers do not gain much, for example, and the trajectories remain parallel by race. Movers gain more by contrast, particularly those exiting to the suburbs, but in a way that just shifts the race gaps in parallel fashion. For example, among movers out of Chicago, whites' advantage over blacks does not narrow—rather, a fractal-like shift occurs. Thus most of the racial and ethnic inequality in neighborhood attainment cannot be explained by changing economic circumstances, life-cycle stage, or other major characteristics of families that influence residential decisions. After accounting for these and other factors not previously considered in the mobility literature—from depression to crime to support networks—the bottom line is that whites attain neighborhoods that are substantially

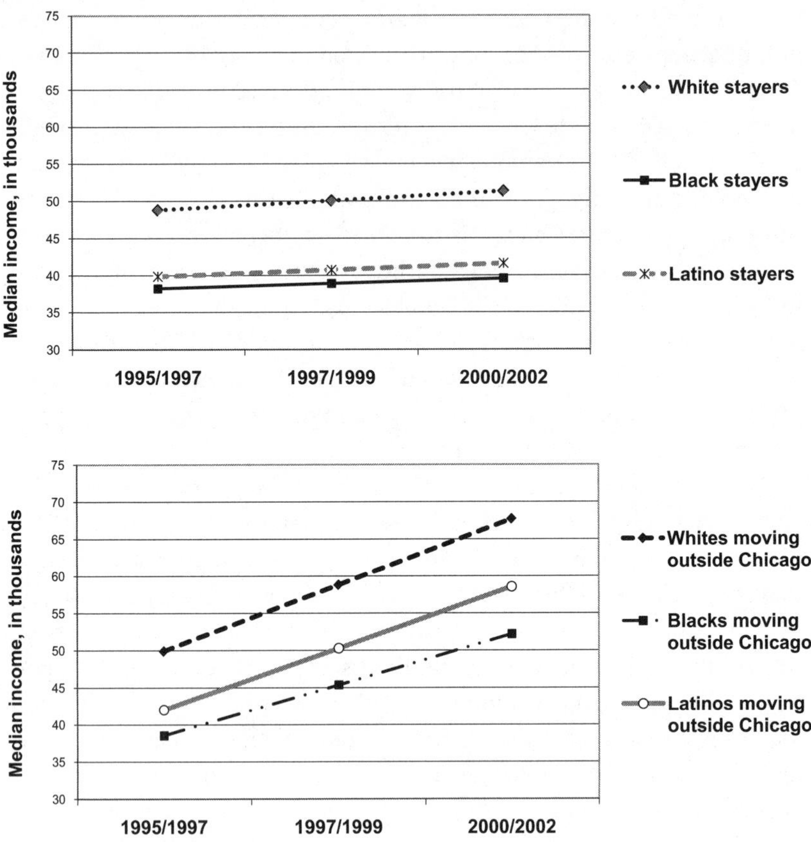

FIGURE 12.1. Trajectories of neighborhood income attainment controlling for stable and time-varying confounders

more affluent than nonwhites, and that residential mobility leads to sharp improvements in neighborhood income for all groups, especially among those leaving Chicago.

Neighborhood Racial Composition

I now examine whether the same patterns arise for racial makeup by modeling changes in the percentage of African American neighbors over time. I present the fully adjusted trajectories in figure 12.2. The extreme racial segregation that characterizes Chicago is immediately apparent. African Americans live in neighborhoods that are composed almost exclusively of members of their own race; this is especially true if they remain within the city. Blacks who exit Chicago, by contrast, enter neighborhoods that are much more integrated than those they left behind in the city, even after controlling for the full set of individual and family-level covariates. Whites live in neighborhoods with lower proportions of African Americans than Latinos no matter where they move over the course of the survey. For both whites and Latinos, exiting Chicago leads to the largest reduction in the prevalence of black neighbors, though the trend lines associated with mobility out of the city are much less steep than they are for African Americans, and are also much less steep than in models predicting neighborhood median income. In other words, moves out of the city bring about only slight changes in the racial mix of Latinos' and whites' neighborhoods. This is partly attributable to the fact that Latinos, and especially whites, tend to originate in Chicago neighborhoods with only small populations of African Americans. The larger result in figure 12.2 is thus unmistakable. With the exception of the few black families (14 percent of total) who moved out of Chicago, mostly to the suburbs, the racial stratification of residential neighborhoods is socially reproduced across the destinations of movers of all races no matter what their individual-level characteristics or changing life circumstances. And even for those black families that did leave Chicago, the logic of this book predicts that the racial integra-

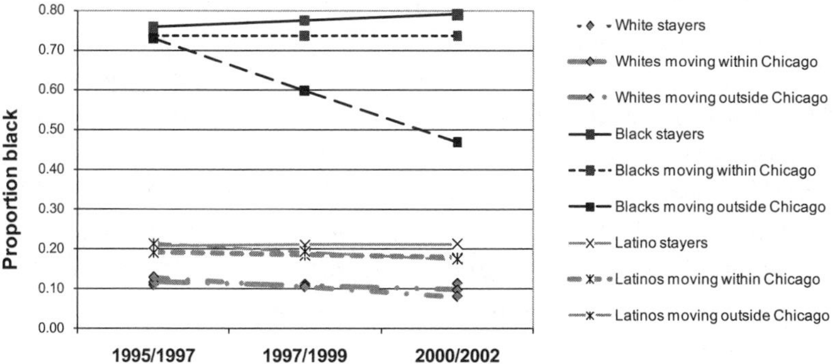

FIGURE 12.2. Trajectories of neighborhood racial composition controlling for stable and time-varying confounders

tion achieved may well be temporary. This possibility brings us directly to the next question I pose.

Who Moves and Why?

Thirty years ago, Peter Rossi asked the question: Why do families move? The basic answer turned on the stage of a family's life cycle and changing housing needs.[18] Rossi's book was widely influential, with later social science literature adding to his argument to incorporate multiple dimensions of economic and social status. In this section I am motivated by Rossi's question and the findings above to pursue the next line of inquiry: What predicts who leaves the city and who does not? More specifically, who moves up and out of poverty and what predicts downward mobility? We can answer these questions by exploiting in a different way the rich set of individual and family-level predictors in the PHDCN, in addition to both the initial status and *change* in the racial and economic composition of neighborhoods during the first half of the 1990s (i.e., up to the first survey wave).

This strategy revealed that families moving outside of Chicago respond to changes in neighborhood racial and ethnic composition.[19] Although the prevalence of nonwhites in 1990 did not have an independent influence on future mobility patterns, *increases* in the percentage of black and Latino neighbors from 1990 to 1995 made it more likely overall that families exited the city after the study started in 1995. The large effect of increases in percentage black on moving out was restricted to whites and Latinos, however, a modern day form of white but also Latino flight. Blacks did not move in response to changes in the percent black (or Latino), a clear indicator that racial composition of the neighborhood is less important for blacks than for the other groups, an interpretation consistent with research showing that blacks are the group most willing to live in integrated neighborhoods. Combined with past attitudinal research, the present empirical finding on the differential effects of racial change thus predicts the "temporary racial integration" phenomena.[20]

Perhaps more interesting is that when I augment this basic model informed by the results in chapter 6, I find that collectively perceived disorder predicts whether a family moves out of Chicago above and beyond race and class composition. Recall my argument that shared perceptions of disorder send a culturally meaningful signal about reputation and confidence in a neighborhood. Recall also that perceptions of disorder were strongly influenced by prior racial/ethnic composition and furthermore that the collectively perceived disorder predicted individual-level perceptions many years later. Accordingly, the test carried out here is whether this contextual property of a neighborhood influences not just perceptions, as in chapter 6, but also influences *individual moving behavior*. The result is that socially perceived disorder in the origin neighborhood not only significantly predicts outmigration from Chicago in the aggregate sample, it does so mainly for blacks and not whites. Recall that only whites and Latinos respond directly by moving when there are increases in neighborhood percent black, and chapter 6 revealed that percent black strongly predicts perceptions of increased disorder among all groups. For moving out of Chicago, what matters for nonblacks, then, is the apparently direct "push" of changes in racial composition. But among blacks, who, like all groups, are susceptible to the racially tinged meanings of disorder discovered in chapter 6, the estimated effect of shared perceptions of disorder in 1995 was significantly positive.[21] For blacks the most proximate influence is thus perceptions—unlike whites, racial and ethnic composition, whether change or baseline level, continued to be insignificant for blacks. Recall too from chapter 6 that the predictive power of shared perceptions on later poverty outcomes at the neighborhood level was stronger in predominantly black and racially mixed neighborhoods than in white areas.

Consistent with the theoretical account in chapter 6, then, the implication is that neighborhood change is shaped by shared perceptions about the neighborhood in addition to its changing demography. In this sense, neighborhood context once again matters—"selection" is in fact occurring on the basis of a web of common meanings and social structures linked to place. However, individual race does interact with this process, with changing racial composition appearing to motivate the behavior of whites and Latinos, whereas for blacks, only the cultural aspect of shared perceptions of disorder appears to count when it comes to mobility behavior.

It is notable that by contrast, few individual or family-level factors had consistent associations with mobility across the three racial and ethnic groups. In the total sample and among Latinos, high occupational status was associated with mobility out of the city, but in general the various measures of socioeconomic status (notably income and education) have a weaker influence than one might have predicted. Among the factors that do predict mobility with some consistency are home ownership and age: homeowners and older caregivers are less likely to move outside Chicago, as are the families of older children in the sample. Caregivers who cohabit are also less likely to exit Chicago, while first-generation immigrants are more likely to leave the city. African American caregivers who report exposure to serious forms of violence are more likely to leave the city. White caregivers who report a period of major depression are also more likely to exit Chicago, providing additional evidence that noneconomic factors may be important for understanding decisions regarding residential location.

To a surprising extent based on prior accounts, then, mobility is not much influenced by individual or family characteristics—the dominant selection bet—but rather changes in the neighborhood of origin and perceptions thereof—whites and Latinos are more likely to exit the city if they live in neighborhoods where blacks and Latinos have a growing presence. This evidence suggests a "white *and* Latino flight" response that serves as another mechanism underlying the racial hierarchy. Considering evidence that Latinos are similar to whites in their desire to live in neighborhoods with few African Americans, the significance of "Latino flight" deserves more attention in the literature on persistent residential segregation. Equally if not more intriguing, the results provide further support for the disorder-based theory articulated in chapter 6, one that rests not on observed conditions as much as consensually shared perceptions, reinforcing the cognitive basis of social stratification and, ultimately, the reproduction of inequality. Cultural meanings of disorder are bound up with racial change as a trigger of migration between neighborhoods and out of the city.

Downward and Upward Mobility

I now take the preceding analysis to the next stage by addressing a phenomenon that those critical of neighborhood effects often raise—downward and upward mobility. The image that comes to mind is the mother who chooses to move out of the ghetto based on her exceptional personal characteristics and individual drive. If these dispositional or "characterological" features are also a cause of her children's outcomes, we are thought to have a problem. I thus extend the logic of prior analyses above to ask a new question: How prevalent is individual mobility of this "Horatio Alger"-type problem?

The answer: much less than commonly imagined. The PHDCN allows me to look at origin neighborhoods and destinations anywhere in the United States. I classified origin and destination in terms of both quartiles and thirds of neighborhood median income in 2000 dollars. Doing so allowed the examination of stability and change in one's relative spatial position in the income hierarchy. Results were similar across definitions, so for simplicity I report here the classification by low, medium, and high (equal thirds). Using this classification, most families stay in the same location type—on or near the "diagonal" of the mobility table. Approximately 70 percent of white and nearly 80 percent of black families in PHDCN that start out in low-income areas (the bottom third) stay there, although there is only a small fraction of whites (39 of 601) at risk in the first place. Of those in low-income areas, only 5 percent of blacks, 5 percent of Latinos, and 15 percent of whites move out of poverty and into the upper third of neighborhoods. *Upward mobility in this sense is thus rare, and, when it does happen, whites are three times more likely to have experienced it than their minority counterparts.* Downward mobility is also rare but with similar racial cleavages: less than 2 percent of whites lose ground (N = 6), defined as moving from the upper third of neighborhood income to the lower third, but about 12 percent of blacks and 10 percent of Latinos make this transition. Somewhat shockingly, compared to almost 70 percent of whites, only 20 percent of blacks and 38 percent of Latinos remain in the upper third of neighborhood income at the end. In all likelihood this is due in part to the "white flight" noted above, given the durable link between income levels and race in American society.

To gain further insight on escaping poverty versus drifting downward, I also examined the prediction of downward and upward neighborhood mobility using the full set of individual and family factors. As for neighborhood income attainment, the lion's share of prediction comes from a small set of stratification factors, such as race, college education, income, and household size. Horatio Algers are not only rare, but when they do appear their route to prosperity tends to unfold along structural pathways rather than those defined by individual differences.

My analysis included not just depression, criminality, and social support, but in a final submodel I examine the "big two" individual differences highlighted by Richard Herrnstein and colleagues in *The Bell Curve* and *Crime and Human Nature* as central to differences in life outcomes—"IQ" and impulsivity.[22] I examined five different model specifications, but the results were all similar. In the final model with IQ and impulsivity, only three factors predicted upward mobility—low exposure to violence at baseline, smaller household size, and higher income. For downward mobility, by far the biggest predictor of losing ground was being black, with an odds ratio over 5. The only other predictor was home ownership, which serves as a protective factor against a declining path of neighborhood income. These results underscore again the durability of spatial inequality by race in the American city—individual factors do not overturn structure and blacks are disproportionately burdened by the downward income mobility that does exist.

Does Moving In Turn Affect Individuals?

Neighborhood residential mobility entails a break with the social relationships and networks developed in one's origin neighborhood and the forced development of (or isolation from) new social ties in another place. It probably also means major institutional changes, such as different schools, police departments, and political systems. While it is thus logical to explore the consequence of moving itself, the logic of inequality and the results so far lead us to expect that moving may be either "good" or "bad" depending on the outcome in question and the larger structural context of the move. For example, a move may mean a loss of social capital available to children through the disruption of intergenerational networks and collective efficacy available for children. But disruption can also mean breaking away from a disadvantaged and violent environment, providing benefits if the new neighborhood is supportive and safe. This appears to be what happened in the forced moves of some ex-offenders out of New Orleans after the housing destruction induced by Hurricane Katrina.[23]

Recent analysis of the PHDCN with Patrick Sharkey supports the idea that the process of moving itself plays an important role in shaping the trajectories of children's violence, quite apart from change in the economic or demographic characteristics of neighborhoods that result from a move.[24] At the same time, however, the results support a "socially conditioned" perspective on the impact of residential mobility, one that avoids treating all moves equally. What I mean by this is that not only do neighborhood characteristics matter, but so does the larger geographic destination (in particular, moving within versus out of the city), a result consonant with the basic argument of chapter 10 on spatial regime effects and the sharp differences reported in this chapter on economic returns to mobility in versus out of Chicago.

In an analysis extending this line of inquiry, Sharkey and I specifically found that whereas moves within Chicago lead to an *elevated* risk of violence, residential moves outside of the city *reduce* violent offending and exposure to violence among children in the PHDCN. The pattern was consistent across three outcomes: moving within the city leads to about a 0.13 standard deviation increase in the measure of violent behavior, and multiplies the odds of being exposed to violence by 1.56 and the odds of being victimized by 1.45 (all significant). By contrast, moving outside Chicago reduces violent behavior by more than a third of a standard deviation and reduces by half the odds of being exposed to violence.[25] In addition, the gap in violence between movers within and outside Chicago is explained not only by the racial and economic composition of the destination neighborhoods, but by the quality of school contexts, children's perceived control over their new environment, and fear of violence.

Considered with prior results from the Gautreaux and MTO housing studies, the PHDCN data suggest a *contextually conditioned* set of relationships that distinguish among residential mobility, neighborhood change, and the wider geography of opportunity. As we saw for adult neighborhood attainment, the lesson is that multiple dimensions of a move must be simultaneously considered if we are to assess how mobility impacts a child's developmental trajectory. In the present case, both internal-neighborhood factors *and* destination matter—"getting out of town," or "knifing off," as it is known in the life-course literature, appears to have important consequences for reducing children's violence, a finding that is consistent with the quasi-experimental results from Gautreaux and a more recent study of violence reduction sparked by the separation of ex-offenders from high-risk environments after Hurricane Katrina. Getting out of town also matters greatly for neighborhood attainment, as shown earlier, although again the gains in attainment may well erode in the future.

Beyond Individual Migration

Residential moves are not only conditioned by the larger context, they help constitute and define it. When a person moves between neighborhoods, much more than an individual outcome occurs—a form of social exchange between places is established, which is part and parcel of how neighborhoods change. Between-neighborhood connections are formed, or not. I thus turn to a more explicit consideration of the higher-order implications of the lessons learned to this point.[26] My motivation is to begin to understand "spatial flows" that are created by individual moves.

The key idea is to imagine the pattern of flows connecting the origin neighborhoods of PHDCN families in Chicago to neighborhood destinations anywhere in the United States. To accomplish this analytically, Patrick Sharkey and I classified all neighborhoods based on location within or outside Chicago (mostly suburban Chicago), the dominant neighborhood racial/ethnic group or mix, *and* poverty status at the beginning and end of the study. Neighborhoods with median income in the bottom quartile of Chicago's distribution are defined as "poor." Significant transitions across neighborhoods are defined as those undertaken by at least 5 percent of the residents in each origin neighborhood. Consistent with the decomposition of change approach, stayer mobility pathways are also denoted as significant if at least 5 percent of residents moved addresses but remained in the given neighborhood subtype over the course of the survey. By focusing on the most prominent transitions, the analysis shows how aggregate movement connects neighborhoods and produces a linked network of stratification.[27]

The graph of these flows was striking, so I display in figure 12.3 our key results.[28] Note first that only tiny flows of Chicago residents produce upward mobility in the sense of crossing the boundaries of the racial and ethnic hierarchy that is present in Chicago neighborhoods and well beyond. The most common outcome is to stay in one's original neighborhood (recall also chapter 11), a crucial ingredient in reproducing the system of place stratification. Moreover, the next most common

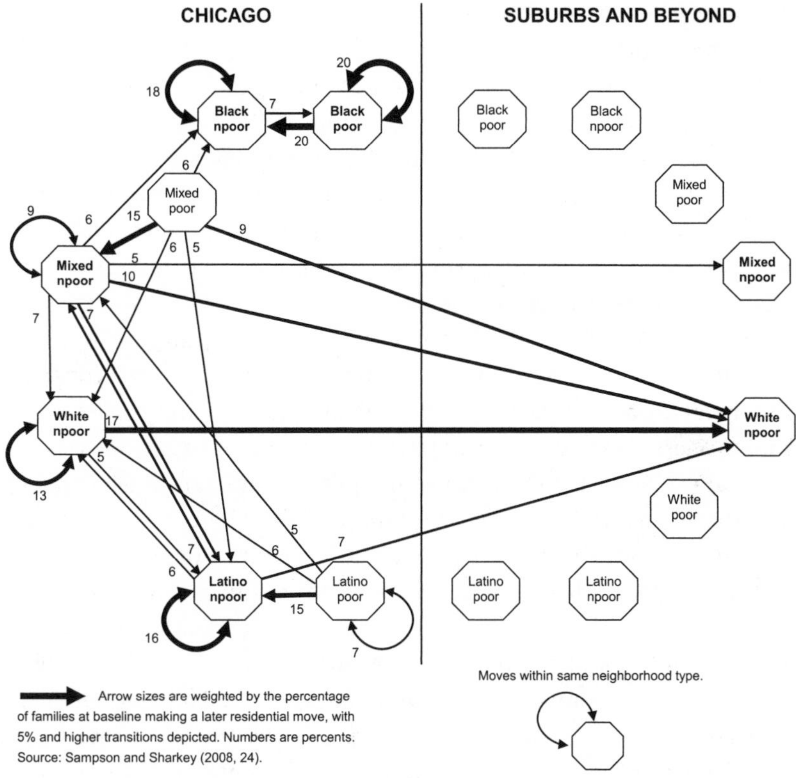

FIGURE 12.3. Mobility flows among white, black, Latino, and mixed ethnic neighborhoods, by poverty typology and Chicago destination status

transition leads movers into neighborhoods *of the same subtype*. Circulation within African American neighborhoods is especially common, as seen in the 20 percent of families in segregated, poor black neighborhoods who change addresses but remain in the "ghetto." Similarly, 18 percent of residents in black nonpoor neighborhoods move into different neighborhoods but of the same type. Twenty percent of families in black poor neighborhoods do leave, but to other segregated black areas. The largest pathway that crosses the black-white divide is from black middle-class areas to white nonpoor areas outside Chicago. This transition is negligible and not drawn in the figure because it represents less than 5 percent of residents.

The dominant flows crossing a racial or ethnic boundary reinforce the hierarchy of neighborhoods rather than undermine it. The data show that four of the five dominant pathways out of Chicago are to white nonpoor areas, and the largest of these pathways originates in white neighborhoods, all of which are nonpoor. White neighborhoods in Chicago are also a favored destination, but do not send to any other neighborhood subtype save one—Latino nonpoor (5 percent make this transition).[29] Considering the improvements in neighborhood quality associated with mobility outside of the city, this pattern reveals one of the major ways in which whites maintain an ongoing advantaged position in the hierarchy of neighborhoods, even in a multiethnic and economically diverse area such as Chicago. Figure 12.3 further reveals considerable neighborhood "exchange" that involves Latino and mixed areas, and, to a lesser extent, Latino and white areas. For example, we see a reciprocal exchange between Latino and mixed (heterogeneous) nonpoor neighborhoods, and between white nonpoor and Latino nonpoor neighborhoods, although the exit pathway from white nonpoor neighborhoods to outside Chicago suggests that Latinos are moving into white Chicago neighborhoods in the process of transition and hence on their way toward becoming Latino enclaves. At the same time, the pathway connecting Latino nonpoor neighborhoods to white nonpoor neighborhoods outside Chicago is composed primarily of Latinos, indicating that nontrivial numbers of Latinos are moving into suburban neighborhoods that are primarily white. A stark reality is thus confirmed: the lack of significant pathways to any poor neighborhoods outside Chicago and to any black or Latino neighborhoods constitutes a hierarchy of racial and economic residential exchange that reproduces neighborhood stratification, a process that in turn bears directly on the lives of children who have no choice in the matter.

Implications

The results of this chapter yield several implications for understanding neighborhood change and thereby neighborhood effects. They also help us make sense of the "Separate Chicagos" introduced at the chapter's beginning, which seem to provoke surprise by many observers. The data here suggest that the culprit is deeply rooted and that surprise is unjustified.

First, a number of previously unobserved factors that represent hypothesized sources of selection bias in studies of neighborhood effects are, despite the numerous suspicions and claims raised in the literature, of minimal importance in actual or revealed neighborhood selection decisions. Residential stratification falls powerfully along race/ethnic lines and socioeconomic location, especially income, education, and home ownership. These are, for the most part, the only factors that explain a significant proportion of variance in neighborhood attainment. Even after introducing a variety of theoretically motivated covariates that captured heretofore unstudied aspects of locational attainment—such as depression, criminality, IQ, impulsivity, and social support—the substantive picture of our results was unchanged. It follows that longitudinal studies, such as the present, that properly account for neighborhood selection decisions along with key individual and family factors may make for a valid test of neighborhood influences.

Second, the data show that context matters for mobility, suggesting that the search for individual explanations may be misguided. Whites and Latinos living in neighborhoods with growing populations of nonwhites are most likely to move out, providing evidence that mobility arises, at least in part, as a response to changes in the racial mix of the origin neighborhood. Blacks are not influenced by racial change, but they appear to be provoked to leave when collectively perceived disorder is high. It is likely that some of the inequality reproduction that lies behind the Separate Chicagos is "chosen," not in the sense of an intended consequence but because some families, especially African Americans, trade more affluent (white) neighborhoods for ones perceived to be more hospitable and racially diverse, a reasonable assumption given the grim history of race relations in Chicago. Taking the full measure of things, it is a mistake to consider white suburbs the yardstick of measurement, as Kenneth Clark argued in 1965 (and as was quoted at the outset of chapter 11). Indeed, the data are consistent with the notion that members of minority groups make residential sorting decisions based on their perceptions of a racialized hierarchy of places—even if they are felt to be unjust—in an era of reduced institutional discrimination. There is no significant exchange between African American and either mixed or Latino neighborhoods in low-income areas that presumably do not present the vigorous opposition or institutional barriers of the sort proposed by place stratification theory, even though anticipated discrimination may motivate nonwhite stayers.

Preferences and constraints thus work together to sustain the self-reinforcing cycle of inequality also reported in chapters 5 and 11. As a result, poverty traps are difficult to escape and likely to continue, absent state-led interventions (e.g., deconcentration of public housing) or cultural changes that yield visions of social life where ethnic and class diversity is seen as an urban amenity rather than a stigma. The election of Barack Obama in 2008 was thought to have gone some distance in promoting this sort of change, especially since his home neighborhood in Chicago is a now a national symbol of racial diversity. Positive change may well be underway, but exceptions provide insights and, as seen in chapter 8, Hyde Park is organizationally dense and has put immense resources for a long time into maintaining stable racial integration.[30] Not every community has a University of Chicago or other institution to anchor its effort to achieve racial diversity; nearly all others are left on their own. For the average neighborhood, the racial and economic hierarchy of neighborhoods is highly durable. In the final section of the book I will return to the question of what explains the repositioning of neighborhood trajectories.

For now we see that a paradox of sorts emerges—even as "Separate Chicagos" remain persistent and visible, there is a constant "churning" and mobility across neighborhood boundaries that intermix a number of social categories such as crime, depression, and other factors not typically considered. Yet even here context matters: people move for a variety of reasons, but rarely are characteristics of origin and destination neighborhoods irrelevant in cognitive appraisals. The meaning of disorder is a case in point, as are changes in the racial composition of a community. Ironically, then, neighborhood conditions matter a great deal for influencing bottom-up selection decisions, suggesting a different kind of social influence than normally conceived—sorting as a social process. The next chapter pursues the structural implications of this idea at the level of the citywide network of residential moves. In the meantime, this chapter has demonstrated that, if anything, *selection bias is itself a form of neighborhood effect.*

13 Network Mechanisms of Interneighborhood Migration

If there is one area of social research that many consider to have resisted "individual reductionism," it is social networks. A prominent and growing field, social networks have captured the public imagination. The phrase "six degrees of separation" is now part of popular culture, and the idea that our friends can make us fat recently made front-page news.[1] This newfound popularity contrasts to the longstanding role that social networks have played in the community and urban literature.[2] Indeed, the density of social ties in a neighborhood is one of the most frequently mentioned characteristics thought to predict outcomes such as better health and lower crime. As chapter 2 showed, this kind of thinking goes back at least to the early Chicago School. So in a real sense the current popularity of networks is an example of rediscovering the past, in this case that of classic urban sociology.

What is surprising, however, is how little neighborhood networks have actually been studied, as opposed to being invoked in metaphorical terms. Even when social ties are assessed empirically, networks typically refer to perceptions about the nature of ties in an area or the aggregation of individual-level ties—not the structure of an actual network. In other words, prior research is dominated by a focus on individual connections and an "egocentric" perception of social structure. Such an analytic move can answer important questions, and I have not hesitated to use ego-derived measures where appropriate. The measures of social cohesion, kin/friendship ties, and reciprocated exchange reported in chapter 7, for example, were based on the aggregation of individual self-reports. Shared expectations, a major component of collective efficacy, are also necessarily linked to variations in perceptions. But while these and other constructs have been shown to have theoretical import for certain questions, rarely has social science documented variations *between* communities in social networks, much less the citywide structure.

In this chapter I therefore present a different approach to "neighborhood networks," building on the findings and logic laid out in chapters 11 and 12 that showed the fundamental importance of selection into and out of neighborhoods. Derived from work in collaboration with Corina Graif, I analyze the structure of residential selection and the social sources of interneighborhood migration.[3] Relations among neighborhoods become the unit of analysis, which in turn allows empirical assessment of how dissimilarity in structural and cultural characteristics influence mobility flows. I examine three sets of competing factors that are hypothesized to explain interneighborhood networks: (1) spatial proximity, (2) differences in race and income composition, and (3) dissimilarity of the social and cultural climate (perceived disorder, collective efficacy, local ties, and organizational participation). The results reveal effects of both spatial and structural distance on the flows of people between neighborhoods, and I further show that dissimilarity in social climate is distinct from the alignment of economic status and demographic composition between communities. In particular, I highlight the salient role of collectively perceived disorder and I examine how individual factors such as depression and criminality are related to patterns of interneighborhood migration. Overall the results show that dyadic patterns of neighborhood movement are fundamentally social rather than individual in nature and thereby form an active ingredient creating the interdependent social structure of Chicago.

In chapter 14, I push the network idea to another level by examining how ties of influence among key institutional leaders in Chicago form connections within and across communities, and in turn how the structure of these networks bears on community-level outcomes. Taken together, these two chapters present what I argue is a novel way to complete this section's bird's-eye view of the neighborhood networks and social structure of the city.

How Residential Mobility Creates a Network

Analogous to international migration, a move between two neighborhoods creates a tie between origin and destination, knitting together the larger structure of residential mobility.[4] In this view, the microlevel selection to a new neighborhood or the decision to stay behind may be seen as a mechanism with structural implications. Although not couched in these terms, Wilson's influential argument about the effects of the outmigration of the black middle class on concentrated ghetto poverty was linked to the social consequences of residential mobility. Consistent with the argument in chapters 11 and 12, sorting or individual selection among neighborhoods thus has emergent or macrolevel consequences.

Figure 13.1 begins to illustrate how the dynamic structure of residential mobility looks, showing connections among Chicago's community areas (circles) arranged in relative geographic position and with arrows sized in proportion to the direction and volume of residential moves.[5] Circles sizes denote the number of different communities in the citywide network to which a focal community is tied, normalized according to the sample size. The network map on the left reflects "indegree," or the number of distinct communities from which a focal area *receives* migrants. "Outdegree," on the right, measures the number of different communities to which a focal area *sends* former residents. Sending ties are only relevant for community areas that contain a sampled PHDCN neighborhood in the first place.[6] I will examine specific communities shortly, but for now the graphs reveal both similarity and variability in receiving and sending patterns of intercommunity migration. There are several communities on the Far Northeast Side, for example, that tend to lose rather than attract residentially mobile families—they are primarily senders. By contrast, a dense clustering of both in-moves and outflows is apparent in a relatively small area on the Northwest Side. Yet overall it is the case that most communities are similar in their indegree *and* outdegree, and that some residential moves reach across the length of the city, thereby connecting far-flung and not just close-by neighborhoods. What are the sources of these structured moves and what communities are central to the story?

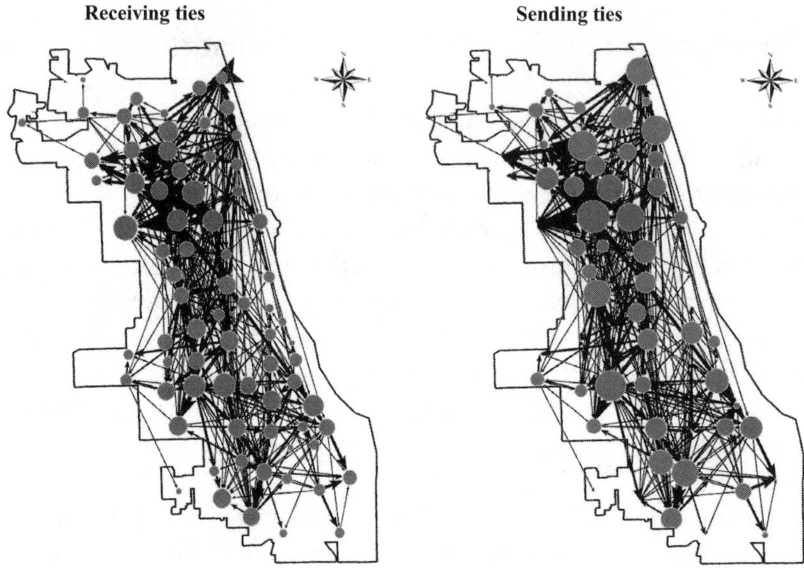

FIGURE 13.1. Dynamics of residential mobility in Chicago, 1995–2002: community-area connectivity by receiving and sending status. Size of circle for indegree valued by the number of communities from which a focal area received in-movers. Outdegree proportional to the number of communities to which it sends movers.

Figure 13.2 breaks down residential moves by black, white, and Latino families over the course of the PHDCN study and situates them in the context of specific places. I do so by identifying every community area, but to reduce clutter I only name key places within each race/ethnic type; the rest are identified by number.[7] Because of the smaller sample sizes by race, I graph binary moves that reflect any tie. I focus on receiving ties (indegree) so as to compare the maximum number of communities across the city. We see that whites and blacks form dynamic connections among neighborhoods within what appear to be almost parallel universes. Whites, for example, move largely among the far northwest communities (e.g., Jefferson Park, Portage Park) and a few, like Clearing, on the Southwest Side. Black migration is highly constrained to the West Side, especially Austin, and the Far South Side. Communities such as West Englewood, South Shore, and Roseland are seeing in-migration from the traditional black belt. As we learned from other maps, these areas are also disproportionately high in concentrated disadvantage. What is equally important and striking to the eye is the large number of communities not connected—where people do *not* move. There is almost no white-black racial exchange across large areas of the city, with many isolates. Black families move within sections of the city that are highly circumscribed by concentrated disadvantage.

The rightmost panel shows that Hispanics form a third sector of mobility, moving back and forth among a set of communities in the northwest area (e.g., Logan Square and Hermosa), the traditional "barrio" of Little Village/Pilsen, and the emerging Latino community of Brighton Park. To the southeast, Hegewisch and East Side are attracting Latino families as well. We see a high degree of movement between Latino immigrant and heterogeneous communities, but virtually no movement to black communities, meaning that the "separate Chicagos" referred to at the outset of chapter 12 extend to black and Latino populations and not just the usual black-white dichotomy. Meaningful mixing does not occur, for all intents and purposes, across sharply drawn racial and ethnic lines: individual selection is a highly structured process.

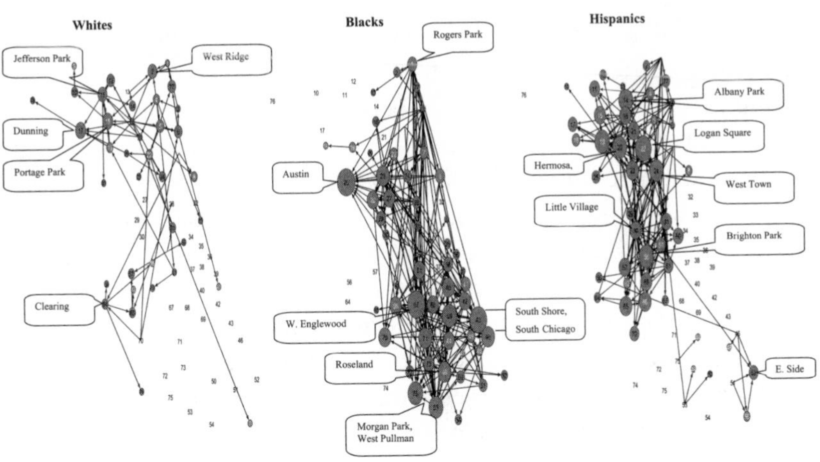

FIGURE 13.2. Moving in separate social worlds: residential ties over time by race/ethnicity of movers. Circles proportional to indegree movement. Binary ties and community-area identifiers shown in graph.

Explaining the Structure of Mobility

The patterns in figure 13.2 and chapter 12 motivate the hypothesis that what sociologists call "homophily" governs residential selection. At its simplest level, homophily is the principle that like attracts like. The implication is that interactions or network ties between similar people or entities will occur at a higher rate than among dissimilar pairings. Because migration is a network in space, it follows that homophily influences not just individual interactions but neighborhood connections as well. The goal is to understand the social processes of homophily.

In reviewing studies on the formation and maintenance of ties between individuals across a variety of dimensions, McPherson and colleagues concluded that "geography is the physical substrate on which homophily is built."[8] Barry Wellman argues that while technology permits distance-free relationships in theory, personal relationships still depend heavily on direct contact at initiation and for their stable maintenance, and as a result they continue to be shaped by geographic proximity.[9] Spatial opportunities for contact are also likely to influence transmission of information about the perceived desirability of nearby neighborhoods. Even in today's globalized world and contrary to the "death of distance" claims reviewed in chapter 1, then, there are strong reasons to expect that there will be greater residential exchange between nearby neighborhoods than between spatially distant neighborhoods. This "spatial logic" implies that geographic distance has direct negative effects on migration networks. Recall from chapter 12, however, that moves traversing long distances, such as to the suburbs, often induce considerable change in the social and physical environment. Distance is often seen as (and is) a positive marker of change, such as when someone moves far away from perceived danger in the inner city. In these cases we might expect a weakened role for spatial proximity. This chapter directly assesses how residential moves play out with respect to the simple fact of spatial proximity, holding constant other differences between origin and destination.

The tendency of people to associate with similar others based on nonspatial social characteristics such as race, income, and education has been well documented in sociology. The homophily of interpersonal ties is reinforced by population homogeneity based on race, ethnicity, religion, and family attributes. To the extent that people actively seek socially similar relationships, similarity in the composition of neighborhoods of origin and destination will be more likely. *Social distance* is thus a second factor hypothesized to influence neighborhood connections defined by residential mobility. There is support for this general idea in studies of other "supraindividual" units of analysis—similarity in status, power, and other social attributes increases the diffusion of norms and information between organizations, for example.[10] And as shown in previous chapters, spatial mechanisms of segregation reinforce the sorting of poor black families into highly disadvantaged and segregated black neighborhoods and high-income white families into more resource-advantaged white neighborhoods.

A counterhypothesis is that residential mobility is associated with social mobility in American cities. An example was shown in chapter 12. The greatest increases in neighborhood income over time were among families that moved outside of Chicago. To the extent that residential mobility is an indicator of upward social mobility, connections between neighborhoods with *dissimilar* income levels or racial compositions may be more likely than between neighborhoods with similar status attributes. "Moving up" is about purposeful dissimilarity, in other words. But as chapter 12 also showed, nontrivial upward mobility was rare, and the vast majority of families remained in the city. Vastly different neighborhood starting points, combined with a similar rate of economic return to mobility by race, led to a social reproduction of inequality whereby destinations were nonconverging (e.g., recall figs. 12.1 and 12.3). These simultaneous patterns suggest that while residential mobility is a mechanism of social mobility, neighborhoods with similar income levels and racial composition will nonetheless be disproportionately connected through residential flows and thus form a kind of higher-order structural constraint that confronts each individual mover.

Perhaps the most interesting but least studied possibility is that the *social climate* based on collective processes emphasized in this book, such as perceived disorder and shared perceptions of control, is an independent trigger of neighborhood sorting and the reinforcement of migration chains. Although focusing on Mexican migration to the U.S., Massey and associates present evidence that local social structures and voluntary associations (e.g., soccer clubs) facilitate mobility between specific communities of origin and particular communities of destination. Other studies show that friends, kin, and local institutions play a role in the residential mobility trajectory of African Americans over long distances.[11] Little evidence exists about residential mobility pathways in U.S. cities, but the neighborhood logic of this book suggests that social mechanisms are at work in important ways. For example, those who value tight-knit communities where residents are involved in voluntary associations may actively seek these same attributes in choosing a new community of residence. Neighborhood associations are often directly involved in efforts to manage public narratives about neighborhood change.[12] Socially cohesive communities may also selectively communicate relevant housing information through organizational and other institutional channels to residents from other cohesive communities, thus connecting residential flows from communities with similar profiles.[13]

Neighborhood reputations matter as well, perhaps especially so with respect to perceptions that a neighborhood is disorderly or "bad." The fame of the "broken windows" thesis is ironic here, for the more the idea that cues of disorder (e.g., graffiti, unsupervised kids hanging out on the street, vacant housing) attract criminals and crime is publicized, the more likely people are to act on its prediction. This reinforcing cycle helps explain why shared perceptions of disorder are implicated in how the character of a neighborhood evolves or is reinforced over time. Chapter 6 showed that shared perceptions were as strong if not stronger in predicting later poverty than a neighborhood's social and demographic composition. Social perceptions of disorder actually had a larger effect on later poverty levels than the inertial path dependence for which prior poverty serves as a direct proxy. Recall also that systematically observed disorder had no independent association with later poverty—the significant pathway was through prior shared perceptions. Because reputations of neighborhoods are bound up with meanings of disorder and reinforced through informal and institutional mechanisms (e.g., gossip, real estate steering, information flows), it follows that similarity in perceived disorder will shape patterns of interneighborhood movement, a form of *cultural homophily*. The resulting hypothesis is that, conditional on the economic and racial composition of a neighborhood, and controlling for associated conditions like the crime rate, similarity in collective ratings of disorder will predict mobility flows between neighborhoods.

In short, this chapter evaluates three claims against the alternative view that spatial proximity and social distance are no longer controlling mechanisms in interneighborhood migration. The first claim extends the spatial logic set out in chapter 10: the geographic proximity between any two communities will directly increase the likelihood (and strength) of a tie based on residential exchange. The second extends chapters 11 and 12 and is about neighborhood composition. Does socioeconomic similarity between any two communities predict the likelihood or strength of a residential tie between them? On average, neighborhoods with similar socioeconomic levels and racial makeup are expected to be connected by residential exchange flows. The third claim moves the debate beyond the material and compositional qualities of a neighborhood to a direct focus on the collective or social quality of life. Although perhaps less visible to the naked eye than demographic composition, the social climate and shared meanings of a place capture important mechanisms reinforcing the social order of neighborhood mobility.

Strategy and Results

To assess these ideas, neighborhood characteristics that are traditionally considered as attributes were redefined as a set of *interneighborhood* matrices of residential exchange. As an illustration of this method, consider a matrix defining the connections among the eighty sampled neighborhood clusters in the PHDCN. This eighty-by-eighty matrix would have 6,320 cells or between-neighborhood relations, not counting the diagonal; the 343 neighborhoods in the entire city yield 117,306 cells. The cells of the matrix were first defined as the spatial distance between each pair of neighborhoods. Distance was calculated as a Euclidian function from the latitude and longitude coordinates of neighborhood centroids. Next, the absolute *difference* in social characteristics between each pair of neighborhoods was calculated. *Median income* is the main indicator of socioeconomic status. *Percent black* is the main indicator of racial composition; both are based on 2000 census data. *Population density* from the 2000 census (persons per kilometer) and the officially reported *crime rate* from 1995 to 1999 are control variables. *Social climate* indicators are based on the combined community surveys and are adjusted for measurement error. They reflect the average level of each indicator corresponding to the time between baseline and final assessment (1995–2002) and as measured in the two community surveys (1995 and 2002). *Collective efficacy, perceived disorder, density of friend/kinship ties,* and *organizational participation* are defined in earlier chapters.

To analyze these data requires a relational methodology that permits estimation of how spatial distance and social (dis)similarity between neighborhoods explain the connections between them formed by residential migration. In the main set of analyses, a valued tie between any two neighborhoods indicates the *volume* of residential mobility between baseline and final assessment. In a second set of analyses, ties were dichotomized such that a value of one indicates *any* residential exchange of households (one or more) between two neighborhoods. Analyses were conducted on relations among all community areas (N = 76, not counting O'Hare) and all neighborhood clusters (N = 343) in Chicago, and on the community areas and neighborhood clusters represented in the baseline PHDCN sample (N = 47 and 80, respectively). I present a summary description of the main substantive picture that emerges across these different specifications, but I place my primary emphasis on the results from the full spatial network that is defined explicitly by the PHDCN study. The eighty sampled neighborhood clusters and forty-seven community areas are by design representative of the city while simultaneously permitting a reasonably large number of neighborhoods as inputs to the analysis and enough within-neighborhood study members to generate reliable mobility estimates.[14]

Figure 13.3 displays a bar chart of the relative magnitude of standardized effects from a dyadic analysis of the volume of residential flows among the eighty sampled neighborhood clusters and the associated community areas (N = 47). Starting with neighborhood clusters, we see that spatial distance strongly depresses direct ties through residential exchange. The association is robust and the standardized coefficient is much larger than for any other predictor—distance clearly matters for understanding the larger structure of moving.[15] So too does economic composition and its correlated resources. Controlling for the spatial proximity between any two neighborhoods, pairwise dissimilarities in median family income leads to a lower volume of direct residential exchange. Among the other structural factors, racial composition (percent black) approaches significance ($p < 0.10$). In models in which racial and ethnic diversity is substituted for percent black, this pattern remains

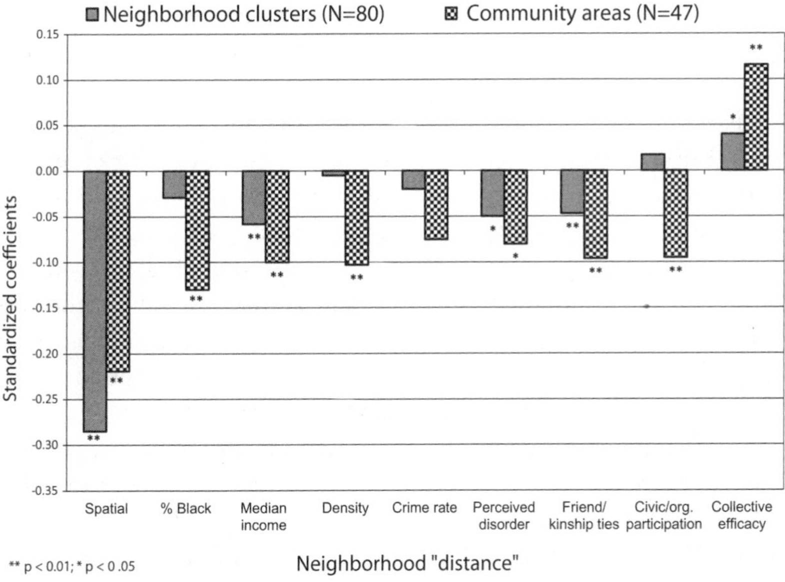

FIGURE 13.3. Explaining interneighborhood flows of residential mobility

unchanged, so it is not just about the measure. The crime rate and population density also do not predict mobility flows.

The most interesting results from a theoretical standpoint pertain to the role of neighborhood social climate and collective processes. After adjusting for the effects of spatial proximity and social distance based on race and income, the volume of ties connecting the eighty neighborhoods in the original sample is directly associated with similarity on friend/kinship networks and perceived levels of disorder. The sign of the coefficients in the figure means that where the level of socially perceived disorder and the density of friend and kin differs between two neighborhoods, there is a significantly lower rate of residential exchange that cannot be accounted for by similarities in the composition of the neighborhoods, their crime rate, or other social factors. The result for friend/kinship ties suggests that homophily at the neighborhood level extends to sorting by social-interactional dynamics. Further analysis also reveals that perceived disorder is robust to controlling for *observed* disorder, suggesting that shared norms rather than physical attributes associated with disorder are what facilitate cross-neighborhood residential connections. Notably, collectively perceived disorder and the density of local social ties rival the effects of demographic composition and income in magnitude.

Perhaps surprisingly, given other results in this book, similarity in organizational participation does not have a direct bearing on migration ties between neighborhoods. Pairwise dissimilarity in levels of collective efficacy predicts *higher* flow volumes, again somewhat unexpectedly. This result means that, all else equal, there is some evidence that residents are moving "up" and "down" with respect to collective efficacy. Graif and I examine this pattern in more detail but do not find evidence that differences in collective efficacy shape the net flows in a particular direction—upward and downward moves are equally likely. We also find that the main pattern in figure 13.3 generalizes to residential ties connecting all 343 neighborhood clusters in Chicago's citywide network, with spatial distance and social distance defined by sociodemographic composition, perceived disorder, and friend/kinship ties all significantly predicting neighborhood exchange.[16]

The duel explanatory power of spatial and social distance maintains when we shift analysis to population flows among community areas in Chicago. These are shown in second set of bars in figure 13.3. Because community areas are larger geographical units, flows between spatially proximate neighborhood clusters within the same community area do not count in the calculation of intercommunity ties, and thus one might expect a weaker role for spatial proximity in shaping network ties. But spatial proximity remains the largest factor, reducing the volume of residential network ties, although less so than for neighborhood clusters. This makes sense, as spatial proximity becomes more salient the smaller the community being considered. In general, however, all the other relationships are larger when the focus is on between-community migration ties. Note that every social distance factor, demographic or social climate in nature, has a stronger effect on migration ties among communities than among neighborhood clusters. Income, disorder, friend and kin network density, and collective efficacy in particular remain significant after adjusting for the spatial effect. Similarity in racial composition becomes stronger in predicting ties and, to an even larger extent, so does similarity in population density and similarity in organizational participation. It appears that sorting among community areas is more patterned according to key stratification and social climate cues, perhaps because, as I argued earlier, these communities have well-defined reputations and social meanings that correspond to these very characteristics, reinforcing social differentiation. Community organizations also typically have referent points or catchment areas that are larger than a single neighborhood. Community sorting is thus more socially structured than by neighborhood.

The reader might be concerned that the analysis has not adequately taken into account family resources in the residential mobility process. While the data indicate that similarity in neighborhood income induces residential exchange, does this pattern hold for all income groups? An economic perspective might argue that household differences in income and available resources drive what only appears to be the contextual effect of median neighborhood income. This concern was addressed by redefining interneighborhood migration according to different categories based on the incomes of PHDCN families at baseline. *Low-income* flows were defined based on households with an income below $10,000 (in 2000 dollars). *Medium-income* flows are based on households with incomes higher than $10,000 and less than $30,000. Because of the skewed distribution and loss of cases at the higher incomes, a *high-income* category was examined in several ways—over $20,000, over $30,000, and over $40,000. The results showed that the similarity of median income predicts interneighborhood ties *within* virtually every household income group, establishing a "contextual effect" of income dissimilarity on mobility exchange at the neighborhood level.[17]

Disorder Flows

The results summarized in figure 13.3 underscore the consistent role of perceived disorder in shaping residential exchange among neighborhoods. This pattern is notable because demographic-economic composition and the crime rate are explicitly controlled. But what is not clear is whether the process is equally present in high- as in low-disorder neighborhoods. The flow of residents from one low-disorder ("well-kept") neighborhood to another may dominate the pattern, given that cleanliness and norms of orderliness are pervasive themes in American neighborhoods.[18] In other words, the cultural sorting might reasonably be expected to be at the high end. I address this distinction and extend the earlier analysis by reclassifying residential moves into high- and low-disorder categories. To preserve the maximum number of nodes and dyadic comparisons in this breakdown, I examine neighborhood clusters. The left panel in figure 13.4 plots neighborhood clusters above the median in perceived disorder (high). The right panel maps counterpart neighborhoods below the median (low). The geographic boundary of Chicago is superimposed on all areas, and arrows reflect binary mobility ties among neighborhoods.

We observe a dense and perhaps surprisingly clustered movement among similarly situated *high-disorder* neighborhoods. Note the two large clusters on the West and South sides of the city that are themselves interconnected along with a smaller cluster on the Northeast Side. Virtually every high-high tie in the city falls within one of these three clusters or connects the clusters. Consistent with the finding that the disorder effect goes beyond spatial proximity, the chains of connection often traverse very distant but otherwise similar high-disorder neighborhoods. Because income and racial composition cannot explain this pattern, these pathways of connections are apparently constituted by their *similarities in shared meanings*, a sort of cultural sorting that produces a structure of homophily. It seems likely that this result is driven by familiarity in norms and practices in the urban environment about use of public space, norms that are reinforced by outside observers. These norms can exist within races and not just between them. For example, ethnographic research in black communities of Chicago has uncovered differing perceptions and sometimes conflicting definitions of orderly or proper behavior (e.g., barbecues on the porch, outside gatherings of teens, working on cars in the street, presence of disorderly family members) within both lower-income and gentrifying black neighborhoods.[19] One imagines also that differing thresholds and levels of comfort for public "disorder" come into play (chapter 6). That there would be residential migration between similarly positioned "high-disorder" neighborhoods is thus socially understandable, even though to my knowledge this phenomenon has not before been shown.

By contrast, the migration flows between *low-disorder* neighborhoods, while geographically shaped consistent with the spatial distance effect, are clustered in two different and largely nonoverlapping regions of the city (e.g., Northwest and Southwest sides) that are highlighted in the right panel of figure 13.4. We see strong sorting at the between-neighborhood level, with a stream of ties connecting low-disorder areas.

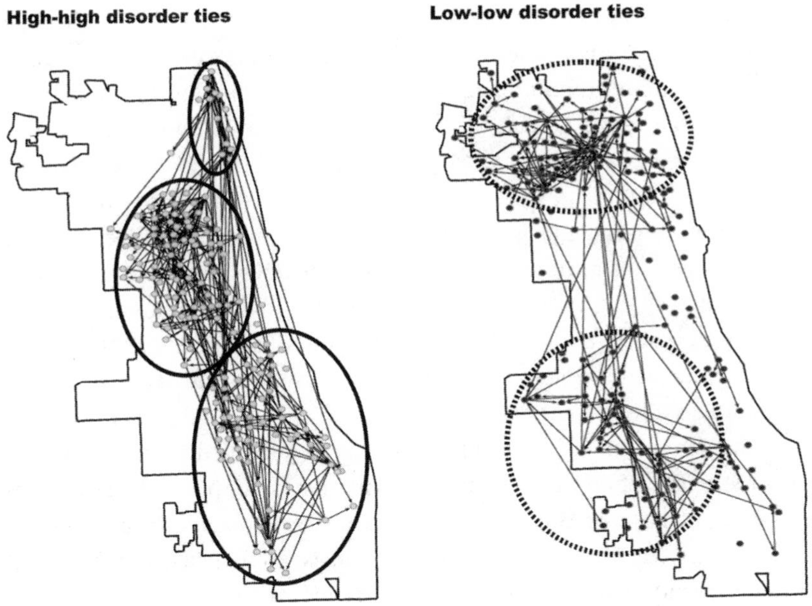

High-high disorder ties **Low-low disorder ties**

FIGURE 13.4. Mobility ties among neighborhoods of similarly perceived disorder

I believe this empirical regularity supports the present theoretical framework that links a demographic-like phenomenon—migration—with the reinforcement of social beliefs and norms. Namely, the steady similarity of origin and destination neighborhoods at the cognitive level of collective beliefs serves to continually reproduce norms about "well-kept" properties and shared perceptions of "order."[20] Although not graphed, it follows that migration flows do not cross the "disorder divide" in significant numbers—social homophily dominates interneighborhood connections.

Individual Propensity and Contextual Homophily

One of the complaints about neighborhood-effects research over the decades has been the notion that people with different individual "propensities" differentially select into and out of neighborhoods. I have dealt with the economic critique rooted in financial resources available to households, but perhaps the bigger worry is about true individual differences. For example, a common worry has been neighborhood selection based on propensity to criminality, a source of considerable disruption and stigma across the life course.[21] Concern has also been expressed about mental health, especially sorting by depression, a concern that reaches back to the "drift" hypothesis noted earlier. The data analyzed in chapter 12 showed that a number of individual factors, including crime, "IQ," impulsivity, and depression, did not change the story when it came to estimating between-individual differences in neighborhood attainment outcomes. But the question remains as to biases that may confound the emerging story of relational connections among neighborhoods. In this section, I thus take the next step of revealing the structure of residential exchange conditional on a core set of individual-level factors.

I consider first how neighborhoods are connected by the moves of people with different criminal propensities, as opposed to the usual strategy of point-in-time geographic concentration of crime events or high-crime individuals. Because so little is known about residential mobility and criminal propensity, I first present basic descriptive patterns. Figure 13.5 shows the spatial trajectories of PHDCN families who moved across the entire metropolitan area, classified by "family crime propensity."[22] The moves of "criminal" and "noncriminal" families follow a similar pattern of outmigration flows even to *suburban* destinations out of Chicago. The only real difference is sample size (there are more noncriminals, as expected)—the patterning is substantively very similar. An almost identical pattern obtains when I compare adolescents (not families) in the upper quartile of violent offending compared to the rest of the adolescent sample. Unlike core stratification factors, then, both violent adolescents and families with a history of criminality spread out quite widely in terms of their penetration into Chicago and the metropolitan region, connecting far-flung neighborhoods with the city core.

I also examined the diffusion of criminality within Chicago, the most common destination of movers. Although some neighborhoods are more likely to be on the receiving end than others, there is a high level of connection between neighborhoods created by the moves of each group. What drives these interneighborhood connections? When the sample is split by those families with and without a criminal history, and following the earlier methodology, we again find that general

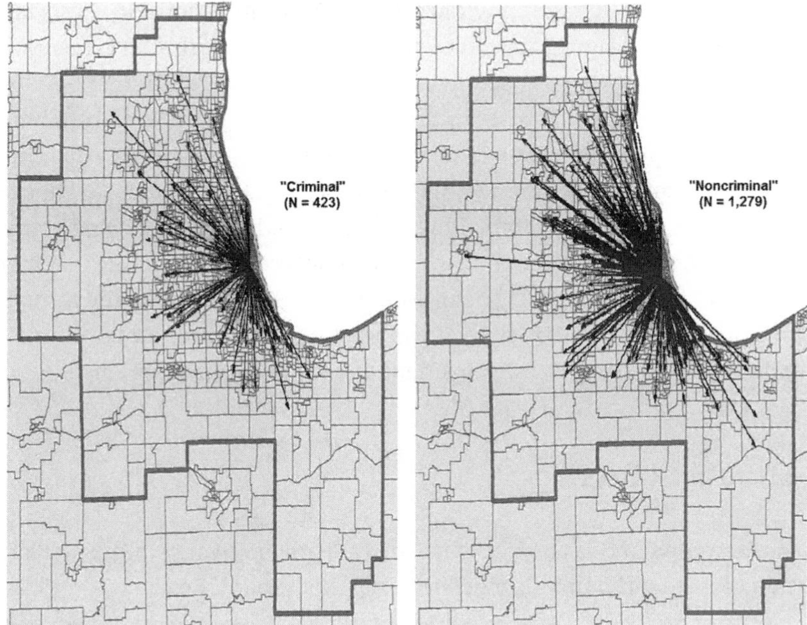

FIGURE 13.5. Criminality on the move: trajectories of suburban moves

processes linked to spatial distance and neighborhood similarities in income, race, friend/kinship ties, and disorder are the key to understanding migration flows. For example, spatial proximity continues to be the strongest predictor of residential exchange for both noncriminal and criminal movers, and the estimated effects of median income and percent black are similar. Moreover, dyadic similarity in the local density of friends/kin and perceived disorder significantly each predict an increased likelihood (and volume) of interneighborhood flows of families, whether or not they have a criminal history at baseline.[23] The consistency and generality of results imply that flows of residential exchange have a *supra*individual component that operates similarly regardless of criminal propensity of the moving household.

Finally, I examined the PHDCN caretakers classified according to those with and without a clinical depression, as defined in chapter 12. Like for criminality, the main results were replicated within groups.[24] Whether or not the head of household was depressed, spatial proximity, similarity in demography/race composition, and similarity in social climate were all significant predictors of interneighborhood residential exchange.[25]

An implication of this set of findings is that network flows of criminally and depression-prone individuals are more hidden from visual inspection than skin color and are in wider circulation among neighborhoods than popular wisdom allows. In colloquial terms, the data in this section suggest that more than a few criminals reside in our midst along with the "down and out." Sorting among neighborhoods by individual risk factors is overwhelmed by the more visible and tangible features of neighborhood stratification that defines the American experience.

Structural Sorting

I have argued in this chapter in favor of a spatial-network conceptualization of residential mobility between neighborhoods. Residential moves reflect an individual action while simultaneously invoking a network of connections among neighborhoods that is both spatial and social in nature. This theoretical logic brings to light a focus on *relations* among geographic entities with social and historical meaning rather than simply their internal attributes. It also clarifies the counterfactual in residential mobility—where residents could have moved to, given the entire range of communities that exist in the city (or potentially, elsewhere). The absence of interneighborhood ties and the concept of "neighborhood isolation" are given real meaning.

The results of this chapter demonstrate that instead of withering away, spatial distance is very much alive in shaping the interneighborhood migration of Chicago families. Accounting for material, demographic, and social-climate differences between communities in addition to income, depression, and criminality, this pattern is likely to reflect a desire of residentially mobile families to retain meaningful physical access to the contacts, social networks, and other resources that are left behind in communities of origin. The time and effort required to build new social networks and gain access to existing social resources in far-flung destinations works as a deterrent against long-distance moves, all things considered. Habits and spatial routines die hard, it seems, and familiarity with one's immediate surroundings is often underestimated as a selection factor, even when the decision has been made to pack up and leave for a new home.

Beyond the brute fact of spatial distance, the results indicate that the greater the similarity between two neighborhoods in demographic composition and the seemingly more nebulous social climate, the higher the likelihood that they are connected through residential exchange. This relational pattern at the neighborhood level was induced primarily by pairwise similarity in median income and social similarity in the density of friend/kinship networks and perceived levels of disorder. At the community-area level, similarity in racial composition and organizational participation emerged as additional predictors of residential exchange, and there was evidence at both the neighborhood-cluster and community level that asymmetry in collective efficacy matters as well. These general results were robust to adjustment according to the spatial flows of households classified by income categories, criminality, and depression, indicating that the patterns are "contextual" and structural at the same time. What I mean by this is that the bird's-eye view of relationships is at the between-neighborhood or structural level, but the approach that defined flows based on subclassification by personal or household factors make them contextual in the classic sense of "above and beyond" the individual. Shared perceptions of disorder and local ties are particularly interesting influences on residential migration that reinforce social boundaries between neighborhoods. Ironically, then, the critique by myself and others that "urban villages" are largely outdated in the contemporary city may be misplaced when we consider the larger structure of population flows. Rather than an effect internal to the neighborhood, as conjured up by the image of the urban village, it appears that dense friend and kinship ties may be more important for the role they play in *interneighborhood* connections.

The results add to the theoretical conceptualization of selection that I have sequentially built up in this section of the book. Social science has adopted a technical and conceptually narrow stance on selection "bias," worried that individuals make choices that demote the significance of social processes. But the opposite is the case, based on my analysis. In fact, the strong version of this chapter and the previous two is that *neighborhoods choose people* rather than the common idea that people choose neighborhoods. This theoretical account points us to the importance of an ongoing social structure that is continually operating and within which any individual or family makes decisions. The flows of movement and the ways in which neighborhoods are linked together are relational and not something that individuals easily control or necessarily are even aware of. I thus believe that it makes theoretical sense to say that individual selection is both a neighborhood effect and a process of higher-order "structural sorting."

14 Leadership and the Higher-Order Structure of Elite Connections

In the last chapter we saw that residential mobility between neighborhoods formed a connective structure, a weblike flow of movement that could not be reduced to the compositional characteristics of individuals. This chapter pursues a conceptually related claim on the idea of the interlocking city. I propose that ties among key institutional leaders form systematic connections of influence within and across communities, and that the emergent structure of these networks bears on our understanding of how cities work. Information exchange and institutional ties among decision makers are a crucial mechanism for getting things done, even if on an everyday basis they might be invisible to the casual observer. My goal is thus to uncover this otherwise hidden structure of elite social action and then connect it back to both internal community characteristics and interneighborhood networks of residential exchange.

To do so, I exploit another original effort of the Chicago Project that I briefly introduced in chapter 4. The Chicago Key Informant Networks Study (hereafter KeyNet) advances the comparative study of social networks by directly probing the ties between community elites and other influential actors. Unlike the vast majority of network studies in single settings, the KeyNet's design is uniquely tailored to an analysis of how leadership structures vary across different communities. Although a pioneering set of community studies has investigated in rich detail the patterning of elite social influence, prior efforts were constrained by a focus on a single community or network or, at most, on a handful of areas.[1] More generally, there is an irony in the literature on social networks—for all the emphasis on "structure," most of the empirical research has focused on interpersonal influences and individual outcomes. That is, the behavior or attitudes of individuals are seen as influenced by others in one's network, what is known as the social influence model. A number of network approaches to social structure makes inferences to the network as a whole (e.g., a classroom or an organization), but rarely are multiple contexts or variability across network structures at issue and almost never in concert with direct measures of social processes and mechanisms.[2]

The KeyNet design addresses these concerns and permits a continuation of our bird's-eye view of the relative position of neighborhoods in the overall social structure. As noted in chapter 2, the overwhelming legacy of the Chicago School has been the community study, with its attendant focus on *intracommunity* dynamics and the between-neighborhood study of variations in local social controls and other internal neighborhood processes in the social disorganization tradition.[3] Across the years, urban scholars have proposed but never fully realized an alternative program of research whereby neighborhoods are regarded as pieces of a larger whole of an interlocking city or metropolis. In this chapter I meet this challenge by studying how social networks link leaders representing the institutional fields that organize much of contemporary social life. My approach to realizing a more holistic vision includes the study of relations both *within* and *across* neighborhoods—not merely as a function of geographical distance but of the interlocking and cross-cutting networks that connect elites, organizations, and ultimately communities throughout (and beyond) Chicago.

The KeyNet study is a large-scale and complex effort that was motivated by a host of questions that could sustain a standalone book. I hope to build on the findings in this chapter to write such a book in the future, with a focus on the social context of governance. For now, however, I strive to be parsimonious by subjecting the KeyNet study to a focused set of five analyses that are directly motivated by the present book's theoretical framework and the results of preceding chapters. My strategy is to first highlight four basic aspects of Chicago's leadership connections: (1) how institutional domains of leadership are interconnected, (2) how the structure of elite networks—such as the density of ties and the centrality of communities in the overall network of ties—

varies across communities, (3) the nature of stability and change in network properties of leadership over time, and (4) whether leadership network structures are explained primarily by the demographic and economic makeup of the community or instead are more fundamentally related to social processes like collective efficacy and a community's organizational life. These four questions cut to the core of our understanding of the community-level context and dynamics of leadership and influence.

Fifth, and perhaps most important, I take a look at how the structure of leadership is related to community wellbeing, and I pursue further the relational approach of the previous chapter by hypothesizing that interneighborhood migration flows are directly related to network flows defined by leadership ties. I argue that if such a link exists and cannot be explained by spatial proximity, demography, or economic status, it would support the ongoing thesis of a higher-order social ordering of the city that simultaneously takes into account individual actions and the composition of each community. Overall I argue that despite the very different empirical terrain, the realization of individual choice—in this case, by elites—is governed by the same systematic properties of the social structure that govern migration flows.

KeyNet-Chicago

The KeyNet was designed to examine community leaders or experts who, based on their position, have specialized knowledge of, and responsibility for, community social action. In a real sense the key informants I study are elite, a group of persons who by virtue of their position exercise power or influence in the community. They are also considerably more educated and make more money than the average citizen; for example, almost half (46 percent) of the key leaders in 1995 had a college or graduate degree, compared to less than 20 percent of the representative sample of adults in Chicago in the same year. We tend to think of elites or leaders only at the very top (presidents, mayors, corporate chieftains), missing the layers of action just below the surface that often do the heavy lifting. Not everybody can be a Mayor Daley, for example, and he is certainly powerful. But his power is nothing without a connective structure that reaches deep into multiple communities and that depends on people who can command action. It is not just the famous aldermen that are at issue, but police captains, school principals, business leaders, ministers, and more. It is these sorts of actors that I study and without whom the workings of Chicago's social order would stall.

The key informant method draws on a distinguished history in cultural anthropology and organizational sociology of using key informants to report on the social and cultural structure of collectivities.[4] The use of positional informants to gather quantitative data on context has also proven to be a reliable, although underutilized, methodology in the social sciences.[5] In the present chapter, I focus on the connections of community leaders within and between communities from a positional perspective, using informants to define, through both nominations of key actors in their network and through snowball sampling, the communitywide context of social organization. KeyNet is a panel-based study that had two major components.

Panel I. The initial design was based on a systematic sampling plan that targeted six institutional domains. We began with the eighty neighborhood clusters in the PHDCN that have been studied throughout this book. These clusters are representative of the city by design and are located in forty-seven of the city's community areas. Because of the sampling design, these forty-seven areas are in effect representative of the city's seventy-seven areas. Targeted domains included *education, religion, business, politics, law enforcement,* and *community organizations.* In most cases the jurisdictions of these domains extend beyond the neighborhood clusters, and so the KeyNet sampling design targeted the larger community area within which the clusters were embedded. As described in earlier chapters, in Chicago most leaders and organizations representing the six institutional domains recognize the boundaries of the city's community areas, which average about thirty-seven thousand residents, and many rely on them to provide services.[6] The sampled communities ranged from ethnically diverse Rogers Park on the Far North Side to black working-class Roseland on the far south, from exclusive Lincoln Park to the extreme poverty of West Garfield Park, from Mexican American (Little Village/South Lawndale) to Puerto Rican (Humboldt Park), and from white middle class (Clearing) to black middle class (Avalon Park). The Loop was also included.

The design required the construction of a geocoded list of over ten thousand positional leaders in Chicago from public sources of information (e.g., phonebooks, directories of businesses and services). Of these, 5,716 were located in the forty-seven sampled community areas. Target informants were defined by the nature of who they were, what they did, and where they were located. Examples of key informants by domain include:

- *Education*: public/private school principal; local school council (LSC) president
- *Business*: community reinvestment officer (banking); realty company owner
- *Religion*: Catholic priest; Protestant pastor; mosque imam; synagogue rabbi
- *Law enforcement*: district commander; neighborhood relations sergeant
- *Politics*: alderman; ward committeeman; state representative; state senator
- *Community organization*: tenant association president; health agency director; community social service manager

Approximately 2,500 cases were sampled, stratified by community and domain before random release for study, with 10 percent turning out to be ineligible (e.g., moved, business closed). NORC at the University of Chicago carried out data collection in 1995, completing 1,717 interviews with sampled leaders in official positions. As seen in the list above, key informants are highly visible actors in the community and easily identifiable, so extreme cautions were taken to protect the confidentiality of data. Occupation alone could identify an alderman, for example.

Following the research tradition established in cultural anthropology and social-network analyses of community influence structures, a "snowball sample" was incorporated as an addition to the original design. We suspected that many of the key actors in a community were new to the position or did not appear on official lists and hence were not sampled. Moreover, some of the influential actors in a community may hold nontraditional positions. To capture the full range of community informants, our interview asked respondents to nominate knowledgeable or influential persons in each of the six core domains of business, law enforcement, religion, education, politics, and community organizations. For the more nontraditional persons who might be able to report on the community, we asked each respondent: "Now, other than the people and organizations that we've already discussed, is there anyone else in [COMMUNITY NAME] that we should speak with, to really understand this community? This could include a longtime resident, a leader of a youth club or gang, a mentor of youth in the community, and so on. Who else would you recommend we talk to?" The sampled positional leaders generated 7,340 reputational nominees, about 3,500 of whom were duplicate nominations—the same individual nominated more than once, or a nominee already in the sample. This finding in itself serves as an important validation of the design.

In all, 1,105 reputational interviews were completed, which, when combined with the positional interviews, brings the final sample size to 2,822. The interviews averaged just under an hour in length, and the overall completion rate was a surprisingly high 87 percent of eligible cases.

Panel II. Just as it is not sufficient to study individual development at one point in time, so it is misleading to rely on snapshots of community-level processes—communities and networks change. A panel-based positional approach to the study of community dynamics allows for the measurement of changes in community leadership (e.g., is there a new leader in the same position?), organizational change (e.g., did the institution itself survive?), changes in the dimensions of social-network structure (e.g., the density of ties), and changes in the content of action (e.g., crime prevention, health promotion). I thus designed the KeyNet panel study to capture (a) reinterviews of 1995 leaders still in the same position, (b) new leaders in the same position or organization as in 1995, (c) leaders in newly formed organizations and positions, and (d) where leaders who exited from 1995 positions went. Organizational and positional sampling frames were updated in 2000 and pretest interviews conducted with fifty-two leaders.

The final sample was constructed in 2002 as a random selection of original positional leaders in 1995, stratified by institutional domain, plus snowball sample nominations designed to capture both new organizations and new leaders. To contain costs, a representative subsample of thirty of the original forty-seven communities was selected for the panel sampling frame. NORC at the University of Chicago was selected to carry out all aspects of contacting respondents and conducting interviews. Over one thousand (N = 1,113) interviews were completed over the summer and fall of 2002 at a response rate of 76 percent of eligibles. Approximately 60 percent of the interviews in 2002 were conducted with new respondents holding the same or similar position as the 1995 respondents, indicating considerable personal turnover in a fairly stable network of positions. The final sample yielded an average of almost forty interviews per community, permitting rigorous examination of how leadership network structures vary across communities.

Assessing Elite Networks

I begin by defining a connection (a tie or an "edge," as it is known in network science) as a nomination that an institutional representative or key informant within a community makes to another individual ("alter"). These ties can be to others within the same community (what I call an "internal alter") or another Chicago community ("external alter"). Ties can and do extend beyond Chicago as well, as, for example, when a leader of a community organization reaches out to a state senator in Springfield, Illinois—yet another kind of external tie. To establish these kinds of leadership ties, the original KeyNet study developed a modified version of Ronald Burt's "name generator," revised by focus groups and then formal pretests in both the 1995 and 2002 studies.[7] In our modified instrument each respondent was asked to identify by name the people they went to in order to "get things done" in the community. Up to five names were allowed. We pretested multiple name generators, but this wording seemed to capture for respondents concrete situations when they formed social ties. Also, by not specifying the type of contact (e.g., asking about a "friend" or "well-known acquaintance") and by not asking for a preset number of contacts (as in, "tell us your three contacts"), we avoided criticisms of commonly used name generators that artificially induce only strong ties or force pseudo-contacts.[8] In fact, many of our respondents were isolates and did not name any contacts, information that is directly relevant to the theoretical problem at hand. The names and addresses of each key contact up to five were recorded, along with their position and organizational affiliation.

In 1995, community leaders nominated almost 5,600 alters as key contacts, but, as theoretically expected, there was overlap in these citations—only about 2,050 of the alters were unique individuals. Respondents nominated 2.5 alters on average, and each distinct alter in 1995 was nominated by 2.72 leaders. The pattern of concentration in 2002 was similar, even though the sample size was smaller—for example, the average number of alter citations was a bit higher, at 3 (over 3,000 nominations and 1,275 distinct alters), and each alter was nominated by 2.4 different respondents on average.

Figure 14.1 shows the flow of ties among respondents and nominated contacts in 2002 for the entire city and without reference to geographic location. Arrows denote direct ties and circles represent individuals with size proportional to "indegree," or the number of distinct ties each person received. The data from 1995 show a similar pattern, but I set that aside in favor of the more recent assessment. At the level of the entire network of individuals, we find a large number of isolated or weakly connected contacts around the periphery (for example, some respondents did not have any contacts) along with a relatively small number of "connectors" in the center who mediate or control much of the action along with a number of cliques radiating outward. There are a number of major players both at the center and in subgroups, including what we might jokingly call "Mr. Big" in the absolute center, but who in fact is big, receiving a disproportionate share of network ties (and who shall remain anonymous, like all leaders).[9]

Although networks like those in figure 14.1 are usually the main story, my major concern is the community-level and temporal variability of ties. Recall the stark differences between the communities of Hegewisch and South Shore introduced in chapter 1 (see fig. 1.4). The former appeared much more "cohesive" than the latter in the picture. I describe here how I capture these differences more formally and for all communities. Because of the systematic and replicable sampling procedures, the KeyNet design allows me to construct network measures for each of Chicago's communities in parallel fashion for both the 1995 and 2002 studies, permitting both comparative and temporal analysis of network structures over time. For simplicity and on grounds of parsimony, I first focus on the *density* of elite ties and the *centralization of the leadership network*.[10] Density captures the idea of cohesion among ties, specifically the proportion of all possible ties that actually exist among

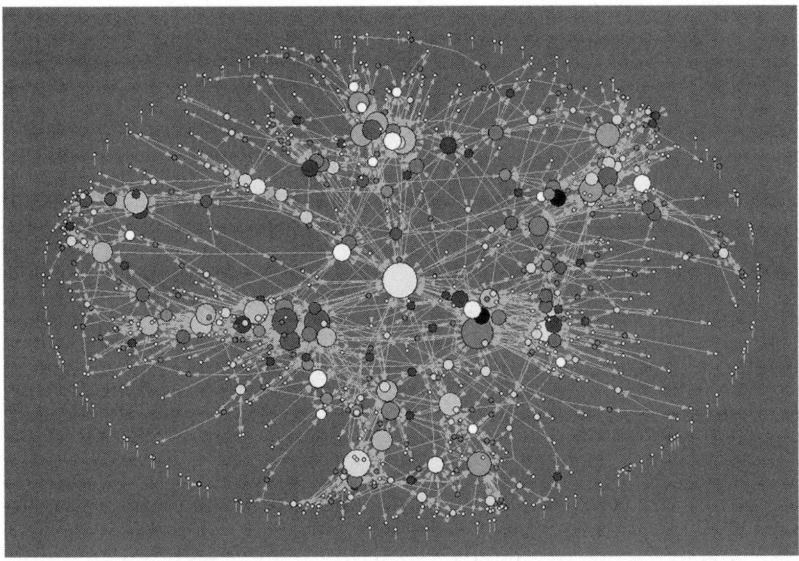

FIGURE 14.1. The structure of ties among leaders in Chicago, 2002

key informants. The opposite of cohesion is fragmentation of ties into cliques. In his seminal paper on weak ties, Mark Granovetter trained his analytic sights on Boston's West End neighborhood, which was unable to fight off urban renewal in the 1950s. Herbert Gans attributed its failure to mobilize mainly to subcultural and political forces, but Granovetter suggested that the ties in the West End lacked structural cohesiveness, a network phenomenon that could only be viewed from what he called the "aerial" perspective—"the local phenomenon is cohesion."[11] In other words, there might be strong ties within interpersonal cliques, as displayed in figure 14.1 or perhaps as in the "urban village" ideal of tight-knit neighborhood groups, but little cross-group or extralocal ties and thus fragmentation at the level of the city's political or social structure.[12] These important ideas have not been systematically investigated at the aerial level across multiple communities over time.

To do this, I first generated a respondent-by-respondent matrix for each community area in which the entries in off-diagonal cells register the number of times respondent i and respondent j cited the same key contact. Density is calculated as the sum of these off-diagonal cells divided by the total possible common cites.[13] Three features of this connectivity measure are worthy of note. First, all leader respondents are included—those who failed to make a single citation are not excluded. This course is taken because the fact of *not* making a citation is meaningful structurally; the respondent is an isolate. On the assumption that the sampling procedure produces a comparable "stain" of networks in different communities, the tendency to pick up peripheral actors will then reflect real differences in the cohesion of these neighborhoods. Second, instead of normalizing by the total possible number of citations, one could normalize based on the actual citations made. This, however, would also mean a loss of information because the fact that someone did not make the full five nominations is meaningful. Across neighborhoods, the tendency to make fewer nominations is an important conceptual component of what we mean by "density."

Third, an important insight of network analysis is that cohesion may not simply be a matter of direct ties. Rather, *chains of indirect ties* may bridge actors, getting closer to the idea that Granovetter originally raised about the West End. The density measure is based on a "path-distance" matrix—the tendency of Chicago's leaders to cite common alters, a two-step tie. Some of these ties can be in the community and others not. If an alderman in Lakeview is connected to a business leader in the Loop that a Lakeview minister is also connected to, for example, they share an indirect tie. The more ties that are overlapping, the more we can say that, in a connectivity sense, the community leadership structure is cohesive. Looking even further at path distances allows us to get a sense of the larger structure of relations in a network. That is, while one- or two-step connections may indicate a relatively sparse network, a look at three-step or four-step or higher-step ties might show that the structure is ultimately quite dense. To the extent that a structure does not appear denser when multisteps are considered, that network is composed of isolated cliques. To capture this idea a higher-order path-distance matrix was generated by taking the density matrix to successive powers, allowing construction of indirect density.[14] A revealing finding is that densely connected communities tend also to be characterized by chains of higher-order indirect ties, suggesting that they are tapping the same phenomenon. For example, the multistep measure correlated with the two-step density measure at 0.87 ($p < 0.01$), and Hyde Park came out on top in both. I thus focus in this chapter primarily on the simpler indicator of two-step ties.

A related network measure that I examine captures more directly the centralization or "agreement" in how key informant ties extend to individual alters. Here the focus is more on the distribution among the cited alters (where the action is going) than on the nominators. At one end of the spectrum we can imagine the unusual situation of a community in which all leaders go to the same and only alter (again, inside or outside the community), which would indicate perfect agreement and overlap. At the other end we might imagine a situation in which leaders are isolated and each nominates a unique individual. To capture these variations, I examine the tendency for a few alters to receive most of the nominating action. For the overall index of centralization, I count all alters, those within the community of interest or outside it, although the nominations can only come from respondents within a given community.[15] The index is based on the Herfindahl formula, a widely used measure of concentration, which in the present case is equal to the sum of the squares of each alter's share of nominations coming from a given community. The centralization index captures the extent to which nominations go to a smaller rather than larger numbers of alters, as well as the variation in the degree of inequality in the number of citations received by all alters nominated by respondents in a community.[16]

A more modern rendering of the ideas that Granovetter raised about Boston's West End is the distinction between what Robert Putnam calls "bonding" ties (strong ties *within* communities) and "bridging" ties (weak ties *among* communities).[17] The density and centralization measures capture a bit of both, depending on where alters are located. Alters outside or external to the community are by definition bridging ties at the community level. Another strategy is to measure the indegree and outdegree of each community similar to the residential migration analysis of the last chapter. A community that *receives* leadership nominations from more distinct communities (indegree) is in a real sense more central to the structure of interlocking ties. A community that *sends* ties to more distinct communities (outdegree) is also connected externally but in a very different way.

Another and perhaps more satisfying indicator of bridging ties at the macro level is the extent to which a community serves as a connector or mediator of ties in the citywide structure. For the sampled network of forty-seven communities in 1995 and again in the thirty communities in 2002, I examined the extent to which leaders were connected to pairs of alters who are not directly connected to each other, putting them in a position to control information and resource flows between leaders with no direct ties. I then extended this concept to the contextual level to derive the number of shortest paths *between pairs of communities* that were generated by Chicago's leaders and that were mediated by a given community. We can think of this type of connection as the brokerage or mediation of intercommunity ties—specifically, the measure taps the extent to which any given community serves as a hub through which leadership connections are flowing, commonly known as "centrality."[18]

Results

The church cannot be an island.

Author interview with the pastor of a leading church on the South Side of Chicago, April 5, 2007

Figure 14.2 recasts the individual connections in figure 14.1 to show how institutional domains in Chicago are interrelated. Recall that six institutional domains were sampled, and a seventh "other" was derived from the snowball sampling. Leaders of community organizations and educational institutions represented about a quarter of all respondents. Leaders in law enforcement, religion, and business represented between about 12 and 17 percent of respondents. By far the smallest domain in absolute number came from politics, representing just 6 percent of the sample. This makes sense, as there are not that many political actors to go around—this domain was quickly "saturated" such that it can be thought of not as a sample from communities but the full population.[19]

It may come as something of a surprise, then, to see how the action among leaders in Chicago is manifested in terms of interdomain connections. Although small in original numbers, the institutional domain of politics looms large in terms of interdomain connectivity and the frequency with which leaders of all organizational affiliations turn to politicians. Indeed, we see in figure 14.2 that of all the domains, politics is the most embedded institutionally. The arrows are proportional to the volume of interinstitutional connections, with politics disproportionately linked across the board. It is perhaps expected that community organizations and politicians are deeply tied, and they are, but politics is

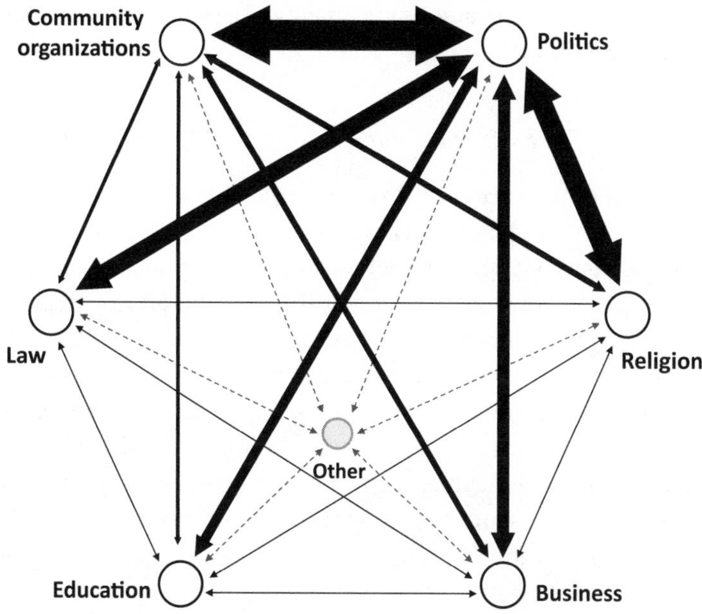

FIGURE 14.2. Interinstitutional connections

nearly as intertwined with religious institutions. The influential pastor quoted above was expressing an apparent reality of how much religion is interconnected with the practical workings of everyday life, which go well beyond matters of faith. The church he led was deeply enmeshed not just with politics and politicians but community organizations, business leaders, educational reformers, and local economic development. Community organizations, which might be thought to be more widely connected, are relatively weakly tied (perhaps unfortunately) to key leaders in education and law. The "other" category is weakly tied to all dimensions, although clearly each kind of institutional domain is connected to this more nontraditional community actor.

In short, figure 14.2 reveals a number of connections that are not part of typical organizational charts. Religious leaders do not do only religion—one of their biggest influences concerns politics. Education leaders are not just about education, and the influential leaders in community organizations have relatively more ties to business than they do to education or law enforcement. Isolated institutional domains would appear to be at a significant disadvantage in the same way that isolated individual leaders are.

Community and Temporal Context

A major goal of this chapter is to explore intercommunity ties, and so I focus for the remainder of analysis on the multiple ways that communities are differentially tied together or isolated as a result of the concrete ties among individual leaders. One of the most helpful strategies is to view the nature of ties at Granovetter's "aerial level," which I present in figure 14.3.[20] Here we see the emergent consequences of individual leader ties for the community social structure of Chicago. Nodes are the sampled community areas, and arrows reflect ties. The size of the nodes is in proportion to outdegree, or the number of distinct communities to which a community sends ties. Only sampled communities can be senders, and so I graph the full network of senders (N = 30 communities). Any community area in Chicago can and does receive ties, as noted by the arrows, but for parsimony the circles and labels are limited to the representative set of sending communities, with the major exception on the left of a non-Chicago type of receiver—the governor, state senators, and other "external" actors who are outside the original sample but nonetheless of considerable substantive interest. Because of the central role that economic status plays in most discussions of social networks and community power, I also classify these communities according to whether they are above or below the median in family income as of 2000.

The results show that certain areas of the city are hubs of activity in terms of connectivity, most noticeably the Loop and Near North Side. But there are regional nodes that are actively connected too on the South Side and Near West Side. There is also a considerable degree of connectivity in the overall citywide network—few communities are islands, although communities do vary in their degree of isolation. It is important to note that while not a large association, income is *negatively* related to outdegree when further standardized by the number of respondents in each sending community (correlation = −0.22). A number of poorer communities thus seem to stand out in terms of their leaders actively reaching outside and making contacts with leaders in many different communities around the city. While this finding goes against

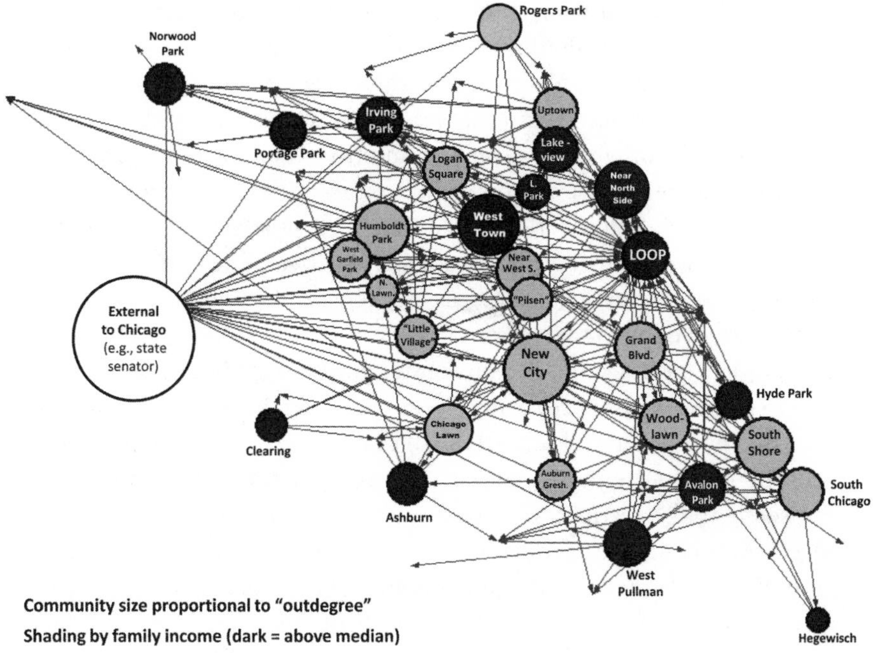

FIGURE 14.3. Community-level structure of influence ties: outdegree of sending communities by income status

a prominent belief that poor communities are isolated in terms of connections to the outside world or the "mainstream," it makes sense to the extent that communities are resource dependent and need to establish external linkages to perceived movers and shakers.

The natural question that arises is how cohesive these patterns are by community. It might be, for example, that a community is resource dependent and its leaders reach out and send a lot of ties to other communities but with virtually no agreement or connections among themselves. Likewise, a community can send a lot of ties but not broker or mediate ties from other communities, another sign of dependence rather than active intervention in the city's web of connections. The data suggest that the density of leadership contacts and the concentration of alter nominations are tapping a similar dimension of cohesive leadership structure, correlating significantly and substantially at 0.73 ($p < 0.01$) in 2002. "Betweenness," which I have defined as a kind of community brokerage indicator, is uncorrelated with the outdegree measure graphed in figure 14.3 and significantly *negatively* correlated with the centralization of nominations within a community (−0.41) despite the relatively small number of cases. Therefore we find two distinct dimensions, one a cohesive internal leadership structure and the other a mediating role in which a given community serves as a junction that ties together otherwise disconnected communities. The Loop, for example, has a high number of external contacts relative to its size and a high number of connections that mediate between other communities but at the same time its leaders are not terribly coherent internally in their mutual or overlapping contacts.

Another key finding concerns temporal stability. The KeyNet study was designed to measure turnover among leadership positions, and in fact turnover was fairly intense, with some 60 percent of respondents in 2002 new to the position relative to 1995. This raises a simple but consequential question: If there is individual turnover, how stable is the overall structure of contacts? It is not inevitable that the churning of individual leaders means fundamental change in the pattern of relations. As I have shown throughout the book, there is often a durability of inequality, social climate, and organizational life, all while the social structure is dynamic. In chapter 8, for example, I showed a high degree of relative stability in the density of nonprofit organizations extending well over a decade. Similarly, there is lots of residential mobility by individuals but a strong inertial quality to neighborhood inequality. This means that any individual leader new to a position is stepping into an ongoing history and structure of relations going well beyond his or her particular background, organizational affiliation, or community.

I directly examine this hypothesis in figure 14.4 by displaying the concentration or cohesiveness of leadership influence by community across time. I also denote each community by whether it is low, medium, or high in resident-level collective efficacy. Two patterns are clearly evident. First, network properties of social organization among elites are quite stable over time (1995–2002) despite considerable turnover in the individuals who occupy the positions. Communities that tend to have a high density of overlap in the contact networks of their leaders—whether internal *or* external to the community—remain densely interconnected even as the individual leaders are replaced. The centrality measure also correlates positively over time (0.54, $p < .01$). Analogous

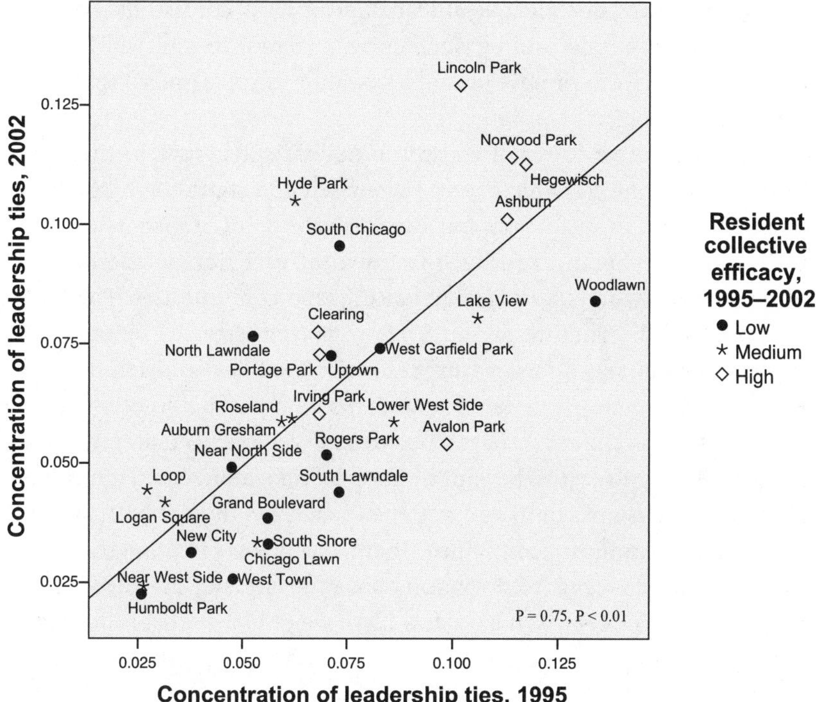

FIGURE 14.4. Persistence of network cohesiveness despite leadership turnover

to residential migration, despite considerable change at the individual level, the underlying structure of relations across communities is remarkably persistent.

Second, figure 14.4 shows that those communities that sit at the upper end of a stable cohesive leadership structure also tend to be high in collective efficacy. A partial exception is Woodlawn, which is low in collective efficacy but saw a significant drop in its relative leadership cohesion over the period. South Chicago is another exception, similarly low in collective efficacy but seeing an increase in its leadership connectivity. Hyde Park and Lincoln Park are medium to high in collective efficacy and saw unexpected increases to the point that they are among the highest in the city in 2002 leadership concentration. Overall, though, communities characterized by fragmentary leadership or low concentration of tie nominations, such as the Near West Side, Grand Boulevard, and

New City, are low in collective efficacy, and several, consistent with the story of the West End told by Gans, have seen radical interventions by the city in the form of new urban renewal (or displacement) that they were unable to stop.

It is instructive to recall again the network structure of the communities introduced in chapter 1, Hegewisch and South Shore (fig. 1.4). These two communities stand at the opposite poles of leadership centralization, further illustrating the range of variation in the density of internal network structures across Chicago communities. The leadership network structure of South Shore is characterized by more external contacts and a larger number of isolated key informants than Hegewisch. Moreover, the few respondents who are tied to others tend to form isolated cliques rather than a dense, well-connected network as in Hegewisch. Interestingly, South Shore is disadvantaged on a number of social dimensions compared to Hegewisch, even though both are not high-income communities. South Shore has a low-birth-weight score that is a full one standard deviation above the citywide average, for example, whereas Hegewisch has a low-birth-weight score that is one standard deviation below the average. This pattern suggests that wellbeing is connected to leader networks.

Taking the larger bird's-eye view suggests an even more general pattern. Where leadership connections are concentrated or less fragmented, we find better health and lower violence across the city. The correlation of the network concentration scores in 2002 with infant mortality rates, percentage of births to teenagers, and homicide rates in 2002–6 is −0.406, −0.309, and −0.527, respectively, across Chicago communities. A concern is that these correlations may be artifically induced by the compositional characteristics of these same communities. But as we saw earlier, economic status is weakly related to leadership network structure. More important, the centralization of leadership ties is a significant predictor of lower homicide and teen birth rates in future years after controlling for the potentially confounding factors of concentrated disadvantage, residential stability, organizational density, *and* the number of communities to which a focal community is tied (outdegree).[21] Thus the level of connectivity of leadership ties in a community is directly related to core outcomes of this book, especially wellbeing in the form of lower violence.

Composition or Social Processes?

The question remains as to what kinds of community characteristics produce variations in leadership connectivity. Is collective efficacy spuriously associated with the density of elite ties in a community? What about concentrated disadvantage and racial composition? And what about the internal versus external nature of community ties? The data tell a simple but powerful story. Namely, the sociodemographic and poverty composition of communities does not determine the kinds of leadership configurations I have charted thus far. Concentrated disadvantage in particular is rather weakly connected to the cohesiveness of leadership and is only modestly predictive of the centrality of a community's position in mediating elite ties. Residential stability, median income, and percent black are weakly correlated as well. But, as we have seen, the cohesiveness and shared expectations of residents is linked to the nature of leadership ties. Because leaders are in a fundamental sense dependent on the residents and organizations they serve, it follows that communities with high shared expectations for social control among their residents would expect or at least help shape a more integrated rather than fragmented leadership style, regardless of the compositional makeup of the community.

I assess these relationships as a whole by examining simultaneous influences. Because of the small number of cases, however, my statistical power is limited. So I examine a parsimonious model that examines those factors highlighted in previous chapters and specified by the theoretical framework I have built up—sociodemographic composition, organizational density, and collective efficacy (see especially chapters 7 and 8). In separate analysis I examined a series of alternative models (e.g., with income and racial composition as controls), but the basic findings were similar. My outcomes of interest are the centrality of communities in mediating leadership contacts and the concentration or density of agreement within communities. To get at the idea of internal versus external ties, I disaggregate the concentration measure into two indices. One taps the concentration or agreement among leaders about alters in the same community. The second restricts the concentration (or Herfindahl index) to shared elite ties *outside* the community. In other words, I ask the question: Do the leaders of a particular community agree or cohere around a set of "go-to" contacts even if those contacts are externally located? I then examine variations in this purely external kind of tie.

The results in figure 14.5 show that disadvantage is modestly connected to lower centrality but not the concentration of leadership ties. Both residential stability and a community's outdegree were insignificant across all three outcomes. For the sake of parsimony, these two factors are thus controlled but not shown in the figure. Once disadvantage, residential stability, and the number of sending communities are taken into account, we see that collective efficacy is significantly and positively related to a more cohesive leadership structure *but only among those alters who share the same community*. Moreover, collective efficacy is negatively related to centrality and unrelated to the external concentration of alter nominations.

The picture seems to be that cohesive communities defined by resident collective efficacy and internally shared alter-elites are not the same ones serving as the largest hubs of intercommunity activity, even though they are not particularly isolated in this regard. What seems to matter most for explaining the centrality of a community in mediating intercommunity ties is the density of its nonprofit organizations, an internal attribute. In further analysis I replicated this finding with the centralization of elite ties in 1995 and the density of organizations in 1994 as the predictor, along with 1990 census data and 1995 outdegree. Consistent with but building on the findings of chapter 8, then, where there is greater organizational density we see more "outreach" and a higher degree of centrality of the community in its city-wide pattern of leadership ties. Organizational effects apparently reverberate within and beyond the borders of any given community.

The bottom line is that community social processes—collective efficacy and organizational density—and not demography or income are doing the major work in fostering connective network structures. This finding reinforces a central claim of the book and also the argument in this section that local and extralocal factors are not necessarily in competition but are mutually contributing to the social organization of the city. More generally, much of the impetus for social network research seems to be in pursuit of the idea that only relational connections matter (i.e., the "structure") as opposed to the social or cultural attributes of

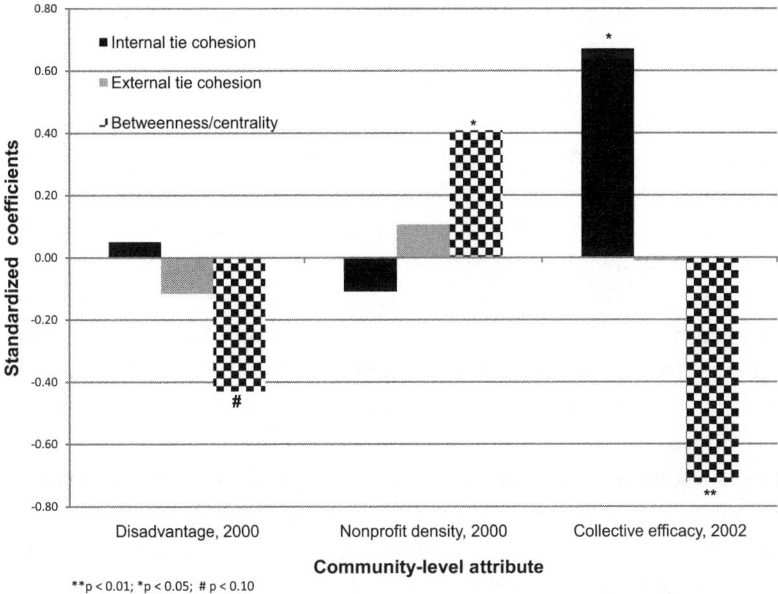

FIGURE 14.5. Community sources of variability in three types of leadership connectivity. (Internal cohesion, $R^2 = 0.34$, $p < 0.10$; External cohesion $R^2 = 0.13$, n.s; Betweenness centrality $R^2 = 0.48$, $p < 0.01$.)

the lower-order units—in this case, communities. I believe this impetus is mistaken—the present theoretical framework argues that both kinds of factors are simultaneously at work and are associated in systematic and mutually reinforcing ways.

Linking Migrations Flows and Elite Connections

In an age of modern communication and asserted placelessness, a dominant view is that elite networks are weakly constrained by the local environment and unlikely to be enabled by mere spatial proximity. Communication, especially among elites, is not seen as limited by geography. Even less attention is typically paid to how the attributes of network actors may play an important role in understanding relational properties of the network dynamics.

To address this gap, I examined the pairwise ties among a representative set of Chicago communities in a manner directly analogous to chapter 13, but here with the tie defined by leadership contact. In addition to the characteristics considered in chapter 13 (see fig. 13.3), I examine pairwise ties previously formed by migration from 1995 to 2002. In other words, the outcome now is the volume of key informant network ties between pairs of communities in 2002 as a function of spatial distance, structural distance, social climate difference, and residential migration pathways up to that point in time.

The results suggest that once again the placelessness critique does not describe how people act, in this case among elites with enhanced options. The effect of spatial distance is highly significant ($p < .01$) as it was for residential mobility and second largest in magnitude, attenuating intercommunity connections. The standard structural characteristics, such as income and racial composition, do not explain patterns of intercommunity leadership ties once spatial distance is accounted for. Neither does similarity in collectively perceived disorder or friendship ties explain key-informant ties between different communities unlike they did for migration ties. Most important, there is a clear and substantial finding that speaks to the importance of intercommunity dynamic flows. Communities that experienced a higher volume of residential exchange in the late 1990s and into 2000 are much more likely to have increased connections among their leaders, controlling for demographic similarities and other social factors. In fact, after alternative explanations are taken into account, the magnitude of the estimated effect of migration networks is larger than all others ($p < 0.01$). It appears that migration flows are tapping the exchanges of people between communities that are productive of informational channels and ultimately elite influence ties. Moreover, similarity in the level of organizational participation generates intercommunity ties as well ($p < .05$). Although smaller in magnitude than spatial proximity or migration ties, the organizational link makes sense based on the findings and theoretical expectations set by chapter 8 and chapter 13.

The mechanism of residential sorting identified in chapter 13 thus appears to be general in nature, reaching all the way to between-community elite variations in influence ties. Although unobserved on an everyday basis, I posit that there is an undercurrent of social interactions connecting communities, residents, and leaders alike across the city, producing a structure that is not immediately apparent or visible from inside a single community.

Conclusion

This chapter has only scratched the surface of the nature of elite connections in Chicago. There are a number of questions to be pursued further and a rich set of analyses that can be imagined.[22] But my present concern is theoretically focused on how leadership ties connect to the broader arguments of this book. I thus pursued a limited set of analyses that followed logically and theoretically from the previous chapters. I believe the results tell a clear story.

First and foremost, the structure of elite network ties varies considerably across communities, as previewed in chapter 1 (fig. 1.4). *Networks can in theory go anywhere, but they go to a somewhere very regularly*—there is little that is random or nonstructured about the networks we have observed. Second, network properties of social organization among elites are highly persistent over time (1995–2002), despite considerable turnover of the individuals who occupy the positions. For example, communities that tend to have a high density of overlap in the contact networks of their leaders remain this way even as the individual leaders are frequently replaced. Analogous to migration, the underlying structure is enduring despite considerable change, lending a further layer of empirical support to the conceptual framework of this book. Awareness of this pattern was also uncovered in my personal interviews with a set of leaders from different domains, including the pastor quoted earlier, the vice president of a major university charged with community affairs, a housing development executive, a law enforcement official involved with crime prevention, and the president of a major philanthropic foundation, among others. The cognitive perception of the stability of key leadership structures over time suggests that reciprocity norms undergird much of the elite influence structure in Chicago.

A third finding is that the variability in leadership network structure by community is not determined solely or even in large measure by the demographic and economic makeup of the community. This is an important point and one not anticipated by standard accounts. Instead of the usual urban suspects, social properties like collective efficacy and organizational density independently predict network structure. Moreover, these vary depending on whether the ties are local or extralocal in nature. Granovetter was right in his intuition that the aerial view produces a different picture, but what is also clear is that the internal view is not irrelevant either—including the kinds of factors that Gans highlighted. Both internal factors, like collective efficacy and a community's organizational infrastructure, bear on the network structures that link communities.

Fourth, there is evidence that the social nature of leadership network structures has independent explanatory power in our understanding of the wellbeing of communities. Controlling for key sociodemographic factors, for example, cohesive leadership structures are directly related to lower rates of violence and teenage births. Because wellbeing along these dimensions is not simply about residents but organizations and leaders, this result is a hopeful signal that, when combined with results of earlier chapters, suggests possible points of intervention. I take this point up in the concluding chapter.

Finally, and perhaps most important for this section of the book, I have shown that migration flows among communities are directly related to the network flows defined by leadership ties. These are radically different behaviors or choices—residents deciding where to move and elites making a connection with other elites. The link between the two is not explained by demography or economic status and thus supports the thesis of a structural sorting that simultaneously takes into account individual actions and social composition. Taken together, the chapters in this section strongly suggest that the higher-order structure of Chicago—or its interdependent social fabric—has an underlying "neighborhood network" logic.

PART V **SYNTHESIS AND REVISIT**

15 Neighborhood Effects and a Theory of Context

Two broad perspectives dominate contemporary thinking among social scientists and the public at large about the causal role of neighborhoods and almost every other social context. One begins and ends with the individual (or "choice") as the unit of analysis and explanation. Individuals autonomously select and decide, so that neighborhoods—and, by implication, much of the social world—are merely an outgrowth of an individual process of selection. Distinct methods flow from this assumption, with priority given to individual-level measurement, individual outcomes, and experiments that attempt to contrive individual choices. In economics, psychology, public policy, and even the discipline of sociology, individuals dominate the unit of analysis in everyday practice.

Another perspective comes at things from the top down. Whether because of globalization, the revolution in communication technologies, or the growth in urban diversity, large-scale structural processes are argued to have flattened boundaries of all sorts and rendered a new, placeless world. One commonly hears that because we can be anywhere, the particulars of our somewhere are of no consequence. With identities "decentered," neighborhoods are seen as an anachronism displaced by global networks of interchangeability. Other factors that have been alleged to neuter local contexts include the economy, politics, and the State. Taking an unrecognized lead from Louis Wirth but with new metaphors, individuals and places alike are viewed cynically—atomized and left bereft of community. This perspective, like the individual selection perspective, leaves little room for neighborhood effects but for a different reason: top-down ("big") processes are an all-encompassing force that overwhelms both individuals and neighborhoods.

In this book I proposed an alternative to these two perspectives by offering a unified framework on neighborhood effects, the larger social organization of urban life, and social causality in general. I did so by melding ideas across intellectual traditions, disciplines, empirical domains, and units of analysis. Contrary to much received wisdom, the evidence presented in this book demands attention to life in the neighborhoods that shape it. I have shown evidence of a deep ecological concentration and marked variability by neighborhood across a wide range of how Americans experience life, whether it is in relation to crime, poverty, child health, public protest, the density of elite networks, civic engagement, teen births, altruism, perceived disorder, collective efficacy, or immigration. I would go as far as to argue that *what is truly American is not so much the individual but neighborhood inequality*. And just because something is "big" does not mean it sits on top in a hierarchical, explanatory sense. Rather than starting with a preordained or deductive theory, or succumbing to pure induction absent an idea, I took seriously the nature of the phenomenon itself, guided by a set of theoretical principles for empirical inquiry. Describing and explaining neighborhood effects writ large became the goal.

To meet the analytic challenges set out in chapter 1, I took the social landscape and continued vitality of contemporary Chicago as my laboratory. Informed by a century's worth of careful scholarship and contextual theory, the Chicago Project is as much an intellectual endeavor as a research one. Chapters 2 and 3 reveal that my analytic argument respects a long tradition of contextual theory and the empirical study of urban social processes, one going back to the famous Chicago School of urban sociology but reaching back as well to European epidemiologists and pioneering scholars of the city, such as Charles Booth. My perspective is not fixed in this tradition but was inspired as well by modern scholars such as William Julius Wilson, Douglas Massey, and a persistent line of criminologists, urban sociologists (of many schools), and, yes, even global and political economy theorists who have also recognized the structural implications of neighborhood inequality along with macrosocial processes.

None of this is to imply the causal irrelevance of the individual. I have taken critics of neighborhood effects seriously and have made individual selection or choice a key element of my inquiry. But I did so not in the manner of viewing individuals as disembodied or isolated decision makers. Humans react to neighborhood difference, and these reactions constitute social mechanisms and practices that in turn shape perceptions, personal relationships, and behaviors that reverberate both within and beyond traditional neighborhood borders, and as a whole define the social structure of the city. Neighborhood effects are thus simultaneously local and extralocal in nature, and reciprocally related to individual actions and choices. The micro and macro barriers erected by disciplinary standard bearers are not sustainable in the final analysis.[1] Ironically, I show that taking choice or selection seriously only reinforces the salience of context.

The main empirical vehicle for my effort has been the Project on Human Development in Chicago Neighborhoods (PHDCN), an original longitudinal study of children, families, and neighborhoods in what is probably the most studied city in America and one of the most American at heart. The PHDCN and its spin-offs, including studies of leadership networks, altruism, organizations, and civic action, represent a long-term commitment and collective investment of labor to a broad vision of neighborhood effects and a fundamentally contextual approach to human development. Because of its far-reaching aspects and large-scale data collection, I tell the story of how the PHDCN was conceived and brought to fruition in chapter 4. Social context matters for research projects, not just individuals, and the making of the PHDCN was no exception. Backed by the intensive effort of the PHDCN and the larger Chicago Project, I followed the core principles of chapter 3 to see how far they could take me. Chapters 5 through 14 contain the results so far. I structured the presentation in a way that rang true to the unfolding of my intellectual confrontation with the idea of neighborhood effects, sequentially pursuing questions about community-level processes, individual processes of neighborhood selection, and the extralocal networks and mechanisms that define the higher-order structure of contemporary urban life.

I must confess, then, that this book is at once an intellectual history of an idea, the story of a major research project, the tale of an iconic city, a systematic theory of neighborhood effects, an empirical account of community-level variations in a range of social processes, an analysis of competing approaches to social inquiry, and a sustained empirical analysis that was designed to uncover new facts while adjudicating and integrating existing hypotheses. Because of these multiple objectives, I mounted what should have been perceived as a relentless analytic march across the social landscape of Chicago. I hope so, because the subject demanded no less. But now it is time to steer a more synthetic path by revisiting the broader ideas and implications of the book. I do so by considering the empirical findings in light of the theoretical principles with which I began, before closing in the last two chapters with a return to the streets and neighborhoods of Chicago in the aftermath of macrosocial changes wrought by the 2008 economic crisis and the city's massive public-housing interventions. Chicago in 2010 provides a unique setting in which to revisit with new data and observations the key arguments of the book.

Principles of Social Inquiry

At a general level I argued that spatial inequality constitutes a fundamental organizing dimension of everyday life, with neighborhoods and local communities a durable and contemporary manifestation of difference. In doing so I rejected intellectual moves toward placelessness and I revised traditional top-down and bottom-up approaches to argue that neighborhoods are not merely the settings in which individuals enact autonomous decisions or follow preset scripts, and that neighborhoods are not merely empty vessels determined by external forces. I argued instead that neighborhood contexts are socially productive—important determinants of the quantity and quality of human behavior in their own right. From this view, this book is an effort to specify the structural and cultural dimensions of neighborhood effects while also attending to the perceptions and choices of individuals and the role of larger social structures. I use the term "effect" in both its verb and noun forms—neighborhood is consequence and cause, outcome and producer. I thus expanded traditional definitions to examine a *family of neighborhood effects* across multiple units of analysis, outcomes, and time scales. In this view neighborhood effects command a broad scope, ranging from individual cognition to the higher-order social structure of the city.

This general argument conforms to the ten principles I set out in chapter 3, the first of which is the most basic: (1) relentlessly focus on *context*, especially neighborhood inequality and social differentiation. The empirical results demonstrate the continuing salience of neighborhood concentration in the American city across a wide range of social phenomena. The other principles flowed from the first in a logical way and were pursued in a multiplicity of ways throughout the book. Abbreviated, they were: (2) Study neighborhood-level variations in their own right and adopt a systematic method of data collection that relies on multiple methods with public standards of measurement. (3) Focus on social-interactional, social-psychological, organizational, and cultural mechanisms of city life rather than just individual attributes or traditional compositional features like racial makeup and class. (4) Study dynamic processes of neighborhood structural change. (5) Simultaneously assess mechanisms of neighborhood social reproduction and cultural continuity. (6) Embed in the study of neighborhood dynamics the role of individual selection decisions and their social consequences and macro outcomes. (7) At the same time, go beyond both the individual and the local to examine spatial mechanisms that cross neighborhood boundaries. (8) Further yet, study the social and cultural organization of the city as a whole, including higher-order links among and beyond constituent neighborhoods. (9) Never lose sight of human concerns with public affairs and the improvement of city life—develop implications for community-level interventions. (10) Last, but not least, emphasize theoretically motivated and interpretive empirical research while taking a pluralistic stance on the nature of evidence needed to assess social causation. Rather than trying to recap the details of all the findings that bear on these principles, I focus here on summary claims from a core set of ideas that I believe are justified by the empirical warrant of the book and that are sufficiently broad to form a theory of context and approach to causality that I hope will inspire a new generation of research on neighborhoods, social life, and the city. As the world becomes increasingly urbanized and the "triumph of the city" expands,[2] a contextual approach to human understanding and causal questions is best equipped to guide social inquiry.

Taking Ecometrics to Scale

In my view, the project of contextual inquiry leads directly to a theory of method. Social science is overwhelmed by nearly a century's worth of careful research methods oriented to individual-level measurement. In facing the challenge of this reality to the study of context, Stephen Raudenbush and I followed principle 2 above in arguing that while the field of psychometrics provides an exemplar to build on, *ecometrics* is just as important.[3] I believe that, taken as a whole, this book provides a roadmap for how context can be studied and with results that motivate taking ecometrics to scale as an equal player in social science. *The important theoretical point is that neighborhood, community, and other collective phenomena demand their own measurement logic and are not stand-ins for individual-level traits.* This is no small task, and it pushes against a strong tradition in the social sciences, including much of sociology.

I hope the PHDCN and the lessons of this book can serve as a model for further development of a metric for the social mechanisms that underlie not just neighborhoods and communities in the American city, but a variety of contexts. Already a number of places around the country have developed systematic metrics for community processes based directly on the PHDCN, as reviewed in chapter 7. Some of these efforts are in rural areas of the South and others in small towns and suburbs. More broadly, there are ecometric efforts to collect social process data from neighborhood contexts around the world, including in places as different as Tanzania, China, England, Australia, and the Netherlands. Ecometrics has direct application to evaluating organizational-level measures in contexts like schools as well.

There is the additional possibility of going to a national-level scale in the U.S. In a surprising but welcome break from past tradition, the Bureau of Labor Statistics pioneered a set of civic engagement questions in the nationally representative Current Population Survey starting in 2008 that capture the kinds of ideas probed in this book.[4] When linked to census data on place and other administrative sources, a new era of contextual research at the national level will be opened up. A national or codified system of measurement, with standard protocols for evaluation, would enhance community-based policy and systematic planning by the government, nonprofit organizations, and foundations. The hope is that such constituencies, including community residents themselves, can use standardized measures for benchmarking or monitoring their progress or capacities in meeting stated goals. The United States has long been propelled by the perceived importance of systematic measures of the GNP and all other things economic. It may well be that the collective health and nonmaterial wellbeing of communities is more important; if so, it is time to buck the dominant trend and engage ecometrics as a tool for progress.[5]

A major breakthrough is also in the offing with respect to systematic observations of the city and the georeferencing of large chunks of everyday life. I described and presented a number of PHDCN results using the method of systematic social observation (SSO) based on videotaping. Some might be concerned that our method was labor intensive, expensive, and limited to Chicago. As luck would have it, however, one of the world's most powerful companies implemented our procedures. Google's Street View advertises itself by showing a car with a video camera sticking out the top (ours was hidden, and we did not advertise). Their vehicles have roamed many of the world's cities with impressive results. Although lacking the SSO precision and investigator control, Google Street View can be and is being used to systematically code a variety of urban street scenes, right down to the level of specific places. When combined with advances in GPS-based digital mapping from the communications revolution (e.g., tracing the physical movement of individuals through cell-phone usage) and new measures of routine activities in time and space, the possibilities are extensive for creating a rich ecometric database of neighborhood and other ecological contexts.[6] Already a number of studies are collecting PHDCN-like measurements using Google Street View, and under my direction the Center for Geographic Analysis at Harvard is creating ChicagoMap, which eventually will include linked SSO, census, survey, administrative sources, and virtually all of the data presented in this book.[7] With additional waves of data, the GIS revolution, and the capacity for real-time analyses of social processes that not too long ago would have taken years, ecometrics is a unifying idea that has the potential to transform how we conduct social science research.

These new forms of data and others certain to come share the feature of spatial flexibility, which matches up well to the principles of inquiry that guided my choice of procedures. Note, however, that my stance departed from the common search for the "best" or "correct" operational definition of neighborhood. Instead I argued that there are multiple scales of ecological influence and possibilities for constructing measures, ranging from microlevel street blocks (or street corners) to block groups to neighborhood clusters to community areas of political and organizational importance to spatial "regimes" and cross-cutting networks that connect far-flung areas of the city.[8] This theoretical framing is consistent with my focus on the interaction of spatial and social logic, especially as manifested in the variable interactions, perceptions, and institutional forces that unfold in ecologically defined areas large and small. Social processes like community reputations, politics, organizational networks, and service allocation, for example, do not fit the push by some to analyze ever-smaller slices of neighborhoods or places. The notion that there is one neighborhood unit or that it must be small is not commensurate with the way people react to and sort themselves on a wide variety of dimensions or outcomes. Ecometrics is thus designed to evaluate the properties of theoretically chosen measures across a range of contextual settings.

Neighborhood Stratification and Reproduction

The great student of the city Lewis Mumford once said, "Neighborhoods, in some primitive, inchoate fashion exist wherever human beings congregate."[9] Half a century later the archaeologist Michael Smith agrees, and, based on research around the world, he claims that the "spatial division of cities in districts or neighborhoods is one of the few universals of urban life from the earliest cities to the present."[10] Neighborhood, in other words, is a near universal theme of human history, and the salience of neighborhood differences has persisted across long time scales and historical eras despite the transformation of specific boundaries, political regimes and the layout of cities. The consistency of differentiation from ancient cities to contemporary Chicago suggests the general and enduring process of neighborhood effects that Mumford and Smith allude to, and hence its theoretical centrality for the study of stratification and social inequality.

Consistent with this idea, this book has demonstrated the deep structure of neighborhood stratification that has persisted in Chicago across multiple units of social ecology in the latter decades of the twentieth century and up to the present day. Key dimensions of neighborhood difference include poverty, affluence, unemployment, and family structure, nationally and not just in Chicago (chapter 5). Racial segregation is unfortunately part of this story, as the spatial isolation of African Americans produces exposure to multiple strands of resource deprivation, especially poverty and single-parent families with children. Ecologically concentrated disadvantage is a powerful form of disparity predicting both individual outcomes and variations in rates of behavior across neighborhoods. For example, across chapters I have presented evidence showing the effects of concentrated disadvantage on violence, disorder, altruism, incarceration, collective efficacy, verbal ability, and other aspects of wellbeing in a way that cannot be attributable to the disposition or composition of individuals. I have examined neighborhood-level associations, contextual effects on individuals, and the role of economic status in explaining interneighborhood migration and information flows. Concentrated inequality thus cuts across multiple scales of influence and across time, and from the individual level of analysis to the structural organization of the city.

Continuity amid Change

Orlando Patterson has argued that one of the great unsolved puzzles in the social sciences is what accounts for the strong continuities in social environments.[11] He argues that the dominant focus on change has obscured the systematic theoretical probing of large-scale historical and cultural continuities. Although he focuses primarily on societies, Patterson's thesis strikes a chord with the literature in community studies and neighborhood effects. From the advent of the Chicago School to the present day, the dominant conceptual focus has been urban change, and I have followed suit up to a point. But I am with Patterson on the fundamental need to interrogate mechanisms of continuity. As shown in chapter 5 and practically every chapter thereafter, legacies of neighborhood inequality are pervasive.

A concern with history and durable inequalities of place does not mean there is an inherent directionality to social life or what many criticize as "teleology." I do not assume, for example, as the classic Chicago School is said to have done, that things are moving toward some master plan like the Donald Trump–designed tower that was encountered in chapter 1. Cities and neighborhoods are constantly changing and in no *inherent* direction. The decline of Chicago in the 1970s when it was losing population actually reversed itself in the 1990s. Many other cities are back from the gloom and doom years of the '70s and '80s as well, with neighborhood vitality prominently on display. Yet we have seen that poverty and its correlates are stubbornly and simultaneously persistent in terms of neighborhood concentration, especially among black and minority-group areas. Despite macro political changes and urban social transformation toward the end of the twentieth century and gentrification in the early twenty-first century, neighborhoods remained remarkably stable in their relative economic standing even as they witnessed considerable inflow and outflow of individual residents. It follows that there is an enduring process of stratification not specific to any one neighborhood and that is not simply a result of individual, demographic, or economic explanations.

To keep the language precise, I have avoided what would otherwise seem to be the useful metaphor of social architecture in explaining the phenomenon of continuity. This concept is appealing but can be read to imply a preprogrammed design. Spatial continuity does not imply such a design nor does it shy away from change—to the contrary, virtually every analysis in this book incorporates a focus on mechanisms of both stability *and* change, including change that often reproduces in new and unintended ways the existing social structure. The idea of *neighborhood social reproduction* is more appropriate in uniting the apparent duality, because while it does not mean cloning or simple replication, reproduction does imply that the future is encoded in the past through a kind of "social DNA"—a set of interacting individuals making choices embedded in a set of interdependent contexts that in sequence produce new forms of interlocking neighborhood processes. The historical reality of the American city is that over time these interactions have reproduced a stable pattern of neighborhood stratification.

My framework on neighborhood reproduction also helps to situate the critique of scholars who argue that neighborhood-effect researchers miss the big picture of history, macroeconomics, and global forces. One of the fundamental insights of Wilson's landmark work in *The Truly Disadvantaged* was to recognize how the social organization of local communities, especially in the segregated ghettoes of American cities, was deeply intertwined with the large-scale changes taking place in society, in particular deindustrialization and the transition to a service economy. Yet some have read Wilson's argument to say that neighborhood effects are misspecified as a result of such outside forces, to which today we can add further globalization and rapid increases in international migration. Such forces matter, but they do not negate the presumed "lower-order" mechanisms of neighborhood any more than individuals are impotent in any social setting.[12] As I have shown and will show anew in the next chapter, even major secular change does not necessarily alter the basics of neighborhood inequality when it is superimposed on a reproducing social structure. My strategy therefore was to examine social mechanisms that link these processes, including individual cognition as a substrate of macro inequality.

Cognitive Inequality and a Place for Cultural Mechanisms

Charles Cooley coined the well-known metaphor of the "looking-glass self," a social-psychological concept positing that a person's individual self grows out of society's interpersonal interactions and the perceptions of others.[13] Over a century later, this book has produced evidence that the *looking-glass neighborhood* is one of the social mechanisms behind continuity, a concept that I believe mediates between individual, community, and large-scale approaches to urban inequality. I showed in several chapters that social-psychological mechanisms interacting with broad cultural processes (e.g., stereotypes and shared expectations on disorder) explain important variations in concentrated inequality, an area of research dominated by structural determinism. In chapter 6, for example, shared perceptions of disorder rather than systematically observed disorder constitute a key mechanism behind durable inequality, especially in predicting the future poverty trajectory of an area and eventual poverty traps.

These results should not be understood to say that concrete cues do not matter or are purely constructivist in nature. Neighborhoods with high concentrations of minority and poor residents have been stigmatized by historically correlated and structurally induced problems of crime and disorder. These persistent and psychologically prominent correlations are not just a mirage—they have deep roots in the concrete history of American stratification and segregation, and are not likely to lapse in the face of short-term interventions. But perceptions take on a new life and cohere into a cumulative texture when refracted through social interactions, practices, and collective reputations.[14] In particular,

I have shown that disorder rooted in intersubjectively shared and thus relational perceptions—rather than simply visible (or "objective") cues—form a meaningful social property of the environment that influences neighborhood-level outcomes. *This is the essence of what I hypothesize as the neighborhood looking-glass self.*

Chapters 11–13 went on to show both individual and higher-order effects associated with processes of cognitive inequality: collectively perceived disorder was found to predict individual residential mobility decisions (whether to move) and the flows of movement between neighborhoods similar in shared perceptions. By this account, selection is contingent on the coordinated perceptions that in turn play a role in shaping the long-term trajectories and identities of places that make up the social organization of the city. If socially interpreted disorder is one of the mechanisms of future population change, migration flows, or the later deepening of poverty, the schema of this book might profitably inform stratification theorists, urban planners, demographers of the city, and even cultural sociologists. Moreover, as the popularity of the "broken windows" thesis expands globally, we have reason to believe that shared perceptions of disorder will increasingly matter in a variety of contexts for reasons that extend far beyond the presence of physical cues in the environment: disorder is about much more than crime.

The concept of moral and legal cynicism reflects another cultural mechanism situated in neighborhood context. In an effort to gauge social norms about moral rules and the experiential relevance of law in the everyday lives of residents, we asked respondents to report their agreement with statements such as "Laws were made to be broken" and "It's okay to do anything you want as long as you don't hurt anyone." In communities with high levels of intersubjectively shared cynicism and the perceived irrelevance of legal rules, violence is higher and lost-letter return rates are significantly lower. This association is largely explained by disadvantage, however, suggesting a feedback loop whereby concentrated disadvantage is corrosive with respect to other-regarding norms, as shown in chapter 9. This process feeds cynicism, which reinforces behavior that is outside of the law (e.g., using violence to settle disputes), in turn further undermining trust and notions of the just community. Legal cynicism also helps explain the persistence of violence in certain communities and racial disparities in violence, with African Americans more likely to condemn crime and violence even as they are disproportionately exposed to greater disadvantage *and* moral/legal cynicism.[15]

I therefore propose that collectively shaped perceptions of disorder and persistent moral and legal cynicism may be underappreciated causes of community wellbeing and of continued racial and economic segregation in the United States, and perhaps cities elsewhere. In this scenario, cultural and structural mechanisms of inequality are considered part of the same dynamic process rather than as rigidly competing ideas. Much has been made in the last few decades on the "cultural turn" in the social sciences, with concepts such as "tool kits" and "scripts" making up a working consensus. While the cultural turn was and is still important, these dominant concepts seem to me individualistic in their typical application and not well suited to understanding persistent cultural mechanisms, deep structures, and macrohistorical cultural continuity. It is interesting, for example, to ask the following question based on the findings of this book: If individuals have so many tool kits to choose from, why is there so much consistency, stability, and *inter*subjective agreement on basic mediators of neighborhood social reproduction? I believe the evidence I have presented supports the notion that "cultural structures" are the fundamental process at work, defined consistent with Patterson's conception of culture as "the production, reproduction and transmission of relatively stable informational processes and their public representations that are variously distributed in groups or social networks."[16] Social norms and coordinated beliefs are rooted in cognitive processes, many of which are implicit or that operate below conscious awareness, and, as implied by this definition of culture, in a structurally patterned and relational manner. Unlike interchangeable tools or contradictory scripts that individuals easily access and then discard, shared understandings and norms imply a greater coherence that has staying power across a wide spectrum of life.[17]

Collective Efficacy Theory (Cosmopolitan Friendly)

A key concept of my analysis is collective efficacy. I made a theoretical claim for the importance of shared expectations for social control and a working trust or felt cohesion among community residents. Indicators of these concepts form a larger construct of collective efficacy, which I showed can be measured reliably and that varies widely across community contexts. It is also significantly linked to a number of behaviors after accounting for social composition. Although questions of causality (to which I will turn shortly) will always remain, the magnitude of results and their consistency across a wide range of considerations reinforce a basic theme that I traced back to social disorganization's forefathers in chapter 7 and then elaborated for the contemporary city. Namely, shared expectations for control processes, or what we can think of as the *efficacy of social regulation*, is important for our understanding of community wellbeing.

The results show that in neighborhoods that are otherwise similar, those with higher levels of collective efficacy exhibit lower rates of crime, not just in the present, but in the following years. I also presented evidence that collective efficacy is relatively stable over time and that it predicts future variations in crime, adjusting for the aggregated characteristics of individuals and more traditional forms of neighbor networks (e.g., friend/kinship ties). More important, highly efficacious communities seem to do better on a lot of other things, including birth weight, rates of teen pregnancy, and infant mortality, suggesting a link to overall health and wellbeing independent of social composition. *In most cases, then, whether rich or poor, white or black, I argue that collective efficacy signals a community on a trajectory of wellbeing.*

One of the distinguishing features of collective efficacy theory is its insistence that human agency and control are not redundant with the dense personal ties that have been of so much interest in a long line of urban inquiry. Dense ties may facilitate collective efficacy, but they are not sufficient and therefore do not form the definitional core of the concept. This assertion was confirmed in analyses across two community surveys and in comparing Chicago with Stockholm, Sweden. The generalization extends to other far-reaching places. A recent publication based on a direct replication of the Chicago-Stockholm study shows that collective efficacy predicts lower crime rates across communities in Brisbane, Australia, controlling for the density of social ties and other compositional features.[18]

Based on theory and empirical evidence, then, we have some confidence to maintain the analytical distinction between collective efficacy and dense personal ties, allowing for what might be thought of as "cosmopolitan efficacy."[19] Shared understandings about control and trust in one's neighbors are foundational to collective action, in other words, whether in the city or countryside. It is ironic but not a surprise that in a big city like Chicago, cosmopolitans are busy exerting efficacy while at the same time decrying the loss of community. In fact, recent research in contemporary cities has shown that even Internet use and connection to the broader digital world are not anathema to collective efficacy. If anything, these seemingly at-odds worlds are *positively* linked—there is recent evidence that wired communities and the Internet promote civic engagement and collective efficacy, especially in contexts of disadvantage.[20] While the lament of community decline is a constant across history, as discussed in chapter 1, the manifestations of community and its aspirational ideal have thus apparently never disappeared and continue to churn in our technologically advanced era.

I conclude that there is something fundamental about neighborhood-level variations in collective efficacy that cut across cities in the U.S. and a number of international boundaries as well, including places as diverse as England, Tanzania, China, the Netherlands, Sweden, and Australia. The emergence of variation in collective efficacy suggests that the capacity for social control and connection to others is a basic social property that goes beyond the aggregated composition of individuals—transcending poverty, race, the State, and even the Internet, predicting lower violence and enhanced public health in a number of studies. By decoupling tight-knit interpersonal ties from control and working trust, collective efficacy theory can also be applied to collective units beyond neighborhoods, such as schools, police forces, financial firms, and societies, a point reinforced in the Chicago-Stockholm comparison.[21]

Although the construct of collective efficacy provides a theoretical roadmap for navigating multiple and overlapping challenges, I would emphasize that it is a social process that has a cultural component in shared expectations, one shaped by context, history, and prior experiences. Collective efficacy is thus simultaneously an outcome itself and a potential causal force, like many things social in nature. When I examined what explains collective efficacy, for example, I found that prior violence can reduce later expectations for control and undermine trust. This finding makes sense from theoretical expectations rooted in self-efficacy theory and our individual lives—past experience matters in how we think about future action.[22] But concentrated disadvantage matters too, and poverty from prior decades predicts concurrent collective efficacy as much or more than recent poverty. Cultural commitment to place matters as well, as I will further probe in chapter 16. And perhaps increasingly the digital revolution will be a force in promoting or undermining collective efficacy. Beyond these economic, demographic, technological, cultural, and historical effects, institutional mechanisms in the form of organizational life play a key role in the transmission of collective efficacy and collective action more generally.

The Organizational Community

Tocqueville observed early in our country's history that America is a society of joiners.[23] The resurgence of nonprofit community organizations in cities around the country in recent decades is the latest manifestation, but urban scholars have been slow to chart the implications. This book has attempted to underscore the importance of what some have called the "missing organizational dimension" in the study of urban life.[24]

In chapter 8, using data from the Chicago Collective Civic Action Project, I examined the explanatory power of nonprofit organizations under a variety of conditions defined by the varying intensity of concentrated poverty, residential stability, racial segregation, and population density along with a number of competing social processes, including friend/kinship ties and civic memberships (voluntary associations). Whether I considered communities high in the *initiation* of collective civic-action events or communities that were *locations* of collective civic engagement or even protest, the density of nonprofit organizations emerged as one of the strongest predictors of all. This basic result maintained when I examined segregated black communities and limited analysis to the reporting of collective civic events by the city's biggest and longest-running newspaper in the black community, the *Chicago Defender*. There seems to be something pervasive about the social appropriation of organizational resources to produce collective civic engagement that cuts across the deep racial and economic divide of Chicago.

Collective efficacy among citizens is primarily about informally activated social control and shared expectations rooted in trust. Chapter 8 showed that collective efficacy of this kind was enhanced by organizational resources embodied in things like neighborhood watches, block groups, tenant associations, and after-school programs. As Mario Small has recently argued, simple activities like childcare are often undertaken in organizational settings that create unanticipated opportunities that often expose parents to collective imperatives, like fundraising or helping to plan group activities.[25] Consistent with Small's study, I believe that nonprofit organizations and the maintenance of organizational resources generate a web of "mundane" routine activities that can lubricate collective life, although seldom planned as such. Something like this is at work all across Chicago—communities possessing a rich organizational life are ahead of the curve.

The importance of nonprofit organizations and their unintended consequences provides a new way to think about intervention and the response to collective challenges. We tend to look at economic aid as the first response. But organizational capacity is often central in how physical and social capital works. There is evidence, for example, that a variety of neighborhood organizations have emerged to help rebuild New Orleans after the devastation of Hurricane Katrina. It may even be that the communities that experienced the greatest trauma from the flooding are the inspiration for a new wave of collective efficacy and city renewal at the ground level. A recent investigation on the fifth anniversary of Katrina, while not a rigorous study, provides a telling clue: "Those who returned found a void of local leadership and set out to rebuild the city from the ground up. The rebound has not been citywide but piecemeal, neighborhood by neighborhood, from Lakeview to Broadmoor to Holy Cross, fueled by newly formed associations and old social clubs, energized residents and out-of-state volunteers, idealists and handymen. Many have become staunch advocates for their corners of the city, collecting local data, organizing committees and even, in the case of the Vietnamese community, drawing up their own local master plan."[26] Thus the rebuilding of New Orleans is taking place neighborhood by neighborhood, propelled in part by an organizational infrastructure that was not designed with Katrina in mind but which has triggered collective efficacy and now collective action. The hurricane reinforced existing inequalities of place, and the rebuilding is structured by those same inequalities and the historical meanings attached to specific neighborhoods. It only makes sense that organizational efforts shaped by neighborhood differentiation are well poised, aided by external help, to have a leading say in the city's rebirth.

The results in chapter 8 and the scenes from New Orleans thus provide a hopeful sign and reassurance about the future of the American city. Despite poverty, racial segregation, and other challenges exacerbated by the truly top-down force of mother nature, community-based organizations provide an opening to enhance collective efficacy and collective civic action, a point to which I will return in chapter 16, when discussing implications for intervention. It is not just one kind of institution that matters, and I showed in chapter 8 that churches are not the answer many believe them to be. It is the totality of the institutional infrastructure that seems to matter in promoting civic health and extending to unexpected economic vitality, whether in the form of rebuilding New Orleans or in rehabilitating vacant houses in economically depressed neighborhoods in cities around the country. Civil society, by this organizational view, is alive and well. Moreover, community-based organizations reflect a strategic site for social policy that is conceptually attuned to our increasingly organizational world and federal policies of privatization that have devolved significant resources to allocation processes mediated by local nonprofit organizations.[27]

The Spatial Logic of the City

A key argument of this book is that the traditional focus on the internal dynamics of neighborhoods is incomplete. I have instead argued for the centrality of extralocal spatial dynamics and mechanisms of spatial advantage and disadvantage. The results were, to my mind, some of the most unambiguous in this book, underscoring the importance of spatial distance in organizing the effects of racial inequality and immigrant diffusion. To put it simply, Waldo Toebler was right about the first principle (not law) of geography. The death-of-distance thesis thus gets it wrong on the fundamentals of present concern—physical distance and spatial processes matter a lot, especially when they interact with social distance. I would go as far as to claim that racial inequality in the American city cannot be understood absent a direct consideration of the role of spatially inscribed social advantage and disadvantage.

Consider a simple example. Taking two middle-income neighborhoods, one black and one white, might to most observers make for a fair match. Allowing that segregation is harmful when it leads to unequal resources by neighborhood, further assume that incomes and all other nonracial characteristics are the same within each neighborhood. Are these two neighborhoods not similar? Doesn't income equivalence resolve the past? My answer is no. I showed in chapter 10 that these two neighborhood types are not even close in character when it comes to the surrounding context. Black neighborhoods in Chicago and most other American cities face a spatial disadvantage with far-reaching implications. The spatial-externalities perspective on racial disadvantage moves beyond the traditional emphasis on internal neighborhood characteristics by conceptualizing how extraneighborhood and citywide spatial dynamics create racial inequalities across a wide range of social processes that are potentially more consequential than the ones already at play within neighborhoods. This book's theoretical framework on spatial inequality helps explain the durability of violence, disorder, and outmigration in poor black neighborhoods, and the ever-present threat of violence in what otherwise would be characterized as middle-class areas. The spatial division of the city comes as dispiriting news to those of us concerned with the betterment of human welfare and reducing inequality.

The good news is that some of this spatial inequality may be breaking down due to the changes that have been introduced to Chicago and America through recent immigration. Inflows of first-generation immigrants reflect a classic example of a diffusion process with spillover effects, including lower crime and economic resurgence of formerly devastated poor neighborhoods. First-generation immigrants in Chicago commit almost 50 percent less violence than the third generation, after we account for their greater poverty and differences along a long list of relevant social characteristics (e.g., income, marital status, and even individual IQ). Not only are recent immigrants (whether white, black, or Latino) less violent, they are more so when living in concentrated immigrant areas, evidence of a contextual effect of immigration.

The spatial logic developed in chapter 10 thus suggests that immigration has a number of positive ripple effects. Independent papers published recently support this hypothesis for crime declines in other American cities and at the national level.[28] At the neighborhood level in Chicago, immigration increases are linked to lower crime, especially in poorer areas and those with histories of racial segregation and exclusion. The analyses in chapter 10 combined with chapter 5 also support the idea that increasing immigration may be working to reduce segregation among blacks, whites, and Latinos.[29] In today's world even more than in the past, it is not tenable to assume that immigration and diversity automatically lead to social disorganization and consequently crime. Stereotypes notwithstanding, I argue that in the United States, at least, the spatial diffusion of immigration is linked to decreases in crime—across neighborhoods, cities, and time.[30]

Selection as a Neighborhood Effect

There is something odd about the way many social scientists approach individual choice, almost as if they are spooked into thinking that choice renders the environment impotent. The stylistic critique that "neighborhoods do not matter" typically comes from those pointing to individuals selectively creating their own environment in a way that is said to bias neighborhood effects. But just as genes do not express themselves regardless of circumstance, individual selection is embedded in and called forth by social contexts. When it comes to residential mobility, it is hard to think of a more relevant factor in selection than the neighborhood itself and even harder to find "rags to neighborhood riches" in the first place—horizontal moves dominate. Thus even as we selectively avoid a neighborhood or are able to choose to live here and not there, we are being influenced by a neighborhood's social position rather than proving its irrelevance, as common wisdom would have it. This interaction helps explain one of the mechanisms of enduring inequality in the United States—spatial separation reinforced by homophily, or the tendency of people to choose to live near like others on valued characteristics, and distant from those disvalued. One can think of this as the demand side of inequality—leading to the mechanism of *contextual hierarchy maintenance*. Actions taken by individuals and institutions to maintain their privileged positions produce the sorts of structural constraints and cultural settings typically emphasized by sociologists. We live in places that have social meanings and structured differences inscribed all over them.

As argued in chapter 12, the result is a seeming paradox. There is segregation by race and income ("Separate Chicagos"), for example, that remains quite durable and visible all while there is a constant churning and mobility across neighborhood boundaries that intermix a number of social categories, such as crime, depression, and other factors not typically considered. *Yet even here context matters*: people move for a variety of reasons, but rarely are characteristics of origin and destination neighborhoods irrelevant in cognitive appraisals. Structural features, such as changes in racial composition, bear on individual appraisals and decisions to move, as do perceptual cues related to social disorder. There is an important implication of selection for redefining neighborhoods; for example, if a black family moves to a racially integrated neighborhood and then that move or moves similar in character induce white families to in turn leave, then the integration of the environment may decline in ways not originally selected by the original mover.[31] Ironically, then, neighborhood conditions matter a great deal for influencing bottom-up selection decisions but they also define contexts of change that set in motion additional selection, suggesting a different kind of social influence than normally conceived—selection as a social process. For these reasons, I sought in chapters 11 and 12 to reframe our understanding of selection bias and rescue it from individualistic fictions. Recall that IQ, depression, and criminality, to name the "big three" of dominant selection complaints, were effectively overwhelmed by larger patterns of sorting by structural characteristics. Consistent with chapter 3's principles for the social inquiry of context, therefore, my thesis turns tables on the standard treatment and offers a new menu of possibilities for future research: *selection bias is itself a form of neighborhood effect.*

The City as Interlocking Social Structure

Taking selection seriously also allowed me to conceptualize and study higher-order structural themes in ways not previously examined. One of the main criticisms of the original Chicago School was that it treated the neighborhood as an isolated entity. Although this critique is not entirely accurate (see chapter 2), the political economy critique makes a similar point. So do structural network theorists—nonspatial or cross-neighborhood relationships are potentially just as important theoretically as internal neighborhood characteristics and spatial dynamics, implying that we should not limit our analytic sights only to a neighborhood's *indigenous* qualities. Spatial analyses of the sort I pursued in chapter 10 get us outside the neighborhood proper but remain within the framework of between-community analysis. While cross-cutting neighborhood networks are tied into the social structure of the city, they are rarely studied.

This challenge was directly addressed in chapters 13 and 14 by considering individual-level actions and how they are implicated in an interlocking layer of structures that connect different neighborhoods. I examined this structural layering in the form of migration and elite influence networks. The idea is that moving between neighborhoods creates a tie, as does one leader going to another leader in a different community to address a problem, even one local in nature. Beyond the direct role of spatial distance, chapter 13 showed that the greater the social similarity between two communities, the higher the likelihood that they are connected through residential exchange networks. This relational pattern at the neighborhood level was induced by various sociodemographic characteristics, especially dyadic similarity in racial composition and median income. Social climate matters too. Similarity in perceived disorder and friendship ties exert independent influences on interneighborhood residential moves, a social form of homophily that reinforces symbolic and spatial boundaries.

Elites are governed by similar processes. Who to contact to achieve an intended outcome is a decision imbued with great autonomy and choice. I studied highly educated and motivated actors, after all—the movers and shakers of the city in law, politics, education, business, religion, and community organizations. But the choices of these institutional leaders vary sharply by community and create links that cross-cut the city in socially structured ways. Despite racial composition, poverty, and the other usual suspects, flows of informational contacts throughout the citywide elite also match up directly to collective efficacy and to patterns of migration flows generated by residents. There is a common higher-order organization and structure to the underlying network dynamics of two disparate behaviors.

Each of these cases—to move, to call on another leader—is an individual choice, but each choice invokes much more than individually independent action. The strong version of chapters 11–14 once again reverses the typical selection-bias critique: *neighborhoods choose people and information flows* rather than people choosing neighborhoods and information flows. What I mean by this claim is that there is an ongoing social structure that is continually operating and within which any individual or family makes decisions. Spatial network flows among neighborhoods are like rivers, with strong currents and whirlpools of activity. The flows of movement and the ways in which neighborhoods are linked together are relational and not something that individuals may be aware of or may easily control. Like an undercurrent, they are out of sight and usually conscious awareness. Information exchange, reputation maintenance, homophily in social ties—these are the kinds of everyday practices that reinforce a chainlike movement of people and feedback loops that solidify neighborhood advantage and disadvantage. Although not by conscious design, the city can thus be said to possess an enduring higher-order structure of stratification and accompanying processes of social organization that are quite persistent despite individual fluidity and neighborhood change.

Whither the Individual?

My approach does not conform to influential accounts in the social sciences and the practices of "methodological individualism" that posit individual choice as the foundation of explanation. I accept the causality of individual action, to be sure, but this book has demonstrated that neighborhood processes and higher-order structures have their own logic and causality. And while I make no claim that neighborhood-level processes are necessarily the most important, like a cog, they mediate bottom-up and top-down mechanisms for many social phenomena. The method of ecometrics and the theory of this book further claim that neighborhood mechanisms and higher-order structures are not subservient to individual selection, as typically conceived. Unlike a hierarchical model, this conceptualization suggests an underlying process that produces chains of effects at all levels—causal processes as conceived in this book do not inherently begin at the top *or* bottom—indeed I have argued that neighborhoods have downward *and* upward reaching influences. This is perhaps a radical view, and no study can simultaneously unpack all the moving parts. But I believe the evidence leads to the conclusion that, in a fundamental sense, individual selection is both a neighborhood effect and embedded in a process of "structural sorting," bringing full circle the findings of the book that integrate individual, neighborhood, and ultimately structure.

Thinking about Causality in a Social World

Social science has experienced a "causal turn," and I would be remiss not to confront its implications for interpreting the theoretical account I have just synthesized. Indeed, the hardnosed critic might still be unsatisfied and ask, *what is the causal status of this book?* In this section I tackle this question directly and summarize my position on social causality, one that follows from the principles of social inquiry that have guided my efforts.

Claims for experimental methods have been particularly strong in the neighborhood effects field but also in social science more broadly. Experiments have been argued to enhance scientific quality, evidence-based policy, and causal inference. Angus Deaton, the former president of the American Economic Association, coined the term *randomistas* to describe those convinced that the randomized clinical trial (RCT) was the only hope for scientific progress.[32] Claims for RCT superiority are not surprising. Experiments have long been cloaked in the mantle of science, especially the paradigm of laboratory randomization in medicine. The common reference to experiments as the gold standard goes a step further, explicitly invoking a claim of hierarchical or superior knowledge.[33] The lure of experiments is growing and much social science has in effect become "medicalized"—experiments and the gold standard of evidence are seen as one in the same.

A parallel movement has promoted the causal inference paradigm for observational studies. Accepting the experimental ideal but armed with advanced statistical tools instead of RCTs, a revolution has occurred in the valorized research procedures for analyzing social science data. Rooted in the counterfactual or "potential outcomes" movement, mathematical and statistical techniques have been recruited to improve causal inferences in nonexperimental research.[34] I applaud the turn to increased clarity about causal questions and I have taken advantage of the new toolkit of methods, including complex techniques if I thought they were an appropriate strategy for the question at hand.

Despite realized gains, however, neither experiments nor advanced statistics alone are the solution to the kinds of neighborhood effect questions that I set forth, nor, I argue, to social life in general. The primary goal of the modern experimentalist, randomista and statistical simulator alike, is to obtain an unbiased estimate of a causal parameter, usually at the individual level and often with individuals "nested" within neighborhoods. But the hierarchy collapses when causality cuts across units and levels. Unlike medical treatments that approximate a closed system, human behavior in social settings is interdependent—nothing is ever "held constant." Although recognition of interdependence is not a new insight, I have shown throughout this book that virtually all social life is interdependent in underappreciated spatial forms—"things go together" in and across distinct places.

As a result, I tackled multiple social behaviors and sought to tease out common mechanisms that accounted for their concentration in time and place, which might be better described as *neighborhood causal processes* rather than a single effect. At the same time I have examined how individual decisions (selection) and perceptions are influenced by neighborhoods, how selection influences neighborhood composition and social dynamics, and how extraneighborhood spatial dynamics and higher-order (or cross-cutting) ties work. This theoretical stance yields a multifaceted analytic approach different than the stylistic or idealized version of much contemporary research, in which neighborhood effect is taken to mean the statistical or experimental "downward" effect of a specific neighborhood characteristic on some individual behavior. This is an interesting question but not necessarily the most important.

Neighborhood-level experiments are an exception to the dominance of individual-level interventions in social science policy. The value of a community-level perspective is that it eschews a simple "kinds of people" analysis and focuses instead on how social characteristics of collectivities can inform policy interventions. There are now community-level experiments in economic development, public health, and violence that may pave the way for a more robust population-level consideration of causality and policy.[35] But while I applaud group-randomized trials and neighborhood-level experiments, they too are subject to the interlocking nature of social life. A key message of this book is that the assumption of an independence or lack of social interactions among neighborhoods is deeply problematic. Analogous to classrooms that are nested in schools and therefore an educational social structure, neighborhoods are embedded in larger communities and a metropolitan structure of inequality (chapters 10–12).[36] Migration flows or social interactions (e.g., leadership ties) that are not only a function of internal neighborhood processes and spatial proximity but instead link multiple neighborhoods across often far-flung sections of the city are further evidence that interdependence is the norm and not the assumed exception (chapters 13–14). More generally, social structure is, by its very nature, a threat to the assumptions of experimental causation. This should not be surprising, because randomization creates, momentarily at least, a nonsocial world.

There is another, more fundamental, issue at stake. Causal inference resides at a theoretical level and is not something that comes directly from the data. Nor, I would argue, is quantitative data inherently more useful in understanding how the world works than qualitative social inquiry. Data never "speak for themselves" and there is no theory-free method—making sense of causal patterns requires assumptions and claims about unobserved mechanisms no matter what the experiment *or* statistical method employed.[37] Causal explanation requires theory, in other words, not a particular method or only one kind of data. I showed this in chapter 11 with the MTO experiment, which in the end is silent on the mechanisms associated with the effects of voucher assignment. Therefore, even if one holds the view that furnishing a scientific explanation consists in locating or displaying causal mechanisms, experimental or statistical results serve as clues, not answers.[38] Sometimes qualitative empirical data can be more informative than what at first glance appears to be more rigorous quantitative data.

Policy Validity

Experiments and the quest for unbiased causal inference are also less relevant for social policy than commonly believed and promulgated. Even if we accept that the internal validity of experiments or causal inferences is strong, effective policy and what we ultimately care about depends fundamentally on *external* validity. The typical causal inference in social science, no matter how carefully crafted through randomization or statistical control, provides a static, marginal effect on a small number of individuals under hypothetical or contrived conditions. External validity in the traditional sense is probably not the best descriptor of the problem, however, as social science confronts contextual variations all the time. The decisive issue is that once we shift from a specific experiment or study result to an institutionalized policy or ongoing social structure, the rules of the game change and social processes spring into action. Analogous to MTO, for example, suppose that a randomized clinical trial finds that moving a small number of poor black families from concentrated poverty to upper-income white or racially integrated neighborhoods in the same highly segregated city improves wellbeing. Suppose further this is a valid causal inference and we grant that all experimental assumptions are met. How policy-relevant is the study? Is it transferable to a macrolevel policy, which is what matters? After all, we want to improve the lives of many children, not just a handful.

History provides a partial and sobering answer. If enough white families choose to withdraw from those neighborhoods because they do not want to live near blacks in any proportion greater than some low threshold, or if black middle-class families depart integrated or changing neighborhoods to maintain higher levels of neighborhood economic status ("black flight"), then the residential and institutional composition of the area shifts in proportion to the scale of the movement. Such changes would not be chosen by the new entrants and at some point planned policy begins to fall apart or must be redesigned as a new social reality is formed. William Julius Wilson's argument on the outmigration of the black middle class is a case in point and sadly, white flight was a reality in many U.S. cities. In Chicago, for example, I showed profound asymmetry in racial change—not one neighborhood in forty years shifted from black to white, but plenty went the other way. Yet in contrast, in some communities like Hyde Park, it is racial *integration* that is reproduced, demonstrating that social interventions have heterogeneous effects depending on the time, place, and in the Hyde Park case, institutions. To understand this process, theory and observational data are again crucial along with a dynamic conception of neighborhood context.

The implication I draw is not that moving someone out of poverty or a busing experiment to improve schooling is bad, only that, unlike fertilizer plots or taking a pill, human reactions to policies are not necessarily aligned to the causal inferences drawn from the original experiment or statistical estimate. The implementation of policy always occurs with interdependent and forward-thinking human beings, in neighborhood or other contextual settings, and with unintended consequences—including those working in ways in direct opposition to what the policy intends. The larger point is that social mechanisms such as sorting, tipping points, hierarchy maintenance, organizational capacity, and collective action—the stuff of social structure—constitutes the stage on which all policies and inference must perform. Policies reflect values and assumptions, moreover, and not everyone in the audience may share them or interpret tradeoffs in the same way as the producers. It follows that policy interventions need to be evaluated in ways that account for social level interdependencies and causation, an argument I return to in the final chapter.

Toward a Contextual Social Science

What I am describing is an effort to nudge social inquiry in a more pluralist yet still rigorous direction. Although perhaps heretical to given trends in the social sciences, I would argue that an unbiased causal inference is not the only or even most important goal, and that we need to broaden our conception of what constitutes explanatory evidence. Put simply, no one methodological technique is dispositive nor can it be, and this book is no exception. This is a positive and not a negative claim against experiments, statistical techniques, or causal clarity. Indeed, throughout my investigation I too estimated "independent" relationships, adjusting for confounding conditions, calling upon a gamut of methods in doing so.

But I would not rest my claims on any single finding I have reported, each of which is bounded with uncertainty and based on data and methods with clear limitations. The evidence must instead be considered in light of the entire project and the substantive nature of the phenomenon before us. Although unwieldy and time consuming, the argument running throughout this book is that theoretically interpretive, descriptive, qualitative, and observational approaches can be combined with ecometrics and rigorous empirical analysis in a holistic way that serves up valid evidence on social causality. In this view theory is not just verbal or a "just so" story, nor is it restricted to a particular mathematical or statistical model; rather it is the analysis of a set of empirical facts in their relation to one another, organized by but informing a set of explanatory ideas. Ultimately, my argument is built up from the commonalities that emerged from many different pieces of evidence looked at under different methodological lamps and with differing angles of projection—more nearly the opposite of the "crucial experiment."

Stanley Lieberson, the author of *Making It Count: The Improvement of Social Research and Theory*, has it right, I think, in arguing that the social sciences have gone astray in trying to mimic a classical physics-like focus on determinism where instead we should borrow the mindset of evolutionary biologists. Darwin's theory was constructed not in a lab or with randomized trials[39] but by "drawing rigorous conclusions based on observational data rather than true experiments" and "an ability to absorb enormous amounts of diverse data into a relatively simple system."[40] Analogous to evolutionary theorists, students of the city are often concerned with causal processes that take on historical and institutional dimensions that range over long periods of time that are not amenable to randomization. For example, to tackle cumulative disadvantage, poverty traps, and altruistic character meant that I had to confront causal processes that unfold across several decades. As I argued in chapters 5, 8, and 13, we thus require a more flexible conception of causality than that offered by individual experiments and their mathematical counterparts. Consistent with a pragmatist philosophy of science and the idea that causality can only be understood in a context, I believe this book taken as a whole has demonstrated a family of neighborhood effects, an example of *contextual causality*.[41]

It is ironic that Lieberson calls on evolutionary biology as a model of investigation, as it was the biological metaphors from ecology that so exercised critics of the early Chicago School.[42] I accept their critique of ecology's functionalism, overemphasis on the physical environment, neglect of political economy, and equilibrium assumptions, but it remains true that a central focus of human ecology is on the interactions of individuals with the environment in a holistic system—properly understood, on social interaction in time and place and its social-level consequences. Freed of functionalist roots and by engaging symbolic and relational structures, it is perhaps not unreasonable to think about neighborhood effects in conceptual terms as social-ecological interactionism; Erving Goffman meets social ecology, as it were.

There is much pragmatic evidence to suggest that observational approaches to contextual causality and social-ecological processes can pass scientific muster and perhaps help redefine contemporary standards of evidence. Consider that some of our most robust causal conclusions in medicine and the "harder" sciences stem from the simplest of methods. The Centers for Disease Control (CDC) has recently noted how the life expectancy of Americans has increased dramatically, lengthening by greater than thirty years since 1900 alone. About twenty-five years of this gain owes to advances in public health policy.[43] What is remarkable is the dominance of observation-based interventions in CDC's top ten causes of the gains. The Salk vaccine is the most famous field trial or experimental success, but motor vehicle laws and improvements in car safety, food regulations, control of infectious disease, and reduction in smoking account for the lion's share of increases in longevity and did not rest on randomized trials. No crucial experiment was needed to conclude that smoking causes cancer, for example. Consensus was achieved after sustained rigorous research of the old-fashioned observational variety. Population policies (e.g., on fertility, infant mortality) are also great successes in many countries around the world, with many of these policies derived from basic nonexperimental research.[44] The early discovery of penicillin was similarly observation based, as was the scientific theory of evolution.

Implication

The larger conclusion from this view of social research is that no technique can be said to constitute the gold standard because there is no gold standard.[45] No method, not an experiment or Darwin in the field, is universally superior, and the common assertion of a gold standard of evidence is merely a rhetorical device. The choice of method depends on the question and the nature of the phenomena under study, and the hard truth is that we have little choice but to adapt in creative ways to the kinds of evidence that social scientists confront.[46] The idea of the "crucial test" of causality is also misleading, as Lieberson and Horwich argue in making a case for "implications analysis."[47] Traced to the great British statistician R. F. Fisher, their idea is that we should trace out as many different consequences of a causal hypothesis as possible, and implement observational studies to discover if these consequences hold up. Although we are taught to prioritize the crucial experiment, even in the hard sciences this is not how things typically work in practice. No one positive finding confirms a theory any more than a negative finding disconfirms a theory, especially in the social world of contextual variations.

The story of John Snow trekking about in Victorian London and discovering the Broad Street pump as the cause of the great cholera epidemic is thus as inspiring a model for good research as any mathematical model or experiment—detective work is a necessary part of our job.[48] Neither pure induction nor pure deduction, diverse strands of evidence must instead be weighed against a theory of the case at hand. It is in this sense that method can never be the answer alone, but neither can theory be divorced from method. In Snow's world and ours, only by piecing together multiple nuggets of information, mixing and matching data sources like a bricoleur, and ultimately organizing empirical findings theoretically does an explanatory argument ultimately emerge.

16 Aftermath—Chicago 2010

In the summer of 2010 I returned to the streets of Chicago that I had walked many times over the years and that were introduced to the reader in chapter 1. Retracing my steps provides a chance to reflect on the empirical findings and general ideas that I synthesized in the previous chapter while grounding them in a context that is propitious for analytical leverage. The fall of 2008, as we now know all too well, saw a calamitous economic crisis that began in the U.S., but that rippled outward. The economic shock hit American cities after a prolonged boom and shattered the confidence of elites and lay people alike—in 2009, poverty rose to its highest level in fifteen years. Like a hurricane or heat wave, an economic crisis provides the analyst with an opportunity to examine how social structure deflects or exacerbates "disaster," in this case one that is decidedly unnatural in causal origin.[1] The large-scale transformation of public housing in Chicago adds another layer of human intervention—here, by the government—that dislocated tens of thousands of families. Chicago has changed in many other ways both large and small, including that, for the first time in twenty-two years, Richard M. Daley is no longer Chicago's mayor.[2]

My aim, then, is to close out the theoretical arguments of the book against the backdrop of recent social change. Returning to the logic of where I began in chapter 1, I take both a street-level and bird's-eye view of the city, situating in specific places, and at the higher-order or structural level, the continuing salience of neighborhood differentiation. This strategy provides a contextualized portrayal of Chicago neighborhoods fifteen years after the PHDCN was launched, while at the same time affording an overall glimpse of how the city has absorbed a global economic crisis and public housing transformation on a massive scale. Motivated by the book's comparative strategy and key findings, I highlight how the linked processes of stability and change have played out across multiple neighborhoods. Of special theoretical interest are communities that have gone against the grain and bucked the trend predicted by their prior histories or that are confronting external challenges in notable ways. For example, what is it about communities that fall on the "off-diagonal" or are otherwise anomalous in their response to the economic crisis, or that have stepped up to increases in crime against great odds? This book has also provided unmistakable evidence on mechanisms of neighborhood social reproduction. Is durable inequality still maintained, and in what ways?

My empirical sources are multifaceted in nature and include personal field observations, housing foreclosures filed during and after the economic collapse, incidents of violence in 2010, newspaper accounts and local reporting, administrative records on the location of public housing and voucher users after the demolition of CHA projects, and a smaller-scale replication of the letter-drop study in a strategically chosen sample of neighborhoods that I conducted in June of 2010. These data, qualitative and quantitative in form, are woven together to paint a final holistic picture of the social organization and deep structure that still defines Chicago.

Seeing Change

It was a warm June day, but the feel was much like my visit to the Magnificent Mile on a cold day in March of 2007 and countless times before that. Cartier, Van Cleef and Arpels, and Tiffany & Co. were sparkling. At Erie and Michigan I noted cranes in action, with apartments being advertised "starting at 1.4 million" (presumably studios on the lower floors) before completion was anywhere in sight. It was hard to tell that a severe recession was in high gear, although upper-end stores expressed their response to hard times in amusing ways: a man stood on Michigan with a huge cardboard tent sign draped over him, advertising Gucci, Armani, Prada, and Dior—"now 10% off." People seemed to take notice.

FIGURE 16.1. Old meets new Chicago: Donald Trump Towers over the classic Wrigley Building. Photograph by the author, June 12, 2010.

But North Michigan Avenue looked as busy as ever and little worse for the wear of the global downturn.

At the Chicago River, Donald Trump's skyscraper is complete and towers high over its neighbors, notably the classic Wrigley Building just to its east. Built in the 1920s, the Wrigley is considered one of America's most famous and beautiful office towers. The juxtaposition of old and new is jarring, but it symbolizes Chicago's simultaneous interplay of stability and change. The photo I took on this June day (fig. 16.1) captures this surreal pairing. As on previous visits when the building was going up, tourists are snapping pictures of the tower and the impressive array of buildings along the Chicago River. Near the Wabash Street entrance, a security man paces outside, keeping an eye on things. Even he looks true to the Trump image of privileged sleekness, well dressed and with the latest in electronic communications dangling from his head. Busyness, importance, and wealth are projected all around Trump's entrance.

After I cross the Chicago River into the Loop, Millennium Park continues to exude the theme of bold and new against a classic backdrop. And it is still drawing crowds. I have to admit that the controversial extravaganza is impressive, and the project does work as a testament to Chicago's audacious ambition and architectural dominance. From Louis Sullivan to Frank Gehry seems almost natural. On this day anyway, Gehry's pavilion reflects the sun and blends in well with the environment. As in the winter, people mill about and the projected faces of average citizens stare out of the fountain's facade alongside Michigan Avenue. The only difference is that instead of skaters gliding about, kids splash in the water. Looking east and continuing through the South Loop and past Roosevelt Road into the Near South Side, one sees additional evidence of the gentrification that has reclaimed the old rail yards and single-room-occupancy hotels. New condominiums are scattered throughout the area, especially in the new "Eastside" (east Loop) and along South Michigan Avenue between 13th and 18th streets.

Further down Michigan Avenue, beginning at around 35th Street, the transformation of the Near to Mid South Side is ongoing. Many high-rise and low-rise housing projects are gone, and mixed-income housing is present where once only concentrated poverty reigned. I see evidence of several new apartment buildings just off South Michigan that I did not recall from less than a year earlier. But as before, there is an absence of vibrant street activity and it is not hard to find trash in the street or vacant and boarded-up buildings as you move slightly west or east. Even directly on South Michigan, around Pershing Boulevard, one sees abandoned lots and apartments with plywood covering the windows, often next to an occupied unit. Mary Pattillo reports that Grand Boulevard (or Bronzeville) is ambivalent about redevelopment, and the physical landscape almost seems to reflect this attitude.[3] Consistent with this view, there is an odd mixture of vacant lots from the former housing projects sitting cheek by jowl with new condominiums and evidence of a thriving black middle class. I noted multiple boarded-up buildings on 47th

Street in March 2007 and saw a group of homeless men sitting around a fire on a trash-strewn lot at Drexel and 43rd and near 47th. Over three years later I cannot say that the feel is much different. The homeless men are not at the same location, but I see smaller groups of men, apparently homeless, in other nearby places. The lot is still empty and 47th Street remains pocked with physical signs of disrepair. The recession seems to have slowed progress, as many buildings along major thoroughfares are empty and appear victims of increased home foreclosures.

Although still in transition, the neighborhoods in Oakland and most of Grand Boulevard nonetheless represent a distinct turning point in the history of Chicago's poor. The major intervention on the part of the city did not have miraculous results, but it did substantially alter the community's trajectory, for better or worse. Change is most pronounced around the areas where the projects once stood. Considering the legacies of inequality I have demonstrated, this is no small feat. But legacies usually do not simply vanish; they linger on and are constantly negotiated. And some challenges were simply passed on to other communities—even if the poor move elsewhere, they are still present. Social service demands must thus always be considered in a larger metropolitan context and cannot be limited to one neighborhood. The south suburbs are already feeling the impact of the city's changes.

Back on South Federal Street, things look today almost exactly like they did in figure 1.1, around the former site of the Robert Taylor Homes. I go to the same spot and find it as before, empty and quiet—dead space, as it were. The only difference is that a Chicago Police officer sits in a cruiser parked about a hundred yards away in what was formerly a street teeming with people. He eyes me carefully as I stroll around. Other than the officer there is no one within sight of me for what seems like a long time. Clearly mine is not an everyday activity, although a green expanse of grass stretches out before me. The space is marked by a strong history, and its stigma apparently lingers on. If the results of this book are any guide, it will be some time before social transformation is complete, if it ever is.

Further south and east, the community of Hyde Park looms large, home to the University of Chicago and the president of the United States.[4] Hyde Park has been stable after its brush with rapid change in the mid-twentieth century and maintains its integrated housing with a mix of organizational and structural advantages. The most obvious is the university, but the community boasts a robust civic life, a density of nonprofit organizations, an educated elite, and connections to power. I looked up the most recent data available I could locate (2005) on the density of nonprofit organizations, using the same sources used in chapter 8. Of all the communities in the city of Chicago, Hyde Park ranked sixth or in the top 10 percent. Its rate of collective civic action events in 2000 (also see chapter 8) was fifth in the city. Using the Key Informant network data from chapter 14, it comes out on top in terms of the density of direct and indirect ties among leaders. These external indicators correspond to the qualitative feel one gets walking in Hyde Park and talking to its residents and leaders, and it comports with my local knowledge of the place gleaned over twelve years. As noted in chapter 1, community input and institutional connections are manifested in visible cues (e.g., signs, churches, bookstores, petitions) and a density of community organizations. Obama's presence has only solidified the organizational identity of the community, both internally and nationally.

Just west of Hyde Park, however, stark differences (again) remain. Across Washington Park the community of the same name has seen attempts at recovery but is still waiting for jobs and economic rebound. Along the major thoroughfare of Garfield Boulevard and spilling into its side streets, vacant and boarded-up buildings, gated stores, and empty lots are not uncommon. As noted in chapter 1, if Kenwood and the gentrification near the lake in Grand Boulevard approach the status of a "Black Gold Coast," then Washington Park and the lingering memories of the areas around the old Robert Taylor Homes may constitute the nearby "slum," as perceived by many Chicagoans. Mayor Daley made a visible point of trying to invest in this area in the form of proposed new construction for the 2016 Olympics, but Chicago failed in its bid. On any given day, many of Washington Park's struggling men may be seen waiting for better days, unemployed and passing the time.

The recession adds to a community's burden in ways that exacerbate prior disadvantage, an expression of how structural forces are mediated by local contexts. I examined data on all housing foreclosure filings in 2009, calculated as a rate per thousand mortgages as of 2007. This measure presents an up-to-date look at the intensity of foreclosures initiated after the economic crisis. Of all communities in Chicago, Washington Park sits at the top. Grand Boulevard, despite the evidence of the middle-class renewal just noted, is ninth highest in the city. The top ten communities in the penetration of foreclosures are all predominantly black.[5]

As I head further south into Woodlawn, I see further disadvantage and physical disrepair of the housing stock on its western fringes. But as in other visits in recent years, heading eastward toward the lake brings evidence of renewal. New housing, both middle income and mixed income, sprouts on a large number of blocks where tenements once stood. To the extent that Woodlawn is an "outlier," I would argue that it benefits from its history of organizational action combined with its spatial proximity to the University of Chicago (with its own network of connections to key players) just north. Despite its continuing poverty, for example, Woodlawn ranks thirteenth (in the top quintile) in the city's distribution of nonprofit organizational density. The Woodlawn Organization (TWO) is one of these organizations, formed back in the early 1960s when distrust of the University of Chicago ran deepest.[6] The Reverend Arthur Brazier, pastor emeritus of the Apostolic Church of God, twenty thousand members strong, was at the center of coalition building in Woodlawn ever since he helped bring about TWO's inception some fifty years ago.[7] Although controversial and in some cases distrusted by local residents and accused of caving in to the interests of economic developers at the expense of long-term residents, there can be little doubt that TWO is a political and organizational force. The Key Informant study independently reveals that Woodlawn ranks highest in Chicago on the centralization of organizational contacts in 1995 and in the upper quartile in 2002—networks of influence converge on a small number of leaders within Woodlawn. The provocative alliances formed by TWO and other community organizations, presumably aided by their structural cohesiveness in network contacts, have combined with intervention from the University of Chicago to have sharply altered Woodlawn—for better or worse.

The contextual example of Woodlawn comports with a larger point I have made: when confronted with stark material deprivation and macro forces, neighborhoods must depend on organizational connections both local *and* that cut across the city and beyond for increasing their capacity in garnering outside resources. These resources are likely to increase in importance as the economic crisis slows housing activity and unemployment lingers at rates most American communities never experience. Hence, consistent with my general findings, stability and change simultaneously exist: Woodlawn's altered trajectory is relative, and it remains a vulnerable and largely poor community. Its rate of home foreclosures in 2009 is eighth highest in the city.

Heading further south, I revisited Avalon Park and Chatham to see how they are faring in the new economic environment brought on by the recession. I reported in chapter 1 that, unlike their neighbors to the north and west, these black communities have been stably working or middle class for many years. As I passed along the same streets in June of 2010, I noticed many scenes similar to those in the past. In the warm early evening, men and women were out watering their gardens, talking, and relaxing on porches. The feeling was peaceful. Along street after street south of 79th and west of Stony Island, I could see neat brick homes, indicators of block-group associations, and children playing happily. On what seemed like every other block, the signs were especially noticeable, warning off those who would dare tread on the willed tranquility. It was not just the expected drugs and gang activity that were admonished. In the 7900 block of South Dante, as but one example, a sign warned against "loud music," "walking a dog without a leash," "ball playing on front," and "car washing." Disorder was nowhere to be found in the stereotypical form commonly attributed to black communities, and if the messages on the frequent signs are to be taken as a cultural expression, then shared expectations are solidly mainstream, even if not overtly conservative in nature. This observation corroborates a larger empirical regularity that emerged from the PHDCN study—blacks (and Latinos) in Chicago are less tolerant of activities like drinking and drug use than whites, a regularity that contradicts frequent portrayals in the media.[8]

But there was change in the air here, as in Woodlawn. The neat brick houses one after another were now interlarded with abandoned or vacant buildings; not every street, but the effect was noticeable enough that it made me take note. In the middle of a block it was not uncommon to see a house or a sequence of two to three houses boarded up or with signs posted on the door, presumably the result of foreclosures. The intrusion of the recession in the form of vacant houses was perhaps not surprising in Washington Park, but in higher-income places like Chatham, to be ranked fourteenth overall in the city in its rate of foreclosures comes as something of a shock to the residents. My visual inspection conformed to the macrolevel data, suggesting that the black working class is experiencing the economic crisis in manifestly negative ways, a qualitative sense of the vulnerable getting poorer. Or, in this case, the working class getting shoved down a notch, with the losses of those foreclosed on shared by the remaining homeowners.

Consistent with a message of this book, the impact of the larger social structure is thus uneven across neighborhoods in ways that are not simply a result of income. In the white working-class or mixed neighborhoods I observed on the same visit in June (e.g., Irving Park, Portage Park, Uptown), I did not see the same evidence of foreclosures, abandonment, or vacancies. Avalon Park and Chatham have seen families raising their kids, tending to their homes, and going about quietly living the American Dream for years, only to be confronted with a new challenge to their housing infrastructures. As if that were not enough, the social infrastructure is being challenged on another more public and explosive front.

Confronting Violence

> When people think of the South Side of Chicago, they think violence. In Chatham, that's not what we see. It's happened, and we're going to fix it, so it doesn't happen again.
>
> Thomas Wortham, president of the Cole Park Advisory Council[9]

Perhaps linked to the economic crisis or perhaps, as some officials and local residents assert, linked to the infusion of poor families with lots of teenagers from the former "projects," violence has encroached on the tranquility of Chatham. Whatever the cause, according to local perceptions and some official statistics, violence was up in Chatham's neighborhoods in 2010, and its threat has become ever more salient, given the proud reputation of the community as a safe haven.[10]

In the spring of 2010 the papers were full of a heartbreaking story that encapsulates a key theme of this book's perspective on violence. Community residents of Chatham came together in May to organize against shootings that had erupted in Nat King Cole Park, located at 85th Street and King Drive. Over the years the park had been the site of basketball games, children playing, picnics, and everyday activities enjoyed by families. But in April, a gunman in a van stopped to open fire on a group of teenage males playing basketball. It was the second shooting in weeks. No one died, but the hoops were shut down and an angry community sought to "take back the park." According to Thomas Wortham, who grew up near the park, as had his father and his grandfather before him, residents were not cowed. Despite the shootings the park was soon filled again with runners, children on swings, and youngsters eager to play ball but now under the watchful eye of adult residents. "Monitoring has to be done," intoned another resident. Police patrols were also increased, but in a nonacademic expression of collective efficacy, the district commander admitted that the police cannot solve crime alone: "but if we all work together—the police, the community, the elected officials—all of us together . . . can make a difference with it."[11]

Tragically, Chatham would soon bear witness that collective efficacy and policing are not always enough. Despite his and others' efforts at mobilization, the same Thomas Wortham would come face to face with predatory violence only a week later and yards away. A Chicago police officer and Iraq veteran, Wortham was gunned down on May 19 during an attempted robbery of his new motorcycle after leaving a family dinner at his father's home, where he had grown up—steps away from Cole Park. Wortham's father was on the porch that night and yelled when he saw a gun pointed at his son's head. A retired police sergeant, Wortham's father went inside to get his own gun and then intervened, in the process shooting one of the three offenders. But it was too late. As his son lay dying, the two other robbers fled in a car, running over the younger Wortham and dragging his body along the block. Shocking the residents of this peaceful neighborhood and across the city, the offenders were allegedly taking part in a drinking game of who could rob someone first. A stunned Mayor Daley was angry: "Here's a young man who served twice in Iraq. . . . It should wake up America."[12] The shocks were not over. In rapid fashion two other Chicago police officers were murdered in July of 2010 in separate incidents on the South Side, one just north of Chatham in a similar "safe haven." The South and West sides witnessed other spasms of violence that took a toll, even if less noticed.[13]

Unfortunately, predominantly black neighborhoods in Chicago, whether poor, working class, or middle income, have always faced spatial vulnerability to crime to an extent that white neighborhoods of all kinds simply have not. Consistent with the theme of racially uneven exposure, the twenty-year-old man shot while attempting to rob

Officer Wortham did not live in the neighborhood, but came from a nearby South Side community, the Wentworth Gardens area just west of the former Robert Taylor Homes. Another apprehended robber came from Englewood, the extremely distressed community to the west of the expressway. Global effects of concentrated disadvantage and spatial vulnerability have been described in earlier chapters, but in this tragic story we see the confluence of mechanisms at work in a single local community. Will Avalon and Chatham Park become the new truly disadvantaged as the black middle class flees, more houses are foreclosed, and poverty rises with the influx of families displaced by the city's housing authority? Recall the women I described in chapter 1, who unfurled a quilt commemorating all the children murdered in the Robert Taylor Homes in the mid-1990s. Things got so bad in their neighborhood that it no longer exists; rightly or wrongly, implosion was considered the only way out. Will Chatham inexorably decline and one day suffer a similar fate?

I contemplated this question when I could not get the Wortham story out of my mind. My answer, rooted in the findings of this book, is no. The data tell a story of resistance to crime, challenge-inspired collective efficacy, and a long-term stability to the area in its social character, despite underlying structural vulnerabilities. Chatham residents express strong attachments to their community and since the murder seem to be more vigilant than ever in not giving in to violence. More generally, the outpouring over the Wortham murder has spurred collective organizational events (e.g., rallies, neighborhood alliances) and what I would broadly describe as "ratcheted-up" efforts to instill collective efficacy. One resident, for example, stated that residents had banded together in response to the murder because "Unless everybody pulls together, it won't work." [14]

It is too early to tell definitively, but two months after the Wortham killing and after the media glare had died down, the park was literally "crimefree." Using geocoded and time-referenced crime data, I did a search for all crimes—minor and major alike—reported to the police occurring within a quarter-mile radius around Cole Park for the two-week period ending July 24, 2010.[15] As the map in figure 16.2 shows, the blocks around the park did not produce a single crime, not even so much as a disorderly conduct. On the major thoroughfare of 87th Street near Vernon Avenue, there was a larceny and theft from a car, and a

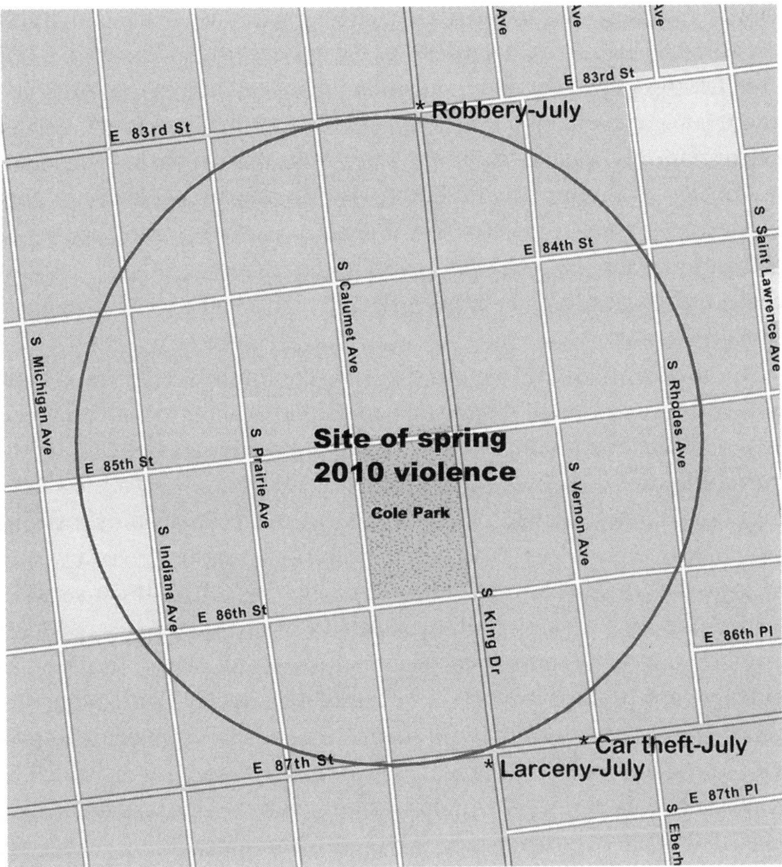

FIGURE 16.2. A crimefree Nat King Cole Park, July 11–24, 2010

robbery occurred up on 83rd Street. But within and around the park, it was crime free, and with a population of several thousand, the crime rate in the neighborhood has been low when prorated over a year.

Why does violence unhinge some communities and draw others together? This book has provided a partial answer. Among the twenty-five predominantly black communities in Chicago (defined as 75 percent or more black), Avalon Park and Chatham rank first and second, respectively, in terms of the level of collective efficacy as independently measured in the PHDCN surveys. In terms of organizational participation, I consulted both the nonprofit density data and the PHDCN. Although they are in the middle of the pack in terms of official density of nonprofits, averaged across the two waves of the survey, Avalon Park ranks fifth or in the top 10 percent of organizational participation in the entire city, and it is second among black communities and Chatham is eighth. This performance is notable because neither community boasts a University of Chicago or anything like it in terms of organizational heavyweights. The evidence, then, indicates that there is a relatively strong pool of organizational activity and latent capacity for collective efficacy in these communities, leading me to be optimistic concerning their struggle to remain vibrant.

In addition, I would emphasize that community legacies are not only negative. It would be a mistake to read into my emphasis on mechanisms of social reproduction the idea that poverty and violence are the inevitable stuff of stability. Quite to the contrary, if one recalls the findings in chapter 5, higher-income and low-violence areas have a strong tendency to reproduce themselves as well. There may be no great wealth to transmit in Chatham or Avalon Park, but by cultivating a sense of ownership and cultural commitment to the neighborhood, residents produce a social resource that feeds on itself and serves as a kind of independent protective factor and durable character that encourages action in the face of adversity. Residents are thus far from being duped; they know full well that the South Side they call home is disvalued by many outsiders. But as Wortham was quoted before he was murdered, Chatham residents do not perceive their community solely within the narrative of violence, they actively seek to transcend it: "we're going to fix it," he said. One can only hope that his murder was not in vain and that he will ultimately be proven correct, that the pattern in figure 16.2 will be sustained.

Roseland is further on the South Side and nearer to the city limits. It too is a virtually all-black community but more disadvantaged than Avalon Park or Chatham. Roseland is not the worst off by any means, but it is a notch down on the socioeconomic rung and showing signs of distress. It has the tenth-highest foreclosure rate in the city, for example, and faces a tenacious crime problem of its own. With this greater risk comes higher stakes, and the residents seem to recognize this in their outlook. Although the density of formal nonprofits in Roseland is neither high nor low—it sits right at the median—the participation by residents is surprisingly high, given its profile of concentrated poverty. Of all communities in the city of Chicago, Roseland ranks tenth in organizational participation measured by the PHDCN survey. Among predominantly black communities, it ranks in the upper quintile in collective efficacy as well as organizational participation, and in the upper third of collective action events. These independent data and the pattern of results throughout the book suggest that residents will activate their shared expectations to address, if not always meet, community challenges.

Roseland's organizational life shone the day I visited. At 6:45 p.m. on June 11 at the intersection of 111th and Wallace, I came across a group of African American men with bright orange shirts standing in the street and approaching passing cars in animated fashion. Curious, I stopped to find out what they were apparently protesting. The men were part of "Roseland Ceasefire," an organization with citywide roots dedicated to preventing crime.[16] On this day they were trying to engage other residents to take increased responsibility for denouncing violence, and also, I suspect, to send a message of hope to local teenagers who were under the threat of gangs. As I watched the action and reactions of passersby, the significance of this spot slowly dawned on me. In the fall of 2009, the nation had watched in horror as Derrion Albert, a sixteen-year-old student, was beaten to death with a wooden plank outside Fenger High School. The beating was part of a large fight among dozens of youth that was deeply unsettling even to those who had seen violence before. Although murders happen frequently in the U.S., this one was videotaped and soon went viral. The video was so chilling that it quickly garnered news attention worldwide, with some claiming the daytime violence outside a school was in part responsible for Chicago losing its Olympic bid soon afterward.[17] Fenger High School is just one block south of where the protesters gathered, at 112th and Wallace.

I passed by the school and reflected on the import of Albert's death and still strong reverberations in the community, given hope by the collective response to violence I had just witnessed but harboring no illusions of a miraculous ending. One of the fundamental principles of collective efficacy is that its interpretation is relative to need and risk. A rich suburban community with little violence usually does not see this type of action, but neither does it need to. The question is what resources are marshaled under what threat, and how to measure latent capacity given that there are many kinds of risk. For example, Hegewisch on Chicago's Southeast Side faced literal destruction in the early 1990s from Mayor Daley's proposal to build a third airport. Enraged, "Citizens against the Lake Calumet Airport" rose up to protest not only a powerful political machine but economic powerhouses behind the multibillion-dollar plan. The effort brought together residents, leaders, and organizations. In 1995, Hegewisch's collective efficacy and density of key-informant leadership ties were among the highest in the city. A residue of increased collective efficacy was likely built up by the airport challenge, but without an underlying capacity in the first place, Hegewisch, like many places before it around the country, would have wilted under pressure. Many runways pave over someone's former house, after all.

The point then is that, without challenge, efficacy loses meaning. That is why this book proposed an empirical strategy for measuring collective efficacy that was grounded in the theoretical insight that shared expectations given a concrete problem constitute the crucial mechanism in the emergence of action. While Roseland is not well off and faces many risks, foreclosures and violence among them in the summer of 2010, at least some of its residents are taking visible action, and the PHDCN data suggest that the reservoir has not been emptied. One wonders what else is taking place behind the scenes.

A photo I took the day of the rally conveys the contradictions of Roseland (fig. 16.3). An apparently homeless man saunters by in the street, passing homes for sale (foreclosed?) one block away from where a student was publicly slain. The latter alone would crush many communities, but, like Chatham, one can only hope that the angry young men also present in the picture are successful in their struggle to reclaim the very same streets.[18] That the protestors are all men should not go unremarked. One of the criticisms of the black community voiced by some observers on the Left and Right alike is that black men in the inner city have not shouldered their responsibilities for raising children and helping to regulate the always difficult road to adulthood of teenagers. Where were the fathers of the boys who stomped Derrion Albert to death, some pointedly asked?[19] The prevalence of female-headed families with children in poor communities like Roseland is undeniably high, over 40 percent. But while one incident does not a trend make, the men of Roseland I observed on this day were out, angry, and quite visibly going against the scripts that had written them off as uninvolved.

FIGURE 16.3. Collective protest against violence in Roseland, June 11, 2010. Photograph by the author.

Heading northwest past the Dan Ryan, we find more poverty stretching for hundreds of blocks, reaching hard into communities like Englewood and West Englewood. The great recession, along with the deconcentration of large projects like the Robert Taylor Homes, heap more challenges on top of long-term vulnerability and threaten to erase hard-won gains. According to the 2009 data, Englewood and West Englewood represent the third- and fifth-highest foreclosure rates in Chicago, respectively. Moreover, because of their cheap housing to begin with, many CHA voucher holders are moving south and west to communities like Englewood, Washington Park, and South Shore. South suburbs such as Harvey, Country Club Hills, and Dolton are also witnessing a surge of lower-income residents moving in from Chicago.

The new influx of disadvantaged residents highlights the cumulative Matthew Effect process I have emphasized—poor communities with the least resources are taking on added burdens disproportionately, in turn reinforcing preexisting inequality. This cycle of disadvantage is not just structural but cultural in its ability to influence behavior over sustained periods of time. As shown in chapter 13, collective perceptions of disorder are as important as income levels (individual or neighborhood) in driving migration networks between communities. Population flows track community reputational histories, which are shaped in the public's eye by racial and immigrant concentration (chapter 6) and unwittingly reinforced by institutionalized identities encoded in the media and even the Chicago *Local Community Fact Book*.[20] A vicious cycle emerges, with structural and cultural mechanisms intertwined in their dynamic effects.[21]

Once again, however, some communities defy simple categorization and the equation in the public's mind of social problems with particular race and income groupings. Widespread racial stereotypes put highly efficacious areas in the white Far Northwest Side, but consider some anomalies. Although Mount Greenwood is nearby to what is widely thought of as the "Southside Ghetto" and is relatively mixed racially by Chicago standards, it produces high collective efficacy. Beverly is a stable middle-class area even more proximate to the same poverty and more mixed—fully one third of its residents were black in 2000, probably closer to 40 percent by mid-decade. Yet the integrated community of Beverly stands out as the most efficacious community in Chicago overall in 1995 and second best in 2002, after Mount Greenwood. In chapter 7 (fig. 7.3), I showed that Ashburn is also a mixed-race community (43 percent black, 37 percent white, and 17 percent Latino) and yet high in collective efficacy. How do these communities do it? That the extremes of low and high collective efficacy are all on the widely denigrated South Side underscores my claim that social processes must be taken as seriously as demographic composition. Embodied in places like Beverly, Avalon Park, and Chatham, a commonality that stands out beyond residential stability in housing and socioeconomic resources is durable organizational density (or capacity) combined with a strong community identity and commitment to place. Recall from chapters 7–9 that residential stability and organizational density explain neighborhood-level collective efficacy and social altruism net of economic and population composition.

While rare, sometimes even the most disadvantaged communities experience notable changes. The low-income black communities of Oakland and Riverdale, for example, witnessed the largest *increases* in collective efficacy over time relative to their historical profiles and social dynamics occurring elsewhere in the city. As discussed in chapter 5 and highlighted above, Oakland was the site of major structural interventions, including the dismantling of segregated high-rise public housing and public investment by the city. Besides the simple poverty declines, these interventions seem to have boosted both internal and external perceptions of its efficacy. Yet most communities that have achieved high collective efficacy or increased collective efficacy have done so absent such "macro" interventions. Edison and Norwood Park on Chicago's Northwest Side, for example, are stable high-collective efficacy areas that are virtually all white and that have been middle to upper income for years. Riverdale is on the Far South Side and similarly experienced no major policy or economic interventions. It presents nearly the opposite profile of Edison and Norwood Park—low income and black—but Riverdale managed to increase more in collective efficacy over time, even if it still sits below the baseline level of the Northwest Side cluster. And Mount Greenwood increased over the late 1990s to become the highest-ranking community on the level of collective efficacy by 2002, again absent an "exogenous" intervention. Drawing directly from the findings in chapter 8, I would argue that this upturn came about as a result of the community's organizational infrastructure. In 1995, prior to the surge in collective efficacy, Mount Greenwood ranked in the top 20 percent (along with Chatham and Avalon Park) in Chicago on the participation of its residents in civic organizations. Beverly was first in organizational participation in 1995, and by 2002 its collective efficacy was second only to Mount Greenwood.

These examples show that while correlations exist between social processes and structural features of economic stratification and racial segregation, they are not isomorphic. Levels and changes in the collective character of communities cannot simply be "read off of demography," in other words. Moreover, because challenges are not the same in every community, the nature of how collective efficacy evolves and how it unfolds over time varies. There is no one single or invariant pathway, and sometimes unplanned events, like the killing of a police officer at his father's home or the video of a murder of a local teen, alter trajectories in ways we cannot uncover with our data, even if pervasive mechanisms overlay and shape the higher-order causal picture. Thus, I would argue that collective efficacy and organizational capacity reflect a deeply social and nonreductionist form of community wellbeing.

Bird's-Eye View Revisited

Using the most recent quantitative data available, I zoom out to take the bird's-eye view of the social processes I have just described more qualitatively. One key question has been stability and change in economic status. Has the economic or housing crisis altered the city's relational character, beyond the stories of the different communities told above? Or has global disaster been superimposed on an enduring structure of inequality, and, if so, at what magnitude?

To answer these questions I first examined two sources of data from 2009, one on housing-voucher holders and the other on families displaced from Chicago Housing Authority (CHA) projects.[22] Both relocatees from the CHA and housing-voucher users directly reflect families in poverty or that are otherwise economically vulnerable. As expected, when I created per-capita rates in 2009, the two indicators strongly overlapped and produced a high correlation (0.84, $p < 0.001$). Thus I created a standardized scale that combined the per-capita presence of CHA and voucher users in a community. I then examined its citywide distribution as predicted by the index of concentrated disadvantage in 2000 that I examined in earlier chapters.[23] Simultaneously I also examined the rate of home foreclosures filed per mortgage in 2009 after the onset of the Great Recession. The act of foreclosure is a distinct marker of economic and social vulnerability, one that is perhaps more visible to the naked eye through vacancies than the poverty reflected in the CHA measure.

Figure 16.4 shows that inequality's spatial distribution remains largely intact after the economic crash and major changes in public housing policy in Chicago. The correlation of concentrated disadvantage in 2000 and its parallel in 2009 is notably high, given the measurement difference in indicators, nearly a decade's worth of race/ethnic change, and much ballyhooed gentrification ($R = 0.86$, $p < 0.01$). What's more, the communities hard hit by home foreclosures after the crash are almost all clustered in the upper-right corner of the figure. Low-foreclosure communities cluster tightly on the bottom left, with a familiar group of names like Beverly and Lincoln Park. There are a few

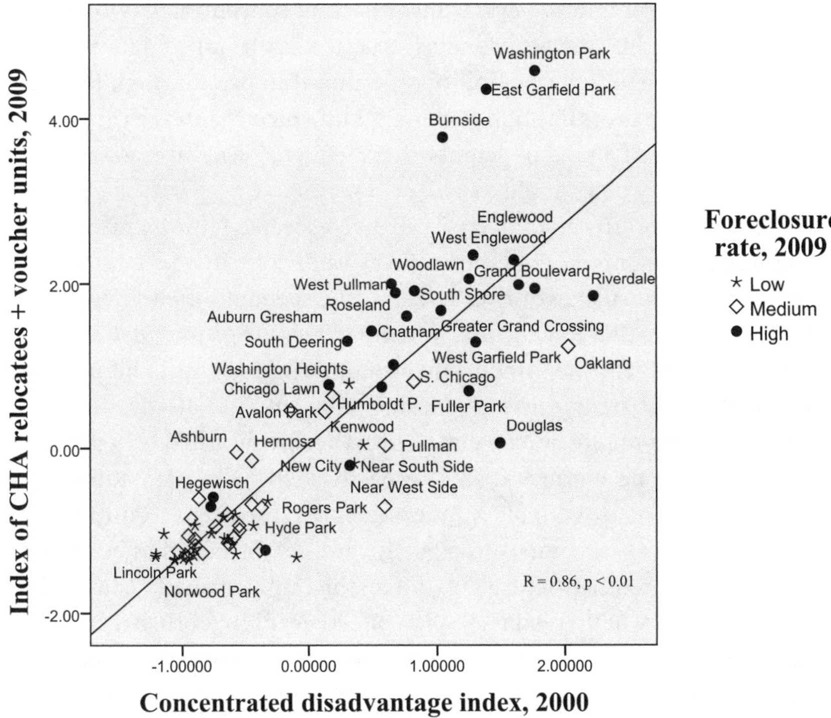

FIGURE 16.4. Inequality's durable imprint before and after the 2008 economic crisis.

anomalies such as Douglas and Oakland seeing relative "gains" from poor starting points, and with Oakland escaping the worst of the foreclosure crisis. By contrast, Washington Park and East Garfield Park were vulnerable to begin with, only to take on a set of new burdens dished up by Wall Street and the city's housing authority.[24] Overall, however, inequality by place remains highly persistent—knowing a community's racially linked disadvantage in 2000 pretty much tells you its allocation of CHA relocatees, distribution of the voucher holders, and intensity of foreclosure filings a decade later and after major structural shocks. Rather amazingly, when I create an index of concentrated disadvantage for 1970, it correlates nearly as highly with the CHA poverty index in 2009 as disadvantage in 2000, at 0.67 ($p < 0.01$). Disadvantage in 1970 also significantly predicts the foreclosure rate in 2009 (0.51, $p < 0.01$). A forty-year persistence despite the radical turnover of residents indicates yet again the community-level transmission of concentrated poverty. As I have argued, this transmission has structural, cultural, and individual underpinnings, with vulnerability reproduced in part through the systematic sorting over time of individuals, but which chapters 11–13 demonstrated is itself a kind of neighborhood effect. The organizational life of a community plays a role too.

To probe the aftermath of crisis further, especially its organizational character, I examined community-level variations in the foreclosure rate per HUD mortgages during and after the economic meltdown. Prior evidence shows that low income, unemployment (e.g., job loss), and declines in home values are important economic ingredients in home foreclosures.[25] Consistent with this finding, concentrated disadvantage in 2000 is highly prognostic, correlated with the foreclosure rate in 2007–9 and in 2009 alone at 0.74 and 0.71, respectively ($p < 0.01$). More interesting is the systematic variability in foreclosure rates after accounting for economic and racial composition. A key thesis of the book has been that organizational infrastructure exerts a distinct influence on a community's wellbeing, whether expressed in collective efficacy, other-regarding behavior, collective civic engagement, or lower violence. I extend this reasoning to foreclosures and the global economic crisis. Homes sit in a neighborhood context, after all, and most nonprofit community organizations take it as one of their goals to improve the local social and physical infrastructure, a component of future resale opportunities. It stands to reason that a community's organizational profile will matter during times of housing crisis. Moreover, many nonprofits directly aim to *prevent* foreclosures by targeting high-risk neighborhoods. The Local Initiatives Support Corporation (LISC) is especially active in this area and coordinates nonprofit housing organizations in Chicago and around the country. Key mechanisms of support include credit screening, postpurchase training, and mortgage-foreclosure-prevention counseling. I hypothesize, then, that in addition to underlying economic and racial causes, there is a neighborhood organizational component to the intensity of housing foreclosures.[26]

Although I do not have the data to conduct a state-of-the-art test or prove causality, I examined the rate of foreclosures across Chicago's seventy-seven community areas as a function of disadvantage (e.g., poverty, unemployment), racial composition, and housing stability. The results confirm the expectation that in areas of greater home ownership there are more home foreclosures, all else equal. Concentrated disadvantage is a major predictor as well, as is racial composition—predominantly black and poor areas suffer disproportionately. But of equal interest and in a further confirmation of the organizational framework put forth in chapter 8, a direct role emerges for the prevalence of nonprofit organizations in a community. I find that communities high in organizational density experienced lower rates of foreclosure, controlling for prior economic, housing, and demographic characteristics.[27] The resulting inference is that foreclosure rates vary sharply by local context and that organizational capacity is a protective factor, with those communities that are organizationally "rich" experiencing significantly lower rates of foreclosure no matter what their economic or demographic profile. Thus a twofold process appears to be at work—foreclosure is grafted onto the city's durable structure of economic and racial ordering, but the organizational capacity of individual communities nonetheless moderates the toll. *Community-based prevention is apparently not just for crime.*

The Enduring Grip of Violence

A recurring theme in my visits to Chicago's communities was violence. Despite the heralded crime decline in the U.S. and Chicago, violence remains a problem and one that is anything but randomly distributed by place. Two hypotheses are popular among the public and many scholars: the recession will increase crime, and its geographic shifts are caused by the movement of public-housing residences. I find neither to be true, supporting a thesis of this book. The overarching story is that violence tracks the same community-level sources that it always has.

I collected the most recent data on violence that I could from Chicago Police Department records covering January to July of 2010. Just fewer than fifteen thousand incidents of violence were reported in the city for this period, with a low of three to a high of 1,189 across communities. I calculated the per-capita rate in 2010 and compared it to a period before the major shocks of the economic crisis and public-housing transformation. I selected the rate of violence from 1995 to 2000, a multiyear period of the most rapid declines in violence in the city's recent history and before the bulk of CHA teardowns. The tenacity of violence's grip is sobering. Ten years after these large-scale changes, the correlation of violence over time is very high ($R = 0.90$, $p < 0.01$),[28] rendering a plot unnecessary, especially since communities near the top, bottom, and "off" the diagonal are by now familiar. Chatham and Avalon Park saw modest increases, for example, and Grand Boulevard (formerly the site of the Robert Taylor Homes) and the Near South Side saw decreases, but with a correlation approaching unity, overall rank is strongly preserved. Places like Beverly, Edison Park, and Mount Greenwood thus continue to enjoy a stable peace while communities like Englewood, West Garfield, and Washington Park continue to suffer violence at city-high rates.

The relative stability of violence by community remains obvious. What about hypotheses from earlier chapters on social mechanisms of explanation? I do not aim in this chapter to descend into technical details, but in light of the new data and recent events, I want to try one last time to replicate and update key results. On theoretical grounds, I began with two social processes that have been shown in several chapters to be salient—collective efficacy and collective perceptions of disorder. I examined the association of these factors with 2010 violence rates, controlling for the temporally proximate indicator of concentrated poverty examined above—foreclosure rates and the CHA/voucher density in 2009. Both collective efficacy and perceived disorder in 2002 continue to significantly predict rates of violence in 2010 ($R = -0.65$ and 0.54, respectively). I then examined simultaneous influences. Low collective efficacy and perceived disorder were independently linked to later rates of violence, even though significantly correlated themselves and both indicators of disadvantage were again controlled.[29]

As a next step I assessed other neighborhood processes examined in earlier chapters, with a theoretical focus on friend/kinship ties, organizations, and leadership ties. Consistent with the "urban village" finding of chapter 7 and the discussion in chapter 15, dense social ties are related to increased collective efficacy, but they do not directly translate into lower violence. The same picture emerges for organizational density and civic participation, suggesting that the influences of organizations and locally embedded social ties on violence are mediated by collective efficacy. When I went on to estimate *changes* in key social mechanisms and violence, collectively perceived disorder lost its explanatory power. *But increases in collective efficacy in the latter part of the 1990s significantly forecast decreases in crime during the decade of 2000–2010, adjusting for the foreclosures and poverty shifts brought on by the economic crisis.*

In a final set of analyses, I examined the variability in violence in the first half of 2010 as a function of both internal neighborhood characteristics and extralocal mechanisms by extending the spatial logic set forth in chapter 10 and the relational concerns of chapters 13 and 14. I found that violence in 2010 continues to have a large spatial correlation that reflects the neighbors of neighborhoods. Still, controlling for the effects of spatial interdependence and the disadvantage index in 2009, both collective efficacy and perceptual disorder measured from 2002 are directly associated with violence in 2010. A one-standard-deviation increase in collective efficacy is associated with approximately a 25 percent reduction in later violence, a magnitude of estimate similar to that reported in chapter 7 and as found in previous work.[30] I also controlled for dimensions of cross-community ties in the form of residential migration networks, but the results were similar in pointing to the continued simultaneous influence of internal and extralocal spatial dynamics: concentrated disadvantage, spatial vulnerability in the city's ecology of violence, and collective efficacy all remained important predictors of future violence. And in the subset of thirty communities in the 2002 KeyNet study, I found that the cohesiveness of leadership ties was directly associated with lower rates of violence in 2010, controlling for concentrated poverty measured in 2009.[31]

In short, major themes in chapters 5–14 are realized in 2010, despite a historic crime drop, a global economic shock, and a housing crisis. The similar patterns suggest, as argued in chapter 15, that mechanisms of social reproduction are fairly general in their operation: communities constantly change, but in ways that regularly follow social and spatial logics. My bird's-eye revisit in this section has thus revealed a pattern that reaffirms the thesis at the heart of this book: *no matter how much our fate is determined by global or "big" forces, it is experienced locally and shaped by contexts of shared meanings, collective efficacy, and organizational responses.*

Altruistic Social Character, Properly Understood

As a final empirical replication, I conducted my own Stanley Milgram–inspired field experiment. In chapter 9 I reported on a large-scale effort to measure other-regarding or socially altruistic behavior in the form of returning letters "lost" in public settings. I argued that retrieving and mailing back a stamped letter is a direct behavioral indicator of anonymous other-regarding propensity. Material payoff and strategic reputation building, common economic explanations of altruism, are implausible. One can argue that returning lost letters is influenced by the location of mailboxes, rain or wind, the season, or the number of people on the street, but these factors can either be randomized by design, controlled, or are randomly distributed across larger communities. Consistent with this claim, I showed in chapter 9 very large differences in letter-return rates across communities after a long list of letter conditions were adjusted. A dropped letter is ignored or not, and this outcome varies substantially by neighborhood context.

The letter-drop field experiment in the early 2000s was carried out over the course of more than a year in conjunction with personal interviewing. More than 3,300 letters were dropped in neighborhoods across the entire city, and an elaborate design was followed. Because of time and resource constraints, I adopted a streamlined plan for the summer of 2010. I chose nine communities on theoretical grounds with the goal of representing variation in key social types. First, I selected the Loop and the Near North Side, examples of dense and seemingly anonymous urban settings. They are often teeming with street life, especially the Loop which is characterized by a very diverse and large daytime population. The Near North alongside the lake is well to do, largely white, cosmopolitan, and almost a stereotype of yuppies (recall also fig. 1.5 and the concentration of high Internet users in this area). Its western edge is poorer and more diverse. The Loop is dominated by businesses and commuters but has an increasingly upscale residence base. Next I chose two middle/working-class communities, one white (Irving Park) and one black (Avalon Park). I then chose two lower-income black areas that also will be familiar to the reader by now. I selected Roseland on the Far South Side and Grand Boulevard on the Near South. Although similar in some respects, there is distinct variation in these two areas according to the pace of gentrification and intervention by housing policy. Next I selected a Latino immigrant community, choosing the Lower West Side (Pilsen). Finally, I chose Uptown and Hyde Park. Although differing in makeup and city location, these communities are heterogeneous or mixed, by most standards, and organizationally dense. Taken as a whole, the nine communities vary by region of the city and a variety of social conditions that capture theoretical contrasts of interest.

My method was purposely simple and designed to control letter-drop conditions and yield similar "ecometric" reliability, as before. I did so through intense concentration of effort, dropping 325 letters over three days, with the number of drops proportionate to the size of each community's population. The average of thirty-six per community was just under the forty-two of the larger study.[32] The overall return rate contradicts narratives of "hunkering down" as a result of the economic crisis, increasing diversity, and a pervasive urban "distance." Nearly ten years after the first study, with cell-phone distraction among walkers vastly increased, nearly a third (31 percent) of dropped letters were mailed back ($N = 102$). For the seven communities where letters were dropped during the day, the return rate was a bit higher, at 35 percent.[33] This is not materially different than nearly a decade earlier, when the return rate was 37 percent in the same communities.

This result, however, does not tell us if communities switched places in the city's social order or whether they maintained their profiles. Despite the small number of cases and constraints on statistical power, there is substantial continuity in the community-level structure of other-regarding behavior. The correlation in letter return rates over time is large and significant ($R = 0.74$, $p < 0.05$). Grand Boulevard seems to be an outlier of sorts, with an outcome considerably lower than expected based on its prior history. When I remove Grand Boulevard, the association increases to 0.78 ($p < 0.05$). Perhaps instability in Grand Boulevard due to housing demolitions have unsettled local norms or otherwise dampened other-regarding behavior. But the main story is a substantial "stickiness" in the altruistic social character of the neighborhoods.

A closer look at how communities are arrayed reveals a third pattern. One might think that the Loop and Near North Side are unwelcome environments for letter returns. On the days I conducted the study, the streets were jammed with people and I was skeptical that anyone would notice, much less mail, a dropped letter. On several occasions I circled back only to watch oblivious pedestrians stepping over my envelopes. Yet notice and return letters people did, in fact at rates higher than all other communities and consistent with the high propensity at the start of the decade. With all due respect to Louis Wirth, the mostly cosmopolitan urbanites of the Near North and Loop are some of the most other-regarding in Chicago. Other than Grand Boulevard, both high-diversity and low-diversity communities (e.g., Hyde Park vs. Roseland) are not far apart in unadjusted rates of letter returns. Altruistic-type behavior appears to emerge from social norms that are not merely compositional, at least with respect to race or ethnicity. It may be that a poverty effect accounts for why places like Grand Boulevard are at the bottom and wealthy areas like the North Side at the top of the return scale. The negative correlation between poverty and letter returns supports this account ($R = -0.73$, $p < 0.05$). A further argument from chapter 9 is that other-regarding behavior derives in part from a community's organizational and cultural context. In support of this notion, letter-drop return rates are higher where there is a density of organizations

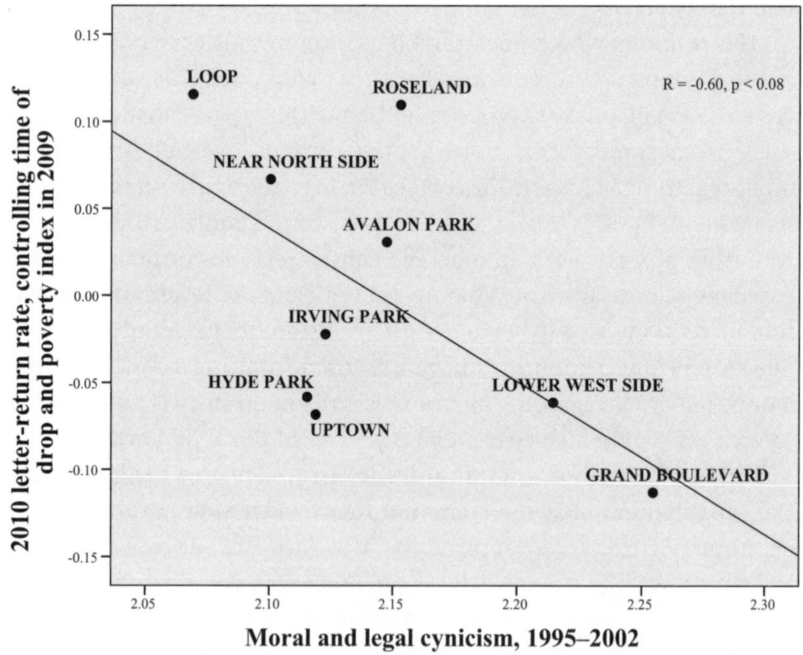

FIGURE 16.5. Moral/legal cynicism and the attenuation of other-regarding behavior: poverty-adjusted rates of letter-drop return in 2010 by community. Letter-drop return rate in 2010 controls for poverty index (CHA and voucher users) in 2009 and night-drop condition. Moral/legal cynicism scale adjusted for measurement error.

($R = 0.58$, $p = 0.10$) and lower in areas of moral/legal cynicism (−0.82, $p < 0.01$). The latter is especially interesting because it taps a cultural mechanism that was predictive of earlier letter-drop returns.

Although the sample is too small to conduct a robust analysis, I probed these ideas further in two strategic ways. First, I examined whether the prior level of moral/legal cynicism is linked to letter returns after controlling for initial (or baseline) propensity. Although the significance levels are compromised by the nine cases, and this is a strict test, given the temporal persistence of letter-return propensity, the negative cynicism coefficient remained significant. Moreover, after I controlled for the indicator of nearly concurrent poverty (the voucher and CHA index of poor residents per capita in 2009), the prior level of cynicism in the community continued to significantly predict a lower 2010 letter-drop return rate while the poverty association was eliminated.[34] Figure 16.5 displays the main result across the nine communities. The altruistic character of a community is thus not only enduring, but in combination with results from earlier chapters there is evidence that it may be reproduced over time by concentrated disadvantage and mediating cultural mechanisms of cynicism about the motives of others.

A Concluding Place

Having shown the 2010 version of the larger citywide pattern behind the scenes from individual communities, I end my street-level observations in the concluding chapter where I did in chapter 1, with probably the most famous contrast in the Chicago School history and the site of a major intervention by the city of Chicago. A revisit to Zorbaugh's classic investigation illuminates in one place the interlocking themes of this book while at the same time offering lessons for how to think about policy and community-level interventions in new ways.

17 The Twenty-First-Century Gold Coast and Slum

The scene of Harvey Zorbaugh's *Gold Coast and the Slum*, published over eighty years ago, has been transformed by history and profound demographic change. But for Zorbaugh the interesting puzzle was social differentiation and not the manifest characteristic or group of the moment. Italians were linked to violence and urban mayhem in the Near North Side's Little Sicily (often referred to as "Little Hell") in the roaring twenties, but in the wake of further European immigration, the great migration from the rural South, neighborhood racial change, and Chicago's decision to build segregated large-scale public housing, the "slum" half of Zorbaugh's contrast was transformed demographically. Cabrini-Green in the late twentieth century became a national symbol of the high-rise containment of the urban poor, housing over four thousand predominantly black families just blocks away from the white wealthy areas of the Gold Coast. In 2003, CBS's national *60 Minutes* program called Cabrini "the nation's most infamous public housing project, synonymous with gangs, drugs, misery and murder."[1]

How does social difference and social distance play out today, if at all? As described in chapter 1, amid great fanfare, most of the Cabrini-Green project has been "removed" under the city's plan for transformation. Thousands of families were displaced to other units (exactly where, no one is really sure) and the buildings demolished, like the Robert Taylor Homes on the South Side. In a fundamental sense, the Zorbaugh contrast has thus been radically and purposely reshaped by governmental intervention. Given its proximity to the Magnificent Mile, many had predicted considerable economic investment and in-migration of the well to do—in essence, that a new neighborhood would emerge in short order. The 2003 CBS report, for example, conjured up an unambiguous image of "beautiful new mixed-income developments—rich and poor living side by side." Several years later, one can argue that in some ways this is true; a case for "positive" change can be made. In the northern part of the neighborhood, market-rate units in the mixed-income North Town Village sold briskly in the mid-2000s. Closer to Cabrini's many housing units, I reported in chapter 1 that in March of 2007 a woman begged for money near a large sign outside new condos and a gym on North Larrabee Street with the bold proclamation: "Look Better Naked." Today that sign is gone, as is the woman begging, and the people going in and out of the building to exercise look like any other health-conscious young professionals in a major American city.

But seen from another lens, those streaming in and out of the gym are the opposite of a racially integrated scene, and two blocks away I observed what appeared to be a homeless woman walking slowly across an empty lot with a torn suitcase, heading toward an abandoned building. Physical decay is still present in many blocks, with a large number of boarded-up buildings near West Oak and North Hudson. Moreover, a remaining unit of Cabrini still showed signs of inhabitation, with people huddled behind wire meshing installed to secure the otherwise open gangways. Even on a sunny day I could not see faces clearly, but I heard a number of women's voices. Middle-aged men hung around outside, apparently unemployed. As I walked around the side of the building, a dead rat that had been bludgeoned lay on its back near an open garbage bin that reeked of uncollected refuse. Two blocks to the east was Munchies Grocery, a convenience store with a hard-bitten look. None of the young professionals I encountered in the far western area of the neighborhood ventured near it on my visit, nor to the nearly abandoned project that was allegedly to be torn down any day. Sadly, on the last day of my final visit to this neighborhood, on October 16, 2010, the owner of Munchies was shot in the back and murdered by an unknown assailant.

Death Corner

Is the glass of community change half empty or half full? According to Zorbaugh, the intersection of Oak and Cambridge in Chicago's Little Hell of the 1920s was "known throughout the city as Death Corner"[2] A short stride from Munchies Grocery, this intersection sits today in the heart of what used to be the Cabrini-Green neighborhood. I thus figured this was a socially and historically strategic site to re-observe up close Zorbaugh's twenty-first-century manifestation. On June 10, 2010, and a stone's throw from Cabrini's rubble, I observed men sitting around a makeshift table on the sidewalk on the east side of North Cambridge about ten yards south of Oak. They appeared to be playing cards, with about four or five other men leaning against nearby cars and an empty lot stretched out across the street. In the distance, new multiunit housing could be seen to the west, and to the east one could see the skyline of the southern Gold Coast.

I took a picture to capture for the reader the feel of this particular intersection. In figure 17.1, one can see an abandoned building with a chain across its entrance door, broken windows, and a "price reduced" sign. The men I noted are just around the corner to the right of the building. Behind the camera is an empty lot, and litter is easily noticed. These multiple signs of "disorder" are not uncommon in certain Chicago neighborhoods, but BMWs parked in front (behind a car with no hubcaps) and upscale new housing (low-rise units visible to the west) are not usually in the same frame. Perhaps this BMW belongs to a local professional who lives in one of the half-million-dollar condos just three blocks away (on North Crosby, extending both north and south of Oak), or perhaps, more cynically, it belongs to a suburban buyer of drugs visiting for a short transaction. I cannot say, and I worry about my findings from chapter 6—context pervades our perceptions about what is, and is not, disorder. The implication is that I am no more unbiased than the reader.[3]

Hence a considerable degree of uncertainty pervaded the public spaces around this particular corner on this day. Was I seeing gentrification in progress? Transformation momentarily stalled? Or is this area too tainted by the past, with the stain of murders in the streets and corner stores too much to overcome? It is rather remarkable, after all, that this is the same area Zorbaugh highlighted in the 1920s Italian slum of

FIGURE 17.1. In the former shadow of Cabrini-Green: 1920s "Death Corner" in 2010. Photograph by the author, June 10, 2010.

his day, cheek by jowl with the Gold Coast. One senses that some things are really not that different when it comes to the concepts of social distance, spatial proximity, violence, and perceptions of difference, both in the physical and social environments.

Bothered by these questions, I made a final trip to Death Corner and the Near North Side in October of 2010 to recheck key observations.[4] The Near North along the Magnificent Mile and Gold Coast looked as opulent as ever. Tourists jammed the streets on a nice fall day but thinned out dramatically once I headed west and crossed the vicinity of North State. Along West Oak Street east of North Cambridge, I found the same vacant units as in the summer. The abandoned building in figure 17.1 remained boarded up and chained, and upon closer inspection I noted a "water service termination" notice on the door. A group of men were hanging out in the late afternoon near the building, but now about eight to ten in number and gathered on the west side of the street about twenty yards from my last visit. Soon after passing the group of men, one asked me directly, "Did you find any?" Walking south on Larrabee a block to the west there were empty storefronts near upscale buildings as I approached North Kingsbury and then West Chicago Avenue. A community garden was active along the south side of Cambridge, near Chicago Avenue. The contrasts were a bit surreal, with a gardenlike atmosphere so close to abandonment.

As I walked north from the garden, I passed a long stretch of low-rise, mostly boarded-up projects. Black plywood covered the majority of doors, especially on the east side of the street. Despite the abandoned feel, I encountered a surprising number of people on the street, all African American. A number of children were playing, and mothers stood in doorways while men and teenagers milled about in the street. I was the only white person for several more blocks—this slice of the Near North Side was completely segregated racially. As I circled back to the abandoned building on Zorbaugh's Death Corner, I felt wary when I came across two men sprawled out near the back side of the empty building, one flat on his back and passed out. The other was drooping and bobbing as if about to fall over, with glassy eyes. But then one man crossing the street greeted me jovially with a "Hey, man" and a wide grin. I returned the greeting and moved on.

The next morning at 11 a.m. the group was in the same spot, only this time a number of apparently homeless men had joined in. Blankets were strewn about, and a grocery cart that was not there the day before was visible. Geese grazed in an empty field across the street while construction hummed in the background on the site of the former high-rises. The field was cleaned up from the summer and now reminded me of the former site of the Robert Taylor Homes (fig. 1.1). A surreal feeling pervaded, as it did in Grand Boulevard when I was similarly strolling in an empty space that once housed thousands of residents in the very recent past. Uncertainty about the future of these remaining inhabitants weighed on my mind as I exited for the last time. Walking through an alley not two blocks from Oak and Cambridge, I came across an arresting stretch of graffiti on the back of a building. The realities of concentrated incarceration, racial inequality, and a life of constrained options was brought to life by the author, perhaps a child, in poignant form.[5] In two sketches were the grim faces of black men behind prison bars. Under one was drawn an open book with the message, "You must have power to fight power." The second message continued, "Intelligence is not fighting the powers that be but developing the powers to be," with a diploma drawn beneath. The images were jarring, but I was struck by the sense of resistance to racial subjugation and the sense of a pathway forward through education.

Lessons of Time and Context

The corner of Oak and Cambridge in the twenty-first century is a work in progress, as it was in Zorbaugh's day. Change has come, to be sure, but in nuanced ways social mechanisms differentiating the Gold Coast and the slum are still churning at some fundamental level. Whether concentrated inequality, race/ethnic segregation, perceptions of (dis) order, shared expectations for social control of public places, cynicism about the future, incarceration's penetration in the black community, spatial proximity to (dis)advantage, imbalanced inflows and outflows of residents (selection), network ties among key leaders over neighborhood economic development, foreclosures, or organizational resistance by residents, multiple layers of individual, neighborhood, and structural effects are simultaneously being negotiated and reproduced.[6] I have also argued that it is difficult to overcome cultural reputations and legacies of severe disadvantage, making it a mistake in the first place to predict a community's trajectory solely on the basis of economic forces. So, under the theory of this book, it is not surprising that the predictions of city officials and pundits alike have not materialized.

Once the economy recovers and the dislocation induced by the takedown of Cabrini fades, however, the social and spatial logic of this book's theory suggests that the transition will ultimately be complete. Cabrini's legacy of disadvantage, deep as it was, has a lower reputational and spatial handicap to overcome than its counterparts on the South Side. To be clear, I am not suggesting that transformation is necessarily a good thing, or that change is inevitably in the direction of progress. Seeming to defy "rational" logic, for example, while some cheered the neighborhood's demolition, other Cabrini residents banded together to protest being forcibly removed from the projects—it was, after all, a place they called home. And the self-interests of developers are hardly virtuous. A website designed to promote neighborhood real estate is perhaps too transparent in its wishes that the Gold Coast will quickly finish the annexation of Cabrini's ashes: "Already infused with chic dining spots, grocery stores and a growing shopping district, Cabrini-Green is the Chicago neighborhood of the future."[7] I thus have no illusions, then, that the rich "living side by side" with the poor will occur in other than a minority of housing units. The side by side will likely be separated by a perceived and actual physical distance, especially for the many men to be released from prison in the coming years. Reintegration into the community will take place in a profoundly altered landscape.

My larger point is analytic—Death Corner and its subsequent manifestations over many years embody in a microcosm the neighborhood mechanisms and interlocking structure of Chicago that I have emphasized throughout the book. One cannot be understood apart from the other, as the fates of both are intertwined. In other words, contextual causality is at work. The twenty-first-century Gold Coast and slum also encapsulate a final set of lessons in thinking about how to intervene more constructively to meet social challenges and reduce urban inequality.

Intervening at the Scale of Community and City

Consistent with the individualist American ideal, the dominant policy approach to reducing inequality by place starts with the premise of promoting individual choice. This dominance is highlighted symbolically and concretely in the voucher movement, one that advocates vouchers as a way to move individuals away from whatever bad school or bad community that inequality has wrought. But more than just move individuals away, an allied policy is to eradicate the damaged community left behind. The stories of Cabrini-Green and the Robert Taylor Homes are emblematic of this logic, where "escape from the ghetto" is followed by its demolition. In a kind of morality play, the disadvantaged communities of origin are first demonized, giving rise to support for their removal, followed by the promotion of vouchers for the individuals displaced. The teardown approach to urban poverty policy is eerily familiar, despite claims that we have learned from the past. Indeed, the urban renewal of the 1950s and 1960s operated on similar assumptions about the need to raze entire neighborhoods of the disreputable urban poor.[8]

Motivated by the findings of this book and building on my argument in chapter 15, a different approach to policy is to intervene holistically at the scale of neighborhoods, communities, and cities themselves. Rather than simply move people out of targeted communities, the idea is to renew what is already there while simultaneously investing in communities on the edge of critical need but not yet deemed policy-relevant. In Chicago and its environs today, this second group of communities constitutes the predictable destinations of public-housing refugees. To be clear, I have no wish to argue against increasing individual opportunities, and I have confronted full bore the undeniable social problems that places like Cabrini-Green and the Robert Taylor Homes endured. Rather than argue negatively, or against vouchers, I wish to make a positive case by emphasizing a point brought to life in this book: communities can serve as a unit not just of social science theory and method, but of holistic policy intervention that prioritizes the interconnected social fabric. When urban infrastructure in cities is discussed in macrolevel or community terms, concerns usually turn first to physical or material manifestations (e.g., roads, economic development, housing designs). Physical infrastructure and housing are crucial, but so too is the social infrastructure.

In short, I want to make the dual case for *community-level intervention* instead of individual-level escape hatches and a government policy focus on the *interlocking social infrastructure* in the neighborhoods of American cities. My intent is not to evaluate or proffer specific interventions but to point the way toward how a new agenda might be conceived. From this view, ideas rather than specific policies should be the guide, and the goal of research should be to provide robust knowledge. Their translation into practice requires the skills and equal partnership of those on the front lines and in positions of power to make things happen.

Based on the theory and research of this book, I believe that we need to first pay special attention to integrating violence interventions with other efforts to rebuild communities at risk. Although "things go together," safety is a fundamental condition for humans to flourish, and, as a result, violence is a leading indicator of a community's viability over the long run. As the children in Cabrini-Green experienced and our research verified, even the basics of cognitive learning ability are harmed in the midst of violence.[9] There is no magic bullet of violence prevention, but there are promising efforts with a community focus that deserve further scrutiny. One is Operation Ceasefire, now in operation in multiple cities, including Chicago. As we saw in action in Roseland, the goal is to reduce the risk of future violence while at the same time promoting adult-teen relationships and attempting to sustain the community's collective efficacy. In a similar vein, there is evidence that "community policing" can work when it genuinely integrates crime policy with efforts to build networks of informal social control, trust, and collective efficacy. One mechanism is the regular meetings of police and residents on neutral turf (e.g., in a school or church) where both sides identify the location of problems (e.g., "hotspots") and targeted place-based solutions are then pursued.[10] Informal social control and citizen input is thus brought into alignment, at least in theory, with official forms of problem solving and crime reduction.

Community reentry programs for ex-prisoners should be added to the safety agenda, given the severe neighborhood concentration of incarceration and the known vulnerabilities of ex-prisoners, especially in the job market.[11] I showed how the nation's experiment with "mass" incarceration is in fact highly stratified locally, transforming some Chicago communities into hyperincarcerated outliers with prison intake rates almost inconceivably high (figure 5.5). Exiting one dysfunctional social system into such stigmatized and resource-disadvantaged communities is virtually a recipe for recidivism. But perhaps a concern with community *preentry* should take precedence. Reducing the number of new admissions to prison is a goal that research shows can be achieved at the same time as reducing crime.[12] The key to success is smarter and more efficient policing yoked to a community-based focus that stresses good police-citizen relationships.[13] The perceived legitimacy of criminal justice institutions is likely to be reinforced with such a policy move, whether among adult ex-prisoners or the children growing up in the neighborhood whose future encounters with the law are at stake. Recall that legal cynicism was a central concept that emerged in my analysis—where mistrust of the law and cynicism about institutions are prevalent, community norms erode and violence is expected as a routine feature of everyday life. Thus the nexus of incarceration, policing, and institutional legitimacy is ignored at our peril, but at the same time the research here suggests constructive options for a holistic counter-response.

I believe it is therefore essential that we take a broader view and integrate public safety interventions with more general *noncrime* policies that address antecedent and mediating processes of social and cultural organization. Whether through the enhancement of age-graded mentorship and monitoring of adolescent activities as a form of collective efficacy, increasing organizational opportunities for citizen participation in decision making, or enhancing the legitimacy of government institutions that have eroded trust among those served, we need a surgical-like attention to repairing or renewing existing structures rather than simply designing escape routes. Sometimes triage is necessary in an emergency, of course, but in my experience Chicago is not on the stretcher—even the worst-off communities command human assets and organizational potential that have not been fully harnessed. In fact, my data support the notion that disadvantaged communities sometimes have rather high levels of other-regarding behavior and latent collective efficacy that are otherwise suppressed by the cumulative disadvantages built up after repeated everyday challenges, Roseland being a case in point (see also fig. 16.5).

The logic of my inquiry clearly moves us beyond the borders of any single neighborhood, however, and to a concern with organizational, political, and macrosocial forces. Citywide or metropolitan policies on *mixed-income housing* and *community economic development* are theoretically relevant because they are inextricably tied to neighborhood-level dynamics of migration and the kinds of leadership connections observed in chapters 13 and 14. The destruction of the Robert Taylor Homes and Cabrini-Green came with offsetting promises of mixed-income renewal, and there is evidence in this direction to the credit of Chicago's leadership. But progress is piecemeal, and communities that are *outside* the orbit of the intervention are nonetheless taking in thousands of families from the old projects and await support. Many destinations are not even in Chicago, as the southern suburbs have discovered, some to their considerable surprise. Taking a more structural or bird's-eye view is thus necessary and consistent with the critics of neighborhood effects who argue for a focus on how factors such as concentrated poverty, racial integration, residential stability, and now home foreclosures are influenced by interconnected housing and school policies, zoning decisions, economic development and banking policy, and a number of other government actions or universal forces that are external to any given neighborhood. But the internal dynamics of a neighborhood remain crucial not least because external institutional actors react to them, as do nonresidents. Such a stance simultaneously respects both the "political economy" and neighborhood traditions but also critiques coming from globalization theorists and those focused on individual choice, drawing on my view that no one level of analysis is necessarily privileged at the outset in terms of a holistic understanding of causality.

In all these potential efforts it follows that individuals are still of concern, especially the most vulnerable among us—children. *Linking investments in early child development with community context* is thus an idea whose time has come.[14] The national interventions now being promoted by the federal government in many cities, such as Choice Neighborhoods and Promise Neighborhoods, along with localized efforts such as the Harlem Children's Zone, provide grounds for optimism that a new generation of social-level thinking for children can be integrated with a more dynamic concern with what happens when we take things to scale.[15] Linking community-level interventions with systematic observational and ethnographic knowledge about the mechanisms of urban change seems an especially promising direction. Properly done, intervening at the community level is not only feasible but more cost effective in the long run than targeting individuals. Predicting individual behavior is notoriously difficult and inefficient, whereas as I have shown that community social structures are highly patterned over time. Ironically, then, policies seeking to promote individual development might better start not with the individual but with the social context, where inequalities at birth are already well in place.

Rethinking "What Works" Structurally

I submit that we need a new definition of what constitutes policy *evaluation* to complement the more holistic approach to intervention I have sketched. If social structure and ongoing neighborhood dynamics are crucial to the long-term prospects of meaningful change, they should be a required part of the evaluation of any social policy, even if ostensibly aimed at individuals or a single community.[16] It is not enough to move residents out of Cabrini-Green or the Robert Taylor Homes and remove the physical evidence of past mistakes, or to erect new housing in their former shadows. The social fabric was fundamentally altered in unintended ways, and displaced residents are moving to other neighborhoods, many with similar problems. If left unattended, these destinations will produce new versions of concentrated disadvantage and social stigma, and in turn new feedback loops of neighborhood social reproduction.

Ultimately, then, my argument is that *intervention is never in just one community* even though it was designed or described as such. Not even a program such as the Harlem Children's Zone (HCZ) can be isolated and set aside as a model for replication, as it has been in the popular press. The very concept of a "zone" implies embeddedness, and two of the mysteries of the HCZ to date is what mechanism is doing the work and whether the program can be taken to scale in other contexts. I suspect it cannot, at least not in the ways currently promoted. Once an intervention takes hold, both formal rules and informal practices change, and interconnected actions cumulate to form new structures. Even the simple act of moving to Harlem to take advantage of its community-wide benefits means that some other community was left behind and thus affected—residential mobility is never just about an individual. These kinds of extralocal effects thus need to be considered in the costs and benefits ("what works") of intervening in any one community. By considering the big picture and how it is drawn by individual actions and structural constraints alike, and by looking to the success of population-level health policies over the past century, we have the tools of ecometrics and the theory to rigorously study these processes, intervene accordingly, and evaluate holistically. Although it may seem obvious in retrospect to bring context and history into the formal evaluation process, in practice this is rarely done in ways that respect interlocking structures and mechanisms. This book thus implies that a rescaled approach to policy evaluation is in order.

Coda

I would like to close by emphasizing that this book is not about a single theoretical hypothesis but rather two fundamentally different ways of looking at the world. Is life a construction of independent self-maximizing individuals, or are the important processes rooted in collective processes—the "we"—that come together in neighborhoods, communities, and other contextual settings steeped in shared understandings? The first image is powerful in contemporary America, both ideologically and in terms of recent developments in genomics, neuroscience, and rational choice models of human behavior. It seems as if a day does not pass without a new report claiming that human behavior has its origins in some individual attribute or condition determined in early life.

I put my theoretical bets on the second idea, however, arguing that the causal forces that organize life chances reside at the social level, even if mediated by individual action. A long-term project in collaboration with many others was constructed to provide original data to test this notion, and these data are now widely available. If my theoretical claim, analysis of the data, and synthesis on how the results have played out are correct then it cannot be said that the origins of behavior are individually based—such a claim is no more viable than saying that context is subordinate to the expression of a gene. The rational actor model is a theoretically elegant alternative to the early-origins thesis and can be formalized, but life is neither elegant nor lived independently. Our selection decisions, thought to be about individual utility, are inextricably dependent on the social environment.

The implication is that the many findings reporting to have established the supremacy of the individual are predetermined. When we only look for (or model) individual effects, the modus operandi of much social science, we are quite likely to succeed. One might say we have already succeeded, but the victory has been Pyrrhic. The response to this dilemma by some social analysts is to retreat into pure structuralism (top-down theory) and deny the importance of individual choice altogether, but that does not fully respect the phenomenon either. In my view and in light of the present results, the field of social science will profit from a turn toward deeper engagement with contextual mechanisms of causality from bottom to top and back again, and how they are shaped by the enduring spatial logic of urban life and the interconnected social worlds we inhabit.

The conclusions of this book also bear hope for social policy. For no matter how much neighborhoods appear stable (and the evidence on this is very strong, as I have shown), *existing continuities are not inherent but are socially reproduced in multiple ways that can be acted upon.* We act on individual incentives all the time, and macronational policies are woven into the identity of the country. There is thus nothing intrinsic about policy to prevent intervening at the scale of the community and citywide social web while attending to the realities of individual choice. My engagement with the streets and neighborhoods of Chicago has convinced me that if we do so, we will discover the logic and power of neighborhood effects—whether looking-glass or structural—in organizing a surprisingly diverse array of everyday life.

NOTES

CHAPTER ONE

1. *Elsewhere USA* explores the seeming fixation of Americans on connecting to everywhere but where they actually are (Conley 2009).

2. Giddens 1990, 19; 1991, 146. Giddens's (1991) treatise on modernity has been cited over 14,000 times in the scholarly literature, perhaps an unparalleled record. For an influential statement on placelessness, cited less but still a citation classic at over two thousand, see Relph 1976. For an argument that the "death of distance" is "changing the world," see Cairncross 1997.

3. Friedman 2005.

4. The seminal empirical adjudication of personal networks in the modern era is Claude Fischer (1982), who showed that urbanism's effects are specified; estrangement occurs in the public sphere—less helpfulness and more conflict—but not in the private sphere of personal relationships and personal wellbeing. See also Tilly 1973, 211.

5. Wellman 1979.

6. Brint 2001.

7. Louis Wirth (1938) was thus one of the first to link diversity with decline. I return to this point in later chapters when delving empirically into the puzzle of neighborhood heterogeneity. Interestingly, as Everett Hughes pointed out in personal communication to James F. Short Jr.: "Louis used to say all those things about how the city is impersonal while living with a whole clan of kin and friends on a very personal basis." Apparently Wirth's theoretical angst about the decline of community was not realized in the social world he inhabited. One wonders if this is true of contemporary doomsayers, including those chatting or texting away.

8. Wellman 1979. See also Fischer 1982, chapter 1. The history of social disorganization theory is addressed in chapter 4; see also Kornhauser 1978.

9. Nisbet 1953.

10. See especially Putnam 2000, 2007.

11. Coleman 1988. The application to urban sociology and community has been widespread. A recent example is Saegert, Thompson, and Warren 2002.

12. Smelser and Alexander 1999; Skocpol 2004.

13. McAdam, McCarthy, and Zald 1996.

14. See the Institute for Communitarian Policy Studies, (http://www.gwu.edu/~ccps/index.html), and its former journal, *The Responsive Community*.

15. McPherson, Smith-Lovin, and Brashears 2006.

16. Putnam 2007.

17. See Simmel, "The Metropolis and Mental Life" (1903), reprinted in Levine 1971.

18. Selznick 1992; Etzioni 1997.

19. Mailer 1969, opening line, Part II

20. Abu-Lughod 1999.

21. The "Los Angeles School" of urban sociology (e.g., Dear 2002) might be thought to be the leading proponent of this view, but I refer broadly to current thinking across the social sciences, including sociology, political science, epidemiology, and perhaps especially economics. Indeed, as will be seen in examples throughout the book (especially chapters 11–12), the idea that neighborhoods "do not matter" in an individually rationalistic and placeless world is commonplace despite the long existence of research on neighborhood effects (chapter 2). The LA School of geography seeks to answer a different but legitimate class of questions (Sampson 2002a; Abbott 2002).

22. Zorbaugh 1929, 13.

23. The tour begins here in Chicago's Near North Side (later, compare fig. 1.2): http://www.mapquest.com/maps?city=Chicago&state=IL&address=N+Michigan+Ave+%26+E+Pearson+St&zipcode=60611&country=US&latitude=41.89757&longitude=-87.62411&geocode=INTERSECTION.

24. Wilson and Kelling 1982.

25. During a street observation on another walk in 2006 (March 10), I witnessed a protest march replete with drummers, chanting, and dissemination of a statement from the Dalai Lama. Leading the march were monks who sought to draw attention to Tibetan dissidents on the occasion of the forty-seventh anniversary of the Tibetan National Uprising Day. The nature and location of this event corresponds to a theory of collective civic engagement pursued later in the book.

26. Emporis Buildings 2007.

27. Algren 1951.

28. One might be forgiven for noting similarities between the man, the building, and the granddaddy of Chicago politics, Richard J. Daley. "He was raucous, sentimental, hot-tempered, practical, simple, devious, big, and powerful. This is, after all, Chicago" (Royko 1971).

29. Gilfoyle 2006.

30. Bridgeport, an iconic working-class white neighborhood that produced generations of political heavyweights, sits south and west of the Dan Ryan, within earshot of the Chicago White Sox's Comiskey Park. The Daleys' move away from Bridgeport to a nearly half-million-dollar townhouse in Central Station Townhouse (in 1994 dollars) was the subject of much consternation among locals and widely reported in the local media. It was not the price so much as the identity of location—the beers and brats of Richard M.'s father in Bridgeport were given a symbolic punch. Daley #2 has been reported as intending to move up even more, quite literally, to a high-rise perch across from Millennium Park, smack in the heart of the Loop. Rising over a former Dunkin' Donuts near the corner of Wabash and Randolph, the Heritage at Millennium Park commands stunning views of the park and Lake Michigan to the east.

31. Nels Anderson's *On Hobos and Homelessness* is widely considered the major "Chicago School" take on the homeless—see Anderson 1998. He studied the West Madison Street Area, but the Near South was another favorite haunt of hobos in the early years. At the current intersection stands a Latin American and Caribbean fusion restaurant, where I dined twice in 2007 with many well-heeled and fashionable people out on the town.

32. I return later to gentrification, but it is not clear the term fits the Near South. Gentrification is commonly thought to mean areas where the lower-income residents are pushed out. Many areas here had no permanent residents. The South Loop has seen a net loss of thousands of SRO units since 1990.

33. For a sociological history of the Robert Taylor Homes, see Venkatesh 2000.

34. Chicago Housing Authority 2007.

35. Whether crime, school dropout, mortality, or disease, the Wentworth district long stood out as a leader in what William Julius Wilson (1987) called "social dislocation."

36. Field observations, 2007.

37. For a description of the changes in the North Kenwood area, especially the "gentrification" conflict between lower- and upper-class African Americans, see Pattillo 2007.

38. Typical is the 8000 South Avalon block club, welcoming visitors but "no ball playing, car washing, speeding, loud music, loitering or littering." Nearly every block declares the same.

39. Zorbaugh 1929, 14.

40. In introducing the bird's-eye view, I map the community areas in Chicago. Lake Michigan is the defining natural feature of the city's border to the east—the city boasts some twenty-five miles of lakefront property. A less beautiful feature of Chicago is O'Hare International Airport extending westward from the city in the northwest corner, a place likely to have been experienced by every reader. Community areas are defined in more detail in chapter 2, and individual communities important to the story of this book will be mapped and described more precisely as the book progresses, as will other ecological areas nested within them. I begin here in figure 1.2 by denoting the names of the communities visited earlier in the chapter, starting with the Magnificent Mile just south of the Near North Side's Gold Coast and stretching down through the Loop and Near South Side all the way to Avalon Park. We ended our tour back up in the Near North Side but west of the Gold Coast in today's manifestation of Zorbaugh's 1929 "slum" in the form of "Death Corner." The reader can examine street referents and match the names of all seventy-seven communities to figure 1.2 by navigating the following website: http://www.cityofchicago.org/city/en/depts/doit/supp_info/citywide_maps.html.

41. I define child health as the standardized combination of infant mortality rates and low-birth-weight babies—these two indicators are very highly correlated (0.81, $p < 0.01$). As expected based on prior research, poverty is significantly correlated (0.78, $p < 0.01$) with poor infant health. I examine in figure 1.2 the predicted infant health rate from its poverty rate across communities (displayed in thirds). The probability that the relationship between predicted infant health and homicide occurred by chance is less than one in one thousand and thus is highly nonrandom.

42. Another way to demonstrate the spatial link is to estimate the association of homicide with infant mortality and low birth weight while directly controlling for poverty. When I do so, the partial correlation is 0.60 ($p < 0.01$). Poverty thus does not explain away the clustering.

43. Population size cannot explain the patterning of events either as that is also adjusted. Interestingly, even *within* the highest-crime-rate community of Chicago, crime is highly concentrated by time and place, almost as if the wider citywide patterns of ecological concentration are refracted onto the microlocal level of a single block. See St. Jean 2007.

44. Drake and Cayton [1945] 1993. See especially maps on pages 203 and 205.

45. For the most thorough review of the intellectual history of the social disorganization tradition, see Kornhauser 1978. I will synthesize this literature in chapter 2.

46. These data will be described in further detail in chapter 8.

47. This is an increasingly dominant viewpoint (McCarthy, Miller, and Skidmore 2004).

48. These measures and data sources will be explained in full in later chapters.

49. Florida 2002. For an assessment of Florida's argument in Chicago, see Graif 2010.

50. The partial correlation of rates of Internet use and bohemians across communities, controlling for median rent and median income, is 0.55 ($p < 0.01$). Keith Hampton also shows that residents who are digitally "wired" and frequent users of the Internet are more connected to their neighbors and more involved in local collective action than their disconnected counterparts (Hampton 2010; Hampton and Wellman 2003). Thus even the digital world is "placed."

51. Sampson 2008a, 133. As of the mid-2000s there were only a handful of Starbucks south of Roosevelt Road in Chicago; most cluster on the North Side. A Starbucks in Wicker Park was visibly defaced with graffiti on a visit in 2007. Clashes of culture were readily apparent. Exiting Myopic Used Books, where one can buy any number of dog-eared radical treatises, a perfectly opulent woman from American Apparel stared down at me from a billboard.

52. As argued by Wacquant 2008, for example.

53. See also Sampson and Wikström 2008.

54. Wikström 1991.

55. "Lax Real Estate Decisions Hurt Starbucks," *New York Times* (Stone 2008).

56. The neighborhood-effects and place stratification literatures represent important exceptions, as reviewed in chapter 2. Still, it seems that jet-set academics and newspaper columnists fall hard for the notion that neighborhoods do not matter. At least, perhaps, until they return to upscale homes in economically segregated communities with high test scores for (private?) schools. Or to the highly secure condominium with elaborate owners' associations set up to protect and enhance neighborhood investments. It is also notable how few of "the world is flat" critics buy homes in the world's violence-ridden slums, where property comes dirt cheap. Doing so would appear to be a quite rational move if individual choice is what matters, not neighbors or neighborhoods.

57. Castells 2000, 697; 1996.

58. Sassen 2001; Massey 1996.

59. Even emotional attachment to place and local interaction, widely considered dead according to contemporary assertions, are not dead according to empirical accounts. When Albert Hunter attempted a replication twenty-five years later in the same Rochester, New York, neighborhood studied intensively in 1950, he found a decline in local facility use (e.g., shopping, entertainment) but no change in neighboring and local interaction. The "sense of community"

actually increased, leading Hunter to reject the idea of a cultural-symbolic loss of community (Hunter 1975, 549). At the national level, Americans continue to derive a sense of identity from their neighborhood with over 50 percent of the population reporting that they talk with their neighbors several times a week or more (Social Capital Community Benchmark Survey 2010). It has also been argued that the widely discussed finding of a shrinkage in Americans' personal networks stems from an error in the data (Fischer 2009).

60. Gieryn (2000, 465) presents an excellent sociological review of the concept of place. For a political science perspective, see Agnew 2002. The geographical view is iconoclastic by the standards of contemporary wisdom and more in line with this book, noting the "power of place" (De Blij 2009), not its disappearance. The intellectual history of geography is interesting in its own right. It went so far out of fashion as a discipline that its departments were shut down in several major universities. Geographical science is now in resurgence in those same universities. The social science literature on neighborhoods, a special kind of place, is voluminous and will be synthesized in the next chapter.

61. I wish to be clear that this book is not an official statement of the project as a whole. Not all participants in earlier stages would necessarily agree with my theoretical framing or analysis. Chapter 4 reveals the diversity of thought that went into the planning of PHDCN.

62. Daniel Burnham, urban planner extraordinaire, famously nudged Chicago at the beginning of the twentieth century, to "make no small plans" (Smith 2006). Nelsen Algren (1951), along with many others before and after, has noted the character of a city always on the make.

63. Small 2009; Sampson et al. 2005; Marwell 2007; McQuarrie and Marwell 2009.

CHAPTER TWO

1. One might even say an unrepentant descendant except that I believe that to adhere rigidly to any one "school" concedes too much intellectual terrain. Fortunately for the Chicago School, this risk is minimized by the nature of what it was not. Howard Becker (1999) makes the useful distinction between schools of *thought* (which imply unanimity of intellectual outlook) and schools of *activity*. If the Chicago School of urban sociology between the two world wars can be said to be a school, it was in forms of empirical activity rather than an agreed upon theoretical commitment. Enforced schools of thought are usually constructed after the fact by outsiders; see Abbott 1999.

2. Molotch 2002. Michael Dear fired the first shot in a symposium declaring an ascendant LA School 2002, with responses by Abbott 2002 and Sampson 2002a among others. For a discussion of the French School and new urban so-

ciology, see Lefebvre 1991 and Gottdiener and Hutchison 2006. The "New York" School has been presented in Halle 2003.

3. See Laub 2004 for a discussion of the application of life-course principles to intellectual ideas. I am particularly interested in the concepts of pathways and turning points in the idea of neighborhood effects.

4. Levin and Lindesmith 1937, 801. On the repeated rediscovery of neighborhood over time, see Sampson and Morenoff 1997.

5. Morris 1958, 51. See also his review of English social ecology in general.

6. Quetelet [1969] 1842, 87.

7. Morris 1958.

8. Rawson 1839, 336.

9. Mayhew 1861.

10. Booth 1889.

11. Shaw 1930.

12. Mayhew 1862, 272.

13. Shaw and McKay [1942] 1969.

14. For searchable access to archive materials from the Booth collections of the Archives Division of the Library of the London School of Economics and Political Science and the University of London Library, see http://booth.lse.ac.uk/ (LSE 2008).

15. Johnson 2006.

16. For further intellectual history, see Abbott 1997.

17. Park and Burgess 1921. For an image of the map: http://www.csiss.org/classics/content/26. On the Green Bible, see Short 1963, xvii.

18. Park 1915.

19. Park and Burgess [1925] 1967.

20. Social workers Jane Adams and Merritt Pinckney vocalized the need to address the deteriorated housing, mental disorder, truancy, infant mortality, and delinquency they deemed a result of rapid industrialization and social change. Sophonisba Breckinridge and Edith Abbott (1912) examined the geographic distribution of cases brought before the Juvenile Court of Cook County (Chicago) on delinquency petitions and showed that a disproportionately large number of cases were concentrated in certain neighborhoods. While these early social workers were not methodologically sophisticated, their emphasis on the relationship between the volume of delinquency and local community characteristics was nonetheless influential.

21. Shaw 1929.

22. For a review of neighborhoods and health, see Sampson and Morenoff 1997 and Sampson and Morenoff 2000.

23. Goldberger, Wheeler, and Sydenstrycker 1920, 2707.

24. Sampson and Morenoff 1997.

25. Kawachi and Berkman 2003.

26. Shaw and McKay [1942] 1969, 106.

27. Faris and Dunham 1939.

28. Literally, in fact. Drake and Cayton's maps on delinquency and insanity published originally in 1945 ([1945] 1993, 203, 205) were borrowed from the Institute of Juvenile Research where Shaw and McKay worked, and from Faris and Dunham, respectively.

29. Kornhauser 1978; Bursik 1988. Social disorganization theory is commonly traced to the work of Shaw and McKay, who in turn drew on Park and Burgess. But equally important influences were Thomas and Znaniecki (1927, introduction, chaps. 1, 3) and Wirth (1938), who argued that ethnic heterogeneity, along with size and density, undermined social integration.

30. Sampson and Groves 1989.

31. See also Janowitz 1975.

32. Whyte 1943.

33. Gans 1962.

34. Jacobs 1961; Stack 1974.

35. Putnam 2000.

36. Bursik 1999.

37. Sampson, Morenoff, and Gannon-Rowley 2002.

38. Robinson 1950. For an interesting contemporary take, see Subramanian et al. 2009.

39. Shevky and Bell 1955. In many ways the social area analysis tradition may be seen as a continuation of the typological work that Rawson promoted in nineteenth-century London.

40. See, for example, Berry and Kasarda 1977.

41. Morenoff and Sampson 1997.

42. Harvey 1973; Castells 1977; Gottdiener and Hutchison 2006.

43. Their argument culminated in the book *Urban Fortunes* (Logan and Molotch 1987).

44. Strip malls, restrictions on mixed-income housing, the separation of stores from residences, minimum lot sizes, gated enclaves, surveillance demands, and the banishment of sidewalks have all been blamed for undermining the authenticity of urban places. For a perceptive analysis of New York in the aftermath of Jane Jacobs, see Zukin 2010.

45. Bursik 1989.

46. Skogan 1990. Nationwide, fully 20 percent of all central-city housing units occupied by blacks were lost in the period 1960–70 because of urban redevelopment alone. This does not include displacement brought about by routine market forces (e.g., evictions, rent increases).

47. Wacquant 1993. For an argument on the "planned shrinkage" of state resources in the case of New York City, see Wallace and Wallace 1990.

48. Wilson 1987.

49. See also Massey and Sampson 2009.

50. Wilson 1996.

51. Wilson 1987, 56.

52. See also Jargowsky 1997.

53. For a critical account that claims Wilson is a conservative because he fails to properly attribute inequality to racism, see Steinberg 1995. Another critique of neighborhood-effects research for being conservative comes from a student of Wilson's. Wacquant asserts that neighborhood effects are really "state" effects. He uses the 1996 Welfare Reform Act in the U.S. as an example of the retrenchment of the state in producing a concentration of urban "outcasts" (Wacquant 2008). Because this action was at the federal level, however, the mechanisms that explain how a national policy that was a constant across localities created neighborhood-level variations beyond those that were already in place are not explained. Macro effects are not incompatible with this book's argument; in fact a macroneighborhood interface was part of the logic of Wilson's original thesis and the idea of concentration effects. I directly address in later chapters the related critique that neighborhood effects research has tended to neglect cross-neighborhood linkages and the mediation of state resources by nonprofit organizations (Marwell 2007). The social isolation hypothesis that is embedded in Wilson's work has also come under criticism for assuming a monolithic culture in the ghetto. I think this criticism is partially valid although I read into Wilson a greater emphasis on forms of spatial isolation that renders contact with diverse outlets—including mainstream values—less likely. I return to issues of culture at several points in this book.

54. Massey and Denton 1993.

55. Morenoff and Sampson 1997.

56. Massey 1990, 337; see also Massey and Eggers 1990.

57. Both also find empirical support in Quillian's (1999) adjudication.

58. Nisbet 1953 argues, correctly I believe, that the real question is not why the decline, but rather why there is such an obsession with community decline that reinvents itself over time. For relevant insight on the fractal nature of intellectual change, see Abbott 2001.

59. Some of the most ambitious foundation efforts in the last decade include those by the Ford, Rockefeller, and MacArthur foundations to increase the capacity of local communities to solve common problems. Nongovernmental organizations (NGOs) have grown noticeably as well, many embracing similar ideas of building community. A notable example is the Community Development Corporation (CDC) movement, which has long privileged community as a meaningful

unit of social intervention to improve the lives of the poor. For further elaboration of this point and especially criminal justice policy, see Sampson 1999.

60. For a review and critique of the new urbanism, see Glaeser 2011.

61. World Bank 2010.

62. Robert Putnam was a well-known advisor to Clinton and Tony Blair in the UK. For an interesting account of the Bush view of community, see Milbank 2001. There is every indication that President Obama is attuned to community issues, coming as he does from a community-organizing background on the South Side of Chicago. I return to this in chapter 8.

63. Interestingly, Nisbet's ideology of lament seems to be pervasive among baby boomers, a group that has achieved widespread prosperity and educational achievement when considered in historical perspective. Seeking an alternative to suburban sprawl, consumerism, mainstream institutions such as old-line churches and fraternal orders, and the atomizing effects thought to stem from globalization, the baby-boom generation appears to be driving much of the demand for things like the new urbanism and a return to city neighborhoods. The NIMBY syndrome takes on new meaning here, pitting old versus new gentrifiers against one another in an attempt by the former to stop the rapid development of the community and the perceived loss of what drew their interest to restoring decaying neighborhoods in the first place.

64. This is not to say philosophical concerns are irrelevant. To the contrary, in a later section of the book I attempt to integrate normative considerations of justice (the "good community") with empirical findings on other-regarding and socially altruistic behavior.

65. Gerald Suttles (1972b) wrote some thirty years ago on how the frenzy over "local control" and community building seemed impervious to evidence on its failures. A more recent example is the widespread popularity of community policing. For critical evidence on both community ideals and their implementation in the form of community policing, see Herbert 2006.

66. Novelists have been more astute than social scientists on the crushing weight of distorted forms of community. Dostoevsky's *Grand Inquisitor* and Nietzsche are emblematic.

67. Sugrue 1996; see also Kaufman 2003.

68. Sampson, Morenoff, and Gannon-Rowley 2002.

69. The social-ecological literature has also considered neighborhood differentiation related to life-cycle status, residential stability, home ownership, density, land use, and ethnic heterogeneity. The evidence is mixed, especially for population density and ethnic heterogeneity (Morenoff, Sampson, and Raudenbush 2001; Brooks-Gunn, Duncan, and Aber 1997). There is research showing that residential instability and low rates of home ownership are durable correlates of many health-related behaviors, but there is evidence that residential

stability predicts negative rather than positive outcomes (Ross, Reynolds, and Geis 2000). A more recent but understudied object of inquiry is concentrated *affluence* (Massey 1996; Brooks-Gunn et al. 1993). Many of these factors will be considered later.

70. Sorensen 1998, 240; Wikström and Sampson 2003. One of the earliest sources of serious sociological attention to the idea of social mechanisms was Robert Merton (1949), who focused on the self-fulfilling prophecy and the "Matthew Effect," among other mechanisms (Hedström and Bearman 2009). The mechanistic turn in the social sciences is in its ascendancy even though there is sharp disagreement on the proper conceptual or methodological approach.

71. Sampson, Morenoff, and Gannon-Rowley 2002, 447. For the most recent assessment of the literature on neighborhood social mechanisms that I could find, see Galster 2011.

72. Jencks and Mayer 1990; Mayer and Jencks 1989.

73. Woodward 2003.

CHAPTER THREE

1. Park and Burgess 1925 [1967], 147

2. Park 1915, 579.

3. Suttles 1972, 8.

4. Choldin 1984. This in part addresses the concern of the political economy critique.

5. Suttles 1972, 59; Reiss n.d.

6. Suttles 1972, 51.

7. Hunter 1974.

8. Gieryn 2000.

9. On the concept of social homophily, see McPherson, Smith-Lovin, and Cook 2001.

10. Suttles 1972. For important work on the defended neighborhood in action against change, see Taub, Taylor, and Dunham 1987; Wilson and Taub 2006.

11. Coleman 1961.

12. Smith 2010; Smail 1999.

13. Smith 2010; Jacobs 1961, 117.

14. Warren 1975, 50.

15. Zorbaugh 1929, 65. He went on to say that in this "neighborly" sense, "there are no neighborhoods" (68).

16. For example, see Powell et al. 2010.

17. Brubaker 1996.

18. The seminal work of Suttles (1968) in *The Social Order of the Slum* shows how differential social organization maps onto territorial forms. See also Tilly 1973, 212.

19. Differential commitment to neighborhood might be thought of as the "community of *differential* liability," a variant on Janowitz's (1975) conception of the "community of limited liability," where attachment to neighborhood is voluntary and often based on instrumental values surrounding investment rather than the constrained interpersonal ties that characterized the "urban villages" of our past. I accept most of Janowitz's reasoning but resist its implication of the seemingly inevitable decline of community.

20. Wilson 1987. For a pre-Wilson analysis, see Massey and Sampson 2009.

21. See, for example, Anderson 1990, 1999; Bourgois 1995; Newman 1999; Sanchez-Jankowski 2008. Notable exceptions to the inner-city poverty restriction include Pattillo-McCoy's exploration of the black middle class (1999,) in Chicago and Lacy's (2007) study of the suburbs of Washington, DC. See also ethnographies by Kefalas (2003) and Carr (2006) of a white working-class area in Chicago and Katz's (2009) comparative study of Los Angeles neighborhoods in the larger Hollywood community. Largely absent in this tradition are studies of mixed or Latino (but see Small 2004; Klinenberg 2002; Wilson and Taub 2006; Katz 2009) and white upper-income areas.

22. Sanchez-Jankowski 2008, 9. See also Pattillo 1998.

23. Somewhat surprisingly, upon close reading one finds that it is not unusual for urban ethnographies to make comparative or even causal claims about neighborhood effects even though empirical observations are within one place. To be clear, however, I am not critiquing the empirical or scientific validity of ethnography, but rather specifying the logic of specific claims.

24. See also the methodological arguments and ethnographic work by Katz 2001, 2009.

25. Firey 1947 is usually considered one of the first to systematically tackle cultural issues in the study of urban ecology.

26. At the level of the nation-state, the classic statement is Benedict Anderson [1983] 1991, *Imagined Communities*. For a fascinating historical study of neighborhoods and the mental use of maps in medieval Marseille, see Smail 1999.

27. Gieryn 2000, 465. See also Katz 2009.

28. Coleman 1994. See also Clampet-Lundquist and Massey 2008.

29. Thus psychometrics turns on the measurement of individual differences, ecometrics on ecological or neighborhood differences. See Raudenbush and Sampson 1999.

30. Park and Burgess [1925] 1967.

31. Wilson 1987.

32. Janowitz 1975; Marwell 2005, 2007.

33. See also Coleman 1986. Again, my consideration here does *not* signal a commitment to methodological individualism or rational choice theory, nor,

I think, was Coleman intent on claiming that there was only one way to study micro-macro transitions.

34. Economists are often viewed as being at the forefront of the selection-bias concern, but the sentiment is widely shared in the social sciences, with the seminal critique of neighborhood-effects research offered by Jencks and Mayer (1990).

35. Heckman 2005.

36. The empirical forays of methodological individualists betray a reductive emphasis on individuals and lack of deep concern with social context in its own right (Abbott 2007; Jackson and Pettit 1992). A possible exception is "analytic sociology" and the associated concept of "structural individualism" (see Hedström and Bearman 2009), although the "supervenience" assumption and associated epistemological stance of analytic sociology has, in my opinion, deflected attention from the ontology of social-level or contextual causality (see chapter 15). Although for different reasons, the classic perspective on ecological context in developmental psychology, that of Bronfrenbrenner (1979), has also in practice focused on the individual despite the theory's emphasis on the "mesosystem" and macrosystem.

37. Sawyer 2005. See also Hedström and Bearman 2009.

38. This framework extends my initial argument in Sampson 2002a combined with my reading of a long line of urban scholarship mainly from World War I to the present. It also builds in part on the vision laid out by the late James Coleman before his death (Coleman 1994, 1986) and Andrew Abbott's intellectual history of *Department and Discipline* (Abbott 1999).

39. Snow 1993.

40. Chapter 2; Abbott 1997, 1152. Such a stance does not rule out generalities, only a fine balancing act between treatment of the city as both lab and social field (see chapter 4). Although not a terribly pleasing phrase, the concept of the "middle range" (Merton 1949) has much to offer in the way of eliding the unhelpful divisions that still rile much of social science, such as basic/applied, theory/research, and positivist/interpretive (Sampson 2010a).

41. We have made virtually all of the major components of the PHDCN data public over the years, within the constraints of confidentiality agreements (see http://www.icpsr.umich.edu/icpsrweb/PHDCN/). Over a hundred scholars have already published papers on the data that we are aware of. There are likely more papers not reported to ICPSR, and others will appear in the future. I will also be making much of the data from this book available through ChicagoMap, a project of the Center for Geographic Analysis at Harvard (see chapter 15).

42. See Burawoy 2003 for his notion of the "revisit" to ethnographic field sites. On an abstract level, one might say here I attempt a targeted revisit to mul-

tiple Chicago communities, a comparative reassessment using an assortment of methods, but mostly quantitative, of neighborhoods that have been studied over the years. My views have evolved as a result of this process, most notably an increased appreciation for historical and cultural processes.

43. Appendices are a common device to present such material, but they tend to reify a false distinction between the main line of theoretical argument and analytic methods. I thus eschew the strategy of multiple appendices and integrate methodological and theoretical arguments into the ongoing flow of the presentation, with additional details provided in footnotes.

CHAPTER FOUR

1. The interpretation of PHDCN offered in this chapter is my own and no doubt is shaped by my intellectual history. Although I make every effort to be accurate and I conducted multiple interviews in piecing together the story, others may of course have seen things differently at the time. I also apologize in advance if not all people with roles in the project are sufficiently recognized in print. This was truly a collaborative project with literally hundreds of participants.

2. The Framingham Heart Study (FHS), conducted in the place known as the "The Town That Changed America's Heart," has long been considered the gold standard in research on health. The FHS was a clustered community-based study that started some fifty years ago and that has followed the original participants over time with intensive measurement. Its influence has been enormous (Framingham Heart Study 1995–2006). The PHDCN, as we shall see, purposefully eschewed the "national sample" approach of most surveys and comes closer to the Framingham ideal of in-depth scientific assessment in a place thought to be broadly representative of the types of problems facing Americans.

3. Cloward and Ohlin 1960; Wilson and Herrnstein 1985. Norval Morris was also important, but my take is that he played more of an administrative rather than intellectual role in the project's design. Although not on the original committee, David Farrington of the University of Cambridge was a major intellectual influence behind the idea of a multicohort longitudinal design, as discussed below.

4. This tension has roiled the study of crime since the days of Cesare Lombroso and the search for the "born criminal" or "criminal man" in the 1800s. He is still being sought. For a new translation of this influential Italian criminologist, see Gibson and Rafter 2006.

5. Wolfgang, Figlio, and Sellin 1972.

6. Published as Laub 2004.

7. The intense intellectual focus in criminology on prediction follows an interesting path over the course of the last century, a topic John Laub and I ex-

plored in "The Sutherland-Glueck Debate: On the Sociology of Criminological Knowledge" (Laub and Sampson 1991). See also Laub 2004.

8. March 31 (p. 1) and November 28 (p. 1), 1994, respectively.

9. Farrington, Ohlin, and Wilson 1986.

10. For a fascinating intellectual history of the Chicago School, including its colorful characters, see Abbott 1999.

11. Reiss and Tonry 1986.

12. The late David Rowe and I spent many hours disagreeing but always with pleasure.

13. For an early case for why a new longitudinal study was needed, see Farrington, Ohlin, and Wilson 1986. For a detailed description of design-related features that went into the planning phases of the PHDCN, see Tonry, Ohlin, and Farrington 1991.

14. The composition of the leadership team changed over time. For example, the psychologist Terrie Moffitt left fairly early on to take up work on another longitudinal study, and Jeanne Brooks-Gunn joined near the end to represent developmental psychology. Elizabeth Susman and Jeff Fagan also helped out in the middle phase, and the late Bob Cairns was a key figure in the early stages of the project's developmental thinking, as was Michael Tonry in the management of the group's early planning activities. I was scientific director for the community design, and Stephen Raudenbush was scientific director for analysis.

15. See also Earls and Buka 1997.

16. Judt 2007. Mailer called New York "one of the capitals of the world."

17. As David Brooks (2009) notes: "All smart analyses of the Obama administration begin with Chicago."

18. Kotlowitz 2004.

19. Whereas NYC, LA, and Chicago, to name the big three, certainly look different, we need to distinguish between surface difference and underlying fundamentals on neighborhood inequality and social processes. Consider Latino immigration. Readers might be surprised to learn that metropolitan Chicago has almost 1.5 million residents of Latino or Hispanic origin, by some estimates the second-largest concentration in the country. The city proper grew during the 1990s and is one of the most ethnically diverse cities in the United States. One might be further surprised that Hispanic-white segregation (the index of dissimilarity, ranging from 0 to 100) is 63 in LA compared to an almost identical 62 for NYC and 67 for Chicago. Asian-white segregation levels are also similar, 48 for LA compared to 50 for NYC and 44 for Chicago. Or consider that violence follows a general pattern of ecological concentration in LA just as in other cities. Solid empirical research on changes in crime in LA County over recent decades has demonstrated a timeworn social-ecological pattern linking neighborhood dete-

rioration and rising crime rates in late twentieth-century LA to concentrated disadvantage and associated neighborhood factors that have predicted crime distributions in American cities going back to early twentieth-century Chicago. It is true that some forms of race-linked segregation are new to American cities in the post-Fordist era (and remain more entrenched in Chicago), but a large research literature has attacked this very issue. Note as well that Mike Davis's (1992) fiery depiction of the coming ruin of Los Angeles runs opposite to the facts. Crime is down and the city is booming like many others. In short, while LA and NY look and feel different than Chicago, and while the LA School is clearly right about the distinctive urban form and ecological routines in LA, the question is how much this matters for the sorts of questions I pose.

20. One of the best papers highlighting the struggle to balance field and laboratory approaches, with Chicago as the case study, is Thomas Gieryn's "City as Truth Spot" (2006). In the present case, I go back and forth in using Chicago as both a field and laboratory.

21. Ever in aggressive overdrive, the headlines in the *Chicago Tribune* when I first drafted this chapter extolled the can-do virtues and American naturalness (versus Los Angeles "phony") that would win Chicago the 2016 Olympics. A few weeks later Chicago was selected as the American representative over LA. Chicago grit again won out, but in the end Rio was the charm.

22. For a history of Chicago community areas, see Chicago Fact Book Consortium 1990. See also Hunter's (1974) important analysis of neighborhood and community identity in Chicago.

23. The Latino community of South Lawndale is known locally as "Little Village," for example, but the area remains distinctive and set apart from North Lawndale. Similarly, the Lower West Side is widely known as "Pilsen."

24. Suttles 1972. See also Hipp's (2007) analysis of variability in ecological definitions and Grannis's (1998, 2009) description of "tertiary communities" that takes into account the layout of streets to comprise areas that are connectable without crossing major thoroughfares.

25. Black poverty is well known. That there were *no* white high-poverty neighborhoods is less well appreciated. High-income Latino and high-income Latino/African American neighborhoods were also nonexistent (Sampson, Raudenbush, and Earls 1997, 919). In this sense the research design itself produces a striking comment on segregation by race and class in Chicago. But the same finding has been replicated in other cities, suggesting that Chicago is not unique.

26. There were over fifty research assistants who carried out screenings and interviews, many in Spanish and Polish. The staff represented a diversity of languages and many were immigrants themselves, reflecting the wide diversity of the Chicago area (Holton n.d.). There were supervisors and separate units for data collection, official records, community relations, tracking, and statistical

analysis. The staff was recruited for the long run, with many research assistants sticking with the same families over the full period of the study, enhancing the participation rate. John Holton was the original site director of the PHDCN; he left in 1999. Alisú Schoua-Glusberg was the director of survey operations and oversaw a revised organizational structure. The manager of field operations was Kelly Martin, the data research manager was Nancy Sampson, and the administrative manager was Cynthia Coleman.

27. For further details on the PHDCN data collection for the cohort study, see Martin 2002.

28. Among the scholars in attendance besides PHDCN investigators were Douglas Massey, Claude Fischer, Richard Taub, Ralph Taylor, Lloyd Ohlin, Mercer Sullivan, and Terry Williams.

29. The Community Survey had three stages. At stage 1, city blocks were sampled within each NC; at stage 2, dwelling units were sampled within blocks; at stage 3, one adult resident (eighteen or older) was sampled within each selected dwelling unit. Abt Associates carried out the screening and data collection in cooperation with research staff of PHDCN, achieving a final response rate of 75 percent. The design produced a representative probability sample of Chicago residents and a large enough within-cluster sample to create reliable between-neighborhood measures. The samples within NCs were designed to be approximately self-weighting, and thus between-neighborhood analyses in this book are, unless otherwise noted, based on unweighted data (Sampson, Raudenbush, and Earls 1997, 924). Descriptive data are weighted. The design of the CS allows me to construct measures at multiple geographic scales, including block group, census tract, NC, and community area. In supplemental work I defined "tertiary communities" (see Grannis 2009) made up of aggregations of block groups wherein streets were connected without crossing major thoroughfares. This definition resulted in 221 areas slightly larger than neighborhood clusters defined in the PHDCN (about eleven thousand residents on average) and that produced virtually equivalent ecometric properties for the community survey measures. In the analyses of this book I rely mainly on three sets of units—census tracts (N = 875), NCs (343), and community areas (77). This provides the largest contrast in sample size and boundary definition, with the middle unit (NCs) most conforming to the PHDCN design.

30. The term "ramping up" was used often by the initial supervisor of data collection, but, as it turned out, more in terms of aspirations than a description of actual progress. He was soon fired by the contractor.

31. For a detailed sociological analysis of the Chicago heat wave, see Klinenberg 2002.

32. I am indebted to John Holton, who was PHDCN site director from 1993 to 1999, for his field notes, permission to quote, comments on this chapter, and

recollection of these and other events as described in a personal interview (conducted March 22, 2007).

33. At about the same time I witnessed an ugly event at a University of Chicago seminar chaired by Christopher Jencks. James Q. Wilson, an early advisor to PHDCN, was slated to give a formal presentation. Before he could start, about a half dozen protestors stood up and starting shouting and chanting that Wilson was a racist in favor of genocide. His work with Richard Herrnstein in *Crime and Human Nature* and on the PHDCN was cited by the protestors. The university police were called and the protesters eventually removed, but as I recall not before the seminar had to be aborted. The politics of race and crime have always been deeply controversial, but the early to mid-1990s was an especially volatile time. In this case, to the best of my recollection, Wilson that day was not even scheduled to talk about race and crime. See Massey and Sampson 2009 on the scholarly politics of race that became a legacy of the Moynihan report.

34. The pragmatics and cost of collecting biological measures, using the technology available in 1995, were the driving reasons the PHDCN did not move forward in this area, although the protests were not insignificant either. In addition we concluded that there was a lack of scientific consensus that biological differences, such as they could be measured reliably at the time, were major predictors of crime. It is surprising how fast some things change—today the drawing of blood and obtaining genetic markers is routine.

35. During a discussion of behavioral genetics with a biologist at a professional meeting at the time, he half jokingly asserted that what is needed is a "Department of Molecular Sociology."

36. With the growing use of cell phones and difficulty of interviewing households in person, combined with the increasing constraints imposed by our human subjects' review boards, I nonetheless worry about the future of big social science.

37. Abbott 1997.

38. Reiss 1971, 4.

39. NORC 1995. As a check on quality control, new observers recoded a random 10 percent of all coded face-blocks, and the results compared. This test produced over 98 percent agreement.

40. Short 1963, xvii, in his introduction to Thrasher 1927 [1963].

41. The probability sample was nested within the NCs defined by PHDCN originally, with oversampling within the eighty focal NCs (of cohort selection). The 3,105 interviews completed include 1,145 respondents in focal NCs (37 percent of the total sample or just over 14 respondents per NC on average), and 1,960 in nonfocal NCs (63 percent of the total sample, or just over 8 respondents per NC on average). For purposes of studying racial-ethnic disparities, the sample is very balanced, including 802 Hispanics, 1,240 non-Hispanic blacks, 983 non-Hispanic

whites, and 80 people of other races/ethnicities. The second community survey yielded a response rate of 72 percent, close to matching the first CS even though personal surveys became harder to conduct over time.

42. To ensure that interviewers made reliable and valid observations, ISR conducted a pilot study in which two raters made independent observations of the same block at the same time for eighty blocks, one in each of the focal NCs. In the second stage of the SSO, ISR collected observations from a single rater on almost every block in Chicago that contained a CCAHS survey sample address. All together 1,664 of the total of 1,672 blocks were assessed (approximately eight blocks per focal NC and four blocks per nonfocal NC), for a total of 13,251 face-blocks nested within 1,379 census block groups, 703 census tracts, and 343 NCs.

43. We also sampled new organizations and determined where occupants of the original leadership positions went. The 1995 Key Informant study was more directly linked to the PHDCN community design. The second panel study in 2002 was a cognate effort independently funded by the American Bar Foundation, the MacArthur Foundation, and the Chicago Community Trust.

44. I was also a Research Fellow for seven of these years at the American Bar Foundation, located on the Near North Side.

45. See also Gieryn 2006, 24.

46. Becker 1996.

CHAPTER FIVE

1. Drake and Cayton [1945] 1993; see the maps on pages 203 and 205.

2. Moynihan 1965. Kenneth Clark was a contemporary of Moynihan who made his own provocative splash in *Dark Ghetto* (1965), apparently originating the "pathology" metaphor.

3. On the intellectual and historical context, see Massey and Sampson 2009.

4. Properly so, I would argue, for pathology too easily conjures up the medical model as the correct paradigm to follow. Criticisms of terms like "pathology" and "disorganization" are noted further in chapter 7. Note, however, that the logic used by as Moynihan was not restricted to the black community. The manifestations of pathology were instead thought to vary by location in the social structure. Thus while the terminology is certainly problematic for social phenomena, we should not lose sight of the structural logic that framed Moynihan's argument.

5. This chapter extends the thesis in Sampson 2009b.

6. Moynihan 1965, chap. 3, p. 1. On variable-based approaches, see Abbott 1997.

7. Bowles, Durlauf, and Hoff 2006; Sampson and Morenoff 2006.

8. Moynihan 1965, chap. 5, p. 1

9. Shaw and McKay 1942; Drake and Cayton [1945] 1993; Wilson 1987; Massey 1990.

10. Sampson, Morenoff, and Gannon-Rowley 2002; Land, McCall, and Cohen 1990.

11. See chapter 4 on the pros and cons of census tracts as neighborhood units of analysis.

12. Sampson, Sharkey, and Raudenbush 2008, 848, table 1.

13. Based on this result, I drop density of children from the scale in later analyses. When I examine concentrated disadvantage without racial composition, the resulting scale correlates 0.99 with the initial scale that included percentage black. Results are thus robust across definitions.

14. The full distribution is shown in Sampson 2009b, 266.

15. For further elaboration, see Sampson, Sharkey, and Raudenbush 2008.

16. Massey and Denton 1993.

17. The correlation is 0.59 ($p < 0.01$) in mixed areas. In black areas it is even larger, at 0.78 ($p < 0.01$). For a chart of this relationship, see Sampson 2009b, 267.

18. Bureau of Justice Statistics 2010.

19. Western 2006.

20. Sampson and Loeffler 2010.

21. We measure the imprisonment rate by the number of unique Chicago-residing felony defendants sentenced to the Illinois Department of Corrections from the Circuit Court of Cook County divided by the number of Chicago inhabitants ages eighteen to sixty-four in the 2000 census. We use adults "at risk" in the denominator in order to rule out confounding variations in the prevalence of children under age eighteen that are not eligible for prison. Similarly, we exclude those at the older end because, while society is aging, very few prisoners are over sixty-five. These data were gathered from the electronic records of the Circuit Court of Cook County (Sampson and Loeffler 2010).

22. Wilson 1987. See also Jargowsky 1997.

23. Koval et al. 2006.

24. Sampson and Morenoff 2006.

25. Wilson and Taub 2006; Hunter 1974.

26. Suttles 1990.

27. See also Taub, Taylor, and Dunham 1987.

28. Massey, Condran, and Denton 1987.

29. Dust jacket of Hyra 2008.

30. The sociologist Malcom Klein, in remarks at a plenary session on the Project on Human Development in Chicago Neighborhoods, American Society of Criminology, 2006. The irony is that Klein is from Los Angeles, not the first city that comes to mind as unweird.

31. Peterson and Krivo 2010.

32. Small 2007; Small and Feldman 2008. Some have also claimed that black neighborhoods in Chicago are "remarkably different than those in the average American city" (http://www.columbia.edu/~jwp70/COMURB_Ghetto-Chicago_discussion_2008.pdf). See also the follow-up symposium in the journal *City and Community* 7 (2008): 347–98.

33. Sampson 2009b, 268. I used a principal-components, regression-weighted scale of the indicators introduced above: poverty, female-headed families, welfare assistance, unemployment rate, and racial isolation (percent black). I also used census tracts as the definition of neighborhood (chapter 4) to provide a U.S. comparison.

34. See also Sampson 2009b.

35. Peterson and Krivo 2010.

36. For a scholarly assessment, see Blumstein and Wallman 2000.

37. See http://www.census.gov/acs/www/Products/PUMS/. I used data from the period 2005–7 to increase precision of estimates, as it contains records for about 3 percent of housing units in each geographic area compared to about 1 percent for the one-year files.

38. http://www.uic.edu/cuppa/voorheesctr/Publications/vnc_woodsrpt_0706.pdf, page 9.

39. Wilson 1996.

40. For a chart, see Sampson 2009b, 271.

41. I estimated the equation: Poverty 2000 = $\alpha + \beta$*Poverty 1960 + ε. The expression ($\alpha + \beta$*Poverty1960) is the 2000 *predicted poverty rate* and ε is the deviation or *residual* from the predicted rate. The residual reflects the amount of change in a given neighborhood's poverty that is unaccounted for or unexplained by its initial level of poverty. Residual change scores have the advantage over raw change scores of being statistically independent of initial levels of poverty. In addition, because all of Chicago was used to estimate the regression equation upon which the residuals are computed, these change scores have the desirable property of incorporating the dynamics of the entire ecological structure (see also Bursik and Webb 1982). The 0.91 correlation between 2000 and 2005–9 poverty at the community-area level means that the pattern in figure 5.6 is virtually identical when the latter is substituted. However, because the 2005–9 data were not available until late 2010 and the sampling is different from previous census decades, I retain the 2000 poverty rate to measure residual change.

42. Not examined here is the growth in suburban poverty in southern Cook County. Towns such as Harvey, Dolton, Country Club Hills, and other south suburbs saw growth in poverty and after the CHA transformation, in-migration from former residents of public housing.

43. Koval et al. 2006.

44. Pattillo 2007; Hyra 2008. I will return to these areas in the final chapter.

45. A recent study of the U.S. reports a robust relationship between income inequality and income segregation, but the effect is larger for black families than it is for white families (Reardon and Bischoff 2011).

46. Moynihan 1965; Clark 1965.

CHAPTER SIX

1. Jacobs 1961.

2. Booth 1889; Charles Booth Online Archive 2010.

3. Quoted in Pfautz 1967, 191.

4. *Economist* 2006, 57–58. My discussion here draws on Sampson 2009a.

5. Sennett 1970. See also his reflections some thirty years later (Sennett 2009).

6. Benedict Anderson later wrote on the "imagined community" and identity formation at a "nation" level, but in broad theoretical terms the mechanisms are similar [1983] 1991.

7. Hunter 1985.

8. Goffman 1963a, 9.

9. Lofland 1973, 22, emphasis in original.

10. Putnam 2007.

11. Skogan 1990, 75.

12. Kelling and Coles 1996, 108–56. For a novel counterpoint, see Duneier 1999.

13. *Economist* 2006.

14. Jordan 2005.

15. Ross, Reynolds, and Geis 2000; Geis and Ross 1998.

16. Sampson and Raudenbush 1999.

17. This framework does not imply that disorder is unimportant for explaining neighborhood social dynamics. Although crime and disorder may reflect common origins, crime may be less relevant for understanding urban processes such as population abandonment because it is largely unobserved. Corresponding to the "text" from which all actors in a neighborhood read, disorder is a visually proximate and immediate neighborhood cue of theoretical interest, even if it is a not a direct cause of further crime. I return to this thesis in a later section.

18. This is an important discovery, as individual reliability (e.g., perceptions of disorder) is not the same thing as the reliability of a measure to detect *between-neighborhood* variance. For further discussion of this methodological issue, see Raudenbush and Sampson 1999.

19. The reason for the robbery link, we proposed, is that disorderly areas serve up vulnerable potential victims, such as drug dealers, drunks, and cus-

tomers of prostitutes. For a fascinating discussion and analysis of the ecology of disorder and robbery, see St. Jean 2007.

20. I set aside for now further consideration of the somewhat narrow question of whether broken windows "cause" crime. Current data cannot resolve the question satisfactorily, and in any case, detailed reviews of the literature are available elsewhere (e.g., Harcourt 2001; Skogan 1990; Taylor 2001; St. Jean 2007). However, I would note here an interesting study that appeared in *Science* in 2008. Researchers using a set of field experiments examined the "spreading of disorder" by manipulating aspects of physical disorder (e.g., graffiti, litter) to see if passersby in the city of Groningen, Netherlands, were influenced to act inappropriately. Keizer, Lindenberg, and Steg (2008) report that "micro" settings of disorder significantly increased the adoption of analogous disorderly behaviors and what they deem stealing. For example, Netherlanders were more likely to litter when collecting their bicycles if the bike park area was covered in graffiti than if it was clean. They were also more likely to open or take an envelope that visibly contained a five Euro bill meant for the mail if the postbox on which it was placed by experimenters was in a disordered condition. Disorder begets disorder, they concluded. The broken windows hypothesis put forth by Keizer, Lindenberg, and Steg is that disorder is a descriptive norm that undermines the tendency of humans to follow injunctive norms of appropriateness. Thus if I see a lot of litter it works to inhibit my resolve and may spread to other deviance. While clever, this study does not explain why disorder is concentrated rather than spread over geographic areas, nor does it demonstrate that disorder spreads to predatory crime, the intended target of the broken windows theory. The study also does not extend to what we might think of as "permanent" disorder. The manipulated disorder of the experiment was temporary, and if it occurred in otherwise stable areas, which seems likely, then subjects may have reasonably assumed their litter would be cleaned up. In this sense it may well be that people litter in temporary situations where there is graffiti, or that people drink more in settings where others are acting wild. Thus the assessment of the neighborhood must be considered as well, and committing murder, burglary, or robbery as a result of littering or signs of decay is another link altogether, one that remains unproven.

21. Ross and Mirowsky 1999, 414.

22. Goffman 1974.

23. Bottoms and Wiles 1992, 16.

24. Lamont 2000.

25. Loury 2002, 17.

26. For a discussion of Bayesian thinking, see Rosenkrantz 1977.

27. Ariely 2008; Thaler and Sunstein 2008. On how the pursuit of goals operates outside conscious awareness, see Custers and Aarts 2010.

28. Fiske 1998.

29. Bobo 2001; Quillian and Pager 2001; Rumbaut and Ewing 2007.

30. Wilson 1987; Massey and Denton 1993; Skogan 1990.

31. Loury 2002.

32. Fiske 1998; Banaji 2002.

33. Devine 1989; Bobo 2001, 292.

34. Correll et al. 2002, 1325.

35. Werthman and Piliavin 1967.

36. Irwin 1985.

37. Goffman 1963b.

38. Hagan 1994, 150.

39. Stinchcombe 1963.

40. Wacquant 1993.

41. Kefalas 2003, 11, 14, 43, 62, 74.

42. I am no exception. One morning a few years ago I stepped outside my home only to notice a fresh swath of painted graffiti on the wall of a nearby apartment building. My first reaction was anger and, I admit, an almost instantaneous fear that my wife and I had bought in the "wrong" neighborhood, one about to decline. But realizing that I lived in a stable, well-off neighborhood despite its dense urban character and proximity to a park and public transit line, I relaxed. I talked with authorities about the defacement as did others and the graffiti was cleaned up. Soon after, the same thing happened again and the process was repeated. After a cycle of four to five episodes, the problem went away. In this instance, "broken windows" were temporary and led to collective action, not crime or decline (Sampson and Raudenbush, 1999, 638), but the experience nonetheless taught me a lesson in the subjective emotions that disorder can inspire.

43. Laub and Sampson 1995.

44. Watt 2006.

45. Sampson and Raudenbush 2004.

46. We assessed in detail the robustness of all results (Sampson and Raudenbush 2004, 333–34, 339–40). For example, we measured and accounted for time of day in all analyses. Not surprisingly, physical disorder was highly stable over time. Even if some social disorder emerged at night (e.g., a bar fight), our results would be overturned only if it occurred in a large number of areas where other social disorder was *not* present during the day. From all we know on the basis of prior research and our knowledge of Chicago, such a reversal of pattern is highly unlikely. Spatial mismatch is another concern. Suppose that a resident, when responding to questions about disorder, recalled an area different from the block group where he or she lived. Our measures, however, reflected the block group as a whole and not differences within or outside block groups in the

degree of observable disorder. The research design also produced a representative survey sample of individuals within block groups. Averaged across multiple residents, idiosyncratic definitions would not produce a systematic influence of racial composition on block-group variations. Furthermore, results were insensitive to controls for spatially correlated errors and variations in the size of neighborhood units, yielding similar patterns up to the community areas of Chicago, which average almost forty thousand residents. The strong similarity of findings implies that spatial mismatch cannot account for the effects of race/ethnic composition. The large magnitude of race/ethnic effects, especially in models in which physical disorder is measured virtually without error, undermines any claim that our results are artifacts of the unreliable measurement of observed disorder.

47. I address these objectives by combining the data from Sampson and Raudenbush with a panel study of the same neighborhoods. The first component of the panel is the multistage probability-based community survey (CS) based on interviews carried out in 2001–2 by the Institute of Social Research based at the University of Michigan with a new sample of 3,105 Chicago residents living in the same neighborhoods as the 1995 study. The core interview schedule from 1995 was repeated and augmented with additional questions. The design is thus a repeated cross-sectional survey that is well equipped to measure stability and change at the neighborhood level and that is representative of Chicago. The second study is also a repeated cross-section, but this time based on systematic social observation (SSO) of all block faces within the neighborhoods within which the 1995 and 2002 community survey residents lived. Based on successful results from a pretest and to save on costs, observer logs, rather than videotapes, were used on over 1,500 block groups (about seven hundred census tracts). The main SSO disorder measure in 2002 is based on the following items observed on the streets: *cigarette or cigar butts*; *garbage/broken glass*; *empty bottles*; *painted-over graffiti*; *gang graffiti*; *other graffiti*; *tagging graffiti*; *political message graffiti*; *abandoned cars*; *condoms*; and *drug paraphernalia*. The minimum level of reliability obtained was 0.93 at the block-group level, with 1 the theoretical maximum. Observed physical disorder is thus highly reliable at all neighborhood levels. The third data source is an integration of the 2000 U.S. census with Chicago police records on crime from 2000 up to 2006.

48. Results are similar when substituting percent foreign born for Latino. This is not surprising, as these two indicators are correlated over 0.70 ($p < 0.01$) at the block-group level.

49. See chapter 7 for further variable definitions. The model estimated was: **Person-Level:** 2002 Perceived Disorder = B0 + B1*(Age) + B2*(Male) + B3*(Black) + B4*(Latino) + B5*(Other Race) + B6*(1st Gen. Immigrant) + B7*(2nd Gen. Immigrant) + B8*(Single) + B9*(Married) + B10*(Separated/Divorced) + B11*(Kids)

+ B12*(Education) + B13*(HH Income) + B14*(Own Home) + B15*(Years in Neigh.) + B16*(# Moves) + B17* (# Languages) + B18*(Perceived Collective Efficacy) + B19*(Neighborly Exchange) + B20*(Perceived Violence) + B21*(Friend/Kinship Ties + B22*(Organizational Participation) + B23*(Trust in Neighbors) + B24*(Personal Victimization) + B25*(Fear) + R.

Neighborhood-Level: 2002 Adjusted Perceived Disorder = G00 + G01*(2000 Density) + G02*(2002 SSO Disorder) + G03*(2002 SSO Physical Decay) + G04*(2000 Poverty) + G05*(2002 % Black) + G06*(% Latinos) + G07*(1995 Socially Perceived Disorder) + U0.

Equations were estimated simultaneously using hierarchical models with robust standard errors that include random individual and neighborhood components (for details, see Sampson and Raudenbush 2004). Person-level covariates are grand mean centered to capture compositional differences when assessing neighborhood-level coefficients. Twenty-four percent of the variance is explained at the individual level and 88 percent across block groups. The t-ratios (coefficient/standard error) for percent black and percent Latino are 6.67 and 9.18, respectively. The t-ratio for the black-versus-white contrast within neighborhoods is −3.66; for first generation versus third, −6.88 (all $p < 0.01$).

50. For example, for survey respondents nested within census tracts, blacks and Latinos were significantly less likely than whites ($p < 0.01$) to report disorder. First-generation immigrants scored almost a half standard deviation lower (0.19, $p < 0.01$) on perceived disorder than the third-plus generation. It is only at the much larger community-area level that we see racial differences within communities diminish after racial composition is controlled. This finding is not surprising because segregation between blacks and whites within community areas can be considerable. Immigrant differences within community areas also diminish but remain significant; all else equal, first-generation immigrants perceived about one-third of a standard deviation less disorder within the same community area than third-generation immigrants.

51. The original study showed an ethnic interaction in that Latinos were significantly more likely to perceive disorder as percent black increased compared to blacks and whites (Sampson and Raudenbush 2004, 335). We did not have a direct measure of generational status in 1995. The magnitude of interaction diminished over the period of follow-up study, which makes sense if we consider the argument of Loury (2002) that it takes time for immigrant attitudes to adjust. And in fact, there is no interaction of immigrant status with either percent Latino or foreign born.

52. Because of the repeated cross-sectional survey, the respondents in 1995 are different than in 2002, a crucial design element that ensures independence of neighborhood measures. The between-area or aggregate reliability of perceived

disorder is 0.91 in the 2002 survey for community areas and 0.64 for tracts. See Sampson and Raudenbush 2004 for 1995 statistics.

53. For the block-group and tract level, coefficients for collective disorder were significant at the 0.01 level (t-ratios of 7.43 and 4.39, respectively).

54. All three variables were standardized to have a mean of 0 and a standard deviation of 1 before the analysis and therefore are directly comparable: the estimated effect of collective priors is more than double the effect of racial composition (0.15 vs. 0.07).

55. N = 47 communities. Over 40 percent and 97 percent of variance explained at the individual and community levels, respectively, in both the full and reduced sample model based on 1995 SSO.

56. Putnam 2000. Surprisingly, however, crime is not a major factor in his account.

57. See Merton's (1968) original discussion of the mechanism of self-fulfilling prophecy.

58. Bursik 1986, 73.

59. Skogan 1990; Morenoff and Sampson 1997; Sampson 1986; Liska and Bellair 1995.

60. To account for the nonlinearity, I transformed percent poverty in 2000 into logit form.

61. One of these, Washington Park, was targeted for improvement if Chicago landed the 2016 Olympics. The city failed in its bid, but the choice gives an indication of the widely shared perceptions of Washington Park's desperate economic and social conditions.

62. More specifically, 68 percent of the variance in the logit of 2000 census tract poverty is explained by just six neighborhood characteristics measured at a prior time. The standardized coefficients (raw coefficient divided by standard deviation) for the four significant predictors are, in order of magnitude, 0.35 (percent black in 1990), 0.33 (collective priors on disorder in 1995), 0.32 (1990 percent poverty), and 0.30 for 1990 percent foreign born. Interestingly, the two predictors that failed both substantively and in terms of significance were prior *observed* disorder and the homicide rate. The results thus confirm that collectively perceived disorder is on par with prior poverty and key demographics in predicting the poverty outcomes at the neighborhood level.

63. With correlations of 0.60 and 0.33, respectively. I also controlled for residential stability and racial composition within the race/ethnic strata, along with prior poverty. Collectively perceived disorder had a significant and larger independent association with later poverty in black and Latino areas (0.35 and 0.26, respectively; $p < 0.01$) than in white areas (0.10, not significant).

64. At the tract level for relative change, for example, the standardized co-

efficient for disorder as perceived in 1995 was −0.49 (t-ratio = −4.70, $p < 0.01$) compared to observed disorderly conditions (B = 0.09, t-ratio = 1.00). At the community-area level there is much more correlation among predictors and thus less precision in estimates along with reduced statistical power. The main pattern of results was similar, however, with shared perceptions of disorder a significant predictor of an area's losing population. The perceived disorder coefficient was −0.35 ($p < 0.05$).

65. A recent examination of household moves and racial transition supports the general hypothesis of this chapter. Using a national study of households, Hipp (2010) reports that whites who perceive more crime in the neighborhood or that live in blocks with more commonly perceived crime are more likely to move out of such neighborhoods. Moreover, whites are significantly less likely to move into a housing unit in areas high in perceived crime, but African American and Latino households are more likely to move into such areas.

CHAPTER SEVEN

1. Bursik and Grasmick 1993, 30.
2. Reiss 1986.
3. Bursik 1988.
4. Warner and Rountree 1997; Sampson and Groves 1989.
5. Wilson 1996.
6. Stack 1974.
7. Pattillo 1998. See also Pattillo-McCoy 1999.
8. Venkatesh 1997. See also St. Jean 2007.
9. Browning, Feinberg, and Dietz 2004.
10. William F. Whyte's *Street Corner Society* (1943) famously asserted that the problem of Cornerville was not that it was disorganized, but that its form of organization clashed with the dominant norms of middle-class society. For a recent essay on differential social organization, communities, and crime that I see as broadly compatible with my approach, see Matsueda 2006.
11. Granovetter 1973.
12. Bellair 1997. For evidence on health, see Kawachi and Berkman 2003.
13. Sampson, Raudenbush, and Earls 1997. See Bandura 1997 on self-efficacy theory.
14. In fairness it is important to note that social disorganization theorists did not equate disorganization with "chaos" or lack of patterning, rather they meant that social controls were variably aligned with the goals, needs, and resources of residents. Hence, misalignment meant disorganization. For a trenchant defense of social disorganization theory, see Kornhauser 1978.
15. Portes and Sensenbrenner 1993, 1323.

16. Hardin 2002.

17. The political scientist David Laitin suggested to me the connection of collective efficacy to the notion of "common knowledge." Usually traced to the philosopher David Hume, the argument of common knowledge is that a fundamental condition for coordinated activity is that humans know what behavior to expect from one another. Without this requisite mutual knowledge, or what I would call shared expectations, mutually beneficial conventions would disappear. Understanding the conditions that lead to common knowledge is critical. A key difference is the amount of common information that all are required to possess.

18. Kobrin 1951. Bob Bursik brought this point to my attention; see Bursik 2009.

19. Pattillo-McCoy 1999; Anderson 1990; St. Jean 2007.

20. Williams and Collins 1995.

21. Raudenbush and Sampson 1999.

22. Thus differentiating our notion of collective efficacy from the aggregation of beliefs about how one's personal efficacy is dependent on others. See also Bandura 1997.

23. Neighborhood reliability is defined as: $\Sigma\ [\tau_{00}/(\tau_{00} + \sigma^2/nj)]\ /\ J$, which measures the precision of the estimate, averaged across the set of J neighborhoods, as a function of (1) the sample size (n) in each of the j neighborhood clusters, and (2) the proportion of the total variance that is between neighborhoods (τ_{00}) relative to the amount that is within (σ^2).

24. Sampson, Raudenbush, and Earls 1997, 922. Analyses were carried out using neighborhood clusters (NCs) and later replicated with tract and community areas.

25. Morenoff, Sampson, and Raudenbush 2001.

26. Browning, Feinberg, and Dietz 2004. To judge whether neighborhood structures serve collective needs, I argue that the theory of collective efficacy must apply the nonexclusivity requirement of a social good—that is, does its consumption by one member of a community diminish the sum available to the community as a whole? Safety from crime is a quintessential social good that yields positive externalities of benefit to all residents of a community, especially its children. So are good schools and clean air. By contrast, we would not consider racial exclusion in the form of racially defended neighborhoods to be a collective good, as for example when neighborhood associations in some American cities in the 1960s and 1970s were exploited by whites to keep blacks from moving to white working-class areas.

27. Small 2009.

28. Morenoff, Sampson, and Raudenbush 2001.

29. Pratt and Cullen 2005.

30. See also reviews in Sampson, Morenoff, and Gannon-Rowley 2002; Kubrin and Weitzer 2003; Leventhal and Brooks-Gunn 2000.

31. Sampson, Morenoff, and Raudenbush 2005.

32. Bernasco and Block 2009.

33. Wikström et al. 2010.

34. Browning, Leventhal, and Brooks-Gunn 2005, 2004. Collective efficacy appears to significantly delay the timing of first intercourse but only for those youth who experience lower levels of parental supervision, suggesting a person-environment interaction.

35. Maimon and Browning 2010.

36. Browning 2002.

37. See Cagney and Browning 2004; Morenoff 2003; Wen, Browning, and Cagney 2003, and Browning and Cagney 2002; and Browning et al. 2006, respectively.

38. Sampson and Wikström 2008.

39. Przeworski and Tuene 1970.

40. Sampson and Wikström 2008, figure 5.3.

41. Sampson and Wikström 2008, table 5.6.

42. For the multivariate model with the structural predictors represented in figure 7.2 controlled simultaneously, the t-ratios of collective efficacy were −4.55 and −3.09 for Chicago and Stockholm, respectively ($p < 0.01$). Disadvantage was significantly positive in both cities ($p < 0.01$) followed by minority-group segregation ($p < 0.10$). I also conducted a multilevel analysis of survey-reported victimization controlling for nine major characteristics of individual respondents in both cities. The odds of violent victimization were higher in neighborhoods characterized by neighborhood instability, disadvantage, and lower collective efficacy, consistent with the picture painted by the independent measures of violence derived from geocoded police records in each city (each of which have unique error sources).

43. Mazerolle, Wickes, and McBroom 2010.

44. Zhang, Messner, and Liu 2007.

45. Kamo et al. 2008.

46. Odgers et al. 2009.

47. Skrabski, Kopp, and Kawachi 2004.

48. Villarreal and Silva 2006.

49. Cerda and Morenoff 2009.

50. http://www.nationalchildrensstudy.gov/Pages/default.aspx.

51. Cohen et al. 2006.

52. Way, Finch, and Cohen 2006.

53. Neighborhood reliability is a function of sample size and the propor-

tion of the total variance that is between neighborhoods relative to that within neighborhoods. The 2002 survey yields lower reliabilities overall, given its substantially lower sample size. For example, at the neighborhood-cluster level the 2002 reliability is only 0.54 compared to about 0.80 in 1995. The corresponding community-area level reliability is 0.92 in 1995 and 0.76 in 2002.

54. For reasons noted above, the correlations are lower but still significantly positive at lower levels of aggregation—0.59 for neighborhood clusters and 0.43 for census tracts ($p < 0.01$).

55. See also Molotch, Freudenburg, and Paulsen 2000; Suttles 1984. The previous chapter tackles the disorder thesis more explicitly.

56. For an analysis of trust and diversity, see Sampson and Graif 2009a.

57. I thank Richard Block of Loyola for providing the data. I examine census tracts as the main operational unit of variation to gain statistical power and reduce the covariation among predictors. As a check, I repeat key analyses on community areas and block groups. Rather than present a welter of results, I focus on dominant patterns with tracts as the lead case. Because homicide is rare, I analyze the natural log of the rates in five-year intervals—1995–99 is the wave 1 outcome and 2002–6 is the wave 2 outcome.

58. For a description of legal/moral cynicism, see Sampson et al. 2005.

59. Lagged dependent variables are subject to criticism and some feel they induce their own bias by controlling away potential causal pathways. The counterargument is that they account for potential causes of crime that are not explicitly measured. I used the "pretreatment" covariate of lagged homicide in 1993 for wave 1 and 2000 crime for the wave 2 lagged control.

60. I estimated a hierarchical linear model using HLM 6.0. At the temporal level I estimated Crime $= \beta_{oj} + \beta_{1j}\ CE_{ij} + \Sigma_{\ (Controls)}\ \beta_q X_{qij} + e_{ij}$, where β_{oj} is the intercept; CE_{ij} is the value of collective efficacy associated with time i in neighborhood j; and β_1 is its partial effect on crime. The $\beta_q X_{qij}$ coefficients reflect time and other predictors measuring time-varying neighborhood characteristics. The error term, e_{ij}, is the unique contribution of time, which is assumed to be independently and normally distributed with constant variance σ^2. At the between-neighborhood level the two parameters of interest are $\beta_{oj} = \theta_{oo} + U_{oj}$, and $\beta_{1j} = \theta_{o1}$, where θ_{o1} reflects the average effect of collective efficacy across j neighborhoods. U_{oj} is the neighborhood-level error term, assumed to be normally distributed with a variance τ. The variance parameter for collective efficacy was not significant.

61. See Kirk and Papachristos 2011. Although they use a modified scale of legal cynicism that includes indicators of police dissatisfaction, the pattern is clear. Communities with low collective efficacy and high legal cynicism are persistently violent.

62. Coefficient $= -0.25$, t-ratio $= -3.12$. The corresponding burglary coeffi-

cient was −0.27 (t = −3.15) with lagged burglary rates as a predictor. Because tract-level data provide more cases and induce less overlap among predictors, as another test I entered percentage black as a separate predictor from the concentrated disadvantage scale. In all models disadvantage remained a strong predictor and percent black was positively significant. The estimated effects of collective efficacy were not materially affected, with t-ratios for homicide, robbery, and burglary, adjusted for race, at −3.25, −3.52, and −3.18, respectively ($p < 0.01$).

63. I estimated a hierarchal model in which years formed the first level and neighborhoods the second. Based on the descriptive trends I examined a quadratic function of time at level 1 (time and time squared, to capture decline and then leveling off), and predicted the slope of the linear part of the crime drop at level 2. In other words, I examined how changes in collective efficacy were related to the magnitude of deceleration in crime, the main component of change. This model controls for time-stable differences between units (heterogeneity of unobserved differences) and examines the trajectory of crime in relation to changes in collective efficacy.

64. Hipp (2009) argues that this applies more to control expectations than cohesion. I agree, but would note that in our formulation "cohesion" refers mainly to trust and perceived helping behavior, not the density of ties, which is measured separately. As Hardin (2002) argues, trust is constituted by shared expectations, so at a theoretical level these concepts are closely related.

CHAPTER EIGHT

1. "Mexicans in Chicago: A New Kind of Politics," *Chicago Tribune*, April 6, 2007. These power brokers are members of Chicago-area "immigrant clubs" that are the "engines behind a new political movement that is making itself felt from Illinois to Michoacan."

2. Obama was director of the Developing Communities Project (Obama 1988, 153).

3. Tocqueville 2000.

4. Putnam 2000.

5. For the initial presentation of the study, see Sampson et al. 2005.

6. For more on this argument, see McAdam et al. 2005.

7. There is a large literature here, but see McAdam 1999 [1982] for a classic source.

8. Wuthnow 1998, 112; Wilson 1987.

9. This thesis harkens back to classic themes in the literature on urban voluntary associations and personal networks as a source of collective capacity (Komarovsky 1946). See the review and more contemporary findings in Fischer 1982 that do not support the declensionist narrative in terms of personal networks.

10. McAdam 2003, 289; Henig 1982.

11. Putnam 2000, 153.

12. Oliver 2001, 202.

13. Alinsky 1946.

14. Marwell (2004, 2007) argues that nonprofit community-based organizations can thus leverage the interests and voting power of their clients. Although Marwell focuses on individual voting, this networking process in principle has the capacity to generate multiple "externalities" of collective civic engagement. A small but important body of recent research supports this idea by showing how nonprofit organizations foster collective action tasks and unanticipated individual gains (Small 2002, 2009; Warren 2004).

15. Earl et al. 2004.

16. Self-help gatherings, unlike a community festival or church pancake breakfast, focus on the individual and are typically not open for public display and consumption. Note that while regularly scheduled meetings (e.g., weekly church services) are excluded, a wide range of nonroutine events that often emerge from the context of regular meetings are included, such as a church fundraiser for AIDS victims, the public claim "PTA Seeks Ouster of Principal," a school's fiftieth-year celebration, and special events like "PTA Dads' Night."

17. Once event identification was completed, the articles were examined to exclude double counting of the same event. In addition, the articles were scanned to determine if there were multiple events reported in one article. We systematically coded each event within an article based on a coding scheme that was pretested on independent years of data. Interrater reliability was established at both stages of the data-collection process: event identification and event coding. Across persons and sites, interrater reliability averaged 90 percent or more.

18. The distinction between protest and civic events can be captured by noting differences in their forms and claims. Unlike protest, civic events typically do not desire to bring about (or prevent) a change in policy, nor do they express specific grievances. Even though they are also collective in nature, civic events take on different forms than the rally or protest, such as celebrating the community (e.g. festivals, community breakfast), procuring resources (e.g., rummage sales, fundraisers), and accomplishing collective goals (e.g. cleanups, preservation).

19. For a more detailed assessment, see Sampson et al. 2005, 685–87; 703–7.

20. For figures on temporal trends and patterns, see Sampson et al. 2005, 688–91.

21. Taub, Taylor, and Dunham 1987, 184–85; Trice 2008.

22. Total civic memberships correlate highly with civic memberships in one's residential neighborhood ($r = 0.83$, $p < 0.01$) across the seventy-seven communi-

ties, suggesting both measures tap the same propensity for civic membership. They also produce similar results.

23. *Friend/kinship ties* is based on the average number of friends and relatives that respondents reported lived in their neighborhood. *Reciprocated exchange* is based on a scale of five items: (1) "About how often do you and people in your neighborhood do favors for each other? By favors we mean such things as watching each other's children, helping with shopping, lending garden or house tools, and other small acts of kindness?"; (2) "How often do you and other people in this neighborhood visit in each other's homes or on the street?"; (3) "How often do you and people in this neighborhood have parties or other get-togethers where other people in the neighborhood are invited?"; (4) "When a neighbor is not at home, how often do you and other neighbors watch over their property?"; (5) "How often do you and other people in the neighborhood ask each other advice about personal things such as childrearing or job openings?" These items tap the kinds of networks and exchanges traditionally thought to underlie mobilization capacity.

24. As control variables we included predictive (1995) survey measures of community-level socioeconomic status, racial composition (percent non-Hispanic black), and the aggregate level of violent victimization in the community. Population density (persons per kilometer) and population size from the 2000 census are also accounted for when modeling 2000 events. See Sampson et al. 2005 for details on the modeling strategy for collective action events. The results were robust to a number of alternative specifications and sensitivity analyses.

25. Employing lagged outcomes is a stringent test because lagged organizational measures are not available and could have accounted for variation in the rate of 1990 collective action. The lack of statistical significance for later organizational services controlling for lagged collective action thus does not necessarily imply a lack of the former's causal salience.

26. We were able to identify and geocode the initiating organization in approximately half of all events given the descriptions in the newspaper, compared to an 87 percent location rate for the events themselves. We did not find any information contrary to the assumption that the availability of initiator address information was distributed more or less randomly across areas.

27. Taub, Taylor, and Dunham 1987, 184.

28. This effort is in collaboration with Doug McAdam (see McAdam, Snellman, and Sampson 2010). The phone fiches list the religious institutions by denomination in addition to telephone numbers and address. We matched the street addresses to a geocoding database maintained by Yahoo and obtained a nine-digit zip code. The addresses that did not match the database were manually checked for spelling errors. Using Google maps, typos and abbreviations

were corrected. The result was a total of 11,057 valid church addresses that were matched to census tracts and eventually to community areas in Chicago. Thanks go to Kaisa Snellman at Stanford for research assistance in collection of the NCCS and church data.

29. Indices based on the first principal component of five highly correlated Herfindahl indexes of concentration (see Blau 1977), where Diversity = $1-\Sigma\Pi_r^2$, and where Π_r refers to a particular group's (e.g., racial/ethnic) proportion of the population. The constituent measures tapped the number and spread of twenty-five language groups, one hundred birth countries of first-generation immigrants, five race/ethnic groups, and both within-Hispanic and within-Asian diversity. A high score on the summary measure reflects multidimensional diversity in the community.

30. Just less than 60 percent of the variance in total initiator/event location rates was explained. The standardized coefficient for the estimated direct effect of nonprofit organizations per hundred thousand on collective action propensity was 0.39 (t-ratio = 3.93, $p < 0.01$). Only residential stability had a larger and perhaps surprisingly negative effect. Stable communities appear to be high in informal but not organizational efficacy, once again suggesting that newer forms of collective action do not conform to traditional patterns.

31. Nonprofit density shows a negative relationship with collective efficacy in figure 8.4, but it is not significantly different than zero and therefore directionality is not meaningful.

32. McAdam 1999 [1982]; Cohen and Dawson 1993.

33. Grossman, Keating, and Reiff 2004, 134.

34. For further details on sampling, coding, and long-term trends, see Sampson et al. 2005. Special thanks go to Heather MacIndoe and Simón Weffer-Elizondo for yeoman efforts in training the coders and managing data collection for the CCCP.

35. Because event counts are highly skewed, with a handful of communities like the Loop dominating the overall count and many recording no events, we calculated nonparametric Spearman correlations of rank-order agreement for each decade and for the aggregate total. Each was significant, with the aggregate coefficient (rho) across the three decades at 0.40 ($p < 0.01$).

36. Sampson et al. 2005, 706. Examples of event overlap include Martin Luther King Day celebrations, Operation PUSH events, fundraisers for UNICEF, a protest over the Contract Buyers League, the Chicago Consular Ball, Hyde Park's Fourth of July Picnic, and a Lawndale art fair.

37. Obama 1988, 4.

38. McRoberts 2003.

39. This pattern holds across the racial divide. In black communities, the coefficients for the density of nonprofits and churches are 0.30 ($p < 0.05$) and 0.00,

respectively. The corresponding coefficients in nonblack communities are 0.22 and 0.00. The church effect is thus nil, even by race.

40. For a more detailed examination of black civil society and the role of the black church, see McAdam, Snellman, and Sampson 2010.

41. *Chicago Tribune*, April 9, 2009.

42. Utica, New York, where I grew up, is a shell of its former self, having lost nearly half its population and with abandoned buildings sprawling block after block from downtown. Yet like countless other small industrial cities—many with large minority and poor populations—it is not on the radar screen of the social science or political elite.

43. Putnam, Feldstein, and Cohen 2003.

44. Skogan and Hartnett 1997.

45. Neighborhood poverty may thus be said to have a conditional relationship with organizational participation. See also Swaroop and Morenoff 2006; Small 2004.

46. Fung 2004.

CHAPTER NINE

1. Abraham 2009. The case received widespread attention around the country and beyond.

2. *Dispatch*: "Were they white, black, or Hispanic?" *Lucia Whalen*: "Uhm, well, they were two larger men. One looked kind of Hispanic but I'm not really sure. And the other one entered and I didn't see what he looked like at all. I just saw [them] from a distance and this older woman was worried, thinking someone's breaking into someone's house. They've been barging in and she interrupted me and that's when I had noticed, otherwise I probably wouldn't have noticed it at all, to be honest with you. So I was just calling because she was a concerned neighbor."

3. "I've had much reflection on that, and yes, I would make the call—I would absolutely do that again," she said. "If you're a concerned citizen, you should do the right thing." Boston.com, July 29, 2009, at http://www.boston.com/news/local/breaking_news/2009/07/911_caller_in_g.html.

4. I set aside further discussion of the validity of Gates's arrest, however, because while important it is not central to my argument.

5. Sugrue 1996.

6. Suttles 1972.

7. Wilson and Taub 2006.

8. Determining whether a crime is motivated by hate, like determining the motive of any behavior, is nonetheless highly problematic. Relying on police accounts renders things even murkier. The finding that neighborhood and county-level social organization are related to the official reporting of hate crimes (Lyons

2007; McVeigh, Welch, and Bjarnason 2003) suggests the difficulty in separating variations in offending behavior from societal reactions.

9. Rawls [1971] 1999, 461; 1993, 37. To Rawls's list we can add safety and security. There is a long literature that comes to the same conclusion—across groups there is a great deal of consensus on rankings of seriousness of crimes and the desire for security (Kornhauser 1978).

10. On his communitarian critics, see Taylor 1989; Selznick 1992; Sandel 2009. Perhaps the most penetrating critique, albeit one that is deeply sympathetic, is found in Amartya Sen's *The Idea of Justice* (2009). Sen takes issue with Rawls by arguing for a comparative and global framework that emphasizes *realized* outcomes in addition to idealized (or what Sen calls "transcendental") institutional principles. In my opinion, however, the critique of Sen does not undermine the basic argument I derive about altruism, much less the essence of Rawls.

11. Rawls [1971] 1999, 458, 463.

12. Gillman (1996) argues that the constitutional law tradition has long sought to balance individual rights against the need to promote the health and safety of communities, and that the very idea of police power signifies the adjudication between individual rights and social order.

13. For a concise explication of the original position, see Rawls 1993, 23–28.

14. For a philosophical analysis that also affirms altruism as a fundamental concept along with prudence, albeit from a different analytical route, see Nagel 1970.

15. Levitt and Dubner (2009) criticize behavioral economic experiments for their artificial setup and maintain that humans can be manipulated to be selfish *or* altruistic. I agree in part but would revise their critique. Humans respond to social context, and the goal, as in this chapter, is to find naturally occurring instances where behavioral aspects of altruism can be systematically observed (and ideally manipulated) across social settings that vary in theoretically relevant ways.

16. A common experimental game gives players A and B a set amount of money. A can offer any amount to B, and, if accepted, both get to keep the money. If B rejects the offer, no one gets a penny. Rational choice theory predicts that because any amount of money is a gain for both, no offer should be rejected, and A should make a low initial offer. But B will reject A's offer if it is perceived as unfair, and the opening offers of A are typically much higher than selfish models predict. For recent reviews on social norms, see Stout 2006; more generally, see Thaler and Sunstein 2008. There is also comparative evidence that a city's rate of helping strangers is a cross-culturally meaningful characteristic of a place (Levine, Norenzayan, and Philbrick 2001).

17. Stout 2006, 14. In terms of political theory, see the discussion by Mansbridge (1990).

18. The main statement on procedural justice is Tyler 1990. The link between Rawls and Tyler's legitimacy principles deserves further scrutiny. For innovative work on bringing "social identity" into mainstream economic theory, see Akerlof and Kranton 2010.

19. This is the essential idea behind social control theory (Sampson and Laub 1993).

20. For an evolutionary theory of group-based selection on altruism, see Sober and Wilson 1998 and Wilson 2002. On cultural selection and varieties of altruism, see Jencks 1990.

21. Rawls 1993, 16.

22. Sampson and Bartusch 1998.

23. Donations to United Way have been proposed (Chamlin and Cochran 1997), but there are sharp disagreements in society over the role of charity versus the State, and this organization in particular has suffered withering criticism. The financial ability to give is also confounded. Healy (2004) provides an innovative analysis of organizational influences on organ donation.

24. Milgram, Mann, and Hartner 1965, 438.

25. Technically, I used a multivariate logistic response model. For further details and analysis of letter-drop conditions, see also Morenoff and House n.d.

26. In general, results were similar regardless of unit of aggregation.

27. Iwashyna, Christakis, and Becker 1999. I thank Nicholas Christakis for his help in obtaining and interpreting the data.

28. Patterson 2004.

29. I used this fact in additional analysis to create another indicator of CPR by specifying witnessing as an instrumental variable because the proportion of witnessed events varies across communities. Specifically, I used witnessing to predict CPR at the cardiac-arrest level, after netting out the effects of age, race, sex, and home location of victim, and then aggregating by community areas to produce an adjusted CPR rate. This technical analysis is beyond the scope of the present chapter, but the results were nonetheless very similar and give me added confidence.

30. Disadvantage and diversity are defined as in earlier chapters for both 1990 and 2000.

31. Specifically, I created an Empirical Bayes Residual scale that simultaneously adjusts for the cardiac-arrest and neighborhood predictors at the time of event from a multilevel model.

32. In this model, the t-ratio for the organization coefficient was 4.64 ($p < 0.01$).

33. Specifically, I estimated a multivariate multilevel analysis of 3,303 letters nested within neighborhood clusters and community areas, but the main re-

sults focus on the latter. As an outcome I estimate the log-odds of letter returns. Formally, the baseline model can be expressed as:

Letter Model: Prob(Return = 1|B) = P log[P/(1-P)] = B0 + B1*(Post-anthrax) + B2*(Sept. or Oct.) + B3*(Nov.) + B4*(Dec.) + B5*(Jan.) + B6*(Feb. or March) + B7*(Afternoon) + B8*(Windy) + B9*(Rain) + B10*(Address type) + B11*(Observed) + B12*(Weekday) + B13*(Suspicious) + B14*(People on street) + B15*(Residential) + B16*(Parking lot) + B17*(Waterfront) + B18*(High-rise private) + B19*(High-rise public) + B20*(Single-unit public) + B21*(Single private)

Level-2 Model: B0 = G00 + G01*(Size 2000) + G02*(Density 2000) + G03*(Disadvantage 2000) + G04*(Stability 2000) + G05*(Diversity 2000) + U0.

34. The standardized coefficient for concentrated disadvantage was −0.71 ($p < 0.01$), controlling for all letter-drop conditions and other neighborhood characteristics. Organizational density and population size were also significant predictors (B = 0.34 and 0.26, respectively), whereas race/ethnic diversity, residential stability, and population density were not significant. To explain the disadvantage finding, one person suggested to me that poor neighborhoods might have fewer mailboxes. I have no way of knowing whether this is true, but the research design works against this explanation, in any case. Letters were randomly distributed throughout the neighborhoods, and thus the majority of drops were not in close proximity to a mailbox. One had to pick up the letter and mail it somewhere different from the point of retrieval. I would further argue that the numerous controls for land use and housing type adjusts for "mailbox proximity" across community areas.

35. The reader will not be surprised to learn that blacks and Hispanics are significantly more likely than whites to perceive legal norms as less than binding, and that low SES respondents are twice as likely as high SES respondents are to report high levels of legal cynicism. This pattern occurs in both the 1995 and 2002 surveys. Yet once neighborhood disadvantage is taken into account, blacks hold views about legal norms and police behavior similar to those of whites (see also Sampson and Bartusch 1998). Blacks are more cynical because they are more likely to live in environments of concentrated disadvantage. At the same time, minority groups are more intolerant of deviance and fighting than whites, even taking into account neighborhood-level factors. The analyses in this chapter were rechecked by controlling for neighborhood differences in tolerance of deviance. The results were not affected.

36. The Kaiser-Meyer-Olkin measure of sampling adequacy indicates the proportion of variance in observed variables that is likely caused by an underlying factor. In the present case this figure is 50 percent, which given the elapsed time is surprisingly high and supports, once again, the theoretically based hypothesis of a latent altruistic character.

37. In this analysis, the first principal component accounted for 68 percent

of the common variance in letter-return rates in 2002 and collective efficacy 1995–2002. Given the much longer passage of time, it is perhaps expectable that the adjusted CPR rate from 1988 did not correlate strongly with the later survey measure of collective efficacy.

38. Crime rates are measured as the log of the rate per hundred thousand residents for the years 2002 through 2006 for homicide. I also examined burglary and robbery rates. These are widely considered the three most valid and reliably measured of all crimes.

39. For more on this link, see Browning, Leventhal, and Brooks-Gunn 2004, 2005. In addition, I would argue that the assumption of uncorrelated error terms between the altruism scale and teen births is reasonable, given the passage of time and the very different nature of the specific acts in question. Once demographic and economic composition is controlled, the assumption of uncorrelated error terms with respect to crime is reasonable as well.

40. Sampson and Bartusch 1998.

41. Because of the relatively small number of cases overall, I opt for theoretical parsimony in figure 9.2, with control variables limited to the major hypothesized confounders in terms of neighborhood composition. That said, I conducted a number of additional tests to explore the robustness of the main pattern of results. For example, I controlled for alternative demographic markers in the form of concentrated poverty and percent black, along with systemic factors such as residential stability and organizational density. I also examined social process variables such as friend/kinship ties, exchange networks, and organizational density, which I showed above was a key predictor of altruism. Although there were some fluctuations depending on the model specification, the basic pattern remained. The results were largely similar for burglary rates and robbery rates in 2002–6 as well, suggesting the crime pattern is especially robust.

42. For homicide, the standardized coefficients for letter drop/CE and CPR were –.039 (t-ratio = –3.80; $p < 0.01$) and –0.11 (t-ratio = –1.93; $p < 0.10$), respectively. The comparables for teen birth rates were –0.23 (t-ratio = –2.50) and –0.20 (t-ratio = –3.78), both $p < 0.05$. The separate indicator of CPR altruism thus has relatively greater predictive power for teen birth rates than homicide.

43. This pattern broadly supports the arguments of Patterson (2004, 2009). It is worth noting as well that I found no evidence that collective efficacy (or trust or cohesion) was associated with selfish norms (so called negative social capital) or anti-altruistic behavior.

CHAPTER TEN

1. Tobler 1970:236.

2. For a debate on the "first law," see Goodchild 2004 and response in Tobler 2004.

3. For what is probably the classic statement on the spatial ecology of interaction, one still alive and well, see Festinger, Schachter, and Black 1950. More recently, see Blau 1977.

4. I am indebted to Jeff Morenoff and Corina Graif for their collaborative work on spatial analyses in earlier papers. This chapter is not an appropriate forum for details on statistical modeling. See Morenoff et al. 2001 and Graif and Sampson 2009 for more on methodology. For a discussion of spatial models, see also Messner et al. 1999; Tita and Cohen 2004.

5. For a primer on spatial statistics, see Anselin (1988). Moran's I is the unstandardized regression-slope coefficient of *y* predicting *Wy*. Like a correlation, it has an upper limit of 1 so that the higher the number, the higher the positive spatial correlation. A "pseudo"-significance test of spatial correlation is calculated by comparing observed correlations with a distribution of randomly permuted ones. Results are similar with weights based on the four closest neighborhoods.

6. This pattern suggests that the spatial interdependence estimates are conservative, although it should be noted that the density of nonprofit organizations is well measured and yet not very interdependent with its spatial neighbors. As will be shown in chapter 14, organizational mechanisms take on a higher-order structure that goes beyond nearest neighbors.

7. Morenoff, Sampson, and Raudenbush 2001. See also Sampson, Morenoff, and Earls 1999 for a spatial analysis of child-related dimensions of collective efficacy and "social capital."

8. In earlier chapters I therefore opted to present the simpler rather than more complex findings when the substantive results were robust to the introduction of spatial errors. This chapter is mainly focused on the "value added" of a direct spatial analysis, especially the roles of spatial lag and spatial heterogeneity, to which I now turn, and the concept of spatial advantage.

9. In technical terms we can define y_i as the homicide rate of Neighborhood (N) i, and w_{ij} as element i,j of a spatial weights matrix that expresses the geographical proximity of N_i to N_j (Anselin 1988, 11). For a given observation i, a spatial lag $\Sigma_i w_{ij} y_j$ is the weighted average of homicide in neighboring locations. This can be defined in different ways, but in the present data the patterns are robust to alternative spatial weights. For the most part PHDCN work has used what is called first-order contiguity, which defines neighbors as those Ns that share a *common border* (referred to as the rook criterion). Thus, $w_{ij} = 1$ if i and j are contiguous, 0 if not. Similar results obtain when using the four or six nearest neighborhoods to a focal neighborhood, as in the Moran's I plots. To test formally for the independent role of spatial dependence in a multivariate model, the spatial lag is treated as an *explanatory* variable. The spatial lag regression model is thus: $y = \rho WY + X\beta + \varepsilon$, where y is an N by 1 vector of observations on the dependent variable; Wy is an N by 1 vector composed of elements $\Sigma_i w_{ij} y_j$, the spatial lags for

the dependent variable; ρ is the spatial autoregressive coefficient; X is an N by K matrix of exogenous explanatory variables with an associated K by 1 vector of regression coefficients β; and ε is an N by 1 vector of normally distributed random error terms, with means 0 and constant variances.

10. Technically, the notion of diffusion implies a process that occurs over time, whereas the spatial autocorrelation we have examined are point-in-time—homicide rates are spatially interrelated across neighborhoods and simultaneously determined. Further details about the maximum likelihood estimation are available in published work (Morenoff, Sampson, and Raudenbush 2001).

11. Although spatial error cannot be definitively distinguished from spatial lags, there are empirical tests to explore which process is more consistent with the data. I conducted these tests and only estimated spatial lag models where the data indicated a better fit and where there was strong theoretical motivation to posit spatial diffusion or exposure-like effects. The fact remains, however, that the assumptions behind a spatial lag model are not possible to prove in the data.

12. Morenoff and Sampson 1997.

13. Sampson, Morenoff and Earls, 1999.

14. Morenoff, Sampson, and Raudenbush 2001.

15. Sampson and Wilson 1995.

16. African Americans are approximately six times more likely to be murdered than whites (Fox and Zawitz 2003), and homicide remains the leading cause of death among young African Americans (Anderson 2002). That alone makes violence surface as perhaps the major challenge to the viability of cities and pursuit of racial equality. Both police records and self-reported surveys continue to show disproportionate involvement in serious violence among blacks, and nearly one in three black males will enter prison during their lifetime compared to less than 5 percent of white males. Even as crime continues to decline, African Americans are at increasing risk of incarceration and subsequent weak attachment to the labor force (Western 2006), reinforcing black disadvantage and involvement in crime.

17. This conclusion is confirmed in two assessments of the available literature from 1995 to approximately 2005 (Peterson and Krivo 2005; Pratt and Cullen 2005). In the meta-analysis of Pratt and Cullen, concentrated neighborhood disadvantage is the largest and most consistent predictor of violence across studies. Peterson and Krivo find substantial similarity in the basic pattern of relationship with both blacks and whites. There are exceptions here and there, as expected, but the general trend is thus more similarity than dissimilarity in basic pattern.

18. Shaw and McKay's ([1942] 1969) observation in Chicago from over half a

century ago is worth repeating: "The important fact about rates of delinquents for Negro boys is that they too, vary by type of area. They are higher than the rates for white boys, but it cannot be said that they are higher than rates for white boys in comparable areas, since it is impossible to reproduce in white communities the circumstances under which Negro children live. Even if it were possible to parallel the low economic status and the inadequacy of institutions in the white community, it would not be possible to reproduce the effects of segregation and the barriers to upward mobility" (614).

19. Pattillo-McCoy 1999.

20. Sampson, Morenoff and Earls (1999) constructed hypothetical simulations in which the mean level of *Wy* in white neighborhoods was assigned to black neighborhoods, thus equalizing the spatial inequalities between the two groups. The results suggested that, all else being equal, giving black neighborhoods the same mean spatial proximity scores as white neighborhoods reduces the racial gap in child-centered social control by 38 percent and the gap in adult-child exchange by 64 percent. Performing the same exercise using concentrated disadvantage rather than spatial proximity reduces the racial gap in child control by 56 percent, but produces no change in the racial gap in adult-child exchange. These simulations provide further evidence that the differing spatial environments of black and white neighborhoods play a role equal to if not greater than that of internal structural characteristics in generating inequalities in collective efficacy.

21. Saenz 2004.

22. Martinez 2002; McNulty and Bellair 2003a, 2003b.

23. Sampson, Morenoff, and Raudenbush 2005.

24. The estimated probability that an average male living in a high-risk neighborhood without immigrants will engage in violence is almost 25 percent higher than in the high-risk immigrant neighborhood, a pattern again suggesting the protective rather than crime-generating influence of immigrant concentration. This finding is broadly consistent with other research (Martinez 2002).

25. Sampson 2006, 2008c.

26. Sutherland 1947.

27. We first constructed a Herfindahl index of the concentration in census tracts of twenty-five distinct foreign languages in order to capture a broad range of immigrant-related diversity. A second measure of percent foreign born yielded a broadly similar albeit somewhat weaker pattern. For details, see Graif and Sampson 2009, from which Figure 10.3 is adapted.

28. Interestingly, the estimated effects of collective efficacy remained significant but did not vary spatially, suggesting a space-invariant process unlike immigrant diffusion.

29. Anderson 1999.

30. Huntington 2004.

31. Nisbett and Cohen 1996.

32. For more on my immigration penetration thesis, see Sampson 2008c.

CHAPTER ELEVEN

1. Briggs, Popkin, and Goering 2010.

2. See "American Murder Mystery" (Rosin 2008).

3. Kling, Liebman, and Katz 2007, 109. See also Oakes 2004. Considering that over a century of neighborhood ecological research forms the baseline, this is high praise for one study.

4. NBER 2006.

5. Clampet-Lundquist and Massey 2008. Destination neighborhoods were still segregated (> 75 percent black on average), whether for the control or experimental group. See also Sampson 2008b.

6. Note that situational effects can still be persistent and form an enduring pattern. For example, our research in Chicago shows that while collective efficacy consistently predicts the event rate of violence in a neighborhood, including into the future (chapter 7), it does not predict rates of offending by neighborhood youth, the latter of which may occur anywhere (Sampson, Morenoff, and Raudenbush 2005).

7. Schlossman and Sedlack (1983) provide a review of the idea and empirical content of the community-level interventions animating the Chicago Area Project (CAP) up until the 1980s, which grew out of the delinquency-related research of Shaw and McKay reviewed in chapter 2. CAP celebrated its seventy-fifth anniversary in 2010. Population-level interventions are better established in public health, including the experimental randomization of macrolevel ecological units to causal treatments (Boruch and Foley 2000; Sikkema et al. 2000).

8. The HOPE VI federal housing program and the New Communities Program of the MacArthur Foundation (http://www.newcommunities.org/) represent two examples of a governmental and private intervention at the macro level, respectively. I make no claims here on success or failure, the point is to further contrast the individual versus neighborhood question. For a counterfactual approach to neighborhood interventions, see Verbitsky and Raudenbush 2006.

9. Orr et al. 2003, appendix C2.

10. Langer and Michael 1963.

11. Although for somewhat different reasons, the indiscriminate use of control variables was the subject of a detailed warning by Stanley Lieberson over twenty years ago (1985, chap. 6).

12. See Clampet-Lundquist and Massey 2008 and Ludwig et al. 2008.

13. Sampson 2008b. This chapter refines my earlier argument and presents new data.

14. Following MTO publications, I begin with census tracts as analytic units because they permit me to link geocoded address data over time. For the city of Chicago *and* the United States as a whole (representing over sixty-five thousand census tracts), one linear factor was extracted on the basis of a principal components analysis of poverty, welfare assistance, female-headed families, unemployment, and percent black (see also Sampson, Sharkey, and Raudenbush 2008). I thus focus on a summary scale of concentrated disadvantage rather than a single item. In later analysis I look at measures beyond disadvantage.

15. Sampson 2008b, figure 1.

16. The racial composition difference was not significantly different across treatment groups. It is important to note that "scaling up" to account for complier status simply scales up standard errors too, and thus does not change the significance (or not) of differences.

17. Linear differences in the principal components scale of concentrated disadvantage, which weights poverty more than race, are significant by treatment group ($p < 0.05$). A z-score scale including all U.S. and Chicago area moves is not significantly different.

18. All t-tests use randomization weights recommended in Ludwig et al 2008. As noted above, adjusting for compliance status does not change any conclusions regarding significance.

19. What about interim moves? I have focused on destination neighborhoods for theoretical reasons, but consistent with MTO publications I found a significant ($p < 0.01$) nine-point difference between the experimental and control group in duration-weighted poverty. However, the duration-weighted difference for percent black is only two points and not significant ($p < 0.05$).

20. This is consistent with prior research showing no effect on neighborhood employment change (Kling, Liebman, and Katz 2007, web appendix, table F14).

21. Residents in the 2002 community survey were asked: "How many close friends and relatives do you have (people that you feel at ease with, can talk to about private matters, and can call on for help)?" "How many friends and relatives do you have to whom you can turn when you need to borrow something like a household object or a small amount of money or need help with an errand?" "How many friends and relatives do you have who you can ask for advice or information?" In each question respondents provided the number of friends. I created an overall scale based on the mean for each Chicago community across the three dimensions.

22. These indicators were highly interrelated and comprised just one factor, so I took the first principal component to reflect the common variance.

23. I selected a random sample of the experimental group to equalize sample sizes and provide a balanced and easier-to-see comparison. Using the full sample produces a similar pattern.

24. See also Sampson 2008b, figure 5.

25. There were no significant differences between treatment and control groups at the community-area level for the eleven survey-based social processes independently measured in PHDCN, both level and change. I also examined spatial "neighbors of the neighborhood" at the census-tract level by calculating the spatial lag of poverty and disadvantage using a Euclidean distance-based measure—the average of neighboring tracts weighted by distance from the focal tract. Neither spatially lagged poverty nor concentrated disadvantage were significantly different between treatment and controls. At destination the magnitude of difference in spatially lagged percent poverty was less than 1.5 percentage points.

26. For a disadvantage map, see Sampson 2008b, 220.

27. For maps of Baltimore moves in MTO, see Clark 2005.

28. Sharkey 2008. According to Sharkey, this means that in a fundamental sense the "ghetto is inherited." He is further examining this notion in a book in progress.

29. Zorbaugh 1929, 134.

30. Basically, SUTVA means that potential outcomes for one unit are unaffected by the particular assignment of treatments to other units. For further discussion, see Sobel 2006.

31. Deaton 2008, 4.

32. Wheaton and Clarke 2003.

33. Shonkoff and Phillips 2000, chap. 8.

34. Sharkey 2008.

35. Sampson, Sharkey, and Raudenbush 2008.

36. I set aside the statistical details here, but the main strategy was to adapt a method pioneered by Jamie Robins for causal inference with time-varying data: inverse probability of treatment weighting (IPTW); see Robins 1999; Robins, Hernan, and Brumback 2000; Hong and Raudenbush 2008. The intuition is that one wants to give more priority to data observations that are unconfounded with observable predictors of selecting into the treatment. In the following chapter I will present validating information on the causes of residential sorting that were used in the model. Because whites and Hispanics were not exposed to concentrated disadvantage in anything near a comparable way, our analysis of verbal ability focused on African American children. For details see Sampson, Sharkey, and Raudenbush 2008.

37. Shonkoff and Phillips 2000.

38. See also Sampson 2008b. The t-ratio for this estimated effect is 2.74

($p < 0.01$). When including twelve-year-olds there is also a significant cohort-by-treatment interaction.

39. Sampson 2008b, 852.

40. Informative models of selection and neighborhood effects can still be applied to MTO. Corina Graif is exploring spatial effects in her Ph.D. dissertation in all five MTO sites, and long-term follow-up of the MTO will allow for a more rigorous test of developmental effects (see also Ludwig et al. 2008). To the extent that significant (although still marginal) differences in the local neighborhood and larger spatial environment are maintained as a result of the original voucher offers, then the chances of observing developmental treatment effects will be increased. Moreover, a recent study comparing the Chicago samples of MTO and PHDCN along with another voucher study found similar negative effects of concentrated disadvantage on verbal ability (Burdick-Will et al. 2011). This relationship thus appears to be sturdy across studies and method of assessment.

41. This section updates my earlier assessment in Sampson 2008b. I return to a discussion of experimental design and social causality in the final section of this book.

42. By following the youngest MTO children further in time, one can gain more leverage on developmental interactions, making the third follow-up of MTO an important scientific investment even though the design limitations analyzed in this chapter will remain.

43. Technically, SUTVA means that the causal effect estimate in MTO is the difference between the average treatment effect and the "spillover" effect on the untreated (Sobel 2006, 1405). Not only are spillover effects of great substantive interest, policy inferences could be led significantly astray by not distinguishing these two components of the treatment effect.

44. Hudgens and Halloran 2008; Rosenbaum 2007; Berk 2005. I set aside here discussion of other and perhaps even more demanding assumptions that analysts of the MTO must adopt in order to make causal inferences, such as the assumption that compliers in the experiment were no more likely to benefit from a neighborhood move than others. This is a strong assumption, as is the assumption of parallel effects of posttreatment mediators. None of these assumptions are subject to direct empirical verification and thus must be asserted as part of a social theory.

CHAPTER TWELVE

1. Ahmed and Little 2008.

2. Ludwig et al. 2008, 150.

3. Heckman 2005.

4. Alba and Logan 1993. See also Logan and Alba 1993; Logan et al. 1996.

5. Massey and Denton 1985.

6. Logan 1978. But see chapter 2, where I noted the nuances in Chicago School theory that, with the exception of Suttles (1972), have gone largely unremarked.

7. See, e.g., Massey, Gross, and Shibuya 1994; South and Crowder 1997, 1998.

8. Crowder, South and Chavez, 2006.

9. This chapter builds on the analysis in Sampson and Sharkey 2008. A later review of selection bias and residential mobility consistent with this chapter is Bergström and Ham 2011.

10. Faris and Dunham 1939 [1965].

11. Clausen 1991.

12. Measure based on the revised conflicts scale (Straus et al. 1996), with reliability 0.84.

13. Walters et al. n.d.; Kessler and Mroczek 1997.

14. Elder, Johnson, and Crosnoe 2003; Settersten and Andersson 2002.

15. For descriptive statistics on neighborhood outcomes and all covariates at the individual and family levels, along with details on the analytic modeling strategy, see Sampson and Sharkey 2008. If individuals dropped out of the study, their information was excluded *only* in the wave(s) in which they did not take part in the survey. We adjusted for any bias that might arise due to attrition by modeling the probability that individuals would leave the study at each wave, and then weighting the data in the time-varying file based on the inverse probability of attrition. Also, for individuals who were interviewed in a given wave but did not provide information for a specific variable, we used a multiple imputation procedure for missing values. Finally, to estimate the effects of within-household change (e.g., in income) on change in neighborhood environments, predictors of neighborhood attainment are decomposed into between-individual (time-stable) and within-individual (time-varying) components. Approximately a quarter of the variance in neighborhood income is due to change over time.

16. The reliability of the slope of change in median income for stayers in the neighborhood is 0.59; for movers out of the city, it is 0.84; and for movers within the city, it is 0.75. These results confirm the substantial "signal" in the data in terms of differences in the rate of change in neighborhood income over time. All results are weighted to account for potential attrition bias.

17. Results were nonetheless consistent with expectations. For example, consistent with the spatial assimilation model, household income and education are strong predictors of neighborhood income. Compared to high school graduates, caregivers with at least a college degree are estimated to live in neighborhoods where the median income is roughly $2,500 higher. Compared to families with total household income in the range of $30,000–$40,000 per year, being in the highest income group (household income over $50,000) is associated with a jump in neighborhood median income of about $7,400. By contrast, being in

the lowest income group (less than $10,000) is associated with a drop in neighborhood median income of $2,500 relative to the reference group. *Change* in household income leads to improvement in the neighborhood environment—individuals who entered the highest income group during the course of the study shifted their residences into more affluent neighborhoods. See Sampson and Sharkey 2008, 15–19.

18. Rossi 1980. On later work, see Lee, Oropesa, and Kanan 1994; Crowder 2000.

19. Sampson and Sharkey 2008, table 4.

20. On racial attitudes, see Charles 2000. For an analysis that provides direct evidence on the reemergence of racial segregation among those who moved to integrated neighborhoods, see Sharkey 2011.

21. T-ratio = 2.15 ($p < 0.05$). I also simultaneously examined measures of other social processes, such as exchange networks, personal victimization, and organizational participation in the neighborhood, but none of these were significant. Shared perceptions of disorder stand out.

22. Herrnstein and Murray 1994; Wilson and Herrnstein 1985. Although IQ and impulsivity measures were only available for children in the household, the "nature" argument rests on the reported high degree of heritability in both constructs across generations. I took the means for those families with two or more children.

23. Kirk 2009a.

24. Details presented in Sharkey and Sampson 2010. This analysis takes into account and adjusts for all the stable and time-varying confounders described earlier in this chapter. Using a dynamic modeling strategy described in Sampson, Sharkey, and Raudenbush 2008, our basic strategy was to first model the predictors of moving and then use these results to inform an analysis that isolated the time-varying effects of moving on later individual outcomes. Analogous to a propensity score method, we obtained balance on the covariate set and describe the pros and cons of assumptions underlying the method. We also used an "instrumental variable" approach that makes different assumptions but yields similar results.

25. There was no significant effect of moving out of Chicago on violent victimization for the propensity-based method, but there was using an instrumental variables approach. Interestingly, further analysis showed that moving was largely unrelated to other nonviolent outcomes, such as school performance, alcohol use, and verbal ability. The specificity of the findings suggests that a method artifact is not driving the consistency of the violence results.

26. With the exception of Quillian's (1999) analysis, studies of change in neighborhood attainment typically focus on individual processes and not their aggregate consequences. There is a rich literature that uses formal simulations

to estimate how neighborhood racial segregation is produced. Schelling (1971) is the classic statement on how individual preferences translate into a segregated residential structure. Through simulations, he showed that collective sequences of mobility decisions made by individual actors responding to their divergent preferences for neighborhood composition can lead to more segregation than any individual would prefer, a "threshold" or tipping-point effect. However, using data on neighborhood preferences, Bruch and Mare (2006) find that the probability of moving increases in a continuous rather than nonlinear manner as more and more members of an outgroup enter the neighborhood. The lower levels of segregation produced by Bruch and Mare's simulations raise the possibility that preferences, by themselves, cannot explain residential patterns in America.

27. Similar to any research design that follows the same individuals as they move over time, we cannot capture changes in neighborhood composition due to inmigration by nonsample members (e.g., migration from Mexico or into Chicago from the suburbs). The analysis of flows is also constrained by the supply of destination neighborhoods, especially nonpoor areas in the suburbs with predominantly minority populations.

28. For details see Sampson and Sharkey 2008, 24. Rather than analyze the difference between the number of a certain race/income group making a transition in one direction and the number making the same transition in the opposite direction (e.g., Quillian 1999), we examined flows between neighborhoods occurring in each direction separately. We chose the threshold of a 5 percent transition to balance a concern for discovery with a concern for emphasizing common, systematic patterns of movement across neighborhoods. In other analyses we explored race-specific flows, different thresholds for transition, alternative definitions of poverty, and applied design stratification weights. The basic flow patterns were robust.

29. This flow consists almost entirely of Latinos moving from predominantly white origin areas into Latino neighborhoods. Race-specific flows also document that 80 percent of whites transition into (or remain in) neighborhoods that are predominantly white *and* nonpoor.

30. The same holds for other communities that have achieved stable integration: "In places like Beverly. . , there are institutions to promote inclusiveness and integration" (Trice 2008).

CHAPTER THIRTEEN

1. Christakis and Fowler 2009; Watts 2003. For a review of the major insights of network research in the social sciences, see Borgatti et al. 2009.

2. See Fischer 1982.

3. Graif and Sampson 2010; Sampson and Graif 2010.

4. Massey and colleagues (1990) present a leading example of international migration as a network.

5. Household address information at all three waves of the PHDCN was geocoded and linked to census-tract codes, allowing us to trace changes in the residential locations of sample members occurring over the course of the study by tracts, neighborhood clusters, and community areas. Ties (arrows) are adjusted to account for sampling weights at the household level, and moves are calculated as a proportion of the sampled neighborhood population at baseline. Sampling weights account for the stratified neighborhood selection and the within-cluster probabilities of selection based on age of child. Weighted data are thus reflective of the targeted Chicago population. Moving flows outside the city are not shown, but analyses below adjust for the differential probabilities of residents in each neighborhood to leave the city. Similar results occur for indegree and outdegree based on the eighty sampled neighborhood clusters (Graif and Sampson 2010: Sampson and Graif 2010).

6. Any community in Chicago can receive movers and so *in*degree reflects all areas. Over 85 percent of Chicago neighborhoods received a PHDCN mover. By contrast, neighborhoods that were not included in the original sample have an *out*degree (and corresponding size) of zero.

7. The reader can thus zoom in on any community of interest. To link names to area identifiers not named in the figure, see Chicago Fact Book Consortium 1990 or http://www.cityofchicago.org/city/en/depts/doit/supp_info/citywide_maps.html.

8. McPherson, Smith-Lovin, and Cook 2001, 431. See also Blau 1977.

9. Wellman 1996.

10. Burt 1987; Galaskiewicz and Wasserman 1989.

11. Price-Spratlen 1999; Massey et al. 1990.

12. Sugrue 1996; Bursik and Grasmick 1993.

13. The thesis of the defended community would also predict this pattern (Suttles 1972).

14. Details for the underlying analyses are elaborated in Graif and Sampson 2010. We applied a multiple regression quadratic assignment procedure (MRQAP) that excludes the diagonals (Krackhardt 1988, 1992) and accounts for network-specific dependencies in the dyadic neighborhood data. The data are randomly permuted to form a reference distribution under the null hypothesis of no relationship, from which parameter estimates are calculated and compared against observed estimates to assess significance. Because of this nontraditional method, I emphasize coefficients significant at the 0.05 level. The analysis explicitly controls for dissimilarity between neighborhoods in the proportion

of original residents that moved out of Chicago and dissimilarities in both indegree and outdegree defined earlier.

15. Tests for the overall model indicate that the proportion of random trials yielding a value as large as or larger than the observed estimate of explanatory power is lower than 1 in 1,000. There was only a 3 in 1,000 odds of observing the spatial distance coefficient by chance.

16. Because the sample size of individuals is smaller in nonsampled clusters, this analysis examined binary ties defined by the presence of any move in any direction. The full city analyses also introduced a sample design control, defined as a matrix whose cells equal unity if neighborhoods within dyads were both part of the initial sample, and zero otherwise.

17. This includes the sampled network and all Chicago NCs, with results significant in each household income category except for the high income, sampled network cell ($p < 0.10$).

18. Kefalas 2003; Carr 2006.

19. Pattillo 2007; St. Jean 2007.

20. See the rich account in Kefalas 2003 on the importance of perceived orderliness and the shared narrative of the "The Last Garden" in one of the Southwest Side communities encircled in the right panel of figure 13.4.

21. Pettit and Western 2004; Sampson and Laub 1993; Western 2006.

22. For the full PHDCN sample, I created an indicator based on domestic violence (self-reported by caretakers) and whether any family member had an arrest record. I define "criminal" households as those with unofficial violence within the family *and* a family member with an official arrest history. I also examined a more restrictive measure of adolescent violence based on a self-reported scale validated elsewhere (Sampson, Morenoff, and Raudenbush 2005), with the violent group defined as the highest quartile. The results are similar, but this measure is only available for those PHDCN subjects over twelve years of age, so I focus on family criminality.

23. With few exceptions, these results hold independent of the definition of ties (weighted or binary) and the network analyzed, whether based on the sampled nodes or all the nodes.

24. Sample sizes are not large enough to reliably examine mobility flows by IQ or impulsivity, as these were only measured on children in selected cohorts (see chapter 12).

25. The probability of moving out of Chicago was invariant by depression like it was for crime, and therefore limiting to the city does not bias the results. Fifteen percent of depressed caregivers moved out of the city compared to 16 percent of nondepressed caregivers (not significant). The main pattern of results was also robust to the type of tie—for example, volume of flows or any connection—and to the network analyzed (sampled NCs or citywide).

CHAPTER FOURTEEN

1. Laumann and colleagues in particular made important contributions to the study of elite influence in a small German town and in two American communities (Laumann and Pappi 1976; Laumann, Marsden, and Galaskiewicz 1977). See also Galaskiewicz 1979 and Knoke 1990.

2. Gould 1991 represents an important exception to this general observation. Perhaps the most direct parallel to the current study at the level of between-community comparison of networks isthe Rang Nong Study of fifty-one village networks in Thailand (Entwisle et al. 2007). More generally, the ADDHEALTH study is a recent innovation that has improved our ability to study networks and social context.

3. Janowitz 1975; see especially the critique in Marwell 2007.

4. Campbell 1955.

5. Houston and Sudman 1975; Laumann and Pappi 1976.

6. For example, 93 percent of KeyNet respondents corroborated the community-area name, and 84 percent reported using its officially designated boundaries in carrying out their work.

7. Burt 1995.

8. Granovetter 1978, 1541.

9. An examination of individual ties in selected communities where I had detailed knowledge of actual connections (e.g., Hyde Park) suggested a high degree of construct validity. The leaders at the center of the figure or in the center of cliques are also well known in Chicago. In follow-up qualitative work I interviewed a set of these leaders, described the KeyNet study, and probed the nature of individual and institutional connections. This project is beyond the scope of the present chapter and will be separately reported.

10. For details on network measures generally, see Burt 1980; Wasserman and Faust 1994. For further discussion of the application to the KeyNet study, see Sampson and Graif 2009a.

11. Granovetter 1973, 1374; see also Gans 1962.

12. But as Gans (1974) responded, it was not that bridging ties within the West End were absent, rather it was that external ties to the city's political elites were missing. Either way the network ties went unexamined empirically by both sides in the debate.

13. Because we allowed up to five nominations, the denominator is (5*n*(n-1)), where n refers to the number of citations.

14. For each exponent k, the number in a cell indicates the total number of k-step ties that connect respondent i and respondent j (Burt 1980, 86–88). A new matrix was computed in which the cells register the minimum number of steps it takes for respondent i to reach respondent j. In no case did more than four steps add to the connectedness of these networks, so I stopped at four. I then

recoded all nonzero equal to 1 and computed a new density measure: total # of direct or indirect ties divided by n(n-1). I thank Ezra Zuckerman for early assistance in creating these measures for the original study and Dave Kirk and Corina Graif for research assistance, especially in the second KeyNet panel.

15. Note that community of home residence is a separate matter. One can be a principal in Logan Square, for example, and live in Lincoln Park. For purposes of the analyses in this chapter, I define internal and external ties not by the home residence of the leader but the community in which he or she works or has jurisdiction over.

16. More formally, $\Sigma_j [(\Sigma_i X_{ij}) / \#NOM]^2$, where $\#NOM = \Sigma_i \Sigma_j X_{ij}$ and i indicates a respondent from community k, j refers to an alter nominated by respondent i in community k, and X_{ij} represents a tie (or nomination) from respondent i in community k to any alter j of all alters receiving nomination from respondents in community k. X_{ij} equals 1 if a tie exists and 0 if it does not.

17. Putnam 2000.

18. Let $p_{bc}(a)$ be the proportion of all shortest paths linking community *b* and *c* which pass through *a*. The "betweenness centrality" of community *a* is defined as the sum of all $p_{bc}(a)$ across all pairs of communities, not including a, where *a*, *b*, and *c* are distinct communities in the citywide network of dichotomized ties and the sum is adjusted for network size. Betweenness centrality is a function of the number of times a given community serves as the shortest pathway between any other two communities (Freeman 1977), hence the idea of centrality.

19. Network analysis raises complex issues of bounding and what one defines as the full network. Based on the sampling design, I argue that the KeyNet study either saturated or nearly saturated each domain and that in the latter case the selected respondents are a representative sample. Given the multistage probability sampling of PHDCN areas to begin with, I further argue that the network variability is comparable across the sampled network of forty-seven community areas (and thirty areas in 2002) and that these areas are reflective of nonsampled communities in Chicago. Another analytic issue that is sometimes raised is the size of the network, as there may be an inherent tendency for larger networks to show less density. Although a particular network measure can be sensitive to design features, I tried to err on the conservative side by examining multiple measures wherever possible and relying on those with evidence of construct validity, a relatively simple interpretation, and that produced similar results despite variations in measurement or model specification and adjustment for network size.

20. Community areas are arrayed geographically but not with the precision of typical GIS maps. The network software positions nodes to accommodate size as well (in this case outdegree), so that in some cases the circles are not in the exact geographic center of a given area.

21. Specifically, a cohesive leadership style as indicated by the higher centralization of elite contacts predicts lower homicide rates in a community (t-ratio = −3.09), second only to concentrated disadvantage. Internal centralization yields a similar but slightly stronger link to lower violence. Cohesive leadership predicts lower teen births as well, but at a reduced level of significance ($p < 0.10$), after concentrated disadvantage and organizational density. By contrast, low birth weight is unrelated to leadership networks once these other characteristics are controlled.

22. Network analysis is frequently criticized for being overly technical and emphasizing measurement at the expense of substance, producing highly refined analysis on networks for which there is little inherent interest. I have tried to steer away from a focus on the technical and have emphasized instead the major patterns in the data for theoretically motivated constructs. But one could certainly go further, such as defining subgroup clusters (block modeling) and more refined embeddedness measures for both communities and organizations. I set this task aside for future work.

CHAPTER FIFTEEN

1. Even the discipline of economics, long thought to be hostile to the idea of social context in general and neighborhood effects in particular, is radically changing in ways that I believe this book furthers (see especially the effort of Akerlof and Kranton 2010).

2. Glaeser 2011.

3. Raudenbush and Sampson 1999, chap. 7.

4. http://www.census.gov/apsd/techdoc/cps/cpsnov08c.pdf (see attachments 7 and 8).

5. The National Children's Study (NCS) in the U.S. is also likely to include ecometric measures of contextual social processes. At the societal level, see Hall and Lamont 2009.

6. See, for example, Wikström et al. 2010.

7. Go to http://worldmap.harvard.edu/chicago.

8. See Galster 2011 for a similar argument on the importance of analyzing neighborhood effects at multiple scales of geography. The work of Grannis (2009) lays out the idea of tertiary communities built up by microlevel social interactions that are shaped by street layout.

9. Mumford 1954, 258.

10. Smith 2010, 1

11. Patterson 2004, 2009.

12. Note that such a critique is teleological and subsumed in a macrostructural determinism. That durable inequalities persist across large-scale political and economic change undermines the idea that we can reduce such continuities to only outside forces.

13. Cooley 1902.

14. Suttles 1984; Permentier, Hamm, and Bolt 2009.

15. Chapter 7; Sampson and Bartusch 1998; Sampson, Morenoff, and Raudenbush 2005; Kirk and Papachristos 2011.

16. Patterson 2009, 1. I make no pretense here to be comprehensive in evaluating culture writ large or the seminal work of Bourdieu on cultural reproduction and "habitus" (Bourdieu 1977). On the post-Bourdieu "cultural turn," see Lamont 2000; Small, Harding, and Lamont 2010; Patterson 2004, 2009; Harding 2010. See also Wilson 2009 on the integration of structural and cultural forces within the context of explaining inner-city life, and Small's (2004) integration of Goffman's (1974) frame analysis with neighborhood narratives on organizational participation. Economists have also begun to take culture seriously (Akerlof and Kranton 2010; Akerlof 1980) and more recently a pushback has emerged among sociologists to reclaim culture as causal motivation rather than just rationalization, a position I endorse (see especially the theoretical and empirical project of Vaisey 2009). My focus here is on neighborhood processes and the explanation of continuity.

17. The apparent rejection of any talk of values or norms by the new cultural sociology is rooted, by my reading, in a "straw-man" version of Parsons. While Parsons certainly overreached, to explain deep continuities in social life without recourse to the role of social norms seems shortsighted and, in the end, unconvincing.

18. Mazerolle, Wickes, and McBroom 2010.

19. See also the analysis in Sampson and Graif 2009.

20. Hampton 2010.

21. Collective efficacy at the school level is studied by Kirk 2009b; see also Bryk and Schneider 2002. It does not seem a stretch to imagine that the theoretical ideas of collective efficacy presented here could even be applied to financial firms and the recent economic crisis, which I would argue stems from a failure of control (social regulation) combined with a weakening of shared expectations about moral behavior (e.g., a cynical maximizing of short-term profit for personal gain at the expense of the long-term wellbeing of a company). Cultural norms and deterrence processes might go a long way toward explaining Wall Street actions.

22. This may explain why, in some societal contexts, the cohesion component of collective efficacy appears less important or even a separate factor. In the favelas of Brazil, for example, historical forces have concentrated forms of severe disadvantage such that cohesion may be necessary for survival, but it may not improve social control, especially in the face of armed militias. Violence in rural Mexico dominated by the drug trade is another context in which cohesion

and violence may be related in complex ways. These are important topics for future research.

23. Tocqueville 2000.

24. McQuarrie and Marwell 2009.

25. Small 2009.

26. Robertson 2010. See also Gratz 2010.

27. See especially Marwell 2004, 2007.

28. Ousey and Kubrin 2009; Stowell et al. 2009; Martinez, Stowell, and Lee 2010.

29. The census reports coming out from 2010 show the continuing spread of immigration to the suburbs and countryside across America (Tavernise and Gebeloff 2010).

30. Canada appears broadly similar in this regard. European immigration presents a very different historical context and as a result an apparently different scenario, although the long-term picture is not yet clear.

31. On the importance of simultaneously modeling individual choice and neighborhood change, see Bruch and Mare 2006. See Sharkey 2011 on unselected neighborhood racial change.

32. Deaton 2008.

33. Cartwright 2007. As if to make the point for neighborhood-effects research, consider the unsubtle claim of a recent observer about the Moving to Opportunity experiment: "MTO is the gold standard" (Smolensky 2007, 1016). Educational research has also seen a strong experimental push (Raudenbush 2008), as has the field of criminology, which I explore in more detail elsewhere (Sampson 2010b).

34. Often called "Rubin causality" after the pioneering work of the statistician Donald Rubin, the counterfactual model has become the dominant conceptual framework for casual inference (Holland 1986). For an excellent book-length treatment, see Morgan and Winship 2007. Tools such as propensity score matching, inverse proportional treatment weighting, and instrumental variables are now common in the social sciences as a way to get at causality.

35. See, for example, Kamo et al. 2008; Sikkema et al. 2000; Weisburd et al. 2006.

36. Student mobility and interactional patterns across classrooms thus bear directly on educational experiments (Raudenbush 2008).

37. Wikström and Sampson 2006, 2003. One often hears that experiments are preferable to observational studies because they require fewer assumptions. But experiments just require *different* assumptions. Depending on the behavior, it may even be that experiments make more heroic assumptions than observational studies, as argued in chapter 11.

38. As the philosopher James Woodward argues: "To the advocate of the causal conception, relations of statistical relevance are *beacons guiding our way to crucial explanatory relations*" (Woodward 2003, 350, emphasis added).

39. It is important to distinguish between the random clinical trial (RCT) and "field experiments" that may or may not include randomization. Darwin conducted what I would call biological field experiments in his backyard garden (Boulter 2008). The letter-drop studies in this book represent another type of field experiment—there is intervention but not randomization.

40. Lieberson and Lynn 2002, 1.

41. Naive positivism is properly derided in many quarters, as it is perhaps the last holdout that views causality in a deterministic fashion and frowns on the idea of unobserved mechanisms. Most practicing researchers go about their work addressing probabilistic outcomes, thinking about unobserved mechanisms, and recognizing contingencies. I am one of them. I reject naive positivism and "scientism" but accept the *aspirations* of science, which, broadly defined, I view as a commitment to principles and procedures for the systematic pursuit of knowledge involving the formulation of a problem, the collection of data through observation or experiment, the possibility of replication (science is "public"), and the formulation and testing of hypotheses by a variety of means (science is catholic on method). For an interesting view on causality from the philosophy of science, see Steel 2004 and Reiss 2009. In sociology, see Abbott 1998. My views on causality are probably best described as pragmatist in a critical-realism tradition (Hacking 1999).

42. Abbott 1999. See also chapter 2. The most explicit theoretical statement of human ecology after the original Chicago School was Amos Hawley (1986). But his account fell into some of the same traps as McKenzie's and perhaps even Park and Burgess's, with an emphasis on sustenance mechanisms and the physical environment to the neglect of cultural symbols, change, and social mechanisms of reproduction. Yet the generative insights of ecology and the idea of interacting community systems were not lost, eventually migrating into anthropology with important results. I thank Gerry Suttles for this insight.

43. http://www.cdc.gov/mmwr/preview/mmwrhtml/00056796.htm.

44. Smith 2009.

45. Cartwright 2007, 11.

46. By this logic the sort of claims we often hear of quantitative over qualitative data, or vice versa, are unsustainable. More generally, see Becker (1996), who makes the correct call, I think, on the real issue being the quality of the empirical inference (e.g., ethnography does not own the study of "process" or culture, and it can be quite systematic; quantitative methods can be as nonsystematic and nongeneralizable as an ethnography, and so on). In fact I would say that, while quantitative in nature, the methods of this book are inspired by some of

the same principles as ethnography, especially the systematic focus on context and social process. Duneier's (1999) ethnography, for example, is obviously very different than mine but it shares a similar impulse and a systematic method of social inquiry that I believe aligns with the sort of quantitative investigation of the city undertaken in this book. While also very different, Katz's (2009) ethnographic effort undertakes comparative neighborhood inquiry with a focus on social process. In my research on the life course, I have taken a dual qualitative-quantitative approach to questions of stability and change in the lives of individuals, and so perhaps I see less tension in contrasting forms of data than commonly argued (Laub and Sampson 2003). For a discussion of the role of systematic theory in ethnography, see Wilson and Chaddha 2009. On causal inference and ethnography, see Katz 2001.

47. Lieberson and Horwich 2008. See also their conception of the jury trial as a metaphor for adjudicating evidence in the social sciences.

48. For a description of Snow's methodology, see Johnson 2006.

CHAPTER SIXTEEN

1. Klinenberg's (2002) study of two communities in Chicago after the heat wave of 1995 showed how a natural disaster was mediated by social context in explaining the death toll.

2. In reporting on Daley's decision to not run for reelection, the *New York Times* asserted that "All cities change over time, but Chicago may be in a class by itself" (Saulny 2010).

3. Pattillo 2007. See also Hyra 2008.

4. Technically, Obama hails from Kenwood near East 50th Street, although many locals consider Hyde Park to include up to 47th Street. What is known as North Kenwood (north of 47th) has traditionally been linked with the poorer community of Oakland.

5. For further details on data sources, see Woodstock-Institute 2010. I also calculated the rate of foreclosures that were filed for the years 2007–9, obtaining nearly similar results in the ranking of high- and low-rate communities. However, Washington Park increased dramatically in foreclosures after the fall of 2008. For 2007–9 overall, Riverdale had the highest rate, and, with Englewood and West Englewood, remains in the top five by either measure.

6. The organization traces its founding to a group of religious and block-club leaders bringing together a coalition of over a hundred neighborhood associations, religious institutions, and civic organizations, aided by Saul Alinsky of community-organizing fame. Over the years the organization grew and mobilized residents for numerous causes. http://www.twochicago.org/.

7. Brazier's influence in Chicago is widely recognized, especially on the South Side but also nationally. In October of 2010, he passed away at the age of

eighty-nine, after which President Obama issued a statement noting that Brazier "promoted spiritual empowerment and economic development through his pastorate of Apostolic Church of God and leadership of numerous community organizations and charitable efforts." See http://www.whitehouse.gov/the-press-office/2010/10/22/statement-president-passing-bishop-arthur-m-brazier. His legacy lives on, literally. The Apostolic Church of God's executive board installed Brazier's son, Byron, as pastor in 2008 after the elder Brazier retired. The younger Brazier appears to be catching up to his father's level of connections, having served in a high-level post at the Chicago Housing Authority and sitting on numerous boards.

8. See also Sampson and Bartusch 1998.

9. Sweeney 2010. "That's not the morals and values we live by," chimed in Marc Robertson, an ordained minister, when referring to the intrusion of violence.

10. Pattillo (1998) reports on an earlier manifestation of spatial vulnerability to crime in a middle-class African American community on Chicago's South Side, reinforcing again the powerful mechanisms of social reproduction.

11. Sweeney 2010.

12. Spielman et al. 2010.

13. Sweeney, Gorner, and Germuska 2010.

14. Spielman et al. 2010.

15. I completed this chapter section in August of 2010, just after a trip to Chicago and my last visit to the community of Chatham. The July crime statistics were thus the most recent available at the time. The reader can produce his or her own map for any area of the city, although the temporal window for searching crimes is limited to the three months prior to the date of access. See http://gis.chicagopolice.org/CLEARMap/startPage.htm#.

16. http://www.ceasefirechicago.org.

17. Although I debated with myself whether including a link to the video was sensationalistic, I decided to err on the side of including all relevant information, consistent with my liberal use of citations and documentation throughout the book. For a news report on the story that includes the video of the melee and a later protest by local leaders, see http://www.chicagobreakingnews.com/2009/09/derrion-albert-vigil-and-march-postponed.html.

18. The criminological literature at times has alluded to the idea that poor communities tacitly support gangs (see Kornhauser 1978). I saw none of this in evidence on this day, at least, and none in the broader surveys of Chicago residents. Gang violence is widely condemned.

19. For just such a critique from the conservative side, see MacDonald 2010. Of course, the liberal Daniel Patrick Moynihan long ago voiced similar concerns of the plight of black men and family structure in the black community (see the

discussion in Massey and Sampson 2009). The issue has been taboo, but with the rise of incarceration it is back on the table.

20. Chicago Fact Book Consortium 1990.

21. A nationally popular song by Jim Croce in the 1970s captured common attitudes:

Well 'ole south side of Chicago
Is the baddest part of town
And if you go down there
You better just beware
Of a man name of Leroy Brown.

So begins a string of racial stereotypes, with Leroy Brown a gun-toting thug who drives a large Eldorado, womanizes, fights, and flashes his diamond rings. Cultural stigma by place is real and, as my findings on the perceptions of disorder show, highly persistent. In 2010, many in Chicagoland would still claim the South Side as the baddest part of town. A larger North/South Side distinction applies to the suburbs as well—the "north shore" is widely deemed to be preferable compared to the south suburbs. I know this firsthand, having lived in southern Cook County for twelve years. Although my kids were raised there and I was (and am) deeply fond of the area, eyebrows were often raised when I declared my residence to those living north of Roosevelt Road (and who often had not ventured south, except perhaps to the University of Chicago).

22. Data released in 2010 from the American Community Survey (ACS) are not up to the present task because they are based on averages from 2005 through 2009 (see chapter 5), meaning that the bulk of the ACS predates the recession. My goal is to examine pre- and postrecession estimates.

23. I examined the disadvantage index of poverty, unemployment, welfare, and female-headed families both with and without percent black. Because racial segregation is so tightly bound up with economic and family status, the results are nearly identical. I graph the full index.

24. Burnside is unusually disadvantaged too, but has the smallest population size of all communities in Chicago (less than 3,500 people in 2000) and so the data are more unreliable.

25. Davis 2010.

26. Neighborhood organizational alliances in New York are said to provide an "old fashioned bulwark in a tide of foreclosures" (Powell 2010). Community-based foreclosure prevention has also been reported to work in Minneapolis (Quercia, Cowan, and Moreno 2005).

27. I examined residential stability (home ownership and tenure length), percent non-Hispanic black, concentrated disadvantage (separating out race), and the density of nonprofits as predictors of foreclosure rates in 2007–9. I

also examined 2009 foreclosures, but with fewer filings, the rates were more skewed and not as reliable overall. Controlling for structural characteristics, all of which were measured in 2000, nonprofit density in 2004 was the second-largest predictor of foreclosure filings in 2007–9 (standardized coefficient = –0.35, $p < 0.01$). The largest predictor was percent black (0.56, $p < 0.01$) followed by disadvantage and stability, which were also significant (0.24 and 0.22, respectively). Over 80 percent of the variance was explained, confirming that, like the other phenomena examined in this book, the risk of foreclosure varies sharply and systematically by community characteristics. When I weighted the regression model with the square root of the number of HUD estimated mortgages to account for variability in precision of estimates, similar results were obtained. I also examined diversity (immigration), median household income, and changes during 2000–2009 in the index of CHA and housing-voucher units that were unexpected based prior disadvantage. The basic pattern was upheld.

28. Similar results obtain for burglary (0.78), robbery (0.91), and homicide (0.84), all $p < 0.01$.

29. Specifically, the standardized coefficients are –0.31 and 0.21 (both $p < 0.01$).

30. Again, my goal is not to present a definitive causal analysis but to ask whether the basic patterns that were uncovered earlier continue. The spatial model is a good test, as the lag of violence measure adjusts for both observed and unobserved predictors of violence in a neighborhood's risk profile (see Morenoff, Sampson, and Raudenbush 2001). As in chapter 7, however, I believe that ultimately there is a reciprocal feedback relationship between crime and collective efficacy, but this relationship is not estimable with current data. I am pursuing this issue in current analysis.

31. Standardized coefficient = –0.35 ($p < 0.01$). The CHA/Voucher index of poverty in 2009 was positively and significantly linked to violence in 2010. The number of communities to which a focal area was connected (outdegree) was controlled, but it was not significant. This basic pattern corresponds to the link between the concentration of leadership ties in 2002 and lower homicide rates in 2002–6 that I reported in chapter 14, suggesting a durable organizational component to the social control of violence in a community.

32. The letters were addressed to a person on the "6th Floor" of a building at a street address in Cambridge, Massachusetts (Harvard University was not named). The text was identical to the 2002 study in the business condition letter. The fictitious names of companies and letter-writer signatures (in case the envelope was opened) were randomly varied for added measure. All letters were stamped and addressed with bold type behind water-resistant cellophane. The only unexpected design variation occurred at the end, when I ran out of time and had to drop letters in two communities (Uptown and Irving Park) at night—

no night drops occurred in the 2002 study. Return rates were possibly attenuated by street-sweeper rounds in the early morning and the fact that a number of hours passed between the drops and when passersby would appear in the day. Otherwise I strived to drop letters the same way and in a random fashion across contexts—on the sidewalk, near a mailbox, near a parked car door, and near a business, in particular. I repeated this systematic drop routine across blocks within all nine community areas, using a combination of walking and driving, depending on the type of drop (e.g., sidewalk vs. near a parked car). Within days of my return to Cambridge, dozens of letters began to appear. Ninety percent of the eventual returns appeared within a week, and after two weeks the letters trickled off to zero.

33. I therefore adjusted the return rate in all analyses below by calculating the residual from a regression with the nighttime indicator (coded 1 for Irving Park and Uptown, 0 for others) as the sole predictor of return rates. I compare the 2010 adjusted return rate with the adjusted letter-drop return rate for the early 2000s, so that, overall, conditions are not confounded.

34. In this regression the t-ratio for moral/legal cynicism was −2.62 ($p < 0.05$). I repeated the analysis, controlling for the 2009 foreclosure rate instead of the CHA poverty index, with the same result—moral/legal cynicism from 1995–2002 had a long-term negative association with community-level propensities for other-regarding behavior as revealed in the letter-drop experiment. In similar tests, neither collective efficacy nor the density of nonprofits was directly associated with the 2010 letter-return rate. Although the sample size precludes a definitive analysis, moral/legal cynicism thus stands out among the neighborhood social processes I have considered. For a recent cultural extension of the legal cynicism theory originally set out in Sampson and Bartusch (1998), see Kirk and Papachristos 2011.

CHAPTER SEVENTEEN

1. Kohn 2003.

2. Zorbaugh 1929, 171. Zorbaugh also reported that in the square half-mile vicinity “every year for the past eighteen years there have been from twelve to twenty murders.” For a map of gangland Chicago in 1931, see http://www.encyclopedia.chicagohistory.org/pages/11538.html, where a symbol for Death Corner, centered on West Oak, is shown with the subtitle “50 murders—Count ‘Em” (Grossman, Keating, and Reiff 2004). Some put Death Corner at West Oak and what is now North Cleveland, but which is only about a hundred feet to the east. See also the map in figure 1.2.

3. The reader can see the same site at an undetermined earlier period (I am guessing 2008 or 2009—Google does not date its pictures). The following address was accessed July 28, 2010: http://maps.google.com/maps?rlz=1T4RNWN_enUS

305US300&q=oak+and+cambridge,+chicago,+il&um=1&ie=UTF-8&hq=&hnear=W+Oak+St+%26+N+Cambridge+Ave,+Chicago,+IL+60610&gl=us&ei=4aFQTMvfCoT58AbH5MCVAQ&sa=X&oi=geocode_result&ct=title&resnum=1&ved=0CBMQ8gEwAA. In Street View at the time, the building in my picture can be viewed by looking south. The Cabrini buildings to the northwest are now gone. Across from the abandoned building in figure 17.1 is a still-empty lot, which can be viewed by looking north. A few blocks to the east, one can clearly see the Trump Towers and Loop skyline to the south. To the west are many new housing units, some mixed income.

4. October 13–16, 2010.

5. The faces of the men were drawn in a shape that suggested to me a youthful source. Pictures that I took of these markings are available on request.

6. A modern-day reading of Zorbaugh (1929) repays the effort. He wrote on the increasing "interlocking directorates" (261) among social agencies; community organization as part of revitalizing democracy in the life of city areas (265); segregation and the rise of social distance (242); community perceptions and "mentalities" (244) underlying organizational capacity; the sequential segregation of ethnic and minority groups (127); the lack of dense ties along the Gold Coast (65); why people return to poverty neighborhoods (134–5); spatial distance and the stigma of the South Side to Gold Coast elites—"People in this neighborhood refuse, as a matter of fact, all invitations to tea or dinner on the South Side" (64); and the concentration of leadership ties in the North Side (62). These and other social mechanisms were richly described in ways that bear import, suitably tailored, for today's city.

7. http://www.dreamtown.com/neighborhoods/cabrini-green.html. As of August 10, 2010, residents still remain in the last Cabrini building "freakishly close to the giant REI store, the glitzy British School and the new Whole Foods cathedral" (Smich 2010).

8. *The Urban Villagers* is perhaps the most famous sociological account of the unintended consequences of urban renewal in the mid-twentieth century (Gans 1962). In this case an Italian slum was eradicated in the West End of Boston, suggesting a general mechanism at work.

9. See also Sharkey 2010.

10. Skogan and Hartnett 1997. This is not "broken windows" policing as typically portrayed in the media.

11. Western 2006.

12. Durlauf and Nagin 2011. The motive for privileging the police over prisons is found in the longstanding evidence that the certainty of apprehension is much more effective than severity in reducing crime. Prisons have become the poster child for severity of response, as the painting found on the wall of the Cabrini-Green neighborhood described above so graphically revealed.

13. This argument is consistent with the philosophical underpinnings of chapter 9. Although beyond the scope of my purpose here, it is quite possible to conceive of the "good police stop" using the conceptual tools I articulated. Empirically, there is also evidence that when the police work in good faith with local institutions as partners rather than as outside enforcers, crime control efforts are more accepted *and* more effective. See especially Berrien and Winship 2002.

14. This idea complements an emerging body of scientific evidence (Heckman 2006; Shonkoff and Phillips 2000) that links children, communities, and schools. See Raudenbush 2009 on school organizational reform and current efforts in Chicago to improve schools and the learning environment within disadvantaged neighborhoods.

15. See Wilson 2010, especially for a description of the multifaceted intervention in the Harlem Children's Zone. See also http://www.hud.gov/offices/pih/programs/ph/cn/ and http://www2.ed.gov/programs/promiseneighborhoods/index.html. The Millennium Villages project in Africa is an interesting non-U.S. example of empowering villages and improving both health and the physical infrastructure, very much in the spirit of a community-level theory of wellbeing. See http://www.unmillenniumproject.org/mv/index.htm.

16. Both the Moving to Opportunity program and mixed-income policies such as HOPE VI are cases in point. These and similar programs tend to assume a static equilibrium and do not account for the interdependencies among neighborhoods in social mechanisms or the macrolevel political and social environments that can reinforce segregation.

REFERENCES

Abbott, Andrew. 1997. "Of Time and Space: The Contemporary Relevance of the Chicago School." *Social Forces* 75:1149–82.

———. 1998. "The Causal Devolution." *Sociological Methods and Research* 27: 148–81.

———. 1999. *Department and Discipline: Chicago Sociology at One Hundred*. Chicago: University of Chicago Press.

———. 2001. *Chaos of Disciplines*. Chicago: University of Chicago Press.

———. 2002. "Los Angeles and the Chicago School: A Comment on Michael Dear." *City and Community* 1:33–38.

———. 2007. Mechanisms and Relations. *Sociologica* 2.

Abraham, Yvonne. 2009. "The Gates Affair: Would You Stand for This?" *Boston Globe*, July 21.

Abu-Lughod, Janet. 1999. *New York, Chicago, Los Angeles: America's Global Cities*. Minneapolis: University of Minnesota Press.

Agnew, John A. 2002. *Place and Politics in Modern Italy*. Chicago: University of Chicago Press.

Ahmed, Azam, and Darnell Little. 2008. "Chicago, America's Most Segregated Big City." *Chicago Tribune*, December 26.

Akerlof, George A. 1980. "A Theory of Social Customs, of Which Unemployment May Be One Consequence." *Quarterly Journal of Economics* 94: 749–75.

Akerlof, George A., and Rachel E. Kranton. 2010. *Identity Economics: How Our Identities Shape Our Work, Wages, and Well-Being*. Princeton: Princeton University Press.

Alba, Richard D., and John R. Logan. 1993. "Minority Proximity to Whites in Suburbs: An Individual Level Analysis of Segregation." *American Journal of Sociology* 98:1388–427.

Algren, Nelson. 1951. *Chicago: City on the Make*. Chicago: University of Chicago Press.

Alinsky, Saul. 1946. *Reveille for Radicals*. New York: Vintage Books.

Anderson, Benedict [1983] 1991. *Imagined Communities: Reflections on the Origin and Spread of Nationalism*. London: Verso.

Anderson, Elijah. 1990. *Streetwise: Race, Class, and Change in an Urban Community*. Chicago: University of Chicago Press.

———. 1999. *Code of the Street: Decency, Violence, and the Moral Life of the Inner City*. New York: W. W. Norton & Company Inc.

Anderson, Nels. 1998. *On Hobos and Homelessness*. Edited by R. Rauty. Chicago: University of Chicago Press.

Anderson, R. N. 2002. *Deaths: Leading Causes for 2000*. Hyattsville, MD: National Center for Health Statistics.

Anselin, Luc. 1988. *Spatial Econometrics: Methods and Models*. Dordrecht, Netherlands: Kluwer Academic.

Ariely, Dan. 2008. *Predictably Irrational: The Hidden Forces That Shape Our Decisions*. New York: Harper Collins Publishers.

Banaji, Mahzarin R. 2002. "Social Psychology of Stereotypes." In *International Encyclopedia of the Social and Behavioral Sciences*, edited by N. J. Smelser and P. B. Baltes. Oxford: Elsevier Science Limited.

Bandura, Albert. 1997. *Self Efficacy: The Exercise of Control*. New York: W. H. Freeman.

Becker, Howard. 1996. "The Epistemology of Qualitative Research." In *Essays on Ethnography and Human Development*, edited by R. Jessor, A. Colby, and R. Schweder. Chicago: University of Chicago Press.

———. 1999. "The Chicago School, So-Called." *Qualitative Sociology* 22: 3–12.

Bellair, Paul E. 1997. "Social Interaction and Community Crime: Examining the Importance of Neighbor Networks." *Criminology* 35:677–703.

Bellow, Saul. 1953. *The Adventures of Augie March*. Fiftieth anniversary edition. New York: Viking Press.

Bergström, Lina, and Maarten Van Ham. 2011. "Understanding Neighbourhood Effects: Selection Bias and Residential Mobility." In *Neighbourhood Effects Research: New Perspectives*, edited by M. v. Ham, D. Manley, N. Bailey, L. Simpson, and D. Maclennan. Dordrecht, Netherlands: Springer.

Berk, Richard. 2005. "Randomized Experiments as the Bronze Standard." *Journal of Experimental Criminology* 1:417–33.

Bernasco, Wim, and Richard Block. 2009. "Where Offenders Choose to Attack: A Discrete Choice Model of Robberies in Chicago." *Criminology* 47:93–130.

Berrien, Jenny, and Christopher Winship. 2002. "An Umbrella of Legitimacy: Boston's Police Department-Ten Point Coalition Collaboration." In *Securing Our Children's Future*, edited by G. Katzman. Washington: Brookings Institution Press.

Berry, Brian, and John Kasarda. 1977. *Contemporary Urban Ecology*. New York: Macmillan.

Blau, Peter. 1977. *Inequality and Heterogeneity: A Primitive Theory of Social Structure*. New York: Free Press.

Blumstein, Alfred, and Joe Wallman. 2000. *The Crime Drop in America*. New York: Cambridge.

Bobo, Lawrence. 2001. "Racial Attitudes and Relations at the Close of the Twentieth Century." In *America Becoming: Racial Trends and Their Consequences*, edited by N. J. Smelser, W. J. Wilson, and F. Mitchell. Washington, DC: National Academy Press.

Booth, Charles. 1889. *Life and Labor of the People of London*. London: MacMillan.

Borgatti, Stephen P., Ajay Mehra, Daniel J. Brass, and Giuseppe Labianca. 2009. "Network Analysis in the Social Sciences." *Science* 323:892–95.

Boruch, Robert, and Ellen Foley. 2000. "The Honestly Experimental Society: Sites and Other Entities as the Units of Allocation and Analysis in Randomized Trials." In *Validity and Social Experimentation: Donald T. Campbell's Legacy*, edited by L. Bickman. Thousand Oaks, CA: Sage.

Bottoms, Anthony E., and Paul Wiles. 1992. "Explanations of Crime and Place: Essays in Environmental Criminology." In *Crime, Policing and Place*, edited by D. J. Evans, D. T. Herbert, and N. R. Fyfe. London: Routledge.

Boulter, Michael. 2008. *Darwin's Garden: Downe House and the Origin of Species*. London: Constable.

Bourdieu, Pierre. 1977. *Outline of a Theory of Practice*. Cambridge: Cambridge University Press.

Bourgois, Philippe. 1995. *In Search of Respect: Selling Crack in El Barrio*. New York: Cambridge University Press.

Bowles, Samuel, Steve Durlauf, and Karla Hoff, eds. 2006. *Poverty Traps*. Princeton: Princeton University Press.

Breckinridge, Sophonisba Preston, and Edith Abbott 1912. *The Delinquent Child and the Home*. New York: Charities Publication Committee.

Briggs, Xavier de Souza, Susan J. Popkin, and John Goering. 2010. *Moving to Opportunity: The Story of an American Experiment to Fight Ghetto Poverty*. New York: Oxford University Press.

Brint, Steven. 2001. "Gemeinschaft Revisited: A Critique and Reconstruction of the Community Concept." *Sociological Theory* 19:1–23.

Bronfenbrenner, Urie. 1979. *The Ecology of Human Development: Experiments by Nature and Design*. Cambridge, MA: Harvard University Press.

Brooks, David. 2009. "The Chicago View." *New York Times*, June 5, A21.

Brooks-Gunn, Jeanne, Greg Duncan, and Lawrence Aber, eds. 1997. *Neighborhood Poverty: Policy Implications in Studying Neighborhoods*. Vol. 2. New York: Russell Sage Foundation.

Brooks-Gunn, Jeanne, Greg Duncan, Pamela Kato, and Naomi Sealand. 1993. "Do Neighborhoods Influence Child and Adolescent Behavior?" *American Journal of Sociology* 99:353–95.

Browning, Christopher R. 2002. "The Span of Collective Efficacy: Extending Social Disorganization Theory to Partner Violence." *Journal of Marriage and the Family* 64: 833–50.

Browning, Christopher R., and Kathleen A. Cagney. 2002. "Neighborhood Structural Disadvantage, Collective Efficacy, and Self-Related Physical Health in an Urban Setting." *Journal of Health and Social Behavior* 43: 383–99.

Browning, Christopher R., Seth L. Feinberg, and Robert Dietz. 2004. "The Paradox of Social Organization: Networks, Collective Efficacy, and Violent Crime in Urban Neighborhoods." *Social Forces* 83: 503–34.

Browning, Christopher R., Tama Leventhal, and Jeanne Brooks-Gunn. 2004. "Neighborhood Context and Racial Differences in Early Adolescent Sexual Activity." *Demography* 41: 697–720.

———. 2005. "Sexual Initiation during Early Adolescence: The Nexus of Parental and Community Control." *American Sociological Review* 70: 758–78.

Browning, Christopher R., Danielle Wallace, Seth L. Feinberg, and Kathleen A. Cagney. 2006. "Neighborhood Social Processes, Physical Conditions, and Disaster-Related Mortality: The Case of the 1995 Heat Wave." *American Sociological Review* 71:661–78.

Brubaker, Rogers. 1996. *Nationalism Reframed: Nationhood and the National Question in the New Europe*. Cambridge: Cambridge University Press.

Bruch, Elizabeth E., and Robert D. Mare. 2006. "Neighborhood Choice and Neighborhood Change." *American Journal of Sociology* 112:667–709.

Bryk, Anthony, and Barbara Schneider. 2002. *Trust in Schools: A Core Resource for Improvement*. New York: Russell Sage Foundation.

Burawoy, Michael. 2003. "Revisits: An Outline of a Theory of Reflexive Ethnography." *American Sociological Review* 68:645–79.

Burdick-Will, Julia Anne, Jens Ludwig, Stephen W. Raudenbush, Robert J. Sampson, Lisa Sanbonmatsu, and Patrick T. Sharkey. 2011. "Converging Evidence for Neighborhood Effects on Children's Test Scores: An Experimental, Quasi-Experimental, and Observational Comparison." In *Whither Opportunity? Rising Inequality and the Uncertain Life Chances of Low-Income Children*, edited by G. Duncan and R. Murnane. New York: Russell Sage Foundation.

Bureau of Justice Statistics. 2010. "Prisoners in 2008." http://bjs.ojp.usdoj.gov/content/glance/incrt.cfm.

Bursik, Robert J., Jr. 1986. "Delinquency Rates as Sources of Ecological Change." In *The Social Ecology of Crime*, edited by J. M. Byrne and R. J. Sampson. New York: Springer-Verlag Inc.

———. 1988. "Social Disorganization and Theories of Crime and Delinquency: Problems and Prospects." *Criminology* 35:677–703.

———. 1989. "Political Decision-Making and Ecological Models of Delinquency: Conflict and Consensus." In *Theoretical Integration in the Study of Deviance and Crime*, edited by S. Messner, M. Krohn, and A. Liska. Albany: State University of New York Press.

———. 1999. "The Informal Control of Crime through Neighborhood Networks." *Sociological Focus* 32:85–97.

———. 2009. "The Dead Sea Scrolls and Criminological Knowledge: 2008 Presidential Address to the American Society of Criminology." *Criminology* 47:5–16.

Bursik, Robert J., Jr., and Harold Grasmick. 1993. *Neighborhoods and Crime: The Dimensions of Effective Community Control*. New York: Lexington Books.

Bursik, Robert J., Jr., and Jim Webb. 1982. "Community Change and Patterns of Delinquency." *American Journal of Sociology* 88:24–42.

Burt, Ronald. 1980. "Models of Network Structure." *Annual Review of Sociology* 6:79–141.

Burt, Ronald S. 1987. "Social Contagion and Innovation: Cohesion versus Structural Equivalence." *American Journal of Sociology* 92: 1287–335.

———. 1995. "Social Capital: Short Form Questionnaire." Chicago: University of Chicago. http://faculty.chicagobooth.edu/ronald.burt/research/QUEST.pdf

Cagney, Kathleen A., and Christopher R. Browning. 2004. "Exploring Neighborhood-Level Variation in Asthma: The Contribution of Neighborhood Social Context." *Journal of General Internal Medicine* 19: 229–36.

Cairncross, Frances. 1997. *The Death of Distance: How the Communications Revolution Will Change Our Lives*. Boston: Harvard Business School Press.

Campbell, Donald. 1955. "The Informant in Quantitative Research." *American Journal of Sociology* 60:339–42.

Carr, Patrick J. 2006. *Clean Streets: Controlling Crime, Maintaining Order, and Building Community Activism*. New York: New York University Press.

Cartwright, Nancy. 2007. "Are RCTs the Gold Standard?" *Biosocieties* 2:11–20.

Castells, Manuel. 1977. *The Urban Question: A Marxist Approach*. London: Edward Arnold.

———. 1996. *The Rise of the Network Society*. Oxford: Blackwell.

———. 2000. "Toward a Sociology of the Network Society." *Contemporary Sociology* 29: 693–99.

Cerda, Magdalena, and Jeffrey D. Morenoff. "The Limits of Collective Efficacy." 2009. Ann Arbor: University of Michigan, Department of Sociology.

Chamlin, Mitchell B, and John K. Cochran. 1997. "Social Altruism and Crime." *Criminology* 35:203–27.

Charles Booth Online Archive. 2010. http://booth.lse.ac.uk/cgi-bin/do.pl?sub=view_booth_and_barth&args=531000,180400,6,large,5.

Charles, Camille Zubrinsky. 2000. "Neighborhood Racial-Composition Preferences: Evidence from a Multiethnic Metropolis." *Social Problems* 47:379–407.

Chicago Fact Book Consortium. 1990. *Local Community Fact Book: Chicago Metropolitan Area*. Chicago: Academy Chicago Publishers.

Chicago Housing Authority. 2007. http://www.thecha.org/housingdev/robert_taylor.html.

Choldin, Harvey. 1984. "Subcommunities: Neighborhoods and Suburbs in Ecological Perspective." In *Sociological Human Ecology*, edited by M. Micklin and H. Choldin. Boulder: Westview.

Christakis, Nicholas A., and James Fowler. 2009. *Connected: The Surprising Power of Our Social Networks and How They Shape Our Lives*. Boston: Little, Brown, and Co.

Clampet-Lundquist, Susan, and Douglas S. Massey. 2008. "Neighborhood Effects on Economic Self-Sufficiency: A Reconsideration of the Moving to Opportunity Experiment." *American Journal of Sociology* 114:107–43.

Clark, Kenneth B. 1965. *Dark Ghetto: Dilemmas of Social Power*. New York: Harper and Row.

Clark, William A.V. 2005. "Intervening in the Residential Mobility Process: Neighborhood Outcomes for Low-Income Populations." *Proceedings of the National Academy of Sciences* 102:15307–12.

Clausen, John A. 1991. "Adolescent Competence and the Shaping of the Life Course." *American Journal of Sociology* 96:805–42.

Cloward, Richard A., and Lloyd E. Ohlin. 1960. *Delinquency and Opportunity: A Theory of Delinquent Gangs*. Glencoe, IL: Free Press.

Cohen, Cathy J., and Michael Dawson. 1993. "Neighborhood Poverty and African American Politics." *American Political Science Review* 87:286–302.

Cohen, D. A., B. K. Finch, A. Bower, and N. Sastry. 2006. "Collective Efficacy and Obesity: The Potential Influence of Social Factors on Health." *Social Science and Medicine* 62: 769–78.

Coleman, James S. 1961. "Social Disorganization." In *Contemporary Social Problems: An Introduction to the Sociology of Deviant Behavior and Social Disorganization*, edited by R. K. Merton and R. A. Nisbet. New York: Harcourt, Brace & World.

———. 1986. "Social Theory, Social Research, and a Theory of Action.' *American Journal of Sociology* 91:1309–35.

———. 1988. "Social Capital in the Creation of Human Capital." *American Journal of Sociology* 94:S95–S120.

———. 1994. "A Vision for Sociology." *Society* (November): 29–34.

Conley, Dalton. 2009. *Elsewhere, U.S.A.: How We Got from the Company Man, Family*

Dinners, and the Affluent Society to the Home Office, Blackberry Moms, and Economic Anxiety. New York: Pantheon.

Cooley, Charles H. 1902. *Human Nature and the Social Order*. New York: Scribner's.

Correll, Joshua, Bernadette Park, Charles Judd, and Bernd Wittenbrink. 2002. "The Police Officer's Dilemma: Using Ethnicity to Disambiguate Potentially Threatening Individuals." *Journal of Personality and Social Psychology* 83:1314–29.

Crowder, Kyle. 2000. "The Racial Context of White Mobility: An Individual-Level Analysis of the White Flight Hypothesis." *Social Science Research* 29:223–57.

Crowder, Kyle, Scott J. South, and Erick Chavez. 2006. "Wealth, Race, and Inter-Neighborhood Migration." *American Sociological Review* 71:72–94.

Custers, Ruud, and Henk Aarts. 2010. "The Unconscious Will: How the Pursuit of Goals Operates Outside of Conscious Awareness." *Science* 329:47–50.

Davis, Mike. 1992. *City of Quartz: Excavating the Future in Los Angeles*. New York: Vintage.

Davis, Morris A. 2010. "Reflections on the Foreclosure Crisis." *Land Lines* (July): 3–8.

Dear, Michael. 2002. "Los Angeles and the Chicago School: Invitation to a Debate." *City and Community* 1:5–32.

Deaton, Angus. 2008. "Instruments of Development: Randomization in the Tropics, and the Search for the Elusive Keys to Economic Development." London: The Keynes Lecture, British Academy, October 9th.

De Blij, Harm. 2009. *The Power of Place: Geography, Destiny, and Globalizations's Rough Landscape*. Oxford: Oxford University Press.

Devine, Patricia. 1989. "Stereotypes and Prejudice: Their Automatic and Controlled Components." *Journal of Personality and Social Psychology* 56:5–18.

Drake, St. Clair, and Horace R. Cayton. 1945 [1993]. *Black Metropolis: A Study of Negro Life in a Northern City*. Chicago: University of Chicago Press.

Duneier, Mitchell. 1999. *Sidewalk*. New York: Farrar, Straus & Giroux.

Durlauf, Steven N., and Daniel S. Nagin. 2011. "Imprisonment and Crime: Can Both Be Reduced?" *Criminology and Public Policy* 10:13–54.

Earl, Jennifer, Andrew Martin, John D. McCarthy, and Sarah A. Soule. 2004. "The Use of Newspaper Data in the Study of Collective Action." *Annual Review of Sociology* 30:65–80.

Earls, Felton, and Stephen L. Buka. 1997. *Project on Human Development in Chicago Neighborhoods, NIJ Research Report, Technical Report I. NCJ 163495*. Washington, DC: United States Department of Justice, National Institute of Justice.

Economist. 2006. "Britain: Soothing the Savage Breast." *Economist*, January 14.

——. 2006. "There Goes the Neighbourhood." *Economist*, May 4, 57–58.

Elder, Glen H., Jr., Monica Kirkpatrick Johnson, and Robert Crosnoe. 2003. "The

Emergence and Development of Life Course Theory." In *Handbook of the Life Course*, edited by J. Mortimer and M. Shanahan. New York: Kluwer Academic/ Plenum.

Ellison, Ralph. 1947. *Invisible Man*. New York: Random House.

Emporis Buildings. 2007. http://www.emporis.com/en/wm/bu/?id=102119.

Entwisle, Barbara, Katherine Faust, Ronald Rindfuss, and Toshiko Kaneda. 2007. "Networks and Contexts: Variation in the Structure of Social Ties." *American Journal of Sociology* 112:1495–533.

Etzioni, Amitai. 1993. The Institute for Communitarian Policy Studies. http:// www.gwu.edu/~ccps/index.html.

——. 1997. *The New Golden Rule: Community and Morality in a Democratic Society*. New York: Basic Books.

Faris, Robert E., and Warren H. Dunham. 1939. *Mental Disorders in Urban Areas: An Ecological Study of Schizophrenia and Other Psychoses*. Chicago: University of Chicago Press.

Farrington, David P., Lloyd E. Ohlin, and James Q. Wilson. 1986. *Understanding and Controlling Crime: Toward a New Research Strategy*. New York: Springer-Verlag.

Festinger, Leon, Stanley Schachter, and Kurt Black. 1950. *Social Pressure in Informal Groups*. New York: Harper.

Firey, Walter. 1947. *Land Use in Central Boston*. Cambridge, MA: Harvard University Press.

Fischer, Claude. 1982. *To Dwell among Friends: Personal Networks in Town and City*. Chicago: University of Chicago Press.

——. 2009. "The 2004 GSS Finding of Shrunken Social Networks: An Artifact?" *American Sociological Review* 74:657–69.

Fiske, Susan. 1998. "Stereotyping, Prejudice, and Discrimination." In *Handbook of Social Psychology*, edited by D. T. Gilbert, S. Fiske, and G. Lindzey. New York: McGraw-Hill.

Florida, Richard. 2002. *The Rise of the Creative Class: And How It's Transforming Work, Leisure, Community and Everyday Life*. New York: Basic.

Fox, James A., and Marianne W. Zawitz. 2003. "Homicide Trends in the United States: 2000 Update." Washington, DC: Bureau of Justice Statistics.

Framingham Heart Study. 1995–2006. National Heart, Blood, and Lung Institute. http://www.framingham.com/heart/.

Freeman, Linton C. 1979. "Centrality in Social Networks: Conceptual Clarification." *Social Networks* 1:215–39.

Friedman, Thomas L. 2005. *The World Is Flat: A Brief History of the Twenty-First Century*. New York: Farrar, Straus and Giroux.

Fung, Archon. 2004. *Empowered Participation: Reinventing Urban Democracy*. Princeton: Princeton University Press.

Galaskiewicz, Joseph. 1979. *Exchange Networks and Community Politics*. Beverly Hills: Sage Publications.

Galaskiewicz, Joseph, and Stanley Wasserman. 1989. "Mimetic Processes within an Interorganizational Field: An Empirical Test." *Administrative Science Quarterly* 34:454–79.

Galster, George. 2011. "The Mechanism(s) of Neighbourhood Effects: Theory, Evidence, and Policy Implictions." In *Neighbourhood Effects Research: New Perspectives*, edited by M. v. Ham, D. Manley, N. Bailey, L. Simpson, and D. Maclennan. Dordrecht, Netherlands: Springer.

Gans, Herbert J. 1962. *The Urban Villlagers: Group and Class in the Life of Italian-Americans*. New York: Free Press of Glencoe.

——. 1974. "Gans on Granovetter's 'Strength of Weak Ties.'" *American Journal of Sociology* 80:524–27.

Geis, Karlyn J., and Catherine E. Ross. 1998. "A New Look at Urban Alienation: The Effect of Neighborhood Disorder on Perceived Powerlessness." *Social Psychology Quarterly* 61:232–46.

Gibson, Mary, and Nicole Hahn Rafter, eds. 2006. *Criminal Man, by Cesare Lombroso*. Durham: Duke University Press.

Giddens, Anthony. 1990. *Consequences of Modernity*. Stanford: Stanford University Press.

——. 1991. *Modernity and Self-Identity: Self and Society in the Late Modern Age*. Stanford: Stanford University Press.

Gieryn, Thomas. 2000. "A Space for Place in Sociology." *Annual Review of Sociology* 26:463–96.

——. 2006. "City as Truth Spot: Laboratories and Field-Sites in Urban Studies." *Social Studies of Science* 36: 5–38.

Gilfoyle, Timothy. 2006. *Millennium Park: Creating a Chicago Landmark*. Chicago: University of Chicago Press.

Gillman, Howard. 1996. "The Antinomy of Public Purposes and Private Rights in the American Constitutional Tradition, or Why Communitarianism Is Not Necessarily Exogenous to Liberal Constitutionalism." *Law and Social Inquiry* 21:67–77.

Glaeser, Edward L. 2011. *The Triumph of Cities: How Our Greatest Invention Makes Us Richer, Smarter, Greener, Healthier, and Happier*. New York: Penguin.

Goffman, Erving. 1963a. *Behavior in Public Places: Notes on the Social Organization of Gatherings*. New York: Free Press.

——. 1963b. *Sigma: Notes on the Management of Spoiled Identity*. New York: Simon and Schuster.

——. 1974. *Frame Analysis: An Essay on the Organization of Experience*. Cambridge, MA: Harvard University Press.

Goldberger, J., G. A. Wheeler, and E. Sydenstrycker. 1920. "A Study of the Relation of Family Income and Other Economic Factors to Pellagra Incidence in Seven Cotton Mill Villages of South Carolina in 1916." *Public Health Reports* 35:2673–714.

Goodchild, Michael F. 2004. "The Validity and Usefulness of Laws in Geographic Information Science and Geography." *Annals of the Association of American Geographers* 94: 300–303.

Gottdiener, Mark, and Ray Hutchison. 2006. *The New Urban Sociology*. Third edition. Boulder: Westview.

Gould, Roger V. 1991. "Multiple Networks and Mobilization in the Paris Commune, 1871." *American Sociological Review* 56:716–29.

Graif, Corina. 2010. "From Diversity to the Rise of Creative Hotspots of Artists and Nonprofit Art Organizations." Cambridge, MA: Harvard University, Department of Sociology.

Graif, Corina, and Robert J. Sampson.. 2009. "Spatial Heterogeneity in the Effects of Immigration and Diversity on Neighborhood Homicide Rates." *Homicide Studies* 13:242–60.

——. 2010. "Inter-Neighborhood Networks and the Structure of Urban Residential Mobility." Cambridge, MA: Harvard University, Department of Sociology.

Grannis, Rick. 1998. "The Importance of Trivial Streets: Residential Streets and Residential Segregation." *American Journal of Sociology* 103:1530–64.

——. 2009. *From the Ground Up: Translating Geography into Community through Neighbor Networks*. Princeton: Princeton University Press.

Granovetter, Mark. 1973. "The Strength of Weak Ties." *American Journal of Sociology* 78: 360–80.

——. 1978. Review of *Networks of Collective Action: A Perspective on Community Influence Systems*, by Edward Laumann and Franz U. Pappi. *American Journal of Sociology* 83:1538–42.

Gratz, Roberta Brandes. 2010. "It Takes a Neighborhood." *New York Times*, September 28.

Grossman, James R., Ann D. Keating, and Janice Reiff, eds. 2004. *The Encyclopedia of Chicago*. Chicago: The University of Chicago Press.

Guerry, Andre-Michel. 1883. *Essai Sur La Statistique Morale De La France*. Paris: Crochard.

Hacking, Ian. 1999. *The Social Construction of What?* Cambridge, MA: Harvard University Press.

Hagan, John. 1994. *Crime and Disrepute*. Thousand Oaks, CA: Pine Forge Press.

Hall, Peter A., and Michèle Lamont, eds. 2009. *Successful Societies: How Institutions and Culture Affect Health*. New York: Cambridge University Press.

Halle, David, ed. 2003. *New York and Los Angeles: Politics, Society, and Culture: A Comparative View*. Chicago: University of Chicago Press.

Hampton, Keith N. 2010. Internet Use and the Concentration of Disadvantage: Glocalization and the Urban Underclass. *American Behavioral Scientist* 53: 1111–32.

Hampton, Keith N., and Barry Wellman. 2003. "Neighboring in Netville: How the Internet Supports Community and Social Capital in a Wired Suburb." *City and Community* 2: 277–311.

Harcourt, Bernard. 2001. *Illusion of Order: The False Promise of Broken Windows Policing*. Cambridge, MA: Harvard University Press.

Hardin, Russell. 2002. *Trust and Trustworthiness*. New York: Russell Sage Foundation.

Harding, David J. 2010. *Living the Drama: Community, Conflict, and Culture among Inner-City Boys*. Chicago: University of Chicago Press.

Harvey, David. 1973. *Social Justice and the City*. Baltimore: Johns Hopkins University Press.

Hawley, Amos O. 1986. *Human Ecology: A Theoretical Essay*. Chicago: University of Chicago Press.

Healy, Kieran. 2004. "Altruism as an Organizational Problem: The Case of Organ Procurement." *American Sociological Review* 69:387–404.

Heckman, James J. 2005. "The Scientific Model of Causality." *Sociological Methodology* 35:1–97.

———. 2006. "Skill Formation and the Economics of Investing in Disadvantaged Children." *Science* 312:1900–1902.

Hedström, Peter, and Peter Bearman. 2009. "What Is Analytic Sociology All About? An Introductory Essay." In *The Oxford Handbook of Analytical Sociology*, edited by P. Hedström and P. Bearman. Oxford: Oxford University Press.

Henig, Jeffrey R. 1982. *Neighborhood Mobilization: Redevelopment and Response*. New Brunswick: Rutgers University Press.

Herbert, Steve. 2006. *Citizens, Cops, and Power: Recognizing the Limits of Community*. Chicago: University of Chicago Press.

Herrnstein, Richard, and Charles Murray. 1994. *The Bell Curve: Intelligence and Class Structure in American Life*. New York: Free Press.

Hipp, John R. 2007. "Block, Tract, and Levels of Aggregation: Neighborhood Structure and Crime and Disorder as a Case in Point." *American Sociological Review* 72: 659–80.

———. 2009. "Collective Efficacy: How Is It Conceptualized, How Is It Measured, and Does It Really Matter for Understanding Neighborhood Rates of Crime?" Irvine, CA: University of California, Department of Sociology.

———. 2010. "The Role of Crime in Housing Unit Racial/Ethnic Transition." *Criminology* 48: 683–723.

Holland, Paul. 1986. Statistics and Causal Inference. *Journal of the American Statistical Association* 81:945–70.

Holton, John. n.d. "Notes from the Field." Chicago: Project on Human Development in Chicago Neighborhoods.

Hong, Guanglei, and Stephen W. Raudenbush. 2008. "Causal Inference for Time-Varying Instructional Treatments." *Journal of Educational and Behavioral Statistics* 33: 333–62.

Houston, Michael J., and Seymour Sudman. 1975. "A Methodological Assessment of the Use of Key Informants." *Social Science Research* 4:151–64.

Hudgens, Michael G., and M. Elizabeth Halloran. 2008. "Toward Causal Inference with Interference." *Journal of American Statistical Association* 103:832–42.

Hunter, Albert. 1974. *Symbolic Communities: The Persistence and Change of Chicago's Local Communities*. Chicago: University of Chicago Press.

———. 1975. "The Loss of Community: An Empirical Test through Replication." *American Sociological Review* 40:537–53.

———. 1985. "Private, Parochial and Public Social Orders: The Problem of Crime and Incivility in Urban Communities." In *The Challenge of Social Control*, edited by G. Suttles and M. Zald. Norwood, NJ: Ablex.

Huntington, Samuel. 2004. *Who Are We? The Challenges to America's National Identity*. New York: Simon and Schuster.

Hyra, Derek. 2008. *The New Urban Renewal: The Economic Transformation of Harlem and Bronzeville*. Chicago: University of Chicago Press.

Irwin, John. 1985. *The Jail: Managing the Underclass in American Society*. Berkeley: University of California Press.

Iwashyna, Theodore J., Nicholas A. Christakis, and Lance B. Becker. 1999. "Neighborhoods Matter: A Population-Based Study of Provision of Cardiopulmonary Resuscitation." *Annals of Emergency Medicine* 34: 459–68.

Jackson, Frank, and Philip Pettit. 1992. "Structural Explanation in Social Theory." In *Reduction, Explanation, and Realism*, edited by D. Charles and K. Lennon. Oxford: Clarendon Press.

Jacobs, Jane. 1961. *The Death and Life of Great American Cities*. New York: Random House.

Janowitz, Morris. 1975. "Sociological Theory and Social Control." *American Journal of Sociology* 81:82–108.

Jargowsky, Paul. 1997. *Poverty and Place: Ghettos, Barrios, and the American City*. New York: Russell Sage Foundation.

Jencks, Christopher. 1990. "Varieties of Altruism." In *Beyond Self Interest*, edited by J. Mansbridge. Chicago: University of Chicago Press.

Jencks, Christopher, and Susan E. Mayer. 1990. "The Social Consequences of Growing up in a Poor Neighborhood." In *Inner-City Poverty in the United States*, edited by L. Lynn and M. McGreary. Washington, D.C.: National Academy Press.

Johnson, Steven. 2006. *Ghost Map: The Story of London's Deadliest Epidemic: And How*

It Changed the Way We Think about Disease, Cities, Science, and the Modern World. New York: Penguin Books.

Jordan, Mary. 2005. "In London, a Feeling of Being Watched: Minority Residents Say Police Harassment on Rise." *Washington Post*, August 26, A15.

Judt, Tony. 2010. "My Endless New York." *New York Times*, November 7.

Kamo, Norifumi, Mary Carlson, Robert T. Brennan, and Felton Earls. 2008. "Young Citizens as Health Agents: Use of Drama in Promoting Community Efficacy for HIV/AIDS." *American Journal of Public Health* 98:201–4.

Katz, Jack. 2001. "From How to Why: On Luminous Description and Causal Inference in Ethnography (Part I)." *Ethnography* 2:443–73.

——. 2009. "Time for New Urban Ethnographies." *Ethnography* 10:285–304.

Kaufman, Jason. 2003. *For the Common Good: American Civic Life and the Golden Age of Fraternity*. New York: Oxford University Press.

Kawachi, Ichiro, and Lisa Berkman, eds. 2003. *Neighborhoods and Health*. New York: Oxford University Press.

Kefalas, Maria. 2003. *Working-Class Heroes: Protecting Home, Community, and Nation in a Chicago Neighborhood*. Berkeley: University of California Press.

Keizer, Kees, Siegwart Lindenberg, and Linda Steg. 2008. "The Spreading of Disorder." *Science* 322:1681–85.

Kelling, George, and Catherine Coles. 1996. *Fixing Broken Windows: Restoring Order and Reducing Crime in Our Communities*. New York: Free Press.

Kessler, Ronald C., and Daniel Mroczek. 1997. "Composite International Diagnostic Interview (C.I.D.I) Short Form." Ann Arbor: University of Michigan, Institute for Social Research.

Kirk, David S. 2009a. "A Natural Experiment on Residential Change and Recidivism: Lessons from Hurricane Katrina." *American Sociological Review* 74: 484–505.

——. 2009b. "Unraveling the Contextual Effects on Student Suspension and Juvenile Arrest: The Independent and Interdependent Influences of School, Neighborhood, and Family Social Controls." *Criminology* 47: 479–520.

Kirk, David S., and Andrew V. Papachristos. 2011. "Cultural Mechanisms and the Persistence of Neighborhood Violence." *American Journal of Sociology* 116:1190–233.

Klinenberg, Eric. 2002. *Heat Wave: A Social Autopsy of Disaster in Chicago*. Chicago: University of Chicago.

Kling, Jeffrey, Jeffrey Liebman, and Lawrence Katz. 2007. "Experimental Analysis of Neighborhood Effects." *Econometrica* 75:83–119.

Knoke, David. 1990. *Political Networks: The Structural Perspective*. New York: Cambridge University Press.

Kobrin, Solomon. 1951. "The Conflict of Values in Delinquency Areas." *American Sociological Review* 16:653–61.

Kohn, David. 2003. "Tearing Down Cabrini-Green. Cabrini-Green Is Gone: Will the Replacement Work?" *CBS 60 Minutes.*

Komarovsky, Mirra. 1946. "The Voluntary Associations of Urban Dwellers." *American Sociological Review* 11:686–98.

Kornhauser, Ruth Rosner. 1978. *Social Sources of Delinquency: An Appraisal of Analytic Models.* Chicago: University of Chicago Press.

Kotlowitz, Alex. 2004. *Never a City So Real: A Walk in Chicago.* New York: Random House.

Koval, John P., Larry Bennett, Michael I. J. Bennett, Fassil Demissie, Roberta Garner, and Kiljoong Kim, eds. 2006. *The New Chicago: A Social and Cultural Analysis.* Philadelphia: Temple University Press.

Krackhardt, David. 1988. "Predicting with Networks: Nonparametric Multiple Regression Analysis of Dyadic Data." *Social Networks* 10:359–91.

———. 1992. "A Caveat on the Use of the Quadratic Assignment Procedure." *Journal of Quantitative Anthropology* 3:279–96.

Kubrin, Charis E., and Ronald Weitzer. 2003. "New Directions in Social Disorganization Theory." *Journal of Research in Crime and Delinquency* 40: 374–402.

Lacy, Karyn R. 2007. *Blue-Chip Black: Race, Class, and Status in the New Black Middle Class.* Berkeley: University of California Press.

Lamont, Michèle. 2000. *The Dignity of Working Men: Morality and the Boundaries of Race, Class, and Immigration.* Cambridge, MA: Harvard University Press and Russell Sage Foundation.

Land, Kenneth, Patricia McCall, and Lawrence E. Cohen. 1990. "Structural Covariates of Homicide Rates: Are There Any Invariances across Time and Space?" *American Journal of Sociology* 95:922–63.

Langer, Bruce, and Stanley Michael. 1963. *Life Stress and Mental Health.* London: Free Press.

Laub, John H. 2004. "The Life Course of Criminology in the United States: The American Society of Criminology 2003 Presidential Address." *Criminology* 42:1–26.

Laub, John H., and Robert J. Sampson. 1991. "The Sutherland-Glueck Debate: On the Sociology of Criminological Knowledge." *American Journal of Sociology* 96:1402–40.

———. 1995. "Crime and Context in the Lives of 1,000 Boston Men, Circa 1925–1955." In *Delinquency and Disrepute in the Life Course: Contextual and Dynamic Analyses,* edited by Z. S. Blau and J. Hagan. Greenwich, CT: JAI Press.

———. 2003. *Shared Beginnings, Divergent Lives: Delinquent Boys to Age 70.* Cambridge, MA: Harvard University Press.

Laumann, Edward O., and Franz Pappi. 1976. *Networks of Collective Action: A Perspective on Community Influence Systems.* New York: Academic Press Inc.

Laumann, Edward O., Peter V. Marsden, and Joseph Galaskievicz. 1977. "Community-Elite Influence Structures: Extension of a Network Approach." *American Journal of Sociology* 83:594–631.

Lee, Barrett A., Ralph S. Oropesa, and Jamie W. Kanan. 1994. "Neighborhood Context and Residential Mobility." *Demography* 31:249–70.

Lefebvre, Henri. 1991. *The Production of Space*. Oxford: Blackwell.

Leventhal, Tama, and Jeanne Brooks-Gunn. 2000. "The Neighborhoods They Live In: The Effects of Neighborhood Residence on Child and Adolescent Outcomes." *Psychological Bulletin* 126:309–37.

Levin, Yale, and Alfred Lindesmith. 1937. "English Ecology and Criminology of the Past Century." *Journal of Criminal Law and Criminology* 27:801–16.

Levine, Donald, ed. 1971. *Georg Simmel on Individuality and Social Forms*. Chicago: University of Chicago Press.

Levine, Robert V., Ara Norenzayan, and Karen Philbrick. 2001. "Cross-Cultural Differences in Helping Strangers." *Journal of Cross-Cultural Psychology* 32: 543–60.

Levitt, Steven D., and Stephen J. Dubner. 2009. *Superfreakonomics: Global Cooling, Patriotic Prostitutes, and Why Suicide Bombers Should Buy Life Insurance*. New York: Harper Collins.

Lieberson, Stanley. 1985. *Making It Count: The Improvement of Social Research and Theory*. Berkeley: University of California Press.

Lieberson, Stanley, and Joel Horwich. 2008. "Implication Analysis: A Pragmatic Proposal for Linking Theory and Data in the Social Sciences." *Sociological Methodology* 38:1–50.

Lieberson, Stanley, and Freda Lynn. 2002. "Barking up the Wrong Branch: Scientific Alternatives to the Current Model of Sociological Science." *Annual Review of Sociology* 28:1–19.

Liska, Allen E., and Paul E. Bellair. 1995. "Violent-Crime Rates and Racial Composition: Convergence over Time." *American Journal of Sociology* 101: 578–610.

Lofland, Lynn. 1973. *A World of Strangers: Order and Action in Urban Public Space*. New York: Basic Books.

Logan, John R. 1978. "Growth, Politics, and the Stratification of Places." *American Journal of Sociology* 84:404–16.

Logan, John R., and Harvey Molotch. 1987. *Urban Fortunes: The Political Economy of Place*. Berkeley: University of California Press.

Logan, John R., and Richard D Alba. 1993. "Locational Returns to Human Capital: Minority Access to Suburban Community Resources." *Demography* 30:243–68.

Logan, John R., Richard D. Alba, Thomas McNulty, and Brian Fisher. 1996. "Making a Place in the Metropolis: Locational Attainment in Cities and Suburbs." *Demography* 33:443–53.

Loury, Glenn C. 2002. *The Anatomy of Racial Inequality*. Cambridge, MA: Harvard University Press.

LSE. *Charles Booth Online Archive* 2008. Accessed October. Available at http://booth.lse.ac.uk/cgi-bin/do.pl?sub=view_booth_and_barth&args=531000,180400,6,large,5.

Ludwig, Jens, Jeffrey B. Liebman, Jeffrey R. Kling, Greg J. Duncan, Lawrence F. Katz, Ronald C. Kessler, and Lisa Sanbonmatsu. 2008. "What Can We Learn about Neighborhood Effects from the Moving to Opportunity Experiment? A Comment on Clampet-Lundquist and Massey." *American Journal of Sociology* 114:144–88.

Lyons, Christopher. 2007. "Community (Dis)Organization and Racially Motivated Crime." *American Journal of Sociology* 113:815–53.

MacDonald, Heather. 2010. "Chicago's Real Crime Story: Why Decades of Community Organizing Haven't Stemmed the City's Youth Violence." *City Journal* 20:16–28.

Mailer, Norman. 1968. *Miami and the Siege of Chicago: An Informal History of the Republican and Democratic Conventions of 1968.* New York: New American Library.

Maimon, David, and Christopher R. Browning. 2010. "Unstructured Socializing, Collective Efficacy, and Violent Behavior among Urban Youth." *Criminology* 48:443–74.

Mansbridge, Jane. 1990. "The Rise and Fall of Self Interest in the Explanation of Political Life." In *Beyond Self Interest*, edited by J. Mansbridge. Chicago: University of Chicago Press.

Martin, Kelly. 2002. "Project on Human Development in Chicago Neighborhoods Longitudinal Cohort Study: Field Data Collection Report." Chicago.

Martinez, Ramiro, Jr. 2002. *Latino Homicide: Immigration, Violence, and Community.* New York: Routledge Press, Taylor & Francis Group.

Martinez, Ramiro, Jr., Jacob I. Stowell, and Matthew T. Lee. 2010. "Immigration and Crime in an Era of Transformation: A Longitudinal Analysis of Homicides in San Diego Neighborhoods, 1980–2000." *Criminology* 48:797–829.

Marwell, Nicole. 2004. "Privatizing the Welfare State: Nonprofit Community-Based Organizations as Political Actors." *American Sociological Review* 69:265–91.

———. 2005. "Beyond Neighborhood Social Control: From Interaction to Institutions." New York: Columbia University, Department of Sociology.

———. 2007. *Bargaining for Brooklyn: Community Organizations in the Entrepreneurial City.* Chicago: University of Chicago Press.

Massey, Douglas, Gretchen Condran, and Nancy A. Denton. 1987. "The Effect of Residential Segregation on Black Social and Economic Well-Being." *Social Forces* 66:29–56.

Massey, Douglas, Andrew B. Gross, and Kumiko Shibuya. 1994. "Migration, Segregation, and the Geographic Concentration of Poverty." *American Sociological Review* 59:425–45.

Massey, Douglas, and Robert J. Sampson. 2009. "Moynihan Redux: Legacies and Lessons." *Annals of the American Academy of Political and Social Science* 621:6–27.

Massey, Douglas S. 1990. "American Apartheid: Segregation and the Making of the Underclass." *American Journal of Sociology* 96: 329–57.

———. 1996. "The Age of Extremes: Concentrated Affluence and Poverty in the Twenty-First Century." *Demography* 33: 395–412.

Massey, Douglas S., Rafael Alarcon, Jorge Durand, and Humberto González. 1990. *Return to Aztlan: The Social Process of International Migration from Western Mexico.* Berkeley: University of California Press.

Massey, Douglas S., and Nancy Denton. 1993. *American Apartheid: Segregation and the Making of the Underclass.* Cambridge, MA: Harvard University Press.

Massey, Douglas S., and Nancy A. Denton. 1985. "Spatial Assimilation as a Socioeconomic Outcome." *American Sociological Review* 50:94–106.

Massey, Douglas S., and Mitchell L. Eggers. 1990. "The Ecology of Inequality: Minorities and the Concentration of Poverty, 1970–1980." *American Journal of Sociology* 95: 1153–88.

Matsueda, Ross. 2006. "Differential Social Organization, Collective Action, and Crime." *Crime, Law and Social Change* 46:3–33.

Mayer, Susan E., and Christopher Jencks. 1989. "Growing Up in Poor Neighborhoods: How Much Does It Matter?" *Science* 243:1441–45.

Mayhew, Henry. 1861. *London Labour and the London Poor: The Condition and Earnings of Those That Will Work, Cannot Work, and Will Not Work.* London: C. Griffin and Company.

———. 1862. *London Labor and the London Poor.* London: Griffin, Bohn.

Mazerolle, Lorraine, Rebecca Wickes, and James McBroom. 2010. "Community Variations in Violence: Social Ties and Collective Efficacy in Comparative Context." *Journal of Research in Crime and Delinquency* 47:3–30.

McAdam, Doug. [1982] 1999. *Political Process and the Development of the Black Insurgency, 1930–1970.* Chicago: University of Chicago Press.

———. 2003. "Beyond Structural Analysis: Toward a More Dynamic Understanding of Social Movements." In *Social Movements and Networks*, edited by M. Diani and D. McAdam. Oxford: Oxford University Press.

McAdam, Doug, John D. McCarthy, and Mayer N. Zald, eds. 1996. *Comparative Perspectives on Social Movements.* New York: Cambridge University Press.

McAdam, Doug, Robert J. Sampson, Simón Weffer-Elizondo, and Heather MacIndoe. 2005. "'There Will Be Fighting in the Streets': The Distorting Lens of Social Movement Theory." *Mobilization* 10:1–18.

McAdam, Doug, Kaisa Snellman, and Robert J. Sampson. 2010. "Churches and Non-Profits: Toward a More Nuanced Understanding of the Link between

Organizations and Collective Civic Engagement." Stanford: Stanford University, Department of Sociology.

McCarthy, Helen, Paul Miller, and Paul Skidmore, eds. 2004. *Network Logic: Who Governs in an Interconnected World?* London: Demos.

McNulty, Thomas L., and Paul E. Bellair. 2003a. "Explaining Racial and Ethnic Differences in Adolescent Violence: Structural Disadvantage, Family Well-Being, and Social Capital." *Justice Quarterly* 20: 201–31.

——. 2003b. "Explaining Racial and Ethnic Differences in Serious Adolescent Violent Behavior." *Criminology* 41:709–48.

McPherson, Miller, Lynn Smith-Lovin, and Matthew E. Brashears. 2006. "Social Isolation in America: Changes in Core Discussion Networks over Two Decades." *American Sociological Review* 71:353–75.

McPherson, Miller, Lynn Smith-Lovin, and James M Cook. 2001. "Birds of a Feather: Homophily and Social Networks." *Annual Review of Sociology* 27:415–44.

McQuarrie, Michael, and Nicole P. Marwell. 2009. "The Missing Organizational Dimension in Urban Sociology." *City and Community* 8: 247–68.

McRoberts, Omar. 2003. *Streets of Glory: Church and Community in a Black Urban Neighborhood*. Chicago: University of Chicago Press.

McVeigh, Rory, Michael R. Welch, and Thoroddur Bjarnason. 2003. "Hate Crime Reporting as a Successful Social Movement Outcome." *American Sociological Review* 68:843–67.

Merton, Robert K. 1949. *Social Theory and Social Structure*. New York: Free Press.

——. 1968. "The Self-Fulfilling Prophecy." In *Social Theory and Social Structure*. New York: Free Press.

Messner, Steven F., Luc Anselin, R. Baller, D. Hawkins, G. Deane, and S. Tolnay. 1999. "The Spatial Patterning of County Homicide Rates: An Application of Exploratory Spatial Data Analysis." *Journal of Quantitative Criminology* 15:423–50.

Milbank, Dana. 2001. "Needed: Catchword for Bush Ideology; 'Communitarianism' Finds Favor." *Washington Post*, February 1, A01.

Milgram, Stanley, L. Mann, and S. Hartner. 1965. "The Lost Letter Technique: A Tool of Social Research." *Public Opinion Quarterly* 29:437–38.

Molotch, Harvey. 2002. "School's Out: A Response to Michael Dear." *City and Community* 1:39–43.

Molotch, Harvey, William Freudenburg, and Krista E. Paulsen. 2000. "History Repeats Itself, but How? City Character, Urban Tradition, and the Accomplishment of Place." *American Sociological Review* 65:791–823.

Morenoff, Jeffrey, and Robert J. Sampson. 1997. "Violent Crime and the Spatial Dynamics of Neighborhood Transition: Chicago, 1970–1990." *Social Forces* 76: 31–64.

Morenoff, Jeffrey D. 2003. "Neighborhood Mechanisms and the Spatial Dynamics of Birth Weight." *American Journal of Sociology* 108:976–1017.

Morenoff, Jeffrey D., and James A. House. n.d. "Lost Letter Experiment." Ann Arbor: University of Michigan.

Morenoff, Jeffrey D., Robert J. Sampson, and Stephen Raudenbush. 2001. "Neighborhood Inequality, Collective Efficacy, and the Spatial Dynamics of Urban Violence." *Criminology* 39:517–60.

Morgan, Stephen, and Christopher Winship. 2007. *Counterfactuals and Causal Inference: Methods and Principles for Social Research*. New York: Cambridge University Press.

Morris, Terrence M. 1958. *The Criminal Area*. London: Routledge and Kegan Paul Ltd.

Moynihan, Daniel P. 1965. "The Negro Family: The Case for National Action." Washington, DC: U.S. Department of Labor, Office of Policy Planning and Research.

Mumford, Lewis. 1954. "The Neighborhood and the Neighborhood Unit." *Town Planning Review* 24:256–70.

Nagel, Thomas. 1970. *The Possibility of Altruism*. Oxford: Clarendon Press.

NBER. 2006. "Improved Neighborhoods Don't Raise Academic Achievement." Cambridge, MA: National Bureau of Economic Research.

Newman, Katherine. 1999. *No Shame in My Game: The Working Poor in the Inner City*. New York: Knopf.

Nisbet, Robert. 1953. *The Quest for Community*. New York: Oxford University Press.

Nisbett, Richard E., and Dov Cohen. 1996. *Culture of Honor: The Psychology of Violence in the South*. Boulder: Westview Press.

NORC. 1995. "PHDCN Project 4709, Systematic Social Observation Coding Manual, June 1995." NORC/University of Chicago.

Oakes, J. Michael. 2004. "The (Mis)Estimation of Neighborhood Effects: Causal Inference for a Practicable Social Epidemiology." *Social Science and Medicine* 58:1929–52.

Obama, Barack. 1988. "Why Organize? Problems and Promise in the Inner City." *Illinois Issues* (August/September).

Odgers, Candice L., Terrie E. Moffitt, Laura M. Tach, Robert J. Sampson, Alan Taylor, Charlotte L. Matthews, and Avshalom Caspi. 2009. "The Protective Effects of Neighborhood Collective Efficacy on British Children Growing Up in Deprivation: A Developmental Analysis." *Developmental Psychology* 45: 942–57.

Oliver, Eric. 2001. *Democracy in Suburbia*. Princeton: Princeton University Press.

Orr, Larry, Judith D. Feins, Robin Jacob, Erik Beecroft, Lisa Sanbonmatsu, Lawrence F. Katz, Jeffrey B. Liebman, and Jeffrey R. Kling. 2003. "Moving to Opportunity Interim Impacts Evaluation." Cambridge, MA: National Bureau of Economic Research.

Ousey, Graham C., and Charis E. Kubrin. 2009. "Exploring the Connection between Immigration and Violent Crime Rates in U.S. Cities, 1980–2000." *Social Problems* 56 447–73.

Park, Robert E. 1915. "The City: Suggestions for the Investigations of Human Behavior in the Urban Environment." *American Journal of Sociology* 20:577–612.

Park, Robert E., and Ernest Burgess. 1921. *Introduction to the Science of Sociology*. Chicago: University of Chicago Press.

———. 1925 [1967]. *The City: Suggestions for Investigation of Human Behavior in the Urban Environment*. Chicago: University of Chicago Press.

Patterson, Orlando. 2004. "Culture and Continuity: Causal Structures in Socio-Cultural Persistence." In *Matters of Culture: Cultural Sociology in Practice*, edited by J. Mohr and R. Friedland. New York: Cambridge University Press.

———. 2009. "The Mechanisms of Cultural Reproduction: Explaining the Puzzle of Persistence." Cambridge, MA: Harvard University.

Pattillo, Mary E. 1998. "Sweet Mothers and Gangbangers: Managing Crime in a Black Middle-Class Neighborhood." *Social Forces* 76:747–74.

———. 2007. *Black on the Block: The Politics of Race and Class in the City*. Chicago: University of Chicago Press.

Pattillo-McCoy, Mary E. 1999. *Black Picket Fences: Privilege and Peril among the Black Middle Class*. Chicago: University of Chicago Press.

Permentier, Matthieu, Maarten van Hamm, and Gideon Bolt. 2009. "Neighbourhood Reputation and the Intention to Leave the Neighbourhood." *Environment and Planning A* 41:2162–80.

Peterson, Ruth D., and Lauren J. Krivo. 2005. "Macrostructural Analyses of Race, Ethnicity, and Violent Crime: Recent Lessons and New Directions for Research." *Annual Review of Sociology* 31:331–56.

———. 2010. *Divergent Social Worlds: Neighborhood Crime and the Racial-Spatial Divide*. New York: Russell Sage Foundation.

Pettit, Becky, and Bruce Western. 2004. "Mass Imprisonment and the Life Course: Race and Class Inequality in U.S. Incarceration." *American Sociological Review* 69:151–69.

Pfautz, Harold, ed. 1967. *Charles Booth on the City: Physical Pattern and Social Structure*. Chicago: University of Chicago Press.

Portes, Alejandro, and Julia Sensenbrenner. 1993. "Embeddedness and Immigration: Notes on the Social Determinants of Economic Action." *American Journal of Sociology* 98:1320–50.

Powell, Brian, Catherine Bolzendahl, Claudia Geist, and Lala Carr Steelman. 2010. *Counted Out: Same-Sex Relations and Americans' Definitions of Family*. New York: Russell Sage Foundation.

Powell, Michael. 2010. "Old-Fashioned Bulwark in a Tide of Foreclosures." *New York Times*, March 5.

Pratt, Travis, and Frances Cullen. 2005. "Assessing Macro-Level Predictors and Theories of Crime: A Meta-Analysis." In *Crime and Justice: A Review of Research*, edited by M. Tonry. Chicago: University of Chicago Press.

Price-Spratlen, Townsend. 1999. "Livin' for the City: African American Community Development and Depression Era Migration." *Demography* 36:553–68.

Przeworski, Adam, and Henry Tuene. 1970. *The Logic of Comparative Inquiry*. New York: Wiley.

Putnam, Robert. 2000. *Bowling Alone: The Collapse and Renewal of American Community*. New York: Simon and Schuster.

———. 2007. "E Pluribus Unum: Diversity and Community in the Twenty-First Century: The 2006 Johan Skytte Prize Lecture." *Scandinavian Political Studies* 30:137–74.

Putnam, Robert, Lewis Feldstein, and Don Cohen. 2003. *Better Together: Restoring the American Community*. New York: Simon and Schuster.

Quercia, Roberto G., Spencer M. Cowan, and Ana B. Moreno. 2005. "The Cost-Effectiveness of Community-Based Foreclosure Prevention." Chapel Hill: University of North Carolina.

Quetelet, Adolphe. [1842] 1969. *A Treatise on Man and the Development of His Faculties*. Edinburgh: William and Robert Chambers.

Quillian, Lincoln. 1999. "Migration Patterns and the Growth of High-Poverty Neighborhoods, 1970–1990." *American Journal of Sociology* 105:1–37.

Quillian, Lincoln, and Devah Pager. 2001. "Black Neighbors, Higher Crime? The Role of Racial Stereotypes in Evaluations of Neighborhood Crime." *American Journal of Sociology* 107: 717–67.

Raudenbush, Stephen W. 2008. "Advancing Educational Policy by Advancing Research on Instruction." *American Educational Research Journal* 45: 206–30.

———. 2009. "The Brown Legacy and the O'Connor Challenge: Can School Improvement Reduce Racial Inequality?" *Educational Researcher* 38: 169–80.

Raudenbush, Stephen W., and Robert J. Sampson. 1999. "'Ecometrics': Toward a Science of Assessing Ecological Settings, with Application to the Systematic Social Observation of Neighborhoods." *Sociological Methodology* 29:1–41.

Rawls, John. [1971] 1999. *A Theory of Justice*. Cambridge, MA: Harvard University Press.

———. 1993. *Political Liberalism*. New York: Columbia University Press.

Rawson, R. W. 1839. "An Inquiry into the Statistics of Crime in England and Wales." *Journal of the Statistical Society of London* 2:316–44.

Reardon, Sean F., and K. Bischoff. 2011. "Income Inequality and Income Segregation." *American Journal of Sociology* 116:1092–153.

Reiss, Albert J., Jr. 1971. "Systematic Observations of Natural Social Phenomena." In *Sociological Methodology*, edited by H. Costner. San Francisco: Jossey-Bass.

——. 1986. "Why Are Communities Important in Understanding Crime?" In *Communities and Crime*, edited by A. J. Reiss and M. Tonry. Chicago: University of Chicago Press.

——. n.d. Personal communication.

Reiss, Albert J., Jr., and Michael Tonry. 1986. *Crime and Justice: An Annual Review of Research*. Vol. 9: *Communities and Crime*. Chicago: University of Chicago Press.

Reiss, Julian. 2009. "Causation in the Social Sciences: Evidence, Inference, and Purpose." *Philosophy of the Social Sciences* 39:20–40.

Relph, Edward. 1976. *Place and Placelessness*. London: Pion.

Robertson, Campbell. 2010. "On Anniversary of Katrina, Signs of Healing." *New York Times*, August 27, 1, 10, 11.

Robins, James. 1999. "Association, Causation, and Marginal Structural Models." *Synthese* 121:151–79.

Robins, James M., M. Hernan, and B. A. Brumback. 2000. "Marginal Structural Models and Causal Inference in Epidemiology." *Epidemiology* 11: 550–60.

Robinson, W. S. 1950. "Ecological Correlations and the Behavior of Individuals." *American Sociological Review* 15:351–57.

Rosenbaum, Paul R. 2007. "Interference between Units in Randomized Experiments." *Journal of American Statistical Association* 102:191–200.

Rosenkrantz, Roger. 1977. *Inference, Method and Decision: Towards a Bayesian Philosophy of Science*. Dordrecht, Netherlands: D. Reidel.

Rosin, Hanna. 2008. "American Murder Mystery." *Atlantic Monthly* (July/August).

Ross, Catherine E., and John Mirowsky. 1999. "Disorder and Decay: The Concept and Measurement of Perceived Neighborhood Disorder." *Urban Affairs Review* 34:412–32.

Ross, Catherine E., J. R. Reynolds, and Karlyn J. Geis. 2000. "The Contingent Meaning of Neighborhood Stability for Residents' Psychological Well-Being." *American Sociological Review* 65:581–97.

Rossi, Peter H. 1980. *Why Families Move*. Second edition. Beverly Hills: Sage Publications Inc.

Royko, Mike. 1971. *Boss: Richard J. Daley of Chicago*. New York: Dutton.

Rumbaut, Ruben G., and Walter A. Ewing. 2007. "The Myth of Immigrant Criminality and the Paradox of Assimilation: Incarceration Rates among Native and Foreign-Born Men." Washington, DC: American Immigration Law Foundation.

Saegert, Susan, J. Phillip Thompson, and Donald Warren. 2002. *Social Capital in Poor Communities*. New York: Russell Sage Foundation.

Saenz, Rogelio. 2004. "Census 2000 Report: Latinos and the Changing Face of America." New York and Washington, DC: Russell Sage Foundation and Population Reference Bureau.

Sampson, Robert J. 1986. "The Contribution of Homicide to the Decline of American Cities." *Bulletin of the New York Academy of Medicine* 62:562–69.

——. 1999. "What 'Community' Supplies." In *Urban Problems and Community Development*, edited by R. F. Ferguson and W. T. Dickens. Washington, DC: Brookings Institution Press.

——. 2002a. "Studying Modern Chicago." *City and Community* 1:45–48.

——. 2002b. "Transcending Tradition: New Directions in Community Research, Chicago Style." *Criminology* 40:213–30.

——. 2006. "Open Doors Don't Invite Criminals: Is Increased Immigration behind the Drop in Crime?" *New York Times*, March 11.

——. 2008a. "After-School Chicago: Space and the City." *Urban Geography* 29: 127–37.

——. 2008b. "Moving to Inequality: Neighborhood Effects and Experiments Meet Social Structure." *American Journal of Sociology* 114:189–231.

——. 2008c. "Rethinking Crime and Immigration." *Contexts* 7:28–33.

——. 2009a. "Disparity and Diversity in the Contemporary City: Social (Dis)Order Revisited." *British Journal of Sociology* 60:1–31.

——. 2009b. "Racial Stratification and the Durable Tangle of Neighborhood Inequality." *Annals of the American Academy of Political and Social Science* 621:260–80.

——. 2010a. "Eliding the Theory/Research and Basic/Applied Divides: Implications of Merton's Middle Range." In *Robert K. Merton: Sociology of Science and Sociological Explanation*, edited by C. Calhoun. New York: Columbia University Press.

——. 2010b. "Gold Standard Myths: Observations on the Experimental Turn in Quantitative Criminology." *Journal of Quantitative Criminology* 25: 489–500.

Sampson, Robert J., and Dawn Jeglum Bartusch. 1998. "Legal Cynicism and (Subcultural?) Tolerance of Deviance: The Neighborhood Context of Racial Differences." *Law and Society Review* 32: 777–804.

Sampson, Robert J., and Corina Graif. 2009a. "Neighborhood Networks and Processes of Trust." In *Whom Can We Trust? How Groups, Networks, and Institutions Make Trust Possible*, edited by K. S. Cook, M. Levi, and R. Hardin. New York: Russell Sage Foundation.

——. 2009b. "Neighborhood Social Capital as Differential Social Organization: Resident and Leadership Dimensions." *American Behavioral Scientist* 52: 1579–605.

——. 2010. "Neighborhood Networks and the City-Wide Structure of Residential Mobility Flows." Paper presented at the 105th annual meeting of the American Sociological Association, Atlanta, GA.

Sampson, Robert J., and W. B. Groves. 1989. "Community Structure and Crime:

Testing Social-Disorganization Theory." *American Journal of Sociology* 94: 774–802.

Sampson, Robert J., and John H. Laub. 1993. *Crime in the Making: Pathways and Turning Points through Life*. Cambridge, MA: Harvard University Press.

Sampson, Robert J., and Charles Loeffler. 2010. "Punishment's Place: The Local Concentration of Mass Incarceration." *Daedalus* 139, No. 3: 20–31.

Sampson, Robert J., Doug McAdam, Heather MacIndoe, and Simòn Weffer. 2005. "Civil Society Reconsidered: The Durable Nature and Community Structure of Collective Civic Action." *American Journal of Sociology* 111:673–714.

Sampson, Robert J., and Jeffrey D. Morenoff. 1997. "Ecological Perspectives on the Neighborhood Context of Urban Poverty: Past and Present." In *Neighborhood Poverty*, edited by J. Brooks-Gunn, G. J. Duncan and J. L. Aber. New York: Russell Sage.

——. 2000. "Public Health and Safety in Context: Lessons from Community-Level Theory on Social Capital." In *Promoting Health: Intervention Strategies from Social and Behavioral Research*, edited by B. D. Smedley and S. L. Syme. Washington, D.C.: National Academy Press.

——. 2006. "Durable Inequality: Spatial Dynamics, Social Processes and the Persistence of Poverty in Chicago Neighborhoods." In *Poverty Traps*, edited by S. Bowles, S. Durlauf, and K. Hoff. Princeton: Princeton University Press.

Sampson, Robert J., Jeffrey D. Morenoff, and Felton Earls. 1999. "Beyond Social Capital: Spatial Dynamics of Collective Efficacy for Children." *American Sociological Review* 64 : 633–60.

Sampson, Robert J., Jeffrey D. Morenoff, and Thomas Gannon-Rowley. 2002. "Assessing 'Neighborhood Effects': Social Processes and New Directions in Research." *Annual Review of Sociology* 28:443–78.

Sampson, Robert J., Jeffrey D. Morenoff, and Stephen W. Raudenbush. 2005. "Social Anatomy of Racial and Ethnic Disparities in Violence." *American Journal of Public Health* 95:224–232.

Sampson, Robert J., and Stephen W. Raudenbush. 1999. "Systematic Social Observation of Public Spaces: A New Look at Disorder in Urban Neighborhoods." *American Journal of Sociology* 105:603–51.

——. 2004. "Seeing Disorder: Neighborhood Stigma and the Social Construction of Broken Windows." *Social Psychology Quarterly* 67: 319–42.

Sampson, Robert J., Stephen W. Raudenbush, and Felton Earls. 1997. "Neighborhoods and Violent Crime: A Multilevel Study of Collective Efficacy." *Science* 277:918–24.

Sampson, Robert J., and Patrick Sharkey. 2008. "Neighborhood Selection and the Social Reproduction of Concentrated Racial Inequality." *Demography* 45:1–29.

Sampson, Robert J., Patrick Sharkey, and Stephen W. Raudenbush. 2008. "Durable Effects of Concentrated Disadvantage on Verbal Ability among African-American Children." *Proceedings of the National Academy of Sciences* 105: 845–52.

Sampson, Robert J., and Per-Olof Wikström. 2008. "The Social Order of Violence in Chicago and Stockholm Neighborhoods: A Comparative Inquiry." In *Order, Conflict, and Violence*, edited by S. N. Kalyvas, I. Shapiro, and T. Masoud. New York: Cambridge University Press.

Sampson, Robert J., and William Julius Wilson. 1995. "Toward a Theory of Race, Crime, and Urban Inequality." In *Crime and Inequality*, edited by J. Hagan and R. D. Peterson. Stanford, CA: Stanford University Press.

Sanchez-Jankowski, Martin. 2008. *Cracks in the Pavement: Social Change and Resilience in Poor Neighborhoods*. Berkeley: University of California Press.

Sandel, Michael J. 2009. *Justice: What's the Right Thing to Do?* New York: Farrar, Straus, and Giroux.

Sassen, Saskia. 2001. *The Global City: New York, London, Tokyo*. Princeton: Princeton University Press.

Saulny, Susan. 2010. "Chicago Is Mayor Daley's Kind of Town." *New York Times*, September 11.

Sawyer, R. Keith. 2005. *Social Emergence: Societies as Complex Systems*. New York: Cambridge University Press.

Schelling, Thomas. 1971. "Dynamic Models of Segregation." *Journal of Mathematical Sociology* 1:143–86.

Schlossman, Steven, and Michael Sedlak. 1983. "Chicago Area Project." *Crime and Delinquency* 29: 398–462.

Selznick, Philip. 1992. *The Moral Commonwealth: Social Theory and the Promises of Community*. Berkley: University of California Press.

Sen, Amartya. 2009. *The Idea of Justice*. Cambridge, MA: Belknap Press of Harvard University Press.

Sennett, Richard. 1970. *The Uses of Disorder: Personal Identity and City Life*. New York: W. W. Norton.

———. 2009. "Urban Disorder Today." *British Journal of Sociology* 60:57–58.

Settersten, Richard A., Jr., and T. Andersson. 2002. "Moving and Still: Neighborhoods, Human Development, and the Life Course." In *Advances in Life-Course Research: New Frontiers in Socialization*, edited by R. A. Setterson, Jr., and T. Owens. London: Elsevier Science Ltd.

Sharkey, Patrick. 2010. "The Acute Effect of Local Homicides on Children's Cognitive Performance." *Proceedings of the National Academy of Sciences* 107: 11733–38.

———. 2011. "Temporary Integration, Resilient Inequality: Race and Neighborhood Change in the Transition to Adulthood." *Demography*, forthcoming.

Sharkey, Patrick, and Robert J Sampson. 2010. "Destination Effects: Residential

Mobility and Trajectories of Adolescent Violence in a Stratified Metropolis." *Criminology* 48: 639–82.

Sharkey, Patrick T. 2008. "The Intergenerational Transmission of Context." *American Journal of Sociology* 113: 931–69.

Shaw, Clifford R. 1929. *Delinquency Areas*. Chicago: University of Chicago Press.

———. 1930. *The Jack-Roller: A Delinquent Boy's Own Story*. Chicago: University of Chicago Press.

Shaw, Clifford R., and Henry D. McKay. [1942] 1969. *Juvenile Delinquency and Urban Areas*. Chicago: University of Chicago Press.

Shevky, Eshref, and Wendell Bell. 1955. *Social Area Analysis: Theory, Illustrative Application, and Computational Procedures*. Stanford: Stanford University Press.

Shonkoff, Jack P., and Deborah A. Phillips, eds. 2000. *From Neurons to Neighborhoods: The Science of Early Childhood Development*. Edited by N. R. Council, Institute of Medicine. Washington, DC: National Academy Press.

Short, James F., Jr. 1963. Introduction to the abridged edition. In *The Gang*, edited by F. Thrasher. Chicago: University of Chicago Press.

Sikkema, Kathleen, J. A. Kelly, R. A. Winett, L. J. Solomon, V. A. Cargill, R. A. Roffman, T. L. McAuliffe, T. G. Heckman, E. A. Anderson, D. A. Wagstaff, A. D. Norman, M. J. Perry, D. A. Crumble, and M. B. Mercer. 2000. "Outcomes of a Randomized Community-Level HIV Prevention Intervention for Women Living in 18 Low-Income Housing Developments." *American Journal of Public Health* 90:57–63.

Skocpol, Theda. 2004. "Voice and Inequality: The Transformation of American Civic Democracy." *Perspectives on Politics* 2:3–20.

Skogan, Wesley. 1990. *Disorder and Decline: Crime and the Spiral of Decay in American Cities*. Berkeley: University of California Press.

Skogan, Wesley, and Susan Hartnett. 1997. *Community Policing, Chicago Style*. New York: Oxford University Press.

Skrabski, A., M. Kopp, and I. Kawachi. 2004. "Social Capital and Collective Efficacy in Hungary: Cross Sectional Associations with Middle Aged Female and Male Mortality Rates." *Jourmal of Epidemiology and Community Health* 58:340–45.

Smail, Daniel. 1999. *Imaginary Cartographies: Possession and Identity in Late Medieval Marseille*. Ithaca: Cornell University Press.

Small, Mario. 2002. "Culture, Cohorts, and Social Organization Theory: Understanding Local Participation in a Latino Housing Project." *American Journal of Sociology* 108:1–54.

———. 2004. *Villa Victoria: The Transformation of Social Capital in a Boston Barrio*. Chicago: University of Chicago Press.

———. 2007. "Is There Such a Thing as 'the Ghetto'? The Perils of Assuming the South Side of Chicago Represents Poor Black Neighborhoods." *City* 11:413–21.

——. 2009. *Unanticipated Gains: Origins of Network Inequality in Everyday Life*. New York: Oxford University Press.

Small, Mario, and Jessica Feldman. 2008. "Is Chicago an Outlier? Organizational Density in Poor Urban Neighborhoods." Chicago: University of Chicago.

Small, Mario Luis, David J. Harding, and Michele Lamont. 2010. "Reconsidering Culture and Poverty." *Annals of the American Academy of Political and Social Science* 629:6–27.

Smelser, Neil, and Jeffrey Alexander, eds. 1999. *Diversity and Its Discontents: Cultural Conflict and Common Ground in American Society*. Princeton: Princeton University Press.

Smich, Mary. 2010. "Slow Change Coming Fast at Cabrini-Green: Last Buildings Are Almost Gone, but Where Will the Last of the Residents Go?" *Chicago Tribune*, August 20.

Smith, Carl. 2006. *The Plan of Chicago: Daniel Burnham and the Remaking of the American City*. Chicago: University of Chicago Press.

Smith, Herbert L. 2009. "Causation and Its Discontents." In *Causal Analysis in Population Studies*, edited by H. Engelhardt, H.-P. Kohler, and A. Fürnkranz-Prskawetz. New York: Springer.

Smith, Michael E. 2010. "The Archaeological Study of Neighborhoods and Districts in Ancient Cities." *Journal of Anthropological Archaeology* 29: 137–54.

Smolensky, Eugene. 2007. "Children in the Vanguard of the U.S. Welfare State: A Review of Janet Currie's *the Invisible Safety Net* and Jane Waldfogel's *What Children Need*." *Journal of Economic Literature* 45:1011–23.

Snow, C. P. 1993. *The Two Cultures*. Cambridge: Cambridge University Press.

Sobel, Michael. 2006. "What Do Randomized Studies of Housing Mobility Demonstrate? Causal Inference in the Face of Interference." *Journal of American Statistical Association* 101:1398–407.

Sober, Elliot, and David Sloan Wilson. 1998. *Unto Others: The Evolution and Psychology of Unselfish Behavior*. Cambridge, MA: Harvard University Press.

Social Capital Community Benchmark Survey. 2010. http://www.hks.harvard.edu/saguaro/communitysurvey/index.html and http://www.ksg.harvard.edu/saguaro/communitysurvey/docs/marginals.pdf.

Sorensen, Aage B. 1998. "Theoretical Mechanisms and the Empirical Study of Social Processes." In *Social Mechanisms: An Analytical Approach to Social Theory*, edited by P. Hedstrom and R. Swedberg. Cambridge: Cambridge University Press.

South, Scott J., and Kyle D. Crowder. 1997. "Escaping Distressed Neighborhoods: Individual, Community, and Metropolitan Influences." *American Journal of Sociology* 102:1040–84.

——. 1998. "Leaving the Hood: Residential Mobility between Black, White, and Integrated Neighborhoods." *American Sociological Review* 63:17–26.

Spielman, Fran, Kim Janssen, Frank Main, and Rosemary Sobol. 2010. "Slain Officer Was 'the Best We Had to Offer': Alderman." *Chicago Tribune*, May 20.

Stack, Carol. 1974. *All Our Kin: Strategies for Survival in a Black Community*. First edition. New York: Harper and Row.

Steel, Daniel. 2004. "Social Mechanisms and Causal Inference." *Philosophy of the Social Sciences* 34:55–78.

Steinberg, Stephen. 1995. *Turning Back: The Retreat from Racial Justice in American Thought and Policy*. Boston: Beacon Press.

Stinchcombe, Arthur. 1963. "Institutions of Privacy in the Determination of Police Administrative Practice." *American Journal of Sociology* 69:150–60.

St. Jean, Peter. 2007. *Pockets of Crime: Broken Windows, Collective Efficacy, and the Criminal Point of View*. Chicago: University of Chicago Press.

Stone, Brad. 2008. "Lax Real Estate Decisions Hurt Starbucks." *New York Times*, July 4.

Stout, Lynn. 2006. "Social Norms and Other-Regarding Preferences." In *Social Norms and the Law*, edited by J. N. Drobak. New York: Cambridge University Press.

Stowell, Jacob I., Steven F. Messner, Kelly F. Mcgeever, and Lawrence E. Raffalovich. 2009. "Immigration and the Recent Violent Crime Drop in the United States: A Pooled, Cross-Sectional Timeseries Analysis of Metropolitan Areas." *Criminology* 47:601–40.

Straus, Murray A., Sherry L. Hamby, Sue Boney-McCoy, and David B. Sugarman. 1996. "The Revised Conflict Tactics Scale (CTS2): Development and Preliminary Psychometric Data." *Journal of Family Issues* 17:283–316.

Subramanian, S. V., Kelvyn Jones, Afamia Kaddour, and Nancy Kreiger. 2009. "Revisiting the Robinson Fallacy: Perils of Individualistic and Ecological Fallacy." *International Journal of Epidemiology* 38: 342–60.

Sugrue, Thomas. 1996. *The Origins of the Urban Crisis: Race and Inequality in Post-War Detroit*. Princeton: Princeton University Press.

Sutherland, Edwin H. 1947. *Principles of Criminology*. Third edition. Philadelphia: Lippincott.

Suttles, Gerald D.1968. *The Social Order of the Slum: Ethnicity and Territory in the Inner City*. Chicago: University of Chicago Press.

———, ed. 1972. *The Social Construction of Communities*. Chicago: University of Chicago Press.

———. 1984. "The Cumulative Texture of Local Urban Culture." *American Journal of Sociology* 90: 283–304.

———. 1990. *The Man-Made City: The Land-Use Confidence Game in Chicago*. Chicago: University of Chicago Press.

Swaroop, Sapna, and Jeffrey D. Morenoff. 2006. "Building Community: The Neighborhood Context of Social Organization." *Social Forces* 84:1665–95.

Sweeney, Annie. 2010. "Chatham Residents Team Up against Violence: Frustration Builds after Shootings Close Basketball Courts." *Chicago Tribune*, May 16.

Sweeney, Annie, Jeremy Gorner, and Joe Germuska. 2010. "31 Days. 303 Shot. 33 Dead." *Chicago Tribune*, 1, 12–13.

Taub, Richard, D. Garth Taylor, and Jan Dunham. 1987. *Paths of Neighborhood Change: Race and Crime in Urban America*. Chicago: University of Chicago Press.

Tavernise, Sabrina, and Robert Gebeloff. 2010. "Immigrants Make Paths to Suburbia, Not Cities." *New York Times*, December 15.

Taylor, Charles. 1989. *Sources of the Self: The Making of Modern Identity*. Cambridge, MA: Harvard University Press.

Taylor, Ralph B. 2001. *Breaking Away from Broken Windows: Baltimore Neighborhoods and the Nationwide Fight against Crime, Grime, Fear, and Decline*. Boulder: Westview.

Thaler, Richard H., and Cass R. Sunstein. 2008. *Nudge: Improving Decisions about Health, Wealth, and Happiness*. New Haven: Yale University Press.

Thomas, William I., and Florian Znaniecki. 1927. *The Polish Peasant in Europe and America*. New York: Alfred A. Knopf.

Thrasher, Frederick. [1927] 1963. *The Gang: A Study of 1.313 Gangs in Chicago*. Chicago: University of Chicago Press.

Tilly, Charles. 1973. "Do Communities Act?" *Sociological Inquiry* 43:209–40.

Tita, George, and Jacqueline Cohen. 2004. "Measuring Spatial Diffusion of Shots Fired Activity across City Neighborhoods." In *Spatially Integrated Social Science*, edited by M. Goodchild and D. Janelle. New York: Oxford University Press.

Tobler, Waldo. 1970. "A Computer Movie Simulating Urban Growth in the Detroit Region." *Economic Geography* 46:234–40.

———. 2004. "On the First Law of Geography: A Reply." *Annals of the Association of American Geographers* 94:304–10.

Tocqueville, Alexis de. 2000. *Democracy in America*. Translated, edited, and with an introduction by H. Mansfield and D. Winthrop. Chicago: University of Chicago Press.

Tonry, Michael, Lloyd E. Ohlin, and David P. Farrington. 1991. *Human Development and Criminal Behavior: New Ways of Advancing Knowledge*. New York: Springer-Verlag.

Trice, Dawn Turner. 2008. "Beverly Block of Chicago Maintains Diversity, Camraderie in a Segregated City." *Chicago Tribune*, December 28.

Tyler, Tom R. 1990. *Why People Obey the Law*. New Haven: Yale University Press.

Vaisey, Stephen. 2009. "Motivation and Justification: A Dual-Process Model of Culture in Action." *American Journal of Sociology* 114:1675–715.

Venkatesh, Sudhir Alladi. 1997. "The Social Organization of Street Gang Activity in an Urban Ghetto." *American Journal of Sociology* 103:82–111.

——. 2000. *American Project: The Rise and Fall of a Modern Ghetto*. Cambridge, MA: Harvard University Press.

Verbitsky, Natalya, and Stephen W. Raudenbush. 2004. "Causal Inference in Spatial Settings." *Proceedings of the American Statistical Association*, Social Statistics Section [CD-ROM].

Villarreal, Andres, and Braulio F. A. Silva. 2006. "Social Cohesion, Criminal Victimization and Perceived Risk of Crime in Brazilian Neighborhoods." *Social Forces* 84: 1725–53.

Wacquant, Loïc. 2008. *Urban Outcasts: A Comparative Sociology of Advanced Marginality*. Cambridge: Polity Press.

Wacquant, Loïc J. D. 1993. "Urban Outcasts: Stigma and Division in the Black American Ghetto and the French Urban Periphery." *International Journal of Urban and Regional Research* 17:366–83.

Wallace, Rodrick, and Deborah Wallace. 1990. "Origins of Public Health Collapse in New York City: The Dynamics of Planned Shrinkage, Contagious Urban Decay and Social Disintegration." *Bulletin of the New York Academy of Medicine* 66: 391–434.

Walters, Ellen E., Ronald C. Kessler, Christopher B. Nelson, and Daniel Mroczek. n.d. "Scoring the World Health Organization's Composite International Diagnostic Interview Short Form."

Warner, Barbara, and Pamela Rountree. 1997. "Local Social Ties in a Community and Crime Model: Questioning the Systemic Nature of Informal Social Control." *Social Problems* 44:520–36.

Warren, Donald. 1975. *Black Neighborhoods: An Assessment of Community Power*. Ann Arbor: University of Michigan Press.

Warren, Mark R. 2004. "What Is the Political Role of Nonprofits in a Democracy?" In *In Search of the Nonprofit Sector*, edited by P. Frumkin and J. Imber. New Brunswick, NJ: Transaction Books.

Wasserman, Stanley, and Katherine Faust. 1994. *Social Network Analysis. Methods and Applications*. Cambridge: Cambridge University Press.

Watt, Paul. 2006. "Respectability, Roughness and 'Race': Neighbourhood Place Images and the Making of Working-Class Social Distinctions in London." *International Journal of Urban and Regional Research* 30: 776–97.

Watts, Duncan. 2003. *Six Degrees of Separation: The Science of a Connected Age*. New York: W. W. Norton and Co.

Way, Sandra, Brian K. Finch, and Deborah Cohen. 2006. "Hispanic Concentration and the Conditional Influence of Collective Efficacy on Adolescent Childbearing." *Archives of Pediatrics and Adolescent Medicine* 160: 925–30.

Weisburd, David, Laura Wyckoff, Justin Ready, John Eck, J. Hinkle, and F. Gajewski. 2006. "Does Crime Just Move around the Corner? A Controlled Study of Spatial Displacement and Diffusion of Crime Control Benefits." *Criminology* 44:549–92.

Wellman, Barry. 1979. "The Community Question: The Intimate Networks of East Yorkers." *American Journal of Sociology* 84:1201–31.

———. 1996. "Are Personal Communities Local? A Dumptarian Reconsideration." *Social Networks* 18: 347–54.

Wen, Ming, Christopher R. Browning, and Kathleen A. Cagney. 2003. "Poverty, Affluence, and Income Inequality: Neighborhood Economic Structure and Its Implications for Health." *Social Science and Medicine* 57:843–60.

Werthman, Carl, and Irv Piliavin. 1967. "Gang Members and the Police." In *The Police: Six Sociological Essays*, edited by D. Bordua. New York: Wiley.

Western, Bruce. 2006. *Punishment and Inequality in America*. New York: Russell Sage Foundation.

Wheaton, Blair, and Philippa Clarke. 2003. "Space Meets Time: Integrating Temporal and Contextual Influences on Mental Health in Early Adulthood." *American Sociological Review* 68:680–706.

Whyte, William F. 1943. *Street Corner Society: The Social Structure of an Italian Slum*. Chicago: University of Chicago Press.

Wikström, P.-O. 1991. *Urban Crime, Criminals and Victims*. New York: Springer-Verlag.

Wikström, Per-Olof, and Robert J. Sampson. 2003. "Social Mechanisms of Community Influences on Crime and Pathways in Criminality." In *Causes of Conduct Disorder and Serious Juvenile Delinquency*, edited by B. Lahey, T. Moffitt, and A. Caspi. New York: Guilford Press.

———, eds. 2006. *The Explanation of Crime: Context, Mechanisms, and Development*. Cambridge: Cambridge University Press.

Wikström, Per-Olof H., Vania Ceccato, Beth Hardie, and Kyle Treiber. 2010. "Activity Fields and the Dynamics of Crime: Advancing Knowledge about the Role of the Environment in Crime Causation." *Journal of Quantitative Criminology* 26:55–87.

Williams, David R., and Chiquita Collins. 1995. "U.S. Socioeconomic and Racial Differences in Health: Patterns and Explanations." *Annual Review of Sociology* 21:349–86.

Wilson, David Sloan. 2002. *Darwin's Cathedral: Evolution, Religion, and the Nature of Society*. Chicago: University of Chicago Press.

Wilson, James Q., and Richard Herrnstein. 1985. *Crime and Human Nature*. New York: Simon and Schuster.

Wilson, James Q., and George Kelling. 1982. "Broken Windows: The Police and Neighborhood Safety." *Atlantic* 127:29–38.

Wilson, William Julius. 1987. *The Truly Disadvantaged: The Inner City, the Underclass, and Public Policy*. Chicago: University of Chicago Press.

——. 1996. *When Work Disappears: The World of the New Urban Poor.* New York: Knopf.

——. 2009. *More Than Just Race: Being Black and Poor in the Inner City.* New York: Norton.

——. 2010. "The Obama Administration's Proposals to Address Concentrated Urban Poverty." *City and Community* 9:41–49.

Wilson, William Julius, and Anmol Chaddha. 2009. "The Role of Theory in Ethnographic Research." *Ethnography* 10:269–84.

Wilson, William Julius, and Richard Taub. 2006. *There Goes the Neighborhood: Racial, Ethnic, and Class Tensions in Four Chicago Neighborhoods and Their Meaning for America.* New York: Alfred A. Knopf.

Wirth, Louis. 1938. "Urbanism as a Way of Life." *American Journal of Sociology* 44:3–24.

Wolfgang, M., R. M. Figlio, and T. Sellin. 1972. *Delinquency in a Birth Cohort.* Chicago: University of Chicago Press.

Woodstock-Institute. 2010. "Chicago City and Regional Foreclosure Activity: Second Half 2009 Foreclosure Figures."

Woodward, James. 2003. *Making Things Happen: A Theory of Causal Explanation.* Oxford: Oxford University Press.

World Bank. 2010. *Social Capital.* http://web.worldbank.org/WBSITE/EXTERNAL/TOPICS/EXTSOCIALDEVELOPMENT/EXTTSOCIALCAPITAL/0,,contentMDK:20642703~menuPK:401023~pagePK:148956~piPK:216618~theSitePK:401015,00.html.

Wuthnow, Robert. 1998. *Loose Connections: Joining Together in America's Fragmented Communities.* Cambridge, MA: Harvard University Press.

Zhang, Lening, Steven F. Messner, and Jianhong Liu. 2007. "A Multilevel Analysis of the Risk of Household Burglary in the City of Tianjin, China." *British Journal of Criminology* 47: 918–37.

Zorbaugh, Henry. 1929. *The Gold Coast and the Slum: A Sociological Study of Chicago's Near North Side.* Chicago: University of Chicago Press.

Zukin, Sharon. 2010. *Naked City: The Death and Life of Authentic Urban Places.* New York: Oxford.

INDEX